Immanuel Kant's moral theory

Immanuel Kant's moral theory

ROGER J. SULLIVAN

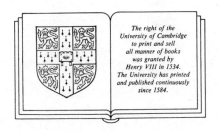

The right of the
University of Cambridge
to print and sell
all manner of books
was granted by
Henry VIII in 1534.
The University has printed
and published continuously
since 1584.

CAMBRIDGE UNIVERSITY PRESS

CAMBRIDGE

NEW YORK PORT CHESTER MELBOURNE SYDNEY

Published by the Press Syndicate of the University of Cambridge
The Pitt Building, Trumpington Street, Cambridge CB2 1RP
40 West 20th Street, New York, NY 10011, USA
10 Stamford Road, Oakleigh, Melbourne 3166, Australia

First published 1989
Reprinted 1990

Printed in the United States of America

Library of Congress Cataloging-in-Publication Data
Sullivan, Roger J., 1928–
Immanuel Kant's moral theory / Roger J. Sullivan
p. cm.
Bibliography: p.
Includes indexes.
ISBN 0-521-36011-0. ISBN 0-521-36908-8 (pbk.)
1. Kant, Immanuel, 1724–1804 – Ethics.
2. Ethics – History – 18th century. I. Title.
B2799.E8S83 1989
170′.92′4–dc19   88–10225
CIP

British Library Cataloguing in Publication Data

Sullivan, Roger J.
Immanuel Kant's Moral theory.
I. Ethics. Theories of Kant, Immanuel.
I. Title
170′.92′4

ISBN 0 521 36011 0 hardback
ISBN 0 521 36908 8 paperback

Contents

CONTENTS

Part II: The moral norm for persons

CONTENTS

CONTENTS

CONTENTS

Preface

I have long been convinced that it is distressingly easy to misunderstand individual strands of Kant's moral thought apart from the context of his entire moral theory. There are some fine brief overviews of Kant's moral theory, such as H. B. Acton's *Kant's Moral Philosophy,* John Kemp's *Philosophy of Kant,* S. Körner's *Kant,* and Roger Scruton's *Kant.* But the very brevity of these studies prevents them from doing justice to the intricate complexity of Kant's theory. Many other books and articles concentrate on only one part of the Kantian corpus, but since no one of Kant's books contains his entire moral theory, those works also tend to be incomplete in important ways. My aim in writing this book is to set out a synoptic and detailed exposition of Kant's entire practical theory.

Others have also felt the need for such a work. John Rawls, for example, has noted that "unfortunately, there is no commentary on Kant's moral theory as a whole."[1] I am grateful that a philosopher of his stature has shared my belief in the need for such a study, but I am also glad I did not come upon his further comment ("perhaps it would prove impossible to write") until I was already so far along in my work that I had decided I would not be deterred by the difficulties Rawls had anticipated and with which I had become familiar.

One of those difficulties concerns just what it was that Kant "really" held. Because even his contemporaries found him hard to understand, Kant once wryly admitted, "I have often been reproached for writing in a philosophical style that is obscure; indeed, I have even been charged with intentionally cultivating and affecting unclarity in order to give the appearance of having had deep insights" (*M.M.* 206). Small wonder, then, that even today there is no firm consensus about many of the most important parts of Kant's theory – such as the nature and the role of Categorical Imperative – much less about the structure of his entire practical theory. To attempt an exposition of his theory as a whole, therefore, requires exceptional bravery – perhaps "foolhardiness" would be a better word. If some readers find my interpretation incompatible with their own, I hope they still find this exposition helpful, if only to clarify their own reading.

Probably more often than any other philosopher, Kant elicits strongly partisan emotional responses from his readers. Lewis White Beck described this characteristic well when he wrote, "Something makes it difficult for most and impossible for many philosophers and students of the history of philosophy to be impartial about Kant and his teachings. . . . It has always been so. In his own lifetime the polemics from his opponents reached a degree of acerbity more characteristic of theological debate than of philosophical."[2] At least part of the reason for this phenomenon can be traced to the fact that Kant hardly ever set out to write simply an exposition. As Hans Saner points out in his *Kant's Political Thought*, almost all of Kant's works were written as arguments against competing philosophical positions. During the course of his philosophical career, Kant managed to attack virtually every major philosophical position – rationalism and empiricism, skepticism and dogmatism, naturalism and supernaturalism. His friend Moses Mendelssohn had good reason to describe him as the "all-destroyer," *der alles Zermalmender*. Kant predictably ended up with many disciples convinced that the new "Critical philosophy" alone was the correct view, but he also alienated almost everyone else who could read him.

Kant believed that the need to do philosophy arises out of conflicting views about how we should understand human nature and the human condition, and he also believed that philosophizing itself, while irenic in spirit, must be essentially polemical in nature. As a result, he often offered only a partial or one-sided statement of what he thought. Occasionally he became so caught up in his arguments against some view or other that he wrote in what today turns out to be a very misleading fashion. Moreover, Kant himself regarded philosophy as a process, and even during his "Critical period," his thinking underwent significant development. It therefore is inevitable that he occasionally seems to contradict himself and that there are passages in which he seems to say something quite different from what I present as his mature doctrine.

Since philosophical thinking today is closely identified with the practice of criticism, it is important for me to say that I have tried to produce, insofar as possible, what admittedly might be regarded as a philosophically unnatural work – in the main at least, an impartial exposition rather than a polemical study. There is an almost universal presupposition that he who is not for Kant must be against him, and vice versa. But, at the cost of considerable effort, I have put aside my desires to engage Kant philosophically in order to attend to what, insofar as I could tell, *Kant* wanted to say.

A sophisticated reader, particularly one with strongly negative views of Kant's theory, will wonder how I can occasionally simply set out what Kant said, in what will surely seem to be a philosophically innocent fashion. Despite appearances to the contrary, my omission of critical comments at various places should not be interpreted as my trying to write a "sympathetic" account that ignores weaknesses and problems in the Kantian theory. I have constantly reminded myself that those reading this book will be far more interested in learning what Kant thought than in learning what I think about what Kant thought. For that reason I also have avoided the common practice of offering "reconstructions" articulating what Kant *should* have said in place of what he did in fact say.

Occasionally it was apparent that some critical discussion simply could not be avoided, that it would have been a mistake to ignore *all* the criticisms commonly made of Kant's theory. Many of these turn out to be without merit because they are based on either a partial or an incorrect reading of his theory. But I still have mentioned some such criticisms to help clarify the exposition. I also have tried to segregate such remarks clearly from the exposition proper, and I have noted those places where my own reading may be particularly controversial.

Although I have not set out to advocate Kant's moral theory, I still have tried to present his theory as strongly and positively as possible. With ample reason: No philosopher could continue to have the impact on such large numbers of thinkers if his theory were not extraordinarily powerful. Whatever problems Kant's theory may have, it still seems to many thoughtful people to be an essentially correct view. This holds true not only for most professional philosophers writing in the field of ethics today but also for many people who do not claim to be philosophers. The Kantian view or something closely akin to it seems clearly to be the way many people think about morality even today, particularly those reared in the Judeo-Christian tradition. Kant often says what they themselves would say about their own moral life, were they to articulate it. As arguably the most important moral philosopher in the modern period, Kant clearly has had the "last and so the best laugh" over his philosophical opponents, just as he once, in a somewhat bitter mood, wrote that he would (*M.M.* 209).

One way to discuss Kant's philosophy has been admirably modeled, for example, by Bruce Aune in his *Kant's Theory of Morals* and by John Atwell in his *Ends and Principles in Kant's Moral Thought*. Each shares his consideration of alternative readings of particular Kantian texts before settling on what he believes to be the best interpretation.

I have set out to write a very different kind of book. I have deliberately suppressed the internal dialogues preceding my contentions about what Kant held, in order to keep Kant himself at the center of the discussions. Some readers, particularly those more sophisticated, are bound to feel dissatisfied, to think that I should have examined some materials more carefully and expanded the exposition, even if doing so meant a longer book. Rather than pay that cost, I have, not happily, decided to discuss a good many topics in an admittedly summary fashion. My main explicit support for my reading of Kant is an appeal to the Kantian texts themselves, and I have included many quotations and references in my book. In this connection, I have found that notwithstanding developments and inconsistencies in Kant's thinking, his moral theory is much more tightly constructed than it appears to be if we read only one or another of his works.

I have had another ambition while writing this book: to present Kant's moral philosophy, insofar as I could, in clear, ordinary language. It must be admitted that this is a highly un-Kantian aim. Kant himself did not think his moral philosophy *could* be paraphrased in a more popular style without distortion or serious oversimplification. (See *Gr.* 30–31/409–10; *Pr.R.* 10.) He held that he had to use the "language of the schools" in order to achieve precision (*M.M.* 206; see 206–8). Consequently, his style reflects both the scholastic German of the eighteenth century and the stilted Latin texts typically found in the classrooms of that period.

Although reading Kant will never be a popular leisure activity, I have tried to state his moral theory so that those who are not already experts will be able to understand it, or at least most of it, without enormous effort. Whenever possible, for example, I have translated Kant's faculty-psychology language into discussions about people, and I occasionally have used more ordinary expressions, such as "moral reasoning," in place of Kant's own technical phrase "pure practical reason." In this matter I think I have been more successful in some chapters than in others. Kant's defense of human moral agency and of the primacy of moral interests, for example, requires excursions into his theoretical philosophy that resist a restatement in ordinary language.

I must make several disclaimers. As I have already indicated, I am aware that the readings I offer may not be the only plausible or legitimate ones. Like others who have worked with Kant, I have found that below one level of meaning, there is another and then still another. It may be as presumptuous for anyone to claim to offer either a "complete" or a "final" account of any great philosopher like Kant as it would be, to quote my late mother-in-law, for anyone to insist there is but one right way to be an Episcopalian. So I will claim only to offer a more comprehensive survey of Kant's practical theory than is now available. It would have been possible for me to say much more than I have on virtually every topic in this book – but the book is already long enough.

Since I have aimed to write an exposition, I have no special theme underlying the order of presentation to give it a thread of continuity, except perhaps my conviction that there is an overall wholeness to Kant's practical philosophy. As much as possible, I have simply let the theory itself dictate the order in which the various topics occur, so that individual sections are preceded by what they logically presuppose, the lines of development within Kant's general argument are made clear, and most of his characteristic repetitions are unnecessary. For example, the discussion of Ideas of reason was originally located in several different chapters until it eventually found a home in Chapter 2. Most of the material has gone through many different versions in various locations before each topic seemed to settle down more or less contentedly where it can now be found.

This procedure has the drawback that it has meant usually neither analyzing different ways in which Kant may have treated the same doctrine in different books nor attending adequately to how his thinking developed and evolved during his philosophical life. But this already has been done (or is being done) by such scholars as Allison, Beck, Cassirer, Gregor, Guyer, Paton, Saner, Schilpp, and Ward.

Further, as interesting as it would have been to do so, I have not tried to determine to what extent various prominent philosophers today are or are not "Kantians."[3] Again, the book is already long enough. Nonetheless, this exposition can provide an opportunity for readers to review the historical Kantian use of such prominent current moral notions as "autonomy," "persons," "respect for persons," "duties," and "rights." Recalling what Kant held does provide a standard against which a knowledgeable reader can assess modern trends in ethical and political theorizing.

In graduate school, like most other philosophy students, I originally studied Kant (as this book shows) with the help of H. J. Paton's commentary on the *Groundwork* and Lewis White Beck's on the second *Critique,* supplemented, because I was enrolled in John R. Silber's seminar, by Silber's articles. Like most other students, I eventually realized that I could judge the value of a commentary only after I had immersed myself in the Kantian texts themselves. Accordingly, while writing this book, I spent my time mainly with those texts, and only after I had a fairly complete draft did I allow myself the luxury of reading some of the vast secondary literature.

Like many others, I quickly found I could not possibly read everything I wanted to read, at least not if I ever hoped to complete the manuscript. Omissions of books and articles from the bibliography may show an un-Kantian lack of cosmopolitan vision, but these omissions are also both a sign of my mortality and an admission that I feel more at home within the Anglo-American analytic tradition than, say, with Continental phenomenology. I have tended to concentrate my reading of secondary literature mainly on classic pieces, such as those by Beck, Fackenheim, Paton, and Silber, and articles representative of a younger group of Kantian scholars of extraordinary talent and insight (many of whom, incidentally, did their graduate work under John Rawls). When I have altered my exposition or felt that the views of another author could enhance the exposition, I have cited the source in the notes.

Finally, I need to acknowledge a large number of debts accumulated while working on this book. I do so not out of duty but out of a deep feeling of gratitude.

While writing the book, I often found myself yielding to a tendency typical of those working with Kant, to develop a peculiarly acrimonious temper. My moral failures in this direction led my wife (who, for better or worse, is an Aristotelian) to threaten me more than once with owl-of-Minerva stew for supper. I hereby acknowledge my guilt and her forbearance, as well as the many times her suggestions rescued me from unnecessary imitations of Kant's difficult and often stylistically ugly constructions.

There are many others to whom I owe large debts of appreciation. Donald Livingston, James Willard Oliver, Edmund L. Pincoffs, and Dwight Van de Vate, Jr., read and critiqued a very early version of the manuscript. Lewis White Beck offered helpful suggestions on the basis of a partial reading of a later version. Sharon Anderson-Gold, Leslie A. Mulholland, and Allen W. Wood then critiqued a still later version. All attended in mutually complementary ways to different parts of Kant's practical theory, and I owe a great deal to their suggestions. I also acknowledge with special gratitude how much the final draft has been influenced by the criticisms of an anonymous reader for Cambridge University Press. None of these people, of course, should be held accountable for any errors in the final draft, which they did not see, nor should their help be construed to mean they necessarily agree with my interpretation of Kant's moral theory. I wish also to thank my copy editor, Mary Byers, as well as my production editor at Cambridge University Press, Martin Dinitz, and Professor Gerda Jordan, who was kind enough to act as my local expert on seventeenth- and eighteenth-century German.

One last note: The title of this volume should properly have been *Immanuel Kant's Practical Theory,* to emphasize that the book includes an examination of such topics as his philosophy of history and political theory. Those who do not already know how Kant used the term "practical" might have been misled by that choice, however; and those who do know this will not be misled by the title I have used.

Key to abbreviations and translators

Publishers and editions are listed in the Bibliography.

Anthr.	*Anthropology from a Pragmatic Point of View* – Mary J. Gregor
Conflict	*The Conflict of the Faculties* – Mary J. Gregor (Part II – Robert E. Anchor)
Cr.J.	*Critique of Judgment* – James Creed Meredith
Ed.	*Education* – Annette Churton
End	*The End of All Things* – Ted Humphrey
Enlight.	*What Is Enlightenment?* – Ted Humphrey
Gr.	*Groundwork of the Metaphysic of Morals* – H. J. Paton
H.H.	*Speculative Beginning of Human History* – Ted Humphrey
Idea	*Idea for a Universal History with a Cosmopolitan Intent* – Ted Humphrey
Lect.	*Lectures on Ethics* – Louis Infield
Logic	*Logic* – Robert Hartman and Wolfgang Schwarz
M.M.	*The Metaphysics of Morals*
	Preface, Introduction, and Part I (205–372) – John Ladd
	Part II (375–491) – Mary J. Gregor
Orient.	*What Is Orientation in Thinking?* – Lewis White Beck
P.P.	*Perpetual Peace* – Ted Humphrey
Proleg.	*Prolegomena to Any Future Metaphysics* – Lewis White Beck
Pr.R.	*Critique of Practical Reason* – Lewis White Beck
Pu.R.	*Critique of Pure Reason* – Norman Kemp Smith
Rel.	*Religion Within the Limits of Reason Alone* – Theodore M. Greene and Hoyt H. Hudson
T&P	*On the Proverb: That May Be True in Theory but Is of No Practical Use* – Ted Humphrey
Theol.	*Lectures on Philosophical Theology* – Allen W. Wood and Gertrude M. Clark

I
Introduction

Although I am absolutely convinced of many things that I shall never have the courage to say, I shall never say anything I do not believe.

Kant to Moses Mendelssohn, April 8, 1766

Immanuel Kant's life

Immanuel Kant's life took place on two very different levels. To all appearances he lived the life of a quiet academician, avoiding even small changes in his routine. But this outer tranquillity was only the setting within which to do his inner, creative work, and there, above all else, Kant was a revolutionary philosophical polemicist, pitting his mind "against the great thinkers of the past, against his contemporaries, and against himself."[1] Kant developed a radically novel philosophical system of such enormous strength and importance that it has dominated the thinking of all who came after him. As was said originally of Plato: After Kant, philosophers argued for him or against him, but no one could philosophize any longer without taking him into account.

Kant was born in Königsberg, East Prussia (now Kaliningrad in the Soviet Union), on April 22, 1724, the fourth of nine children of a harnessmaker. He lived in or near that city all his life, and died there on February 12, 1804. After attending the University of Königsberg, he acted as a private tutor for families living nearby until he was appointed an instructor at the university. There he taught an astonishing variety of courses, including mathematics, geography, anthropology, the natural sciences, metaphysics, logic, natural theology, ethics, and pedagogy. In 1770 he was appointed professor of mathematics, and later professor of logic and metaphysics, a position that more accurately reflected his academic interests. Although he regularly taught fourteen hours a week, he found the time to think through the philosophical ideas that would become an intellectual revolution.

Had he died before 1781, Kant would have been just another obscure eighteenth-century German professor. But that year, when he was fifty-seven, he published the first edition of his monumental *Critique of Pure Reason,* a work that would irrevocably change the future of Western philosophy. During the next seventeen years he continued to develop, elaborate, and defend his ideas in an impressive series of books and articles.[2]

As his ideas spread throughout Europe and England he became more and more deeply involved in philosophical controversy (see, e.g., *M.M.* 208–9), but he continued to live an otherwise quiet academic life until his characteristic vigor began to fail and he was forced to give up lecturing.[3] When he retired in 1797, his presence at Königsberg had transformed the small provincial university into an institution of widespread fame.

Throughout his adult life Kant impressed his contemporaries as a person with a serene and cheerful heart. According to his biographer Cassirer, however, this cheerfulness "was not for Kant a direct gift of nature and fate, but . . . was won instead by hard intellectual struggles."[4] Kant was not naturally gregarious, but he learned to take pleasure in the company of others. He never married (apparently believing that marriage would threaten his freedom – see *Anthr.* 309), but he cultivated many friends and often dined with them or had them and his students as guests in his home for meals and long conversations afterward. His mental acuity showed itself extremely well in urbane and stimulating conversations (and in his lectures), which were described by former student Johann Herder as "witty" and "entertaining" (words hardly applicable to his written works!). Characteristically, Kant even drew up a series of Dale Carnegie–like maxims for how best to conduct dinner conversations so everyone would go home feeling warmly toward his dinner companions. (See *Anthr.* 178–82.)

His years of enforced pious exercises at parochial school had taught Kant to mistrust the "soft" sentiments and their displays. Except for a brief attraction to the French style of dress as a young instructor, he lived simply and avoided all but the plainest pleasures. The emotions he respected were those that had been recommended by the ancient Stoics as reflecting and promoting a strong will and high principles. So, for example, he strengthened his naturally frail constitution by a stern discipline directed against ease and indulgence. For the same reason he seemed always to have kept a certain reserve, even in his closest relationships. He continually confounded those who thought they knew him well enough to anticipate the direction his philosophical development would take. The motto he borrowed from Bacon for the second edition of his *Critique of Pure Reason,* "De nobis ipsis silemus" (About ourselves we are silent), reflects his reticence about himself. Fame apparently meant little to him compared with the importance of working out the implications of the Critical philosophy, which he never thought of as completed.

In Kant's moral theory the dignity of persons and their right to respect is grounded in their freedom – their ability to subordinate their particular desires and inclinations to the universal law of morality.[5] To live up to this freedom is the meaning of integrity, and so it is understandable that more than anything else Kant treasured intellectual and moral integrity, both in himself and in others. He is remembered by those who knew him as the best model of his own moral doctrines: He valued the impersonal universal in all those with whom he dealt more than their individuality or particularity. An incident occurred about a week before his death that has often been used to illustrate how Kant guided his relationships with others by the disinterested interest of moral respect, which he nonetheless called the "courtesy of the heart."

Desperately weak, mentally unable to concentrate, and virtually blind, Kant insisted on rising and remaining standing until his doctor had seated himself. With great effort Kant then remarked that at least "the sense of humanity has not yet abandoned me."[6]

Kant's audiences

In his philosophical writings on morality Kant addressed several different audiences, each presenting its own special problems.[7]

The audience with which he was chiefly concerned consisted of those educated people who had been so impressed with Newtonian science that they believed, as logical positivists and behaviorists in our own century have contended, that cognitively significant statements are to be found only in the physical sciences. They therefore relegated moral (and aesthetic and religious) claims to the inferior status of merely emotional utterances. Kant aimed to defend morality against these moral skeptics by showing that because science suffers certain unavoidable limitations, moral claims not only have their own rightful cognitive status but ultimately enjoy *primacy* over scientific knowledge.[8] We will examine the challenge to morality that these people represented in the next chapter.

What can hardly be overstressed now, however, is that Kant did *not* write about morality because he thought it was a philosophically intriguing topic that he simply wanted to explore systematically. Those who had questioned or attacked the significance of moral claims were always first and foremost on Kant's mind. As a consequence, almost all of his works on ethics, particularly his *Groundwork,* are best approached by thinking of them as long arguments against moral skepticism rather than as simply expositions.[9] Doing so goes a long way toward helping us understand Kant, particularly when he presents his claims in a one-sided fashion – a polemical trait that probably has caused more misinterpretations than even his turgid style.

A second audience and the group against which Kant directed his strongest language consisted of other philosophers. (See, e.g., *Gr.* 30–32/409–10; *Pr.R.* 24.) Most of these thinkers were not professional academics as they are today; they were to be found in the leisured, educated class and particularly in the clergy. According to Kant, they and all their predecessors had analyzed the nature of human morality incorrectly by trying to base it on experience They thereby had not only played into the hands of the skeptics but also had tended to subvert the moral convictions of ordinary people. To counteract what he saw as their pernicious influence, Kant set out to explain how and why their analyses had been seriously defective.

Kant also disagreed with philosophers in the rationalist tradition who had sought final answers about reality and the meaning of life – what went under the title of "metaphysics" – by claiming it is possible to learn about ultimate reality on the basis of what we first know about the world. That this methodology needed to be abandoned, Kant argued, could be shown by the fact that it had resulted only in contradictions and confusion. Yet he did not believe that we can or should try to give up our metaphysical yearnings, our search for final answers, and he also thought he had discovered the only right way to go about doing just that.

Finally, although Kant realized that most of his works were far too complex and philosophically sophisticated ever to be widely read or understood by ordinary and relatively uneducated people, he still kept those people in mind. Philosophical views do tend to sift eventually into the domain of public thought. Kant had enormous respect for the prephilosophical moral convictions of ordinary people, and he in fact based his entire analysis of morality on what he refers to as "ordinary moral consciousness." He believed that people do have a fundamentally reliable, if not always clear, grasp of what morality is about, certainly better than that of most philosophers. The main moral problem ordinary people have, Kant thought, is keeping faith with their moral ideals and, to help them do so, he set out to formulate the ultimate moral norm as clearly and precisely as possible. Through his discussions illustrating the force of that norm, he also aimed to offer some hardheaded advice about what is morally and politically right and wrong.

It is Kant's very mixed agenda that largely accounts for the fact that some passages – those that set out and appeal to the moral beliefs of ordinary people – seem clear and straightforward while others – directed at one or another of his more sophisticated audiences – may seem nearly incomprehensible. As we shall see, however, the various levels within Kant's explanations and arguments are so closely interwoven that it often is not possible to understand one without also understanding the others.

Kant's respect for ordinary moral thinking

Kant frequently wrote that the ultimate data for his analysis of the nature of human morality were drawn from the moral thinking of ordinary people with ordinary intelligence. The Greeks, he held, had been wrong to think that knowledge *is* moral virtue, and so they (and Leibniz) were wrong in believing that morality can be the possession only of a leisured, educated elite. On the contrary, morality is no discriminator of persons; it binds everyone. Since one cannot have moral obligations that one does not and cannot know about, moral norms and ideals must be available to working people of the most ordinary intelligence. Philosophers do not have access to moral insights that are not also available literally to everyone else. (See, e.g., *Pu.R.* Bxxxiii; *Gr.* 22/404.) In fact, the egregious errors of philosophers seem to indicate only that they too often confuse themselves with extraneous considerations.

Everyone, he concluded, must have a fundamentally correct prephilosophical understanding of morality, even if that understanding lacks clarity and adequate expression. The task of the philosopher, therefore, and Kant's chief claim on behalf of his own analysis, is to set out clearly, correctly, and precisely what already is "inherent in the structure of every man's reason," particularly the ultimate moral norm (*M.M.* 376; see, e.g., *Pu.R.* A730/B758, A807/B835, A831/B859; *Gr.* vi/389, 8/397, 17/402, 20–24/403–5, 34/411; *Pr.R.*

8n, 30, 36, 87, 91–92, 126; *M.M.* 206). In response to the criticism that he had not said anything new when he stated that principle, he wrote: "Who would want to introduce a new principle of morality and, as it were, be its inventor, as if the world had hitherto been ignorant of what duty is or had been thoroughly wrong about it?" (*Pr.R.* 8n).[10]

Kant's morality, then, is the morality of the ordinary person, and this helps to account for the continued influence of his writings in any country with democratic ideals. Friedrich Paulsen, one of Kant's biographers, attributes this sympathy for the ordinary person – the peasant and laborer – to a harsh lesson Kant had learned in his parents' home. What the peasant class could mainly look forward to was an austere life of hard work with little chance of adequate reward in this world. Their greatest personal achievement would be the conscientious performance of their duties. By contrast, the advantages to which the aristocracy were born offered them a wider variety of pleasures but did not necessarily enhance their moral character. On the contrary, a life of privilege often produced only a morality of selfish egoism, at whatever cost to the "lower" classes.

A morality of the people would allow no such attitudes; it would hold equally for everyone. No one would have the political right *merely* to use others. The moral law would also not tolerate the sort of discriminations between people historically made by the titled and not uncommonly even by tradition-bound peasants. It would not estimate the worth and dignity of a person by that person's natural talents or wealth or family or social status or brilliance or accomplishments, however earthshaking.[11]

An examination of the moral consciousness of ordinary people also shows, Kant wrote, that the human moral condition is a state of constant inner conflict between two warring elements – the unyielding demands of morality and the insistent lure of temptations against those demands. In fact, it is through this conflict that we come to know the reality and nature of morality. (See *Pr.R.* 31, 35.)[12] We find our desires pressing on us, demanding our attention and their satisfaction, as if the only choices available to us concern the selection of whatever promises us the most pleasure. Yet, as soon as we consider actually pursuing pleasure, Kant went on, we find our reason challenging the moral acceptability of what we are considering doing. What we subjectively *want* to do is always called into question by a rational and objective ideal of what we *ought* to do. (See *Pr.R.* 30, 44, 66, 74.)[13]

Because we are self-conscious, Kant continued, we also become aware that moral obligations claim our obedience in a categorical fashion. The categorical or lawlike character of moral obligation, Kant explains, shows the objective nature of morality. Natural or physical laws are called objective "laws" precisely because they hold universally and necessarily; they are not person dependent in the sense that they are laws for everyone. Likewise, the moral law is objective and not person dependent; it holds universally, without regard for any contingent conditions that may subjectively differentiate one person from another. Actions are judged as obligatory, wrong, or permissible, without regard for our feelings and inclinations. Our desires and aversions provide

5

no justification for ignoring or disobeying moral mandates; there is nothing we can do to free ourselves of moral judgments. (See, e.g., *Gr.* vi/389, 2/393, 16/401, 27/407–8, 38/413, 49/414; *Pr.R.* 31–32, 152.)[14]

From this brief analysis of common prephilosophical beliefs about human nature and morality (what he called "ordinary moral awareness"), Kant derived nearly everything else that he says about the nature of morality – and of religious belief and practice as well.

Kant's debt to Pietism

More specifically, who were most of the "ordinary" people with whom Kant was most familiar? They were those Protestant Christians he knew at Königsberg, most of them Pietists. His parents were devout Pietists, and for eight years, until he was sixteen, Kant attended an intensely Pietistic school. (It was called the Collegium Fridericianum, because the emperor, Frederick the Great, was so convinced by the Enlightenment's insistence on the importance of education that he subsidized even parochial schools.) The young Kant then enrolled in the University of Königsberg, a center of Pietistic theology, where Martin Knutsen, also a Pietist, was the faculty member who was to have the most influence on him.

Pietism was a religious movement within eighteenth-century Lutheranism that emphasized practical faith: The moral world is to be found in the ordinary everyday details of human living, not within rigidly structured, otherworldly, monastic, ascetic practices.[15] From Pietism Kant learned his populist Protestant respect for the moral capacity and dignity of the "ordinary person."[16] True to the Pauline-Augustinian-Lutheran religious tradition, Pietists also had a profound belief in Original Sin and the consequent human proclivity toward evil, joined with at least as strong a belief in the biblical doctrine that through atonement and spiritual rebirth, we all have a vocation to moral perfection. Today many people have great difficulty deciding what is morally right, but the main problem in the Pietists' view was to *do* what is right. What is right and what is wrong can easily be known from biblical injunctions: pride and injustice, for example, are vices; humility, purity, and loving-kindness are virtues.

Kant reacted strongly against the obligatory regimen of religious practices at the Fridericianum – daily prayer, a daily examination of one's inner spiritual life, and public displays of religious feelings. He believed that too often such exercises degenerate into hypocritical, denigrating grovelings – impotent attempts to ingratiate oneself with God. (See *Rel.* 184n/172.)[17] He also developed a complete lack of patience with evangelical and sentimental piety. But from Pietism he did develop his conviction that the morally good character of a person depends only on that person's moral disposition of dutifulness or conscientiousness.

In Kant's analysis, because morality characteristically is pitted against desires, moral requirements appear to us most frequently as negations and constraints, as our duty, limiting what we may do and telling us what not to

6

do. The virtuous person is one who does what he *ought,* not because it is in his interest to do so but because it is what he ought to do, his *duty.* In this tradition the emphasis is on the purity of our intentions, not on the effective use of power in the world. Through no fault of their own, good people who were not part of a wealthy aristocracy did not usually have much worldly power. Their lack of power should not be considered as detracting from the value of their morally pure intentions, nor should the ability of some people to act effectively be thought of as necessarily enhancing their moral character.

Kant was convinced of the rightness of this kind of moral and religious consciousness; it needed only to be explicated and defended.[18] One of his early biographers quoted him as saying:

Even though the religious ideas of that time and the concepts of what they called virtue and piety were anything but clear and adequate, still they really got hold of the basic thing. You can say what you want about Pietism – the people who were serious about it were outstanding in a praiseworthy respect. They possessed the highest thing men can possess, that calm, that serenity, that inner peace, undisturbed by any passion.[19]

It would not do, however, merely to generalize a view of the human moral and religious condition from those instances with which Kant was acquainted.[20] One would then end up with only a sociology of religious and moral beliefs in eighteenth-century Königsberg. Such an account could not justify moral requirements presenting themselves as binding us absolutely, independently of historical conditions. Kant had to show how morality can be universally and necessarily true for all human beings for all time, and, indeed, in its most fundamental outlines, for all other rational beings as well, if there are any besides us. It was this requirement that led him to construct an analysis of the nature of morality that is deliberately ahistorical, a characteristic of his theory that has often been criticized.[21]

Throughout his moral writings, Kant supports the rightness of his analysis of morality by appealing to Everyman's own moral self-awareness. This may seem a very bold move, for anyone can then dismiss what Kant says merely by contending that he does not set out that person's moral thinking correctly. But in Kant's theory there can be no court of higher appeal, and he was confident that his analysis would ring true with everyone sufficiently sensitive to and honest about his own moral life (see, e.g., *T&P* 285).

Kant and the Enlightenment

The second major influence on Kant was the Enlightenment (in Germany it was called *Aufklärung*). Great advances in science (or "natural philosophy") – physics, astronomy, mechanics, and mathematics – had transformed the traditional views about the nature of the universe. This also had generated a new and optimistic faith in the power of reason not only to explain all physical reality with relatively few fundamental and purely mathematico-mechanical laws of enormous scope and power but also to create a new, thoroughly rational, Newtonian-like science of humankind. In place of the Christian teleocosmic view that saw the end of human beings as something to be attained in another world, the Enlightenment put its faith only in this world and in the power of reason and of culture to make unending progress in the material and spiritual condition of man. (See, e.g., *Rel.* 19–20/15–16.)

The new ideal for politics was a secular, rational order in which the rights of the individual would be recognized, as in the social contract and natural rights theories of Thomas Hobbes, John Locke, and Jean-Jacques Rousseau. The Enlightenment also saw the beginnings of modern psychology and sociology, the rational study of and effort to understand and control human behavior, based on empirical investigations. (See, e.g., *Pu.R.* A347/B405–6, A550/B578, A848–49/B876–77.)[22] Finally, in philosophy it meant both a new and critical examination of the power of human reason and a rejection of the old style of rationalistic metaphysics that had claimed that our knowledge can transcend the limits of experience (see, e.g., *Pu.R.* Ax–xii, xia). The method to be used in philosophy, as in psychology, was Newtonian, applied to inner experience, to human consciousness.

Insofar as it was based on Newtonian science, the Enlightenment also suffered a deeply ambivalent attitude toward both nature and humans as part of nature. On the one hand, the New Science had rejected Aristotelian final causalities in favor of a mechanistic view of all objects in the world including human beings. But on the other hand, the Enlightenment pinned all its hopes on the human capacity to engage in rational, purposive activity; and then "Nature" was considered, as by Rousseau, to be the basis for all our ethical and aesthetic standards. As we shall see later, Kant's solution to this paradox – his doctrine of the two viewpoints – was both brilliant and perplexing.

Kant considered himself not only part of but a custodian of the Enlightenment. In his pamphlet *What Is Enlightenment?* (1784), he answered the question in the title in terms of the process of "man's emergence from his self-imposed immaturity" to have the courage to live his life on the basis of his own thinking. The only condition necessary for beginning the process of enlightenment, for actually beginning to use our reason, Kant wrote, is freedom – externally, the absence of institutional restraints on independent thought and public debate, and internally, the courage to think for ourselves rather than let others do it for us. (See *Enlight.* 36; *Orient.* 144–45, 146n; *Rel.* 188n/176–77.)

Progress through the rational study of nature requires that individuals be free to develop through education their ability to think and that governments protect the peace and promote intellectual freedom. The enemies of progress, then, are those social customs and institutions that are intolerant of rival views and systematically try to keep people in ignorance: totalitarian governments that forbid scholarly research and discussion, and churches that authoritatively denigrate reason, putting mysteries, miracles, and purported revelations in its place. Such tyrannical uses of power "trample on the holy rights of mankind" (*Enlight.* 39). "Religion through its sanctity, and lawgiving through its majesty, may seek to exempt themselves from [criticism],"

Kant wrote, "but they then awaken just suspicion, and cannot claim the sincere respect which reason accords only to that which has been able to sustain the test of free and open examination" (*Pu.R.* Axia).[23] The Enlightenment, then, not only marked the beginning of modern science but also contained the seeds of contemporary faiths – positivism, behaviorism, materialism, and humanism.

Kant had to bridge the distance between, on the one hand, his profound belief in God and, on the other, his commitment to the Enlightenment, which valued reason and human progress over religious faith. He would have felt the tensions between the two worldviews while still a student, for Martin Knutsen, who introduced Kant to Newton's work, somehow managed to be not only a Pietist but also a disciple of Christian Wolff (1679–1754), a Leibnizian and a rationalist.[24] So also was the metaphysician Alexander Baumgarten, whom Kant admired and whose texts Kant used in his own courses. Strangely enough, though, Pietism itself also helped make Kant receptive to the Enlightenment:

Both [Pietism and the Enlightenment] constituted reactions to the clerical, legalistic, and institutional Christianity of the day. Both shared the accents of individualism and religious freedom, and the view that life is to be changed in a practical way. Primarily, it was the [Pietistic] focus on life and ethics in an atmosphere of tolerance which did the most to prepare the way for the dogmatic indifference of the Enlightenment and the pluralism of modern times.[25]

Pietism and the Enlightenment therefore complemented each other in Kant's theory, which stresses the life of practice and the freedom of the individual and opposes dogmatic and authoritarian social structures. But there remained many differences between Pietism and the Enlightenment. Kant would have seen the process of resolving these conflicts into a single unified view of human life as a paradigmatic exercise of philosophizing. Still, his loyalty to both reason and religion had to have made the reconciliation of the two emotionally difficult for him personally, however little he usually let this show in his published works.

As we would expect, Kant's mature ethical and religious views are not completely at home with either Pietism or the Enlightenment. On the one hand, he rejected the Pietistic beliefs that morality consists in unquestioning obedience to the revealed will of God and that the ultimate motive for being moral lies in the religious sentiments we have toward God. But on the other hand, contrary to the prevailing view of Enlightenment thinkers such as Voltaire, Diderot, Bacon, Locke, and Wolff, he also held that teleological theories of morality, which see the highest human good only as happiness, corrupt morality at its very foundations. He also never gave up his Pietistic conviction that our highest faculty is our will, not our intellect, for the highest good we can achieve is not theoretical knowledge (as the Greeks had thought) but a practical goal: moral virtue and happiness commensurate with virtue. Further, despite his later attacks on Shaftesbury and Hutcheson for holding that the basis for acting morally lies with some special moral sense, Kant never entirely renounced his pre-Critical conviction that within strict limits, those British moralists were correct in saying that sentiment does play an essential role in human morality.[26] Contrary to the prevailing Enlightenment temper, Kant also defended our need and right to religious faith (stripped of practices he found both unnecessary and morally harmful). In fact, he defined his own monumental philosophical efforts as, above all, a program to silence forever "all objections to morality and religion" and to do it "in Socratic fashion, namely, by the clearest proof of the ignorance of the objectors" (*Pu.R.* Bxxxi). Despite his exaltation of human moral reasoning, Kant concluded that, even with our best efforts, our *ultimate* hope for the achievement of the moral destiny of the human race must lie with our religious faith, with God's salvific will and divine grace.

2
The context for Kant's moral philosophy

Throughout most of the *Groundwork,* Kant's analysis consists of a hypothetical argument: If there is such a thing as morality, then this is what it is and what it must be. For ordinary people, who do not question the validity of moral demands, that is enough. The moral skeptic, however, requires more: evidence that the demands of morality are not illusory but should be heeded.

The main problem confronting Kant arose out of the New Science developed by Galileo, Kepler, Newton, Descartes, and others. They viewed the universe as an enormous machine governed inexorably by precise physical laws that can be discovered by observation and experiment and that ultimately are mathematical in nature. Freedom and responsibility disappear from this picture of the world – and with them morality. Such a world has no meaning, no purpose, no intrinsic value; it simply *is.* If we are to have a science of human behavior, we need to give up the belief that at least part of us – our invisible "souls" – is exempt from such laws. Human beings must be regarded as nothing more than things like all other things, insofar as we are completely determined by causal laws of nature.

Kant had no desire to oppose the New Science, but to defend belief in morality (and religion), he would have to show that theoretical or scientific knowledge has limitations that prevent it from reaching all of reality. It therefore leaves room for and so does not necessarily undermine morality (or religion). Without professing either emotivism or moral relativism, Kant then could defend the claim that human agents can have motives and perform actions that are exempt from the world of causal determinism. As we shall see, he also would need to argue that the moral worth of an action does not depend on its consequences.

We therefore must take seriously Kant's statement in the preface to the second edition of his *Critique of Pure Reason:* "I have therefore found it necessary to put aside [theoretical/scientific] knowledge in order to make room for [moral and religious] faith [*Glaube*]" (*Pu.R.* Bxxx; see Bxxii, A295–96/ B352–53; *Pr.R.* 11n; *M.M.* 378).[1] Kant's moral philosophy is not an afterthought to his epistemological analyses.[2] On the contrary, he *defined* philosophy as the study of humankind and of its essential and ultimate purpose, and he identified that purpose, the "whole vocation of man," as a *moral* destiny. (See *Pu.R.* A838–40/B866–68; *Logic* 343/29.) But first he had to analyze theoretical knowledge, to explain how we come to know the world and what counts as such knowledge. Only then would he be in a position to show the limits of knowledge.

Kant's response to skepticism

The most urgent philosophical question of the seventeenth and eighteenth centuries concerned what we are rationally entitled to believe.[3] Although this question had preoccupied thinkers from the beginning of Western philosophy, it had become especially pressing before and during the Enlightenment in the writings of Descartes and of the three great British empiricists – John Locke, George Berkeley, and David Hume. All had concluded that at least much of the way the world appears to us – colors and sounds, for example – is contributed, not by the world itself, but by the manner in which our own sensory organs "take up" the world.

The most skeptical position was held by Hume, who argued that we can know *only* our own sensations. Whatever certainty we feel about anything beyond the sensations we experience is just that – a feeling. We live in a "commonly shared world" only in the sense that we apparently and happily have the same general psychological makeup and so experience similar sensations and feelings.

Kant agreed that we can learn about the world only through our senses and that our perceptual processes do radically affect the way the world appears to us. (See, e.g., *Pu.R.* A50–51/B74–76, A68–69/B92–94, B131ff; *Pr.R.* 42, 45, 107.) But he also was convinced that Hume's skepticism is unacceptable. The success of Newtonian science simply could not be explained in terms of how people subjectively happen to feel. (See *Pr.R.* 12–13, 51.) There must be some *objective* basis or "ground" that can explain how scientific theories can set out laws governing the world and why it is that science works. (See, e.g., *Pr.R* 12–13.)[4] (In general, subjective claims hold only contingently, and they tell us more about the subject or person for whom they do hold than they do about the world. By contrast, objective claims are not person dependent; they hold universally, for everyone, and they do so necessarily.) If moral judgments are not merely enunciations of subjective feelings, they too must have an objective foundation. Kant therefore set out to refute Humean skepticism about the possibility of objective human judgments, both theoretical and moral.[5]

Briefly, Kant argued that we can avoid skepticism only by embracing two doctrines. First, since sensory impressions occur independently of our will, we must attribute their ground (*Grund*) to what objectively exists outside of and independently of us. (See, e.g., *Pu.R* Bxl–xlin, B49, B274–79, A491–97/B519–26, A535–41/B563–69; *Gr.* 105–6/451.) Second, we must understand the critical roles both our perceptual and mental processes contribute to our knowledge of the world. In order to know the world – to have either scientific knowledge or the knowledge of ordinary persons (which Kant took to be a kind of crude version of the disciplined experiences of scientists in their laboratories), not only do we need to be able to perceive the world, but our reason must also contribute the rational structure of thought necessary to make those perceptions coherent.[6]

Once we become aware of how much our perceptual and mental processes contribute to our knowledge of the world, we cannot help *thinking* about that world apart from those contributions. (See, e.g., *Pr.R.* 42.) But we simply cannot know what things are like "in themselves," apart from the contributions our senses and our mind make to the way in which we know the world. (See, e.g., *M.M.* 226.) Such knowledge obviously is beyond all possible experience. So Kant called things-as-they-are-in-themselves "the noumenal" (or "intelligible" or thinkable) world, in contrast to the "phenomenal" world, that is, the world we come to know through sensory experience. (This is the basis of Kant's doctrine of the two viewpoints, which plays a crucial role in his explication and defense of morality.)

Since we can know nothing about what the world is like in itself, as far as human knowledge is concerned, both "subjectivity" and "objectivity" must be defined on the side of the knower.[7] The question now is, What enables us to have objective knowledge? One requirement, as we have just seen, is that objective empirical knowledge must have a "given," that is, contributions from the world in what Kant called the "sensible manifold of perceptions." But the structural conditions necessary for making sense out of those perceptions, and thus for the very possibility of experience of the world, cannot themselves be *based on* experience, even though we can become aware of them only by reflecting on our experience. Further, universality cannot be grounded either on our subjective desires and inclinations or on even an indefinitely large number of perceptions. Consequently, objective knowledge of the world must depend on reason and its contributions. The question now is, What are the contributions of our reason that enable us to have experience and acquire objective knowledge?

Answering that question, Kant contended, requires us to "critique" our reason (see *Pu.R* A841/B869). Positively, such a critique aims to defend the validity of theoretical reasoning against skeptical positions like that of Hume. Negatively, it aims to show why science must leave room for morality and – this actually amounts to the same thing – why the pretensions of the old metaphysics are empty (although our theoretical reason still asks ultimate questions it cannot answer; see, e.g., *Pu.R* A11/B25).

This enterprise requires a special methodology – what Kant called a "deduction." A "metaphysical deduction" begins with what is certain, our experience, and is intended to uncover those concepts or other mental structures we must presuppose as an "absolute rational necessity" both for the possibility of the experience we in fact have and for the validity of scientific laws. (See *Pu.R.* B38; *Pr.R.* 11n.) A deduction is "transcendental" that requires us introspectively to step back, as it were, from all our particular experiences in order to defend the right of our understanding to make such contributions so that we can *have* experience and knowledge of the world. These contributions of reason cannot *be based* on but, rather, must "transcend" experience that reason makes possible.[8]

13

A priori and a posteriori knowledge claims

What we gain from this transcendental analysis is knowledge learned a priori, that is, "not knowledge independent of this or that experience, but knowledge absolutely independent of all experience" (*Pu.R.* B2–3; see A840–43/B868–71).[9] So, Kant writes, "We can know a priori of things only what we ourselves [our reason] put into them" (*Pu.R.* Bxviii). By contrast, empirical knowledge is knowledge possible only a posteriori, that is, through experience.[10] A priori judgments are characterized by necessity and strict universality, while a posteriori judgments are not; "experience teaches us that a thing is so and so, but not that it cannot be otherwise." (See *Pu.R.* B3–4, A734/B672, A840/B868.)

Much of Kant's *Critique of Pure Reason* is devoted to what he calls "transcendental logic": the analysis of the a priori contributions of our mind – concepts and rules – that constitute the "formal conditions of experience," that is, which enable us to have experience and know objects of experience (*Pu.R.* B284; see A52/B76, A56/B80–81; *Pr.R.* 42).[11] In his Critical writings Kant was led to take such a radical position about the extent of the contributions of reason that he himself likened it to the Copernican revolution in astronomy. Copernicus had made the revolutionary suggestion that the explanation of the observed motion of celestial bodies should be sought "not in the heavenly bodies, but in the spectator" (*Pu.R.* Bxxiin; see Bxvi–vii). In a far more sweeping claim, Kant held that *all* objects we can know must conform to our mind, rather than, as had always been thought, our mind conforming itself to those objects. (See *Pu.R.* Bxvi–xxiii, xxiin.)

Kant called his position "transcendental idealism"; and it still may seem implausible to readers today, for he argued that the order we "find" in the world originates not with the world but with our own mind. (See, e.g., *Pu.R.* A490–97/B518–25.) Kant understood how his readers might react: "However exaggerated and absurd it may sound, to say that the understanding is itself the source of the laws of nature, and so of its formal unity, such an assertion is none the less correct, and is in keeping with the object to which it refers, namely, experience" (*Pu.R* A127). What we may naively think of as laws of nature to be discovered "out there" in space and time are actually rules of our own understanding, "synthesizing," as Kant puts it, our perceptions. Without this organizing framework, we would have no coherent experiences. Instead, the world would seem to us to be, in William James's words, "one great blooming, buzzing confusion."[12]

Of themselves the categories and rules originating in reason are "empty," without content. What gives them "content" depends on the subject matter involved. (See *Gr.* i–iii/387–88.) The various theoretical sciences (then called natural philosophy) deal with what is the case and what does happen – nature and the laws of nature. What is required, as we have seen, to give them content (actual referents in the world) is for us to have sensations of them (or of "matter"). By contrast, practical thinking (ethics or moral philosophy) concerns what "ought to happen," and its objects are those actions we *should* perform and ends we *should* adopt, even if we in fact do not (*Gr.,* iii/388; see also 62/426–27; *Pu.R.* A633/B661, A840/B868; *Pr.R.* 14–15, 120; *Lect.* 243–44/1–2). So the objects of moral thinking cannot be based on what does happen but must be identified by reason; it alone is able to determine what ought to happen.[13]

Both theoretical and practical thinking employ concepts and principles or rules by which we rationally organize our thinking, and so both have a systematic foundational part, which Kant also calls "metaphysics." (See *Pu.R.* A841/B869; *Gr.* i–iii/387–388; *Pr.R.* 45; *M.M.* 215–18, 375.) The metaphysics of nature and the metaphysics of morals each consists of the basic laws for their respective kinds of objects. These laws, as Kant points out, are "synthetic" statements because they contain logically distinct concepts. But they also are laws because they hold necessarily and universally – characteristics that only our reason can contribute and that can be known only a priori. Understanding what this means and why it was crucial for Kant to defend this characterization of the laws both of nature and of morality is the burden of the next section.

Can there be synthetic a priori judgments?

Kant's question "How are synthetic a priori judgments possible?" sets what is arguably the most important task of his entire philosophy. But before we examine exactly what Kant is asking here, it should be noted that even asking this question presupposes such knowledge, and that in itself was a highly controversial claim.[14] It looked too much like the discredited view that we can learn about the world merely by thinking about it, a claim that, as Kant well knew, David Hume already had demolished.

Kant understood Hume as holding, in effect, that there are only two kinds of meaningful judgments.[15] Analytic claims such as "All bachelors are unmarried males" are true if an analysis of the concepts involved shows that the predicate concept enunciates (at least part of) the meaning of the subject concept. We do not appeal to experience to confirm or falsify analytic judgments. Their rightness must be confirmed by reflection, that is, in an a priori fashion. If they are true they also are necessarily and universally true, for their truth can be tested merely by the principle of noncontradiction, which underlies them. (See *Pu.R.* A718/B746; *Proleg.* 267.) They can be true even if the universe contained no referents for them (such as bachelors). But this also means that they only explicate concepts and tell us nothing about the *world.* Kant wrote that "analytic judgments really teach us nothing more about the object than what the concept we have of it already contains; they do not extend our knowledge beyond the concept of the object, but only clarify the object" (*Pu.R.* A736/B764; see also A6–7, B2–3 and 10–11; *Proleg.* 266–68; *Logic* 63, 111).

Synthetic judgments, on the other hand, are ampliative. They do inform us about the world by asserting a real connection between logically distinct objects or events, such as "This book was written in Columbia, South Carolina." In the Humean view the truth of all such claims can be learned only a posteriori, through either personal or vicarious experience with the world. True assertions about matters of fact offer us information that is only contingently true, so that any generalities we infer from experience can be, at best, only probabilities. Claims about specific causal relations are not analytically true, not logical relations (as the rationalist tradition from Plato on had held); they too can be learned only from experience. (See *Pu.R.* B3–4 and 10–11.) Since that is so, Hume held that the "necessity" we commonly think we find in causal connections is groundless. Our belief in necessary relations between different existing things must therefore be only a matter of the way in which we have been accustomed to *feeling* under certain conditions. (See *Pu.R* A760–69/B788–89; *Pr.R* 50–51.)

Because this analysis can be extended to every field of human knowledge, Kant concluded Hume's account makes human experience not only inexplicable but impossible, and Hume's stance must be rejected. If all synthetic claims could be known only a posteriori, we would be completely unable to explain the necessity and universality we find not only in pure mathematics, such as geometry, and in scientific laws but also in our ordinary moral judgments. (See, e.g., *Pu.R.* B4–5, 19–20, 127–28, A718/B746.) The claims made in these disciplines are not all merely analytic, yet their lawlike quality also means they cannot be merely inductive generalizations based on experience.[16]

One of the main philosophical tasks for Kant's "Copernican revolution" in the theory of human knowledge, then, was to explain and defend the possibility of synthetic judgments known independently of experience, that is, a priori, and their rightful use by both theoretical and moral-practical reason. (See *Pr.R* 53–54.) Defending morality, Kant wrote, is the more difficult task, for no one seriously doubts the existence of science, even if they do not understand how or why it works, whereas no appeal to experience can support the validity of moral claims. (See *Pr.R* 46, 91.)

Finally, without synthetic judgments known a priori, we would have to do what Kant considered to be impossible, namely, give up the "metaphysical quest" in the traditional sense of the search for ultimate reality. (See *Pu.R.* A842/B870; *Pr.R.* 52–53.) Kant was convinced that as rational beings we simply cannot be satisfied by partial, conflicting, or only conditionally necessary explanations and goals. We have an unavoidable, rational need for absolutes. We cannot avoid wondering about our own true nature, about the origin of the universe, and about an ultimate ground that might explain everything. We find ourselves thinking of the universe as what has come to be called "a great chain of being." Our reason inherently longs for complete and ultimate answers, for what transcends the temporal and is absolute, universal, necessary, and final – a self-existent systematic unity or totality, what Kant called "the unconditioned." (See, e.g., *Pu.R.* A305/B362, A322/B379, A326–28/B382–85, A645/B673, A647/B675, A681/B709, A797/B825, A804/B832, A832/B860; *Gr.* 127–28/463; *Pr.R.* 107; *Cr.J.* 401.)

Yet this search may never be successful, because the answers that can fully

satisfy our curiosity lie beyond all our possible sensory expe
A333/B390, A565/B593).[17] The old way of doing metaphysics -
about the nature of ultimate reality on the basis of our experien
world – clearly needed to be rejected. (See, e.g., *Pr.R.* 15, 42; (
41.) It yielded only the "dialectical illusion" of knowledge. (See *Pu.*
B397, A642/B670.)[18] Unless we are content with empty claims or ir
mysticism, we apparently need to see things from God's point of viev
speak, which of course we cannot do.

Nonetheless, as Lewis White Beck wrote, Kant

. . . was in love with metaphysics, and he never was really faithless to her; we "ret
to metaphysics as to a beloved one with whom we have had a quarrel" [*Pu.R.* A8\
B878]. So deep-rooted in man is this metaphysical urge – rooted not just in huma
nature, but in the very structure of his reason itself – that it is as little to be expected,
Kant tells us, that men will cease to breathe in order to escape the dangers of getting
infections. Kant could not believe that a faculty like pure reason could have been
made a part of man's endowment if it had had no proper function.[19]

As a consequence, underlying all of Kant's other philosophical aims was
the reintroduction of metaphysics – but what Beck calls a "practical-dogmatic
metaphysics." (See *Proleg.* 366–67; *Pr.R.* 5, 54–55; *M.M.* 376.)[20] For, Kant
argued, metaphysics must lie behind and guide the advance of all philosophic
inquiries. (See *M.M.* 376–77.) Since Kant held that the supreme (though
not the total) goal for human beings is moral in nature, all of his philosophy,
including his metaphysical quest, is aimed finally at the promotion of that
moral goal. (See, e.g., *Pu.R.* A801/B829.)

Ideas of reason

One contribution of reason (*Vernunft*) is especially important to Kant's ethical
theory. As we have just seen, our reason is essentially purposive and, whether
we seek truth or goodness, continues to pursue ultimate and absolute reality,
which it identifies through what Kant calls "Ideas of reason." (See *Pu.R*
A310–32/B366–89.)[21] Ideas of reason are transcendental concepts because
they refer to what transcends all our experience – what is perfect, unlimited,
and unconditioned. By contrast, nature always appears to us in limited chains
of causally conditioned events. Ideas, therefore, cannot originate in experinc
or be verified by it. We can find neither a perfect nor even an adequa
example of any Idea in any possible experience. (See, e.g., *Pu.R.* A311/B3f
A320/B377, A326–27/B382–84n2, A533/B561, A571/B599, A845/B873;
100/447, 120–21/459; *Pr.R.* 47; *M.M.* 221; *Anthr.* 199–200.) As we shall
however, for our moral purposes we also may and must regard some a/
and actions as incomplete and imperfect embodiments of those Ideas
Pu.R. A315/B371–72, A328/B384–85; *Pr.R* 47.)

Since they cannot be generated from any empirical information, th
tions must be constructed by reason alone. Reason does not presupp
any of the referents of these Ideas actually exist; they are only i/

enable us to *think* about, as in geometry, perfect circles and perfectly straight lines. (See, e.g., *Pu.R* A576–78/B604–6.) That is why Kant calls them "merely Ideas" (*Pu.R.* A328/B384, A644/B674; see *Gr.* 108/452; *Pr.R.* 124). Even so, the limitations of theoretical thinking prevent us from categorically denying that there are or can be objects corresponding to such Ideas. (See *Pur.R.* A320/B377; *Pr.R.* 132.) Because these Ideas are not self-contradictory, however transcendent (beyond all possible experience) their possible objects may be, we are still able at least to *think* about them, using the categories of the understanding to define at least negatively the nature of those referents. (See *Pr.R.* 127n.)

As we shall see in Chapter 8, some of these Ideas are required for scientific inquiry – to help guide our efforts to enlarge our knowledge of the world. (See *Pu.R.* A311/B368, A327/B383–84, A644/B672.) Yet those same Ideas are all theoretically "empty" in the sense of lying beyond all possible experience. So they themselves remain "problematic": We must use them (if only "regulatively") when we think theoretically, but we can neither comprehend them nor show that they have any objective validity, that is, real referents. (See, e.g., *Pu.R* A254/B310, A323/B380, A338–39/B396–97, A641/B669, A644/B672, A663/B691, A671–73/B699–701, A701/B729; *Gr.* 108/452, 122–26/459–62; *Pr.R.* 3, 97, 120, 133, 144–45.)[22] In fact, all efforts to do either only generate contradictions within reason, showing that any such project is ill-conceived and should be abandoned.

What is important for our purposes now is the crucial role Ideas of reason play in Kant's analysis of morality. Since moral reasoning is concerned with the way we *ought* to behave, our moral life is defined by a whole range of standards or ideals or models of perfection, none of which is or can be found (or "exhibited") in the world of theoretical experience. (See *Pu.R.* A548/B576, A569/B597; *Gr.* 36/412, 121/459.) That is, they are not the sort of data scientists might come upon and measure in their research; they are not things we can see or touch or taste. They are not scientific names of classes of individuals in the world but norms on which we are to *act*. So indispensable are they to morality, Kant writes, that denying that they have any possible validity means, in effect, denying morality itself. (See *Cr.J.* 447, 471, 531, 553.)

For example, to be moral agents, we must have a free will, or what Kant calls "pure practical reason," which will also lead him to try to analyze and defend the Ideas of freedom and autonomy.[23] His explication of human morality also requires him to use the Ideas of practical lawfulness,[24] morally obligatory ends,[25] persons,[26] the good will, duty, holiness, and virtue.[27] There are still other Ideas of reason essential to his moral theory: the "kingdom of ends,"[28] personal immortality and God,[29] and the total, highest end for human beings.[30]

To understand Kant's moral theory we also need to understand his philosophy of history,[31] his political philosophy,[32] and his philosophy of religion,[33] and there we encounter still other Ideas of reason, such as history (or Nature)

as a teleological process, an original social compact, the ideal (republican) form of government, perpetual peace, divine providence, and grace.

All particular moral norms, such as friendship, truthfulness, and honesty, also are Ideas of reason. (See, e.g., *Pu.R.* A315/B371–72, A569/B597; *M.M.* 469.) Even if there has never been, say, a genuine instance of friendship, Kant writes, our reason still requires us to use the Idea of friendship as an ideal or standard against which we are "to estimate and to measure" how we should act so as to be a friend. (See *Pr.R.* A570/B598; *Pr.R.* 127n; *M.M.* 469–70.)

Briefly, the argument (or "transcendental deduction") Kant uses to justify the use of these Ideas of reason begins with and rests on his claim that the ultimate law of morality appears in our awareness as an undeniable "fact of reason." The reality of that law guarantees the legitimacy of our adopting and using *whatever* concepts are absolutely necessary for us to function as agents subject to that law – whether those concepts refer to conditions necessary for the possibility of moral reasoning itself or of its objects. (See, e.g., *Pr.R.* 132, 142n, 143.)[34] In fact, Kant claims that our belief in the realities that the Ideas of God, freedom, and immortality name has a more secure basis than our acceptance of scientific claims, for the moral law is irrefutable whereas the observations scientific theories are meant to explain often depend on those theories, which are reformable.[35]

Questions of methodology

Kant used two interrelated and, he thought, mutually supportive methods to understand the nature of morality. (See, e.g., *Gr.* xiv/392; *M.M.* 403, 412–13.) The first, the "analytic" or "regressive" method (which in effect involves one or more deductions), begins with ordinary moral consciousness and consists in exhibiting those concepts and principles we must presuppose for the possibility of the moral awareness we have and the moral judgments we make – and in defending the validity of using those concepts and principles. (See *Pr.R.* 91.) In the first chapter of the *Groundwork,* for example, Kant begins with the judgment of ordinary people that nothing is superior to good moral character (having "a good will"). On the basis of his analysis of this judgment, he concludes that good moral character for human agents must consist in their acting dutifully because it is their duty. That in turn leads to the "Principle of Autonomy," which he argues is the only possible ultimate practical norm they may use. The second method, which Kant uses in his second *Critique,* is based on definitions and principles arrived at through his previous analyses of the contents of ordinary moral reasoning. It involves systematically (or "synthetically") clarifying what morality must be to be morality and then in defending the claim that human beings are moral agents.

Whichever method we use, when discussing the derivation of particular duties, Kant described the only correct philosophical method this way: "The reasons must *proceed* in *one series,* as *ground* and *consequent,* to a conclusive reason, and only in this way can they constitute a proof" (*M.M.* 403–4). When we feel a need to pile arguments on one another, he went on, we can be sure that we either are confused or have not yet got the argument straight. But in none of his books did Kant himself offer a single *and* complete account of his analysis of human morality, from "ground" to "consequent." What I have tried to do in this book, then, is to present his entire moral theory in a single line of development, showing how one doctrine leads to others. What this will also show is that Kant's moral theory as a whole has an internal coherence that his method of presentation may conceal.

In Part I, "The Nature of Morality," I shall begin with an introductory exposition of Kant's "theory of human action," that is, a general analysis of those beings and events to which we ordinarily think we can apply moral predicates. Doing this will help to avoid misreading him later on.[36] I then shall systematically contrast his analyses of the two different norms by which an agent or an action may be assessed – prudence and morality. In this section I also shall examine Kant's defense of the possibility and the reality of human morality against the claims of mechanistic Newtonian science. In the concluding chapter of this section I shall set out Kant's arguments for holding that morality and its interests are preeminent over all other interests and goals we may have.

In Part II, "The Moral Norm for Persons," I shall explain Kant's analysis of moral motivation and of good moral character, with special attention to his notion of "dutifulness" and his doctrines concerning the role of moral emotions in human moral life.

In Part III, "The Norm for Moral Judgment," I shall examine in detail the general rationale for Kant's famous Categorical Imperative, the meaning of each of its three formulas, and the application of that norm to human moral problems. The discussion of the third formula in Chapter 15 will include Kant's doctrine concerning the meaning of human life in terms of its ultimate highest end.

In the final section of the book, "Kant on History, Politics, and Religion," I shall show how Kant introduced a historical dimension into his analysis of human morality, and I shall examine the connections between his political, religious, and moral views.

There are also two appendixes. The first presents a discussion of Kant's doctrine of the two viewpoints,[37] and the second briefly examines his views concerning moral education.

I
The nature of morality

3
The nature of human action

We do not think that every kind of agent or every kind of behavior should be appraised in specifically moral language. We do not, for example, make moral judgments about chemical reactions or animal behavior. Our moral judgments, therefore, presuppose that there is something special about human beings that justifies our thinking of at least most of them as "persons" in the full sense, that is, as agents "whose actions can be imputed to" them so that they can be held responsible for what they do (*M.M.* 223; see *Rel.* 32–34/ 27–30). An adequate moral theory must set out an analysis of what that something is.

Within the rationalistic tradition of Western philosophy that distinctive feature of our agency has always been taken to be our ability to reason practically, that is, our ability both to deliberate about how to act and then to act on the basis of our deliberation. (See *M.M* 223, 227.) But not all our practical thinking is specifically moral in nature, and for this reason any analysis of moral reasoning needs to be preceded by a more general account of practical thinking. This is called a "theory of action," and it provides the conceptual framework within which a moral theory can be developed.

So much of Kant's moral writing consists of either an analysis or a defense of our ability to reason practically that it might seem it should be an easy task to set out his more general theory of action. But Kant himself explicitly refused to offer such a theory and, in fact, held that he should not be criticized for not doing so. (See *Pr.R* 9n.) He wished to avoid what he saw as a fundamental mistake made by other authors such as Christian Wolff, who, he thought, offered a theory of action that by its excessive dependence on empirical information, corrupted any analysis of morality following it. (See, e.g., *Gr.* ix–x/390; *Pr.R.* 9n.) But Kant still needed to *use* a theory of human action, which he gradually developed during the course of his moral philosophy. That theory of action can be pieced together but only from remarks scattered throughout his writings, often in footnotes.[1]

Although Kant's theory of action is developed only within his moral theory, it nonetheless is crucial to set it out now. One of the reasons why Kant's ethical theory is so difficult to understand and so easily subject to misinterpretations is precisely that he did not first provide a clear context for his later, more particular claims about the nature of human morality.[2]

Stated in general terms, Kant's view of the nature of human agency agrees fairly well with our "commonsense" convictions as well as with the doctrines held by most philosophers before Kant. As we saw in the preceding chapter,

relate to the world in different ways. We do so theoretically, as spec-
~~~~vhen we seek only to *understand* the world, and we do so practically,
~~ ~~~~~s, when we try to *change* the world.[3] According to Kant, then, human
beings considered in the latter way, as agents, (1) have the power to act (2)
so as to aim at goals of their own choosing (3) according to rules (or "maxims")
they themselves have adopted.

In his discussions of human agency Kant could not completely avoid using
terms also used by psychology, but he made it clear that he intended to engage
in a conceptual analysis only – not an empirical, psychological study. (See
Pr.R 9n.) He was eager to be as independent as possible of psychology, for
to the degree that it aspires to be an empirical science, psychology necessarily
begs the most important questions about the nature and possibility of morality.
To be a science within the Newtonian tradition, psychology must regard all
human conduct as causally determined, and this denial of freedom automatically entails the denial of the possibility of morality as we ordinarily think
of it. Kant therefore insisted that, insofar as he had to use a theory of action,
it must be ethically neutral: It must not contain definitions or descriptions
that rule out ahead of time even the possibility that we are moral agents.

Kant also believed that we need to understand what a moral agent is and
must be before we can appreciate what is involved in defending the claim
that we actually are moral beings. His analysis as presented in this chapter
(and in Chapters 4–6 as well), therefore, needs to be understood as a hypothetical claim: *If* we are moral agents, we must be able to act only on the
basis of our own thinking; we must have the power Kant called "pure practical
reason."

The exercise of causal power

The idea of "agency in general" is broader than the notion of human agency,
and the most fundamental notion in agency in general is that of causal power
(*Kraft*). In his first *Critique,* Kant wrote that the concept of action (*Handlung*)
is derived from the concept of causality (*Kausalität*), since an action consists
in the exercise of causal power or force by an agent to effect some change or
alteration (*Wechsel*) in the world. (See *Pu.R* A204–6/B249–52; also A82/
B108.)

Since (as David Hume had already pointed out) we do not see causal power
itself but only its impact, perceived changes in the world are not actions but
the effect or result of actions. So, Kant wrote, "All alteration is thus only
possible through a continuous action of the causality which, so far as it is
uniform, is entitled a moment. The alteration does not consist of these mo-
ments, but is generated by them as their effect" (*Pu.R.* A208–9/B254).[4]

Always goal directed

Whether rational or not, any agent *is* an agent precisely by virtue of possessing
the ability to exercise causal power. (See *Pr.R* 9n.) The actions of all nonrational agents are themselves caused by other, temporally prior causes. The

actions of nonrational living agents (e.g., animals) are simply reactions to sensuous stimuli. (See *Gr.* 122n/460n.)

What makes human agency distinctive, Kant wrote, is our ability to act on the basis of reasons, that is, our ability to conceptualize goals, whether they be external or internal states of affairs, and act so as to achieve them. (See *Gr.* 36/412, 82/437, 97/446; *M.M.* 357.) Kant defined the kind of causality belonging to rational beings so far as they are rational as the "capacity of being, by means of one's representations, the cause of the objects of those representations" (*M.M.* 356; see also 211). He referred to it interchangeably as "practical reason" (*praktische Vernunft*), "the faculty of desire" (*das Begehrungsvermögen*), and "the will" (*der Wille* and *die Willkür*). (See *Gr.* 36/412, 97/446; *Pr.R.* 9n; *M.M.* 211.)[5]

Before we act, Kant held, we must always take an interest *in* something – he called it the "agent's end" (*Zweck*) or "object" (*Gegenstand*) or the "matter" (*das Material*) of an action. (See *Gr.* 122n/460n; *Pr.R.* 24–25, 89.) Since all specifically human actions are goal directed, it is a function of practical reasoning to identify and define the goal of acting. We regard something as a goal or "practical good" that "is to be made real by our will . . . one that is possible through action" (*Pr.R.* 113).[6]

As we shall see in the next two chapters, Kant held that we have two general kinds of practical goods or ends: natural or prudential goods, based on our desires and learned from experience; and ends that are morally good in the sense of being either morally permissible or morally obligatory. These latter we define and project only on the basis of our own thinking and we regard them as goods we ought to recognize, whether or not we want to.

Kant also argued that the morality of an action cannot be *based* on goals or ends of *any* kind, for, in his analysis, doing so destroys the very possibility of morality. (See *Gr.* 128/463.) Having renounced a precise theory of action by which to control his vocabulary, however, his manner of stating this claim (as, for example, in *Gr.* 40/415 and 64/427) can be and often has been misinterpreted to mean that morally good action requires us to act without *any* end in view.[7] So it may not be possible to insist too strongly now that, in Kant's own words, "there can be no will without an end in view" (*T&P* 279n). "It is certainly undeniable that every volition must have an object and therefore a material," he wrote, for "in the absence of all reference to an end no determination of the will can take place in man" (*Pr.R.* 34 and *Rel.* 4/4; see *Gr.* 63/427).

As the details of Kant's moral theory gradually emerge, it will become clear that *no* idea is more important both to the theory and to the systematic unity of his entire philosophical enterprise than his insistence on the essential purposiveness of *all* rational activity. Reason, he wrote, has its own immanent or inherent "interests." He in fact defined philosophy as "the science of the relation of all knowledge to the essential ends of human reason" (*Pu.R* A839/B867).

Some of Kant's clearest and strongest statements about the goal-directed nature of practical reason in particular occur in *The Metaphysics of Morals:*

No free action is possible unless the agent also intends an end (which is the matter of choice [Willkür]) [389]. . . . An *end* [*Zweck*] is an *object* of free choice [*Wille*], the thought of which determines the power of choice [*Willkür*] to an action by which the object is produced [384]. . . . Every action, therefore, has its end [385; see 381]. . . . The power to set an end – any end whatsoever – is the characteristic of humanity (as distinguished from animality) [392]. [As a rational agent,] man has, in his reason, something more than [mere animals] and can set his own ends. [434]

To summarize, then, according to Kant rational human action is *always* intentional. It involves our deliberately acting so as to bring into being (or prevent) some state of affairs (object or end) of which we are aware and in which we have taken an interest.

Kant repeatedly defined practical goals as "possible," not just in contrast with "actual" but in contrast to "impossible," thereby implying that it is irrational for us to try to pursue unattainable goals. (See, e.g., *Gr.* 41/415, 44–45/417; *T&P* 280; *Anthr.* 236.) This does not mean he thought that we have so much power that we always can achieve the changes we intend in the world, or that we always can do so by ourselves. We frequently need the help of others, and our intentions, which are regarded by Kant as actions, can be and frequently are frustrated, for we do not have full control over the world and so over the outcome of our actions. What we always have control over, however, is the way in which we form those intentions themselves, and what we must always believe when we pursue a goal is that it somehow is attainable.

The presence of desires

Centuries before, Aristotle had written: "Thought alone moves nothing," and he then went on to define choice as "thoughtful desire" or, alternatively, "desiring thought" (*Nicomachean Ethics* 6.2.1139a36). As he saw it, we are agents only because we can both think *and* desire. Although Kant is commonly interpreted as not agreeing at all with Aristotle, here he is at least very close to Aristotle when he holds that human agents will act only when and because they first are *interested* in some goal. (See *Pu.R.* B166a.)[8] Because the notion of "being interested in" implies not just the presence of an impulse but a consciousness *of* something *as* a possible goal, Kant holds that an interest (*Interesse*) "can never be attributed to a being which lacks reason" (*Pr.R.* 79; see *Gr.* 122n/459n).

Without a systematic theory of action, Kant does not always clearly delineate the relations between "interests," "feelings," "desires," and "motives." This is extremely unfortunate, for these are just the concepts he will use shortly to draw a crucial distinction underlying virtually everything else in his analysis of human morality.

As Kant uses the terms, "feeling" in a general sense (*Gefühl*) signifies a person's capacity to experience attraction and aversion, pleasure and pain (see *M.M.* 211), whereas "feelings" (*Gefühle*) refer to particular sensations experienced at some definite time. Sometimes, as in aesthetic appreciation, we simply enjoy contemplating an object. But, Kant argues, since practical

26

interest always is aimed at attaining or avoiding something, we humans will not act at all in the complete absence of all feelings, whether they be temporary surges of desires ("agitations" – *Affekte*) or more settled emotions ("inclinations" – *Neigungen*) (see, e.g., *Gr.* 38n/413n; *Cr.J.* 189, 228; *Anthr.* 251). "All that is practical," Kant writes, "so far as it contains motives [*Bewegungsgründe/Triebfedern*], relate to feelings" (Pu.R. A15/B29).[9] For us actually to exercise our agency so as to pursue what we see as good in some sense or to avoid what we see as bad in some sense, our will (*Willkür*) must therefore be a "faculty of desire" (*Begehrungsvermögen*). (See *Gr.* 38n/413n; *M.M.* 211, 399.)

Since we normally are not compelled by our feelings, it is our choice whether we act on the desires we experience. (See *Rel.* 24/19.) When we do, Kant identifies our faculty of desire with appetite (*Begierde*) and calls our interest "an interest of inclination," for we are motivated to act by a desire for what promises us pleasure or the avoidance of pain. (See *M.M* 211; *Anthr.* 251.) In this sense, "an end is always the object of an inclination" (*Rel.* 6n/6). The anticipation of pleasure (or absence of pain) is our incentive or motive (*Triebfeder*) for acting.

Kant now makes a radically novel claim: There are, he argues, some feelings that are caused entirely by our own reasoning, by our will as a "higher faculty of desire." (See, e.g., *Pr.R.* 62.) We then take an interest *in* acting without acting *from* a merely sensuous motive; and only then do we have a distinctively *moral* interest – that of a "sensuously disinterested reason" (*Pr.R.* 62). In Kant's analysis, there still must be a feeling side to practice. So that we will *care* about acting as we should, we need to feel respect for the demands of morality. But this sentiment of respect itself rests finally and only on our prior recognition of the law of our own reason, the moral law (*Gr.* 38n/413n; *M.M.* 211–13, 407).[10]

Kant's claim here can be stated in terms of our having either two kinds of interests or two kinds of feelings. In having prudential interests, we have only a "mediate interest" in any particular action; we are interested in its consequences (for example, the promise of pleasure) rather than in the action itself.[11] By contrast, in morally good action, we take an "immediate interest" in the action itself as being the right way to act, regardless of its consequences. (See *Gr.* 122n/460n.)

In terms of feelings, desires are *merely* "pathological" or sensuous (or natural or nonmoral) when we pursue what we have found on the basis of experience to be *simply* pleasurable.[12] Our anticipation of pleasure precedes and motivates our action; we think of something as "good" only because we first experience a desire for it. The expectation, say, of pleasurable feelings can and often does occur independently of and prior to our considering any moral questions about how we should behave. Moral feelings, on the other hand, are generated by our consciousness of having moral obligations. (See, e.g., *M.M* 399.) Since they are felt somatically, they are also sensuous, but not merely so, for they occur only *after* and *because* we first have recognized that we are bound by the law of morality (see *Pr.R.* 59n). So it is that law that finally is our motive or incentive. As we shall see in Chapter 10, moral sentiments not only can motivate us to act as we ought; they also can follow on our recognition that we have acted morally rightly or wrongly. (See *M.M.* 378, 399.)

Without further explanation, the distinction set out here may not seem very clear, and examining it in detail will be part of the burden of the following chapters. What is at stake can be put this way: The manner in which the relationship is formed between a person's will and feelings determines for Kant – as it did, albeit in a different fashion, for moral philosophers before him – the moral quality of that person's character.

Practical rules

In his *Critique of Pure Reason* Kant defined reason as preeminently "the faculty of principles" or rules (*Pu.R.* A299/B356; see also *M.M.* 214). When used practically, reasoning is a power to formulate and act on principles of conduct. It is, in fact, just this power, Kant argues, that sets us apart from the rest of creation: "Everything in nature works in accordance with laws. Only a rational being has the power to act *in accordance with his idea* of laws – that is, in accordance with principles – and only so has he a will. . . . the will is nothing but practical reason" (*Gr.* 36/412; see also 97–98/446; *Pr.R.* 15, 32, 59–60, 125).[13]

The first function of practical reasoning is to identify possible goals to be attained, and the second consists in a union of reason and emotions causing us to take an interest in goals. The third function of practical reasoning is to form and adopt rules for achieving such goals in certain situations. Kant describes the will as a power to act on rules it itself has framed and made its own. (See *Gr.* 53/422, 63/428; *Pr.R.* 19, 27; *M.M.* 231.) If we find our rules are correct, we then tend to make them general policies or principles (*Grundsätze*) to be acted on when appropriate. Kant calls practical rules we either are considering adopting or actually have adopted our "maxims": "A *maxim* is a subjective principle of action [that] contains a practical rule determined by reason in accordance with the conditions of the subject . . . it thus is a principle on which the subject *acts*" (*Gr.* 51n/421n; see also 15n/400n).[14] Since Kant so frequently writes about them, it is important to understand that there is nothing mysterious about maxims. Maxims simply articulate an agent's intentions or disposition (*Gesinnung*), that is, the rules a person adopts and on which a person actually acts, unless, of course, that person is acting nonrationally, say, absentmindedly or while delirious. Kant does not claim that a rational agent either always does or always must have an explicit maxim consciously in mind while acting. But an agent's maxim normally could be stated by that agent if he or she were asked to set out the reason for acting in a particular way.

Since all rational actions are goal directed, Kant calls all our maxims "material" rules, in the sense that "every maxim contains an end" (or matter or object), at least implicitly (*M.M.* 395). Generally speaking, therefore, we tend to presume that a person intends to pursue a particular end when he adopts and acts on a maxim appropriate for attaining that end. Every maxim "represents a possible action as good," but prudential maxims represent an "action as a *means* to an effect which is its purpose," and moral maxims represent a possible action as *good in itself*, "without reference to . . . any further end" (*Gr.* 39/414, *Pr.R.* 20, and *Gr.* 39–40/414–15; see *Gr.* 88/441; *Pr.R.* 31).[15]

Contingently rational agents such as we humans need not and do not always act rationally. We can and do act nonrationally to some degree or other when we act impulsively, passionately, carelessly, absentmindedly, and so on. Consequently, *all* practical rules (both prudential and moral rules) appear to us at least tacitly as commands or imperatives, telling us how we should act in order to act rationally. (See *Gr.* 8/397, 15n/400n, 36–39/412–14, 122/460; *Pr.R.* 20; *Lect.* 245–46/3–4.)[16]

The task ahead

So far, Kant seems to offer us a "commonsense" view that, though incomplete and in need of elaboration, makes perfect sense. Human action consists in a person's taking an interest in and causing changes in the world for the sake of some end he sees as good. Our acting is guided by our reasoning, which both identifies the end of the action and sets forth a rule for attaining it. All such rules appear to us as rational constraints against any tendency we may have to act irrationally. Kant's complete theory is, of course, far more complex and sophisticated than this introduction. It may be helpful, therefore, to indicate in a general way the route he will follow.

Kant believed that the main task for a moral philosopher is to clarify what everyone already knows, if only in a confused way; and what needs clarification above all else, he thought, is the great difference between moral and nonmoral (or prudential) reasoning. He harshly criticizes all other moral philosophers for not making this distinction, for their failure to do so in effect had helped to subvert morality. (See *Gr.* viii–ix/390, 22–24/404–5, 30–32/409–10; *Pr.R.* 24.) Large portions of his moral writings are directed to drawing the distinction between prudence and morality as sharply as possible and to setting out his reasons for doing so. The next two chapters, therefore, will be concerned with Kant's analyses, first of prudence and then of morality, and of the differences between them.

Before going on, however, it may be helpful to mention a peculiarity about Kant's way of presenting his views that can create difficulties for readers trying to keep the line of reasoning clear. There are two questions that, it can be argued, should be considered separately before a unified theory is constructed: What makes an action morally right? And, what makes an agent morally good? That these questions can be considered to be logically distinct is shown by the fact that we can conceive of a morally evil person performing a morally acceptable action (e.g., paying a debt) as long as his immoral purposes are served by his doing so. We also can conceive of a morally good person mistakenly believing he is acting rightly when in fact he is not.

Kant believed we can make this distinction, for he thought there is an objective nature to types of actions such as telling the truth and making false promises. Within his own theory, they can be described and assessed as morally acceptable or not, independent of the motivation leading an individual to do them. This is the force of distinctions he makes between "merely legal" and genuinely moral actions, and between "juridical" and "ethical" duties. (See, e.g., *M.M.* 214; *Lect.* 274–75/36–37.)

But Kant also often thinks of an "action" as a person's intention rather than as the person's behavior and, when he does, he describes actions so as to include the agent's end and motive.[17] For example, instead of saying that moral *agents* act prudentially when they act so as to satisfy their desires, Kant typically writes that all prudential *actions* are done out of inclinations of one kind or another and all moral *actions* are done out of the motive of dutifulness. Likewise, in the first chapter of the *Groundwork* he sets out to state the supreme principle for morally right *actions,* but he does so by analyzing the nature of morally good *character,* including a brief discussion of the moral incentive of respect for morality. (See Kant's review of his argument in *Gr.* 81–86/437–39.) Consequently, a person reading Kant can become very confused about just what question Kant is addressing. John Stuart Mill must have had this tendency of Kant's in mind when he later praised Utilitarian writers for "affirming that the motive has nothing to do with the morality of the action, though much with the worth of the agent" (*Utilitarianism,* Chapter 2).

4
Prudence: taking care of our own interests

We human beings are not self-sufficient. We have a wide variety of needs we must meet not only to survive but also to lend quality to our lives. Doing so is a "problem imposed upon us by our own finite nature" (*Pr.R.* 25). Kant writes:

Man is a being of needs, so far as he belongs to the world of sense, and to this extent his reason certainly has an inescapable responsibility from the side of his sensuous nature to attend to its interest and to form practical maxims with a view to the happiness of this and, where possible, of a future life. (*Pr.R.* 61; see also 61–62; *Gr.* 12/399)

By "happiness" (*Glückseligkeit*) Kant means our well-being in general, conceived ideally as the maximum satisfaction as a whole of our needs and desires as rational but finite beings – and our enjoyment of and contentment with such a life now and in the future, along with a reasonable confidence that it will continue. (See *Gr.* 1/393, 12/399, 23/405, 42/416, 46/418; *Pr.R.* 22, 61, 124; *M.M.* 387, 480; *Pu.R.* A806/B834.) "Happiness," Kant writes, is an Idea of the imagination because it refers to a completeness that we can try to imagine but that we can never encounter in our experience. (See *Gr.* 11–12/399, 46–48/418–19; *Cr.J.* 430.) For Kant, concern for our own welfare (*Wohlleben*), for what seems in our best interest, falls under the heading of "prudence" (*Klugheit*).

Saying that all human beings have "the strongest and deepest inclination toward happiness" is not, for Kant, merely an empirical generalization (*Gr.* 12/399; see also 42/415). Rather, the claim makes explicit what a priori reflection shows holds necessarily for all rational beings who are, by their "very being," finite (see *Gr.* 42/415): "To be happy is necessarily the desire of every rational but finite being, and thus it is an unavoidable determinant of its faculty of desire [or will]" (*Pr.R.* 25; *T&P* 278; also *M.M.* 387, 480). Occasionally, when he is extolling the absolute worth of good moral character (as in *Gr.* 4–6/395–96), Kant may seem to be arguing that our only legitimate practical interests are all moral in nature. But as the preceding quotations show, he in fact insists that our own happiness is a legitimate need and a genuine, if nonmoral, good. (See, e.g., *Gr.* 1/393, 7/396.)

Desires, inclinations, and self-interest

When he analyzes the notion of happiness, Kant uses a fundamentally hedonistic terminology. Everything we seek to attain is subsumed under the rubric of pleasure (*Lust*), and everything we seek to avoid is subsumed under

31

that of pain or displeasure (*Unlust* or *Schmerz*; see, e.g., *Pr.R.* 58–59; *Anthr.* 230–31).[1] Feeling, as we saw in the preceding chapter, is our ability to experience pleasure and pain, and enjoyment (*Vergnügen*) is the subjective experience that follows from the fulfillment of our desires (see *Pr.R.* 9n; *M.M.* 212). Desires include both attraction to what promises pleasure and contentment, and aversion to whatever may frustrate our desires or threaten pain or discomfort. (See *Gr.* 16n/401n; *Pr.R.* 25, 44, 58–61.)

To have everything go the way we want it to, Kant writes, is our "greatest, in fact our whole, desire in life. . . . The force in you that strives only toward happiness is inclination" (*M.M.* 480, 482). That is why Kant also describes enjoyment as a feeling that our life is prospering and pain a feeling that it is being hindered. (See *Anthr.* 231.) Desires, then, always provide the incentive (*Triebfeder*) in our pursuit of happiness. (Kant calls the motive for an action the "incentive" or "subjective ground" of that action; see *M.M.* 218.) In all such actions we not only take an interest *in* an object; we act *out of* our interest in and our desire for it so that what we do can always be explained by what it is we want to attain or avoid and why (see, e.g., *Gr.* 16n/401n; *Pr.R.* 9n, 24, 44, 58–61). As we saw in Chapter 3, when a desire (*Begierde*) becomes a settled or habitual disposition, Kant calls it an "inclination" (*Neigung*). (See *M.M.* 212.) Only agents with a finite, sensuous nature such as human beings can have desires and inclinations.

When our interest in an object is based on our feelings and inclinations, Kant calls our interest "merely pathological" and "pathologically determined." (See *Gr.* 38n/413n; 122n/460; *Pr.R.* 120.) As we also saw in the preceding chapter, the term "pathological" carries no implication that our desires and inclinations are somehow diseased. Kant intended the term to mean only that desires and inclinations and their fulfillment or frustration are the sort of psychophysical phenomena that psychologists use to explain our actions.

Given this analysis, it follows that when we act prudentially our motive is always self-interest. Conceptually, for Kant, it is not possible for us to act prudentially from anything but a self-serving motive; we would not act as we do unless we found it in our own interest. (See *Gr.* 10–11/398–99; *Pr.R.* 22.) Such a motive, Kant holds, is equivalent to what we ordinarily mean by self-love (*Selbstliebe*), which he conflates with selfishness (*Eigenliebe*), that is, caring mainly or only about ourselves and our own welfare, however we conceive of it. (See *Pr.R.* 73–74.)[2]

Prudential reasoning

Kant calls the thinking we do when we consider how to satisfy our prudential concerns, "empirically conditioned reasoning." (See *Pr.R.* 16; *Rel.* 45n2/41.) It is empirically conditioned because both its functions depend so heavily on empirical matters. (See *Gr.* 38n/413n, 122n/460n; *Pr.R.* 21, 33, 44, 58; *M.M.* 215–16.) One function of empirical practical reasoning is concerned with the ends of prudential actions, the second with the means to attain those ends. (See *Lect.* 246–47/4–5.)

Stated in general terms, the goal of all prudential thinking is to promote our own welfare or happiness. We learn what gives us pleasure and pain and so learn from experience what we want and what we do not want. (See *Pr.R.* 58, 62; *M.M.* 215.) Each of us therefore must imagine, as best we can, what in the long run will make us happy – what combination of pleasures will satisfy our desires and inclinations as a harmonious whole. Some pleasures may be incompatible with our notion of happiness, and the fulfillment of some desires may clash with the fulfillment of others. So we are forced to frustrate some desires and to "tame" others for the sake of what we take to be our best welfare. The ability to do this with some success, Kant writes, is the meaning of prudence in the sense of "personal wisdom" (*Privatklugheit;* see *Gr.* 42n/416n; *Pr.R.* 44, 120; *Rel.* 58/51).

Once we have decided what we want, we need to figure out how to get it. Since only our reason can discern causal connections, empirical practical reason must also be a faculty of desire in the sense of supplying general rules, or "maxims," learned through experience, to get us what we want. (See *Gr.* 38n/413n, 122n/460n; *Pr.R.* 20–21, 28, 68; *M.M.* 225.) The acceptability of such rules depends on their *effectiveness,* and that in turn depends on our having accurate information about both how the world works and what kind of power we ourselves need. (See *Gr.* 41/415; *Pr.R.* 20, 25–26, 25n.) We also must rely on experience to find out whether the conditions actually hold for us to get what we want. (See *Gr.* 41/415; *Pr.R.* 37, 51.) Here, to be rational means to learn from experience so that we do not persist in unnecessarily painful or counterproductive behavior.

So prudence also involves skill in using whatever means are at our disposal to attend to what we consider to be in our best welfare – whether we need only our own power or also (Kant identifies this as prudence in the sense of "worldly wisdom" or *Weltklugheit*) the help of other people. (See, e.g., *Gr.* 42n/416n; *M.M.* 455.) Anyone, Kant writes, who wills and not merely idly wishes for something "wills also the means (so far as reason has decisive influence on his actions)" (*Gr.* 45/417). Consequently, all particular prudential maxims presuppose and instantiate the same ultimate, formal prudential principle: Insofar as an agent acts rationally, willing an end also means willing whatever means are within that agent's power and (which the agent knows) are necessary to get it. This very general principle, Kant writes, is analytically true, following from an analysis of what it means for fully rational but finite agents to will something they can get by acting. (See *Gr.* 45/417, 48/419.)[3] Kant himself did not explicitly put it this way, but the principle of prudence may be reworded without distortion as: It is prima facie rational for us as finite beings to act so as to fulfill our needs and promote our own happiness.

However, because we do not always act rationally even in matters of self-interest, both the ultimate prudential rule and all more specific rules conforming to it appear to us in the form of imperatives. (See *Gr.* 39–40/414.) Moreover, they all also hold *hypothetically* because they all presuppose a condition: Each is relevant to and binds us individually only on the condition that we have and do not give up our desire for the specified end. (See *Gr.*

39–46/414–18.)[4] Stated as an imperative, then, the ultimate prudential principle reads: If you genuinely want something, then, to be rational, you ought also to use whatever means are available and necessary to obtain it. (The "ought" here is a prudential, not a moral, word.) More particular prudential imperatives have the form: If you really want x (this end), then do y (the means to that end).

We can desire an almost limitless number of different things, and there often are several different but equally effective ways to attain the same goal. There are thus an indefinitely large number of such imperatives. (See *Gr.* 39–41/414–15; *Pr.R.* 31.) They are all "of one and the same kind and belong under the general principle of self-love or one's own happiness," but they also can be divided into two classes, because the ends to which they are relevant are all of two general kinds (*Pr.R.* 22; see also 34, 73–74). In the case of definite states of affairs that we may or may not want, Kant calls the rules for attaining them "technical rules" and "rules of skill [*Kunst*]," for they all involve theoretical knowledge. (See *Gr.* 40–44/414–16.)[5] When the end is happiness in general, then, as we have seen, we may presume that is something everyone wants. Kant calls the rules for attaining happiness "assertoric," "pragmatic," and, most commonly, "prudential" rules in a more restricted meaning of "prudential."

Technical imperatives

Technical principles are actually empirical propositions about the world, supplied by theoretical reason. (See *Gr.* 41/415; *M.M.* 217.) They are the sort of principles contained in the applied part of the theoretical sciences. Stated only as theoretical rules, they set out the means (the cause) to some end (the effect), and their rightness or correctness is judged only in terms of the effectiveness of the means in attaining the stated end. (See *Gr.* 41/415.) Insofar as they are correct, they are all objectively valid; that is to say, they accurately describe causal connections in the world and so should be accepted by everyone as true (though we might wish things were otherwise).[6]

Technical principles simply describe the world. What makes such information practically relevant to us, so that we *use* it to guide our actions, is and must be something else, namely, our desires for whatever that information will help us to get. Then, for example, the purely theoretical *statement* "Water boils at 212° F at sea level" is transformed (because we are imperfectly rational agents) into the practical *imperative* "If you want to boil water at sea level, you must raise its temperature to 212° F."

The consequence of this analysis, Kant writes, is to show that the expression "empirical practical reason" is a misnomer. Insofar as technical imperatives incorporate rationality, that rationality is supplied by theoretical reason. (See, e.g., *Pr.R.* 25–26.) The impetus (or motivation or ground) for our adopting those principles as practical rules is not reason but our desires. (See *Pu.R.* A548ff/B576ff; A823–24/B851–52; *Gr.* 41/415; *Pr.R.* 19, 21, 33, 59; *Cr.J.*

172, 195–97.) Thus our use of technical imperatives does not show that our *reasoning* by itself is a genuinely practical power. (See *M.M.* 217.)

Moreover, the introduction of desires into technical principles causes them to lose their objective validity. Technical imperatives can be only subjective rules, for they hold only contingently; that is, they hold as rules only for those agents who happen to have the desires and aims that makes those rules relevant to them. We can ignore or reject these imperatives anytime we wish, if, for example, we decide that the cost of trying to get something is simply too high and so we give up its pursuit. (See *Gr.* 38/413, 50/420.)[7]

Prudential imperatives

Even if we agree in the main with Kant's analysis so far, we may be tempted to think that at least prudential imperatives can be objectively valid and hold necessarily for everyone. After all, they aim at happiness, which every rational finite person necessarily wants. And we normally are far better off thinking about our welfare than not doing so. Kant in fact writes: "Reason does, indeed, allow us to seek our advantage in every way possible to us, and it can even promise, on the testimony of experience, that we shall probably find it is in our interest, on the whole, to follow its commands rather than transgress them" (*M.M.* 216).

However, even though prudential imperatives prescribe actions as a means to something actually desired by every human being, Kant argues that they still hold only contingently and hypothetically. (See *Gr.* 42–43/416, 46–47/418–19.) In fact, he maintains that they turn out to be even more subjective than technical imperatives (which they may contain), so much so that he prefers not to call them rules at all, but only counsels. He offers several reasons for his view.

First, it is easy enough to give an abstract definition of happiness, and it is true that we all necessarily desire our own happiness. When, however, we try to give content to that idea, no matter how powerful and thoughtful we may be, we still find we cannot form a definite, firm, and self-consistent notion of what happiness consists in for ourselves, much less for others. (See *Gr.* 12/399, 46–47/417–18; *Pr.R.* 25, 36.) We know that the satisfaction of one desire often means the frustration of other desires and that happiness as a whole may require us to give up some individual pleasures we still really want. Also, the more we concern ourselves with what we want and what we might want, the more we tend to multiply our desires. Because we cannot satisfy them all, we may easily end up being less, not more, happy. (See *Gr.* 4–7/394–96.) Any attempt we might make to devise a sort of calculus of satisfactions quickly shows us how recalcitrant our desires can be. They resist our best efforts to organize them. So, Kant argues, prudential reasoning turns out to be a singularly unsteady guide to happiness. It cannot hope to offer us reliable maxims for the attainment of a goal it cannot focus on clearly and consistently. (See *Gr.* 12/399; *Cr.J.* 430.)[8]

35

Further, different people have different desires and count different things as more pleasurable than others, as contributing to or constituting part of their notion of happiness; and their preferences about such things can change from one moment to the next. (See *Gr.* 38/413, 44/416; *Pr.R.* 25, 28, 36.) No substantive principle of happiness, therefore, can be objective, that is, "prescribe the same practical rule to all [finite] rational beings, even though the rules go under the same name – that of happiness" (*Pr.R.* 36; see also 20–22, 25–26, 33, 36, 63, 126; *Gr.* 25/417).

Because we do have common needs, we all in fact also often happen to want many of the same things. But when we do, our agreement is still only a contingent affair, and the relevant imperatives are still only subjectively valid. In fact, nowhere is that subjectivity so evident as when there is a *consensus* of desires. Such a contingent agreement does not provide the basis for a necessary and rational harmony between individuals. Instead, the fact that some things that happen to be widely desired are frequently in short supply means that agreement among desires tends only to lead to enormous conflict and unhappiness. (See *Pr.R.* 25–26; also 20–22, 27–28, 33, 63; *Cr.J.* 400.)

Moreover, no matter how well we develop our talents and skills, actually achieving our goals in this life often depends on what Kant calls "nature and its beneficence" – external circumstances that "by and large are not under man's control" (*M.M.* 482; see *Cr.J.* 430). Nature places many obstacles in our way – "plague, famine, flood, cold, attacks from animals great and small, and all such things" (*Cr.J.* 430). So, too, do other people, because, as we shall see later, Kant thinks we all have a natural tendency to be hostile and antagonistic toward one another.

Finally, as Kant points out when assessing the prudence of making a false promise, the rules for achieving our goals all turn out to admit of exceptions. (See *Gr.* 18–19/402–3.) Their effectiveness depends on the individual circumstances in which a person finds himself, and even the best rules hold only for the most part. (See *Pr.R.* 36, 126; *M.M.* 216.) The maxim that we should save for our retirement, for example, may hold for the most part, but others can ignore it because they luckily have inherited enough money not to need a savings program. (See *Pr.R.* 20.) We also may find that changing circumstances make it more advantageous for us to break rather than keep a rule that has served us well in the past. (See *Gr.* 18–19/402–3.)

Kant's conclusion is that we have no principle for deciding how to attain any lasting happiness in this world. Given the complexity of life and all the facts we need to know in order to decide what is and what will continue to be in our best interest, given the limitations the world imposes on our having the means to get what we want, given all the unexpected contingencies that can arise, and, finally, given the inherent ambivalence of human nature, Kant concludes that human "nature is not so constituted as to rest or be satisfied in any possession or enjoyment whatever" (*Cr.J.* 430; see 430–31; *Pr.R.* 36, 62). We should not expect any lasting happiness.

So prudential imperatives are at best only counsels or advice that it is often, but not always, best to follow. (See *Gr.* 47–48/418–19; *M.M.* 389.) They turn out to say something like this: If you happen to count such and such as part of what will make you happy, then many people have found this a good rule to follow. But of course your situation may be different, the best laid plans can go awry, and you may not want to follow this rule if it jeopardizes other things you happen to count as part of your well-being. So this general rule is only advice that you should consider but that you may decide to reject. Whether you decide it is or is not good advice on which to act, your decision may backfire. But that is true no matter what you decide to do. There are no guarantees in this life, something we all learn from acting imprudently and even from acting prudently. (See *M.M.* 216.)

The amorality of prudence

Having completed Kant's analysis of the nature of prudence, we can now turn our attention to his consideration of its value.[9] As Kant sees it, whether we examine the actions prudence recommends or the qualities of the prudential person or the goal of happiness, nothing about prudence (or what Kant also calls "heteronomy") gives us reason to think it has *any* intrinsic moral significance. (See *Gr.* 88–89/441; *Rel.* 45n2/41.) As we would expect, Kant's doctrine here was later found to be outrageously unacceptable by hedonists such as Jeremy Bentham and John Stuart Mill.

Kant's assessment of prudence rests either tacitly or explicitly on "ordinary moral consciousness," that is, on how ordinary people differentiate between merely natural or pragmatic good (*das Wohl*) and moral good (*das Gute*) and between natural evil (*das Übel* or *das Weh*) and moral evil (*das Böse*). (See *Pr.R.* 58–60.)[10] Consequently, the full force of Kant's claims in this section depends on his elucidation of the nature of morality in the next chapter. But to complete in this chapter our discussion of his examination of prudence, we will examine his arguments now rather than later.

Clearly, Kant begins, prudentially motivated actions and the hypothetical rules articulating them can be called good in the sense of helping us satisfy our needs and desires. But to say they are good insofar as they are effective is also to say that such actions are good only instrumentally. They have no intrinsic value in themselves, much less any intrinsic moral value. In fact, as we all know, prudentially good actions may also be violations of moral norms, such as justice. (See *Gr.* 13–14/399–400, 16n/401n, 38n/413n, 40/414, 63/427, 122n/460n; *Pr.R.* 35, 58, 62; *T&P* 282.)[11]

Similar remarks can be made about the personal qualities of prudential persons. They may have native gifts such as intelligence, wit, and good judgment; well-developed skills; and natural temperamental traits such as courage, resoluteness, constancy, self-control, and thoughtfulness.[12] They also may possess an abundance of the "gifts of fortune," such as power, wealth, health, and good reputation. All of these can contribute to a person's happiness. But again, they all are only instrumentally good, valuable only insofar as they help us get what we want, and they all can be used either for morally good or morally evil purposes. (See *Gr.* 1–3/393–94; *Pr.R.* 4, 64.)[13] However helpful they may be in promoting our happiness, they are not morally good; they are not of themselves even morally significant.

For the same reason, those desires that motivate us to pursue our own welfare also lack intrinsic moral significance. Prudential desires, inclinations, and aversions are all "merely pathological"; that is, they are based on our anticipation of somatic pleasure or pain. Of themselves, such desires and aversions are neither morally good nor morally evil; they are simply indifferent to the categories of moral right and wrong. So the sheer fact that we have certain desires and aversions does not mean we are either morally good or morally evil.[14] Some people, for example, may have a sympathetic temperament so that they naturally enjoy helping others. Such characteristics may deserve "praise and encouragement" when they happen to promote genuinely moral ends, but they still do not deserve moral esteem (*Gr.* 10/398, 14–16/400–401). Because they all finally are aimed at what gives us pleasure and makes us happy (or at avoiding pain or unhappiness), they can just as easily lead us to act immorally when that is what gives us pleasure (see *Gr.* 90–91/442). Moreover, as we saw in the preceding section, desires and aversions vary subjectively from person to person and from time to time for the same person. They are by nature unstable and cannot be a reliable and objective ground for morality, which often requires their frustration rather than their fulfillment. (See *Lect.* 276/38.) For all these reasons, merely pathological or somatic desires and inclinations do not belong to the moral world; they have "no genuinely moral worth" (*Gr.* 10/398; see 13–14/399–400).

If prudence is to have intrinsic moral worth, then, since moral value cannot be found either in the acts it generates or in the personal qualities of the prudential person, that worth must be found in its end, in the concept of happiness or, alternatively, in the prudential principle that it is rational for us to act so as to promote our happiness. Whenever a maxim of conduct is based on some object or goal, there are only two ways in which that maxim might bind a person: Either the person must be causally determined to seek that goal, or he or she must be willing to adopt it as his or her own goal. Under the first condition, the maxim is a law but a law of natural causal necessity, so that the agent acts under compulsion, without freedom. Such actions obviously can have no moral significance. Under the second condition, the maxim holds only if the person in fact subjectively *wants* whatever he or she may get by acting on that rule. Then prudential ends can have value for us only insofar as they fit into our wants. (See *Gr.* 65/428.) So even though the general principle of prudence itself is objective and holds for all dependent rational beings like us, *specific* prudential rules can oblige us only subjectively and contingently. (See *Gr.* 51/420; *Pr.R.* 25; *Lect.* 276/38.) Since our experience with moral laws shows they *all* must hold objectively and absolutely, maxims adopted to obtain some end or other can never attain the status of moral rules. (See *Gr.* 61/426, 63–64/427–28, 90/442; *Pr.R.* 21, 34, 63–64; *Rel.* 4/3–4.)[15]

Kant admits that we may, and we often in fact do, approve and, if it is important to our own welfare, we can even cherish what we and others desire and enjoy. (See *Gr.* 14/400.) But we all also know that happiness and good moral character are entirely different notions. (See *Gr.* 90/442; *Pr.R.* 87–88.)[16] We may be pleased, for example, to see others happy, but that certainly does not mean we think they are by that fact also morally good. (See *Pr.R.* 37.) We would laugh at a person who tried to characterize his pursuit of his own advantage as his moral duty. (See *Pr.R.* 35.) We also know people can be very unhappy even when they are morally good, as well as happier than they deserve to be when they have not been morally good. (See *Gr.* 1–2/393; *M.M.* 480.) When people err in prudential matters, we do not therefore judge them to be immoral; we often say only that they made a mistake. (See *Gr.* 122/460; *Pr.R.* 60–61.) Moreover, many things such as simple good luck can give us pleasure and make us happy, but we do not therefore think such nonrational causes should be considered morally good (see *Gr.* 15/401). This listing of typical ordinary judgments in which people sharply distinguish between morality and happiness could be continued indefinitely. The point is clear: Analysis fails to reveal anything of moral significance about happiness (or any of its components), just from the mere fact that it is the end of prudential conduct. (See *Gr.* 13/399–400, 90/442.)

Kant's conclusion, then, is that there is nothing about prudential behavior that justifies our thinking it has intrinsic moral value.

Past errors

Kant now turns his attention to the analyses of other philosophers, who, he writes, showed they knew less about morality than ordinary people by mistakenly trying to locate morality within the domain of prudence.[17]

They all held (correctly) that merely thinking about something does not necessarily lead to any action; before we act, we first must take an interest in doing so. But they then presumed (incorrectly) that the motivation for actions must always be found in our merely pathological desires, and if that is the case, then nothing can be considered good unless it first is desired. (See *Gr.* x–xi/391.) So they concluded that the only way to discover what is morally good is to inventory and classify all the various things human beings empirically have desired and therefore may be considered good in the sense of "desirable." The "best" or "highest" or "noblest" will then be given the honorific title of "morally good." Some philosophers ended up defining the concept of "moral good" in terms of pleasure and happiness, others in terms of a special kind of feeling or "moral sense," and still others in terms of perfection, either human or divine. (See *Gr.* 89–90/441–42.)

However they differed on their conclusions, they all agreed that we can know which actions are morally *right* only by first determining what should be considered *good*. To put it another way, all other moral philosophers believed that a moral theory must begin with the notion of what is "good" and then derive from it the notion of what is morally "right."[18] Those actions are morally right that promote the best, natural (that is, nonmoral) goods.

Because all these theories defined the notion of good as fundamental, Kant argues, they could offer only "material principles," that is, rules for attaining what they had defined as good. Such theories all fall into one of two types. The first group consists of theories that base morality on the purely subjective phenomena of desires and inclinations. Here belong both those theories that consider feelings only insofar as they are subjective internal phenomena – whether sheer feelings (Epicurus) or apparently moral feelings (Hutcheson) – and those theories that rely on some external agency, whether education (Montaigne) or the civil constitution (Mandeville), to generate the right feelings. (See *Gr.* 91/442.) The second group comprises theories of "ontological perfection." They regard morality as objective in the sense of originating either in nature, particularly human nature (Wolff and the Stoics, and, although Kant does not explicitly include him here, Aristotle), or in a supernatural being (Crusius and all other theological moralists). (See *Gr.* 92–93/ 443; *Pr.R.* 40–41, 64.)

In the first group, as we have just seen, any effort to base morality on feelings of whatever kind ends in what Kant calls "moral egoism" and "eudaemonism" – a prudential, not a moral, theory. (See *Anthr.* 130.) It was common for members of the second group to claim that their notions of what is good – whether perfection or moral contentment – are superior just because they originate in our understanding. (See *Gr.* 90/442, 92–93/443; *Pr.R.* 22– 24, 40–41.) These norms may be more refined than merely sensuous pleasure, but the proponents of all such theories still base morality on our attraction to some end or other. They all, therefore, must hold that people have to be *induced* to pay attention to and to strive for perfection. Theological theories of perfection (which commit the added error of presuming that we can have direct knowledge of God's will) still must appeal to subjective desires or aversions, and therefore remain prudential, not moral, theories. (See *Gr.* 92–93/ 443.)

Moreover, naturalistic theories turn out to offer such general descriptions of what is practically good as to result in only empty and useless norms of instrumental effectiveness, such as: "Do good; avoid evil." If they try to give more definite content to the notion of perfection, they have to recommend physical or mental development, which can be only conditionally good, that is, good only insofar as it does not conflict with the moral law. They thus end up presupposing the very morality they are intended to explain. (See *Gr.* 73–74/432–33, 86–87/440, 91–92/442–43; *Pr.R.* 41; *Rel.* 3n/3; *Lect.* 275/ 37–38.)[19]

Kant condemns all these moral theorists in the harshest terms. Their initial error made it impossible for them to understand correctly the nature of morality, which their analyses in fact portrayed only as a high species of prudence. (See *Pr.R.* 109.) *Any* attempt to base a moral theory on some conception of what is good can offer only hedonism, a compilation of rules falling under the general principle of self-love or happiness. (See *Pr.R.* 22.)

If all the incentives for practical goals are based on desires, then (contrary to what Mill later argued) qualitative differences are not important. All the different versions of what is good are still alike in the way in which they can motivate a person to act. When we compare pleasures as pleasures, "it is not a question of where the conception of this enjoyable object comes from, but merely of how much it can be enjoyed. . . . how great, how long-lasting, how easily obtained, and how often repeated this agreeableness is" (*Pr.R.* 23; see also 22–25, 72; *Gr.* x–xi/391). Everything identified as good is good only in that it promises pleasure; a theory must therefore rely on the desire for pleasure to motivate people to adopt the appropriate maxims of conduct. This, Kant concludes,

. . . explains once and for all the reasons which occasion all the confusions of philosophers concerning the supreme principle of morals. For they sought an object of the will in order to make it into the material and the foundation of a law . . . instead they should have looked for a law which directly determined the will a priori and only then sought the object suitable to it. (*Pr.R.* 64)

If all the past efforts to understand morality had exhausted the possibilities, Kant writes, then there could be no such thing as human morality. (See *Pr.R.* 22–24.) But what all other philosophers had failed to consider is the possibility that man could be subject "only to *laws which are made by himself* and yet are *universal*" (*Gr.* 73/432; see *Pr.R.* 41). As we shall see in the next chapter, these are the only kinds of practical rules that can bind us as laws and therefore be genuine moral principles. This claim lies at the very center of Kant's moral theory, and explaining it will take up most of the rest of this book.

Kant realized that it sounded "arrogant and egotistic" to say that all his predecessors and contemporaries were wrong in their analyses of the nature of morality, but, he argued, there can be only one correct systematic analysis. (See *M.M.* 206–7.) In fact, contending that there can be several incompatible but equally correct analyses of *any* subject, whether chemistry, medicine, or morality, is simply "self-contradictory" and incoherent. So Kant defends himself by pointing out that he is doing nothing more than what anyone else does and must do who claims to have the correct understanding of any topic (*M.M.* 207).

Kant concludes, then, that all other philosophers ended up not with a moral theory but merely with a psychosociological study, an "empirical anthropology" of human hopes and fears and of the heteronomous behavior they engender. (See *Gr.* x–xi/390–91, 38n/413n, 42/416, 44/417; *Pr.R.* 21, 64–65; *M.M.* 405–6.)[20] But this much at least can be said for them: By their very mistakes they did prepare the way for the correct analysis. (See *Gr.* 89/441; *M.M.* 207.)

What can be learned

To avoid merely repeating the errors of the past, we need to learn several important lessons. First, Kant writes, the moral rightness of an action cannot depend on what it might or actually does accomplish, and the moral goodness of a person's character cannot depend on motives based on such expected results. (See *Gr.* 15/401; see also *Pr.R.* 34.) Morality is impossible if practical reason is always heteronomous and, as Hume had held, always plays the role of servant to our desires, whether those desires aim at pleasure or at conformity to societal standards or to the will of another (even God). And any moral theory that tries to base morality on desired changes that we might cause by our actions is doomed to failure, for all such natural goods also could have been caused by chance or whatever. (See *Gr.* 15/401.) So there is no special value in our being rational beings if reason only serves our desires, if we are only able to accomplish what nonrational and thus nonmoral natural events also can bring about. (See *Cr.J.* 434, 443, 448–49; *M.M.* 435–36.) Kant writes:

That [man] has reason does not in the least raise him in worth above mere animality if reason only serves the purposes which, among animals, are taken care of by instinct; if this were so, reason would be only a specific way nature had made use of to equip man for the same purpose for which animals are qualified, without fitting him for any higher purpose. (*Pr.R.* 61; see *Ed.* 442/2, 447/13)[21]

Second, a lesson to which Kant repeatedly returns in his writings is that *morality cannot be based on or drawn from experience,* and to think we can do so is to expose ourselves to "the grossest and most pernicious errors" (*M.M.* 215; see also 405). "Nothing is more reprehensible than to derive the laws prescribing what *ought to be done* from what *is done*" (*Pu.R.* A319/B375). Kant takes Aristotle to be "the chief of the empiricists" in the matter of the origin of our moral knowledge, and against him argues that "anthroponomy," that is, what today we would call psychology and sociology – empirical knowledge of human behavior – tells us absolutely nothing about how we ought to behave (*Pu.R.* A854/B882; see A547/B575, A734/B762; *Gr.* 27–28/ 407–8; *M.M.* 406).

Aristotle had argued that we learn our moral ideals mainly by imitating models or paradigms of good conduct. Kant admits that here Aristotle is right: Children do in fact learn how to act by imitating others. But he argues, we still can recognize conduct *as* morally good only if we first have norms given only by reason for identifying it as such. (See *Gr.* 29/408; *Pr.R.* 158; *M.M.* 479–80; *Ed.* 453/26–27.) Examples may be helpful in moral education by showing that morally correct behavior is possible and by encouraging us to act rightly. However, examples are unnecessary and unhelpful in learning what morality requires of us, for moral norms cannot originate in experience. (See *Gr.* 29–30/408–9; *Pr.R.* 154, 160–62; *Rel.* 62–63/56–57; *M.M.* 479–80.)

Experience, Kant writes, leaves us without any "certain moral principles, either to guide judgment or to discipline the mind in fulfilling our duty" (*M.M.* 217). As we have just seen, experience can offer practical rules that at best can hold for the most part because they may or may not apply to individuals, depending on their inclinations and circumstances. (See *Pr.R.* 25–26.) Given the meaning of morality based on common understanding, Kant argues, its imperatives must be objective, that is, universal and apodictic, and obligate everyone equally, not taking into account the inclinations or circumstances of any individual persons or groups (*M.M.* 216). A practical rule to which exceptions must constantly be made is clearly unfit to serve as a moral law of conduct. (See *Pr.R.* 126.)

Further, morality commands actions we may never have encountered in experience, such as true friendship, and so it cannot be based on psychological or sociological observations about how people do in fact behave. (See *Pu.R.* A548/B576; *Gr.* 27–28/407–8; *M.M.* 216.) "All is lost when empirical and therefore contingent conditions of the application of the [moral] law are made conditions of the [moral] law itself" (*T&P* 277). An adequate analysis of the absolute nature of morality can never be based on contingent facts we know about human beings. (See *Pu.R.* A318–19/B375; *Gr.* vi/389, 25–30/406–9, 59–63/425–27, 63–64/427–28, 90/442, 94–95/444; *M.M.* 215–16, 481.)

Finally, neither experience nor introspection can offer us even one sure example of genuinely moral motivation. (See *Gr.* 25–26/406–7; *Rel.* 63/56–57.) Since empirical studies of human beings (e.g., psychology) must regard all human actions as originating in prior determining causes and so in nonmoral desires, experience can offer only "spurious and impure motives" for morally right behavior. If we were to try to base morality on experience, we would have to conclude that there is no specifically moral motivation. (See *Gr.* 27–28/407–8, 48–49/419; *M.M.* 216–17; *T&P* 284–85.) Kant therefore concludes that any effort to base morality even partly on experience actually undermines morality and, if pursued, can only "degrade mankind" and result in "the death of all morality" (*Pr.R.* 71 and *T&P* 285; see *Gr.* ix/390, 30–34/409–11; *Pr.R.* 22–26, 110–19; *M.M.* 377–78).

What Kant concludes, positively, is that morality is possible only if our reason *itself* can be a "higher faculty of desire," which, through reflection on its own power and requirements, independent of experience and of all our desires for pleasure, can develop a system of moral concepts and principles, determine what is good, and then motivate us to pursue it. (See, e.g., *Gr.* iii–ix/388–391, 32–35/410–12; *Pr.R* 9n, 15, 24, 31–32, 62–63, 118; *M.M.* 214–17, 375–76.) What this in effect means is that Kant is convinced that we need what no philosopher has yet offered – a purified "metaphysics of morals" to serve as the foundation of a correct moral theory. It is to the a priori foundation or "groundwork" (*Grundlegung*) for such a metaphysics that we now turn.

5

Morality: living autonomously

Since we can have no theoretical insight into the claim that we are moral beings, since that claim cannot be supported by any appeal to experience, Kant contends that it is only by reflecting on our ordinary notion of "moral agency" that we can determine what an agent must be to be a moral agent.[1] And only then are we in a position to support the claim that we are such agents.[2] So in this and the following chapters of this section we first will examine Kant's analysis of the nature of human moral agency, and then go on to his defense of our status as moral agents.

We have already seen that Kant believed that contrasting morality with prudence displays, as no other method can, the distinctive nature of human morality, while also refuting the errors of other philosophers (see, e.g., *Gr.* 8/397). But he could not have critiqued prudence as he did had he not already taken the defining difference between it and morality to be the subjectivity of the former and the objectivity of the latter. It is the objectivity of morality that requires its rules to be formally and substantively impartial, fit to bind everyone equally; and it is the objectivity of morality that justifies its claim to be overriding, that is, to have rightful priority over all other interests of individuals and groups.

Kant claimed to draw this contrast from ordinary moral consciousness, for he was convinced that if we really are moral agents, we must be aware of what that means, even if most of us can articulate our knowledge only in a somewhat disorganized and unclear way. Consequently, he regarded our common moral convictions as the ultimate data for an analysis of morality, and he frequently validated his claims by corroborative appeals to those convictions. In the following pages, we will roughly imitate Kant's own strategy in the first chapter of the *Groundwork* – drawing the Categorical Imperative from what he takes to be our ordinary understanding of what makes a person morally good (or have a "good will"). (See *Gr.* xiv/392, 8/397, 59/425.)[3]

Freedom

In his philosophy of action Kant granted that human beings will exercise their power to act only if they take an interest in doing so. So, as we saw in the preceding chapter, he characterized prudential actions as those actions we perform when we try rationally to meet the needs of our dependent nature. We are interested *in* acting because we are motivated *by* our various desires for what we hope acting will get us. In all such cases, when we act *from*

44

interest, reason is "empirically conditioned," and its sole role is to serve our desires by helping us get what we want. Since prudential actions have no moral value, we can be moral agents only if our ability to act rationally is not limited to prudential considerations.

This means that when we *judge* how to act morally, we may not base our decisions on what we do or do not want. We may determine how to act morally only by judging in what Kant describes as a "sensually disinterested" fashion, that is, according to norms given by our own reasoning, norms that set aside our individual desires and aversions and any consideration of possibly adverse consequences of obeying those norms. Likewise, to *be* morally good, we must act because we take an immediate interest *in* acting, without acting *from* interest. That is to say, we must be able to exercise our causal power without being influenced to do so by *any* causes lying outside our own reason, including our own desires and inclinations. (See, e.g., *Gr.* 88–89/441, 93–94/443–44; *Pr.R.* 15–16, 24–25, 33–34, 44, 63, 160–61; *M.M.* 213.) By itself, our power of reasoning must be able to affect our feelings in two related ways: It must be able to cause us to take enough interest in acting morally so that we can do so, and if necessary, it must be able to frustrate any opposition from our desires. (See *Gr.* 14–16/400–401.)[4]

In the language of Kant's faculty psychology, we must possess the power of "pure reason" or "pure practical reason" (*reine praktische Vernunft*). (See, e.g., *Pr.R.* 22, 24, 55–56.) (I also will call this power "moral reason," although Kant himself does not use that expression.) As "a higher faculty of desire," moral reason must be both a *cognitive* and a *conative* power, *entirely by itself* able to determine how we should act and also able to motivate us to act on those judgments without relying on any prior desires. (See *Pr.R.* 15, 41–42, 46, 67–68; *M.M.* 213.) This is *the* central thesis of Kant's moral theory.

Today it is virtually impossible for us to appreciate how radically Kant broke with traditional moral theorizing with the claim that pure reason can be practical. (See, e.g., *Gr.* 63/427; *Pr.R.* 15, 23, 41–42.) In fact, this constitutes what may be called Kant's Copernican revolution in moral philosophy. No one before Kant had thought to suggest that human reason could be so powerful. By contrast, as we have seen, all other philosophers had based the motivation or conative power of practical reason on desires, and they had identified what is morally good as grounded in those feelings that either have the greatest strength or are "higher" (rather than "lower"), a distinction revived almost a century later by John Stuart Mill. (See *Gr.* xi/391.)

Today it also is difficult for us to appreciate how novel was Kant's understanding of the nature of freedom. Most philosophers before Kant would have agreed that we can be moral beings only if we are free in some sense or other, but no one before Kant had thought (and few after him have thought) that we can and must possess as radical freedom as he did.[5]

In our ordinary way of speaking, we often take freedom to be what Kant calls "psychological freedom," that is, the absence of both internal and external impediments to doing what we *want* to do. In his political writings Kant himself tends to use the word "freedom" in this sense. But for the purposes of ethics he holds that such an understanding of freedom is completely in-adequate, for it is based on experience and describes only prudential, not morally worthy, conduct.

For Kant, "freedom" in the full, moral sense is a transcendental Idea of reason, for it refers to what (purportedly) lies beyond all possible sensory experience and therefore can originate only in our own reason. Negatively, by "freedom" Kant means our ability to act in *complete* independence of any prior or concurrent causes other than our own will or practical reasoning, our "power to restrain and overcome inclinations by reason" (*M.M.* 481). Positively, freedom is the power of *absolute* causal self-determination, enabling us to judge and act autonomously, only on the basis of our own reasoning. (See *Pu.R.* A532–34/B560–62, A554/B582; *Gr.* 97–98/446–47; *Pr.R.* 29, 33, 100; *M.M.* 213–14, 226.) To be free, therefore, *is* to be a morally responsible person. "A free will and a will under moral laws are one and the same" (*Gr.* 98/447). Kant also defines the ultimate principle of morality *as* the principle of freedom – the power of an agent to act on objective laws of his or her own adoption.

Autonomy

In Kant's moral theory it is usually possible to use the word "autonomy" in place of "freedom." An autonomous person is one who judges and acts freely in both the negative and positive senses of "freedom," by principles of reason alone. (See, e.g., *Conflict* 27/43.)

Today the term "autonomy" is often used not only as a moral but also as a psychological "pro-word." In the humanistic theories of Abraham Maslow, Carl Rogers, and Lawrence Kohlberg, for example, it is used to designate the main characteristic of the psychological ideal of a mature – a "self-actualizing" or "fully functioning" – person. However, in those theories, the term tends to function more like Kant's principle of prudence than the law of morality. The emphasis is mainly on the particularity of each person, and further, on each person's unique complex of subjective needs and desires: Each of us should be aware of our own desires and needs, and it is up to us to develop norms for taking care of ourselves by satisfying them.

"Autonomy" is also used to refer to what is often regarded as an absolute *right* (variously identified as psychological, legal, and/or moral) of persons to make their own decisions and to control their own lives without interference by others. During disagreements, the term "autonomy" has such powerful connotations that it is often used as an "argument stopper"; to accuse someone of not respecting another's right of autonomy is to condemn the first person's actions as bad – often as morally bad.

By contrast, persons described as lacking autonomy are called "heteron-omous" in the sense of being excessively other directed. They are described as uncritically willing to shape their feelings and behaviors so as to conform to the norms and expectations of others, whoever or whatever the "others" may be: parents, a social group, a state, a church, or even God. The road

away from heteronomy and toward autonomy is often described, occasionally
with a nod in Socrates' direction, as "therapy."

These contemporary uses of "autonomy" do bear some resemblance to their
Kantian ancestor, for, like Kant's notion, they require the exercise of practical
reasoning. They also reflect the conviction that the autonomous person must
be responsible, that is, self-governing; and, further, they rule out certain
kinds of coercion by others. But here the similarities end, for Kant's idea of
"autonomy," like that of "freedom," is far more precise and restricted than
the present-day notion. For Kant, the term "autonomy" denotes our ability
and responsibility to know what *morality* requires of us and our determination
not to act immorally. Rather than being a norm for promoting and satisfying
our desires, then, the law of autonomy functions fundamentally as "the supreme limiting condition of all subjective ends" (*Gr.* 69–70/430–31). It is
precisely the fact that morally right maxims qualify as universal laws that
shows they are not and cannot be essentially self-seeking (*M.M* 451). Therefore, the autonomous person is one who, by enacting objective principles of
conduct, is not only self-legislative but also universally legislative.[6] For Kant,
then, the road to autonomy is through that self-imposed discipline or self-
mastery necessary to adopt rules by which we transcend individuality in favor
of universality.

The consequence, as we shall see in Chapter 16, is that Kant does not
regard autonomy itself as a right but as an ability and an obligation that
provides the moral basis for political rights. Our obligations toward others
are not based on their rights; rather, their rights are based on our prior obligations. What it means to hold autonomy as a moral absolute must be examined very carefully, for in his political theory Kant holds both that external
coercion may be not only compatible with but even essential to autonomy,
and that civil punishment may involve the loss of civil liberties without also
entailing the loss of a person's autonomous personality.

The obligations autonomy imposes on us can all be stated in moral rules,
and it is to Kant's discussion of the special nature of those rules that we now
turn.

Moral rules

"The concept of causality carries with it that of *laws* [*Gesetze*] in accordance
with which, because of something we call a cause, something else – namely,
its effect – must be posited" (*Gr.* 97–98/446). To be a cause *means* to exercise
power in a law-regulated way. An agent of *any* kind can be an efficient cause
only in a law-governed world, only by following a law or laws determining
its "character" in a broad sense, that is, how its causality is exercised. (See
Pu.R. A539/B567.) Therefore, to say that a moral agent acts freely does not
mean that such an agent acts lawlessly. In a lawless (i.e., completely ruleless)
world, anything could follow from anything, and that would make the notions
of causality in general and of free, moral agency in particular totally meaningless. (See, e.g., *Rel.* 35/30.) To say that a moral agent is one who acts

freely must therefore mean that such an agent can exercise causal power on the basis of a law or laws given by his own reason alone.

Earlier we saw that Kant defined reason as preeminently "the faculty of principles" (*Pu.R.* A299/B356). It should be no surprise, then, that he defines practical reason as a causal "power to act in accordance with [one's own] idea of laws – that is, in accordance with principles" (*Gr.* 35/412; see *M.M.* 214). It must be through a law or principle that it supplies by itself that pure practical reason can give us an ultimate moral criterion by which to guide our conduct. We now need to examine this aspect of morality: action according to a rule originating in reason alone.

Once again Kant explains his doctrine by contrasting morality with prudence (see, e.g., *Gr.* 43–44/416–17). As we have seen, all prudential rules are material maxims learned from experience: They set out the means to desired ends. Because they serve desires, which lie outside reason, Kant calls all such rules "heteronomous." For the same reasons, they can bind us only conditionally and subjectively – when we in fact have desires they can help satisfy; otherwise we are free to ignore them. Rules provided by reason *alone* clearly must be radically different from prudential maxims. For one thing, such rules must all be objective: They must be rules that hold without exceptions, both necessarily and universally for all rational agents and for all human beings simply because they are rational. (See, e.g., *Gr.* 13–14/399–400, 17/402, 51–52/420–21, 96/444; *Pr.R.* 25, 27–29.)[7]

We also have seen that all particular hypothetical rules conform to one ultimate, abstract formula of prudentially practical rationality that may be stated in abbreviated form as, "Whoever wills an end, wills the means necessary to it." Prudential rules are "right" insofar as they are effective in helping us get what we want. But, as we also have seen, if morality is not just a high species of prudence, the rightness of moral rules must be independent of any considerations about whether they effectively promote our advantage.[8] So it must be some other characteristic of the maxim of an action that makes that maxim morally right (*Gr.* 15/400, 38n/413n, 39–40/414–15, 43/416, 94–95/444, 122n/460n).

Because all the desires that ground prudence have been set aside and because moral rules originate in reason alone, the only remaining characteristic of such rules is their *form*. Just as all prudential rules conform to an ultimate norm of empirically conditioned rationality, so all substantive moral rules conform to a single ultimate formula of pure rationality. That can only be a principle setting out in a purely formal way what it is to be a rational agent. Kant calls it the Law of Freedom or of Autonomy, and it articulates in a single formula what we have already learned about the nature of morality: A moral agent is an agent who can act autonomously, that is, as a law unto himself or herself, on the basis of objective maxims of his or her reason alone. (See, e.g., *Gr.* 98/447.) This law requires but one thing, namely, that we be "law-abiding," that we act only on the basis of maxims that can function as laws. It may seem that this requirement is too abstract to be very helpful

as a moral guide, but it in fact turns out to be a surprisi
norm.

The Categorical Imperative

In his analysis of human agency in general, Kant maintaı.
we are only contingently rational, all practical rules always appeஃ
commands or imperatives, telling us how we should or should not act in oı
to act rationally. (See *Gr.* 37–39/413–14.) Since we are often tempted to act
contrary to reason even in matters of self-interest, all prudential rules appear
to us in the form of imperatives, albeit hypothetical ones that we can rationally
avoid following merely by altering our desires. Since we also are often tempted
to act immorally, the Law of Autonomy and all particular moral rules also
appear to us as imperatives. But because moral imperatives are grounded
only in our own reason and because they require us to regard our desires as
irrelevant to what we should do, we cannot escape the right of moral rules
to obligate us. They are genuine laws. (See *Gr.* 50/420.)

There is only one legitimate reason that can exempt an agent from the
Law of Autonomy,[9] namely, the excuse "This is not a rational agent." We
in fact do use this plea to exempt animals, small children, and profoundly
emotionally disturbed or mentally disabled adults from moral responsibility.
But we may not use this excuse for ourselves. The claim "I need not act
morally, because I am not rational" is incoherent, for a person cannot consistently both offer a reason for what he or she says and also claim to be a
nonrational agent, one who cannot recognize the action-guiding nature of
reasons. Moral rules, therefore, obligate us unconditionally or absolutely or
categorically – and not hypothetically or conditionally. (See, e.g., *Gr.* 71/
431; *Pr.R.* 31.)[10] That is why Kant calls the Law of Autonomy, as it appears
to us, "the Categorical Imperative."

With imperfectly rational agents such as ourselves in mind, Kant defines
an objective practical principle as "one which would also serve subjectively
as a practical principle for all rational beings if reason had full control over
the faculty of desire" (*Gr.* 15n/400n).[11] In its form as the Categorical Imperative, the Law of Autonomy commands us: "Act autonomously, that is,
on the basis of your own reason alone." Since it also obligates everyone like
us, it can be paraphrased as: "Act in such a way that the maxims of your
actions can serve at the same time as universal laws, that is, as maxims on
which all other autonomous agents may also act." (See, e.g., *Gr.* 52/421.)
Although we also have positive duties, the Categorical Imperative so frequently
obligates us to deny our desires that we typically become aware of it as a
prohibition. (See *Gr.* 37–39/412–14, 102–3/449; *Rel.* 42/37.) Stated negatively,
then, that same imperative is: "I ought never to act except in such a way
that I can also will that my maxim should become [i.e., also hold as] a universal
law," a law binding everyone else as well (*Gr.* 17/402).

As we shall see in more detail in Chapter 11, the Categorical Imperative

49

.lows necessarily and analytically from Kant's conceptual analysis of what
.t is to be a rational agent, even if only contingently so. He also repeatedly
reminds us that his analysis is not novel and is not meant to be. Although
this may not seem obvious at the moment, Kant argues that he is only elucidating our ordinary notion of morality, clarifying the norm ordinary people
use when they make their ordinary moral judgments correctly. (See, e.g.,
Gr. 20–22/403–4, 88/440, 95–96/445.) When we think morally, Kant writes,
we all necessarily presume the Categorical Imperative as our ultimate norm.
It is present in the inherent structure of human reason, and its presence there
gives us our moral personality, or what Kant calls "personality itself (the
idea of humanity considered quite intellectually)" (*Rel.* 28/23; see *M.M.* 376).

Consequently, he maintains, we can confirm his analysis merely by in-
trospecting our own moral consciousness and by listening carefully to the
way in which other people make their moral judgments. For example, we
will find that, once people are convinced something is their moral obligation,
they invariably experience their own reason as commanding them absolutely
to fulfill that obligation, without any regard for their desires and inclinations.
(See, e.g., *M.M.* 216.) This is why any compromise of a moral principle
seems immoral.

Obligatory, forbidden, or permissible

Kant almost always describes the Categorical Imperative as generating either
negative or positive duties; in all his ethical works, the stress is on the concept
of "moral obligation." For example, in one passage he writes that the Categorical Imperative represents "an action as objectively necessary in itself"
(*Gr.* 39/414), and in another, that if we attend to the way in which people
make their moral judgments, we find that "everyone does, in fact, decide by
this rule [the Categorical Imperative] whether actions are morally good or
bad" (*Pr.R.* 69).

It is all too easy to conclude that the obligation to act only on maxims that
can hold as universal laws means that the maxim of any kind of action *not*
violating the criterion of universality should be understood to be morally
obligatory. Such an interpretation makes Kant's moral theory so harsh as to
be ludicrous, for there are all sorts of maxims that *could* pass the test of
universality but that it would be absurd for us to consider obligatory for
anyone, much less for everyone (such as tying the laces on my left shoe first).
Likewise there are an indefinite number of apparently morally acceptable
maxims that we clearly cannot will that everyone should adopt (such as trying
to become a philosopher, or whatever).

Not surprisingly, Kant's actual views reflect his respect for ordinary moral
thinking. In the *Groundwork,* he writes that an action "which does not harmonize with [the Categorical Imperative] is *forbidden* [*unerlaubt*]," whereas
"an action which is compatible with the autonomy of the will is *permitted*
[*erlaubt*]" (*Gr.* 86/439). And in the *Critique of Practical Reason* he sets out
three categories of modality, which he points out conform fairly well to "pop-

ular usage": the permitted and the forbidden, duty and what is contrary to duty, and perfect and imperfect duty. (See *Pr.R.* 11n, 66.)

In contemporary deontological logical systems, "permissible" is commonly and simply *defined* as "neither forbidden nor required," as Kant also does in *The Metaphysics of Morals* (223). But he also argues that strict obligation arises only negatively. So the fact that a maxim does not conflict with the Categorical Imperative is a sufficient condition for holding that an action with that maxim is *permissible* (*"licitum"*) and in that sense is "fit" to be or "qualifies" as a *possible* maxim in an ideal moral world. (See *M.M.* 214, 221–22, 388–89.) A merely permissive law (*"lex permissiva"*) makes such an action morally arbitrary, not obligatory. All other things being equal, once we judge that a maxim is not morally forbidden, we have what Kant calls a "moral title" either to act on or not to act on that maxim in the pursuit of our well-being. (See, e.g., *M.M.* 222, 247; *T&P* 283.)

As a little reflection shows, most of the choices ordinary people make turn out to be morally permissible behaviors aimed at promoting their morally legitimate welfare and well-being. At any given moment there may be and usually are an indefinite number of permissible maxims on which we may act. Although we may wish Kant had offered a more balanced presentation of his moral theory, one that placed more emphasis on this doctrine, it is clear that this is his doctrine.

Narrow and wide duties

Kant also shows that he is not the harsh moralist he occasionally has been portrayed as being, when he holds that our moral duties do not all obligate us in exactly the same way. He divides our moral obligations into those that are "narrow" and those that are "wide."

Kant describes narrow duties as "strict," "rigorous," and "perfect," for *any* action that violates them is morally wrong, its maxim – when conceived of also as a universal law – always generating a contradiction. (See *Gr.* 57/424.)[12] Our strict duties may be interpreted positively, such as the requirement to keep contracts, but they are fundamentally *negative* or limiting, specifying what Kant calls "duties of omission," namely, what is morally forbidden (e.g., "Do not break your contracts"), and requiring us to limit our pursuit of happiness by the demands of morality. (See, e.g., *Gr.* 53n/421n, 57/424; *M.M.* 382, 385, 390–91.)[13]

As we have just seen, our negative and narrow duties typically have co-ordinate positive and wide duties. Positive duties of virtue oblige us just as seriously as negative duties, but the Categorical Imperative is indeterminate about them in the sense of not specifying exactly what or how much we must do to fulfill them.[14] Rather than require us to perform particular actions, positive duties require us to adopt a policy, a self-imposed law, to act on some maxim or other instantiating that policy. (See *M.M.* 382, 385, 388–90, 392–93, 410.)

We cannot even *conceive* of the violation of a negative duty without generating a contradiction. But we do not similarly generate an internal contradiction if we conceive of a world in which everyone adopted a maxim or policy of ignoring, say, their positive obligation to help others, *as long as* they can adopt such a policy while still observing their coordinate negative obligations. Kant did not explicitly include this latter condition, because he did not discuss at any length the logical connections between negative and positive obligations. However, he does insist that we cannot rationally *will* a world in which everyone adopted a policy of ignoring any of their positive duties, because, as we shall see, we *eventually* will have to contradict such a maxim. (See, e.g., *Gr.* 55–57/423–24, 89/441; *Pr.R.* 34.)

While it is impermissible for us to be completely indifferent to or to ignore our positive obligations, a decision to obey such obligations in one way rather than another usually is morally permissible. (See *M.M.* 389–90.)[15] This is why Kant calls such duties "wide," "broad," "limited," and "imperfect." (See *Gr.* 53n/421n, 57/424; *M.M.* 446.) They leave us, Kant writes, "a play-room [or elbowroom – *Spielraum*] (*latitudo*) for free choice in following (observing) the law" (*M.M.* 390; see also 383, 393, 411, 432n). The more general a positive duty is, the more arbitrary it is exactly how we are to act on it. (See *M.M.* 390.) Because of this, there is no systematic way to offer an exhaustive and a priori account of how we are to fulfill our positive duties. (See *M.M.* 205, 389–90, 468–69.)[16]

Kant offers several reasons why positive ethical duties can and must be "wide" in obligation, reasons closely conforming to our ordinary moral judgments.

First, they cannot prescribe exactly how a person should behave because different actions can fit equally well under the same general positive maxim or policy. (See *M.M.* 389–90.) For example, there are an indefinite number of ways in which we can fulfill the morally obligatory policy to develop our talents. (See *M.M.* 392.) The general maxim to do so does not specify what Aristotle called "the particulars" of actions falling under it – what, where, when, to what extent, by what means, in what manner, and so on. (See *M.M.* 392–93.)[17]

Second, such maxims are limited or imperfect in the sense that we may limit one such maxim by another. Kant writes, for example, that we may limit the extent to which we exhibit obligatory beneficence toward others by the obligation to love our parents. The obligation of benevolence is clearly a duty, but as a general rule *particular* benevolent acts are "not an absolute obligation" (*Ed.* 490/104; see *M.M.* 390).

Third, wide duties require us to take into account empirical facts about the various situations in which we find ourselves, and exactly how an individual should do that is a matter of judgment. (See *M.M.* 205, 392, 411.) How one shows respect for one's parents, for example, obviously will be quite different, depending on whether they are alive or deceased, living nearby or far away, healthy or ill, and on and on. Exactly how one shows respect for anyone will also depend on cultural differences specifying how respect is to be demonstrated.

Despite occasional passages that seem to identify morality with rule following, Kant's discussion of wide duties illustrates how deeply he respected the important role of judgment in human moral life. He should not be faulted for failing to offer some procedure for arbitrating between different ways of fulfilling wide obligations. As he points out, we cannot rely here on some further maxim to help us apply a particular maxim to a particular case, for then we would need a maxim for using that maxim, and so on, ad infinitum. Moreover, each new maxim would still require the exercise of judgment. There simply is no substitute here for the exercise of judgment.[18]

When, in the case of wide duties, we cannot rely on moral principles for procedural guidance, Kant holds that our decisions both can and must be made "according to rules of prudence (pragmatic rules)" (*M.M.* 433n). Taking circumstances into account now is not only not immoral but even morally necessary in order to fulfill wide duties. We cannot act at all until we choose between an indefinitely large number of alternative courses of action. (See *M.M.* 223, 392; *Lect.* 258–60/18–19.) This is why, for example, Kant suggests that differences in social rank, age, sex, health, economic situation, education, cultural level, and even personality traits may all be taken into account when we fulfill wide duties. (See *M.M.* 468–69.)

Kant's doctrine concerning the moral indeterminacy of positive duties therefore supplements his doctrine concerning morally permissible actions to provide a defense against one set of criticisms based on a mistaken or incomplete understanding of his moral theory. It has been alleged, for example, that the Categorical Imperative mandates a radical egalitarianism requiring us to do for everyone whatever we do for one, or to do only and exactly what everyone else should and can do, or forbidding us to do what not everyone can do. On this mistaken view, for example, it would be immoral for educators to provide enrichment courses for students with exceptional mental abilities. Likewise, it supposedly would be immoral for anyone to practice, say, almsgiving, if not everyone can do so. But Kant advocates common sense and holds that in the matter of positive duties we are obligated to adopt a *policy* of, for example, beneficence. People with limited financial resources can still fulfill their obligation of benevolence by giving their time and talents. What each person should do must be left to the judgment of the individual. To put it somewhat differently, we are all obligated by the same specifically moral maxims, but decisions about how to act on positive obligations involve our choosing *prudentially good* maxims. As we shall see in Chapter 11, just as it is a blunder to try to judge the morality of a maxim by the prudential criterion of effectiveness, so it is a practical mistake to try to judge the prudential advisability of a maxim by the moral criterion of universality.

Kant's analysis of morally indifferent actions and morally wide duties also means that, strictly speaking, the most precise as well as most general way to state the notion of moral obligation is to put it negatively: The requirement that the maxims of our actions must be able to *qualify* for being a universal law means that our maxims must not "come into conflict with a law as such," that is, violate the Categorical Imperative. (See *M.M.* 389.) If we represent Kant as saying (as he in fact does) that we ought to act *only* on maxims that can serve as laws for everyone, it is important to add that these are not all laws of prohibition.[19] Many are positive duties that allow a wide variety of choices, and many others are laws of permission, which insist only that all other things being equal, what is morally permissible for one person must also be morally permissible for everyone else. It is unfortunate that Kant does not sufficiently emphasize this point.

Moral judgment

We have just seen the important role of judgment in fulfilling positive moral duties. But it may still be that Kant's emphasis on moral reasoning as an ability to formulate moral rules tends to obscure the crucial role he gives reasoning in the form of moral judgment.

In the first *Critique* Kant described judgment (*Urteilskraft*) as the ability of our understanding to determine whether and how particulars stand under a given law or universal, or, alternatively, whether a universal stands over a given particular and, if so, which universal. (See *Pu.R.* A19, A79/B105, A132–34/B171–74, A178–81/B221–24; see also *Pr.R.* 53, 68–69, 89; *Cr.J.* 179; *M.M.* 438; *Anthr.* 139, 199.) In general, moral judgment has two very different tasks. It must determine which practical principles – or possible *maxims* of kinds of actions – are morally acceptable and may or should be adopted as practical policies. It also must enter into decisions about how actually to *act* here and now. Throughout his moral works Kant's main attention is given *only to the first task,* a peculiar feature of his moral theory that to the best of my knowledge has been totally overlooked because he misleadingly but typically begins discussing his individual cases *as if* what is at stake is the second kind of decision, even though it is the acceptability of the agent's maxim with which he is concerned.

Before Kant, the Western philosophical tradition had tended to follow Aristotle by analyzing all practical deliberation in terms of what had come to be called the "practical syllogism." Kant also does this when he explains the tripartite division of the branches of civil government:

These three parts [of government] are like the three propositions in a practical syllogism: the law of the sovereign Will [the Legislature] is like the major premise; the command to act according to the law [the Executive] is like the minor premise that is the principle of subsumption under the Will; and the adjudication (the sentence) [the Judiciary] that establishes what the actual Law of the land in the case under consideration is, is like the conclusion. (*M.M.* 313)[20]

The following schema represents this kind of moral deliberation by means of which all substantive moral principles or "imperatives of duty can be derived from this one imperative as their principle" (*Gr.* 52/421).

54

I. **Major premise:** The Categorical Imperative.
 Minor premise: The maxim of an act type.
 Conclusion: A substantive moral principle in the form of a substantive categorical imperative.

In Part III we shall see in much greater detail how such judgments are made. For now the schema is sufficient to show that Kant thinks of practical rationality primarily in terms of what has come to be called an "administrative model," for this kind of thinking concludes to practical rules, like the policies or directives an administrator might promulgate.[21]

To bridge the gap between our practical maxims and our actual decisions about how to act here and now, we need to make still another sort of judgment. (See *Gr.* vii/390; *Pr.R.* 67.) Kant virtually ignores this last kind of judgment, but he also happens to appeal to it, almost casually, to describe part of the organization of the second *Critique:*

The division of the Analytic of Pure Practical Reason must turn out to be similar to that of a syllogism, i.e., proceeding from the universal in the major premise (the moral principle), through a minor premise containing the subsumption of possible actions (as good or bad) under the major, to the conclusion, viz., the subjective determination of the will (an interest in the practically possible good and the maxim based on it). (*Pr.R.* 90)

Here Kant follows much more closely the way in which a "practical syllogism" traditionally had been constructed according to Aristotle's description in *De anima* 3.11.434a16–19. An example of this kind of practical judgment, syllogistically schematized, would be as follows:

II. **Major premise** (a substantive universal moral principle): Making false promises is a morally wrong practice in which conscientious people do not engage.
 Minor premise (the particular facts): This action is a case of making a false promise, and I am not the kind of person who makes false promises (the subsumption of a proposed action under its description as a possible maxim of the agent, who has already adopted his fundamental "moral disposition," given in the major premise).[22]
 Conclusion: Therefore, I will not do this action ("the subjective determination of the will").

Syllogism II schematizes the kind of practical deliberation that occurs when an individual has already adopted either the ultimate principle of morality or the ultimate principle of prudence as his or her ultimate maxim. Now, in order to decide how to act here and now, that person needs to judge how a particular way of acting falls under the policies or principles he or she has already adopted. Kant rarely explicitly discusses this kind of practical deliberation. He simply presumes that his readers will know what it is all about and, in fact, in the *Critique of Practical Reason* (90, quoted earlier) he uses it to explain something else he regards as less clear.

Since this last kind of judgment obviously plays a crucial role in human moral life, we need to understand *why* Kant does not pay more attention to

55

it. The first reason is that he simply believes there is very little to be said about such judgments.[23] Kant thinks of this kind of judgment as a native endowment, like eyesight, calling it "so-called mother-wit." He writes that if we are lucky enough to have it, we can develop it by experience, whether personal or vicarious, through the use of casuistry. (See *Pu.R.* A132–34/B171–74, B172–73n; *Gr.* vii/389; *Pr.R.* 67; *T&P* 275; *M.M.* 411, 468; *Anthr.* 199.)

Kant's second reason reveals again the essentially *polemical* motivation behind almost all his philosophical writings. He typically did not write about morality simply because he was fascinated by the topic and wanted to offer a systematic exposition of it. Rather, throughout his ethical works he is chiefly concerned to defend morality against skepticism, to silence forever "all the objections to morality" engendered by the Newtonian revolution in science (*Pu.R.* Bxxxi). He therefore set out to show that there is a *rational* answer to the question *Why* should I be moral? As the title of his most famous work on ethics indicates, that required him particularly to investigate what he called the *Grundlegung* of morality, variously translated as the groundwork or grounding or foundation of human morality.

To answer the skeptical question *Why* is *this* kind of action morally right (or wrong)? Kant's defense of morality requires him to show that substantive moral principles can be objective judgments. Once again he is concerned to show that such judgments, rightly made, are based on reason, not merely on emotions or on sociological factors such as one's moral upbringing. So he offers the various formulas of the Categorical Imperative, as well as detailed accounts of the procedure for using the Categorical Imperative, to show that we do have rational criteria for deciding whether a maxim is morally acceptable. But he pays little attention to the kind of moral deliberation that was not under attack and therefore not in need of any particular defense.

Kant himself does not explicitly recognize the difference between the two kinds of reasoning, and the unfortunate consequence has been a great deal of controversy over the proper role of the Categorical Imperative.

Many readers have been led to think that Kant claims we need to use the Categorical Imperative in all our everyday decisions about how to act here and now, when we generally *already* know in principle what is right and what is wrong. It can be argued that Kant did know that in such decisions we simply act on the appropriate moral principles – substantive categorical imperatives – we have already adopted as our own policies. But because he does not explicitly discuss such decisions, his readers may take him to be claiming that all our moral decisions about how to act here and now must look something like this:

III. **Major premise:** The Categorical Imperative.
   Minor premise: The maxim of a possible action; for example, I wish to try to become a philosophy teacher (or whatever). (Implied reasoning process: If everyone did that, there would be no one to tend to all the other things that need doing and there wouldn't be enough teaching jobs available, etc.)
   Conclusion: Therefore, I should not try to become a philosophy teacher (or anything else, nor should anyone else, for that matter!).

56

This, of course, is a ridiculous conclusion, and those readers who have interpreted Kant in this manner quite naturally are led to think either that the Categorical Imperative is a completely unworkable moral norm or that it needs radical revision.

What has gone wrong here? First, we encounter the error discussed in the preceding section: judging in an inappropriate manner specific actions that fulfill general positive obligations. Second, syllogism III confuses the kind of deliberation appropriate only to testing maxims for their moral acceptability (syllogism I) with the form of deliberation appropriate to decisions about how to act here and now (syllogism II). As we shall see in Part III, the first kind of deliberation requires us to test the maxims of possible actions within the context of a law-governed, ideal moral world. Apart from that context, the deliberation may pretend to make a judgment on the basis of the purely formal, moral criterion of universality, but the conclusion is in fact based on the empirical and prudential consequences of everyone acting alike because they all have the same desire.

So as it turns out, the Categorical Imperative plays only a background role in our everyday moral life. We usually already have substantive moral maxims or adequate policies to guide our everyday decisions, such as the principles Kant sets out in the *Groundwork* and the *Metaphysics of Morals*. We need only judge when and how to act on them in various situations. But we do need to use the Categorical Imperative when we are having difficulty deciding whether a problematic maxim *is* morally right and we wish to avoid rationalizing our desires, or when, like Kant, we need to defend maxims from the attacks of moral skepticism.[24]

Erroneous moral judgments

In Kant's theory, we have no higher moral guide than pure practical reason and its norm, the Categorical Imperative. To claim that there is some forum or authority beyond or above the individual person's own moral reasoning destroys autonomy and, with it, morality. Putting the entire burden for moral decisions on the autonomous judgment of the individual person presupposes that each of us *can* know what is right and what is wrong. And this in fact is Kant's claim: "We must be able, in every possible case, in accordance with a rule, to know what is *right* and what is *wrong*, since this concerns our obligation, and we have no obligation to that which we cannot know" (*Pu.R.* A476/B504; see *Rel.* 186/174). It is not absolutely necessary, he tells us, for everyone to know "concerning all possible actions, whether they are right or wrong" (*Rel.* 186/174). But we must be able to determine *with certitude* what *our* obligations are. (See *M.M.* 440.)[25] As we have seen, Kant insists that determining with certainty what is right and what is wrong is not only possible but also not especially difficult. Moreover, in this regard no one has any special access to moral knowledge not also available to everyone else. (See, e.g., *Gr.* 20–22/404.) Therefore, we must conclude that what a person decides is his duty must *be* his duty.

It is obvious, however, that not every moral judgment is correct. Here the problem of evil appears as a historical litany of enormously evil acts committed by people like Hitler and Eichmann, claiming that their grossly mistaken moral judgments were morally correct. On a lesser scale, our personal moral experience leads us to believe that normally conscientious people can and do form incorrect moral judgments and act wrongly but from the motive of duty. (How frequently this happens and how often it is due to a lack of care in making judgments can only be guessed, since we have no sure access to anyone's actual reasoning; see *Rel.* 20/16.) In any case, however, we can distinguish between objectivity – what accords with the Categorical Imperative– and subjectivity – the moral judgments we actually adopt because we think they are objectively right, judgments that can be mistaken. (See *M.M.* 483–84.)

Kant clearly did not wish to deny that people can and do make wrong moral judgments. For example, he argues against any social union (such as a church) enacting unchangeable laws, because its doing so may only perpetuate old errors. As his *Religion* makes clear, Kant holds that the moral authoritarianism of historical religious bodies is badly in need of progressive enlightenment. (See *Rel.* 186/174; *T&P* 305; *M.M.* 327.) Moreover, as we saw in Chapter 4, Kant was certainly convinced that it is possible for people to be in error about the nature of human morality in general. This belief in fact helped justify his writing most of his moral works. He was convinced that, by falling into "the extravagances" of philosophical "genius," all other philosophers had misunderstood the nature of moral demands – consistently and universally, not just "at times" or "occasionally." (See *M.M.* 206–7, 163.)

His discussions of *how* it is possible for moral judgment to go amiss are not sufficiently prominent, for above all else, in his Critical writings he wanted to defend the *power* of pure practical reason. Moreover, what he does say seems internally inconsistent, partly because he did not distinguish carefully among (1) errors about the nature of human morality, (2) errors about maxims, and (3) errors about how to act. So we need to piece together what we can from what he says in various places.

On the one hand, there is the view that moral reason has sufficient power that errors cannot be inculpable. Speaking about moral maxims in his lectures on ethics, Kant maintained that "in respect to his natural obligations no man can be in error; the natural moral laws must be known to all; they are contained in our reason; no man can, therefore, err innocently in respect to them, and in the case of natural laws there can be no innocent errors" (*Lect.* 355/132). In this context, the "Natural Law" is equivalent to the a priori Law of Autonomy, and "natural moral laws" specify mainly negative duties that can be determined by reason alone, using the Law of Autonomy to examine the maxims of actions. (See *M.M.* 237–42.) (By contrast, positive juridical laws are laws only because they are civilly enacted.) Because the Categorical Imperative is a purely formal criterion, our proficiency in making judgments about our duties may benefit from practice, but those judgments pose no special difficulties and, like pure mathematics, require no special methodology. (See *M.M.* 411.)

Kant holds here that everyone *can* know the Natural Law and the obligations it generates. (See *Lect.* 355/133.) It follows, then, that erroneous moral judgments about obligations imposed by the Natural Law *must* be culpable. Hence, regardless of any protestations to the contrary, those committing gross crimes against humanity *cannot* do so in good faith: Their maxims and the actions they supposedly justify must have been adopted in bad faith and be due to bad moral character. (See *Lect.* 355/132–33.) This is exactly why we cannot conceive of such people as having a good will – the only unqualifiedly good thing "in the world, or even out of it" (*Gr.* 1/393).

On the other hand, Kant did not seem to want to deny that it is possible for a person, when making moral judgments, to make an "honest" mistake, without necessarily being an evil person. For example, he holds that errors in general may be due to "a crude and unpracticed judgment" (*Pr.R.* 163). And he still thought it possible for Epicurus, as mistaken as he may have been, to merit the judgment of being "virtuous" (*M.M.* 485). He even admits (but not often), "I can indeed err [note: *not* "I have erred"] at times in my objective judgment as to whether something is a duty or not"; and the principles a person of good character adopts "might occasionally be mistaken and imperfect" (*M.M.* 401; *Anthr.* 292).[26]

Finally, because he regards our judgments about what maxim to act on here and now as an exercise of our understanding, he tends to think of errors here mainly as simple errors in reasoning. (See *Pr.R.* 69; *Rel.* 186/174.) When he does discuss problems with practical errors, he tends to think mainly about issues irrelevant to this problem, for example, possible impediments (such as our own recalcitrant will) to our carrying out what we have *already* determined to be a duty. (See, e.g., *M.M.* 227–28.) He also says that, when deciding how to fulfill wide duties, anyone may "make a mistake (a *peccatum*)," literally, "a sin," by doing "more or less than prudence prescribes" without, however, committing "a vicious act (*vitium*)" or incurring moral blame (*M.M.* 433n). These are simple errors, which methodical study and thoughtful reflection on our experience, whether personal or vicarious, generally can remedy.

In any case, our best safeguard against errors is to follow what Kant calls dialectical rules for arriving at truth in our moral judgments. These rules emphasize that autonomy is both an impersonal and a social ideal: (1) think for oneself; (2) think from the standpoint of every other person; and (3) think consistently. (See *Cr.J.* 294; *Logic* 367/63; *Anthr.* 228.) Such conditions, taken together, amount simply to a restatement of the Law of Autonomy in the form of the Categorical Imperative. They are best fulfilled in the forum of open and public debate, where (particularly in difficult cases) the thinking of one person, one group, or even one culture can be tested for errors and idiosyncrasies from the standpoint of others also using the Categorical Imperative. (See *Orient.* 144–45; *M.M.* 314; *Anthr.* 219.)[27] As we shall see in

Chapter 18, all sincere moral disagreements, including those arising from different religious traditions, are subject to these dialectical rules and to the ultimate norm of pure practical reason.

Even with the most careful safeguards, however, it is still possible that at least *some* of the moral judgments of conscientious people may be wrong. There is always the possibility that in some moral matter we may suffer invincible ignorance, that is, be sufficiently unenlightened as not to realize that we are in error. In that sense moral enlightenment is always a process in progress. Even universal agreement does not guarantee that a particular maxim does in fact conform to the criterion of universality. It is the other way around: Universality or objective validity is the basis for correct universal and rationally necessary agreement. (See *Pr.R.* 12–13.) If we have conscientiously applied the Categorical Imperative, if we have followed every safeguard available to us, especially the dialectical rules, then we must regard our judgments about our duties, however unenlightened they in fact may be, as our actual duties. Our moral character depends on our fidelity to those judgments.

Given his faith in the Enlightenment, Kant is confident that, in the forum of public debate, reason and truth will triumph. The main problem, as he saw it, is not knowing what is right; it is doing what is right. There are never any guarantees that individuals will actually follow the correct dictates of reason in their lives.

The infallibility of conscience

We may tend to think of our judgments about what is morally right and wrong as paradigmatic exercises of conscience, but in Kant's analysis, conscience is not primarily a person's judgment about what is morally right or wrong; that judgment is already presupposed. (See *M.M.* 400, 437, 440; *Rel.* 186/174.) Instead, conscience is a "second-order" type of moral reflection – the sort of moral reasoning we do about ourselves – about our own moral character, whether we have used sufficient care in determining which maxims are morally acceptable, and whether we have conscientiously followed those judgments in our actions. (See *M.M.* 400, 437–38; *Rel.* 186/174.)

Kant holds that "man cannot so scrutinize the depths of his own heart as to be quite certain, in even a single action, of the purity of his moral purpose and the sincerity of his attitude, even if he has no doubt about the legality of his action. . . . It remains hidden from the agent himself how much pure moral content there has been in the motive of each action" (*M.M.* 392–93; see *End* 329–30). Although we can never be sure that we *have* acted from the proper moral motive, we can know whether we have *tried* to do so. (See *M.M.* 387, 392–93; *Rel.* 51/46, 68/62.) But we cannot reach any certain verdicts about our character. (See, e.g., *M.M.* 392–93, 441; *End* 329–30; *Anthr.* 295.) Kant, in effect, concludes that the judgments of our conscience are mainly limited to questions about the moral *legality* of our behavior and about our effort to act dutifully.

For this reason, Kant describes conscience by legalistic expressions. It is a "tribunal," "the consciousness of an inner court in man," in which we think of ourselves as prosecutor, accused, defense counsel, and judge. It leads us to a "judgment about what a person has or has not done," "a verdict of [moral] reason" – "condemnation or acquittal" (*M.M.* 438 and 440). Such judgments about whether we have acted in a morally legal fashion inevitably give rise to moral feelings such as guilt or moral contentment. (See *M.M.* 400.)

An individual's actual moral virtue – or lack of it – is irrelevant to the authority of that person's conscience. *Having* a conscience is not something we affect by our conduct; it is "an inevitable fact," part of our very being as rational agents (*M.M.* 379n, 400, 438). Since "conscience speaks out involuntarily and inevitably," we cannot have an obligation to acquire or have a conscience (*M.M.* 401; see 400). We also do not have a duty to live so as to merit the approval of our conscience, for then there would have to be another conscience to make us aware of the first, and so on. (See *M.M.* 400–401.) But Kant writes, we do have a duty to "know ourselves," by cultivating our conscience and sharpening our attentiveness to it. (See *M.M.* 401, 441.) Conscientiousness, therefore, means fidelity to one's moral judgments.

Kant's doctrine here reflects our ordinary moral thinking, for we commonly say that to be morally good, we must be true to our own convictions about what is right and what is wrong. But we also regard conscience as a *corrigible* expression of a person's character. Kant is extremely reluctant to admit this, since a "good will" is always and unconditionally good and since there is and can be no more ultimate moral authority than our own conscience. So, he writes, "we can only reverence" the judgments of our conscience and hold them to be as sacred as divine verdicts (*M.M.* 439n; see 439–40).[28] As a consequence, he also holds that, for the individual person, such judgments, conscientiously made, *cannot* be wrong. Errors can be identified as errors only when we can distinguish between what is true and what another person subjectively and mistakenly believes to be true. In the case of judgments about *our own* conscience we cannot make such a distinction. In *this* sense, Kant concludes, an erroneous conscience is "a logical impossibility" (*M.M.* 401).[29] "I cannot err in my subjective judgment as to whether I have compared my action with my practical reason," that is, with the objective judgment of pure practical reason (*M.M.* 401). In this matter, he concludes, "nothing more can be required of" a person (*M.M.* 401).

It also follows that people we describe as "lacking a conscience" actually are hypocrites. They cannot be sincere; they are lying to themselves by pretending to themselves that what they know to be false is true – for example, that an immoral action is morally good or that the ultimate prudential principle is the ultimate moral principle. (See *M.M.* 400, 430–31.) At the very worst, Kant writes, a person can become unconscientious, that is, "in the extremity of corruption, induce himself to pay no more attention to [his conscience], but he still cannot help *hearing* it" (*M.M.* 438; see 400–401).

In only one passage in his *Religion* does Kant partly balance the one-sidedness of his teaching. There he writes that from the viewpoint of an *objective observer,* persons who habitually perform morally legal actions but from merely prudential motives can eventually fall into self-deception about their moral disposition, believing themselves to be morally virtuous when they in fact lack moral worth. (See *Rel.* 38/33–34.) We can only wish he had discussed this and similar cases more thoroughly.

6
Morally obligatory ends

As we have seen, in prudential conduct, we make something an end because we find it desirable. In Kant's analysis, the sheer fact that we have adopted something *as* an end does not mean that it therefore can serve as the basis for moral choice: "Now it is certainly undeniable that every volition must have an object and therefore a material; but the material cannot be supposed, *for this reason,* to be the determining ground and condition of the maxim" (*Pr.R.* 34; emphasis mine). On the contrary, "when it is a question of duty, morality is perfectly able to ignore all ends, and it ought to do so" (*Rel.* 4/ 3–4). For the mere fact that because we have reason, we can set our own goals only gives us added "*extrinsic* value in terms of [our] usefulness (*pretium usus*)" (M.M. 434). Consequently, if "we assume any object, under the name of good, as the determining ground of the will prior to the moral law, and then derive the supreme practical principle from it, this always produces heteronomy and rules out the moral principle" (*Pr.R.* 109; see *M.M.* 376– 77, 382).

It may therefore seem to follow that we can act morally only when we act with *no* end in view. Kant occasionally is interpreted as believing this, but such a reading cannot be correct, for as the preceding quotation from the *Critique of Practical Reason* shows, he held that every maxim must be a "material maxim," that is, "contain an end" (*Pr.R.* 34 and *M.M.* 395). To make a rational choice means that a person has decided that something is worth pursuing as an end (or "object" or "matter"). There can be no rational actions that are completely aimless, much less aimless actions that are morally good. Moreover, our adoption of a material maxim always indicates that we have an interest in the end of that action. (See *M.M.* 230, 381, 384, 389; *Pr.R.* 20.) So, Kant writes, "Pure practical reason is a power of ends as such, and for it to be indifferent to ends or take no interest in them would be a contradiction, because then it would not determine the maxims for actions either (since every maxim contains an end) and so would not be practical reason" (*M.M.* 395).

Since Kant's theory may now seem simply incoherent, let us recapitulate his thinking so far. Whenever we act and so whenever we act morally, he holds, we *must* act on material maxims, that is, maxims incorporating ends. Prudential ends are merely subjective and extrinsic in value; they are ends for us only if and because we happen to want them. (See, e.g., *Gr.* 38/413, 64/427, 70/431; *Pr.R.* 44–45, 62; *M.M.* 388–89.) As we have seen again and again, if we could choose only subjective ends, then all our maxims would be hypothetical rules, and all our actions would be merely means – assessable only by the norm of effectiveness. (See *Gr.* 63–64/427–28; *Pr.R.* 58–59.) In that case "a *categorical* imperative would be impossible. And this would do away with all moral philosophy" (*M.M.* 385; see 382, 395).

Consequently, Kant concludes, the very existence of morality depends on there being *objectively* good ends (or "matter"). These are ends whose value does not depend on anyone's or everyone's desires and inclinations (*Pr.R.* 60–61). An objective or moral end is one that is "determined by reason alone" and so is "universally valid"; it is necessarily an end for every agent insofar as that person's actions are determined by reason. (See *Gr.* 7–8/396, 38–40/413–14, 63/427, 74/433; *Pr.R.* 44–45, 58, 60–61; *M.M.* 376, 380.) (This also means that whatever is morally forbidden is objectively wrong, regardless of anyone's desires.) So important are such ends to morality, Kant writes, that ethics can be defined *either* as a system of universal laws *or* as "the system of the ends of pure practical reason" (*M.M.* 381; see 394, 406).

Since morality always appears to us human beings as an "ought," moral ends always appear to us as morally obligatory (and whatever is objectively wrong necessarily appears to us as morally forbidden). Yet the expressions "morally obligatory ends" and "ends that also are duties" should *not* be interpreted to mean that any of our moral duties are ultimately *grounded* in these ends, for, once again, that would be to fall into heteronomy. (See, e.g., *Gr.* 88/441.) Neither moral motivation nor the moral rightness of maxims may ultimately be *based* on ends – even on objective ends.

Objective ends

The question now is, How is it *possible* for there to be objective ends?[1] This question in turn needs to be divided into two others. First, if we cannot appeal to our desires, by what criterion can we identify some objects (or matter) as intrinsically and objectively good? Second, even if we can identify something as objectively good, what can motivate us subjectively to adopt it as our end if we do not desire it?

Given what we have already seen of Kant's analysis of reason, we could have anticipated that he would call pure practical reasoning a "power of ends as such" (*M.M.* 395). Kant answers both of the preceding questions by maintaining that in its role as a higher faculty of desire, moral reason must be able both to identify whatever is objectively good and to motivate us to adopt it as an end. (See, e.g., *Pr.R.* 31, 58, 65.)[2] Let us examine first the cognitive power he claims for pure practical – or moral – reason.

To determine what is objectively good, we cannot appeal to experience or to any of the social sciences. (See, e.g., *Gr.* 62–63/426–27; *M.M.* 371.) We must be able to identify objectively good ends by a norm given a priori, that is, by our own moral reason alone. Once again, then, Kant turns to "the judgment of every reasonable man," to the norm already "inherent in the structure of every man's reason" (*Pr.R.* 60–61; *M.M.* 371). That norm, of course, is the Law of Autonomy, the purely formal requirement of universality. (See *Pr.R.* 34; *M.M.* 382, 385.) It identifies the objectively good simply as that which is good in the judgment of any and every rational being. Then, Kant writes, whatever "*can* be an [objective] end . . . *is* an end for pure practical reason" (*M.M.* 395).

This is how Kant resolves the problem of incorporating ends into morality without falling into heteronomy. The identification of what is morally good is grounded in the moral law; it is never the other way around. "The mere form of a law," Kant writes, "which limits its material, must be a condition for adding this material to the will but not presuppose it as the condition of the will" (*Pr.R.* 34).

The discussion of morally good ends belongs to the metaphysics of morals, but some ends are objectively good for specifically human moral agents, and identifying them requires us to take our "humanity" into account. Kant's discussions of human morality frequently do not draw the line clearly between, on the one hand, what can be said in a *pure* a priori way and applies to all rational beings, and, on the other hand, what necessarily must be said in a *mixed* a priori way because it applies specifically to human persons.[3] He spends so much effort contrasting the a priori basis of morality with the empirical foundation of prudence that it is not difficult to overlook the degree to which he also believes that claims about human morality must take into account special features of human nature and human life.

For example, as far as we can know, the notions of "duty" and "virtue" are specific only to moral agents with traits such as we human beings have but that other moral agents, if there are any, may or may not possess. (See *M.M.* 217.) Likewise, it is within human social practices such as promising that the recognition and respect due human moral agents take place, making such practices morally permissible. Finally, as we shall see in Chapters 12 and 13, some morally obligatory ends turn out to be also natural human goods, such as the development of one's talents. So Kant holds that the second formula of the Categorical Imperative is a synthetic a priori proposition because it adds nonformal material to the will. (See *M.M.* 396.) But the goodness of moral ends for specifically human agents may not depend on empirical information to make them desirable to us and in that sense our ends; their goodness depends only on the formal law of moral judgment.

Once we identify objectively good ends, how can moral reasoning motivate us to adopt them as our own ends? As we saw in the preceding chapter, Kant holds that only rational beings can "take an interest in" something as an end and, further, that finite and contingently rational beings like us *need* an incentive to be interested in, to care about doing what we ought. (See *Pr.R.* 79.) "Moral interest must be a pure nonsensuous interest," Kant insists, and yet, because we have a sensuous nature, for us at least, "an end is always the object of an inclination" (*Pr.R.* 79 and *Rel.* 6n/6). Kant therefore concludes that this originally nonsensuous interest of moral reasoning must give rise to special sensibly felt incentives on which we shall act. (See *M.M.* 398.)

We will examine the moral sentiments generated by moral reason as a conative power in Chapters 9 and 10. For now, it is enough to state that Kant insists they have essential positive and negative roles in human moral life. Positively, they must be sufficiently powerful for us to take an efficacious interest in specifically moral ends, apart from any merely pathological interest, that is, without any anticipation of pleasure. Negatively, they are needed as a moral limit on our prudential ends; they must be powerful enough for us to frustrate, when necessary, any and all merely subjective ends we may have. (See *Gr.* 63/427; *M.M.* 380, 389, 395.)

Right actions

If moral or pure reason actually is practical, Kant writes, "it will show its reality and that of its concepts in actions" (*Pr.R.* 31; see also 38, 67). To explain the notion of a "morally right action," Kant again contrasts morality with prudence. We learn prudential rules from experience with the world; they are "right" or "correct" insofar as they accurately set out what we must do to get what we want; and actions are prudentially good only insofar as they are instrumentally effective in getting us what we want. By contrast, moral rules are based on reason alone, they are correct only insofar as their maxims do not violate the Law of Autonomy, and morally correct actions as such are intrinsically good, irrespective of any possible or actual consequences. (See *Pr.R.* 60.)

Our ability to act on prudential rules and achieve prudential ends depends on and so is limited by various empirical contingencies, such as our own capabilities and conditions in the world. (See *Pr.R.* 36, 57; *M.M.* 482.) If our ability to act morally rightly were similarly dependent on empirical conditions, many of which we cannot fully control, moral rules could hold only conditionally, like prudential rules. But that would make the notion of a *categorical* imperative meaningless, and that would be the death of morality. (See *Pu.R.* Bx, Bxxi–xxii, B578ff, A800–804/B828–32; *Pr.R.* 20–21, 29–34, 42–47; *T&P* 283n.) What moral reason commands *must always* be within our power to do. (See *Pr.R.* 32, 36–37, 121–22; *M.M.* 380.) So the power of moral reason to cause morally good actions must not be dependent on empirical conditions, which may have no direct relevance to moral possibility. (See *Pu.R.* A319/B375, A547–48/B575–76; *Gr.* 40/415; *Pr.R.* 31, 45, 58, 66, 113.)

What is always possible for us to do is to shape our *intentions* in a morally acceptable manner, "whether the physical power is sufficient to this or not" (*Pr.R.* 15; see also 20, 45–46, 68–69).[4] Morally significant actions, then, for Kant, are *not primarily* performances in the world. Essentially, they are those "inner actions" or intentions that precede and cause our physical movements as their effects – *if* the latter are not frustrated by some external agency or other.[5] Having the right intention means conscientiously adopting morally acceptable maxims of conduct, "even before I ask whether I am capable of achieving a desired effect or what should be done to realize it" (*Pr.R.* 20; see also 15, 21, 44, 58, 60, 62; *Gr.* 13–14/399–400; *M.M.* 218–19). In this sense,

66

there is no need to teach anyone how to perform morally good actions, for "whatever [a person] wills to do he also can do" (*Pr.R.* 37).[6]

Kant uses many different terms to refer to moral action proper: "volition," "willing," "intention," "the manner of acting," "the maxim of the will," "the determination of the will," "the inner legislation of reason," "principle of volition," "mental disposition," and "character." (See, e.g., *Gr.* 3/394, 13–14/399–400, 43/416; *Pr.R.* 15, 60, 66, 82–84, 86, 98, 123, 152; *M.M.* 227.) He expresses this doctrine peculiarly in the *Groundwork* when he describes the practicality of pure reason (*Vernunft*) as consisting in its ability to "have influence on the will [*Wille*]" (*Gr.* 7/396; see also *Pr.R.* 15). Since he identifies pure reason and the will, in effect he is saying that our practical reason must be able to be completely self-determining, so that we can form our intentions by the Law of Autonomy. (See *Gr.* 1/393, 3/394, 98/447; *Pr.R.* 16, 20, 45–46, 60, 66, 71, 114–15.)[7]

That Kant considers moral life to be primarily "a morality of intentions" (*eine Moralität der Gesinnung*) can be obscured by the fact that he also takes "practice" to be "cases that come up in experience" (*Pr.R.* 152 and *M.M.* 205). He states, for example, that moral practice concerns what a person does "*in concreto* in his conduct of life," namely, "actions which are events occurring in the world" (*Gr.* vii/389 and *Pr.R.* 68; see also 119).[8] Moreover, his examples commonly refer to actions in the sense of observable conduct. (See, e.g., *Gr.* 9–10/397–98, 12–14/399–400, 18–19/402–3, 55–56/421–23; *Pr.R.* 30.) Finally, in his political writings, Kant holds that the subject matter of civil responsibilities consists in "outer duties" or "duties of outer freedom," that is, behavior subject to coercion by the state. The moral-political category of justice also concerns behaviors affecting others. (See *M.M.* 218–19, 230.)

Kant did believe that external, visible performances can have moral significance as a sign of our moral sincerity. We do not satisfy the apodictic demands of morality merely by insincere wishes, by taking "a wish for the deed" (*M.M.* 430; see also 441). We always need to strive with all our power to carry out our moral decisions in our conduct, for such effort indicates the genuineness of our intentions (*Gr.* 3/394).

In an ideal world we always would have the physical power and skill to carry out our intentions effectively. (See *Pr.R.* 43.) But the world in which we happen to live is not so ideally constructed. Too much depends "on circumstances that, by and large, are not under man's control," and then our inability to carry out our intentions does not detract from our moral quality (*M.M.* 482). Because that is the case, our power – or lack of it – to effect changes in the world is not necessarily a moral matter at all, and inculpable ineffectiveness may be disregarded in assessing a person's character. (See, e.g., *Gr.* 85/439.)[9]

We therefore need to keep in mind that when Kant describes actions as "the object" (*Gegenstand*) or "the end" (*Zweck*) of moral reason, he may be thinking of "an action" in either of these two senses.[10] In the first sense, our moral willing is its own immediate object, to be shaped autonomously by the

Law of Freedom. (See *Gr.* 98; *Pr.R.* 16, 45–46, 60, 63, 66, 71.) In more ordinary language, our intentions deserve to be considered morally good (the kind of intentions grounded in morally good character) when they are autonomous decisions; and having such intentions may be sufficient for us to be morally good people. When we do have the power to carry out those decisions in observable conduct – "actions" in the second sense – then moral reasoning must also inform and guide our behavior as its object. (See *Pr.R.* 83, 86–87.)

A "good will"

Although morally significant actions may be considered one by one, each is also but a momentary expression of an underlying and unifying moral character. The supreme individual practical end or good to be produced is a morally virtuous character or what Kant calls "a good will." (See *Pr.R.* 44, 58–60.) Unlike the qualities of the prudential person, a morally good will is "absolutely and in every respect good and the supreme condition of all good" (*Pr.R.* 62; see 60).[11] As Kant's "first proposition" in the *Groundwork* states, a good will (i.e., a morally good person) is "good through [his or her] willing alone – that is, good in [himself or herself]." His or her character is intrinsically and unconditionally good. It has "inner worth" (*innern Werth*) or dignity (*Würde*) because the person's willing is good in itself, not because of what the person actually "effects or accomplishes" in the world (*Gr.* 3/394 and 77/435; see 13–16/399–401, 63/427, 82/437, 85/439; *Pr.R.* 15, 21, 45–46, 58, 60, 62, 156–57; *M.M.* 228). What makes a person's willing intrinsically good is that person's ultimate moral disposition – the adoption of the Law of Autonomy as his or her overriding practical maxim. We shall discuss the nature of the good will in more detail in Chapter 9.

Kinds of practical goods

The ends of moral reason are not all alike. Some morally obligatory ends, such as moral perfection, are ends to be achieved. Others, such as morally good actions, need to be done. Still others already exist and are to be recognized and respected as having intrinsic, unconditional, or absolute value merely by their existence. These include all rational beings or "persons," not only human beings but whatever other rational beings there might be. (See *Gr.* vi/389; *M.M.* 385.)[12] However, we only have experience with and knowledge of *human* persons, and so it is only to them that we actually have duties. (See *M.M.* 442.)[13]

In Chapter 3 we saw that it would have been a great help to his readers had Kant offered a clear theory of human action. It would have been an equally great help had he offered, particularly in the *Groundwork*, a general division of objective goods, for the moral world we will examine is heavily populated by such goods.[14] According to Kant, we humans all have two general kinds of practical goods: As natural beings, we all necessarily want to be happy; as moral agents, we all should develop a morally good character. In anticipation of more detailed discussions later, the following outline roughly schematizes those practical goods.

I. Natural and conditionally good (prudential) goods, to be promoted and, if possible, to be achieved by us (see Chapters 4, 14, and 15):
   A. Happiness – an intrinsic good for us as *natural* beings; its pursuit is morally permissible when not contrary to the moral law; its achievement is our right insofar as we are virtuous.
   B. Natural perfection, that is, mental and physical development and whatever external and social goods are extrinsically good in the sense of being necessary conditions for or instruments in helping us achieve happiness.
II. Unconditional (moral) goods:
   A. Intrinsically good ends to be promoted and, if possible, achieved by us:
      1. as moral beings: moral virtue (see Chapters 9 and 10);
      2. as moral-physical beings: natural perfection insofar as that is a constituent of moral virtue (see Chapter 13);
      3. as social beings: the kingdom of ends, in the form of a just political state, as perpetual political peace within a league of nations, as an ethical society, and finally in its perfect form as the Kingdom of God in a life after death (see Chapters 15–17).
   B. Intrinsically good self-existent ends to be recognized and not acted against: all human persons or, more specifically, the moral law present equally in the reason of every person (see Chapter 14).

As we saw in Chapter 4, happiness is an Idea of the imagination – the complete and lasting satisfaction of all our needs and desires as a whole and our enjoyment of and contentment with such a life. Because our pursuit of happiness is subject to restraints imposed by morality, however, happiness is only conditionally good. So also are those helpful means to, or necessary conditions for, happiness that Kant lists in the first paragraphs of Chapter I of the *Groundwork:* mental and emotional traits and "gifts of fortune" such as health, power, wealth, and honor. (See *Gr.* 1/393.) But the moral law does recognize that, because we are by nature dependent beings, we have a moral right to such happiness as is not contrary to the Law of Autonomy.

Moral perfection or holiness is the ultimate supreme good for every moral agent, but our moral agency is characterized by two ineluctable limitations: imperfection and embodiment. For us as imperfect (i.e., only contingently moral) agents, morality always must appear as our duty, and virtue is the highest moral accomplishment of which *we* are capable. (See *M.M.* 379–80.)[15] As embodied and dependent agents, we also have a moral duty to develop and sustain whatever natural capacities form part of human virtue or are necessary for us to strive for virtue. (See *M.M.* 387, 395, 418, 420, 423, 429, 444, 456.)[16] So, as the outline shows, we can and must regard some natural goods, such as human life, the development of talents, and a just state, from two different viewpoints. We can pursue them only for prudential purposes, and then they are only conditionally good. They also have only instrumental value insofar as they help us achieve desired ends. But they also can be regarded either as *part* of human virtue or necessary *means* in our pursuit of virtue, and in either case Kant holds that those same goods should also be regarded as objectively good and as morally obligatory. (See *M.M.* 387–92.) If we do not keep these distinctions in mind, we may be puzzled by his contention that some natural goods are also moral duties.

A system of obligatory ends

Kant regards ethics as, equivalently, a system of morally obligatory ends and a system of moral duties. When discussing the latter, he divides and organizes his materials in different but often overlapping ways: duties to self and duties to others; duties to persons (both self and others), considered either as imperfectly moral beings, as moral beings with a physical nature, or as social beings; duties that are narrow and negative and those that are wide and positive; and juridical duties and "ethical" (or nonjuridical) duties. Depending on which division he takes to be the most general, the others are then regarded by him as subdivisions. One approach does not seem obviously better than another.[17]

The following outline takes that division of duties to be most general that separates our duties into those that are negative and mainly narrow and those that are positive and mainly wide. Each of these headings then is divided into duties to ourselves and duties to others, both as imperfectly moral beings and as embodied natural beings. It is, of course, possible to arrange these materials differently, as Kant himself did on occasion. (See, e.g., *M.M.* 398, 412.)

OUR FUNDAMENTAL MORAL DUTIES[18]

NEGATIVE (AND NARROW) DUTIES	POSITIVE (AND WIDE) DUTIES
To myself as an imperfectly moral being: my virtue	
I may not violate my own moral integrity by heteronomously –disobeying the moral law –refusing to limit self-love by respect for the moral law, e.g., by lying, avarice, servility[19]	I must cultivate my autonomy – my dignity and self-respect; I will maintain a virtuous moral character by trying –always to do my duty –because it is my duty[20]
To myself as a moral-physical being: natural perfection necessary to my virtue[21]	
I may not completely neglect self-development or misuse sex or cause myself physical harm, e.g., by excessive food or drink, by self-mutilation, or by suicide[22]	I must both develop my natural talents and promote my physical health and self-preservation[23]
I may not neglect my happiness when doing so is detrimental to my virtue[24]	I have an indirect duty to tend to my happiness when that is necessary or helpful to my virtue[25]

To others as imperfectly moral beings: their virtue

I may not tempt others to do wrong, e.g., by scandal (a negative but wide duty), nor may I treat them disrespectfully, merely as things, e.g., by lying to them[26]

(I have no positive duties to others' achievement of virtue; each person is responsible for his or her own moral character)[27]

To others as moral-physical beings: their happiness

In general: I may not be indifferent to the happiness of other human beings[28]

In general: Out of duty I must, insofar as I can, make others' permissible happiness my own end[29]

Duties of inner freedom: I may not allow myself mean attitudes toward others' pursuit of happiness[30]

Duties of inner freedom: I must be benevolent by wishing for and taking satisfaction in the happiness of others[31]

Duties of outer freedom:
–I may not act unjustly, disobey civil laws, or treat others merely as a means to my own ends[32]
–I may not refuse to help others in need, insofar as I can do so[34]

Duties of outer freedom:
–I must be beneficent, i.e., contribute to the morally legitimate happiness of others (a nonjuridical ethical duty)[33]
–I must help provide the basic needs of those unable to do so for themselves (a juridical ethical duty)[35]

When organizing our various duties, Kant had two aims in mind. First, he wanted to reflect faithfully the judgments of ordinary moral reason. Second, he believed that organizing any complex subject matter into a schema, outline, or "architectonic" is just what can raise our ordinary judgments to the rank of science. Showing the interrelationships of the various parts can help ensure completeness and promote our understanding of that subject. (See *Pu.R.* A832/ B860; *Proleg.* 263.) But as it turns out, the verdicts of ordinary moral judgment prove surprisingly recalcitrant to systematization. So, for example, Kant claims that all negative duties are narrow, but, as the outline shows, not tempting others is a negative but wide duty. He also claims that all duties of virtue are of wide obligation (see *M.M.* 390), but as the outline shows, we also have narrow and negative duties of virtue. But Kant was so enamored of schemata that he usually ignores the exceptions to his generalizations. None of the exceptions is in fact so important *as* an exception as to justify our setting aside his distinctions, say, between narrow and wide duties.

However, Kant's tendency to force materials into neat categories can cause serious confusion when he seems to claim that different kinds of duties fall under and are justified *only* by one or another of the formulations of the Categorical Imperative. For example, in the *Metaphysics of Morals* he occasionally seems to describe all juridical and external duties as falling under, and thus as justifiable only by, the first formula, and all ethical, inner, and nonjuridical duties as falling under and justifiable only by the second formula. (See, e.g., *M.M.* 380–81, 395–96, 410.) On this reading, the first formula

71

of the Categorical Imperative is what he calls the "supreme principle of justice," requiring that the maxims of external actions must be fit to serve as civil laws for everyone and only limiting or ruling out behaviors that do not fulfill this requirement. (See *M.M.* 231.) By contrast, the second formula is the "principle of the doctrine of virtue," requiring of us positive and wide duties not subject to any external legislation.

But Kant also claimed that he used different formulas only because he thought that, from a purely subjective and heuristic point of view, one might be more appealing to, and thus more effective with, some readers than another. (See *Gr.* 79–80/436.) (So, when discussing each formula later, I shall follow Kant in this matter and discuss duties in the terminology appropriate to that formula.) He also insists that there is but *one* Categorical Imperative with different but equivalent formulas. (See, e.g., *Gr.* 51–52/420–21.) If they are formally equivalent, then the duties required by one formula cannot be different in any significant way from those generated by another. As we shall see when we examine the first and second formulas in more detail, they do turn out to be equivalent, or at least they can be so interpreted. Either can be used and in fact both are used by Kant in other books to support the same claims concerning what is required, what is forbidden, and what is permissible.

Conflicts between moral rules

What generally most impresses his readers, particularly those who read mainly the *Groundwork,* is Kant's emphasis on the rule-making-and-following character of reason. We cannot understand rational activity or moral agency, he writes, unless we think in terms of practical rules, including both the Categorical Imperative and more particular maxims of possible act types. (See, e.g., *Gr.* 36–37/412–13; *Logic* 14.)

It is understandable, then, that Kant's critics have commonly been led to think that a singularly embarrassing problem for his theory is its inability to deal with conflicting moral obligations or rules. There is no particular problem with "conflicts" between a narrow obligation and a wide one. Narrow obligations admit of no exceptions, but wide duties may be satisfied in any number of ways. So in such cases one would fulfill the narrow obligation and simply look to fulfill the wide duty in another way at another time.

But how can we understand those problematic circumstances in which we must choose between what we take to be conflicting narrow or rigorous moral obligations? We may be able to avoid wronging another person, for example, only by telling a lie. Conflicts between strict maxims of conduct do present special problems for Kant. If there could be a genuine conflict between strict moral duties, then it would seem that one obligation would have to override the other. But Kant insists that strict moral obligations are obligations to which *no* exceptions may be made. It also might seem that such conflicts are in principle simply not possible, since Kant has argued that the ultimate norm of morality is and must be pure practical reason, which cannot generate logical incompatibilities without destroying itself. As Kant holds elsewhere, the one condition necessary for the very existence of reason is the principle of noncontradiction. (See, e.g., *Pu.R.* A151/B190; *Pr.R.* 120; *Logic* 49–51/ 55–57.)

We therefore might try to maintain that the ultimate moral norm cannot and does not generate conflicting moral rules. But such a claim is contrary to common moral experience; it fails to account for the facts of our moral life, just as did Socrates' denial of the reality of moral weakness. Alternatively, we might conclude that moral reason does in fact generate contradictions and so is *not* a reliable moral guide. But that admission is untenable for Kant, for it would destroy morality.[36]

There are at least two reasons why Kant did not pay sufficient attention to this type of problem. First, he believed that the most crucial moral conflicts occur between duty and inclination, and those are the conflicts with which he is mainly preoccupied. Second, as we saw in Chapter 5, he says very little at all about those deliberations preceding decisions about how to act here and now, for they cannot be schematized in an a priori way.

Kant does confront this problem, but only once and then only in a very summary fashion. The very brevity of his discussion means we need to reflect very carefully on what he says. He writes, "Two conflicting *rules* cannot both be necessary at the same time: if it is our *duty* to act according to one of these rules, then to act according to the opposite one is *not* our duty and is even *contrary to* our duty" (*M.M.* 224; emphases mine). So Kant admits what he cannot deny – that moral *rules* can and occasionally do conflict in the concrete situations of life. (See *M.M.* 297.) He apparently saw no particular difficulty in this admission. As long as such conflicts are not logically *necessary* and can be resolved, they are no more a threat to reason as a competent guide than are the conflicts between the moral and prudential interests of practical reason.

But since the ultimate moral norm commands us to act self-consistently, it *is* "inconceivable," Kant writes, that we could be obligated to act inconsistently. He therefore insists, as he must, that there *cannot* be a genuine conflict between *duties* (*ein Widerstreit der Pflichten*), a conflict such that we would have a duty to act at the same time on conflicting rules.

In the case of a conflict between moral rules, Kant maintains that what determines our actual duty is what he calls "the ground of obligation (the *ratio obligandi*)," which is to be found *either* in the agent *or* in the moral rule itself (*M.M.* 224; see 222). For any particular duty, "there can be *only one* ground of obligation" (*M.M.* 403), and in the case of conflicting rules, "one or the other of these grounds is not sufficient to oblige" the person, and therefore obedience to one or the other rule is "not a duty" (*M.M.* 224). In such instances, he argues, it is not correct to say that the stronger obligation takes precedence or that one is more obligatory than the other, for all moral obligations are absolute. (Even wide obligations do not admit of exceptions, only of a wide range of ways to fulfill them.) Rather, the stronger *ground* of obligation prevails. (See *M.M.* 224.) And then "it is not only not a duty but contrary to duty to act according to the other" rule (*M.M.* 224). Negative

73

and strict duties as a rule thus carry more weight than positive duties, and positive duties to self have more prima facie weight than positive duties to others. (See, e.g., *Lect.* 432–33/211.)

It is easy to interpret Kant harshly, as engaging here merely in verbal magic. Even H. J. Paton, normally a sympathetic interpreter, describes Kant's distinction as merely "a matter of terminology."[37] We cannot help wishing that Kant had discussed these issues in more detail, but it is not too difficult to give him a more plausible reading than Paton does. What Kant has in mind here is the necessary and ineluctable role of judgment in the application of moral rules. One of the things our judgment tells us, for example, is that we do not have a moral obligation actually to *act* on every moral rule at every given moment. We can hold that a particular rule is a narrow moral rule, like the injunction against lying, which does bind us without exceptions (is a *lex obligandis*, as Kant puts it), and yet judge that it is not a law actually obligating us (a *lex obligans*) here and now to act on it. (See *Pr.R.* 159.) When, for example, I am reading a book or working in the garden, the moral injunctions, say, of benevolence and against lying still weigh against me, but, in the absence of other considerations, I may not be obligated actually to obey either injunction at that moment.

Now imagine a person who seems obligated to perform two different actions simultaneously by the same moral rule to keep his word. He has promised to meet another person, fully intending to do so, but finds out, just before the appointed time, that he needs to take his wife to the hospital. Unless there are other morally contravening considerations, clearly he is entitled to judge that *his* sole duty *at that moment* is to take care of his wife. It would be contrary to his duty to ignore his obligations to his wife in order to keep his appointment, and he should simply break it. He may *regret* having to do so without warning, but he need not feel morally *guilty* about it. The other person planning on the appointment may be irritated and feel inconvenienced, but he has no reason to judge the husband to be morally blameworthy.

This is the sense of Kant's saying that the stronger *ground* of obligation – here that of a husband who has special strong contractual obligations to his wife – takes precedence. The ground of obligation cannot here be based on the rule of promise keeping, because that rule cannot arbitrate between the two courses of conduct. This is also the bite in Kant's contention that there is no genuine conflict between moral duties: Such a person does not say that he made an *exception* to the rule of promise keeping; he says, rather, that *at this moment and under these circumstances* he was not obligated to keep his appointment.[38]

This explanation may not satisfy a critic who believes that moral virtue for Kant consists only of a blind and absolutistic following of rules. Certainly in many passages Kant does give the impression that he thinks the "carrying out of rules" is what morality is all about. (See, e.g., *Pu.R.* A328/B385, A476/ B504; *Gr.* 36–37/412–13.) But as we saw in the preceding chapter, he also has great respect for the importance of ordinary moral judgment. (See, e.g., *Pu.R.* A133–34/B172–74; *Gr.* vii/389; *Pr.R.* 67; *T&P* 275; *M.M.* 411, 468.)

His respect for the subtlety of ordinary moral consciousness could hardly have led him to develop a moral theory that would reduce autonomous moral judgment to a mindless following of moral formulas. (See *Gr.* 21/404.) In fact, in his *Answer to the Question: What Is Enlightenment?* Kant himself attacks mechanical rule following as diametrically opposed to the ideal of the Enlightenment that each of us should act autonomously; that is, we should make our own moral judgments and live our lives by our own reason: "Rules and formulas, those mechanical aids to the rational use, or rather misuse, of his natural gifts, are the shackles of a permanent immaturity," which is the antithesis of our having "a rational appreciation for both [our] own worth and for each person's calling to think for himself" (*Enlight.* 36).

We may conclude that Kant did take into account the possibility of conflicts between moral rules and incompatible courses of conduct following from the same rule. It may further be argued that he introduced clarity and precision into our description of such conflicts by refusing to allow them to be described as conflicts between moral duties. Finally, his theory recognized the critical place of judgment in human moral life. The connection between a moral theory's principles and the actual moral decisions we must make requires judgment, which as we saw in Chapter 5, Kant maintained cannot be reduced to a schematized procedure but can only be fostered and promoted by careful reflection, by casuistry, and by experience. (See, e.g., *Gr.* vii/389.)

7
The defense of morality

Kant has set out what it must *mean* to say that we human beings are moral agents. He has also concluded that all other philosophers were badly mistaken in thinking of human morality as a high species of prudence. What he has not yet shown is that we *are* moral agents. His analysis has yielded hypothetical claims only: *If* there are moral agents, this is what a moral agent must be – one who can act autonomously; and *if* there are contingently moral agents, the Law of Autonomy necessarily appears to them as a categorical imperative. (See *Gr.* 124/461.) Kant therefore has offered only this claim about our own purported moral agency: If our common belief that we are moral agents is true, we are bound by the Law of Autonomy as a categorical imperative. (See, e.g., *Gr* 72/432.) But he also remarks that getting this far should not be underestimated; by itself it represents "a quite considerable gain" (*Gr.* 103/449).

Clearly, people commonly believe that they have a moral nature, that they can make moral judgments, and that they are obligated to act morally. Most do not feel any great need for a defense of these beliefs. In fact, they would find it odd that anyone thought such a defense necessary. As we know, Kant had enormous respect for the ordinary person's ability to think about moral matters. Had such people been his main readership, in all probability he would have been content simply to offer a clear and correct analysis of the nature of morality in general and of human morality in particular. (See *Gr.* 109/453.)

Nonetheless, because the new Newtonian science regarded the natural world of which human beings are a part as completely governed by inexorable causal laws, it inevitably generated moral skepticism. In a causally determined world the notion of an "ought" can have no meaning. (See *Pu.R.* A547/B575; *Pr.R.* 95–96.) Moral skeptics could readily admit that belief in our free and moral nature is widespread, and they could even admit that they found themselves deliberating and acting as if they were free. But they also would maintain that these beliefs are as illusory as the once common belief that the earth is flat and, like that belief, can be explained (away) by sociological and anthropological causal accounts. Against such a radical skepticism, therefore, Kant must find an adequate defense of the reality of human moral nature. (See *Pu.R.* Axi, Bix–x, Bxxi–xxii, Bxxviia, Bxxx, A822–23/B850–51; *Gr.* 120–21/458–59; *Pr.R.* 4–5, 11n, 28–29, 48, 50–57, 91.)[1]

Philosophers before Kant had typically held that theoretical reasoning is not only our most powerful faculty but also our only access to reality.[2] If we cannot show by standard theoretical criteria that something actually is so, we are not entitled to believe that it is. In his defense of the reality of our moral agency, Kant stands this view on its head by arguing that although theoretical reasoning has its own rights, moral or pure practical reasoning is in some significant ways a more powerful faculty, able and entitled, within certain strictures, to go beyond the limitations of sense experience and so of theoretical reasoning. (As we shall see in the next chapter, Kant uses this same argument to contend that moral interests are finally more important than theoretical interests.)

How is morality possible?

As we have seen, if we humans are rational agents, we are the sort of agents to whom the Law of Autonomy must appear as an imperative. Such an imperative, of course, can make sense and actually bind us categorically if and only if we can obey it by acting autonomously. Kant therefore states that the defense of human morality requires us to answer the question: "How is the imperative of morality possible?" (*Gr.* 48/419). He restates the problem in two other, equivalent ways: "How can an imperative be categorical?" and "How can pure practical reason be possible?" (*Gr.* 124/461; *Pr.R.* 42). Answering this question will be especially difficult, he writes, because "we have here a synthetic a priori practical proposition" (*Gr.* 50/420; see 95/444).

To understand this last statement, we need to review some of the materials covered in Chapter 2. There we saw that Kant holds that propositions or judgments can be either analytic or synthetic. In analytic judgments, the predicate merely repeats, perhaps in a partial but more explicit fashion, what already is contained in the (meaning of the) subject concept. If an analytic judgment is true, it is universally and necessarily true. In more contemporary terms, to say that a statement is analytically true is to say that it is true by definition. By contrast, in synthetic judgments the predicate is ampliative; that is, it adds new information about the subject.

In Chapter 4 we saw that Kant holds that the ultimate principle of prudence is that insofar as an agent is rational, willing an end also means willing whatever means are known by that agent to be necessary to get that end. This claim, Kant states, is analytically true, for it simply explicates the notion of (finite) rational agency: The concept of "willing the means to an end" is contained in and so is part of the concept of (or the meaning of) rationally "willing an end." (See *Gr.* 45/417, 48/419.) But formulated as a principle for rational agents who can still act irrationally, the ultimate "law" of prudence states that a contingently rational agent who wills an end *ought* also to will the means he knows are necessary to get it. This is a synthetic priori claim, for the predicate is ampliative and is joined to the subject by a verb exhibiting necessity.[3] To agents like human beings, who can and often do act counterproductively, this principle appears as an imperative of prudential rationality. If we ask, in Kantian fashion, How is the imperative of prudence possible; that is, how can such an imperative oblige a person hypothetically? the imperative's binding power for agents like us depends on our having desires we genuinely want to satisfy and having ways to do so.

The Principle of Autonomy – "A moral agent is one who can (and, insofar as that agent acts morally rightly, *does*) act autonomously, on the basis only of that agent's own reasoning, that is, independently of any merely pathological desires" – is also an analytically true proposition.[4] The predicate, Kant tells us, only makes explicit our ordinary notion of what it is to have the nature of the subject, a moral agent. (See *Gr.* 20/403, 88/440, 95–96/445.) Given the way in which Kant uses the terms "free," "moral," and "autonomous," the following claim *about* human agents is also necessarily and analytically true: If human agents are free, they can act autonomously, which means they are moral agents bound by the Law of Autonomy. (See *Gr.* 98/447, 110–11/453–54; *Pr.R.* 31.)

Kant has given us a rule for deciding in an a priori fashion which statements are analytically true: Their denial results in a contradiction. (See *Pu.R.* A7/B11, A151/B190–91.) The Law of Autonomy is analytically true, for if we try to deny it, we end up with self-contradictory and meaningless sentences such as: "It is not the case that a free agent is an agent who can act autonomously, on the basis of his own reasoning alone" and "An agent is morally good insofar as that agent does not (always) act morally rightly, that is, autonomously."

By contrast, Kant holds that this claim or definition is *not* necessarily analytically true: "A rational agent *as such* is an agent who is necessarily under the Law of Autonomy." (See, e.g., *Gr.* 50n/420n.) Kant's position here may strike a reader today as strange, for it would seem that a rational agent as rational is just the kind of agent who would always act on the basis of reason alone. But in the preface to the *Groundwork,* Kant explains that philosophers like Christian Wolff had begun their moral philosophy with an empirical psychological analysis of the concept of "rational agency as such" or "in general" or "willing as such." That is, they defined agents as rational only in the sense of being able rationally to fulfill their desires and inclinations. (See *Gr.* ix–xi/390–91, 62–63/426–27.) They thereby excluded any recognition or consideration of pure willing, that is, of pure practical reason. Given *that* meaning of "rational agent as such," Kant is clearly right: It is not analytically true that the concept of "rational agency as such" and therefore the concept of "all rational agents" would include the idea of being free in the transcendental sense and therefore under the pure Law of Autonomy. (See, e.g., *Gr.* 87/440; *Rel.* 26n/21.) This sort of beginning is flawed by a question begging that in effect rules out even the possibility of a categorical imperative, for any imperative binding such agents apparently could only be hypothetical.[5]

But Kant writes, if we could know that human agents are *free* (that is, given the meaning of transcendental freedom, agents with a pure practical will), then we would also know that we are moral agents, bound by the Law of Autonomy. (See *Gr.* 98/447; *Pr.R.* 31.) This, however, is precisely the question at issue: *Are* we free in that sense, able to act only on the basis of our own reasoning? Or, alternatively, "How is a categorical imperative possible?" (*Gr.* 124/461).

We are now in a position to understand Kant's saying that the Categorical Imperative is "a synthetic a priori practical proposition." The Categorical Imperative is a judgment in the form of a *command* directed at humans, who purportedly have a pure practical will but who act on its law only contingently and in *that* sense are only contingently rational agents. (See *Gr.* 111/454.) If we reconvert the Categorical Imperative into a synthetic a priori *principle,* it then reads (put negatively and most precisely): A human agent is an agent who should never disobey the Law of Autonomy (that is, ought to be an agent who never acts contrary to the Law of pure practical reason). Since the predicate (an agent who never acts contrary to pure practical reason) expresses an idea that does not merely unfold what we may claim to know about human agents, the principle is ampliative and synthetic, joining two logically distinct ideas.

In many synthetic judgments, what justifies our connecting concepts is sensory experience (*Erfahrung*). To say, for example, "The main campus of the University of South Carolina is located in Columbia" is to make a claim about a relation of place between two distinct entities. This synthetic statement can be verified in an a posteriori fashion, that is, on the basis of experience, but the statement lacks the necessity found in a priori judgments. It is only a contingent claim. Other school campuses have been moved and, however unlikely, it is still possible that the main campus of this particular university could be relocated.

By contrast, however, whether as a practical principle about or as an imperative addressed to human beings, who purportedly can obey the Law of Autonomy but do so only contingently, that law is not only synthetic but also asserts a necessary (or a priori) relation between the subject and predicate concepts with the connective "ought to be." In his first *Critique,* Kant had agreed with Hume in holding that synthetic judgments expressing *necessity* cannot be shown to be true on the basis of experience, which can tell us only what happens to be so, not what *must* be so. As the first step in his defense of morality, Kant devotes a good deal of effort to explaining why it is detrimental to human moral life to try to elicit the Law of Autonomy and its analogue, the Categorical Imperative, from experience. At the risk of some repetition, let us examine his analysis.

Why this is a problem

For centuries, Kant writes, philosophers considered freedom to be a *psychological* concept, and they thought they could show on the basis of experience that we are agents who can act in responsible ways. (See, e.g., *Gr.* 100/447; *Pr.R.* 94.) Kant has no argument with the claim that we can act voluntarily in Aristotle's sense: being the intentional cause of our own actions, without being coerced contrary to the springs of action within us. (See *Ni-*

comachean Ethics 3.1.) Still, he continues, it is futile to try to generate moral freedom from this kind of "freedom," for as we saw in Chapter 4, any appeal to experience must portray human agency as heteronomous. (See *Pu.R.* A533/ B561; *Gr.* 48–49/419, 114/455, 120/459; *Pr.R.* 96–98.)

From the point of view of Newtonian science, we must regard ourselves as "animal creatures" with a pathologically determined nature. (See *Pr.R.* 88, 96–97, 105, 114, 161.) Insofar as we can "be moved by reasons" – the sort of empirically conditioned reasoning involved in prudential thinking – we may be entitled to claim that we have "psychological freedom." (See *Rel.* 26n/21.) Our reasoning then can be regarded as one among various kinds of natural causes affecting our behavior, albeit a special kind of cause, but we must still regard our thinking (apparently somewhat like the operations of a computer) as phenomenal "impulsions" and "concatenations of ideas of the mind," and, like other natural causes, bound by physical laws. (See *Pu.R.* A801–4/B829–32; *Gr.* 25–30/406–9, 101/448, 107–8/452–53; *Pr.R.* 47–48, 55, 97, 141; *M.M.* 418.) Kant therefore concludes that psychological freedom is heteronomous, for an agent is "free" to exercise power rationally when and only when moved to do so by some prior causally effective factors such as desires.[6]

Allowing that we can and do act as rational agents because and insofar as we can act on hypothetical imperatives, therefore, provides no support for the claim that we are bound by the Law of Autonomy. (See *Gr.* 50n/420n, 62–63/426–27; *Pr.R.* 94–95.) As we have seen, Kant insists that "autonomy" is uncaused causality, complete self-determination, and a categorical imperative is one that directly and immediately commands us how to act, completely independently of *all* prior and present empirical conditions. (See *Pr.R.* 97.)

Consequently, we cannot expect to support the claim that we humans are (transcendentally) free and responsible moral agents by finding the freedom necessary for morality exhibited in or confirmed by sensory experience (*Gr.* 100/447; see 124–28; *Pu.R.* Bxxx–xxxi, A776/B804; *Pr.R.* 4, 47; *T&P* 285n). In fact, it is "absolutely impossible" *in principle* to find any example of such freedom theoretically "exhibited" among the heteronomously determined objects and events of our experience. (See, e.g., *Pu.R.* A533/B561; *Gr.* 100/ 447, 120–21/459; *Pr.R.* 47; *Rel.* 26n/21; *M.M.* 221.) The notion of this kind of freedom is an Idea of reason that, like all such Ideas, enables us to think about reality that is not bound by the laws of the phenomenal world of experience. (See *Gr.* 108/452, 114/455; *Pr.R.* 94.) Genuine freedom therefore is a notion that, as far as science is concerned, is "transcendent."

It is likewise true that any effort to understand how our reasoning might be autonomously practical is futile. Any theoretical explanation of human moral agency would necessarily consist in setting out the temporally prior determining causes for human agents and their actions. And that, of course, amounts to the denial of freedom and, with it, of morality. (See, e.g., *Gr.* 125–26/461–62; *Pr.R.* 94–95.) So any theoretical argument on behalf of human freedom must end in a self-contradictory and incoherent claim: Human agents are free and autonomous because they are determined heteronomously according to absolute physical laws by events not under their control. (See *Pu.R.* Bxxxix, B234ff; *Gr.* 120–21/458–59; *Pr.R.* 47–48, 55, 94–95; *Rel.* 49n/ 45; *M.M.* 225–26, 431.)

As far as science is concerned, then, moral freedom is theoretically unknowable and in that sense theoretically "empty." (See *Pr.R.* 97.) For that reason, any judgments expressing either the apodictic Law of Autonomy or its analogue, the Categorical Imperative, are regarded as meaningless. (See *M.M.* 225.) There is and can be no scientific rationale for asserting that we have pure reason that can be practical of itself, or for ordering causally determined agents to act freely and spontaneously, on the sole basis of their own reasoning. Finally, if scientific claims can exhaust reality and if natural causal laws determine all agents and events, then heteronomy and determinism triumph, and autonomy is but an empty figment of the imagination. (See *Pu.R.* A536/B564; *Pr.R.* 33.)[7]

There may be a way out of this quandary – *if* it is possible to show that scientific claims do not exhaust all reality so that natural causal laws do not determine all reality. This was an essential part of Kant's program in writing his monumental *Critique of Pure Reason,* and also why he called his work a critique. There he set out not only to show how our reason provides an objective basis for our knowledge of the world but also, by delineating the limits of scientific knowledge, to defend the possibility that human beings are free and therefore moral agents. (See *Pu.R.* Bxxx, A11–14/B28, A19–22/B33–36, A841–42/B869–70.)

If we cannot in principle appeal to knowledge gained in an a posteriori fashion, through our senses, where else can we look to find support for the contention that we are free moral agents? Obviously that support must be sought in an a priori way. We have no alternative save to look inward, at our own inner rational awareness of our spontaneity when we think practically. (See *Gr.* 21/404, 100/448.) This is not "experience" in the strict sense of that word, for it is an awareness of what cannot be understood in terms of the laws of the empirical world. However, if human freedom cannot be explained theoretically without denying its existence, then it must be that it cannot be grounded on anything, whether "in heaven or on earth," but itself (*Gr.* 60 425). Again, we have no alternative but to look to purported inner "moral experience," the self-consciousness of the ordinary person.

Briefly, what Kant contends is that, negatively, our claim to be transcendentally free is immune from all theoretical attacks and, positively, the Law of Autonomy verifies its own existence by its appearance in our moral awareness. Our belief in the reality of our moral agency is therefore certified in two ways. The first is Kant's conclusion in the *Groundwork,* and the second is his contention in the *Critique of Practical Reason.*

Kant's first argument: Part I

It is indisputably true that we do believe ourselves to be free and therefore obligated by the moral law. (See *Gr.* 101–4/448–50.) But the mere *belief* that we are free and moral agents clearly does not seem sufficient for us to claim that we have any *right* to take ourselves actually to be such agents. Our conviction may be a persistent but still only subjective and illusory one. Kant himself calls attention to this objection, but he thinks it can be met, and his first argument in fact is based on our common belief. (See *Gr.* 109/453.)[8]

Kant presents his first argument in the third chapter of the *Groundwork*, and at first reading it may seem to be only verbal magic. Before actually offering his "transcendental deduction" of the reality of our freedom, he first tells us what his claim will be. This initial statement is often taken to be his argument on behalf of his thesis and then criticized for not providing any such support. But I think it makes much better sense to understand Kant's opening words "Now I assert that . . ." ("Ich sage nun . . .") as meaning what today's philosophers mean when they write, "What I now want to claim is that . . ."

Every being who cannot act except *under the idea of freedom* is by this alone – from a practical point of view – really free; that is to say, for him all the laws inseparably bound up with freedom are valid just as much as if his will could be pronounced free in itself on grounds valid for theoretical philosophy. (*Gr.* 100/448; see also 124/461)[9]

Kant admits that up to now he has treated freedom as only an assumption. He states, however, that what is "given" in our self-awareness is the absolutely fundamental conviction that we *are* free and morally responsible for what we do. It is a presupposition whose truth we all find we *must* believe whenever we deliberate about how to act and whenever we do act. (See *Pu.R.* A548/B576; *Gr.* 101–2/448–49, 124/461.) This belief is not subjective in the sense that we think it holds only for us. On the contrary, the same claim we make on our behalf is and "must be equally valid for all rational beings" in general and for all other human beings in particular (*Gr.* 100/447–48, 102/449; see 66–67/429).

It is impossible to destroy this belief by counterarguments. (See *Gr.* 114–15/455–56.) If there were some theoretical presumption to the contrary, it would be simply irrelevant, completely unhelpful. We still would be utterly *unable* to live our practical life without presuming that we are free and responsible agents. (See *Pu.R.* A803/B831; *Gr.* 112–15/454–56, 120/459, 124–25/461.) Even "the most hardened scoundrel," if he is not completely irrational, cannot avoid the conviction that he is morally free and should be a better person than he is. (See *Gr.* 112–13/454.)

Moreover, since we have but one reason with different functions, this presumption is not peculiar to moral-practical judgments. When we think theoretically we also find we must presuppose we are transcendentally free so as "not to deny [our] consciousness of [ourselves] as an intelligence" (*Gr.* 119/458; see 108–9/452). Theoretical reason, too, "must look upon itself as the author of its own principles independently of alien influences" (*Gr.* 101/448).[10]

These statements have frequently led commentators to believe that Kant meant to offer a theoretical argument for our freedom in *Groundwork* III.

But it is highly unlikely that Kant himself meant to do so. It is clearly in the *interest* of our theorizing that our belief in transcendental freedom be defensible, but, as we have seen, theoretical thinking is dependent on sensory experience to show that objects have actual existence. As we also have seen, that is just where the problem lies: No appeal to the "manifold of sensibility" can show that transcendental freedom is actual; there can be no positive theoretical evidence on behalf of our freedom. At best we can look to that kind of reasoning only to "clear a ground" for morality.[11] Fortunately, science cannot provide any compelling evidence to show that such freedom is *not* possible. Consequently, as theoretical thinkers we both can and must remain agnostic about our freedom.

Any argument that we must presuppose that we are transcendentally free when we think theoretically is inconclusive. The mere presupposition cannot by itself show that transcendental freedom is not an unavoidable illusion; it may still be that psychological freedom is all there is. So an appeal to the self-consciousness of a person making judgments does not rebut agnosticism about freedom. What we are entitled to say is only what Kant himself says: Transcendental freedom is a presupposition of our awareness of ourselves, *both* just as thinkers making judgments and as agents deliberating about how to act.

It may not yet be clear why the presumption of freedom by us as agents has any more strength than that same presumption by us solely as thinkers. But we do know that Kant has specifically said that he intends to defend our freedom from a *practical* point of view; he plans to offer a transcendental deduction on behalf of our moral agency. He means to argue that the "given" fact that we all necessarily presume we are free agents grants us a *practical* entitlement and necessitation to *take* ourselves to be free and subject to the Law of Freedom – an entitlement just as strong as if we could claim to know we are free on the basis of empirical evidence.

As we saw in Chapter 2, a transcendental deduction consists in asking what conditions *must* hold true in order that the admittedly "given" may be possible, even if not completely explained or understood. (See *Gr.* 99/447, 112/454, 128/463.) Kant's argument in the *Groundwork* bears some similarity to the "demonstration by way of refutation" that Aristotle had used in Book Gamma of his *Metaphysics*. Aristotle had wanted to defend the principle of noncontradiction from attacks by radical skepticism. But that principle is so fundamental that it cannot be inferred from any prior truths. So rather than try to provide some sort of positive proof – an impossible task – Aristotle undertook only to *defend* that principle, by pointing out that any attack on it presupposes it as a premise and is therefore self-defeating.

In a similar way Kant wants to defend a viewpoint so fundamental it cannot be based on anything else. He does not analogously argue that the claim "We are free" is an unavoidable presupposition in any theoretical argument against freedom, because, as we have just seen, such a contention is inconclusive and, besides, there are no theoretical arguments against the possibility of freedom. But, like Aristotle, he concludes that "nothing is left but *defense*," here the defense of our right to take ourselves to be moral beings (*Gr.* 121/ 459). This is an argument not for a theoretical claim but for a point of view we must take of ourselves, how we must regard ourselves for purposes of moral practice. (See *Gr.* 100n/448n.) Kant will argue that we are entitled, for all purposes involving moral deliberation and choice, to regard ourselves as free moral agents. Kant is convinced that this is the best conclusion his deduction can produce.

But why should the presupposition of moral reasoning have any greater cogency than the identical presupposition of theoretical reasoning? Because pure reason is practical, Kant argues, it has a unique power to cause its own objects – free actions. When we reason practically, therefore, we may do what we may not do when we reason theoretically: legitimately appeal to our own rational self-consciousness to determine what is objectively real. (See *Gr.* 101/ 448.) Doing so does not entitle us to claim we have theoretical knowledge *that* we are free or that we understand *how* we are free. (See *Pr.R.* 107–8, 120–22, 135–36.) It does, however, give us the right to *believe* we are moral agents, the ground of our free actions.

Kant put off the actual deduction of freedom because, he writes, this argument may involve an undesirable and "hidden" circularity. He had first described his task as making "intelligible the deduction of the concept of freedom from pure practical reason and so the possibility of a categorical imperative" (*Gr.* 99/447). But he also defined freedom and morality as "reciprocal concepts" when he wrote, "What else then can freedom of will be but autonomy? . . . A free will and a will under moral laws are one and the same" (*Gr.* 98/447; see also 104–5/450).

Concepts are "reciprocal" when they have the same "sphere" or "extension," that is, refer to the same object (*Logic* 96–98/102–4). One such concept may be used to "explain" the other only in the sense of showing that what may *seem* to be different ideas about the same object are really a "single concept" (*Gr.* 105/450). So, in the second *Critique,* Kant writes that freedom (in its positive sense) and the moral law (or our consciousness of having pure practical reason) are "identical" concepts (*Pr.R.* 29; see 93–94; also *Rel.* 35/30). This is why, as we saw earlier, it is analytically true to say that a free agent is a moral agent. But for the same reason neither concept can be used to explain the other in the sense of accounting for or being its cause (*Gr.* 104–5/450).

The deduction would be misconceived, then, if it were taken to be an effort to show that the exercise of our moral agency requires, "in the order of efficient causes," that freedom be "the ground" for or "explanation" of our autonomous, moral actions (*Gr.* 104–5/450; see also 99/448, 109/453).[12] Such circularity would not be very well hidden after all; it would consist in trying to give a *causal explanation* of one assumption by another that in fact is conceptually identical to the first. Such an "argument" obviously explains nothing.

Was Kant actually concerned that he might offer a circular argument? Most commentators seem to think so. But it seems completely implausible that the author of the first *Critique* as well as of the first two chapters of the *Groundwork* might have been tempted to commit such an obvious error, especially if it meant violating the limits of empirical knowledge that he had so recently, carefully, and repeatedly delineated. It is far more likely that Kant raised this possibility in order to make clear to those reading the *Groundwork* that there is and can be no positive theoretical explanation of our moral agency.

Later, in the second *Critique*, Kant again pointed out that it is not possible to avoid a conceptual move from freedom to the moral law, just because they are logically equivalent – freedom "has no other meaning than" pure practical reason – and each is necessary and sufficient for the other (*Pr.R.* 46):

Nothing more could be done than to show that, if we saw the possibility of freedom of an efficient cause, we would see not only the possibility but also the necessity of the moral law as the supreme practical law of rational beings, to whom freedom of the causality of their will is ascribed. This is because the two concepts are so inextricably bound together that practical freedom could be defined through the will's independence of everything except the moral law. (*Pr.R.* 93–94; see 29)

What is important for our purposes now is that in the *Groundwork* Kant maintained that it is possible to defend human freedom while avoiding circularity (and self-contradiction) *only* by using the doctrine of the two viewpoints. (See *Gr.* 105/450, 109–10/453.) Let us now examine the argument Kant actually offered in *Groundwork* III.

Kant's first argument: Part II

In the *Groundwork* Kant argues that even persons of the "most ordinary intelligence," if they reflect at all, realize, at least vaguely, that the world we know through experience and scientific inquiry does not exhaust reality (*Gr.* 105/450; see also 107/451–52). All our knowledge of the world is radically dependent on the ways in which our senses and our understanding organize our sense perceptions. As a result, what we may claim to *know* theoretically about reality is limited to appearances, to reality-as-it-appears-to-us, that is, to what Kant called the "sensible" or "phenomenal" world. (See, e.g., *Gr.* 105–6/450–51.)

Once we become aware of how radically our own perceptual and mental operations affect the way we know the world, Kant writes, we find we not only can but must think of reality-as-it-is-in-itself (Kant's famous *Ding an sich*), that is, reality apart from all the contributions we make. Although there is but one real world, when we think theoretically, we find our reason (*Vernunft*) insists that we assume there is a "supersensible" reality that is somehow the ground of the world appearing to us. (See *Gr.* 108/452.) We may use the "categories of the understanding" (like ground and consequent) just to *think* about the existence of reality-as-it-is-in-itself, because these categories originate in our reason and are not derived from or based on experience. (See *Pu.R.* A76ff/B102ff.) But we may not claim to have any theoretical knowledge of noumenal reality, because, once again, we can *know* reality only insofar as we encounter it in our sense experience. So Kant calls the Idea of this world as a whole the "noumenal" or "intelligible" or "thinkable" (and in that sense "intellectual") world. (See, e.g., *Pu.R.* A535–37/B563–65; *Gr.* 105–7/450–51.)

Since we can have no theoretical insight into things that by their very nature lie beyond all our possible sensory experience, the noumenal world must remain forever theoretically "problematic" for us. (See *Pr.R.* 104–5.) But this much is clear: Without intuitions of supersensible reality, we must think of the noumenal world as free from all the "conditions of sensibility," such as having a spatiotemporal existence and being subject to the causal rules of a temporal order. For these – the forms of space and time and the temporally schematized notion of ground and consequent – are ways in which our sensible intuition and our understanding take up and organize how the world of sense appears to us. (See, e.g., *Pu.R.* Bxxxvii–xxxviii, A539/B567, A551/B579; *Gr.* 107–9/451–52, 119/458, 125/461–62; *Pr.R.* 4–6, 42–43, 48–49, 55, 95–96, 102.) These conditions all lie with *us,* not with the world apart from us.

By this strategy, Kant denies both the epistemological claims of the old metaphysics and the causal theory of perception held by Cartesians and Lockeans. *This* agnosticism is crucial to Kant's argument for the possibility of freedom and morality, as well as, to use Beck's phrase, a new "practical metaphysics."

More to the point, when we think about ourselves, Kant writes, we find we must take one or the other of those two viewpoints. When we reason theoretically – when, as spectators, we regard ourselves as objects to be understood – we must take the viewpoint that, insofar as we belong to the sensible world, we are ourselves heteronomously bound by deterministic laws of causation. (See *Pu.R.* A536/B564; *Gr.* 106–7/451.) But when we reflect on ourselves as agents, thinking about acting or actually acting, we also find ourselves "involuntarily constrained" to "transfer ourselves into the intelligible world"; that is, we think of ourselves as members of the noumenal world of freedom, as noumenal agents possessing transcendental freedom and therefore as autonomous, moral agents (*Gr.* 110–11/453–54 and 113/455; see also 105–12/450–54; *Pu.R.* A532ff/B560ff; *Pr.R.* 104).

Exactly how, in Kant's view, does the noumenal-phenomenal distinction help him keep from falling into the circularity he needed to avoid? Although he does offer an explanation in the *Groundwork* (109/453), his manner of presenting it has served to confuse rather than to clarify things for most of his readers, and there is little agreement about what he was trying to say there.[13] Let me offer a suggestion that I believe has substantial textual support.

What the noumenal-phenomenal distinction makes clear is that the Ideas of freedom and of a pure practical will can refer only to a nonphenomenal, purely noumenal world. Now freedom is in some sense the *sine qua non* of moral agency, its *"ratio essendi"* (*Pr.R.* 4n). Yet it would be a mistake for anyone to try to offer a positive description of our noumenal agency, that is, try to "furnish its ground" or foundation *theoretically* in any *causal* way (*Gr.* 104–5/450; see 108–9/453, 120/458, 124–26/461). Hence, we must give up any hope of *understanding* pure practical reason and the possibility of the Categorical Imperative; we can only "comprehend its incomprehensibility" (*Gr.* 128/463; see 120–26/458–62). But now we can see that there is no *need* to try to use freedom as a theoretical explanation of the reality of our moral agency. (See *Gr.* 100n/448n.) For what we *can* do is to show that our necessarily thinking of ourselves as noumenal agents leads inevitably to our rightly taking ourselves to be both free and moral agents, and we can do so without being guilty of circular reasoning.

We finally can set out Kant's actual deduction.

We begin by *reflecting on* ourselves as rational beings, thinking either theoretically or morally. When we do so, as we have already seen, we immediately find we cannot avoid making a distinction between passivity and spontaneity. By virtue of the power of reason, even those with "ordinary human reason" can distinguish, "however roughly," between the two points of view, between the sensible world and the intelligible world, between appearances and things in themselves. (See *Gr.* 106/451, 117/457.) We not only can but *must* regard ourselves from both points of view, as belonging to the sensible world and as part of the supersensible world.

The problem is that we can have absolutely *no* theoretical knowledge of the intellectual world. Apart from sensibility, our understanding, although in itself spontaneous, "would think nothing at all" (*Gr.* 108/452). All theoretical reasoning can do is think of the intelligible world in terms of negations, for example, as free in the sense of being independent of determining causes that define the world of nature. (See *Gr.* 117/457, 119/458.)

As moral *agents,* however, we can and must think of the causality of our own noumenal will positively. Like any world, the noumenal world must be law governed, and like any cause, the causality of our will must be under some law or other. (See *Gr.* 97–98/446.) The only possible law for free wills in a free world, Kant writes, is the self-imposed Law of Freedom or of Autonomy – the universal principle of morality.

Kant now makes the same appeal he uses later to claim primacy for pure practical reason. Whereas theoretical reason is dependent on experience to support the claim that its concepts enjoy objectivity, moral reason causes its special objects – free actions. So the claims of moral-practical reason can be confirmed by appealing to our own self-consciousness to determine, for the sake of practice, what is actual. (See *Gr.* 101/448.)

"When we think of ourselves as free," Kant therefore writes, "we transfer ourselves into the intelligible world as members and recognize the autonomy of the will together with its consequence – morality" (*Gr.* 110/453; see also 117/457). To conceive of ourselves "thus would not be possible if the influences of sensibility were able to determine man" (*Gr.* 119/458). So our very ability to exercise spontaneity by thinking of ourselves as members of the noumenal world (and, more strongly, the *necessity* that we do so) is equivalent in cogency, for practical purposes, to the strength of a theoretical proof of our being such members (if such a proof were possible; see *Gr.* 119/458). It then follows that we have the *right* to believe that we are free, moral agents, *which is all that it can mean, within the Kantian system, to say we really are such agents.* (See *Pr.R.* 93.)

So, by that very act of thinking of ourselves as noumenal agents, we also necessarily regard ourselves as bound by the Law of Autonomy. Therefore, "the same laws as would bind a being who was really free [that is, for whom we could provide a theoretical proof of that claim] are equally valid for a being who cannot act except under the Idea of his own freedom" (*Gr.* 100n/ 448n). "This," Kant concludes, "is the extreme limit of all moral inquiry" (*Gr.* 126/462). The deduction of the Law of Autonomy has not failed. Although we are unable to understand *how* pure practical reason is possible, within "the very limit of human reason" the deduction has succeeded in defending our *right* to regard ourselves as free, as having the power of pure practical reason, as being moral agents, and as bound by the Law of Autonomy (*Gr.* 128/463).

It is important to add that we still must also regard the world we see – and ourselves in it – as causally determined in order to understand that world. We have both the right and the need to think of ourselves, for different purposes, from two different points of view, as members of both the noumenal and the phenomenal worlds.[14] In this way, "freedom and nature, in the full sense of these terms, can exist together, without any conflict, in the same actions, according as the actions are referred to their intelligible or to their sensible cause" (*Pu.R.* A541/B569; see A557/B585).

Kant's second argument

Three years after the publication of the *Groundwork,* Kant again defended the ability of pure reason to be practical. There is a good deal of discussion and disagreement among commentators about how this second argument in his *Critique of Practical Reason* does or does not differ from his first argument and why Kant offered it. To keep the structure of the second *Critique* similar to that of the first *Critique,* Kant entitles the relevant section "Of the Deduction of the Principles of Pure Practical Reason" (*Pr.R.* 41), but he then repeats what he had already stated in the *Groundwork,* namely, that "the objective reality of the moral law can be proved [positively] through no deduction" (*Pr.R.* 47; see also 91, 93).[15]

However, this limitation is no loss, for now, in the second *Critique,* Kant argues that the reality of our moral agency is supported in a positive way by the moral law revealing its own reality to us. What we find in our practical self-consciousness, he writes, is what sensory experience cannot give us: *the moral law itself.* (See *Pr.R.* 4n, 29–31, 47, 132–33.) What we find "in the reason of all men and embodied in their being," whenever we deliberate about how to act, is the Law of Autonomy in the form of the Categorical Imperative, questioning our desires and commanding our obedience, and thereby establishing both that it is actual and that we are moral agents (*Pr.R.* 105; see 32, 49; *M.M.* 225, 418). The moral law itself "is given, as an apodictically certain fact, as it were, of pure reason, a fact of which we are a priori conscious" (*Pr.R.* 47; see also 30–31).[16] "The objective reality of a pure will [*Wille*] or of a pure practical reason (they being the same) is given in the moral law a priori, as a fact" (*Pr.R.* 55; see 42). We now have not just a defense of our right to our belief in our own moral agency but positive and indubitable support for that belief: The moral law "is firmly established by itself," and it therefore is in no need of any further proof (*Pr.R.* 47; see also 48, 105, 132, 142; *M.M.* 221, 418).

"Matters of fact (*res facti*)," in Kant's system, are those "whose objective reality can be proved" (*Cr.J.* 468). In his analysis of what we can claim to know, Kant had held in the first *Critique* that Ideas of reason, like freedom, "are only ideas," and in this sense the only "facts" we can know are those that come to us through sensory experience of the world. (See, e.g., *Pu.R.* A19/B33, A329/B385.) Within this context Kant wrote in the *Groundwork* that it is difficult to show the possibility of a categorical imperative, and even more its objective validity, "since here we do not enjoy the advantage of having its reality given in experience" (*Gr.* 49/419–20). But in a footnote to the preface to the second edition, the "B edition," published the year before publication of the second *Critique,* Kant added that before we have the right to ascribe "objective validity" to a concept in the sense of claiming that there really *is* something corresponding to an idea we have, we "must be able to prove its possibility, either from its actuality as attested by experience, *or a priori by means of reason*" (*Pu.R.* Bxxvin, emphasis mine; see *Pr.R.* 54–55).

As Lewis White Beck points out, Kant identifies this unique fact of pure reason in various ways: as "the consciousness of this fundamental law" (*Pr.R.* 31 and 42), as "the moral law" itself (*Pr.R.* 31 and 47), and as "autonomy in the principle of morality" (*Pr.R.* 42).[17] Because Kant tends to use these expressions interchangeably, there is no reason to see this as problematic. The appearance of the Law of Autonomy in our moral awareness is "the sole fact of pure reason," because it is only law that practical reason by itself can give to itself and that therefore can be known a priori. It thereby shows that in us "pure reason is practical of itself alone" and that we are moral agents (*Pr.R.* 31). We do not have an immediate apprehension or intuition (*Anschauung*) of this fact of reason, at least not in Kant's use of that term to signify an "object given to us" in experience (*Pu.R.* A19/B33), for by definition it is not possible for us to have an a priori intuition of supersensuous nature. Rather, we become aware of its presence in our reason in the very process of finding ourselves obligated by it. (See *Gr.* 107/451; *Pr.R.* 42, 45.)[18]

Kant's view of freedom in the second *Critique* is significantly more sophisticated than his discussions in the *Groundwork*. Morality and freedom are equivalent concepts and the law of morality *is* the Law of Freedom. So the practical "fact" of the moral law is sufficient ground to infer that we are free. (See *Pr.R.* 29, 33, 42, 93–94; *Rel.* 58n/45n.) But it does not work the other way around. Thinking of ourselves as free does not necessarily show that we are bound by the moral law, for the freedom we think we have still might be merely a psychological concept denoting a lack of opposition to our acting on hypothetical practical rules. (See *Pu.R.* A303–6/B359–63, A548–50/B576–78; *Pr.R.* 47, 96; *Rel.* 58n/45n.) Kant therefore holds that we are dependent on our consciousness of the moral law for assurance of the reality of our freedom. (See *Pr.R.* 30.)

For Kant, freedom remains the ground (but not the causal ground) of the possibility of the moral law, its *ratio essendi,* but "the moral law is the only condition under which freedom can be *known,*" its *ratio cognoscendi (Pr.R.* 4n; see *Rel.* 138/129). "The mutual opposition involved in self-constraint [the internal moral conflict generated by the Categorical Imperative commanding our obedience in opposition to desires and inclinations] and the inevitability of such opposition leads us to recognize that we are free" (*M.M.* 379n). We cannot help being conscious of our freedom in the sense of having the "power to master [our] inclinations when they rebel against the law – a consciousness which, though not immediately given, is yet rightly deduced from the moral categorical imperative" (*M.M.* 383; see *Pr.R.* 47). We "know that we *can* do it [that is, are free and so able to do what the moral law commands] because our own reason acknowledges [that law] as its law and says that we *ought* to do it" (*Pr.R.* 159; see *Rel.* 49n/45, 50/46).[19]

At other times, when he is not concerned with these issues, Kant continues to regard the concepts of freedom and morality as "reciprocal," as he did in the *Groundwork.* For example, he writes that the "Analytic" section of the second *Critique* shows that the Law of Autonomy is "inextricably bound up with the consciousness of freedom of the will, and actually [is] identical with it" (*Pr.R.* 42; see also 29, 93–94).[20]

Despite the distinction he sometimes makes between freedom and morality, Kant always insists that the reality of our freedom is just as certain as that of the moral law itself. We still, of course, cannot understand *how* we can be free. (See *Pr.R.* 133; *M.M.* 379n.) Freedom – the power of pure reason to be practical – remains theoretically incomprehensible and so a transcendental Idea, beyond the reach of theoretical reasoning. (See *Pr.R.* 4, 55–56.) From the point of view of theoretical knowledge, then, our freedom remains only a subjective postulate and our belief in our freedom a faith (*ein Glaube*). (See *Pr.R.* 4.) But to moral reasoning our freedom is an objectively valid Idea, which we know a priori because it is based on the appearance of its law in our own rational consciousness. It is as undeniable as anything we can know theoretically. (See *Gr.* 120–21/458–59; *Pr.R.* 4, 54–56, 126; *M.M.* 221, 225.)

Relating the two viewpoints

Kant was convinced that the noumenal-phenomenal distinction is the only rational means for avoiding claiming in a self-contradictory way that we are both determined and free. (See, e.g., *Pu.R.* A537ff/B565ff; *Pr.R.* 97, 114.) Since our own reasoning insists that we take both viewpoints of ourselves, we must rationally suppose that we can do so without contradiction. (See *Gr.* 115–16/456.) Kant does not argue that there are two worlds *ontologically* distinct from each other – a phenomenal reality and also, somehow lying behind it as its cause, another and corresponding noumenal reality. Instead, he argues that there is but one world, which we must regard from different *viewpoints* when we think for different purposes. (See *Pu.R.* A534/B562; *Gr.* 108/452, 115–18/456–58; *Pr.R.* 5–6, 6n, 30, 42–43, 65–67, 104, 114, 162.) The laws our understanding contributes to the phenomenal world do not affect the noumenal world, so "both may exist, independently of one another and without interfering with each other" (*Pu.R.* A557/B585). Yet Kant was also convinced that there must be a final single principle that can combine the two apparently incompatible viewpoints. He believed that this principle must be divine, yet he also admitted that the existence and nature of this final explanation must remain theoretically unknown to, and unknowable by, us. (See *Cr.J.* 392–95, 454–57.)

Earlier it was mentioned in passing that pure practical reason may claim insight into the noumenal world only within severe limitations. One such limitation is imposed by logic, the pure science of all thinking: Moral reason may not violate the ultimate logical norm of rationality by making self-contradictory claims. The doctrine of the two viewpoints would be self-contradictory if we were to claim that human beings are both free and determined in the same respect – as phenomenal beings. (See *Gr.* 121/459.) But to regard human beings as determined is to think of them as members of the phenomenal world, and to regard them as free is to think of them from a different point of view, as members of the noumenal world. (See *Pr.R.* 114.)

As our power to know the world, theoretical reasoning has the right to impose a second limitation: Moral reasoning may not overstep the boundaries of knowledge by claiming the ability to "intuit or feel itself into that [noumenal] world" (*Gr.* 118/458). Practical reason also may not claim that it can comprehend *any* noumenal object, including its own free causality, or try to explain how free agency is possible, for "we are unable to explain anything unless we can bring it under laws which can have an object given in possible experience" (*Gr.* 120/458).

Within these limitations, through moral reasoning and for moral purposes only, we do have a limited title to apply the categories of the understanding to noumena. We therefore have *some* insight into, if not understanding of, the noumenal world insofar as we are a part of that world and act in it. (See *Pr.R.* 6–7.) We can define that world "positively" and we also are able "to know [*erkennen*] something of it, namely a law" (*Pr.R.* 43; *Gr.* 118/457).[21] That law, of course, is the purely formal law of that world, the law of rationality and freedom: negatively, the law (which theoretical reasoning also must assume) that noumenal agents are free from determination by the causal laws of the phenomenal world; and positively, the law (which theoretical reason must admit is possible) that noumenal agents have the power of will or pure practical reason, able to act on universal laws of their own adoption. (See *Gr.* 118–20/457–58.)

Nonetheless, if we can avoid making self-contradictory claims by taking the two viewpoints, we seem to be left with a schizophrenic view of human life. On the one hand, we must regard ourselves as only a part of the great mechanism of nature, robots governed mechanically by natural causal laws; and on the other, we must think of ourselves as free, autonomous, rational agents. The laws of heteronomy and of autonomy remain completely exclusive and incompatible. Kant seems to have avoided self-contradiction only at the cost of a single, unified, coherent view of human life. We seem to be left without a way in which to relate free (noumenal) decisions to causally determined (phenomenal) performances. Human moral agents are not and cannot be psychological subjects found in the world of experience. Morality can exist only in a world we cannot see, and the world we can experience is amoral. Since morality admits of "no empirical exhibition," "it is absolutely impossible to give an example of [moral action] from experience" (*Pr.R.* 15 and 48; see also 30; *Gr.* 25–30/406–9).

We therefore seem to end up with no practicality as we typically think of practicality, for our ordinary view is that our decisions can and often do result in performances in the world. Despite the fact that he claims to have begun with ordinary moral judgments, Kant seems to end up giving us an analysis that seems very far removed from such judgments. He himself admits this may look like a serious problem: "It seems absurd to wish to find a case in the world of sense, and thus standing under the law of nature, which admits the application of a law of freedom to it, and to which we could apply the supersensuous ideal of the morally good, so that the latter could be exhibited *in concreto*" (*Pr.R.* 68; see *Cr.J.* 343).

Yet, as he points out, we must regard our actions in the world from the same two viewpoints we must take about ourselves. (See *Pu.R.* A538–58/B566–86; *Gr.* 110/453.) We must regard them theoretically as events causally conditioned by other appearances, but we also must regard our actions as ordinary moral consciousness does, as moral actions, completely unconditioned, as "freedom in its external exercise" (*M.M.* 214; see *Pr.R.* 30, 42–43, 65–67, 104; *Rel.* 50/46). Even though "virtuous action" is an Idea of reason that can neither be drawn from experience with the world nor adequately displayed in the world, our morally legal actions still can and must be regarded as examples, albeit imperfect ones, of virtuous action. (See *Pu.R.* A315/B371–72, A328/B384–85; *Pr.R.* 47.)

For our moral purposes and from the moral viewpoint we must think of our noumenal self both as the archetype of its phenomenal counterpart or ectype and also as the ground underlying our phenomenal actions in the world. (See *Pu.R.* A538–58/B566–86, A807–8/B835–36; *Gr.* 108–20/452–59, 125–26/462; *Pr.R.* 43, 48–50, 97–100, 105, 114–15, 119.) As we have seen, we achieve theoretical knowledge by restricting the use of the categories to possible data in sense experience. Yet since the notions of ground and consequent are categories of the understanding, we still may *think* of our noumenal self as a kind of efficient causality responsible for our empirical self in the world. (See *Pr.R.* 49, 67; *Pu.R.* Bxxvin.) The concept of a noumenal efficient cause specifies a will free from prior causal determination and able to act only on its own Law of Autonomy. (See *Pr.R.* 55–56.) We also necessarily take our noumenal causality as extending to our actions in the world. (See *Pr.R.* 48–50, 54, 86–87, 119.)[22] (We cannot, of course, claim to know any of this or to understand how the two worlds interrelate.)

From the moral viewpoint, therefore, Kant writes, we can and indeed must hold that, as the consequences of our intentions, our free and effective moral decisions are "made visible in example" and so "belong to this world," the world of sense (*Pr.R.* 76–77, 119; see also 66–67, 97–99, 155n, 162–63; *Gr.* 118/457; *Idea* 17). We may regard human actions as "manifestations of the disposition [*der Gesinnung*] which is of concern to the moral law (i.e., appearances of character)," and then we can judge moral character "according to the absolute spontaneity of freedom" (*Pr.R.* 99; see also 66–67; *Idea* 17). From this point of view we regard our phenomenal actions as the "consequence" of the efficient causality of our noumenal character. (See *Pr.R.* 98–99.) So, for example, it is entirely proper to praise the actions of others "which display a great, unselfish and sympathetic disposition and humanity . . . in so far as there are clues which suggest that they were done wholly out of respect for duty" (*Pr.R.* 155n, 85; see also 99).

Nonetheless, actions we see are always only "clues" to a person's moral character, and our judgments always only inferences about which we cannot be certain (*Pr.R.* 85). "When moral value is in question, we are concerned, not with the actions which we see, but with their inner principles, which we cannot see" (*Gr.* 26/407). We cannot be *certain* that any action, even an action of our own, has been done from the right moral intention. (See *Gr.* 25–29/406–8; *Rel.* 5–6/16.) (We shall discuss moral character at more length in Chapters 9 and 10.)

Metaphysical questions

The practical insights we have achieved do not alleviate our inability to comprehend how we can be free, how pure reason can be practical, how a noumenal ground operates, or how a noumenal efficient cause can manifest itself in the world without interfering with physical causal laws. (See *Gr.* 110/453, 120/458, 125–26/461–62; *Rel.* 21/17, 39–40/34–35, 59n/52, 62/56, 138/129, 144n2/135, 170n/158.) However successful Kant's defense of morality may or may not be, his doctrine concerning the limitations of theoretical reasoning and his doctrine of the two viewpoints do render most "metaphysical" questions about the unity of human life simply unanswerable in principle. We cannot achieve any more ultimate unified theoretical understanding of how the noumenal and phenomenal viewpoints can find a common basis in a person's consciousness. (See *Pr.R.* 65.) In fact, any attempt to do so only generates contradictions and, as we have seen, if it were successful, it would mean the destruction of morality. (See *Pu.R.* A532–58/B560–86; *Pr.R.* 43, 49, 54–56, 99–100; *M.M.* 439n.) Finally, we cannot pretend to a *third* underlying point of view about ourselves and the world that might enable us to understand how to relate the two mutually exclusive viewpoints.

Kant acknowledges that some people find they cannot accept an idea they cannot understand, whereas others are unwilling to admit that scientific explanations have their limits. (See *M.M.* 378.) He simply responds that there are limits to inquiry, and that is all that can be said. As much as we may want to satisfy our speculative curiosity, we do not *need* to do so. (See, e.g., *Pu.R.* A803/B831.) The purpose of this entire analysis, after all, has been to define and defend our ability and obligation to act morally – not to understand or explain that power. This is a practical, not a theoretical, inquiry. We know what we need to know for the sake of moral practice. We are moral agents, and as such we are indeed subject to the Categorical Imperative and obligated never to violate it in our actions.

In an extremely emotional passage, which deserves to be read in full, Kant states that when a person becomes aware that, unlike other creatures, he can act freely and morally, "he can look upon himself only with the greatest wonder. . . . And if he takes it to heart, the very incomprehensibility of this self-knowledge must produce an exaltation in his soul which only inspires it the more to keep its duty holy, the more it is assailed" (*M.M.* 483).

8
The primacy of morality

Like all previous philosophers within the Greek rationalistic tradition, Kant regarded reason as so transcending the rest of creation that it is uniquely worthy of awe and respect. Reason alone can discern what is true and good; the rest of creation simply *is*. Reason is the ground of intelligibility, necessity, and universality, and thus also of harmony and peace; by contrast, what Kant called "sensibility" is the ground of surdness, contingency, and particularity, and thus also of conflict.

In his first two *Critiques* Kant set out to clarify the sources, the reach, and the limitations of the different uses of human reason. (See, e.g., *Gr.* i–iii/387–88; *Pr.R.* 120.) He devotes so much care to analyzing the different functions of our reason that it is easy to forget that theoretical and moral reasoning are not different entities. It is the same person, the same rational being, who both thinks and wills: "In the end there can only be one and the same reason, which must be differentiated solely in its application" (*Gr.* xii/391; see also *Pr.R.* 8, 89, 91, 121; *M.M.* 207). In its theoretical use, our reasoning contributes the structure for organizing experience and enables us to have knowledge of the world we experience. That same faculty, in the form of moral or pure practical reason, extends both our agency and our practical insight into the noumenal realm of freedom.

Although there are no *inherent* conflicts between the two uses of reason, they are always in danger of conflicting if the special interests or rights of one or the other are not respected. (See *Pr.R.* 119–20, 143.)[1] Unresolved conflicts within reason attack the soundness of reason, thereby endangering its very existence. (See *Pr.R.* 120–21.) We therefore need an ultimate principle, a norm that can safeguard all our rational interests by arbitrating conflicts between them. (See *Pu.R.* A840/B868.) Resolving such conflicts "is not a part of its interest," that is, not a distinct end of reason; rather it "is the condition of having any reason at all" (*Pr.R.* 120).

Kant therefore specifies the meaning of primacy this way:

By primacy between two or more things connected by reason, I understand the prerogative of one by virtue of which it is the prime ground of determination [*der este Bestimmungsgrund*] of the combination with the others. In a narrower practical sense it refers to the prerogative of the interest of one so far as the interest of the others is subordinated to it and it is not itself inferior to any other. (*Pr.R.* 119)

So far, Kant has shown that in all conflicts between competing moral and prudential interests, the Law of Autonomy ensures the internal unity of *prac-*

95

tical reason by mandating that moral interests should always take precedence. But he still needs to define the relationship between theoretical and moral reasoning. Until that has been done, he has not yet constructed a unified view of human rational life.

For example, the theoretician may be tempted to claim that his enterprise extends to all of reality and is the only thoroughly rational activity open to us. (The need to establish its limits, Kant had said, was just why theoretical reasoning needs a critique; see *Pu.R.* A339/B397, A643/B671, A796/B825.) All practical reasoning would then be viewed as second-rate thinking, lacking the objectivity of science; and morality, as Kant analyzed it, would be regarded as mere fantasy. (See *Pr.R.* 120–21.)

Any failure, on the other hand, to respect the rights of theoretical reason would have equally disastrous consequences. We would open the door to "every nonsense and delusion of the imagination" if we disregarded the admonitions of theoretical reasoning. No limits would restrain those claiming to have insight into, or understanding of, self-contradictory and unthinkable ideas (*Pr.R.* 120; see *Pu.R.* Bxxix).[2] Moreover, there would be no restrictions on claims about sensory experiences of and knowledge of reality lying beyond all possible human experience, say, of God and of life beyond death (see *Orient.* 143; *Pr.R.* 135–36). Religious fanatics would be free to find naturalistic scientific theories radically unsatisfactory and to insist that we must always appeal to the will of God for our theoretical explanations. (See *Pr.R.* 107–8, 138–39.) Finally, political zealots would tyrannically insist that their practical interests give them an unlimited right to regulate the scientific pursuit of truth. (See *Pr.R.* 121.)

It is very much in the interest of both morality and of science to respect each other's rights. When the rights of either are disregarded irrationality triumphs. This is precisely why Kant argues that it is crucial for us to find a way to preserve the unity of reason while protecting the rights of both its uses. The rights of *neither* theoretical nor moral reasoning can be protected and promoted if each is allowed to remain independent of and only contingently and arbitrarily coordinated with the other. To ensure that all possible conflicts between them can be overcome, their unity must be attained in a necessary, a priori manner. That means that our own reason must achieve its own ultimate integrity by giving priority to one of its interests. (See *Pr.R.* 121.)

A brief history

The dominant tradition in Western philosophy had maintained that the best human life consists, insofar as possible, of theoretical thinking, and if one *must* concern oneself with practical activity, it is only at the sacrifice of what is far better.[3] According to Diogenes Laërtius, Pythagoras was the first Western philosopher to liken the activity proper to the philosopher to what was done by those who participated in festivals, such as the Olympic games, purely as disinterested spectators. They, unlike those actually competing, could see and appreciate the entire spectacle spread out before them. Later the two Greek philosophical giants Plato and Aristotle agreed that there is no higher activity available to human beings than what by then had come to be called *theoria* – contemplating and appreciating reality and its laws. They argued that it is our only fully rational activity. The objects of theoretical knowledge in the strict sense – unlike the contingent, changing objects involved in practice – enable us to achieve the highest kind of truth – truth that is necessary and universal. Moreover, theoretical contemplation best imitates what philosophers thought to be the only activity proper to God, who, lacking nothing, does not engage in practical activity.[4] But the cost of giving primacy to theoretical activity was very high. For neither Plato nor Aristotle was then able to construct a coherent, unified view of the best human life, an integrated conception that could reconcile the tensions between theory and practice, between being a rational spectator and a rational agent.[5]

Against this philosophical tradition Immanuel Kant argued for what amounted to another Copernican revolution: He stood the traditional doctrine on its head by insisting that moral practice – or a good will – has supreme value. It is "to be esteemed beyond comparison" as far more valuable than anything else, including theoretical understanding. (See *Gr.* 3/394, 20/403, 81/437; *Pr.R.* 110–11; *Cr.J.* 442.) Kant went even farther and argued that of itself theoretical activity is neither unconditionally nor intrinsically good; it is valuable only insofar as it enhances moral practice and offers morally permissible maxims of happiness!

So powerful has been Kant's influence that most moral philosophers today virtually take it for granted that moral interests should take precedence over all others. Kant's enormous influence gives us good reason to examine his arguments for the primacy of morality.[6]

The grounds for primacy

Since the existence of reason can be safeguarded only by reason itself, we are faced with three possible alternatives. We might base the integrity of reason on pure reasoning, on theoretical reasoning, or on moral reasoning.

The closest we come to the meaning of "pure reasoning" within this context is logic, which is completely formal, concerned only "with the universal rules of thinking as such without regard to differences in its objects" (*Gr.* i/387). Because the laws of logic are necessary conditions for "the possibility of any employment of reason," they are "valid for all thinking" (*Pr.R.* 120 and *Gr.* ii/387; see *Pu.R.* Bix, A330/B386). But "the logical interest of reason (interest in promoting its own insight) is never immediate [for its own sake], but presupposes purposes for which reason can be employed" (*Gr.* 122n/46on). Logic always takes on the interest of the kind of reasoning in which it is used. (See *Pr.R.* 120.) It can, for example, point out violations of the principle of noncontradiction within or between the "material" uses of reason, thereby signaling that something has gone wrong, but it cannot by itself determine which use of reason must yield to the other.

97

Since "human reason has two objects, nature and freedom," either theoretical or moral reasoning must have primacy in the sense of providing a norm by which to arbitrate conflicts within reason. What is especially striking about Kant's argument for the primacy of moral reasoning and interests is that he uses exactly the same criteria as his predecessors had used to give primacy to theoretical reasoning and interests.[7]

Because only reason can accomplish its own systematic, internal unity, primacy must be given to the use of reason that is more powerful. That use of reason is more powerful that is purer, less dependent on conditions outside itself. This was the argument Kant had used to establish the right of moral interests to restrict prudential interests.[8] Now he concludes that moral reasoning rightly enjoys primacy over theoretical reasoning because, in his analysis, moral reasoning is far less dependent on empirical conditions and so is both cognitively and conatively the more powerful faculty.[9]

The limitations of theoretical reasoning

As we have seen, Kant argues that when we think theoretically, the categories of pure understanding can only organize whatever content is given in sensuous experience. Only experience can "give reality to our concepts; in its absence a concept is a mere idea, without truth, that is, without relation to any object" (*Pu.R.* A489/B517). Consequently, our understanding of the world is not spontaneous through and through. (See, e.g., *Pu.R.* A418/B446, A533/B561.) Objective theoretical knowledge also depends on passivity, our receptivity to stimuli. (See, e.g., *Gr.* 108/452; *Pr.R.* 45, 89, 103–4.)

Some philosophers have argued that, within Kant's own theory, moral reasoning is in no better a position: It is not more independent of sensibility than theoretical reasoning but only has a different relationship with it. They point out that moral reasoning supplies only the form of universality, and that the matter of human morality must still come from sensibility by means of prudential judgments. In this respect, they argue, theoretical and moral reasoning are more alike than different.[10] Moreover, our human condition is such that moral reasoning also must be dependent on sensibility for its practicality; for before we take sufficient interest in morality to act dutifully, our moral reason must generate the moral (but still pathological) emotion of reverence or respect (*reverentia* or *Achtung*). (See, e.g., *Gr.* 122–23/460; *Pr.R.* 72–79, 92.)

Kant would have given little time to this argument, for in both of these relationships with the world, moral reasoning does not passively rely on the world to help fulfill its interest. Instead, it judges when subjective prudential maxims are fit to be objective practical laws, and of itself it generates moral emotions, which therefore are never *merely* pathological. "The will is never determined directly by the object and our conception of it; rather, the will is a faculty which can make an object real" (*Pr.R.* 60).

Moreover, Kant argues that theoretical reasoning suffers from still another radical limitation: Both its existence and its functioning depend on its use of several nonempirical norms – speculative Ideas of reason that can neither be understood nor defended theoretically. As we saw in Chapter 2, "Ideas of reason" are transcendental concepts that refer to reality that is unlimited (unconditioned) in some sense.[11] Since Ideas can neither originate in our limited experience nor be verified by it, they are theoretically "empty"; they are and must remain scientifically "problematic." They can be thought, for they are not self-contradictory, but we have no theoretical way to show either that their referents actually exist or that they do not exist. Because theoretical reason cannot *dis*prove the reality of their referents, they are what Kant calls theoretically "allowable hypotheses." (See *Pr.R.* 3–4, 105, 122, 133–34, 144–45.)

Nonetheless, they are not merely arbitrary or optional hypotheses, Kant argues, for we *must* use these Ideas (at least implicitly) to help us extend our empirical understanding of the world. (See *Pu.R.* A311/B368, A314/B371, A327/B383–84, A333–35/B390–92, A339/B397, A644/B672.) But since they refer to reality that transcends the limits of all our possible experience, these Ideas may not be used "constitutively," that is, *in* our explanations of the world. (See, e.g., *Pu.R.* A644/B672, A798–99/B826–27.)[12] We must use them, but only "regulatively" or heuristically, as maxims or "schemata"; we may use them only hypothetically, *as if* (*als ob*) we knew they have objective validity. (See, e.g., *Pu.R.* A323/B380, A642–44/B670–72, A647/B675, A663/B691, A671/B699, A681/B709, A701/B729; *Pr.R.* 134–45.)

The first Idea of reason we must presuppose when we think is, as we saw in the preceding chapter, that of freedom in the negative sense of not being bound by chains of prior causal determinants. (See *Pr.R.* 42.) We can claim to be thinking only if we also presume that we are free and able to make theoretical judgments on the basis of our thinking:

> We cannot possibly conceive of a reason as being consciously directed from outside in regard to its judgments; for in that case the subject would attribute the determination of his power of judgment, not to his reason but to an impulsion [*Antrieb*]. Reason must look upon itself as the author of its own principles independently of alien influences. (*Gr.* 101/448; see also *Pr.R.* 3, 6–7, 47–49, 104)

Just as thinkers, then, we are caught in a dilemma we cannot resolve. We *must* presume we are free enough to be able to think. We can *think* of ourselves as efficient causes, free from causal determination in our thinking, because the concept of causality originates in our own understanding and the concept of a free cause is not intrinsically self-contradictory. (See *Pr.R.* 55.) But we have no way in which to support such an Idea theoretically. (See *Pu.R.* B66–71, A533/B561; *Gr.* 101/448; *Pr.R.* 48.) Since we can know that things actually exist only by finding them in our sense experiences, the notion of a free cause is theoretically empty. There is nothing in any possible sensory experience that can show that there are such causes. Further, we can understand events in the world only insofar as we regard them as causally determined, and so we also cannot understand how we can be free causes even in a merely negative sense of freedom from laws of causal determination. (See *Pu.R.* A444–47/

B472–74, A569/B597; *Gr.* 125–26/462.) So any self-awareness of having the ability to think gives us no *theoretical* grounds for claiming either that we are free or that we can understand how that can be so.[13] As a consequence, just as thinkers, we can neither define nor defend our own activity in a theoretical way.

This is not the end of theoretical reasoning's embarrassment, Kant holds, for scientific inquiry depends on the use of three other Ideas of reason as regulative norms. To understand anything is to be able to exhibit connections and rules governing them, the conditions for a conditioned event or object. So when we think theoretically, we find we need to use Ideas of reason that can act as a "canon" for guiding our efforts to understand the world – ideals of what is completely unconditioned. (See *Pu.R.* A322/B379, A329/B385–86, A651/B679.) Beginning with "what is immediately given" in our internal awareness, these are the Ideas of the soul, the Idea of the world, and the Idea of God. (See *Pu.R.* A333–36/B390–93, A337n/B395n.)

First, as thinkers we persist in existence throughout continuous changes both in our bodies and in the states of the world around us. To account for this continuity we must regard ourselves as the enduring source of the unity of our cognitions. Doing so generates the Idea of the noumenal or supersensible "I" as a thinking personality, which rational psychology then views as a substance grounding the unity of experience. The thinking self, regarded as a permanent, simple, immaterial, intellectual substance persisting through all the changes we undergo, is, in effect, the "rational doctrine of the soul." (See *Pu.R* A342–44/B400–402, A535–37/B563–65, A672/B700, A682–84/B710–12; *Pr.R.* 140–41.)

Second, Kant holds that, for our theoretical purposes, we must regard the empirical world with all its complexity and diversity as "Nature," that is, as a dynamic and self-subsisting whole, a purposive unity that is "organized and self-organizing" (*Cr.J.* 374; see *Pu.R.* A418–19/B446–47, A648–68/B678–96, A684–85/B712–13; *Gr.* 7/396, 80n/436n; *M.M.* 443; *Idea* 18–19). Kant already used the term "nature" as a concept of the understanding when he held that we can understand individual matters of fact only by regarding everything in the world of experience as necessarily taking place according to causal laws, specific examples of which can be confirmed in experience. (See *Gr.* 114/455.) Now, he writes, we also find that we can understand the world in general and organic nature in particular only by assuming the speculative Idea of Nature and thinking of the world of experience as a systematic whole, "as a kingdom of ends," incorporating the teleological principle: Nature "organizes itself, and does so in each species of its organized products" (*Gr.* 80n/436n and *Cr.J.* 370–75; see *Pu.R.* A684–85/B712–13; *Gr.* 114/455).[14] Neither this noumenal view of Nature nor the teleological principle it contains can be confirmed by experience, but we can indicate partial instances of finality, as we do when we attend to the design of organic nature, say, in an acorn or a blade of grass. It would be "absurd" to hope that "another Newton may some day arise, to make intelligible for us even the genesis of a blade of grass from natural laws that no design has ordered" (*Cr.J.* 400).

Kant therefore argues that the scientist must use the Idea of Nature, which is the object of "rational cosmology," in order to have some standard of unified completeness (or truth). (See *Pu.R.* A329/B385–86, A333/B390, A647/B675; *Pr.R.* 142.) He writes.:

> The law of reason which requires us to seek for this unity, is a necessary law, since without it we should have no reason at all, and without reason no coherent employment of the understanding, and in the absence of this no sufficient criterion of empirical truth. In order, therefore, to secure an empirical criterion we have no option save to presuppose the systematic unity of nature as objectively valid and necessary. (*Pu.R.* A651/B679)

But how can a revival of the old Aristotelian notion of finality fit into a Newtonian universe of total causal determination? Kant insists the two views of the universe do not conflict but rather are complementary as long as (1) the principle of finality is used only as a subjective principle to guide theoretical inquiry, (2) only the principle of causal determination is used to explain the world, and (3) neither principle is used as the basis for speculative claims about ultimate reality in the manner of the old rationalistic metaphysics. (See, e.g., *Pu.R.* A671–74/B699–702; *Pr.R.* 134ff; *Cr.J.* 385, 417.)

When they investigate the world, then, physical and social scientists may use the principle of teleology only as a methodological and heuristic device. (See, e.g., *Pu.R.* A671/B699, A685–89/B713–17.) They may not use the principle constitutively; that is, they may not claim to know that any part of the world of experience, organic beings included, is actually purposive, nor may they use the principle of finality in their explanations. But given the limitations on what we may claim to know, Kant writes, it also would be presumptuous for us to think there cannot be purposiveness in nature. As an Idea of reason, finality in nature can be neither proved nor disproved empirically, but it is still a principle we find we must use. (See *Cr.J.* 387–88.)

Finally, we can have experience of and so know the world only in limited series of causal chains, but "for every series of conditions there must be something unconditioned, and consequently a causality which is entirely self-determining" (*Pr.R.* 48; see 48–49). To measure progress in science, then, we need to assume there ultimately is reality that, because it is permanent, can transcend, control, and finally explain all transience. This also is an ideal of successful explanation – an explanation that can be absolutely final because it is internally unified, simple, comprehensively powerful, necessary, and so a completely rationally satisfying explanation of the world and its laws. This speculative Idea of a final and self-explanatory explanation, requiring changeless duration, leads us to regard all the order in the world as if it had originated in the purpose of a supreme reason. This is the transcendental object of rational theology, the theoretically regulative Idea of a noumenal or supersensible Ultimate Reality, the deistic Idea of God – a single, final, supreme, uncaused Cause of all that exists, a necessary and self-explicable Cause in whom all chains of causal explanation can rest. (See, e.g., *Pu.R.*

A571–83/B599–611, A672–75/B700–704, A685–88/B713–16; A700–701/B728–29, A866–67/B714; *Gr.* 127/463; *Orient.* 139; *Cr.J.* 379.)

So in order to pursue its own proper interest, theoretical reasoning is forced to adopt as regulative norms the transcendental or nonempirical notions of freedom, soul, Nature, and God. The referents of all four are "beyond any possible insight of the speculative reason (although not contradictory to it)" (*Pr.R.* 120; see 49, 133–35). They therefore are theoretically incomprehensible and indemonstrable. (See *Pu.R.* A322/B379, A361–66, B406, A576–78/B604–6; *Gr.* 127–28/463; *Pr.R.* 7.) If we try to understand these Ideas, we only involve ourselves in insoluble difficulties that demonstrate conclusively why the old metaphysics was a mistake: With regard to immortality we generate what Kant called "paralogisms"; with regard to freedom (or the intelligible world), "antinomies"; and with regard to God, only an "indeterminate idea." (See *Pr.R.* 5, 132–33.)

Kant's analysis of theoretical reasoning in the first *Critique,* therefore, led him to conclude that although such reasoning can give us genuine knowledge of the world, its limits prevent it from functioning as the ultimate source of the unity of reason. The Greeks, such as Aristotle, had thought that the objects of *theoria* were "by their nature the most valuable." (See *Nicomachean Ethics* 6.7.1141b3.) Because those objects were necessarily and eternally what they were, they enjoyed ontological superiority over the objects of *praxis,* which were only contingencies and suffered change and dissolution. But when Kant argued that theoretical reasoning cannot transcend the limits of the senses, he in effect reduced its objects to ontological inferiority. Theoretical reasoning is able to reach only phenomenal reality, which has no meaning and exists only in the shape of appearances. (See *Pu.R.* A804/B832; *Gr.* 108/452, 127–28/463.) As a result theoretical reasoning is an intrinsically incomplete and rationally unsatisfying activity. It cannot satisfy our inevitable metaphysical wonder about ultimate reality. (See *Pu.R.* Bxix–xxv; A797/B825.) In fact, it cannot even defend its own existence without using concepts that are theoretically both indemonstrable and incomprehensible. In this regard, Kant writes, Nature has treated theoretical reasoning like a stepchild. (See *Pr.R.* 146.)

Showing the limitations of theoretical reason is not enough. Kant must also show that moral reason can supplement "the impotence of speculative reason," thereby securing its right to primacy (*Pr.R.* 122; see 120).

Superior cognitive power

If, Kant writes, we could take as real only what we can reach through sensory experience, then theoretical reason would have the right to primacy. So the first of his positive arguments for the preeminence of moral-practical reason appeals to its superior cognitive power. This, in fact, constitutes the main contention of the section entitled "On the Primacy of the Pure Practical Reason in Its Association with Speculative Reason" in the second *Critique* (*Pr.R.* 119–21).

Kant's argument is as follows: We know that pure reason can be practical, that we can think and act morally, because its law, the Law of Autonomy, is "given" as a unique a priori "fact." (See *Pr.R.* 121.) That law necessarily presupposes freedom as the condition of its possibility, and, as we shall see in Chapters 10 and 15, its necessary ends – moral perfection and happiness proportionate to our virtue – require both God and the immortality of the human soul. These Ideas of God, immortality, and freedom, which theoretical reasoning must use in an incomplete form without comprehending them, therefore are given both positive meaning by moral reasoning and conclusive support for our belief that they have real referents. (See *Pu.R.* Bxxii, Bxxv, B424–26, A800/B828, A828–31/B856–59; *Orient.* 137–40; *Pr.R.* 1–6, 50–51, 66, 103, 120–21, 132–36.) In a sense, then, moral reasoning does "widen our knowledge [*Erkenntnis*] beyond the limits of the world of sense" (*Pr.R.* 50; see 43, 103, 133; *Rel.* 170n/158). It therefore has the power to fulfill our metaphysical yearnings, at least as much as they can be fulfilled.[15]

We still have no objective *theoretical* insight into the nature of things as they are in themselves, and we still have no title to try to develop a theoretical theory about supersensible reality. (See *Orient.* 137; *Pr.R.* 135, 137.) Nonetheless, our belief in the objective reality of the referents of those concepts is now warranted by practical reasoning, so that their legitimacy as regulative assumptions of theoretical reasoning has been made subjectively certain. (See *Pr.R.* 49, 120–21, 134–38, 145–46.) From the point of view of theoretical reason, they may still be postulates and their acceptance still is a faith, but now it is not a blind faith but a rationally justified faith (a *Vernunftglaube*), certified by moral reason. (See *Pu.R.* A818/B846, A822–27/B851–56; *Pr.R.* 4, 44, 47–60, 120–21, 126, 134–35, 143–46.)[16] So, Kant concludes, "Thus in the combination of pure speculative with pure practical reason in one cognition, the latter has primacy" (*Pr.R.* 121).

Admitting that moral reasoning is a metaphysically superior mode of cognition and therefore has primacy does not do violence to the interest of the scientific enterprise or force it to yield any of its rights. (See *Pr.R.* 120.) On the contrary, it is very much in the interest of science that primacy belong to moral reasoning, which can justify and "fill out," so to speak, those Ideas of reason that theoretical reasoning must use but cannot defend or understand. (See *Pr.R.* 132.) Moral reasoning thereby safeguards the very existence of theoretical reasoning. (See *Pu.R.* A444–51/B472–79, A532–38/B560–86; *Pr.R.* 3, 42–43, 46–48, 56–57; *Pr.R.* 3, 94, 120–21, 144.)

Superior conative power

We might still object that moral thinking is in no better position than theoretical thinking, for both must equally presuppose the reality of transcendental freedom. Answering this objection introduces Kant's second positive argument for the primacy of moral reason, which rests on the superior *conative* power of such reasoning.

In the second preface to his *Critique of Pure Reason*, Kant had noted that a priori knowledge "may be related to its object in one or other of two ways, either as merely *determining* it and its concept (which must be supplied from elsewhere) or as also *making it actual*" (*Pu.R.* Bix–x). As we have seen, theoretical reasoning depends on the senses to give it content, whereas moral reasoning is dependent only on itself and defines itself in opposition to and "independently of alien influences" from inclinations (*Gr.* 101/448; see *Pr.R.* 89). This is the point of Kant's saying that "the philosophy of nature deals with all *that is,* the philosophy of morals with that which *ought to be,*" independently of what in fact does and does not occur (*Pu.R.* A840/B868; see also *Gr.* ii–iii/387–88, 27–28/407–8). Moral reasoning has the unique power to *bring into existence its own proper objects,* free decisions that conform to the requirements of reason alone. (See, e.g., *Pr.R.* 60, 66.)

So there is this radical difference between theoretical and moral-practical thinking: Pure practical reason is not dependent on anything "which must be supplied from elsewhere" in order for the referents of its concepts to enjoy existence. What happens to be has no relevance to what ought to be, that is, what moral reason mandates. We reason practically not to *know* objects but to *cause* those objects – morally significant intentions. (See, e.g., *Pr.R.* 66, 89.) It is this conative power to make its objects real that means that the claims of practical reasoning can be confirmed in a way not open to theoretical reasoning. When we reason morally, we can do what we cannot do when we reason theoretically: legitimately appeal to our own rational *self-consciousness* to determine, for the sake of practice, what is actual, namely, our ability and effort to shape our intentions according to the moral law. (See *Gr.* 101/448.) What we must presuppose for the possibility of the moral law and its demands, we also have the right at least to believe must be objectively true. The moral law reveals its reality in our self-consciousness, and with it the condition (freedom) necessary for its existence and the conditions (God and immortality) necessary for its own proper object (virtue and happiness proportionate to it).[17] Once again, because moral reason has more power than theoretical reason, it also has the right to primacy.

What primacy means

As we have seen, there must be a necessary and inseparable connection between theoretical and practical reasoning, between their respective interests – truth and goodness, and between their respective activities – belief and action. To say that moral-practical reason must be given primacy is to identify pure practical reason as the ground for the relation between the two uses of reason. This means that moral interests are preeminent, subordinate to no other interests, while every other end or interest of reason is subordinate to that of moral reason. Consequently, in cases of conflict, pure practical reason may override not only the claims of prudence but also those of theoretical reasoning. (See *Pr.R.* 110–11, 119; *Cr.J.* 206; *Logic* 86–87/94–95.)

Since "the highest ends are those of morality," moral perfection is our supreme ultimate good (*Pu.R.* A816/B844). This is exactly what we would expect, given Kant's initial claim in the *Groundwork* that the *only* end having unconditional value is morally good character – the "good will." There is no nonmoral good that can provide the ground for or basis of the moral good. There are other goods, but they are only conditionally good; that is, their value *ultimately* is not independent of but is derivative from the good will. They are good finally only if they are properly qualified by being either commanded or at least permitted by the good will.

But Kant's claim here is even stronger than that. He has repeatedly insisted that by its very nature, our reason has a profound need (a *Bedürfnis*) for an ultimate, necessary, and comprehensive explanation or justification of everything conditioned that we encounter. (See, e.g., *Orient.* 136.) When he seeks what is absolutely primary in the realm of ends, then, Kant is seeking a final unconditional goal not only for human beings but for the whole of creation, for the universe itself. He, in effect, is asking, Why is there a world at all? In Aristotelian terms, What is its final cause? (See *Cr.J.* 425–26, 434–36.)

Metaphysicians of the old school had speculated about whether the universe had a beginning or first cause that might also reveal its final cause, but as Kant showed in the first *Critique,* their efforts only generated paradoxes, showing that their enterprise was shaped wrongly from the beginning. (See *Pu.R.* A426–33/B454–62.) Since scientific explanations can be framed only in terms of prior and determining causes, after Newton no scientist would even try to answer a question about the "final cause" of the universe. (See *Cr.J.* 415, 417–18, 426, 429.) In fact, Newtonian science made a much stronger claim: Since the universe is explicable only in terms of mechanical laws and mathematical formulas, the universe appears to have no meaning or value at all; it just *is*.

Kant agreed with the Newtonian view, at least of the material universe. So if there is any final purpose to the world, any value in the fact that it exists, Kant therefore argued, that purpose and that value must be given it by beings, who, by virtue of their rationality, have the power to *confer* meaning and value on the universe. The only rational beings of whom we have any knowledge are human beings. (See *M.M.* 491.) So Kant concludes that, without human beings, "the whole of creation would be a mere wilderness, a thing in vain, and have no final end" (*Cr.J.* 442, 448). Today we may be tempted to reject such a claim out of hand as being hopelessly anthropocentric. Compared to the immensity of the universe, we seem so tiny – mere specks, with no significance. But this point of view depends on the primitive assumption that power and importance are only or mainly a function of *size*. An enormous universe may be meaningless by itself but still have meaning conferred on it by some higher power, but a power not dependent on size. What power might our reason give us that can justify the claim that our very existence confers ultimate value on the universe?

Theological theories, of course, attribute our value and dignity – and so also that of the universe – to God. However they have differed doctrinally, all such claims seek the ultimate meaning of the universe outside of us, with God. But Kant refused to go this way, for in his first *Critique,* he also had showed that knowledge of such ultimate Being lies beyond all the capacities of our theoretical reasoning. When officially plying his craft, the scientist must be an agnostic about the existence and nature of God. Further, as we shall see when we examine his philosophy of religion in Chapter 18, Kant holds that none of us can ever be certain that any of the many conflicting claims to some historical revelation really are of or from God. (See *Rel.* 153n/ 142.)

Even as they searched for a nontheological way in which to understand value in the world, the ancient Greek philosophers still looked outside of us to find meaning in human life, and they thought that what can give us worth is only our ability to imitate divine activity – say, by engaging in theoretical contemplation. In the first *Critique* Kant spent so much effort understanding *how* we can know the world of experience and delineating the limits of our theoretical knowledge that it is easy to overlook the question he addresses later – why it *matters* that we have knowledge. He argues that contemplation of the world can have value only if the world itself is first *worth* contemplating. But insofar as we can know it, the world of nature appears to us merely as a chain of contingencies, of conditioned objects and events, and it therefore gives us no reason to think it could itself have a necessary, final, and unconditioned value (*Cr.J.* 435). Since a meaningless world gains no worth merely "from the fact of its being known," contemplation cannot be the final end of human life or the ultimate justification for the world (*Cr.J.* 442).

Nonetheless, Kant does hold that there *is* unique value in our having reason, and he also holds that it is a defining characteristic of rational beings to be able "to form a conception of an end" (*Cr.J.* 426–27, 435). So we know that Kant must hold that whatever we can rationally adopt as an end is at least a candidate for having unconditional, intrinsic value (see *Cr.J.* 429–34). Surely one candidate for such value is the disciplined development of that very power of rationality. As we shall see in more detail in Chapter 13, education and growth in "culture" – in the sense of expanding the range and depth of ends, "any ends whatever of [our] own choosing" – was a goal especially dear to the Enlightenment (*Cr.J.* 430–31, 435).[18] But as Kant somewhat ruefully admits, if culture amounts only to a development of our ability to understand and appreciate nature, it comes down to theoretical contemplation, with the same value. Further, on the level of practice, increased knowledge by itself is only extrinsically valuable, and it may contribute only to chaos rather than to order. It gives us more power to fulfill our natural but unsociable desire to win superiority over others, and it may help us develop only the self-control of the "cool" criminal. (See *Gr.* 2–3/394; also *M.M.* 434.)

We have another end, and necessarily so: happiness, that is, the fulfillment of our needs taken as a harmonious whole. (See *Cr.J.* 431.) Clearly, Kant writes, imperfect and dependent beings like we humans do value our happiness as an intrinsic good. But, as we saw in Chapter 4, insofar as we are but one of many organisms able to feel emotions and to fulfill desires, using reason to satisfy needs and desires gives *us* no worth "above mere animality." Reason is then only serving "the purposes which, among animals, are taken care of by instinct" (*Pr.R.* 61; see *Cr.J.* 429–30). So *of itself* happiness is only a *natural* good, which, like the natural universe itself, can at best have conditional value. (See *Cr.J.* 442–43.) A universe, whether it contains only inanimate matter, or living but irrational beings, or beings who have reason but are capable only of rationally pursuing the conditional end of happiness, Kant argues, is equally without unconditional intrinsic worth. (See *Cr.J.* 449.)

Kant's contention, then, is that every candidate-for-meaning but one ultimately fails us. We can and often do value knowledge, culture, and happiness – and other things, too, such as talents and "gifts of fortune" – for their own sakes. (See *Gr.* 1–2/393–94.) But they are only conditionally or relatively good, too, since the world of nature within which we seek various satisfactions is itself at best extrinsically good and in need of further justification. (See *Cr.J.* 435, 443.) Only one end can be "final and perfect," Kant writes, because it is the one end that we as rational beings can achieve completely independently "of all animality and even of the whole world of sense." (See *Pr.R.* 120.)

By virtue of our having pure practical reason and therefore a moral personality, we have the unique ability to be self-governing, self-creative, self-determining, and autonomous. We are able to act completely independently of nature and its laws, for we can live in the supersensible world as free, moral agents. (See *Cr.J.* 435, 443.) We are thereby able and therefore entitled to project purposes that are *intrinsically and unconditionally* good, entirely on the basis of our own rational choices. We also therefore have the responsibility ourselves to define the meaning and value of human existence, and, with it, the ultimate – because unconditioned – purpose of the universe. Further, because the end we project (i.e., virtue and happiness proportionate to it) is intrinsic rather than extrinsic to us, it follows that *we* are the final end (*Endzweck*) of creation. (See *Cr.J.* 435.) That is why Kant wrote that "it is, then, only as a moral being that we acknowledge *man* to be the end of creation" (*Cr.J.* 444; see 436n). That is also why he penned those famous lines: "Two things fill the mind with ever new and increasing admiration and awe, the oftener and more steadily they are reflected on: the starry heavens above me and the moral law within me" (*Pr.R.* 161; see *Rel.* 23n2/19). As awesome as the heavens may be, the moral law within us has incomparably greater significance and worth.

This is a stunning doctrine, for by it Kant gives us metaphysical claim to the place inhabited by God in both theological and other philosophical systems. By virtue of our supersensible freedom, *we* are not only the first causes of our own moral actions but also the *only* first causes available to serve as an objective ground for the final end of the universe. It is true that the same moral law that reveals to us our freedom also insists that we believe in the existence of ultimate Being beyond the universe. (See *Orient.* 137–38.) But such Being is completely transcendent to and therefore inaccessible to any theoretical inquiry. If meaning is to be given to the universe, it must be a meaning immanent in us and not transcendent to us.

The rightness of this claim is confirmed in the most striking manner, for we have the awesome ability *and* therefore the vocation and the duty to do for other beings with pure practical reason precisely what nature does for phenomenal reality: formulate universal laws. The power to shape laws of autonomous practice for all free beings so transcends the world of nature as to give us the right to believe that we must have a destination that reaches beyond this life "into the infinite" (*Pr.R.* 162; see also 87ff; *Cr.J.* 431, 449–50).[19]

As Kant explains it, to talk of human persons as "moral beings" means to think of ourselves as "*under* moral laws" of our own making and adoption.[20] Our end, which for us is obligatory because contingent, is, of course, good moral character – a good will. Moral goodness is *the* unique, supreme good. (See *Cr.J.* 435.) The goodness of the good will is unconditional, for, as we have seen, our reason identifies its goodness as absolutely final and not derived from or dependent on any other good. (See *Cr.J.* 435, 443.) Its goodness is completely intrinsic to it, for a good will is good of itself. It alone "cannot be evil," because its goodness does not depend on its being an instrumentality, useful in the pursuit of anything else (*Gr.* 81/437). Finally, the goodness of the good will is necessary in the sense that it is an end required by the apodictic law of pure practical reason. (See *Cr.J.* 435–36, 450.) So Kant's opening statement in the *Groundwork,* enunciating what he took to be so fundamental a belief of ordinary moral consciousness in the supremacy of moral virtue that it could serve as the starting point of his analysis of the nature of morality, turns out to be also the culmination of his argument for the primacy of moral reason. (See *Gr.* 1–4/393–94; *Cr.J.* 443.)

Appealing to the Idea of Nature as a symbol of divine providence, then, Kant writes that "it is evident that the ultimate intention of nature in her wise provision for us has indeed, in the constitution of our reason, been directed to moral interest alone" (*Pu.R.* A801/B829). This does not mean that a good will is the only good in the world. (See *Gr.* 1–2/393, 7/396.) It does mean, first, that the world would ultimately be valueless without the good will. Second, all other – nonmoral or natural – goods are only conditionally good; that is, they need some further justification. Moreover, that justification must consist in conformity to – and in case of conflicts, submission to – moral interests. Since moral goodness must be *the* condition of all other things being objectively good, "everything good that is not based on a morally good disposition . . . is nothing but pretense and glittering misery" (*Idea* 26). And, finally, whatever else is objectively good must either contribute to and sustain that ultimate end or be assimilated into and become a constitutive part of that end.

Of all our possible and only conditionally good ends, Kant insists that one can and must be regarded as a distinctive part of our final goal: Because we are all sentient beings with constant needs, that goal is our natural well-being or happiness. When subordinated to the moral law, the originally purely natural and subjective value of happiness is transformed into a self-love of objective and moral quality. (See *Pr.R.* 115; *Rel.* 45n2/41–42; *T&P* 279n.) In that sense, when properly conditioned by the morally good will, human happiness is also part of the ultimate justification of creation.[21]

As for culture, it may be regarded as objectively good if it represents and prepares us "for a sovereignty in which reason alone shall have sway," that is, insofar as we make it part of the exercise of the good will. (See *Cr.J.* 431, 434n.)

Finally, theoretical knowledge turns out to be only conditionally and, ultimately, only extrinsically valuable. Since Kant holds that the final human good consists of virtue and happiness proportionate to it, in effect he leaves no room for theoretical activity as an integral, distinctive, and necessary part of our final good. This does not, of course, mean that Kant denies either the special interest or the rights of theoretical activity, nor does it mean that he denies that we can regard theoretical activity as having intrinsic value, as did the ancient Greeks. But it does mean that our knowledge of the phenomenal world is finally *not* for the sake of knowledge; it is valuable ultimately only insofar as, in the form of technical-practical rules, we use it to contribute to, support, and sustain the "final and perfect" end of human existence – the development and exercise of a good will (*Pr.R.* 120; *Cr.J.* 442–43). Since pure practical reason enjoys primacy, "every interest is ultimately practical, even that of speculative reason being only conditional and reaching perfection *only in practical use*" (*Pr.R.* 121, emphasis mine; see also *Cr.J.* 206). Given his rejection of the ancient Greek ideal of the leisured life and his scorn for social discriminations that favor an aristocratic nobility, Kant's conclusion here echoes his moral egalitarianism, his profound respect for ordinary people, who, however uneducated they may be, still have the same worth as anyone else, because they share the moral vocation and destiny common to all humanity – a good will.

Unity under a common principle

How does Kant think pure practical reason should exercise its primacy so as to preserve the integrity of reason? His doctrine here undoubtedly needs to be critiqued in the light of contemporary scientific practice. But in effect he holds that pure practical reasoning best defends its own primacy by protecting the rights of science. First, moral reason has both the right and obligation to defend the scientific enterprise against dangers posed by the desires or ambitions of individuals and by political or religious ideologies. Scientists are, of course, moral agents, and if they pervert evidence for the sake of their subjective interests, it is precisely because they are guilty of moral failure that they also fail to promote the aim of science to understand the world.[22]

Further, moral reason opposes stagnation in science and promotes the advance of scientific inquiry by defending the right of theoretical reasoning to use those Ideas of reason that we saw are necessary in the pursuit of knowledge.

Finally, moral reasoning has the right and duty to combat anyone who would claim it is possible to go beyond the limits of sense experience and achieve knowledge of supersensible reality. Ironically, moral reason secures the integrity of the scientific enterprise by insisting on the latter's limitations. As we have seen, doing so also protects pure practical reason, for it makes clear that there is no possibility that science will discover anything that might falsify legitimate moral claims.

Moreover, if moral reason enjoys primacy, then the moral Law of Freedom, appearing to us as the Categorical Imperative, must be the ultimate criterion of acceptability for theoretical activity, both in general and in particular. It is the "one principle on which a will can never be in conflict with itself" (*Gr.* 81/437).

As we have seen, the Categorical Imperative commands that any and all conflicts between our two *practical* interests – happiness and morality – be resolved, not by trying to work out a compromise between them or by denying our right to seek happiness, but by systematically subordinating the principle of self-love to the Law of Autonomy. In so doing, the Categorical Imperative functions as an rational imperative of *objectivity* for practice, demanding that we ignore our desires and inclinations – the source of mere subjectivity – when they threaten to pervert our decisions. (By contrast, objectivity is grounded in reason alone – for purposes of practice, in what would be valid for the will of any rational agent; see *Pr.R.* 19.)

Scientists commonly say they practice science because they find it fascinating and intellectually fulfilling. Kant does not dispute this, but he argues that if that were all there is to science, it could be regarded merely as highly sophisticated recreation. Kant always discussed the value of knowledge within the wider context of enlightenment, which, he wrote, is never *merely* a matter of information. Often the person "who is overly rich in information is least enlightened in the use of it" (*Orient.* 146n). Knowledge can be ignored or misused, and its ultimate value and justification must lie in the way it is used.

One way to express Kant's point is to say that science is not and cannot be value free. As Nathan Rotenstreich has observed, science as an enterprise is "ultimately subservient to the standard of truth."[23] It is, in fact, this characteristic that helps define the difference between science and nonscience. Yet "truth" is not a scientific concept with referents to be discovered in possible experience. It is a metascientific norm – essentially a *moral* norm legislating for both the aim and the methodology of scientists as scientists.

In Kant's view, then, the interest of scientific activity – the pursuit of empirical truth – should be viewed ultimately as a moral enterprise. Accordingly, he offers what he variously calls maxims for enlightenment, "dialectical rules" for arriving at truth, "general rules and conditions of avoiding error," and "maxims of common human understanding" (*sensus communis* or the public nature of judgment): (1) Think for yourself, (2) think from the standpoint of every other person, and (3) always think consistently. (See *Cr.J.* 293–94; *Logic* 57/63; *Anthr.* 228.) Kant did not mean to claim that these "maxims" are in fact commonly observed. That is why they are imperatives – rules we *should* adopt, legislating autonomous impartiality and disinterestedness, so we will avoid falling into errors generated by subjectivism, whether emotivism or some other antirationalistic ideology. (See *Orient.* 144–46.) Since it is always a failing to ignore any one of them in the search for truth, they are also categorical in form. So it turns out that these rules are simply a restatement of the purely formal but supremely powerful Categorical Imperative, the law of autonomy, universality, and consistency. What it requires has become so much a part of our thinking today that it may seem obvious and simplistic.

1. *Autonomy: Think for yourself.* As we saw at the beginning of the chapter, scientists traditionally were described as spectators of, rather than as actors in, the world. But this can be a misleading depiction, for even as "spectators" they are never merely passive: They must make decisions and act on them; they must project goals and select ways to try to attain them. In its formulation as the Imperative of Autonomy, then, the Categorical Imperative requires scientists to take it as a professional responsibility to think for themselves and to learn "what they ought to know" (*Enlight.* 40; see 36).

2. *Universality: Think from the standpoint of every other person.* In its formulation as the Imperative of Universal Law, the Categorical Imperative also mandates that, however methodologies might otherwise differ from science to science, they all must be objective (or universal) in at least two different senses. For one, theoretical claims must be objective in the sense of being based on grounds any rational person could accept as constituting sufficient support for such claims. (See, e.g., *Orient.* 141, 146n.) For another, the support for scientific claims must be objective in the sense of being public and replicable.[24] Science must be done from the "standpoint of everyone" in the sense that anyone with the right training and equipment should be able to reproduce the experiments, with the same results, of anyone else.

3. *Consistency: Always think consistently.* Subjectivity is characterized by inconsistency, whereas objectivity and rationality depend on consistency. Consequently, reason cannot feel satisfied with the appearance of any anomalous finding, but pushes for its resolution (while still requiring observance of the first two general rules), even if this will entail radical adjustments in previous theoretical commitments.[25] The fact that the Categorical Imperative here enunciates the originally purely logical principle of noncontradiction as a practical imperative for theorizing means, for Kant, that theoretical consistency is ultimately a moral requirement.

There is one other way in which moral interests override theoretical interests. In terms of the second formula of the Categorical Imperative, moral reason has both the right and the obligation either to "impel the understanding to explore a truth or restrain it therein" (*Logic* 385/82). Invoking this maxim tells us that the ultimate moral justification for seeking truth is respect for our worth and rights as moral beings. (See *Enlight.* 40.) For example, even if the genetic and other medical experiments at German concentration camps had been carried out with impeccable methodology, they were still absolutely unacceptable, for they involved treating people immorally, as mere things.

All scientific experimentation with human subjects is rightfully subject to moral codes of conduct and to reviews to ensure that the dignity of those subjects is not violated.

This, then, is Kant's response to the skeptical reaction of followers of the New Science to morality. In summary, first, given its limitations, science can say nothing at all about morality; and second, the promotion of the interests of the enterprise of science in fact depends on moral standards.

Another quest

In the preface to the *Groundwork*, Kant identified the ultimate aim of his philosophical analysis of morality this way: "A critique of practical reason, if it is to be complete, requires, on my view, that we should be able at the same time to show the unity of practical and theoretical reason in a common principle, since in the end there can be only one and the same reason, which must be differentiated solely in its application" (*Gr.* xii/391).

Now it may seem that Kant has already identified that principle as the Law of Freedom when he determined that pure practical reason enjoys primacy because it has the power to satisfy the need of reason as a whole for coherence and unity. For example, in the second *Critique* he stated that "the concept of freedom, in so far as its reality is proved by an apodictic law of practical reason, is the keystone of the whole architecture of the system of pure reason and even of speculative reason" (*Pr.R.* 3).[26]

Nonetheless it is clear that Kant did *not* believe he had yet accomplished his goal, for in the "Analytic" of the *Critique of Practical Reason,* he wrote that what he has set forth only *supports* "the expectation of bringing some day into one view the unity of the entire pure rational faculty (both theoretical and practical) and of being able to derive everything from one principle. The latter is an unavoidable need of human reason, as it finds complete satisfaction only in a perfectly systematic unity of its cognitions" (*Pr.R.* 91). Moreover, in his third *Critique,* he entitles Part III of his introduction "The Critique of Judgment as a Means of Connecting [a *Verbindungsmittel*] the Two Parts of Philosophy [the theoretical and the moral-practical] in a Whole" (*Ganze; Cr.J.* 176; see 171–79).

So it turns out that Kant's program, first projected in the *Groundwork* and carried out in the third *Critique,* was not intended only to provide us with a principle to arbitrate possible conflicts between theoretical and moral reasoning. Kant is still concerned with what he calls the "great gulf" between the noumenal and the phenomenal viewpoints and the laws of each. (See *Cr.J.* 168–77.) He is not content with the discussion of the relation between the two that ended Chapter 7. He is, above all, a synoptic philosopher, and the most fundamental question, What is man? requires a a single coherent view of human existence. (See *Logic* 25/29.)[27] This means a completely unified view of our rational life. (See *Pu.R.* A840/B868.)

Kant therefore investigates the ability of judgment to provide a subjective "middle term" between theoretical and moral reasoning, a principle to unite the functioning of the two. The principle of judgment that he deduces in that book is the principle of teleology or finality. Although we do not have the space to consider the third *Critique* in any detail, the first part of that book concerns how the principle of finality bridges the gap between reason and desire, thereby providing the basis for a theory that can account for both aesthetic taste (as a "disinterested liking") and judgments about beauty (as symbols of moral goodness). In the second part of that volume Kant repeats the argument we saw earlier in this chapter – that the teleological principle unifies the two viewpoints of reality. It supplements the mechanical viewpoint of Newtonian physics by operating as a methodological and heuristic device to guide theoretical inquiries about the world, by viewing organic nature as if teleological, with natural ends finally to be achieved "in it according to the laws of freedom" (*Cr.J.* 176; see also 442–47).

I I
The moral norm for persons

9
Moral character: Part I

Any ethical theory must address two distinct but related questions: What makes an action morally right? and What makes a person morally good? Since Mill, asking the first question generally has been understood as asking what *behaviors* are morally acceptable. By contrast, questions about the nature of good character traditionally have been taken to be queries about the inner structure of an individual's personality, with emphasis on a person's motivation.

Kant holds that ordinary people do not find it difficult to recognize that these are different questions. (See *Lect.* 279–80/47–48.)[1] Yet, as we saw at the end of Chapter 3, Kant himself tends to treat them as a single question, because he regards moral worth as prior to and so as definitive of what is morally right, and also because he so often thinks of actions primarily as intentions rather than as behaviors. He does just this, for example, in the first chapter of the *Groundwork,* where he defines the supreme principle of morality in terms of a person's intentions: What makes an action morally right is that it originates in a person's good will, that is, with the adoption of a maxim fit to serve as a universal practical law.

Under this description, *mere* moral legality occurs when a person's behavior does not violate the Categorical Imperative and in that sense can be said to be "moral in form" or "morally good in letter"; but the action is "not morally good in spirit or intention" because it is done from an "ulterior" or nonmoral incentive, to satisfy some desire or aversion, and not because it is what one ought morally to do. (See, e.g., *Pr.R.* 72n, 117.) So just "doing the right thing" is in itself not morally wrong.[2] But it also is not "morally good" in the sense that by itself it is not a sufficient condition for the *person* performing such actions to merit thereby the judgment of being, to that extent at least, a morally good individual. (See *Gr.* 9–10/397–98; *M.M.* 219, 227, 390–91; *Pr.R.* 72n, 81–82, 85, 159.)

Kant is forced to separate questions about the quality of actions and the quality of a person's character in his political philosophy, because civil laws can regulate a citizen's conduct but they cannot require obedience from any particular motive or for any particular aim. Kant then calls behavior, considered apart from its motivation, "right" (in a "juridical" – *rechtskräftig* – sense) or "lawful" or "legal" (*gesetzmässig*) or "according to duty" (*pflichtmässig*) when it conforms to what he calls the Universal Principle of Law (or of Justice – *Recht*): An action is right if it is right for anyone to do, or, in Kant's words, if "the free use of your will is compatible with the freedom of everyone according to a universal law" (*M.M.* 231; see 219, 225, 229–32; *Pr.R.* 81).[3] In effect, this principle is a restricted statement of the first formula of the Categorical Imperative, the Formula of Universal Law.[4]

When we turn to his answer to the second question, we find that Kant holds that it is only one's motivation that determines whether one is a morally good person. For us and our actions to have genuinely *ethical* worth, we must act from specifically ethical motivation, which Kant describes as a "submissive disposition" and acting "from duty" – *aus Pflicht* (*M.M* 214 and *Pr.R.* 81–82; see *M.M.* 218–19). Only this is ethics, strictly speaking: adopting maxims with the form of law "out of respect for" and "for the sake of the moral law," that is, *because* they conform to the Categorical Imperative (*Pr.R.* 81 and *Gr.* viii/390; see 10–11/398–99; *Pr.R.* 45–46, 71, 72n, 85, 117, 125, 152; *M.M.* 214, 219, 225).

So radically different is moral motivation from the urge to satisfy desires that Kant calls the former a "reason [for acting]" (a *Bewegungsgrund,* or principled motive) and the latter only an "incentive" or "stimulus" (a *Triebfeder*), a term having causal connotations (*Gr.* 63/427).[5] The former is objective, that is, a motive valid for every rational agent, whereas the latter can be only subjective, for it depends on each person's desires. (See *Gr.* 63/427.) The ultimate law of pure practical reason obligates us categorically not only to do what it commands but also to do so because that is what it commands. The ground of the moral motive, therefore, is the moral law itself, commanding us to do what we ought *because* it is what we ought to do. (See *Gr.* 14–15/400–401; *T&P* 282; *M.M.* 219.)

Merely pathological desires

Underlying Kant's treatment of human moral character is his analysis of "merely pathological" feelings and desires.[6] In the first *Critique* Kant had divided our mental life into its matter and its form. The matter is "given" to us through our senses in what he called the "manifold of sensibility," and we impose the form or rational structure on this matter by our mental activity. While there is and logically can be only one manifold of sensibility, there are two different kinds of "givens": sensations (*Empfindungen*) through which "objects are given to us," and feelings (*Gefühle*), which are not cognitively revelatory of objects but rather are the subjective effect on us of our sensations and representations of objects. (See *Pu.R.* A15/B29, A28n/B44n; *M.M.* 211–12, 211n1.)

Feelings belong to what is given, but strictly speaking they are not part of the manifold of sensibility, for they are not objects we can observe with our senses, and in that sense they lie "outside our whole faculty of knowledge" (*Pu.R.* A801n). Some feelings give us no reason to act, such as aesthetic pleasure, but other feelings – desires or aversions – typically are focused on objects to be pursued or avoided. Desires and aversions function for practical reasoning much as sensations do for theoretical reasoning. Without sensations, the human thinker lacks a world to know; and without desires, the human agent lacks a world on which to act.

Purely pathological desires and aversions all concern the pursuit of pleasure and the avoidance of pain. As we saw in Chapter 4, they are the stimulus for prudential reasoning (*Pu.R.* A15/B29; see also A49/B66, A801/B829). Because Kant takes all such feelings to be part of the given and so of "passivity" – what simply happens to us, "something we merely passively feel" – he classifies them all as heteronomous (*Pr.R.* 116; see *Rel.* 31–32/26–27, 34–35/ 30; *Anthr.* 293). Since they are caused by prior events over which we now have no control, our desires are "no more subject to direct rational control than sensation itself."[7] "I cannot [generate the feeling of] love," Kant writes, "because I *will* to, still less because I *ought* to. . . . So a *duty to love* is logically impossible" (*M.M.* 401; see 401–2, 449; *Gr.* 13/399; *Pr.R.* 83).

As a consequence, Kant regards our desires and inclinations as all equally part of the causally determined natural world and so as amoral – neither morally good nor evil. It makes no difference whether they are felt urgently or underlie a cool deliberate commitment, whether they encourage us to sympathize with or to take advantage of another person. Desires are not the cause of moral evil, which can be attributed only to our will. (See, e.g., *Gr.* 10/ 398; *H.H.* 117; *Pr.R.* 32–33; *Rel.* 34–35/30, 57–58/50–51.) It follows, then, that the sheer fact that a person has and may continue to have certain desires, whether supportive of or contrary to the moral law, is, morally speaking, neither praiseworthy nor blameworthy.

What is required of us is "the a priori subjection of the manifold of desires to the unity of consciousness of a practical reason commanding in the moral law, i.e., for a pure will" (*Pr.R.* 65; see *Gr.* 13–16/399–401). In other words, we are morally responsible only for our willing, for the manner in which we react to our desires. Morality requires us to act independently of and, if necessary, in opposition to all our merely pathological feelings.

Conflicts between reason and desire

In Chapter 3 we saw that Kant aimed to avoid relying on psychology, for doing so could easily distort his analysis of human morality. What he could not avoid, however, was committing himself to a particular view of human nature: Human beings are essentially and ineluctably ambivalent.[8] We all seek what we cannot have – both unlimited happiness and merited moral self-esteem. "Nature has given us two different dispositions for two different purposes, the one for man as an animal, the other for him as a moral species" (*H.H.* 116). Our prudential and moral interests not only are distinct but, as our everyday moral consciousness confirms, also often "make antagonistic claims" that are "diametrically opposed to each other" (*Gr.* 24/405; *M.M.* 378).[9]

Although desires "afford the occasion for" virtue, they also represent a constant rivalry with and threat to morality (*Rel.* 35/30; see *Pr.R.* 79). Since they simply are what they are, desires and inclinations are not themselves morally evil, but we experience them as "subjective limitations and obstacles" to our striving for good moral character (*Gr.* 8/397; see also 37–38/413). Whenever we do act immorally, it is only because we have yielded to the lure of our inclinations, which seek only their own satisfaction. (See, e.g., *Gr.* 9/397, 27/407.)

Consequently, Kant writes, all given inclinations and desires, even those we think of as good-natured, are "blind and slavish," "the subjective antagonists" of, "obstacles to," and "a powerful counterweight to" the moral law, a subversive force that "secretly works against it" (*Pr.R.* 118, 73, 76, and 86, and *Gr.* 23/405; see also *Gr.* 8/397, 37–38/413; *Pr.R.* 32; *M.M.* 380). They are "insatiable" and "tyrannical" and represent "either a hindrance, which we have to overcome, or an allurement, which must not be made into a motive" (*Cr.J.* 433 and *Pu.R.* A15/B29; see also *Gr.* 8/397; *Pr.R.* 128; *M.M.* 430–31).[10]

The opposition between the interests of inclinations and those of pure practical reason, according to Kant, gives rise to a "*natural dialectic* – that is, a disposition to quibble with these strict laws of duty, to throw doubt on their validity or at least on their purity and strictness, and to make them, where possible, more adapted to our wishes and inclinations; that is, to pervert their very foundations and destroy their whole dignity" (*Gr.* 23/405). Even though we can always resist our desires, we still cannot avoid feeling them; we cannot avoid being, as Kant puts it, "pathologically affected" by them. Because the temptation to yield to our desires is "inextirpable" by us, we experience morality as an ongoing inner struggle against the allurements of pleasure (*Pr.R.* 32 and *Rel.* 51/46; see *Pu.R.* A534/B562; *Pr.R.* 25, 83–84, 117). This is a conflict infecting us all because we are not only rational but also physical beings, and we cannot alter our nature. (See *H.H.* 116n.) We all seek our own happiness, and we all continue to want that happiness even when it is inconsistent with the strictures of morality.

Within the context of this struggle, the Law of Autonomy or of Freedom always and necessarily appears to us as an unconditioned and unconditional imperative. The Categorical Imperative commands us, negatively, not to allow ourselves to be ruled by our feelings and inclinations; we must "set aside altogether the influence of inclination, and along with inclination every object of the will" (*Gr.* 15/400; see 7/397; *Pr.R.* 72). Positively, that law requires us to obey it *because* it is the law of our own reason. (See *Gr.* 36–39/412–14, 102–3/449, 122/460; *Pr.R.* 80; *M.M.* 379, 408.)

Because the moral law appears to us within the context of conflict with our desires, it is not accurate to refer to what it requires only as "what is *right*" or to describe virtuous moral motivation only as the disposition to do what is "morally *right*." The term "right" does not acknowledge how our wants clamor for satisfaction so that morality always appears to us, not just as what is right, but as what is our *duty,* our obligation, what we *ought* or *ought not* to do.

Duty

Out of the dialectic between inclinations and pure practical reason, morality always appears to us in the "dry and earnest" form of *duty* (*Pflicht*) (*Pr.R.* 157; see *Gr.* 111/453–54). No moral philosopher before Kant had placed so much emphasis on the notion of duty, and few concepts have greater prominence in his theory.[11] Moreover, in this regard he continues to exercise a profound influence on both the vocabulary and thought of moral philosophers, so it is crucial for us to know what Kant meant by this term.

"If the will is exposed to subjective conditions (certain impulsions) which do not always harmonize with objective ones, the determining of such a will in accordance with objective laws is *necessitation* [*Nötigung*]" or obligation (*Gr.* 37/412–13; see 8/397, 51n/420n, 102–3/449; *Pr.R.* 32; *M.M.* 394). We do not necessarily always do what we ought, and even when we do what is right, we often do it reluctantly. We often would much rather pursue some pleasure or other than do what morality requires of us. (See *Pr.R.* 80; *M.M.* 379–80.) Because we are never completely free of the propensity to pursue pleasure rather than virtue, we always experience morality as *constraining* us, mandating what we ought (not) to do, independently of what we may or may not want to do. (See *Pr.R.* 80, 83–85.)

Under the term "duty," Kant elides three distinct but related ideas, all presupposing the context of conflict between the moral law and desires.

First, he defines duty as "nothing other than the will's *limitation* and the requirement of a universal legislation" (*T&P* 280). In this sense, the term "duty" refers to the Categorical Imperative itself and to its constraining relation to our will. (See *Gr.* 76/434; *M.M.* 379–80.) Since there is but one ultimate moral law, there is but one duty in this sense. (See *M.M.* 395, 482.)

Second, Kant also calls all the actions, the maxims of actions, and the ends commanded by the Categorical Imperative our "duties" (see, e.g., *M.M.* 218, 222, 225, 405). There are many such duties – fidelity to contracts, beneficence, honesty, and so on. (See *M.M.* 395; *Ed.* 492/107–8.)

Finally, Kant uses the term "duty" to refer to the only motive of specifically moral quality, consisting of a law-abiding disposition (*Gesinnung*) of respect for and submissive obedience to the Categorical Imperative in the face of opposition from desires and inclinations. (See *Gr.* 14/400, 86/439; *Pr.R.* 158; *M.M.* 225, 383–84, 387, 389, 392, 395, 406, 410, 446, 482; *Rel.* 24n/20.) Since dutifulness or conscientiousness (*Gewissenhaftigkeit*) abstracts from any ends we may desire, it, like the moral law itself, is a purely formal requirement for morally good choice. It requires us to comply with the moral law *aus Pflicht, because* it is the moral law, out of respect for it, regardless of anything further we may or may not achieve by doing so. (See *Pr.R.* 81; *T&P* 282n; *M.M.* 218, 375.)[12]

If we are to act as we ought, then, our duty (in sense 1), that is, the "universal moral command," is: "Do your duty [in sense 2] from the motive of duty [in sense 3] – *Handle pflichtmässig aus Pflicht*" (*M.M.* 391).

Virtue

The constraint morality places on our choices can coexist with freedom only if we place it against ourselves. So Kant calls dutifulness – here he again borrows a term from the Stoics – "virtue" (*virtus* or *Tugend*), meaning both power and self-mastery. Virtue is an acquired characteristic (a *habitus*).[13] However, the notion of "self-mastery" by itself could designate merely a prudential control over and ordering of our desires (see *M.M.* 394). So, more precisely, virtue consists in the power of autonomy – self-control based on the free legislation of our own reason and of its law, the Categorical Imperative. (See *Gr.* 95/444; *Rel.* 23/19.) It therefore requires the free exercise of human moral reason in both its cognitive and conative roles: negatively, the power systematically to judge and act independently of the influence of all merely pathological desires and inclinations; and positively, the power to bring our decisions (*Willkür*) under the law and rule of moral reason (*Wille*) and to motivate us to act only from a dutiful attitude. (See *M.M.* 214, 218–20, 225, 379–81, 383, 389, 394, 396, 405, 407–9, 410, 437–38, 477.)

Like the notion of duty, the notion of virtue implies a "consciousness of a continual propensity to transgress it or at least to a defilement, i.e., to an admixture of many spurious (not moral) motives to obedience to the [moral] law" (*Pr.R.* 128; see 33; *M.M.* 380, 394, 405, 407; *Anthr.* 294). Kant therefore characterizes virtue as moral strength or moral courage (*fortitudo moralis*) (*M.M.* 405). "We can recognize strength of any kind," he goes on, "only by the obstacles it can overcome," and with regard to virtue the obstacles we must combat are not only our own desires and inclinations but, as we shall see in a moment, also our own corrupted will (*M.M.* 390, 394, 405). Virtue, then, is a strength we must cultivate, both by attending to the dignity of the moral law within us and by active exercise (*exercitio*). (See *M.M.* 228, 397, 401, 405, 435.)[14]

Mixed motivation

As a motive, dutifulness is most evident just when it costs us happiness by requiring us to act directly contrary to our desires and aversions. (See, e.g., *Gr.* 8/397, 10–11/398; *Pr.R.* 156.) But when people reading Kant for the first time measure themselves against his theory of moral motivation, they invariably find that many of their actions that have conformed to duty also have set out the means to some end that they in fact desired. They therefore conclude that they have often acted from "mixed motivation," that is, both from the motive of duty and from prudential motives. What, according to Kant, is the moral worth of actions done from mixed motives?

Because the motive of duty is the only specifically moral motive, Kant holds that actions from mixed motivation are and can be morally good and virtuous *only insofar as* they are ultimately motivated by the moral law; and our actions are fully morally good only if we would have done them out of duty even if there had been no other, prudential incentives. (See *M.M.* 220,

393.) Kant writes, "The proper worth of an absolutely good will . . . lies precisely in this – that the principle of action is free from all influence by contingent grounds" (*Gr.* 61/426). So, when we also have nonmoral reasons for acting morally rightly, say, affection for another person, we should try to regard that action fundamentally as what morality requires of us or permits us to do rather than as what we merely happen to want to do. (See *Pr.R.* 81–82.) (Yet, as Kant also acknowledges, we can never be absolutely sure that we have acted from duty in any particular instance.)

Kant admits that inclinations that happen to support morality may "facilitate the effectiveness of moral maxims" by adding incentives to do what is right (*Pr.R.* 118; see also *End* 338).[15] But he still insists that they do not deserve moral esteem, for insofar as actions are motivated by them, they have no moral worth (*Gr.* 10/398; see 2/393, 65/428; *Pr.R.* 82, 155n). More, because all inclinations and temperamental traits are still heteronomous, aimed only at pleasure and happiness, they all at bottom remain rivals to moral motivation. Any harmony between them and the moral law is only subjective and accidental. (See *Gr.* 2/394; *Pr.R.* 33; *T&P* 288.)

In fact, those desires and inclinations may be morally the "riskiest" that seem to support rather than openly conflict with moral obligations. It is just when we also happen to want what is morally obligatory that we may be most tempted to deny that "all admixture of incentives which derive from one's own happiness [is] a hindrance to the influence of the moral law on the human heart," and then we may begin to waver between acting on moral and amoral motives (*Pr.R.* 156; see 72; *Gr.* 33–34/411). Under other circumstances those same inclinations could as easily lead us to want to do what is morally wrong if that seems to our advantage. Indeed, since inclinations "grow with the indulgence we allow them," insofar as we become used to relying on them, we also risk acting on them when it is immoral to do so (*Pr.R.* 118; see *Gr.* viii/390, 2–3/394; *M.M.* 446–47; *T&P* 282; *Rel.* 30–31/26). Therefore, Kant concludes, "everything empirical added to [moral incentives] is just so much that takes away from their genuine influence and from the absolute value of the corresponding actions" (*Gr.* 34/411; see *Pr.R.* 25, 88–89, 93). All desires for pleasure "must be separated from the supreme practical principle and never be incorporated with it as a condition, for this would destroy all moral worth" (*Pr.R.* 93).[16]

Kant occasionally may seem to take a more lenient view of those natural inclinations that support morality. In the *Groundwork* he allows that a sympathetic temperament may deserve "praise and encouragement," if not moral esteem (*Gr.* 10/398). And in the second *Critique* he writes:

It may even be advisable to connect [the] prospect of a merry enjoyment of life with that supreme determining motive which is sufficient of itself . . . only in order to hold a balance against the attractions which vice on the other side does not fail to offer and not in order to place in these prospects even the smallest part of the real moving force when duty is what we are concerned with. (*Pr.R.* 88)

It is important to note that in all such passages Kant still insists that duty is the only motive with moral quality and that in those cases when we should promote our happiness, we should do so because we have an indirect *duty* to tend to our happiness in order to preserve and promote our virtue. In his *Metaphysics of Morals,* for example, he states that if we can more easily attend to our moral obligations by providing ourselves with such morally permissible "comforts as are necessary merely to enjoy life," then doing so "is duty to oneself" (*M.M.* 452; see 216). But "every duty implies . . . constraint. . . . and what is done from constraint is not done from love," including self-love (*M.M.* 401).

Kant therefore unequivocally condemns any tendency to mix the radically different incentives of happiness and duty, even when "done with good intent and under maxims of the good" (*Rel.* 29/24; see 37/32–33, 83/78). "We cannot give a warning too strongly or too often," he writes, against relying on "alien" empirical inducements to help motivate us to act rightly (*Gr.* 61/426). Deliberately introducing nonmoral, prudential motives to support dutifulness contaminates a person's motivation, making his will morally "impure," precisely because that person "should have adopted the [moral] law alone as [his] *all sufficient* motive" and acted "purely for duty's sake" (*Rel.* 30/25; see 77/71). Cultivating an impure will is worse than suffering occasionally from moral weakness, for it is but one step away from becoming morally evil and giving nonmoral incentives precedence over the moral incentive of duty. (See *Rel.* 42/37.) So the central claim of Kant's moral philosophy is still that pure reason *by itself* is and must be a practical power, sufficient of itself to interest us in acting as we ought, independently of all prudential influences. (See, e.g., *Gr.* 36–37/412–13, 97–98/446–47, 124–25/461; *Pr.R.* 74–75.)[17]

The "radical evil" in human nature

The more he meditated on the comparative strength of reason and of desire in the internal struggle between them and on the frequency of moral failures, the more Kant became convinced that "man shows more propensity [or tendency – *Hang*] to listen to his inclinations than to the [moral] law" (*M.M.* 379n; *Rel.* 492/168; *Anthr.* 332n). We do not just experience choices between the moral law and our desires. Instead, we all find ourselves always at least potentially opposed to the moral law within us. The history of the human race as a whole is a long litany of moral barbarisms, showing a continual proclivity of the members of the species to commit the most terrible crimes imaginable against each other. We all seem to be inclined to act immorally, and we have to make a positive *effort* to act dutifully.

Particularly in his *Religion Within the Limits of Reason Alone,* then, Kant pushes his analysis of the human moral predicament farther and maintains that, as a species, the human race has a depraved nature. Contrary to Rousseau's contention that we are by nature only good, Kant maintains that the human race has a natural inclination to vice. There is "a *radical* innate *evil* in human nature," a propensity that is "inextirpable," at least by any human power (*Rel.* 32/28, 37/32). So inevitably do people deviate from the moral law that "we may presuppose evil to be subjectively necessary to every man, even to the best" (*Rel.* 32/27–28; see 29–32/24–27, 38–39/34). We all find ourselves in an "ethical state of nature," with an innate propensity (*angeboren Hang*) to resist the moral law and to adopt as our ultimate maxim the "evil principle" of systematically giving our desires precedence over the moral law. (See *Rel.* 33/28–29, 39/34.)

We particularly tend to pervert our naturally good "predisposition to humanity," Kant writes, that is, our need to live together in society with others, by regarding our social relationships in a radically individualistic manner. Then we look on ourselves as isolated from and set against all others in an amoral and antisocial Hobbesian world of unrelenting hostility toward and competition with others to satisfy our desires. (See *Rel.* 19/15.) In that world everyone else, in particular those with whom we have personal relations, is regarded either as a means or an obstacle to satisfying our desires, especially to gaining possessions and power. (See, e.g., *Rel.* 27/22; *M.M.* 459.) Not only do people then tend to avoid their own moral obligations to contribute to the happiness of others; they "devilishly" look for ways to violate that obligation and even to discourage others from leading virtuous lives. This morally perverse behavior occurs not only in primitive societies but also in "civilized" interpersonal relations as well as in relations between states.

Our reason finds the origin of this propensity to evil completely incomprehensible. It cannot be discovered simply from an a priori analysis of our nature as imperfectly moral beings, and so the propensity cannot be an objectively necessary part of human nature. Yet saying that the human race tends to evil is not to make merely an empirical generalization, for it is a genuinely universal claim. Moreover, it is a claim about the moral quality of maxims, which do not appear in our experience. The claim that the human species has an evil predisposition is, Kant in effect holds, a necessary transcendental view of the universal tendency of the human will to oppose the moral law.

Having a tendency to evil does not mean that human moral agents are *totally* depraved and *irrevocably* evil, unable to do anything morally good, as some historical religions have interpreted the traditional doctrine of Original Sin. Kant insists as strongly as he can that our moral character depends only on our own free decisions, not on any part of human nature (such as the inclinations) or on the decisions of any other person (such as a biblical Adam) (*Rel.* 37/32–33, 41–42/37, 44/40; *Anthr.* 324; *Ed.* 448/15). He therefore holds that all human beings must be thought of as born in a "state of innocence," that is, without any specific moral character. (See *H.H.* 110–11; *Rel.* 44/40; *Ed.* 492/108.) An infant "is not by nature a moral being. He only becomes a moral being when his reason has developed ideas of duty and law" (*Ed.* 492/108).

Because the moral law within us inexorably commands us to obey it, we can be certain that we are free and able to do so. This means that each of us also has an innate "predisposition [*Anlage*] to personality," that is, the capacity and tendency to respect the moral law and to adopt it as our ultimate practical principle. (See *Rel.* 27/22–23, 44/40, 46/42; *Ed.* 492/168.) In that sense, Kant writes, the human species may also be considered "good by nature" (*Anthr.* 324). "There is no man so depraved as not to feel an opposition to" transgressions against the moral law and "an abhorrence of himself" if he does violate it (*M.M.* 379n; see 441, 464; *End* 331). As long as we retain our reason, we can never totally lose this good disposition, and each person *can* emerge triumphantly from this internal moral struggle.

Where does the predisposition to evil arise, if it is a predisposition of our own will for which each of us must take responsibility? Kant concludes that it must be that we all initially succumb to wickedness, so that the effort to adopt a morally virtuous disposition always begins with a will that each person has *already* committed to the pursuit of pleasure as the supreme good. (See *Rel.* 51/46, 57n/50–51.) (That apparently is why Kant calls the tendency "innate," although it cannot actually be so.) The Stoics (and most other philosophers as well) had underestimated the strength of the opposition to the moral law. They had thought that moral development begins with a simple absence of virtue and a need to curb undisciplined desires. (See *Rel.* 57/50.) On the contrary, "we cannot start from an innocence natural to us but must begin with the assumption of a wickedness of the will in adopting its maxims contrary to the original [good] moral predisposition" (*M.M.* 440; *Rel.* 51/46; *Ed.* 492/108). We begin the pursuit of virtue with a need "first to remove the inner obstacle (an evil will actually present in [us])" and with the moral law already condemning us for initially choosing the evil ultimate maxim (*M.M.* 441; see *Rel.* 57–58/50–51, 59n/52–53, 72/66).

The internal moral conflict everyone experiences, therefore, is a war within our will, on the one hand exhibiting a radical tendency toward evil and on the other a fundamental predisposition to good based on the inexorable commands of the moral law in each person's reason. Kant therefore describes the human species as one that "strives, in the face of obstacles, to rise out of evil in constant progress toward the good" (*Anthr.* 333). Each individual battle can always be won, and in each such victory, the "innate evil propensity in our species is indeed censured by ordinary human reason and perhaps even restrained, but still not eradicated" (*Anthr.* 327; see *Rel.* 57n/50–51).[18]

The nature of moral character

If we are to understand Kant's doctrine of the nature of moral character, we first need to review his claim that, depending on our purposes, we can regard the character of human agents either from a phenomenal or a noumenal point of view. (See *Pu.R.* A538–58/B566–86.)[19]

A person's "physical" or "psychological" or "empirical" self or character consists of inherited dispositional or temperamental traits modified by complexes of acquired habits as well as by the influence of a wide variety of external influences, such as one's family and education. (See *Anthr.* 285–91.) When we take this theoretical point of view, we necessarily regard the character of human agents as part of the phenomenal world. Insofar as we do that, as we saw in Chapter 7, we also must regard "psychological freedom" simply as a kind of causal determinism. From this point of view, Kant writes, we regard character as explicable by prior relevant causal factors, including reason and accompanying mental states. If we could know them all, we would be able to predict exactly how a person will act and react in various situations. (See *Pu.R.* A538–41/B566–69, A550/B578; *Anthr.* 286.) As a consequence, from this point of view, genuinely moral character cannot be found anywhere in the everyday world of theoretical experience.

To regard character as free and moral, Kant writes, we therefore must regard it as purely noumenal and spontaneous, as part of the supersensible, free world of things-in-themselves. So regarded, moral character cannot be perceived, but it certainly can and must be thought about. Given Kant's analysis of the limitations of our knowledge, it is surprising how much insight he thinks we can have into it.

When thinking about moral character, it is very difficult to avoid using empirical terms altogether, and Kant occasionally does use such categories and schemata. (See, e.g., *Rel.* 47–48/42–43.) But since moral character is not part of the phenomenal world, it is subject neither to the forms of space and time nor to the causal laws that our understanding imposes on appearances. (See *Pr.R.* 97–99, 114.) If outside of time, our moral character cannot be affected or conditioned by temporally prior conditions, then it must be *thought of* (even though we cannot understand this) as not subject to change so that nothing can happen *to* it. Likewise, "no action begins *in* this active being itself," for "in respect of the intelligible character . . ., there can be no before and after; every action . . . is the immediate effect of the intelligible character of pure reason" (*Pu.R.* A553/B581; see A539–40/B567–68; *Rel.* 25/20).

Positively, the nature of noumenal character follows conceptually from Kant's previous analysis of the nature of free agency. An agent of *any* kind can be an efficient cause only in a law-governed world, that is, only by following a law determining what kind of a cause it is – how its causality is exercised: "Every efficient cause must have a *character* [*Charakter*], that is, a law of its causality, without which it would not be a cause" (*Pu.R.* A539/B567). Agents with a free will or pure practical reason are unique in that they have the power to adopt and act on laws they themselves as rational beings have formulated. (See *Gr.* 36/412.) They alone can be responsible for the kind of character they have, for the quality of their character depends not on what nature makes of them but on what they make of themselves.

Out of the internal moral conflict everyone experiences comes either virtue or vice, for inevitably either reason or desire will dominate our decisions (*M.M.* 408). "Between its a priori principle, which is formal, and its a posteriori motive, which is material," Kant writes, "the will stands, so to speak, at a parting of the ways" (*Gr.* 14/400; see *Pr.R.* 35). It is not possible for us to give equal weight to both moral and prudential incentives. If we do not deliberately adopt the motive of duty, we inevitably end up acting only on maxims of self-love, that is, on prudential motives. "Unless reason holds the reins of government in its own hands, man's feelings and inclinations assume mastery over him" (*M.M.* 408). There can be no middle ground here.

Kant therefore claims that we all inevitably must choose a fundamental disposition to subordinate one incentive to the other, and this choice determines our basic moral character. (See *Rel.* 12–14/20, 20/16, 24/20, 30/25, 36/31–32.) The "act of establishing character," Kant believes, requires adopting an "absolute unity of the inner principle of our conduct generally" (*Anthr.* 294–95). Each person's "moral constitution" (*Beschaffenheit*) depends on that ultimate disposition (*Gesinnung*), which is enunciated in the overall ultimate maxim, or principle of action, that person has freely adopted and on which he or she acts. (See *Pr.R.* 152; *Rel.* 20/16; *Anthr.* 285, 292.)

Because no one can avoid making this ultimate choice, no one can have a morally indifferent character. Further, since the law of the noumenal world is the Law of Autonomy, a person's ultimate practical principle will be *either* to conform to that law and subordinate everything to it *or* not to conform to it but, instead, subordinate it to the principle of self-love. (See *Rel.* 30/25, 36/31; *Lect.* 43.) In the first condition a person is morally virtuous; in the second, morally evil. (See *M.M.* 390; *Rel.* 20/16, 35/32, 45/41, 45nn1,2/40–41, 85/60.)[20] A person with a good will still has nonmoral incentives but strives always to disregard any and all advantages he or she may stand to gain or lose from doing his or her duty. (See *Gr.* 33/410–11, 33n/411n; *T&P* 279; *M.M.* 408.) As we shall see in the next section, such a person also, through moral weakness, may act wrongly but will not for that reason be genuinely evil.

The adoption of the supreme practical maxim is a unique exercise of our power in that it does not presuppose any more ultimate ground, such as the adoption of some end or other; instead, it is the ground for whatever ends we do adopt. Likewise, our disposition is not determined by incentives but instead is the ground for deciding which maxims are justifiable and which incentives should be acted on. (In that sense the good principle is our *Bewegungsgrund,* our motive and the ultimate objective, overriding ground of all other morally good motives.) We already know that we cannot understand any act of freedom, certainly not by using naturalistic terms; so it is no surprise that we cannot hope to understand how anyone goes about making an ultimate moral commitment. "The ultimate subjective ground of the adoption of moral maxims is inscrutable." (See *Rel.* 30–31/26; see also *Gr.* 122/460, 126/462; *Pr.R.* 72, 80; *Rel.* 21n/17.)

As we just saw, from the noumenal point of view we must think of our agency as not bound by the form of time and so as changeless, and the original choice of principle therefore as "unchangeable" (*Pr.R.* 100, 102). Yet it must be somehow possible for a person to change that ultimate moral disposition. For we also have seen that Kant holds that everyone initially adopts a morally evil principle, and since "the moral law commands that we *ought* now to be better men, it follows inevitably that we must *be able* to be better men" (*Rel.* 50/46). But we cannot understand how anyone can change, much less radically change from an evil to a good disposition. (See *Rel.* 45/40.) Moreover, we cannot appeal to our own self-consciousness for certain evidence that we our-selves have changed for the better, for we do not have an intuition or im-mediate consciousness of our own moral disposition. We can only hope and trust that this is true, since we have made an honest intention and effort to do so. (See *Rel.* 21n/17–18; see also 50–51/46.)

From the intelligible standpoint, a person's rejection of the original and morally evil principle requires a radical change of heart so fundamental that it cannot be done gradually but must be a single decision, which Kant calls a self-redemptive "revolution" in one's disposition. (See *Rel.* 47/42–43.)[21] But from the empirical standpoint, it takes both time and effort to *develop* our character (*virtus phaenomenon*). (See *Rel.* 47–48/42–43; *Anthr.* 294.) Moral reformation "is won little by little" and characteristically requires long practice, aided by education and examples. "Moral strength of mind may be [only] gradually won" (*Pr.R.* 147).

Since adopting an ultimate moral intention means acting on it, Kant also holds, as we saw in Chapter 7, that, for our moral purposes only, we may and must regard a person's perceivable behavior as containing "manifestations" of that person's moral character. (See *Rel.* 67/60–61.)[22] "Regarded as the causality of a thing in itself, [moral character] is *intelligible* in its *action;* regarded as the causality of an appearance in the world of sense, it is *sensible* in its *effects*" (*Pu.R.* A538/B566; see also A541/B569, A546–50/B574–78). For our moral purposes, we therefore must regard a person's noumenal moral character as somehow (*how* we obviously cannot know) the ground for that person's empirical character in the phenomenal world. (See, e.g., *Pu.R.* A539–41/B567–69; *Pr.R.* 107.)

A consistent pattern of morally legal or illegal actions, especially over the course of a person's whole life, gives us some grounds – Kant occasionally even uses the word "proof" – to infer or estimate a corresponding ultimate internal maxim (or a change in that maxim). (See, e.g., *Pr.R.* 99; *Rel.* 71/65, 76–77/71–72.)[23] But we may still err in making such judgments. Although we can usually judge behaviors as morally legal or not, we cannot be certain about the quality of the moral character in which they originate, for character always depends on an ultimate maxim that we cannot see. (See *Gr.* 26/407; *Rel.* 20/16, 31/26, 71/65.)[24] It is possible, for example, for an individual sys-tematically to perform legally correct actions only because they happen to fit into that person's conception of happiness, and, regarded from a moral point of view, "the empirical character is then good, but the intelligible character is still evil," although in individual cases we cannot know this (*Rel.* 37/32; see 30/25). As a corollary, our own "salvation" is never assured and we need constantly to avow anew that ultimate maxim of good character even while we hope we are only reaffirming a commitment already made.

Kinds of moral character

There are, then, only two possible fundamental kinds of moral character: morally virtuous and morally vicious character. From our own moral experience we also are aware that people trying to be virtuous can suffer temporary moral lapses. For this reason, Kant writes, we might think that people can be morally good in some respects and morally bad in others, and we may believe that most people are in fact "partly good, partly bad" (*Rel.* 20/16). But Kant insists that a rational analysis of the necessary nature of noumenal moral character must lead us to reject this view. Here he is proud to call himself a rigorist. The ultimate moral maxim is an either/or affair. Each person can and must adopt one and only one such universal disposition. (See *Rel.* 22–24/18–20, 39n/34.) Each person is and must be fundamentally either morally good or evil.

Yet Kant still has a sensitive appreciation of the moral frailty of human nature. He is well aware that virtuous people will always have a difficult time remaining faithful to their good ultimate maxim. Even the best of us will occasionally fail to live up to his or her intention to obey the moral law. Episodic lapses can coexist, Kant believes, with the "best will," with one's having an ultimate morally good disposition (*M.M.* 408; see 407–8; *Rel.* 29/24–25, 37/32). Worse than moral weakness is an "impure will," when we deliberately act from a mixture of moral and prudential concerns. But even so, both such failings, Kant writes, are still more a matter of lack of virtue than of being morally evil. (See *M.M.* 384, 408; *Rel.* 37/32.)

The real opponent and opposite of virtue is vice – the "monster" that moral reason has to fight. (See *M.M.* 384, 405.) Vice consists in adopting as one's basic principle the intention or disposition (*Gesinnung*) to transgress the moral law whenever it conflicts with the possibility of pleasures one wants. (See *M.M.* 390, 405; *Rel.* 42/37.) Like moral weakness and moral impurity, vice involves acting on inclinations, but the desires here have been allowed to coalesce into settled immoral passions (*Leidenschaften*). (See *Anthr.* 251, 265.) The evil person has calmly and deliberately adopted immoral policies to serve his inclinations. (See *M.M.* 408.)[25] That is why his inclinations and passions are "morally reprehensible"; "they are consistent with the calmest reflection" and "even with subtle reasoning" (*Anthr.* 265 and 267). Moral vice seems virtually incurable, because, as Aristotle had already said centuries before, "the patient does not want to be cured" (*Anthr.* 266).

10
Moral character: Part II

We often explain our actions by saying something like, "I wanted to," or "It made her happy and that made me feel good," or "I enjoyed doing it," or "It helped me get what I wanted." Acting on technical imperatives or counsels of prudence can always be explained by citing the desires and inclinations on which we have acted. However, Kant holds that moral motivation is correctly represented only by saying, "I did it because it was my duty." When contrasted with prudential motivation, there seems to be something lacking in the motive of dutifulness.

Moral interest

Some contemporary philosophers have argued that it does not make sense to ask, Why should a person do his or her duty? They maintain that the answer is already given in the question: A person should do his or her duty because it *is* his or her duty. But within the framework of Kant's moral theory, even when we know what our duty is and that it is our duty, we can still reasonably ask, But why should anyone *care* about doing his or her duty? Since dutifulness may require us to set aside considerations of our own happiness and welfare, it does seem to make sense to ask what can possibly *interest* us in acting dutifully. Put in terms of Kant's analysis of moral reasoning, what can bridge the distance between the cognitive and the conative functions of pure practical reason? How can our moral reasoning actually become practical and motivate us to act on its commands?

In the case of a purely rational being, there is no distance between the two functions of reason, for it is the nature of such a being always and necessarily to act on the Law of Autonomy. But the two functions of pure practical reason are not necessarily united in imperfectly rational agents such as human beings; we can refuse to do what we know morality requires. Moreover, as we saw in Chapter 3, Kant is convinced that we sensuous agents will not take any interest in acting unless we first have desires or aversions as an *incentive* for acting. So, in terms of his faculty psychology, Kant holds that pure practical reason – our will – must be a "higher faculty of desire," able to "supply a motive [*Triebfeder*] and create an interest [*Interesse*] which could be called purely *moral*" in doing our duty (*Gr.* 125/461; see 38n/413n).[1]

But this only creates another problem. Moral willing must be based on the categorical moral law. Basing an action on desires is just what makes our maxims merely hypothetical rules and actions merely heteronomous. If we cannot act except on the basis of desires and aversions, how can we ever act autonomously and morally?

Kant frequently has been misread as claiming that we therefore can and must act in the complete absence of desires of any kind. But his actual position is clear: Although there may be other moral agents (God, for example) for whom this claim may not hold, there *must* be a feeling side to *human* morality. (See *Gr.* 122–23/460; *Pr.R.* 72–79, 92; *M.M.* 221, 406.) He argues that we should be able to see in an a priori fashion that for finite and sensuous beings like ourselves, not only *can* moral reason impact on that part of us that it judges and, when necessary, frustrates, but it *must* do so. (See *Pr.R.* 73–74.) This is confirmed both by the universal human experience of inner moral conflict and by the emotions we all feel when we are confronted by duty, when we act dutifully, and when we do not. (See *M.M.* 399.)

Kant therefore contends that, for agents like us, the moral law must be able to generate specifically *moral sentiments* that can overpower every other incentive that happiness might offer in opposition. (See *Gr.* 122/460; *Pr.R.* 75–76; *M.M.* 399, 406, 408.) Since Kant classifies all feelings under the headings of pleasure and pain, moral sentiments must involve a particular *kind* of pleasure or pain or a combination of the two.

Moral sentiments

As feelings, moral sentiments are both pathological and subjective. (See, e.g., *Pr.R.* 76–77; *M.M.* 399.)[2] They are pathological in the sense that they all are felt as somatic or bodily occurrences, affecting us in various ways and degrees as sensuous beings. They are subjective because they are conditions necessary for agents like us, who need sensuous moral incentives to feel morally obligated. They would not be necessary for moral agents (if there are any) who do not suffer the limitations our nature imposes on us. (See *Gr.* 38n/413n, 102–3/449; *Pr.R.* 72, 77, 80; *Rel.* 64n/58.)

However similar they may be to *merely* pathological feelings and desires in other respects, moral sentiments are radically different in one critical respect: They do not have their origin in empirical sources outside our own reason so that we only passively feel them. (See *Gr.* 16n/401n; *Pr.R.* 75–76, 80, 116–17; *M.M.* 212–13, 399.) Rather, they are the subjective effect of our *prior* recognition of the objective and absolute binding force of the moral law. It is just because they are caused by reason alone that they can be moral feelings. (See *Gr.* 16n/401n, 60–61/426, 122/460; *Pr.R.* 75–76, 80, 116–17; *M.M.* 399; *T&P* 283.)[3]

Kant makes the contrast between the two this way: Our desires are *merely* pathological when we "represent something to ourselves as good, if and because we desire (will) it," whereas when we experience moral desires, "we desire something because we represent it to ourselves as good" on the basis of a prior judgment of the moral law within us (*Pu.R.* 59n; see 92; *Gr.* 38n/413n, 122n/460n; *M.M.* 378, 399). Morality does not obligate us because we first find ourselves interested in it; rather, we find we are interested in doing our duty because we first recognize that it is our duty. (See *Gr.* 102/449, 123/460–1.)

We cannot act dutifully without moral desires, yet we do not have a duty to have any such feelings, since we already have them and irresistibly so by virtue of our consciousness of the moral law within us. (See *Gr.* 72/432; *Pr.R.* 77; *M.M.* 399–403.)[4] Even "the most hardened scoundrel" cannot totally avoid feeling moral emotions. (See *Gr.* 112–13/454–55.) But because we can be more or less sensitive to morality, we can experience such feelings in different degrees, and it therefore *is* our duty to cultivate and strengthen them. (See *Pu.R.* A823/B852, A829/B857; *Gr.* 14–15/400, 16n/401n, 51n/421n, 57/424, 79/436, 86/440, 91/442–43; *Pr.R.* 38, 79, 117; *M.M.* 79, 221, 387, 399–400.)

The external effect – we act as duty requires – may not appear to be different from engaging in the same behavior for prudential reasons, but we still are not acting *out of* desire. (See *Pr.R.* 117.) Moral emotions are not ultimate but are based solely on our consciousness of the moral law. Because dutiful actions are ultimately based on the Categorical Imperative, it therefore can be said to be both the objective and the subjective norm and incentive of morality for us. (See *Gr.* 20/403, 38n/413n, 102/449, 120/460, 122/460; *Pr.R.* 38–40, 72, 75–76, 79, 81, 86, 116–17, 151–58; *M.M.* 221.)

As important as moral emotions are, they may not serve either as the ultimate basis for moral principles or in place of moral judgment, nor can the concept of duty be derived from them. (See *Gr.* 91/442, 122/460; *Pr.R.* 76; *Rel.* 114/104–5; *M.M.* 221, 376–77, 387, 402; *Conflict* 33/55.) It is therefore misleading to call any moral feeling a "moral sense," which implies we have some special sensitivity for recognizing good and evil. (See *Gr.* 60/425.) Kant is not a "moral sense" theorist. Moral emotions are still only subjective feelings, not objective judgments about what we should or should not do. (See *M.M.* 221, 376–77, 387, 400, 402–3.)[5]

Kant admits that what he calls an "illusion of the inner sense" is an error that is difficult for even careful thinkers to avoid. (See *Gr.* 91/442–43, 91n/442n; *Pr.R.* 116; *M.M.* 297.)[6] Yet those philosophers seriously misconstrued our interior moral life who claimed that moral sentiments are the ultimate ground of morality. If the basis for acting morally were a desire, even what might seem like a moral desire, morality would be reduced to prudence. Actions motivated by desires may have "legality but not morality" (*Pr.R.* 71, 76; see 38; *Gr.* 91/442–43, 123/460; *Orient.* 145–46).

Respect for the moral law

The *only* incentive that can motivate us to adopt and act on the motive of duty, Kant writes, is the reverence (*reverentia*) or respect (*Achtung*) we feel for the moral law. (See *Pr.R.* 74, 78, 117, 158; *Rel.* 6n/6.) This is not a feeling we need to try to "will" ourselves to have, for it arises irresistibly from our unavoidable recognition of the moral law. In fact, it is because we all inevitably

133

experience respect for the moral law that we can be said to have a "predisposition" (*Anlage*) to be morally good. (See *Rel.* 27–28/23.) Moreover, it is an incentive of such "herculean strength" that it enables us, when necessary, to offset the influence of all the "vice-breeding inclinations" (*M.M.* 376; see 402; *Gr.* 14–15/400, 16n/401n, 20/403, 38n/413n, 85/439, 102/448; *Pr.R.* 75–76, 158; *T&P* 283). Because it follows from our recognition of the Law of Autonomy, it is the only motive that can give our actions genuine moral worth. (See *Gr.* 86/440.)

For us, then, respect for the moral law is the subjectively necessary side of our consciousness of duty. (See *Pr.R.* 72, 75–76, 80–81, 102; *M.M.* 402, 449, 464.) As an emotion, respect resembles fear (aversion) in that we recognize that the moral law may rightfully demand the denial of self-love; it also is like love (attraction) in that we recognize that this law originates in our own reason and is something we impose upon ourselves. (See *Gr.* 16n/401n; *M.M.* 438, 439n.) Finally, it is like nonmoral emotions in that it *is* a feeling that gives us an "impulse to activity" on which to act. But it is not just a feeling of attraction or of aversion, for it is not just a feeling like sympathy or empathy or love, all of which can be understood in naturalistic terms. (See *Gr.* 16n/401n; *Pr.R.* 80.)

So important a role does respect have that, in his third "proposition" about the human good will in the *Groundwork,* Kant defines duty as "the necessity to act out of reverence for the law" (*Gr.* 14/400; see also 38n/413n, 122/460; *Pr.R.* 73–75, 87–88, 116–17; *M.M.* 387). In his defense of human moral agency in the third chapter of that work, he again discusses moral interest, to try to ensure that his readers do not interpret their moral agency as pathologically caused. (See *Gr.* 121–23/459–61.) As we saw in the last section, moral sentiments must not be invoked as causal explanations for any part of our moral life. Regardless of how an empirical psychologist might interpret respect, from the moral point of view it represents a ground that is not explicable in naturalistic terms. Because acting from duty means acting out of reverence for the moral law, that law remains the ultimate objective motive (*Bewegungsgrund*) of moral action. (See *Rel.* 24/19.)

Since the moral law is the law of our own reason, the virtuous person is one who acts out of self-respect (*Selbstschätzung*). (See *M.M.* 402.) *Any* violation of the Categorical Imperative is a violation of our own dignity, for it involves treating ourselves merely as a thing, as a plaything of our inclinations. Consequently, self-respect is the subjectively necessary ground for our fulfilling *all* our duties. (See *M.M.* 403, 419–20, 429, 483.) Likewise, since "love for one's neighbor" expresses the same moral esteem in which, according to the universal requirement of the Categorical Imperative, we must hold all other persons, respect for others rightfully limits our self-esteem. (See *Pr.R.* 76–78; *M.M.* 402, 449.) The ultimate subjective moral appeal in human moral life, then, is to our self-respect and to an equal respect for all other persons. By virtue of the moral law within us, each of us has a dignity that prevents us from ever legitimately regarding ourselves or others as only conditionally valuable, that is, valuable only to the extent of possibly being the object of someone's inclinations. (See *M.M.* 434–36.)[7]

The range of moral emotions

Kant offers us a well-developed "aesthetic of pure practical reason," that is, a phenomenological survey of the range of moral feelings. (See *Pr.R.* 90; *M.M.* 406.) Besides respect, which is the most fundamental moral emotion, other such emotions Kant discusses include the following:

Humility. Our awareness that we have a "sensuous propensity," an innate tendency to pursue pleasure even when contrary to the moral law, inevitably strikes down any tendency we may have to self-conceit and produces a feeling of humility before the moral law, a feeling of inadequate moral worth in comparison with the strict demands of that law. (See *Gr.* 16n/401n; *Pr.R.* 73–75, 78–79, 87; *M.M.* 435–36, 441.) In this connection, it is important for us to compare ourselves only to the moral law itself, not to other people, since doing the latter only leads to either pride or envy. (See *Lect.* 349–51/ 126–29; *Ed.* 491/105–6.)

Pain. "By thwarting all our inclinations," the moral law necessarily makes us feel sensuously frustrated; we can see a priori that it "must produce a feeling which can be called pain" (*Pr.R.* 73; see 78, 116; *Gr.* 15/401; *T&P* 283n).

Moral contentment. Despite the pain caused by dutiful actions, we also feel relief when we have acted dutifully – what Kant calls self-satisfaction or self-contentment (*Selbstzufriedenheit* and *Selbstbilligung*) over having done our duty (see *Gr.* 7–8/396, 122–23/460; *Pr.R.* 80–81, 87–88, 117–18).[8] Kant also calls this feeling "intellectual contentment" and "moral happiness," although he admits that, strictly speaking, the concept of an intellectual feeling or of moral happiness is self-contradictory (see *Pr.R.* 38, 80–81, 88, 116–18; *M.M.* 212, 377, 387–88, 440). Not only is virtue intrinsically good, but the dictum "Virtue is its own reward" is also correct in that the good feelings following dutiful action can rightly be called an "ethical reward" (*M.M.* 391; see also 396, 406).

Guilt and remorse. When we disobey the moral law, we necessarily experience feelings of guilt, and we regard ourselves with contempt for our actions. (See *Pr.R.* 37–38, 87–88; *M.M.* 379n, 420; *T&P* 283n, 288.) Such feelings also help prevent a virtuous person from enjoying whatever pleasure might otherwise be gained from acting immorally.

Empathy. We identify with the joys and sorrows of others, not on the basis of natural sympathy for or friendship with them but because we recognize their moral worth as well as our duties of benevolence toward them as fellow moral beings. (See *M.M.* 402, 456–58.) Kant approvingly quotes Terence's "noble Chremes": "I am a man; whatever befalls man concerns me too" (*M.M.* 460).

Finally, Kant discusses other moral emotions that are fitting only in special situations, such as gratitude to benefactors, grounded on the will to respect others in appropriate ways. (See *Pr.R.* 72–89; *M.M.* 406, 456.)

The spirit of virtue

When he writes about "dry and earnest" duty, Kant seems to paint a very bleak picture of human moral life. "To command that someone do something gladly is self-contradictory," for commands are necessary only within a context of at least potential reluctance and opposition (*Pr.R.* 83; see also *Gr.* 13/399; *M.M.* 379, 379n). Moreover, the moral law "enjoins its commands relentlessly, and therefore, so to speak, with disregard and neglect of" all the claims of our inclinations (*Gr.* 23/405; see *Pr.R.* 89).[9] Understandably, many of Kant's readers have been repelled by his apparently gray and cheerless delineation of our moral life. Who could be attracted to such an existence?

Kant does wryly note that we are not volunteers in the moral world; instead, we find ourselves conscripted into the discipline of duty. (See *Pr.R.* 82–86.) But even though it is typical of our fallen nature to react to the demands of morality with reluctance, Kant also insists that what a person does unwillingly, morosely, or cheerlessly, "he does poorly" (*End* 338; see also *M.M.* 484–85; *Rel.* 11–12n/19). Consequently, he writes, a virtuous person should "aim at a frame of mind that is brave and cheerful in the observance of duty," much like the attitude described by "the virtuous Epicurus" (*M.M.* 484–85; see *Rel.* 23n2/19).

Kant's ideal moral personality turns out to be very much like the ancient Stoic ascetic ideal of the man of practical wisdom (*ho phronimos*) who was characterized by *apatheia* and whose disciplined way of life could be captured in the maxim *"sustine et abstine"* – endure and forbear (*Conflict* 100/181; also *Ed.* 486/96; see also *Anthr.* 235–36, 249–50; *Lect.* 378–81/157–59, 393–99/171–78, 405–6/184–85). When Kant recommends the "duty of moral apathy," it is important not to misunderstand what he (or the Stoics) meant by that expression (*M.M.* 408; see 484; *Anthr.* 252–53). As he notes, even in his day the word "apathy" was used to refer to total indifference to *patheseis*, to pleasures and pains. Today it is still frequently applied to a person suffering from severe depression. But that is not at all what Kant means by the term.

Kant intends *apatheia* to refer to a learned moral characteristic, both a sensitivity and a strength in attending to pleasures and pains only in the right way, as one should, and a willingness to forgo luxuries and superfluous pleasures. (See *M.M.* 484.) Its opposite consists in being too susceptible to emotional disturbances (*Affekte* and *Leidenschaften*) such as anger and hatred, which, by challenging the sovereignty of reason, can affect one's choices in morally adverse ways. (See *Anthr.* 251–53.)

The person who has developed apathy in the sense of moral self-constraint is one who has resolved to dominate the passions by the law of reason and has developed an inner, disciplined tranquillity. (See *M.M.* 407–9, 484.) Such a serene and joyous frame of mind, Kant believes, is the best phenomenal evidence that a person really has "attained a love for the good, i.e., of having incorporated [the moral law] into his maxim" (*Rel.* 23n2/19).

Kant therefore sees the spirit of morality through a pair of spectacles ground to fit the eyes of an eighteenth-century, enlightened, Christian, Stoic moral teacher. From that perspective he tries to remain true to his initial aim to reflect ordinary moral beliefs as he knew them. He does not believe that human moral life may be characterized as hedonistic, but he also does not believe that a truly virtuous life should be dreary and bleak. He in fact spends a good deal of time discussing ways in which a good person should cultivate and practice sociability as "a garment that dresses virtue to advantage" (*Anthr.* 282). Since we have an obligation to promote the happiness of others insofar as we can, virtue *should* be accompanied by those social graces and manners that give pleasure to one's friends and companions.

Moral fanaticism

It is within the context of his discussion of moral apathy that we can best understand what Kant considers to be perversions of the spirit of virtuous morality.[10]

The first type of "moral fanaticism" (*Schwärmerei*) Kant condemns is the belief that we can become so confirmed in goodness that we no longer experience morality as our duty. (See *Pr.R.* 84–85; *Lect.* 78.) This error gives rise to two different forms of zealotry. The first consists in thinking that we can achieve moral perfection in the sense of developing our emotional dispositions to the point that we can be good-hearted enough to act rightly simply because it is "noble, sublime, and magnanimous" to do so (*Pr.R.* 84; see 81–86, 122, 128, 155–57; *M.M.* 432n; *Conflict* 81–82/145 and 147). The second consists in trying to develop and maintain an intense moral enthusiasm. Such fervor cannot last, and it only leaves a feeling of flat depression in its wake. Even if that were not the case, enthusiasm of any kind is merely an emotion and not a moral phenomenon at all. If there is a place for the Stoic ideal of moderation, it is here: Genuine virtue requires a calm and firm intention to act as one should. (See *M.M.* 409.)

Another form of fanaticism is what Kant calls a "monastic asceticism," that is, the insistence, out of superstitious fear of a vengeful God, that we must engage in rituals and penances to atone for moral faults, in place of a genuine repentance and a change of heart requiring future self-improvement. (See *Rel.* 76/71, 83–84/78.) Such asceticism, he writes, "cannot produce the cheerfulness that accompanies virtue, but rather brings with it secret hatred for virtue's command" (*M.M.* 485).

In a related way, it is fanaticism about dutifulness itself to *over*discipline our inclinations and try to renounce all enjoyment of life. For the sake of our own virtue, we even may have an indirect duty to promote our own happiness in morally acceptable ways, for too many unfulfilled wants create their own temptations to transgress our duties. (See *M.M.* 388, 452.)

Finally, it also is a type of moral fanaticism, Kant writes, to refuse to admit that some choices can be morally indifferent. Here he borrows another Stoic term – *adiaphora* – to designate morally indifferent or insignificant matters. (See, e.g., *Lect.* 356/134.) This error consists in regarding morally trivial differences, for example, between meat and fish or between beer and wine, as of serious moral import. An attitude of finding duties everywhere – what Kant somewhat sarcastically calls "fantastic virtue" – turns "the sovereignty of virtue into a tyranny" (*M.M.* 409; see 222–23).

Morally indifferent and permissible actions

Although this discussion may seem out of place here, it is only now that we are in a position to consider fully Kant's view about morally indifferent actions. His remarks on this topic may seem inconsistent because in different passages he considers this topic from two different points of view. In Chapters 3 and 9 we saw that Kant sometimes thinks of actions primarily as action types or behaviors, identifiable apart from an agent's motives for doing them. This, for example, is the view he takes of actions when he discusses the meaning of a merely "legal" action (one that simply accords with the moral law) and a "juridical" duty (a morally legal action mandated by civil law). Other times Kant thinks of actions primarily as a person's intentions and as the exercise of a person's character, and then the nature of the action depends on the agent's aim and motive in acting.

Kant takes the first position when he adopts the Stoic view that some choices are morally indifferent and depend only on what most "agrees with me" (*M.M.* 409). For example, in the matter of positive duties, such as the duty to develop one's talents, as long as there are no further complicating moral considerations, the choice between becoming an accountant or a computer programmer is a morally indifferent matter.[11] Either equally fulfills the same positive duty, and so each is morally permissible, that is, "neither commanded nor forbidden" (*M.M.* 223; see also 222). Likewise, Kant holds that belief in the specifically historical claims of a church, as long as that belief is not detrimental to a person's virtue, "belongs to the class of *adiaphora,* which each man is free to hold as he finds edifying" (*Rel.* 43n/39). Likewise, sacramental rituals, which historical churches have claimed to be grace-bearing, are, at best, "morally indifferent acts" (*Rel.* 106/97). Finally, Kant writes from this point of view when he holds that *merely* legal actions, that is, morally legal actions done out of desire, are not morally wrong but also have no moral worth.

But in his *Religion* Kant also takes another and more rigorous point of view when he holds that the only morally indifferent actions are those determined by causal natural laws. (See *Rel.* 23, 23n/18.) There are no genuinely morally indifferent actions attributable to human moral agents, for "between a good and evil disposition (inner principle), according to which the morality of an action must be judged, there is no middle ground"; we never have a morally indifferent ultimate disposition (*Rel.* 23n/18).

Regarded this way, morally permissible actions cannot be morally indifferent. (See *Rel.* 23, 23n/18.)[12] They are either morally good or evil, and that depends entirely on the ultimate moral maxim of the agent. Those actions that arise out of a morally virtuous will are morally good, not merely morally indifferent; for even though specific permissible choices must be determined by prudential considerations, the morally virtuous person still chooses what to do only within the range of possibilities compatible with the moral law. Likewise, those actions that arise out of a morally evil will (which gives systematic priority to self-love) are morally evil, even though, in themselves, they may lack moral goodness simply by being merely legal actions or juridical duties. (See *Rel.* 23–24/18–20.) In such cases Kant distinguishes between a person's "intelligible character" and "empirical character." (See *Rel.* 37/32.)

Further, if an agent with a morally good ultimate maxim performs a morally legal action mainly out of a natural sentiment like love or loyalty, then he must be judged in that instance as having a morally impure will, but the action has *some* positive moral worth insofar as he still is acting on that ultimate maxim. Likewise, if the same agent were to commit a morally weak action, there would still be some moral goodness in that action flowing from the agent's continuing character, even though the agent acted wrongly. So critical is the person's ultimate moral maxim that Kant considered moral weakness as closer to virtue in its fullness than moral impurity, even though the former but not the latter involves acting wrongly. This is also why Kant insisted that both moral weakness and a morally impure will should be thought of more as a lack of virtue than as genuinely evil.

Holiness an obligatory end

In the opening words of Chapter 1 of the *Groundwork,* Kant characterizes "the good will" (*der gute Wille*) as always intrinsically good – good absolutely and in every respect, without qualification and regardless of what it can or cannot accomplish in the world. (See *Gr.* 1/393, 3/394; *Pr.R.* 74; *Rel.* 57/50; *M.M.* 396–97, 430.) This description of moral goodness belongs *originally* to what Kant calls the "metaphysics of morals" in the strictest and purest sense, for it applies to all rational beings of whatever kind.[13]

Likewise, the Law of Autonomy, which gives formal content to the notion of a good will, is an a priori principle of pure morality shared by all moral agents. It defines a person as having a "perfect" good will when that person *always* follows the moral law and is "holy" in the sense of always doing so *because* it is the moral law (*M.M.* 392, 446; see also *Rel.* 66/60).[14] This description holds for a completely rational being like God, and it also expresses the supreme end that is a duty for contingently rational agents like ourselves. Kant explains, "This principle of morality . . . is declared by reason to be a law for all rational beings in so far as they have a will. . . . It is thus not limited to human beings but extends to all finite beings who have reason and will; indeed it includes the Infinite Being as the supreme intelligence" (*Pr.R.* 32).

Any failure to pursue a morally obligatory goal signals a moral failure of substantial magnitude. (See *M.M.* 392, 447.) Since holiness is an obligatory moral ideal or end for us, it would seem that its pursuit should be a narrow and perfect duty. Nonetheless, Kant argues that this obligation, like our other positive duties, is not narrow and perfect but subjectively, for *us*, wide and imperfect. (See *M.M.* 391–93, 432n, 446–47.)[15] As strange as this may at first seem, he holds that, strictly speaking, we are *not* bound to act from the motive of duty. What we are bound to do is to adopt the *maxim* of acting from the motive of duty and then to *try* with all the power we have actually to do so. It is important to understand the reasons that led Kant to his position.

What enables God to be holy and necessarily so (or, alternatively, to have "bliss" or "blessedness") is that God is by nature subjectively constituted so as always to act spontaneously according to the objective law of reason. God enjoys "complete independence from inclinations and desires" as possible impediments to following the moral law, and therefore has a will "incapable of any maxims which conflict with the moral law" (*Pr.R.* 118 and 32; see 123n; *Gr.* 36/412, 86/439).

Because God is never tempted to transgress the moral law, that law would never appear to God as a constraining imperative of duty. For the same reason, the notions of "incentive," "interest," and "maxim" (in the sense of a merely subjective practical rule) have no meaning in relation to a divine will. (See *Pr.R.* 79.) By contrast, the Law of Autonomy always appears to us as a constraint, an imperative, because we are *always* "pathologically affected" by our own desires and inclinations, and we also must struggle against an innate propensity to evil, which we cannot completely eradicate. (See *Pr.R.* 32–33, 122–23.) So a good will for us means a "moral disposition in conflict" (*moralische Gesinnung im Kampfe*) (*Pr.R.* 84; see *M.M.* 383–84, 387, 389, 392, 446). For God "there is no doctrine of virtue but merely a doctrine of morality, since morality is an autonomy of practical reason," but for us, autonomy in the face of internal obstacles and opposition is virtue (*Tugend*) or conscientiousness, which requires not just autonomy but "also an *autocracy* of practical reason" (*M.M.* 383; see 227, 396–97, 405; *Gr.* 36–39/412–14; 38n/413n, 76/434, 86/439; *Pr.R.* 32, 82; *Cr.J.* 403–4; *M.M.* 405).[16]

The notion of a morally good disposition (a virtuous will) is an Idea of reason that we cannot locate at all in the world of sense experience and that, with no "immediate consciousness" of it, we cannot find with any certainty even in our own inner moral experience. (See *Rel.* 70–71/65.) Because "the depths of the human heart are unfathomable," a person can never "be quite certain, in even a single action, of the purity of his moral purpose and the sincerity of his attitude" (*M.M.* 446–47 and 392; see 392–93; *Pu.R.* A551n/B579n; *Gr.* 25–27/406–7; *Rel.* 20/16, 21n/17, 63/56; *T&P* 284). Kant contends that we can be obliged to do what we know we can do – try to act from the right moral motive. Since we can never be sure we have actually succeeded in doing so, the obligation actually to act from the motive of duty is a wide, not a strict, obligation.

However, we also can and must believe that we always *can* act from the motive of duty. Our awareness that we are free and thus able to do so is not "immediately given" but "rightly deduced" from the fact that moral reason categorically commands us to do our duty (*M.M.* 383; see 383–84; *Pr.R.* 47; *T&P* 285–88).[17] We therefore are duty bound to constancy or resoluteness, that is, to fidelity to our moral duties. (See *Pr.R.* 158; *M.M.* 477.)

Even when we are virtuous, we still are only contingently so. The continuing presence of inclinations prevents us from simply adopting the good moral principle once and for all, and we must constantly reaffirm it. (See *M.M.* 409.) We are never so confirmed in virtue that we can be confident we will not fail morally in the future, and we always need to be apprehensive about doing so. (See *Pr.R.* 32–33, 122, 127n; *Rel.* 48/43, 51/46, 68/62, 71/65; *M.M.* 379n, 383.) In a sense, we are always just beginning on the road to virtue, and the value of virtue is in the intention, not the accomplishment. (See *Pr.R.* 108–9.) We can only *hope* for constancy in a morally good disposition. (See *Rel.* 51/46, 67–68/61–62; *M.M.* 387, 392–93.)

Kant therefore concludes that, for us human beings, the notion of a good will can mean only becoming all that we *can* become. Holiness or moral perfection is, strictly speaking, not a possible achievement for us, and our obligation to adopt it as our supreme goal is, accordingly, a wide and imperfect duty. (See *Pr.R.* 32–33, 122–23.) "Man's greatest moral perfection is to do his duty and this *from a motive of duty* (to make the law not merely the rule but also the motive of his actions)" (*M.M.* 392; see also 389). But moral perfection in the sense of holiness is not something we are morally obligated to *achieve;* it is an end we are morally obligated to *strive toward.*

The postulate of immortality

Although the moral law commands us to be holy, the human moral condition allows us only to progress *toward* holiness (*Pr.R.* 122–23; *M.M.* 391, 407, 432–33n, 446–47). We cannot actually ever finally win the moral battle; we cannot actually achieve holiness. Kant is forced to conclude that the ultimate moral goal for human beings must therefore consist in a relative but continual increase in strength of character, in growth in virtue, in progress *toward* holiness.

Since we cannot be freed of the obligation to *be* holy, we can never say that we are all that we should be (*Rel.* 67/60). Consequently, Kant argues, obedience to the moral law requires "an endless progression" toward holiness. (See *Pr.R.* 122–23; *Rel.* 67/60–61.) But that is possible "only under the presupposition of an infinitely enduring existence and the personality of the same rational being; this is called the immortality of the soul" (*Pr.R.* 122; see also 118, 122–24, 128). Since moral constancy is a demand of reason, Kant concludes that personal immortality is an Idea of reason that we must postulate to support the necessary end of moral reason. (See, e.g., *Pr.R.* 132.)

By a "postulate," Kant means a "necessary hypothesis," but not what that term meant in mathematics as he knew it, that is, something accepted as intuitively certain; nor does he mean a scientific hypothesis that eventually may (or may not) be confirmed theoretically (*Pr.R.* 11n). "By a postulate of pure practical reason, I understand a theoretical proposition which is not as such demonstrable, but which is an inseparable corollary of an a priori unconditionally valid practical law" (*Pr.R.* 122). Postulates are judgments about what is true, but they are not "theoretical dogmas" that extend our speculative knowledge (*Pr.R.* 132). They are claims about supersensible objects we cannot know theoretically. (See *Pr.R.* 54–56, 136.) They are hypotheses that our moral reason both entitles and inexorably commands us to believe to be true, for they are required in one way or another by the moral law in our reason. (See *Pr.R.* 4, 119, 132–33, 145; *Orient.* 137–38, 137n.) So the expression "postulate of reason" means not a claim resting on evidence insufficient for certainty or a claim inferior to a knowledge claim but a "wholly different" kind of claim. (See *Orient.* 141–42.)

As with all claims about noumenal reality, theoretical reason can neither prove nor disprove that we have a soul in the sense of a "spiritual substance" that is distinct from our body and that can survive our death. (See *M.M.* 418.) Science can only allow that personal immortality is a possible hypothesis, but problematic; we have no theoretical grounds for knowing one way or the other. But the moral law has objective reality and validity, and it requires immortality as "the practically necessary condition of a duration adequate to the perfect fulfillment of the moral law" (*Pr.R.* 122).[18] For our practical purposes, then, we have the right and the duty to have what Kant called a "rational faith" in personal immortality (*Pr.R.* 125–26). This faith, however, still does not entitle us to claim that we thereby have extended our speculative knowledge. What it does entitle us to, Kant holds, is the rationally based hope that if we are morally constant in this life, we will continue to live in constancy "beyond this life," and so be able to fulfill our moral obligation to progress toward the ideal of moral perfection. (See *Pr.R.* 123–24, 123n, 128.)

The infinitely long progress toward holiness is a requirement for our *empirical* character, but it presupposes an inner and nontemporal transformation and a constancy of disposition in our *noumenal* character that is essentially similar to the character of a holy agent. So we can also hope, Kant writes, that our commitment to the good principle will be regarded by God in his atemporal intuitions "as equivalent to possession" of holiness. (See *Pr.R.* 123, 123n; *Rel.* 47–48/43, 66–67/60–61.) This remark in the second *Critique* may seem perfectly gratuitous on Kant's part, particularly given his strong admonitions against appealing to heteronomous sources to support morality. However, it both indicates Kant's dissatisfaction with the "solution" he offered in that book and adumbrates a later and final stage of his thinking on this subject.

The postulates of God and of grace

As Kant was well aware, progress *toward* holiness, however long, is simply not equivalent to *being* holy, and the command of the moral law is to "*be* perfect" (*M.M.* 446). It would seem that this command would be a constant reproach to us for not being all we should be, not because we have not tried to obey it but because we *cannot* be all we should be. But this would mean that rather than providing the ground of dignity for our humanity, our own moral reason would seem to be making an irrational demand that we adopt an end we cannot attain and then unjustly condemning us for our ontological status of being only human moral agents. Moreover, if the supreme good that conditions the second component of our total final end cannot be achieved, then the happiness we deserve proportionate to our moral worth remains indefinite and to that extent unattainable. (See *End* 335.) This is a genuine antinomy of reason if there ever was one, even if Kant seems reluctant to identify it as such (but see *Rel.* 116/107). He could hardly have been content with his doctrine in the second *Critique,* however little dissatisfaction he shows with it there.

The problem can be stated in the following steps: (1) It is not rational for us to strive for an end we do not believe can be attained. (2) What the moral law commands must always be possible. "We must not determine ethical duties according to our estimate of man's power to fulfill the law"; rather, "we must estimate man's moral power by the standard of the law, which commands categorically" (*M.M.* 404; see *Pr.R.* 122). (3) Pure reason commands us to fulfill the moral law perfectly by becoming holy. (See *Pr.R.* 122, 132.) (4) We therefore must believe that holiness is attainable. To doubt its attainability is, in effect, to cast doubt on the moral law itself. (5) Therefore, we are bound to adopt holiness or moral perfection as our practical end toward which we must strive "with all [our] might" (*M.M.* 393; see *Pr.R.* 32–33, 83, 119, 124, 126). (6) Although we can make continual progress toward holiness, we cannot actually attain it by ourselves. Holiness remains beyond *our* capability, no matter how hard or long we strive toward it. (See *Rel.* 45/40.)

It is only in his *Religion Within the Limits of Reason Alone* that Kant indicates how the inconsistency in the preceding reasoning might be resolved. In that book he comes to the same conclusion he had already reached in the second *Critique* when discussing the attainment of the total final good (a doctrine we shall examine in Chapter 15): Morality "leads ineluctably to religion," for God alone can and must supply what we cannot (*Rel.* 6/5; *Gr.* 126–28/462–63).

Interpreted morally, Kant writes, the Christian religion teaches what no ethical philosophy, whether Cynic, Epicurean, or Stoic, had recognized: The moral law in all its purity not only holds us responsible for our own moral reformation but also apodictically commands us to be holy. (See *Rel.* 47/43, 75/70–71; *Pr.R.* 128; *Lect.* 250–51/9–10.) Christianity also supports the hope of our own reason that "if we act as well as lies in our power, what is not in our power will come to our aid from another source, whether we know in what way or not" (*Pr.R.* 127n; see also 131). When we have made ourselves as worthy as we can by having done all *we* can do to progress toward holiness, we then may confidently hope that somehow God will actually transform virtue into holiness, by providing his "grace," namely, "a means of supple-

menting, out of the fullness of His own holiness, man's lack of requisite qualifications" for holiness (*Rel.* 52/47; see 45/40–41, 75–76/70, 117–18/108–9,
120/110–11, 143/134, 171/159, 174/162, 183/171, 189–92/179–80, 194/182;
Lect. 251/10, 294/66, 317–18/92, 321/95–96; *Conflict* 43–44/75 and 77, 47/
83; *Ed.* 494/112).

What this "grace" is or how it can be be added by God to make us holy,
we cannot know or understand. Because any relations of God to man are
transcendent and incomprehensible, we may not claim we have any understanding of them. (See *Rel.* 118/108, 174/162, 190–91/178–79.) Nor can we
understand how it is possible for a human being with an innate propensity
to evil to be holy. What we do know is that, whether we think of it as positive
assistance or as the abatement of hindrance, grace may *not* diminish our power
to act autonomously and dutifully. We must remain free, with the dignity to
which our freedom entitles us. (See *Rel.* 23/19, 44/40, 143/134, 192/180.) So
we may not try to make any practical use of the Idea of grace; our trust in
God requires us to act as if everything depends on us alone. (See *Rel.* 52–
53/47–49; see *Lect.* 320/95.) Understanding this constitutes true religious
enlightenment. (See *Rel.* 179/167.)

The fulfillment of our morally obligatory goal of moral perfection, therefore,
requires us to have a moral faith in the postulate of a personal God to give
us the help we need. Although Kant did not identify the latter as such, we
have good reason to agree with Allen Wood that at least the later Kant, in
effect, did maintain that divine grace must be regarded as a necessary postulate
of pure practical reason (*Rel.* 52/48; *Cr.J.* 451).[19]

Metaphysical questions

Kant's analysis of character raises a number of critical theoretical questions.
How can our atemporal moral character act at all, much less make a spontaneous, ultimate choice between heterogeneous practical principles? How
can an immutable and noumenal cause not only itself change but also initiate
changes that are moral actions in the world of nature? How can a nonsensuous
Idea of pure reason give rise to phenomenal but moral emotions such as
respect, so powerful as to be able to overcome any and all resistance to the
moral law? In a word, how can pure reason by itself be practical?

As we already saw at the end of Chapter 7, Kant has enormous sympathy
for our rational interest in seeking the answers to such questions. But as his
epistemological inquiries showed, *explanations* are in principle simply not
possible. Just as freedom is inexplicable, so also is the power of moral reasoning
and the genesis of moral character. (See *M.M.* 379n, 431, 439n.) Neither
moral virtue nor moral evil of *any* dimension can be *explained* or *understood*
in naturalistic, theoretical terms by appealing to some temporally prior cause.
(See, e.g., *Rel.* 39–40/34–35, 44–45/40, 47/43, 59n/52, 121n/111–12.) So,
many of the most fundamental metaphysical questions about morality cannot
be answered; such matters are incomprehensible. (See, e.g., *Gr.* 121–23/

459–61; *Pr.R.* 72; *Rel.* 21/17, 25/20, 45/40.) Our wonderment is fated to remain unsatisfied.

For our moral purposes, however, we need not be concerned about the limitations of our understanding. We need only believe that our moral reasoning does enable us to obey the moral law. Our right to that belief is grounded, as we saw in Chapter 7, on the Law of Autonomy, which shows its own objective reality in our moral consciousness. (See *Rel.* 45/40.)

III
The norm for moral judgment

11
The Categorical Imperative

Kant's primary purpose in writing the *Groundwork* was to "seek out and establish" the ultimate principle of morality – to formulate that principle and to show that we are bound by it.[1] It is understandable, then, that he devotes more space in that book to the Categorical Imperative than to any other topic. He offers three different formulas of that law, but because there logically can be only one ultimate moral law, he also asserts that the "three ways of representing the principle of morality are at bottom merely so many formulations of precisely the same law" (*Gr.* 79/436; see 51–52/420–21, 57/424, 79/436, 88/440; *Lect.* 252/11).[2] Nonetheless, each of the three formulas emphasizes a different aspect of the same moral law. (See *Gr.* 80/436.) The value in offering alternative versions is to help "reason attend, as Socrates did, to its own principle," particularly by making the very abstract first formula more appealing (*Gr.* 21/404; see 79–81/436–37).[3]

Kant believed that its very formality makes the first formula the most precise, enabling it best to exhibit what it means to say that morally acceptable maxims must be fit to serve as universal laws. (See *Gr.* 80/436.) The second turns out to be as formal as the first, but it emphasizes what Kant nonetheless calls the "matter" of moral principle – persons and their worth. The third combines the first two and sets out the complex, social nature of our final moral goal. (See *Gr.* 70/431, 80–81/436–37.)

Kant refers to the Categorical Imperative in general and to the first formula in particular as the "principle of the autonomy of the will" in contrast to the ultimate principle of happiness, which he calls "the principle of heteronomy." (See *Gr.* 74/433, 87/440.) He also calls attention to the special emphases of the first two formulas by referring to the first as "the universal principle of justice [*Recht*]" (*M.M.* 230–31), and to the second as "the ethical law of perfection," "the principle of the doctrine of virtue," and "the principle of benevolence" (*M.M.* 450). But he did not give "official" names to the three formulas, and so I have given them titles that suggest the emphasis of each:[4]

Formula 1: The Formula of Autonomy or of Universal Law: "I ought never to act except in such a way that I can also will that my maxim should become a universal law" (*Gr.* 17/402).

Formula 2: The Formula of Respect for the Dignity of Persons: "Act in such a way that you always treat humanity, whether in your own person or in the person of any other, never simply as a means, but always at the same time as an end" (*Gr.* 66–67/429).

149

Formula 3: The Formula of Legislation for a Moral Community: "All maxims as proceeding from our own making of law ought to harmonize with a possible kingdom of ends as a kingdom of nature" (*Gr.* 80/436).

Ease of use

We commonly face two problems in our moral life: deciding what is the right thing to do and having the moral strength to do it. Today we might debate which is the harder task, but Kant was convinced that it is having a sufficiently good character. "What duty is, is plain of itself to everyone," even to those of the "commonest intelligence" (*Pr.R.* 36; see 87–88, 163). Once the Categorical Imperative is clearly understood, Kant believed that using it as a norm for moral judgment does not involve any special difficulty: "Human reason, with this compass in hand, is well able to distinguish, in all cases that present themselves, what is good or evil, right or wrong . . . there is no need of science or philosophy for knowing what man has to do in order to be honest and good, and indeed to be wise and virtuous" (*Gr.* 20–21/404; see also xi/391, 19–20/403). Although few of his readers have been convinced that this "compass" is that easy to use, Kant himself believed that "the simplicity of this law, compared with its great and manifold implications, must seem astonishing" (*M.M.* 225). He argues for that claim in an a priori fashion. The moral law, he writes, apodictically "commands the most unhesitating obedience from everyone; consequently, the decision as to what is to be done in accordance with it must not be so difficult that even the commonest and most unpracticed understanding without any worldly prudence should go wrong in making it" (*Pr.R.* 36).

Despite his contention, the Categorical Imperative remains one of the most puzzling parts of Kant's moral theory. Among contemporary philosophers it is widely accepted as the ultimate norm of justice, and yet there seems to be little agreement about just what kind of test it is.[5]

Problems in interpreting Kant can always be attributed at least partly to his writing style; so often he can be read in widely different ways. Moreover, as we saw in Chapter 5, the Categorical Imperative should be applied as a norm only when we are making judgments about the moral quality of problematic *maxims*. Once we have adopted the right maxims, it normally plays no role in our judgments about how to *act* here and now. As we saw, misunderstanding this point can cause all kinds of absurdities. Another reason for interpretative problems with the Categorical Imperative may be traced to the failure of some readers to recognize and the reluctance of others to admit that Kant was, in some sense, a "natural law" moral philosopher. Most authors within the Kantian tradition today reject a natural-law approach to moral theory and find Kant's use of the natural law philosophically embarrassing. But, as we shall see in Chapter 13, Kant believed that there is no way in which to apply the Categorical Imperative so as to generate many of our moral obligations, particularly positive duties to ourselves, without reliance on the natural law.

Whatever the reasons for lack of agreement about the Categorical Imperative, I will present an interpretation of that norm that has substantial textual support and seems to me to be faithful to Kant's own intentions. It may not solve all the problems associated with the Categorical Imperative, but it can solve many of them. This interpretation requires us first to examine the rationale that is common to all three variations of the Categorical Imperative and that underlies its power to be our ultimate moral norm.

The problem

As we saw in Chapter 5, Kant appeals to ordinary moral reasoning to support his claim that the Categorical Imperative is our ultimate norm for making moral judgments. (See, e.g., *Gr.* vi/389, 17/402, 20/403.) But the claims of ordinary moral consciousness may be confused, partial, and even misleading. Moreover, the truth of analytic judgments must rest not on our ordinary moral consciousness but on the principle of noncontradiction, and that of synthetic a priori judgments on reason alone. Consequently, in the preface to the *Groundwork* Kant states that a metaphysics of morals must derive the moral law (as a principle) *analytically* from the Idea of a rational agent, one with pure practical reason. Since the Law of Autonomy appears to contingently moral agents as a synthetic a priori judgment, that is, in the form of an imperative, the necessity expressed in that judgment also must be grounded "solely a priori in the concepts of pure reason" (*Gr.* vi/389). At the end of the second section of the *Groundwork,* Kant summarizes what he has done so far as "merely analytic"; he has elicited the moral law from an analysis and clarification of the ordinary "concept of morality," that is, of moral agency (*Gr.* 95–96/445; see also 88/440). This is just the program he had projected in the preface. (See *Gr.* xiv/392.)[6]

It may not be clear exactly how Kant thinks the moral law can be derived analytically from the concept of moral agency, for in the *Groundwork* he is continually distracted by his concern to explain and defend specifically human moral agency. As a result, he frequently clouds the difference between the Law of Autonomy as a principle analytically elucidating the concept of a moral agent as moral and that same principle as a synthetic a priori norm obligating imperfectly moral human agents. In the following two sections, therefore, I will try to show how Kant derived the Categorical Imperative from the Idea of moral agency.[7] Doing so will help to explain how he believed the Categorical Imperative can and should be used, but it also will indicate that there are serious problems with the conceptual framework of Kant's moral theory.

The principle of noncontradiction

Again and again Kant insists that a metaphysics of morals must have a pure a priori foundation and that the ultimate moral criterion must be completely formal. As we have seen, the only completely formal, pure a priori science is logic. (See *Gr.* i–iii/387–88.) Further, when Kant discusses applications of the Categorical Imperative, he calls it the "principle of contradiction" and the "merely formal condition" of "thoroughgoing consistency." (See, e.g., *Gr.* 55/422, 57/424; *M.M.* 396.) Violations of that norm result in a contradiction (*Widerspruch*) within the will. (See, e.g., *Gr.* 54/422, 55/423, 58/424.) Kant therefore clearly considered the Categorical Imperative to be a practical application of the logical and purely formal principle of consistency or, alternatively, the principle of noncontradiction.[8] Since that principle is "propaedeutic" to all thinking, it obviously holds for all practical thinking, that is, the deliberations preceding, controlling, and expressed in rational actions. (See *Pr.R.* 32.) To understand the Categorical Imperative, then, we must review Kant on the principle of noncontradiction.

That principle states that "no predicate contradictory of a thing can belong to it" (*Pu.R.* A151/B190). It is, Kant thinks, the one condition necessary for the very *existence* of reason. (See *Pr.R.* 120; *M.M.* 231; *Logic* 49–51/55–57.)[9] Given its importance to his theory, Kant's explicit discussions of this principle are surprisingly brief. (See *Pu.R.* A150–52/B189–91; *Logic* 116–17/121–22.) According to the principle of the excluded middle, he argues, contradictory judgments cannot be both true or both false. Whichever one is true, the other must be false. Consequently, the principle is a completely formal law that sets out a universal, if primarily negative, requirement for *every* use of reason: No self-contradictory claim can be true. (See also *Gr.* i–iii/387–88.)[10]

The principle also has limitations. Synthetic judgments, which contain information that can be learned only empirically, must not merely pass the test of the principle of noncontradiction to establish that they are true. Synthetic a posteriori claims need further support from sensory experience. Claims about the world may be self-consistent but still not be known to be true because they lack empirical confirmation, or they may be known to be false by the criterion of what is usually called the "correspondence truth test." (See *Pu.R.* A150/B190.) In the case of synthetic a priori judgments, the defense or ground of their extraordinary necessity and universality must come from reason alone, in the form of a transcendental deduction (or, in the unique case of the moral law, its appearance in our practical self-consciousness as a "fact of reason").

There are, however, some statements for which the principle of noncontradiction acts as both the necessary and sufficient condition of truth, and their truth-value can therefore be determined by that principle alone. These are analytic judgments in which the predicate only makes explicit (at least part of) the meaning of the subject. As we saw in Chapter 2, the denial or contradiction (*Widerspiel* or *Gegenteil*) of an analytically true judgment results in a judgment that as Kant put it, is "null and void" (*Pu.R.* A150/B189). For analytic claims, then, the principle of noncontradiction determines in a purely a priori way both what cannot be true and what must be true. (See *Pu.R.* A151/B190–91.)

In summary, then, the principle of noncontradiction is the fundamental logical determinant of what *cannot* be true. It is a necessary, if only negative, criterion of truth for synthetic claims, but it is both the necessary and sufficient norm of truth for analytic claims, which, if they are true, are necessarily so. As the ultimate law of rationality in general, the principle of noncontradiction may be stated thus: Insofar as one thinks correctly, one observes the principle of consistency; that is, one does not make claims that are self-contradictory or that contradict one another.[11] Because this principle is purely formal, without any specific content, it is an objective law, holding for all rational beings, including God as "the supreme intelligence."

The derivation

Although we humans obviously are not ourselves perfectly rational beings and although we have no experience with perfectly rational beings, Kant maintains that we cannot avoid thinking about the Idea of a perfectly rational being. It seems completely noncontroversial and analytically true to say that a perfectly rational being is a being who always thinks rationally. Since the logical principle of noncontradiction underlies all coherent thinking, a perfectly rational being is, at a minimum, one who always observes the principle of noncontradiction or, alternatively, never thinks inconsistently. That this is itself an analytically true claim can be shown by the fact that denying it generates an absurdity.

Theoretical thinking involves assenting to or withholding assent from judgments, while the exercise of agency involves projecting goals and forming and acting on maxims to achieve them. So the meaning of "contradictory" must be adjusted appropriately when used within the context of practice: A perfectly rational *agent* must be one who never *wills* in violation of the principle of noncontradiction. (See *Gr.* 110–11/453–54.)[12] That this is an analytically true principle is shown by the fact that its denial generates what may be called a "practical absurdity." We may state that denial in a number of different ways; for example, a perfectly rational agent forms and acts on some maxims that that agent does not will.

As we saw in Chapter 4, Kant uses the Idea of a rational but finite agent (one with needs and desires) to explain the analyticity of the ultimate principle of prudence: Insofar as a finite agent is rational, all other things being equal, that agent uses those means known to be available and necessary to get whatever he or she genuinely wants. (See *Pu.R.* A823–24/B851–52; *Gr.* 44–45/417, 48/419.) That this claim is analytically true can be shown by the fact that its denial generates an absurdity: A rational agent who genuinely wants something as an end is one who acts in a practically inconsistent way, by deliberately *not* doing what is both available and necessary to get what is wanted. (See *Gr.* 45/417.)[13]

To act contrary to the principle of prudence may be a violation of the principle of noncontradiction, but it is not of itself a form of immorality. As we saw in "The Defense of Morality," Christian Wolff and virtually every other moral philosopher had mistakenly thought it possible to derive freedom, and so also the moral law, simply from the concept of a rational being as such. But the demand of the moral law cannot be equated in a simplistic way with the demand of logic for consistency; "incoherent thinking is simply not of a piece with moral evil."[14]

Since we already examined them in Chapter 4, we need not rehearse all of Kant's arguments on behalf of the thesis that prudential rationality has no intrinsic moral significance or value. But this at least should be said: Prudence is a limited and partial form of rationality because it is ineluctably dependent on constituents that are not purely rational – desires and experience. As a consequence, an agent with only empirical practical reason would in fact be unable to be perfectly rational in the sense of following the ultimate principle of prudence perfectly. It is just because substantive prudential maxims are grounded in desires and have only arbitrary purposes that they hold only subjectively and contingently; by contrast, substantive moral laws hold objectively and categorically, for both the maxims and the ends of moral actions are grounded in reason alone.

Kant therefore holds that the Idea of a *thoroughly, perfectly* rational agent must be the Idea of an agent that by its very nature always acts on the basis of reason *alone*. (See *Gr.* 29/408–9, 39/414, 50n/420n, 81–82/437–38.) We may not understand exactly what would lead such an agent to exercise the power of agency, particularly if it had no needs, but, Kant writes, the will of such an agent is "a power to choose *only that* which reason . . . recognizes to be practically necessary, that is, to be good" (*Gr.* 36/412; see also 36–39/412–14, 38n/413n, 76/434, 86/439; *Pr.R.* 32, 82, 118, etc.).

The ultimate law of *pure* practical rationality is and must be the practical application of the purely formal principle of noncontradiction. It may be stated as: Insofar as an agent is completely, perfectly rational, that agent adopts and acts *only* on maxims given by his or her own reason alone, maxims that are both self-consistent and consistent with one another. Because this principle is also an objective law, it may be expanded to read: Insofar as an agent acts *purely* rationally, that agent adopts and acts only on maxims that are formally fit to function also as maxims for all rational agents – that is, rational in the sense of possessing pure practical reason.

The ultimate law of pure practical rationality therefore turns out to be the Law of Autonomy, which Kant also derived analytically from what he had taken to be the commonplace notion of moral agency as such. A moral agent as such is and must be one who acts or at least is capable of acting autonomously, only on maxims that can at the same time contain in themselves their own universal validity (i.e., the purely formal requirement of consistency) and therefore are fit to be maxims for any and every moral being as moral. (See *Gr.* 82/437–38.)

Some commentators have maintained that Kant needed to offer an explicit argument for the connection between morality and rationality. But Kant, in effect, holds that such an argument is unnecessary, since the Idea of a perfectly rational agent is analytically the same as our ordinary Idea of a perfectly good or holy agent. Analysis shows that the Law of Autonomy is both the ultimate law of morality and the ultimate law of pure practical rationality (which of course also presupposes the ability of an agent to act freely in the transcendental sense and so also morally). This contention should be no surprise. If the Idea of (objective) moral good is beyond the identifying reach of (subjective) inclinations and desires, that Idea must originate with reason alone. (See, e.g., *Gr.* 38/413–14.) And if good moral character cannot be grounded on a person's desires, there then is nothing else that can ground moral goodness but reason alone.

We now must face a problem that has generated deep disagreements among Kantian scholars: how the relations between various fundamental Kantian terms should be understood and how those relations might best be expressed in modern logical terminology.

There is a fair amount of agreement that Kant himself held that autonomy and the positive concept of freedom are synonymous. "What else then can freedom of will be but autonomy – that is, the property which will has of being a law to itself?" he asks. "Thus a free will and a will under the moral law are one and the same. Consequently, if freedom of the will is presupposed, morality together with its principle, follows by mere analysis of the concept of freedom" (*Gr.* 98/447). "Freedom and the will's enactment of its own laws are indeed both autonomy – and therefore are reciprocal concepts" (*Gr.* 104–5/450).

Consequently, the Law of Freedom and the Law of Autonomy must be the same law. "Freedom and unconditional practical law reciprocally imply each other. [The latter is] merely the self-consciousness of a pure practical reason, and thus *identical with* the positive concept of freedom" (*Pr.R.* 29, emphasis mine; see also 31, 42). "Autonomy of the will is the sole principle of all moral laws," and pure "practical reason *is* freedom in the positive sense" (*Pr.R.* 33, emphasis mine). Freedom and the Law of Autonomy "are so inextricably bound together that practical freedom could be defined through the will's independence of everything except the moral law" (*Pr.R.* 94).

Throughout Kant's moral philosophy, however, the term "freedom" remains problematic, for Kant refuses to identify moral evil as an *expression* of freedom or of autonomy. He also refuses to identify freedom of choice (*Willkür*) as a freedom to choose between good and evil. Yet he clearly also holds that there is and must be a heteronomous mode of freedom: Moral evil does exist, and moral agents are free to do and therefore be responsible for evil. To keep Kant's theory minimally coherent, we must at least read the words "free," "moral," "autonomous," and "rational" (each in its full, transcendental sense) as, for example, *either* the "power to act rationally" *or* the exercising of the power to "act rationally."[15]

If we set aside for now Kant's problematic treatment of evil, this much at least seems relatively noncontroversial: He cannot envisage the possibility that any one of the following claims or sets of claims about *transcendental agency* could not be true. As we would expect, he then uses these claims to offer a number of variations of the Law of Autonomy:

I. A rational agent is a free agent.
   A rational agent is a moral agent.
   A rational agent is an autonomous agent.
II. A free agent is a rational agent.
   A free agent is a moral agent.
   A free agent is an autonomous agent.
III. A moral agent is a rational agent.
   A moral agent is a free agent.
   A moral agent is an autonomous agent.
IV. An autonomous agent is a rational agent.
   An autonomous agent is a free agent.
   An autonomous agent is a moral agent.

So far, we have progressed from (1) the pure a priori principle of non-contradiction, to (2) an analysis of the Idea of a perfectly rational agent as an agent who never wills in violation of that logical norm, to (3) an analysis of the partial adoption of that norm by an agent who has only psychological freedom and empirically practical rationality, to (4) the Idea of an agent who is transcendentally free and perfectly rational and holy because it by nature follows the norm of noncontradiction in its form as the Law of Autonomy. Kant now needs to make the transition from the Law of Autonomy as a law holding analytically for such an agent, to (5) that law as a synthetic a priori principle for all contingently rational/moral agents like us (that is, agents who have pure practical reason and can act morally well but do so only contingently) and, finally, to (6) that law as an imperative actually and categorically binding us.

Since we are not by nature holy, when the otherwise analytically true Law of Autonomy is restated as the ultimate moral-practical principle for us, it then becomes a synthetic a priori and prescriptive principle, a norm for all our possible maxims: A contingently rational/moral agent *should* always act morally/rationally, in other words, only on maxims that do not violate the Law of Autonomy. (See, e.g., *M.M.* 230–31.) This is a synthetic principle because the predicate – one who always acts on maxims that do not violate the Law of Autonomy – goes beyond the meaning of the subject – an agent who can but need not always act on that principle. This is also an a priori claim, because the subject and predicate are joined with a necessity – "should" – that can only be justified by reason alone. (See *Gr.* 50n/420n.)

The transition from the descriptive to the prescriptive version of the Law of Autonomy presents no serious difficulty. Since that principle is a law, it holds objectively and universally. Descriptive laws state what necessarily is the case, and prescriptive laws state what ought to be the case, regardless of what in fact is the case. Both are a priori judgments, but descriptive laws may be either analytic or synthetic whereas all prescriptive laws are synthetic a priori. The subject concept contained in prescriptive practical laws is an agent (or agents) who may or may not obey them; and the predicate concept (the "formal matter" – what is commanded as a universal norm) is not contained analytically in the notion of the subject concept. The Law of Autonomy is an analytically descriptive law for perfectly rational and moral agents, and Kant was thinking of this when he called the first formula "an analytic proposition" (*M.M.* 396). But that law becomes a synthetic, prescriptive law for only contingently moral agents.

So far the Law of Autonomy is still only a principle, albeit an objective and universal one, even when it is stated as a prescriptive and so as a synthetic a priori principle for all contingently moral agents, if there are any such agents. Therefore, Kant writes, if we could *know* that we are free and able to obey it, the claim that we are under that law would be analytically true. (See *Gr.* 98/447.)[16] But we cannot know that we are free, and we clearly may not claim that we are bound by the Law of Autonomy merely on the basis of a conceptual analysis. (See *Gr.* 50n/420, 98/447; *Pu.R.* 55–56.)

However, as we saw in Chapters 5 and 7, we are in fact bound by that law. Because we are only contingently rational/moral, it appears to us not just as a principle but as an imperative, categorically commanding us to respect it. (See, e.g., *Gr.* 37–39/413–14, 111/454; *M.M.* 214, 220, 227, 379.) Like the principle from which it is immediately derived, the Categorical Imperative is a synthetic a priori judgment. (See *Gr.* vi/389, 59–60/425.) We may not *want* to obey that law; we may prefer to act merely on our desires. We can in fact choose to ignore it, because we are obligated but not determined by it. But it is our own reason that formulates and mandates the Law of Autonomy, and therefore, Kant argues, we cannot evade the prescriptivity of that law, no matter how inclined we may be to try to do so. The moral law is still present in our rational awareness, and it inevitably condemns us if we violate it.

One question may still linger. How can the violation of a purely logical norm be morally evil? We obviously would not condemn a person as immoral for deliberately violating the logical rule *modus ponens*. Kant's answer is that logic always takes on the interest of the activity in which it is used. (See *Pr.R.* 120.) When used by pure practical reason, then, the principle of noncontradiction does not remain simply a logical norm. Instead, it becomes the measure of our willingness to recognize and respect our own freedom and rationality and that of every other person. Within a moral context, it becomes the ultimate standard of justice and the ground for a just political life. In the form of the Categorical Imperative, it is even our ultimate norm for judging how we conceive of the meaning and significance of human existence. In the following chapters we will elaborate on these claims.

Problematic texts

The interpretation offered so far may not be completely without problems, but this is not a particularly upsetting admission, for it seems to hold true of *any* interpretation of the Categorical Imperative. Several passages in the *Groundwork* may seem particularly perplexing. But as we shall see, any difficulties with them lie not with the preceding derivation. They arise mainly because Kant did not always carefully distinguish between the Law of Autonomy as an analytic principle describing agents who are completely rational by nature, as a synthetic a priori principle for imperfectly rational agents (if there are any), and as the Categorical Imperative actually addressing us contingently moral agents.[17] Moreover, even though he frequently uses phrases such as "the will of a rational being as rational" and "a rational being as such," throughout Kant is thinking mainly of *our* agency. Human beings are the only rational beings with whom we have any acquaintance, and it was only the reality of our moral agency that was under attack and needed explaining and defending. (See *Gr.* 48/419.) In any case, trying to make sense of such passages has caused his readers enormous problems, and it is little wonder that they have come to widely different conclusions about what Kant actually held.

Groundwork 87–88/440 may seem incoherent, but, given the proper distinctions, it presents no problems. Kant begins by offering an analytically true definition of autonomy: "Autonomy of the will is the property the will has of being a law to itself." Yet, because he is thinking here about the *human* will, Kant then states the Law of Autonomy, not merely as a principle (although he still calls it a principle), but as the Categorical Imperative, which he rightly identifies as a synthetic a priori proposition. (He actually writes about that law binding "the will of every rational agent," but the fact that he thinks of the Law of Autonomy only as an imperative shows he is concerned only with us.) He then makes these claims: An analysis of the concept of morality can show both that the Law of Autonomy is the sole principle of ethics and that this law must appear as a categorical imperative to contingently moral agents; but because it is a synthetic claim, mere conceptual analysis cannot show that this imperative actually does obligate us. He then contends we need an a priori argument – the transcendental deduction he eventually offers in the third section of the *Groundwork*. Until that defense, however, whether that imperative binds us remains an open question. (See also *Gr.* 62/426.)

A passage that may seem even more bewildering occurs in the third section of the *Groundwork:* "The principle of morality is still a synthetic proposition, namely: 'An absolutely good will is one whose maxim can always have as its content itself considered as a universal law'; for we cannot discover this characteristic of its maxim by analyzing the concept of an absolutely good will" (*Gr.* 98–99/447). This is confusing, because Kant had earlier derived the Law of Autonomy *analytically* from the concept of an "absolutely good" or "holy" will. (See *Gr.* 36ff/412ff, esp. 39/414.) He in fact defined such a will as one in which "reason infallibly determines the will" so that the latter is necessarily "a power to choose *only that* which reason independently of inclination recognizes to be practically necessary – that is, to be good" (*Gr.* 36/412). For that reason, "there are no imperatives" for a holy will (*Gr.* 39/414). Now Kant seems to insist that that same analytic principle is a synthetic proposition.

Kant is not doing that, but he is surely guilty of using the expression "absolutely good will" ambiguously. Sometimes he defines such a will as a "holy" will – a status he also claims we human beings cannot achieve. (See *Gr.* 36–39/412–14, 81/437, 86/439.) At other times he uses the expression "absolutely good will" to refer to a virtuous *human* will; then the Categorical Imperative is "the formula of an absolutely good will." (See *Gr.* 81–83/437–38; 95/444.) So, when stated as a prescriptive law for us and requiring us to strive for virtue, that law is, as he claims, a synthetic (a priori) proposition.

But is Kant right in claiming that we cannot arrive at that imperative by analyzing the Idea of morally good character, even if it is only a virtuous rather than a holy will? That, as we have seen, was just his program in the first section of the *Groundwork* – to isolate the ultimate moral norm by analyzing the Idea of a "good will." If we are inclined to be generous in interpretation, we might remember that this problematic passage occurs in the third section of the *Groundwork,* where Kant is preoccupied with defending the reality of our moral agency. Perhaps, then, what he intended to say here is that such a defense cannot rest merely on a conceptual analysis.

Empirical content

However it is stated, the ultimate moral norm is a purely formal law, completely empty of all content, like a statement form written in logical notation. We therefore cannot know how it actually applies to us, that is, what it may substantively command, apart from common knowledge about what it is to be a human being. (See *Pr.R.* 8; *Lect.* 244/2.)[18]

In several places Kant describes specific moral principles as being "derived" (*abgeleitet*) from that ultimate norm. (See, e.g., *Gr.* 32n/410n, 35/412, 52/421, 57/423.) But he notes elsewhere that "the particular cannot be derived from the universal law alone" (*Cr.J.* 407). In order to use the Categorical Imperative to "derive" specific morally acceptable maxims, then, we must apply it to the *human* condition – to the maxims of possible human actions, that is, practical rules we are considering acting on to get what we want. (See *M.M.* 225.) So in the preface to the *Groundwork* Kant describes moral philosophy as having "an empirical part," since its purpose is to formulate laws "for the will of man so far as affected by nature" (*Gr.* ii/37). Its use *always* "presupposes . . . objects as given" empirically (*Pr.R.* 65; see also 31, 34).

As all of Kant's own examples show, the actual use of the Categorical Imperative to determine whether a maxim is morally permissible requires us to begin with what it is that we want or might possibly want and how we propose to go about getting it. (See, e.g., *Pr.R.* 67; *M.M.* 382.) Because we have a sensuous nature, "the material of the faculty of desire (objects of the inclination, whether of hope or fear) *first* presses upon us," and the moral law then judges the moral acceptability of the maxim for attaining that goal (*Pr.R.* 74; emphasis mine).

Moral deliberation therefore requires us to know empirical facts (what Kant called "anthropology" and "empirical psychology") but usually only facts that are commonplace and readily accessible to everyone of ordinary intelligence.[19]

This information is of various kinds. We need, for example, to have theoretical knowledge of the ordinary causal laws of the world in which we live; we need some fundamental insight into the nature of human beings; and we need to be acquainted with everyday social practices. More specifically, we need to be aware, for example, that we are dependent physical beings with needs to be met with the help of our reason. We need to know we are emotional as well as rational beings, so that we have to take an interest in something before we will act so as to attain it. We need to know what sorts of things can be considered desirable and by what means they can be attained. (See *Pu.R.* A54/B78–79; *Gr.* 35/412, 62–63/427; *Pr.R.* 8; *M.M.* 205, 216–17.) We need to be aware that we can and do experience internal conflict between our prudential and our moral interests, so that morality always appears to us as our duty. (See *Gr.* 86/439.) We need to recognize that we are only contingently rational and do not always act intelligently even in prudential matters. Only within the context of such information can we understand how the principle of autonomy functions for *us* as a principle of unity and internal integrity, as an a priori law for arbitrating conflicts within ourselves and between us and others.

That the application of the Categorical Imperative to human life requires us to *take into account* features about human beings that we can learn only from experience does not mean that Kant's theory is therefore *based on* experience or anthropology. (See *Gr.* v–viii/389–90, 32n/410n; *T&P* 277; *M.M.* 216–17.) His theory retains its objectivity because it remains an analysis of what it means to act as a rational agent, albeit now an agent who is contingently rational, dependent, physical, emotional, and so on. Moreover, particular ethical principles, which must take such things into account, are still not subjective, for their validity or binding force does not depend on contingent facts but is grounded only on the ultimate Law of Autonomy, given by reason alone.

Finally, as we have seen, our decisions also require us to exercise judgment. After we have determined what maxims are morally right, we still need to make moral judgments, as described in Chapter 5, about how to act here and now. For those kinds of decisions, we need what Kant calls "pragmatic skills," that is, "judgment sharpened by experience . . . in order to distinguish the cases to which [the various maxims] apply" (*Gr.* vii/389; see *Pu.R.* A132–36/B171–75; *Pr.R.* 67; *Cr.J.* 346–47; *T&P* 275, 289).

Problems with maxims

Commentators have often pointed out that there are serious problems with the formulation and use of maxims of conduct. They commonly note that there is not a one-to-one correlation between maxims and behaviors, so that the "same behavior" may be subsumed under more than one maxim. Each would have its own description, and each would then be regarded as a different action. If one action is morally permissible and another not, it would seem that we can be led to precisely what the ultimate norm of consistency is supposed to rule out – practical contradictions.

Unfortunately, Kant himself did not explicitly discuss such problems. I have not set out to try to solve problems with Kant's theory, but I can at least try to clarify the nature of some of the problems here by pointing out again that our moral judgments are of two kinds. As we have seen, some concern the adoption of maxims of actions, and others concern decisions about actions to perform. Each type of judgment has its own problems. Let us look at each in turn.

If we consider the first kind of practical reasoning, that concluding in a judgment about the moral acceptability of a particular maxim, we may find that a person's intentions are too specific to be formulated as a maxim that can be tested for its suitability to function as a possible law for everyone. (To insist on an untestable maxim would surely be a sign of bad faith.) What is needed is maxims of conduct that have sufficient generality. Onora (Nell) O'Neill calls these our "underlying" or "fundamental" intentions because "to a considerable extent [they] express the larger and longer term goals, policies and aspirations of a life."[20] They therefore lie under our more specific "surface" intentions (even when the latter can be universalized).

There are potentially an indefinitely large number of such principles of action, because of all the various purposes we can have. (See *Gr.* 41/415.) However, judging by Kant's own moral writings, when substantive maxims are stated in a sufficiently general way, the number of *morally* significant maxims applicable to our ordinary moral life seems to be rather small.

Whatever their number, we normally begin by examining rules that can help us get something we want. (As O'Neill states, it is not the purpose of the moral law to come up with plans of action for people who do not already have any.) Even so, maxims to be tested by the Categorical Imperative must be formulated as genuine candidates for practical laws. This means that a maxim must be general in form, containing no references to any particular individuals or circumstances but only to general kinds of actions that all agents, including agents having generally described positions or roles, may (or may not) or must (or must not) do in certain generally described kinds of situations.[21] Moreover, the maxim must be stated so that, when restated also as a universal, it can apply to all moral agents in the kinds of circumstances to which it is meant to apply, and not merely promote or protect the interests of particular individuals or groups. But since there are morally good (even obligatory) ends, maxims clearly may be disinterested and still promote or protect the morally sanctioned interests of classes that are generally described.

When it has or can have these characteristics, a maxim can be formulated with the generality necessary to be tested for its suitability as a universal moral law. If it in fact does pass the test of the Categorical Imperative, we know that it is a maxim that a person with a good will would adopt and on which that person would act. Consequently, the ultimate disposition to adopt such maxims and, when appropriate, to act on them characterizes the intentional life of a morally virtuous person. In this matter, Kant holds, we can attain the certainty necessary for morally correct decisions.

However, when we are concerned with intentions, we also know that there is no *necessary* correlation between them and the moral legality of a person's behavior. The possibilities here are complex, for, as we have seen, we can perform morally right (legal) *or* morally wrong actions from a morally good will as well as from a morally weak or a morally "impure" or a morally evil will. (See, e.g., *M.M.* 422–25; *Anthr.* 258.)

Moreover, Kant repeatedly reminds us that our judgments about anyone's actual motivation are ineluctably beset by uncertainty. We can never be sure of our own motives and aims in any particular instance, much less those of others. The best we can do is to make inferences on the basis of our own genuine efforts or the behavior of others, and the best we can hope to get is a high degree of probability or what is often called moral certainty.

These problems are particularly troublesome to the second type of moral reasoning, done from the standpoint of the agent himself and concerning decisions about how to act here and now, that is, what sort of behavior is morally required or permissible, given that one has *already* chosen maxims on which to act. A similar kind of reasoning is required of the spectator who is trying to decide exactly what action an agent has in fact performed. From each viewpoint we also can concern ourselves with an action in either of two senses – with a person's behavior or with his or her motivation; the first concerns an agent's "empirical character," the second the quality of a person's ethical character.

In all these cases, however, we still must try to decide under what maxim a particular action either has fallen or will fall. We have already discussed one reason why it apparently did not occur to Kant to discuss this kind of judgment: There is no formal procedure to which we can appeal to help us make such judgments. However, we all normally go through a socialization process in which we learn what Barbara Herman has called the "moral range" of salient features to which we should attend in various situations. We are not fated to approach each new day and each moral context without a store of moral experience to help us know how to discriminate between those factors to which we should be sensitive and those which we can ignore.[22]

Nonetheless, even as an agent, our deliberations about how to act may be flawed by factual errors as well as by plain ignorance or by a significant lack of sensitivity to the features to which we should attend. Here we may not claim certitude about our judgments, only that we have tried to do the best we can, and it is clearly possible for reasonable people to disagree among themselves.

What is not clear is that any of these problems are specific only to Kant's moral theory. Rather, since they arise from our epistemological limitations, it would seem that they must occur in any moral theory.

The necessary and sufficient norm

Since the Categorical Imperative is the practical principle of noncontradiction, we may tend to think that it functions only as a *negative* moral norm, telling us what we may *not* do. Kant himself stresses that we first become aware of the moral law "in the form of a prohibition," and he in fact most frequently describes morality as a negation, a limitation on our desires and inclinations (*Rel.* 42/37; see *Pr.R.* 4n). But he also insists that the Categorical Imperative can tell us not only what is morally unacceptable (*illicitum*) but also what is morally permissible (*licitum*) and what is morally obligatory (*obligatio*). (See, e.g., *M.M.* 221–22.) To do that, the Categorical Imperative must be able to function as both the necessary *and* sufficient condition for the moral quality of possible maxims. It can do so *if and only if* maxims being tested by it are formulated as analytic judgments.

In the next chapter we will see exactly what this means. For now, there may appear to be an obvious objection to the preceding claim. How can we test maxims as analytic judgments when the Categorical Imperative – and all substantive moral rules (or categorical imperatives) – always appear to us as synthetic a priori judgments? We can do so because the Categorical Imperative in effect asks, Is this a maxim that a purely rational agent may adopt? As we have seen, the ultimate norm of pure practical rationality is the purely formal principle of noncontradiction: Such an agent acts only on maxims that are both self-consistent and consistent with one another. *This,* then, is the question by which we test maxims of conduct: Is it analytically the case that a purely rational agent could adopt this maxim? For purposes of judging the moral acceptability of maxims, we need not and should not be distracted by the fact that *we* still might not adopt or act on a moral maxim. The fact that we are only contingently morally good is, as we have seen, the main reason morally acceptable norms appear to us as synthetic a priori imperatives.

Not a prudential norm

Before considering how Kant thought we *should* use the Categorical Imperative, it may be helpful to show how *not* to use it. As we shall see, the Categorical Imperative does require us to assess the *logical* consequences of the adoption of a particular maxim. But we may not appeal to the *desirability* of the possible or probable empirical consequences of the (universal) adoption of a particular kind of action or the unity of those consequences under the title of happiness. We also may *not* substitute the verbs "want" and "wish" in place of "will," for the first two verbs belong to the vocabulary of desires.[23] Either usage would change the purely formal moral test into a prudential question. (See *Pr.R.* 70–71.)[24]

So, for example, testing the maxim of lying promises as a universal law does not mean that we have any expectation that our choosing to act in a certain way will actually have the consequence of causing everyone to act the same way. (See *Pr.R.* 69.) We obviously have no such power. Nor does using the Formula of Universal Law require us to try to predict what will contingently and empirically happen when people do make lying promises. As a matter of fact, we do know what empirically happens when people at least frequently make lying promises in the form of bad checks: The practice of check writing does not disappear, but as the use of bad checks makes commerce riskier, people become less trusting and it becomes much more difficult to use checks as currency. As we also know, ordinary prudence counsels us to weigh all the foreseeable consequences of our actions, and writing bad checks usually turns out to be an imprudent practice because we thereby can ruin our credit rating (see *Gr.* 18/402). All of this we learn from experience, and it all is completely irrelevant to the morality of lying promises (here in the form of bad checks). (See *Gr.* 20/430.)

Unfortunately, it is all too easy unwittingly to turn the Categorical Imperative into a prudential norm. Note, for example, what happens when we misuse the Formula of Universal Law to test a maxim such as "I want to become an engineer." If we were to ask, What if everyone did that? we could answer that question only by imagining the empirical possibilities and their impact on our interests.[25] And if we were to do that, we would generate an absurdity – a picture of what would happen if everyone in fact decided to try to become an engineer. Obviously, no one could either want or rationally will such a world. By misusing the Categorical Imperative in this fashion, we can generate an indefinitely large set of such conclusions, which rule out either too much or not enough or both. Rules generated in this fashion tend to be both morally absurd and to produce contradictions, such as the two maxims: "Everyone should tie the laces of their left shoe first" and "No one should do so."

There is no possibility of a nonchaotic world governed by *prudential* rules holding universally. The "laws" of such a world would be based on desires, and desires, as the source of inconsistency and conflict, cannot provide the basis for universal rules of conduct. In fact, Kant points out, it is just in those cases in which there happens to be the greatest coincidence of desires that we also tend to have the most conflicts. (See, e.g., *Pr.R.* 28.) As it turns out, the norm of universality is exactly the wrong way to assess maxims from a prudential point of view. (See *Anthr.* 277.)

So it cannot be stressed too strongly that the Categorical Imperative can function only as a *moral* criterion and then only as a *purely formal requirement of consistency*. All considerations of empirically given interests and consequences must be ignored as irrelevant. (See *Pr.R.* 69–71.)

12

The Formula of Autonomy or of Universal Law: Part I

Stated as an imperative, the Law of Autonomy commands us to "act only on that maxim through which you can at the same time will that it should become a universal law" (*Gr.* 52/421). This is also the first formula of the Categorical Imperative, the Formula of Autonomy or of Universal Law, which exhibits its origin in the logical principle of noncontradiction by obligating us to adopt and act only on maxims that are consistent with themselves when considered also as laws for everyone. Only such maxims are formally fit to serve as maxims for autonomous agents.

Kant calls this formula the "supreme principle of right" because it obligates us to recognize and respect the right and obligation of every other person to choose and to act autonomously (*M.M.* 231). Since moral rules have the characteristic of universality, what is morally forbidden to one is forbidden to all, what is morally permissible for one is equally permissible for all, and what is morally obligatory for one is equally obligatory for all. We may not claim to be exempt from obligations to which we hold others, nor may we claim permissions we are unwilling to extend to everyone else.

Kant offers some twenty variations of the first formula.[1] Some stress that we act autonomously only when we act on maxims fit to be universal laws: "I ought never to act except in such a way that I can also will that my maxim should become a universal law" (*Gr.* 17/402). Others are more explicit about what it means to say that a maxim can function as a universal law: "Maxims must be chosen as if they had to hold as universal laws of nature" (*Gr.* 80/436).[2] Kant also uses a restricted variation of the formula as the foundation for lawmaking in his political philosophy; in that form, it is the Principle of *Recht,* which commands us to "act externally in such a way that the free use of your will is compatible with the freedom of everyone according to a universal law" (*M.M.* 231; see 229–32; *Cr.J.* 295).[3]

Self-constraint

As the title I have given to it stresses, the most fundamental requirement of the first formula is that we act autonomously and respect the right and obligation of everyone else to do the same. We act autonomously, that is, freely in the positive sense, as a law unto ourselves only if we are neither constrained by our own desires for pleasure nor coerced by the will of another person. That this claim is analytically true is shown by the fact that its denial results in the self-contradictory claim that freedom can be compelled. Because the

Formula of Autonomy requires the exclusion of any determining influence from outside of our own reason, the only kind of constraint consistent with our freedom is self-constraint, self-control imposed by our own reasoning. (See, e.g., *Gr.* 73–74/432–33; *M.M.* 481.) The actual formulation of specific norms may originate with others; we each do not have to begin everything anew, as if no one before us had ever understood anything about morality.[4] But if we are to act as moral agents should act, our adoption of moral rules and our obedience to them must be based only on our own rational deliberation and assent. (See *Gr.* 70–71/431; *M.M.* 227, 380–81.)

Because the Categorical Imperative is a norm of self-constraint, its most obvious role is to function as a negative test of possible or actual maxims of happiness. Kant repeatedly makes this point, for example, when he describes that imperative as the "supreme limiting condition of all subjective ends" (*Gr.* 70/431), and when he states:

In itself, no matter what the will's object or end may be (consequently, even happiness), duty is nothing other than the will's *limitation* to the requirements of a universal legislation that is made possible by adopting a maxim [the Law of Autonomy]; however, one completely abstracts from both happiness and from every other end that one may have. (*T&P* 280)

To conform to the Categorical Imperative, then, we must judge maxims in a *disinterested* fashion, particularly in those cases in which we happen to have the greatest interest. (See *Gr.* 2/393–94, 7–8/396–97, 103/449; *Pr.R.* 31, 34, 62; *M.M.* 213–14.)

Practical lawfulness

Since the Formula of Autonomy obligates us to adopt only maxims that are fit to serve also as objective laws, intentions formed autonomously must be not only self-legislative but also universally legislative. (See, e.g., *Gr.* 52/421.) It is therefore appropriate also to call the first formula the Formula of Universal Law.

Kant holds that we can understand how to use the abstract and purely formal Law of Autonomy only if we first know what it means to say that maxims must be fit to be *laws*. (See *Pr.R.* 67–70.) "The existence of things under laws," he argues, is just what we mean by the idea of "nature" in the most general sense of that term (*Pr.R.* 43; see *Pu.R.* A126, A216/B263, A418/B446, A546/B570, A693/B721; *Proleg.* 294; *Gr.* 36/412, 52/421, 81/437). In this regard it does not matter what kind of nature we are talking about: Genuine laws are all alike in that they all hold without exception. If they did not do so, they simply would not be laws. Moreover, laws must also be consistent with one another. A world in which things do not happen with any regularity, according to rules, or a world with laws in constant conflict with one another would be chaotic and self-destructive. (See, e.g., *Lect.* 346/123–24.) We of course already know what laws are like from our knowledge of the world of experience. In fact, the new Newtonian science insisted that our world can be understood just because it is law governed.

Because laws considered just as laws are all alike in holding universally, or, as Kant puts it, in their *form*, he tells us to take the form of the laws of the phenomenal world as a "typic" or type or model of what *any* "nature" must be like, including a world or nature governed by laws of freedom. (See *Pr.R.* 69–70.)[5] As the procedural norm for moral judgment, the first formula prescribes that our maxims must be able to fit together coherently and with harmony (*Einstimmigkeit*) in a moral world.[6] We therefore can test the moral status of proposed maxims by asking whether they can fit together as laws in a world of freedom and morality (*Gr.* 57/424; see *Pr.R.* 27, 44, 69–70). This, Kant writes, is an exercise of our understanding (not of our imagination), for we must test maxims, not by their imagined possible consequences, but by the purely logical norm of consistency. (See *Pr.R.* 69.)

Such a world – an ideal moral world – is only an Idea of reason; it is only a possibility. But what *is* real is the unconditional command of reason: "Ask yourself whether, if the action which you propose should take place by a law of nature of which you yourself were a part, you could regard it as possible through your will" (*Pr.R.* 69).[7] In its first formula, therefore, the Categorical Imperative forbids us to act on maxims that cannot *also* be *conceived* of as laws without contradiction or that are incompatible with other lawful maxims and so cannot be *willed* as laws without contradiction. (See *Gr.* 57/424.) In either case, such maxims would not be fit to serve as laws in a possible moral world. (Even when Kant words a maxim as only giving a permission, what is universal – that maxim taken as a law – is best represented by considering the intention of everyone in relevantly similar circumstances to act on the same maxim as the agent intends to act upon.)

If we attend to the way in which ordinary people make their moral judgments, Kant believes, we shall find that this is, in effect, just the way they do so. "Even common sense judges in this way, for its most ordinary judgments . . . are always based on natural law" in the sense of assessing maxims for their fitness to serve as laws for everyone, as do the laws of the physical world. "Thus people ask: If one belonged to such an order of things . . ., would he assent of his own will to being a member?" (*Pr.R.* 69; see *Gr.* 57/ 424). Put in a different if still somewhat stilted way, the ultimate moral test for maxims is: Could we all rationally agree to live in a world in which everyone adopted that maxim? As we saw in Chapter 11, addressing this issue requires some care so that we do not turn it into a prudential rather than a moral question. But using the Categorical Imperative cannot be so complex that only a professional logician can deal with it. Not, at least, if Kant is right in claiming that ordinary people can and do use it with astonishing ease.

Testing the maxim of a lying promise

To see how Kant thought we should use the first formula, let us examine his well-known discussion of a lying promise.[8] The question at issue, he writes, is: "May I not, when I am hard pressed, make a promise with the intention of not keeping it?" (*Gr.* 18/402; see 18–20/402–3, 54–55/422, 76/434, 81/437).

At the end of the last chapter, it was stated that we need to regard maxims as analytic judgments so that the principle of noncontradiction in the form of the Categorical Imperative can function as the necessary and sufficient moral criterion. In modern propositional logic that principle is usually stated as $\sim(p \cdot \sim p)$. Notwithstanding the controversial status today of symbolizing the logic of intentions, only a primitive formal characterization should be sufficient to display how the Categorical Imperative functions. What can be said now in general terms is that, within the moral context of choosing maxims, a contradiction (*Widerspruch* is the noun Kant most often uses) consists in holding both that a practical principle should hold universally and that it "subjectively should not hold universally but should admit of exceptions" (*Gr.* 58/424). In terms of the Aristotelian "Square of Opposition," which Kant of course knew, the opposition is either between A (universal positive) and O (particular negative) judgments or between E (universal negative) and I (particular positive) judgments. It is impossible to will (*unmöglich zu wollen*) contradictories, because, given the principle of the excluded middle, they are mutually exclusive. (See *Gr.* 55/423, 56/423; *Logic* 117.)

Let us now look at Kant's example. If we symbolize an individual's maxim, such as, "I will make lying promises when I am in need and when it is advantageous to do so," as "m^i," there is no way to test it by the norm of the Categorical Imperative. This is exactly why Kant holds that the Categorical Imperative requires us to "act only on that maxim through which you can *at the same time* will that it should become a universal law," or, put negatively, "Never choose except in such a way that in the same volition the maxims of your choice are *also* present as universal law" (*Gr.* 52/421 and 87/440; emphases mine). To test the original maxim, then, we must restate it as a universal law or what Kant calls a "law of nature" (which I will symbolize as "m^u") and join it with the maxim of the individual to form the conjunction $(m^i \cdot m^u)$. The Categorical Imperative then requires us to see whether *this* conjunction, $(m^i \cdot m^u)$, generates a contradiction.[9]

In the case of Kant's example of a lying promise, we now have the following conjunction:

> I intend to make lying promises whenever it is advantageous to me to do so, and I also will a world in which everyone else makes lying promises, even to me, whenever it is advantageous for him or her to do so.

Clearly, we need commonplace knowledge of what the practice of promise making is all about. To make a promise is to engage in verbal behavior consisting in giving one's word to perform some future action, and to accept a promise means believing that the other person is telling the truth and will fulfill that promise. Kant simply presumes that we all are aware "a priori by reason" that in the absence of any contravening moral considerations, this is a morally permissible social practice. There is no conflict between an individual's intention to engage in the practice of promise making and keeping and everyone else's intention also to do so. (See *M.M.* 224.)

We obviously can make lying promises, and it may also be that we can thereby promote our prudential interests. To test the *moral* quality of a maxim to make lying promises, however, the Categorical Imperative requires us "at the same time" to will a world in which *everyone* has adopted the same maxim. As only a little reflection shows, the logical consequence of that universal law would be that no performance could count any longer as "making a promise," for no one could rationally believe anyone else's "promises." (See *Gr.* 55/422.) So the practice of promise making would disappear, along with all practices that depend on promises. Because lying promises are parasitic on the practice of promise making, we also could no longer make lying promises. The conjunction of our maxim with that same maxim as a universal law therefore generates a practical contradiction; it necessarily "destroys itself" (*Pr.R.* 27–28; see 35, 44, 69, 87–88; *Gr.* 19/403). To put it in another but equivalent way, we generate a "contradiction in our will"; it is not rationally possible to will both our own maxim and that same maxim as a universal law of conduct. If we cannot consent to everyone's also adopting the maxim on which we want to act, our maxim is morally unacceptable.[10]

As this example indicates, morally wrong choices are typically characterized by the adoption of two different standards of conduct – one for ourselves and another for others. With regard to the lying promise, we require or expect others to follow *their* appropriate role in promising, namely, believe we will keep our promise; and at the same time, although we engage in promise-making behavior, we also intend from the start to violate our role in that social practice by not keeping our promise. If we attend to how we think in such cases, Kant explains, we find that we still will the morally acceptable law of conduct but only as a general rule, and we think of ourselves as making only a few exceptions in favor of our own particular situation. (See *Gr.* 58–59/424.) This is not so much a contradiction within reason, he explains, as a conflict between reason and our inclinations. (See *Gr.* 59/424.) As a consequence, we may not be interested in testing the morality of an action we very much want to do. But our virtue or lack of it is irrelevant to the judgment of reason about what a morally good person does and does not do.

So, as the ultimate norm of practical consistency, the first formula is a law of justice, telling us that we do not have the moral right to expect or demand that others use one principle in dealing with us while we are free to use another, incompatible, principle with them. It is immoral for us to make exceptions of ourselves on the basis of our own special interests. The Formula of Universal Law therefore can tell us which maxims are contrary to strict or narrow moral duty and so are morally forbidden. (See *Gr.* 57/424.)

The contradiction generated in Kant's example may be understood in any of three different and equally correct ways. It may be understood as a "practical contradiction," because, when made a universal law, the agent's maxim is self-defeating. It also may be interpreted as a contradiction in conception, for practices are defined in two incompatible ways. Or it may be interpreted as a "teleological contradiction," because the agent's purpose in engaging in the social practice of promising is inconsistent with the given end of that practice.[11]

There are some cases, particularly those involving wide duties, in which an unacceptable maxim does not generate a contradiction in conjunction with that maxim stated as a universal law. A morally good world, however, must be a world formally defined by mutually consistent laws. So even if a maxim is consistent with itself regarded also as a universal law of conduct, it is still morally unacceptable if it contradicts *other* laws of conduct that we must adopt, which are morally obligatory. In the final section of this chapter we shall see in more detail how this test operates.

For now it should be added that the moral rejection of lying promises does not *of itself* also imply that there must be a practice of promise making and keeping.[12] It also does not address the question, Can situations arise in which I may break a promise I earlier made with the intention of keeping? (So it is misleading to call this a "duty of promise keeping.") Applied to the maxim of a lying promise, the Categorical Imperative is a negative norm, insisting *only* that when we do make promises, we may not make lying promises.

Kant's doctrine concerning lies

Lying promises are but a species of lies, and Kant's readers often single out his condemnation of lying to argue that his moral doctrine is excessively rigorous. It is appropriate, then, for us now to see what Kant says about lying.[13] Lies violate the duty of benevolence, Kant writes, when they unjustly injure others (e.g., *M.M.* 403, 430; *Lect.* 449/229). But not all lies wrong individuals. So, as is his custom, Kant suggests we imagine a situation in which we can reap the greatest conceivable benefits for ourselves or our friends by telling a "little lie that would harm no one" (*M.M.* 481). What, he asks, does our reason say about our doing so?

When we use the first formula to see if that maxim can serve as a law in a possible moral world, we generate the following conjunction:

> I will tell little lies that do not harm any individual and may have good consequences, and I will a world in which everyone will lie under similar circumstances.

Once again, we must have some everyday knowledge of the practice relevant to lying. Kant holds that there is a given end or "natural purposiveness" to those kinds of speech acts within which lying can occur. "The intrinsic end [*Zweck*]" of such speech acts is "the communication of one's thoughts" (*M.M.* 430 and 429; *Ed.* 489/102).[14]

In conjunction with itself as a universal law, the maxim of lying – even telling "harmless" lies for "good" reasons – contradicts itself, and therefore generates as its logical consequence the complete frustration of the given purpose of that kind of speech – the conveying of factual information, whether in ordinary conversations or in more formal settings. Kant concludes that "it cannot hold as a universal law of nature that an assertion should have the force of evidence and yet be intentionally false" (*Pr.R.* 44). Truthful assertions cannot survive any universal violation of the essential point of such speech. Once everyone lies for what each considers a "good" reason, we can never know when any verbal behavior counts as "telling the truth." If no statements can be rationally believed to be truthful, it is also no longer possible for anyone to tell a lie.

Because its essential evil lies in the nature of lying itself rather than in any empirical consequences, a person's purpose in lying is irrelevant to the intrinsic morality of lying. (See *M.M.* 238, 403, 429–30, 481.) Within the context of a teleological, law-governed world of free agents, the Categorical Imperative functions as a necessary and sufficient test of the moral acceptability of the maxim of even frivolous "little" deceptions and shows that the maxim to allow lies generates contradictions just as does the maxim to allow lying promises. (See *M.M.* 430.) Because the commands of moral reasoning are unconditional, the prohibition against lying allows *no* exceptions. In the face of that prohibition, Kant writes, "All my inclinations must be silent. . . . I ought not to lie, no matter how great the benefits" from doing so (*M.M.* 481).

However tempted we may be to do so, we may not turn the absolute moral rule against lying into a conditional rule by making exceptions to it "whenever it seems necessary to do so." (See *M.M.* 235–36, 471–72.) Kant surely had read Niccolò Machiavelli; we know that Frederick the Great had done so. And Kant surely would have remembered that the infamous Machiavelli had recommended that the prince "should not deviate from what is good if that is possible, but he should know how to do evil, if that is necessary" (*The Prince*, XVIII). Understandably, Kant was convinced that once we accept "necessity" (*Notfall*) as a valid excuse for *any* exceptions to the moral law – and it is, of course, up to each person to decide what will count as "necessary" – there is no reason to limit that justification only to "a few" exceptions. Sooner or later it will sanction the violation of any and every moral rule, and in the end, "necessity has no law" (*M.M.* 236; see *T&P* 300n; *Lect.* 448–49/ 228–29; *Ed.* 490/104).

This is not all Kant had to say on the topic of lying. But what first needs to be added is something Kant himself did not explicitly say, apparently thinking it too obvious to mention: It would be a gross error for us to confuse the rule "I may never lie" with the quite different rule "I must always tell the truth."[15] As we have seen repeatedly, Kant held that (most) strict or narrow obligations arise *only negatively*. So the moral rule forbidding lying *is* an unconditional and negative law that like all other negative laws, allows no room for any legitimate exceptions. But this narrow and perfect duty never to lie does *not* entail a corresponding positive and equally strict – and obviously ridiculous – moral obligation *always* to be completely open with everyone, to tell *everything* one knows to *everyone* at *every* opportunity. (See *M.M.* 471–72.)

As Kant sensibly recognizes, much of our verbal behavior has some function other than the transmission of factual information. Gallantry and common courtesies of conduct, such as shows of affection for others, may be only role playing, but "this still does not make them deceptions, because everyone knows how to take them" (*Anthr.* 152; see 151–52; *Lect.* 445/225).[16] Moreover, the obligation to tell the truth is a positive obligation and, as we saw in Chapter 5, in the matter of (most) such duties, we are obligated only to adopt *general maxims*. We do have to act on them, but we normally have a moral title to exercise prudential judgment about exactly when and how we actually do so. (See *M.M.* 383, 389–90, 393; *Lect.* 445/225.)[17]

So it is no accident that, in his lectures on ethics, Kant prefaced his examination of the duty of truthfulness with a long discussion on the value of prudent reserve, that is, restraint in expressing one's mind. Such restraint would not be necessary, he said, if everyone were good. But because they are not, were we always scrupulously to tell the truth, we would lay ourselves open to anyone who might want to injure us or our loved ones. (See *M.M.* 471–72.) We have a moral right to a prudent reserve, a right to the privacy of our own thoughts that we also should respect in others. (See *Lect.* 446–49/226–29.) "We do not press our friends to come into our water-closet," Kant told his class, "although they know we have one just like themselves" (*Lect.* 445/225). And so, he concludes, "No man in his right senses is completely candid" (*Lect.* 445/224; see 448/228).

Discretion or "worldly wisdom" (*Weltklugheit*), as Kant explains it, is only another word for prudence (*Klugheit*) in the sense of being able to "use our fellowmen for our own ends" (*Ed.* 486/95; see *Gr.* 42n/416n). So important is discretion to our welfare that it ranks second in importance only to morality itself. And prudence advises a person "to disguise his feelings and to be reserved. . . . We have to hide our faults and keep up an outward appearance. This is not necessarily deceit . . ., although it does border closely on insincerity" (*Ed.* 486/95–96).

One of the few recorded instances when Kant gave normative moral advice to an individual can be found in a famous letter he wrote to Maria von Herbert, who had told Kant that her confession of a relatively innocent deception had cost her the love of a man who had been the center of all her affections. Undoing a deception, Kant wrote her, may be a moral duty, but it is also true that everyone keeps some things to himself, for "everyone fears that to reveal himself completely would make him despised by others." He then noted that there is a critical moral difference between discretion and deceit: "What the honest but reticent man says is true but not the whole truth. What the dishonest man says is, in contrast, something he knows to be false."[18] Elsewhere Kant points out that there are many morally acceptable ways in which we may avoid telling the truth without telling a lie. They include simple silence, mental reservations, noncommittal answers, evasions, and equivocations. (See, e.g., *M.M.* 471–72; *Lect.* 446/226, 449/229.)

In his lectures on ethics Kant also distinguishes between an untruth (a *falsiloquium*) and a lie (a *mendacium*). This distinction may seem jesuitical to some readers, and Kant admits that ordinarily we rightly ignore it. However, in a few isolated cases, it can be an important and morally useful distinction: Every lie is an untruth, but not every untruth is a lie. A *falsiloquium* occurs when (1) I intend to mislead someone or at least to hide what is on my mind (2) because the other person means only to misuse the truth, say, by stealing my money, and so (3) I act or speak in such a way that he draws the conclusion I wish him to draw. "The thief knows full well that I will not, if I can help it, tell him the truth and that he has no right to demand it of me" (*Lect.* 447/226–27). Under such circumstances, as long as I do not *say* that I am telling the truth, such a *falsiloquium* is *not* a lie. An untruth *is* a lie, Kant writes, only if we expressly give another person to understand that we *do intend* to tell the truth and then do not do so (see *Lect.* 448/228). Only the latter is always morally wrong.[19] He adds, however, that in civil law, any falsehood that violates the civil rights of another and causes unjust injury is called a lie, is litigable, and is legally punishable. (See *M.M.* 238n; *Lect.* 447–48/227–28.)

This, then, is what Kant's view about lying comes down to: We may *never* state outright that we *will* tell the truth when we have no intention of doing so. Oaths, for example, must be taken and kept with the utmost seriousness.

There also is one case in which the strict negative duty not to lie is equivalent to a positive obligation to tell the truth. This case, an instance of which we now turn to, is peculiar simply because we usually can either avoid answering or simply refuse to answer.

Kant's infamous reply to Constant

Writers who attack Kant's views on lies generally cite his 1797 work *On a Supposed Right to Lie from Altruistic Motives*.[20] Despite its brevity, this essay has had so deleterious an impact on interpretations of Kant's moral and political theory that it needs to be examined with particular care.

A Swiss-French liberal philosopher of some fame, Henri-Benjamin Constant de Rebecque (1767–1830), had argued that we should tell the truth only to those who have a right to it and then only when the truth will not injure others. "The moral principle, 'It is a duty to tell the truth,'" Kant quotes Constant as having written,

would make any society impossible if it were taken singly and unconditionally. We have proof of this in the very direct consequence which a German philosopher [presumably Kant] has drawn from this principle. This philosopher goes so far as to assert that it would be a crime to lie to a murderer who asked whether our friend who is pursued by him had taken refuge in our house.[21]

Constant then concluded that "to tell the truth is a duty, but it is a duty only toward one who has a right to the truth."[22]

Kant was convinced that civil governments are institutionally constituted to recognize and protect the freedom of their citizens only if the governments are contractarian in nature. A civil law tolerating or mandating lies would undercut all contracts and so make a just state impossible. Kant therefore took Constant to be mounting a particularly dangerous, consequentialist attack on the possibility of a just society. However, his brief answer to Constant has been given harsh treatment by the majority of commentators. For example, H. J. Paton, usually Kant's defender, simply concedes that Kant here fell "into the rigorism with which he is so often charged," a view that has now become the standard opinion.[23] He also condescendingly suggests that Kant's reply was only the "petulant" reaction of a 73-year-old man.

To understand Kant's response, several introductory comments are essential:

First, Constant tacitly equated the rule, "I may not lie," with the quite different rule, "I must tell the truth." Kant did not object to this, because the case Constant proposes happens to be that unique one in which the strict, negative duty not to lie *is* equivalent to a positive obligation to tell the truth. This is a situation in which it is "given" that no other alternatives are available, so that as Kant puts it, a person "cannot avoid answering 'Yes' or 'No.' "

Second, Kant had no objection to Constant's choosing what today we would call "desert island" circumstances, involving a potential murderer seeking information about the whereabouts of his intended victim. As the "Casuistical Questions" he posed in his *Metaphysics of Morals* show, Kant *wanted* people to consider cases, however fanciful, in which "the greatest imaginable good" might be accomplished (or at least hoped for) by breaking the moral law. It is in just such instances, he thought, that we will be the most sorely tempted to say, "Here, at least, it is permissible to make an exception to the usual moral rule." That, for Kant, always signals the beginning of the death of morality. So he saw Constant's case as a litmus test for whether people understand and accept the claim that moral rules *must* be genuinely universal laws.

Nonetheless, and this is the third point, in his response Kant was *mainly* concerned with that kind of practical reasoning underlying the acceptance or rejection of possible *maxims,* for he describes Constant's proposed *maxim* as (in Greek) the "fundamental error." Kant was *not* seriously trying to do casuistry, that is, the kind of practical reasoning aimed at deciding how to act here and now (the second kind of practical reasoning examined in Chapter 5).[24] In the preface to the *Groundwork,* published twelve years earlier, Kant had warned that it could be dangerously misleading to try to draw practical principles from cases. Doing so, he wrote, awakens "a certain bias against examining and weighing [the ultimate principle of morality] in all strictness for itself without any regard to its consequences" (*Gr.* xiii/392). Constant had done just what Kant had warned against, with exactly the result Kant had predicted.

Fourth and last, Constant had argued that his maxim concerning truthfulness was necessary for the very existence of any society, including presumably, a just state. Consequently, Kant's response is primarily a political discussion of *juridical* legislation.[25] Civil lawmaking must be grounded on the Principle of *Recht,* which asks if actions according to a particular maxim will be "compatible with the freedom of everyone according to a universal law" (*M.M.* 231). So in this article Kant is doing exactly what he did in the *Groundwork,* asking once again whether a maxim could "harmonize with itself if everyone, in every case, made it a universal law" (*M.M.* 376).

Kant focuses first on Constant's contention that the questioner has no "right" to the truth so that there can be no duty to answer him truthfully. Kant concedes that the potential murderer has no legal right to the truth, so that a lie would not do him any juridical injustice. But Kant still maintains that lying is wrong. Again, this does not mean he is so foolish as to hold that we have a duty to *volunteer* information to potential murderers. But with reference to this case, Kant does say what most readers, Paton included, have found objectionably rigorous: "Truthfulness in statements which cannot be avoided is the formal duty of an individual to everyone, however great may be the disadvantage accruing to himself or to another."[26] Kant always – not just here – held that we have a strict, negative duty not to lie. If there are no other alternatives available, then truthfulness is an unconditional duty, holding "in all circumstances" in the sense that it does not discriminate between persons "having a right" or not having a right to the truth.

Consider for a moment, Kant in effect proposes, a civil society with a public law based on Constant's maxim – a law that allows or, more strongly, legally *requires* people to tell the truth *only* to those "having a right to the truth" and then *only* when doing so does not violate a duty of benevolence. As we saw in the preceding section, Kant argues that such a law would completely undermine the credibility of all contracts and promises, thereby destroying the possibility of a just society. No one could believe anything any government officials might say, for they may have decided that they legally must lie, either because benevolence requires it or because the citizens have no right to the truth. This is the sort of maxim a benevolent tyrant could adopt, but not a just society of free citizens.

Kant reacts predictably to Constant's suggestion that a duty of veracity could have harmful consequences. It is *only* a possibility, Kant argues, and lying could just as easily lead to the intended victim's death as telling the truth. (This is always a problem if we try to make moral or political judgments on the basis of consequences, which cannot be known with any certainty in advance.)[27] Even if harm does occur, it is a confusion to regard accidental harm as a civil injustice when it is the result of lawful actions. (See also *M.M.* 228, 431; *Lect.* 289–90/58–60.)[28] But if we act lawlessly, then we "must answer for the consequences, however unforeseeable they were, and pay the penalty for them even in a civil tribunal."[29]

If Kant's claim sounds implausible and inconsistent with the judgment of ordinary reasoning, consider this example. While driving, a person scrupulously observes all appropriate traffic laws. Unfortunately, a child darts out into the road from between parked cars. The driver is unable to stop the car, and the child is killed. The driver may feel deep regret for the accident but has no reason to feel any moral guilt. Moreover, civil law does not hold the driver legally liable for the child's accidental death. By contrast, if a person drives while drunk, that person becomes criminally responsible not only for driving unlawfully but also for any and all consequences of doing so, however unforeseen they may be.

It therefore is plausible to argue that Kant's response to Constant is not merely what Paton called "a temporary aberration" of a cantankerous old philosopher but is perfectly consistent with the rest of his moral and political theory. By the criterion of the first formula, Constant's maxim simply cannot function as a law in a just society. This contention has given rise to the suggestion that "one of the great difficulties with Kant's moral philosophy is that it seems to imply that our moral obligations leave us powerless in the face of evil. . . . It is not feasible always to live up to the ideal set by the Categorical Imperative," especially in those circumstances in which "the attempt to live up to it would make you a tool of evil."[30] We need a "two-tiered" moral theory to take care of those instances in which others are already acting immorally toward us.

How might Kant have responded to this criticism? He could have offered at least five different objections to any such "reconstruction." First, he could have argued that we seldom, if ever, find ourselves in a situation in which we are *not* confronted by evil, both in ourselves and in others. Living in an ethical state of nature is not an extraordinary situation but, rather, our *normal* moral condition, and we often can act rightly only at considerable consequential cost. Second, another person's immorality clearly does not provide a *moral* justification for our emulating his or her unethical standards. Kant might very well have quoted Saint Paul here: "Do not return evil for evil." Third, as we have already seen, any argument based on any "necessity" but moral necessity inevitably starts us on the slippery slope toward the complete abandonment of morality. Fourth, moral necessity is defined by a purely formal – not a consequential – norm. And finally, all moral laws must be genuine universals. So integral is this last claim to Kant's thought that its rejection amounts to rejecting most of his analysis of both morality and politics.

Nonetheless, the most telling evidence against Kant here is that virtually no one thinks his position tenable, even when he points out that "truthfulness is a duty which must be regarded as the ground of all duties based on contract."[31] If something has gone drastically wrong here, exactly what is it? Let me suggest that this is an extreme case of what Kant typically did in his polemical writings: present only a very one-sided view of the matter under consideration.

How else might Kant have answered Constant? It would have been helpful had he distinguished clearly between the kind of deliberation that precedes the adoption or rejection of a maxim and the deliberation preceding a decision on how to act in a particular instance. But as we have seen several times, Kant simply failed to make this distinction clearly anywhere in his moral writings, even though he presumed its correctness. In this matter he can be faulted for lack of clarity. Had he separated these two types of deliberations, he could still have argued that Constant's rule is unacceptable as a public juridical norm. The arguments Kant gave against a civil law mandating the policy Constant proposed are not obviously absurd.

Once having made that point, Kant could (and should) then have turned his attention to the case itself. He could have begun by pointing out that Constant's is an extraordinary case, that we rarely face a situation in which we *must* answer a question, and that in the vast majority of cases not lying is not equivalent to telling the truth. He might then have ironically conceded that the case could be interpreted as a conflict between rules, to be settled by judging where the stronger ground of obligation lay. As we saw in Chapter 6, under less polemical circumstances Kant freely admitted that there can be conflicts between moral rules. In this particular case, however, the conflict would not be between two rules against lying, one allowing exceptions and the other not allowing exceptions. Instead, one rule would be the prohibition of lying and the other rule would presumably be a positive rule of benevolence, of contributing to the welfare of others, particularly that of a friend.

Kant is often taken to imply that we should always choose a negative (narrow) obligation over a positive (wide) one. In fact, however, in his discussion of conflicting rules, he rather seems to deny that claim, for he holds that since *all* moral obligations are absolute, we should *not* say that one obligation is more binding than another. Instead, the stronger *ground* of obligation should prevail. (See *M.M.* 224.) And then the other rule is regarded as not actually obligating the person here and now. In fact, Kant believed that acting then on the other rule "is even contrary to duty" (*M.M.* 224). Given a virtually unanimous adverse reaction to what are usually understood to be the implications of his article, it seems reasonable to conclude that in Kant's own terminology, ordinary moral reason judges that here, protecting another person's life provides the stronger ground of obligation so that *in this case* following the rule against lying would in fact be "contrary to our duty."

Since all of this can be maintained within his own theory, why did not Kant respond in this manner? Surely at least in part because he was so intent on protecting the purity of the moral law that he simply refused to introduce *any* considerations that might even *look* like he was compromising on what must not be compromised. Perhaps there is some merit after all in the accusation that here he was being cantankerous!

A last note on one way to check claims like Kant's about what is or is not logically possible or necessary: Simply look at what is the case, for what actually *is* the case obviously is also logically possible. What *is* the case in the matter under discussion can be explained in various ways. If we prefer Aristotle's theory, for example, we may say that morally good people in fact follow Aristotle's view of *epieikeia* (or "equity") by at least tacitly approving exceptions to their normal moral and civil rules in extraordinary cases. If we think Kant has the better theory, we can say that in those cases in which two moral rules conflict, we must judge where the stronger ground of obligation lies, and then the rule with the weaker ground simply does not obligate us. Both alternatives involve the exercise of moral judgment, and both obviously can be abused. But in neither is obedience to our usual rules in normal situations necessarily or obviously undermined, nor is the possibility of a just state seriously jeopardized.

Consistency with other maxims

A maxim that fails the first test of consistency is thereby shown to be contrary to strict or narrow duty and so is morally forbidden. But if we attend to the judgments of ordinary moral consciousness, Kant maintains, we find that this use of the first formula is not of itself a sufficient test, for it does not rule out *all* immoral maxims. Not every maxim that is internally consistent with itself as a universal law is thereby morally acceptable. Nor does the first test tell us whether we have any positive moral obligations or what they are – which the Categorical Imperative must be able to do as our necessary and sufficient moral norm. So we need to apply the first formula in somewhat different fashion to test some problematic maxims, particularly those concerning our positive and wide duties.

The second way in which the Categorical Imperative acts as a test of prudential maxims also follows from Kant's analysis of the requirements for laws in a possible moral world of human beings. The laws of that world must be laws we can rationally will. We cannot rationally will a maxim that when also made a law, contradicts another law (or a system of other laws) we *must* rationally adopt.[32]

We have already seen the rationale for this second test. If we follow Kant in thinking of the form of the laws of the natural world as a prototype of the laws of a moral world, it is clear that the physical world is an enormously complex whole with many different but compatible laws. Since the moral law is a law of practical consistency, it requires not only consistency within an individual's willing but also a formal universal harmony among the rational wills of all those inhabiting a moral world. (See, e.g., *Lect.* 257/17.) Without compatibility *among* its laws, a possible moral world of rational agents would be so full of conflict as to frustrate completely whatever ends such agents might rationally set for themselves. Since rational actions are all teleological, to say that the laws of the moral world must be consistent with each other is also to say that the ends of such laws must be consistent with each other. Therefore, both an individual's moral way of life and the moral world itself must be characterized by a complex wholeness; neither can consist of an incoherent and lawless concatenation of conflicting laws or ends.

It was this second test that Kant had in mind in his fourth example in the *Groundwork,* of a person who, when his life is flourishing, adopts the maxim of simply ignoring everyone else. He will neither contribute to nor detract from their welfare, and he is willing to have everyone else treat him in exactly the same fashion. (See *Gr.* 56–57/423.) Such a maxim would not be inconsistent with itself as a universal law. "It is possible that a universal law of nature could subsist in harmony with this maxim. . . . If such an attitude were a universal law of nature [$m^i \cdot m^u$], mankind could get on perfectly well," certainly better than in an ethical state of nature in which people treat each other antagonistically and unsociably. (See *Gr.* 56/423.)[33] But Kant still denies that it is possible for us rationally to *will* that such a principle hold as a law. (Once again, to "will" such a law is not the same as to *want* such a law. Kant always suspects that in such cases we always would prefer to have others help us without our being obligated to help them in return.)

If we are to make rational practical decisions, we obviously must take into account the fact that we are finite agents with needs constantly to be met.[34] And we have seen, it also is clearly rational for us to will the means to our goals. (See *Gr.* 46/417–18; *M.M.* 393, 451, 453.) We therefore cannot reasonably make the universal claim that we can continue always to be independent of everyone else's benevolence and beneficence. When everything is going well and our needs are all met, we may abjure dependence on others. But we know that there will come times in the future when, because we are by nature creatures of constant needs, we *must* rely on others. We will need their help both to promote our natural welfare and happiness (which we cannot totally renounce) and to help us fulfill our moral obligations to develop and sustain ourselves *as* rational agents with a non–self-sufficient nature, for example, by caring for our health and enhancing our abilities. Eventually we all would (or should) have to contradict the maxim under examination by *having* to ask for the help of others.

Even if, *per impossibile,* that did not turn out to be true, Kant also argues that according to the requirement of universality, we are morally entitled to pursue our own otherwise morally permissible happiness only if we recognize the moral right of others to pursue their happiness as well. As we shall see, their right involves a corresponding obligation on our part to empathize with and contribute to their pursuit of happiness insofar as we can do so. (See *Gr.* 60n/430n, 89/441; *Pr.R.* 26–27, 34.)[35] Since we all *necessarily* seek our own happiness, we cannot will that such a maxim of never helping anyone be a permissive law for *all* rational agents. (See *Gr.* 56–57/423; *Pr.R.* 19, 44, 69–70; *M.M.* 393, 453.) In this way, then, the Formula of Universal Law can and does generate positive as well as negative obligations – here the obligation to help others.

Special features of positive duties will be examined in Chapters 13–15. That we may need the help of others, for example, does not mean they always will be able to give it to us or that we always and necessarily have a strict entitlement to their help to get what it is we need or want.[36] Likewise, there are morally legitimate limits on how much help we are obligated to give others, and there is also a good deal of discretionary room in our decisions about exactly whom to help and when. This is why Kant describes positive duties as "wide"; a decision not to act on the maxim of helping others in any particular instance is in itself neither an exception to nor a violation of that obligation.

13
The Formula of Autonomy or of Universal Law: Part II

In the preceding chapter, we saw that Kant maintained that the Categorical Imperative is the only norm we need to guide our moral judgments: By itself, it is both the necessary and sufficient criterion for correct moral judgments. But using that norm properly requires us to observe three procedural protocols. First, we must take the laws of the world of nature as a model of the universal form of and consistency between laws in a possible moral world. Second, we must test maxims for their moral acceptability only within the context of that ideal world already formed by morally obligatory laws. Finally, since reason is an intrinsically teleological faculty, the ideal moral world, which is based on reason alone, must be a world of objective and mutually compatible ends. So every morally acceptable action-type must have an end compatible with all other ends in that world.[1] One of the variants of the Categorical Imperative reads: "Act according to a maxim of *ends* which it can be a universal law for everyone to have" (*M.M.* 395). Kant himself thought of this as a variation of the second formula, but since every maxim at least tacitly contains an end, this could just as easily be taken to be a version of the Formula of Universal Law.[2]

Thus far, we have tested maxims against common human social practices such as promising, each having its own given "natural" purpose. Promising, for example, is not only morally permissible but also, in some unavoidable cases, morally obligatory. As a consequence, promising and practices like it may neither be acted against nor abandoned. But some maxims are problematic just because there seems to be no "standard" practice with an inherent end against which to test them. Then, even for maxims we take to be immoral, the conjunction of such maxims with themselves as universal laws does not generate a contradiction. Kant therefore maintains that moral reasoning has no alternative save to *construct* a system of morally obligatory and mutually compatible *ends* (or "matter") against which to measure such maxims. (See *Pr.R.* 87.) When doing so we must regard ourselves from two different viewpoints: (1) simply as moral-rational agents and (2) as embodied rational agents with a finite and dependent nature. Each viewpoint generates its own kind of morally obligatory ends.

In the first case, Kant argues, the ends moral reason identifies as morally obligatory are all those agents possessing the power of pure practical reason – "persons." Since the only such agents of which we have any knowledge are human persons, our moral reasoning commands us to regard all human persons (or "humanity") as having intrinsic moral value. The Categorical Imperative then uses the Idea of a person to set limits on what we may and may not do, and also projects the total ultimate end both for each person and for the human species as a whole. These parts of Kant's moral theory are most appropriately discussed in connection with the second and third formulas, which we will examine in the next two chapters.

In the second case, a substantive moral theory for human beings must take into account that we are moral agents with a particular kind of *natural* constitution. Kant therefore argues that moral reason must project morally obligatory ends for human beings *as* moral-physical agents – or, as he puts it, "as an *animal* (natural) and at the same time *moral* being" (*M.M.* 420; see *Gr.* vi–vii/388).[3] To be morally obligatory these ends must be objectively good, that is, good because moral reason mandates that they can and should be adopted and willed by everyone as a rational but also a finite physical and dependent being. (See *Lect.* 264/24.) Individual actions can then be classified by moral judgment as instances of more general practices having "natural" ends that moral reason has identified as morally obligatory. Each person has a duty to promote those ends, Kant holds, and any maxim to ignore or pervert them is immoral.

Kant must therefore be counted as belonging in some important ways to the "natural law" tradition, for he does contend that we must regard ourselves as having natural purposes or ends that we must respect. Kant in fact is willing to rest his claims about the simplicity and the power of the Categorical Imperative on his commitment to morally obligatory natural ends when he writes, "By reason of the ends which all men naturally have it is easy to state what one's duty is" (*M.M.* 375n).

Perhaps because it is so commonly misunderstood, this is one of the more unpopular parts of Kant's moral theory, and it is typically regarded as an unfortunate aberration and a philosophical embarrassment.[4] Nonetheless, Kant's doctrine in this matter is not restricted to a few isolated passages but permeates his moral writings. It plays an apparently indispensable role in his application of the Categorical Imperative.

The principle of physicoteleology

In Chapter 1 we saw that the Enlightenment had two radically different attitudes toward the world of nature. On the one hand, following Newton, it rejected any effort to understand the natural world in terms of final causes and instead regarded that world as a mechanistic and deterministic system, explicable by mathematical laws – and so as completely value free. On the other, following Rousseau, it looked to nature to provide the basis for both ethical and aesthetic standards. Several times we have seen these same two viewpoints in Kant's philosophy.

On the one hand, Kant regards the world of nature theoretically as completely causally determined and morally empty and the condition of man living in a "state of nature" as amoral. Yet on the other hand, as we saw in Chapter 8, he insists that, for our theoretical purposes, we also must regard the natural world or "Nature" as a teleological system – a dynamic whole, purposive, "organized and self-organizing" (*Cr.J.* 374; see *Gr.* 114/455). For example, in the *Groundwork* Kant writes that "teleology views nature as a kingdom of ends," which "is a theoretical Idea used to explain what exists" (*Gr.* 80n/436n).

Kant uses these same two viewpoints in his moral writings. On the one hand, he regards the natural world as amoral and any effort to base morality on empirical, contingent grounds as futile. Nature is just what free moral agents must transcend. Yet, on the other hand, he uses what he calls the principle of "physicoteleology" to interpret nature as purposive, with an essential role in helping us make moral judgments about human behavior. "In distributing her aptitudes, Nature has everywhere gone to work in a purposive manner" (*Idea* 19; *Gr.* 7/396; *Ed.* 456/34). "By a natural purpose [*Naturzweck*]," Kant explains, "I mean such a connection of the cause with an effect that, without attributing intelligence to the cause, we must yet conceive it *by analogy* with an intelligent cause and so *as if* it produced the effect purposefully" (*M.M.* 424, emphasis mine; see also *Pu.R.* A620ff/B649ff, A691–92/B719–20; *Gr.* 4/395, 69/430, 84/439; *Cr.J.* 359–81). Morality is the main purpose of practical reason, for example, because that was "the purpose of nature in attaching reasoning to our will as its governor" (*Gr.* 4/395; see 4–8/394–96, 73/432).

When he finds it is necessary to do so in order to assess the morality of a given kind of behavior, then, Kant uses the theoretically regulative principle of physicoteleology as a moral guide. Like the theoretician, he does not claim to *know* either that this principle is a law of nature or that man as a natural, organic being has natural ends. He claims only that we must *assume* the teleological principle and, when making many of our moral judgments, regard it *as if* we knew it were true. The principle of teleology is given a priori by our understanding; it is what Kant calls a "*subjective* a priori principle," that is, one we find we must use, given the demands of our own reason.[5] However, any distinction between "regulative" and "constitutive" uses of such Ideas of reason collapses when used by moral reasoning, which aims to produce the reality of its own objects. (See *Rel.* 123n/114.) When used practically, Ideas of reason like the teleological principle of Nature function not only as regulative but also as *immanent* and constitutive norms. (See *Pr.R.* 48, 135, 145; *Cr.J.* 454).[6]

Kant's transformation of the tradition

Most natural-law philosophers had thought that Nature exhibits purposes originating with its Creator whose will must be respected. Along with most other eighteenth-century philosophers, Kant believed that God lies behind Nature as a teleological system – a faith that reappears in his philosophy of history.[7] But Kant had rejected the old rationalistic metaphysics. No amount of information about the sensible world entitles us to claim we have any theoretical knowledge of a supersensible world. (See, e.g., *Pu.R.* A603–14/B631–

42, A638/B666; *Cr.J.* 436–42; *M.M.* 226.) Consequently, he held that we find within Nature a wholeness – an order, beauty, and finality – that may and must be regarded *as if* it all originated in the intention of a supersensible Author. (See *Pu.R.* A685–701/B713–29.)

Moreover, any attempt to base moral duties on the will of God, whether in some purported revelation or in natural laws supposedly originating in the divine will, signals a relapse into heteronomy. Obligatory natural ends are not, therefore, ends that *Nature* makes obligatory. Kant did appropriate the teleological language of the old natural-law philosophies, but he did not repeat their ancient blunder: Morality and morally good ends cannot be *derived* from or based on anthropology. A theory of human morality must take human nature into account, but that theory, like morality itself, must be grounded only in reason and its ultimate law. Kant took up the natural-law tradition, but he discarded its rationally ungrounded metaphysical claims and transformed it into an integral part of his critical moral theory by giving it a reasoned foundation.

The validation of natural goods binding universally on human moral agents requires an a priori deduction. (See *Pu.R.* A336/B393, A669–70/B697–98.)[8] In his deduction of the right of moral reason to assert that we must regard some natural goods as morally obligatory, Kant begins with the moral law, which, as an undeniably given "fact of reason," commands our absolute obedience. Clearly, it would be irrational to hold that we are obligated to obey that law unless we are able to know what it requires of us: "We must be able, in every case, in accordance with a rule, to know what is *right* and what is *wrong,* since this concerns our obligation, and we have no obligation to that which we cannot know" (*Pu.R.* A476/B504; see *Pr.R.* 55–57). Since we must be able to make moral judgments, we have the right, indeed the obligation, to assume what we *must* assume to be able to judge what it is that the moral law requires of us. (See *Pu.R.* A633–34/B661–62, A806/B834.) Obligatory anthropological matter cannot be derived from a purely formal law; yet the ultimate ground of that matter still must be the Law of Autonomy, the only foundation of morality.

What we may and must assume are those ends that can and should be ends for *everyone* as a rational but also sensuous being. This is what Kant means when he offers the principle that "what, in the relation of man to himself and others, *can be* an end, that *is* an end for pure practical reason" (*M.M.* 395; see *Pr.R.* 61–62; *Lect.* 264/24; *Ed.* 450/20). Because they are necessary presuppositions for the possibility of many moral judgments, Kant concluded he had the transcendental justification necessary to hold that, for our moral purposes, we must regard some natural goods as morally obligatory. (See *M.M.* 386–87.)

Furthermore, an examination of the human condition shows that the pursuit of certain ends is necessary to fulfill our positive and wide duty to sustain and strengthen our humanity – or, equivalently, our capacity for virtue.[9] "All our mental powers and characteristics can have a bearing upon moral conduct," so that "insofar as the perfections of our mental powers are bound up with the essential ends of mankind, it is a duty to ourselves to promote them" (*Lect.* 364/142). The same claim applies also to our physical condition, for "the functional completeness of all our powers is required in order that the dictates of the will should be made operative" (*Lect.* 266/26). Actions done out of respect for those ends as morally obligatory not only are instrumental in promoting our ability to do our duty but also are intrinsically good, an exercise of our will to do our duty. This is how what initially is merely naturally good is taken up and becomes part of our pursuit of moral perfection.

Obligatory natural ends

As we would expect, Kant's use of a teleological conception of Nature is especially strong when he discusses the duties we have to care for ourselves as moral-physical beings. Natural instincts provide animals with a reliable guide to their physical preservation and welfare, and instincts could have more surely secured the same goods for us, without any intrusion by empirically conditioned practical reason. (See *Gr.* 4–5/395; *Ed.* 441/1–3.) But we have no instincts, and so we have "to work out a plan of conduct" for ourselves (*Ed.* 441/2; see *Gr.* 5/395).[10] But because we have the ability to reason practically, we also can act "unnaturally," that is, contrary to those ends that must be regarded as morally obligatory.[11]

As a consequence, we find ourselves under an imperative (a variation of the Categorical Imperative to be so general a moral principle) that can be stated either positively or negatively. The imperative of positive duties toward ourselves, he goes on, is to "*make yourself more perfect* than mere nature made you," that is, to "be worthy" of your moral vocation (*M.M.* 419; see also 386–87). The imperative of negative duties to self is the ancient Stoic principle to "live according to nature . . ., i.e., *preserve* yourself in the perfection of your nature"; which imperative prohibits actions and attitudes such as lying, avarice, and servility (*M.M.* 419; see 386–87).[12] Natural but obligatory purposes may be neither frustrated nor perverted.

Although he uses the principle of physicoteleology in both cases, Kant uses the term "nature" in two very different senses here. In the imperative of positive duties he regards Nature as having the limited (or nonmoral) aim of spurring individuals, through their innate social tendencies, to develop their prudential reasoning and psychological freedom. In this sense Nature can only bring us to the threshold of negative freedom in terms of stirring us to want to be rid of dependence on and interference by others in the pursuit of what we take to be happiness and components of happiness. (See *Anthr.* 267–68.) It then is up to us to *transcend* Nature by acting freely and morally. By contrast, in the principle of negative duties, Kant projects Nature's plan or goal as the preservation and promotion of the capacity of the human species for achieving moral perfection, even though the species itself must realize this goal. (See, e.g., *Cr.J.* 448, 448n.) (If Nature were responsible for the realization of "moral character," that would counterproductively result in determined, that is, amoral, character; see *Cr.J.* 429, 432.)

Applied to us as moral-physical beings, Kant explains, these commands obligate us to recognize and respect what he describes as "impulses" of "drives" of our "animal nature" (*die Antriebe der Natur, was die Tierheit des Menschen betrifft*) (*M.M.* 420; see 421). Since these "impulses" are not instincts, Kant regards them as the most fundamental expressions of that innate, irradicable, and very general concern we have for our own welfare as natural beings called "self-love."

There are, Kant believes, three general ends, based on self-love, which moral reason can identify as objective teleological criteria against which to measure problematic maxims: self-preservation, the preservation of the species, and cultural development.[13] "One's love of life is intended by nature for the preservation of his person" (*M.M.* 423); the exercise of specifically "sexual love is intended [by Nature] for the preservation of the species" (*M.M.* 424); and the natural function of our love for self in general requires the acquisition of culture, the perfecting of our physical and mental abilities, particularly the latter, so we can live "purposefully." (See *M.M.* 384–86, 420, 443–44; *Cr.J.* 430; *Idea* 19–20.) Considered as a process, "perfection" was an Enlightenment ideal, for it could provide us with "the means to all sorts of possible ends," that is, both happiness and virtue.[14] As we saw in Chapter 3, Kant regards the power to set ends and strive for them as so distinctive a power of human agency as to set us in some ways over mere animality (*M.M.* 444; see 392; *Gr.* 55–56/422–23).

As Kant has pointed out, considered only within the context of Newtonian nature, the goodness of naturally good ends can be grounded only in self-love. As we have seen, the ultimate principle of self-love is the analytic principle that a rational agent with needs wills both the fulfillment of essential needs and "the means (so far as reason has decisive influence on his action)" (*Gr.* 45/417). Obviously, the fulfillment of our basic needs presupposes that we continue to exist, as a species and as individuals, and that we have whatever physical and mental capacities we require. Self-love, therefore, requires us to recognize these as goods we *ought* to value on the basis of our concern for our own welfare. (Since we act irrationally even in matters of self-interest, the principle of self-love appears to us as an imperative, directing us to acknowledge these fundamental natural goods.)

It is true both that self-love inevitably leads us to want and to seek our own happiness, and that caring for our physical and mental well-being enhances our capacity to get and enjoy what we want. But there are significant differences between happiness (or pleasure) and perfection, at least for beings like ourselves, however closely they sometimes may be related. Happiness, as we saw in Chapter 3, is an Idea of the imagination, whereas human perfection is a practical concept, referring to "the fitness or sufficiency of a thing to any kind of ends" (*Pr.R.* 41). (Although Kant calls them "ends," at this provisional stage of the argument, the relevant human perfections are good mainly as instrumentalities.)

As a consequence, we always value happiness for its own sake and seek it as an end, whereas at least in the beginning stages of the process of perfecting ourselves, we often see perfection only as an onerous instrumentality. Too often the process of developing our abilities *conflicts with* our pursuit of immediate pleasure and comfort. But neglecting to develop our natural potentialities can also severely limit the range of pleasures an individual may hope to enjoy during a lifetime. Since this conflict can be understood as a contest between long- and short-range pleasures, neglecting our perfection only shows that even in matters of self-love we do not always act as rationally as we might. But as we also know, insofar as the natural goods Kant has stressed merely promote happiness, they cannot be considered morally obligatory, for of itself our own happiness is *not* a morally obligatory natural end. (See *M.M.* 384–87, 391, 420, 443–44, 451; *Cr.J.* 430; *Idea* 19–20.)[15]

In his defense of the claim that perfecting our nature is a moral duty, Kant makes it clear that its ground "is not regard for any *advantage* that can be gained" by doing so; such a ground is empirical, prudential, and heteronomous, and not fit to be regarded as a moral reason (*M.M.* 444–45; see *Pr.R.* 41). Further, as Aristotle had pointed out, all our powers and skills are capacities for moral opposites; they all can be used for either morally good or bad purposes. (See *Nicomachean Ethics* 5.1.1129a12–15.) But the aristocratic Greeks are not among Kant's philosophical heroes, and he credits Rousseau for reminding him that any "advantage might turn out to be [only] on the side of [our] crude natural needs" (*M.M.* 445; see *Gr.* 1–3/393–94).

Since the only ground for moral obligation is and can be the moral law, that law must identify natural goods as both a means to and an exercise of our *moral* character and therefore demand that we recognize those goods as obligatory ends. Regardless of any desires we may have and any prudential advantage to be gained, the preservation and "development of all the capacities which can be achieved by mankind" are necessary to moral judgment and moral virtue. As such they fulfill our positive moral obligation to "be worthy of the humanity" in us, to be "equal to the end of [our] existence." The perfection of our abilities is therefore a "duty in itself," an integral part of the process of striving for "the highest purpose of Nature," our moral perfection (*M.M.* 387, 444–45; *Idea* 22).

Kant's examples

In the *Groundwork,* all four of Kant's examples of how the Formula of Universal Law tests proposed maxims require us to regard some end as morally obligatory. We have seen how the rejection of the maxim of lying promises depends on its incompatibility with the inherent end of the morally acceptable social practice of promising. Kant's other three examples of immoral maxims also depend on a conflict with one or another morally obligatory natural end. The first two concern our duties to ourselves as moral-physical beings, and the last concerns our duties to others as moral-physical beings.

In his first example Kant contends we have a strict negative duty not to commit suicide in order to avoid a life promising more pain than pleasure. (See *Gr.* 54/422.) He argues that the maxim of arbitrarily destroying one's own life from the motive of self-love, if made a universal law, would generate a teleological contradiction with the already given, natural function or role or purpose (*Bestimmung*) of the same self-love "to stimulate the furtherance of life" (*Gr.* 53–54/421–22; see *Lect.* 369–78/148–57). Because the maxim under review would then generate a world (*eine Natur*) in which the same self-love would have two universal but contradictory functions – both to promote and to destroy one's own life – it could not function as a law in a possible moral world. (See *Pr.R.* 44.) Therefore, that maxim is "entirely opposed to the supreme principle of all duty" (*Gr.* 54/422).[16]

Likewise, in his *Metaphysics of Morals* Kant holds that our positive, wide obligation to preserve our physical integrity entails a correlative, negative and strict duty not to do anything that might contribute to or cause the "destruction of our animal [i.e., physical] nature," whether by the excessive consumption of food or drink, by self-mutilation (the removal of healthy organs), or by suicide (*M.M.* 321; see 420–23, 427).

In his third example in the *Groundwork*, Kant argues against neglecting the development of our natural abilities, particularly our mental powers. A maxim of doing so *could* also be a universal natural law (as, he thought, was actually the case among the "South Sea Islanders") without generating a contradiction. Yet, Kant maintains, as rational beings, we "cannot possibly *will*" that such a maxim should be a universal law (*Gr.* 55–56/423). Insofar as we are rational, we finite agents necessarily adopt the ultimate imperative of prudence (or self-love): to use those means known to be necessary to fulfill our needs. Likewise, for our moral purposes, to fulfill our moral interests, we also must "regard the development of our talents as a duty" (*Gr.* 17n/401; see also 55–56/422–23, 69/430; *End* 332). Like all other positive duties, the obligation to promote our natural perfection allows us latitude to judge exactly how to do so. What is forbidden is the teleological contradiction generated by the maxim that we completely neglect the development of our talents.[17]

Finally, in the fourth example in the *Groundwork*, Kant again regards us as beings who, insofar as we have a physical and dependent nature, rationally should act on the ultimate imperative of self-love. (See *Gr.* 56–57/423.) As we saw in the preceding chapter, a maxim of neither contributing to the welfare of others nor asking for their help is not internally inconsistent, but it is incompatible with the fact that, because we are incapable of renouncing our own happiness, we cannot rationally will a maxim to ignore the means necessary to that end, that is, the help of others when we need it. Likewise, because our moral destiny is irrevocably tied up with the moral destiny of others, with their help and with our obligation to help them, we also cannot morally will that the maxim under examination be a universal law for all human agents.

It is mainly in his *Metaphysics of Morals* that Kant considers the obligation to preserve the species. There he condemns contraception as well as all sexual activities not between marriage partners, for moral reason identifies "Nature's purpose in the intercourse of the sexes [as] procreation, i.e., the preservation of the race" (*M.M.* 426; see also 424–26; *H.H.* 112; *Anthr.* 303). Solitary sex, therefore, is "unnatural" (*unnatürlich*) and "contrary to morality in the highest degree" (*M.M.* 424–25; see 240, 420; *Ed.* 497–98/118).[18]

As we have seen, Kant characterizes the obligation to the preservation of the species as a serious, positive one, like the duties to preserve our physical life and to develop our talents. Yet he does not discuss whether or when anyone might have a positive duty to engage in procreative sexual activity. He limits his remarks about this obligation to *negative* duties, arguing only that when people engage in sexual activity (after, of course, entering into a marriage contract), they "may not, at least, act contrary to that end" (*M.M.* 426). Kant here seems merely to reflect the way in which other philosophers in the natural-law tradition treated this obligation, and he does not try to explain how or why this supposedly positive duty is somehow different from the others.[19]

As with the proposed maxims of lies and of lying promises, the contingent fact that a person may not *care* about the relevant morally obligatory natural end is irrelevant to the *use* of such ends to test the morality of that person's maxim. It may, however, be relevant to the person's moral character, if it shows that the motive to adopt and act on a particular maxim is based not on reason but on desires.

Another example

Chapter 11 ended with an example of how the Categorical Imperative can be misused as a prudential norm. We now are in a position to see how, in that case, the Categorical Imperative should have been used. Doing so will also help show the role that Kant believed natural but morally obligatory ends play in the ordinary moral decisions of human life, particularly when we are using the Categorical Imperative to determine our positive and wide moral obligations. So let us reconsider the example of a person wanting to become an engineer. Let us add the further detail that the same person also wants to practice engineering in State College, Pennsylvania.

Moving to State College has no obvious relevance to any morally obligatory ends and, unless some relevance can be shown, is properly judged to be not a moral issue at all. For it to be a moral issue, we should have to show that moving to State College is relevant to some other moral duty. But the maxim of becoming an engineer clearly falls under the obligatory natural end of developing our talents.

Because, as Kant insists, the Categorical Imperative is fundamentally a negative test, we may begin by asking if the Categorical Imperative forbids one to adopt the maxim of developing one's talents by becoming an engineer if one so desires. We find there is no inconsistency between a positive permissive law allowing anyone wanting to become an engineer to try to do so and our wide obligation to develop our talents, particularly our mental abilities. But a maxim forbidding *everyone* wanting to do so, that is, to try to become an engineer, *is* incompatible with the general obligation to develop our talents.

Therefore, we may conclude it is not morally forbidden and so is morally permissible for a person – any person who wants to do so – to try to become an engineer. If the individual's situation is uncomplicated and there are no other relevant moral questions to be raised, this is as far into the decision process as the Categorical Imperative can take us. The moral law does not tell us precisely what we must do to develop our talents, or how we must do it. (See *Lect.* 363/141.)

Since there are no moral objections to the maxim under consideration, we now have what Kant calls a "moral title" to do as we wish. Like all other judgments about fulfilling wide duties, here "judgment can only decide this according to rules of prudence (pragmatic rules)" (*M.M.* 433n). Since we now are in the morally permissible and in that sense morally indifferent realm of prudence, we have what Kant describes as morally permissible "elbowroom" or "playroom" (*Spielraum* – see, e.g., *M.M.* 433n). Taking circumstances and consequences into account now is not only not immoral but necessary if we are to make as rational a decision as possible. (See *M.M.* 223, 383, 392–93, 411.) What we in fact *should* decide to do (and the "should" here is now a prudential matter) depends on empirical conditions in the world. We now need to ask questions such as: Are jobs in engineering available? Do I have sufficient talent and perseverance to be successful? Can I be reasonably happy in engineering? And so on. Whatever a person's eventual decision, there is no way to be certain that that is the best choice. Prudential judgments always leave us with some uncertainty.

Nonetheless, we are still well advised to consider the most likely consequences. Obviously, it would be imprudent for *everyone* to try to practice engineering (or any other single profession) – in State College (or any other particular geographic location). So if a person finds out that both State College and the field of engineering are in fact getting overcrowded, it may still be morally permissible to keep that goal, but it is probably imprudent to do so. If a person finds that there probably is *no* way to make a living as an engineer, then, in the absence of other relevant considerations, it can be argued that trying to do so is incompatible with the general obligation to self-preservation, in which case he or she would have a moral obligation to consider a different career. There are many other ways in which a person can fulfill the general natural obligation to develop his or her talents. (Of course, we can complicate the story, say, by introducing a sudden inheritance, but there is no reason to think Kant's procedures cannot accommodate such ingenious casuistry.)

If we reflect on the manner in which people make such decisions when they try to do so conscientiously and intelligently, we can understand why Kant thought he was doing just what he said he intended to do, explicate our ordinary practical reasoning. Further, Kant is also correct, in this case at least, in holding that the Categorical Imperative is not all that difficult to use. But all this presupposes that we use the Categorical Imperative as our ultimate moral norm *always and only* within the context of an ideal teleological order, in which the ends of that system of nature are approved or mandated by our own moral reasoning.

Problems with such ends

Living in the pre-Darwinian and relatively homogeneous Christian society of eighteenth-century Königsberg, Kant seems not to have been aware that there might be any problems in using the notion of "natural purposes" in a morally constitutive way. Certainly a strong belief in the natural law characterized the religious moral world in which Kant was raised.[20] Here, as elsewhere in his moral theory, Kant must have seen himself as reflecting both a demand of reason and an already existent moral consensus exhibiting each person's innate ability to reason morally. He seems not to have anticipated that there might be controversy about his interpretations of natural purposes.

If we find a natural-law approach to moral theory unpalatable, we may be tempted to ignore Kant's reliance on obligatory natural ends. But just by itself, apart from the context of an ideal rational order exhibiting not only the form of lawfulness but also morally obligatory ends and a systematic coherence and harmony among those laws and ends, the Categorical Imperative has no criteria against which to measure many maxims. Kant himself offers the example of the tyrant who does not generate a contradiction when he openly promulgates his unjust intentions. When power and not lawfulness prevails, the tyrant can state his intentions openly without worrying about generating a practical contradiction in the form of political opposition. (See *P.P.* 385.)

Outside the context of a system of morally obligatory natural ends, we also run a serious risk of misusing the Formula of Universal Law as a prudential rather than a moral norm, without it being immediately obvious that we are doing so.[21] For example, as we saw in Chapter 12, the *empirical* and generally undesirable consequence of everyone making lying promises (and everyone knowing that everyone is doing so) would be that neither promises nor lying promises would be possible. It just so happens that in this case there is a coincidence – for the purpose of moral clarity, an unhappy coincidence – between the logical and the empirical consequences, between the demand of reason and a person's desire, for *whatever* reasons, to reject a universal practice of making lying promises. The cool scoundrel, for example, would not want a world in which he could not operate his scams by making lying promises, but his unwillingness to make his maxim a universal law would be based on desires, not on reason, and on his wish to use others merely as means, not on any respect for them. As Kant points out, morality may never be so endangered as when it is easy to confuse moral and prudential considerations and interests because there happens to be a coincidence between them. This is exactly why he held that the nature of duty stands out most clearly in those instances in which duty conflicts with our desires. (See, e.g., *Gr.* 8/397.)

It may be that most people today would hold that we need to rethink the specific obligatory natural ends Kant invokes as well as their interpretation, but Kant himself apparently did not believe it is possible to do away completely with all such ends without reducing the Categorical Imperative (which is a merely formal norm) in many crucial cases either to impotence or to a prudential, utilitarian norm. The necessity for such objective ends is implied in the claim that there can be no categorical imperative without ends having intrinsic and absolute worth – whether they be human beings themselves or obligatory ends that moral reason indicates we have by virtue of our human nature. (See *Gr.* 63–64/427–28.)

Culture and morality

Kant's discussions of culture may indicate that this was an area in which he experienced some tensions between his Pietistic background and his deep commitment to the Enlightenment. On the one hand, he reflected Pietism by upholding the dignity of the ordinary and, surely in his time, uneducated person. We see this side of Kant in the *Groundwork,* where he insists that "ordinary moral reasoning" needs little formal education in order to be a competent and even subtle moral guide. (See *Gr.* 20–22/403–4.) But, taken alone, that discussion is misleading, for Kant also believed that human moral enlightenment necessarily presupposes cultural development.

This latter part of Kant's moral theory also provides a balance for those passages, both in the *Groundwork* and elsewhere, in which Kant insists that the goodness of a good will is not dependent on what it actually can accomplish in the world because being able to carry out one's intentions is so dependent on empirical circumstances that "by and large are not under man's control" (*M.M.* 482; see *Gr.* 21/404). A person who read only those passages might conclude that Kant's moral theory licenses well-meaning incompetence. But that is far from the truth. Kant was too committed to the Enlightenment to think that ignorance should ever be considered a moral virtue. When he characterizes the development of man's natural powers as valuable "for all sorts of possible purposes," he is using a phrase that his contemporaries would have understood as referring to the Enlightenment's ideal of progress in moral development by means of cultural development. (See, e.g., *Gr.* 56/423; *M.M.* 392, 444.) Again, "the functional completeness of all our powers is required in order that the dictates of the will should be made operative" (*Lect.* 266/26).

Kant maintains that the achievement of at least a certain level of culture must underlie moral achievement. He defines "culture" as the developed capacity of our "humanity" deliberately to select goals – "any ends whatever of [our] own choosing" (*Cr.J.* 431; see also *M.M.* 444). The process of learning to understand and appreciate the sciences and the fine arts requires us to think about and set goals. (See, e.g., *M.M.* 391–92; *Ed.* 449/19.) Because it promotes reasoning, including deliberation and choices, culture represents an important development of the "aptitude" to act morally, on the basis of reason alone. (See *M.M.* 392; *Cr.J.* 432–33.)

Further, the necessity to develop reason, even if only to serve desires, also impels us to make reason the master of our desires. To *that* extent, then, cultural development represents the emergence of at least an enhanced capacity for (negative) freedom (*M.M.* 392; see 387, 421, 441). Because it requires a person to develop the abilities and discipline (*Zucht*) to pursue and achieve such goals, cultural development requires a person to develop "cultural freedom," that is, to gain control over the "despotism" of desires by rejecting merely impulsive behavior and developing self-discipline (*Cr.J.* 432; see 431–35; *Orient.* 144; *Idea* 22; *Ed.* 443/5).

Moreover, Kant argues, the achievement of culture also requires polish and sociability (*Geselligkeit*) that include but also go beyond simply the development of skills (*Kunst*). (See *Pu.R.* A709/B737.) Culture requires discretion (*Weltklugheit*) and refinement (*Civilisierung*), for we need to learn how to accommodate ourselves "to living in society," to make others like us enough to help us achieve our ends. (See *Ed.* 450/19, 455/31, 484/92, 486/95.) By requiring dependence on others, culture also requires rules of cooperation that often are also rules of morally legal conduct occurring only within the context of social life. Like morality itself, cultural development is aimed not so much at the individual as at the evolution of the human race. (See *Idea* 18–19.) Learning to act in a well-mannered way may constitute only the semblance of moral behavior, but it also may lead to the eventual formation of the moral dispositions appropriate to it.[22]

Finally, culture encourages us both to reflect on the *grounds* for accepting claims as true and to accept only objective grounds, that is, grounds that can hold publicly, for all rational beings, which can be sufficient to support the assent of anyone who thinks rationally. So culture also is a critical protection against superstition and fanaticism (*Orient.* 146n).

In a word, the better educated we are, the greater is our *capacity* for autonomy – for the freedom to set morally permissible ends we might adopt and to help others achieve their ends. Normally we have more power to carry out our moral intentions in the world, and that enables us to act more effectively in fulfilling the obligation we have to promote the ultimate total human end of happiness proportionate to virtue.[23]

The ability to set and pursue goals may be an essential prerequisite to being a rational agent, able to act for moral purposes. But Kant does *not* believe that morality grows naturally out of culture so that culture *of itself* will make people morally good. (Culture, Kant adds, also does not automatically make people contented, as Mill later echoed; see *H.H.* 112.) In fact, the very effort to base morality on culture rather than devising a "culture designed to conform with morality" tends to pervert rather than promote morality, for morality cannot be based on the natural, nonmoral development of human powers (*Anthr.* 328; see *M.M.* 434). Moral goodness "lies in the perfection, not of the faculties, but of the will" (*Lect.* 266/26). Moreover, the main drive to the development of culture, if there is any such single direction, is the unsociable desire to win superiority over others. (See *Idea* 22; *Cr.J.* 453.)[24] Because desires in general and this desire in particular tend to generate conflict, ultimately culture alone may only give us greater potential for destructiveness.

14
The Formula of Respect for
the Dignity of Persons

Throughout his moral writings Kant tends to hypostatize our various powers or "faculties." Empirical practical (prudential) reason does this, and pure practical (moral) reason does that. Although his analyses mainly concern specifically human morality, we seldom find flesh-and-blood *people* in the pages of his books. But Kant did recognize that there is an important emotional side to human morality, and he hoped that the Formula of Respect for the Dignity of Persons, with its emphasis on people (or persons), would "bring an Idea of reason . . . nearer to feeling" (*Gr.* 79/436).[1] In this second formula of the Categorical Imperative he deliberately uses more emotional language than he generally allows himself, and he also stresses that the *subjective* foundation of human morality consists of the dispositions of self-respect and respect for others.

What the first formula does not recognize explicitly but the second formula does is that the class of "moral agents" includes (in fact, to the best of our knowledge, is coextensive with the class of) all *human* beings because of, as Kant put it, the "humanity in our person" in contrast to our "animality." (See *Gr.* 66–67/429.) In general, what he means by the term "humanity" is that functional complex of abilities and characteristics that enables us to set ends and make rational choices. (See *Gr.* 82/437; *Rel.* 26/21; *M.M.* 392, 447–48.) In some passages Kant claims that this acknowledgment that human beings are "morally obligatory ends" (or "matter" or "objects") adds something lacking in the purely formal requirement of universality in the first formula. Then he holds that the first formula is an analytic and the second formula is a synthetic (but still a priori) proposition. (See, e.g., *M.M.* 380, 395.)

But it is simply because the first formula requires us to act only on maxims that can function as universal laws, that is, as laws for *all* rational agents, that it does in fact *imply* that we should recognize and respect not only our own autonomy but also that of all other persons, whether human or not. (See *Gr.* 82–83/437–38; *M.M.* 385.) The imperative that we should act only on maxims capable of being universal laws, Kant writes, inevitably "will lead to" our recognizing that we must respect every human person as having objective and intrinsic worth or dignity (*Würde*). (See *Gr* 80/436, 82–83/437–38; *M.M.* 382.)[2] Consequently, Kant also holds that the two formulas are otherwise "at bottom the same," and the second formula is but a different way to "represent" the original ultimate moral Law of Autonomy (*Gr.* 82/437; see 79/436). Each formula will generate the same moral judgments about the moral acceptability of maxims, and both therefore function as the same ultimate moral principle.

Perhaps the best way to show the equivalence of the two formulas and at the same time discourage any tendency to what Kant would have regarded as a "moral mysticism" about the Formula of Respect for the Dignity of Persons is to point out that the second formula simply restates the requirement that moral actions should conform to the Law of Freedom in both its negative and positive meaning. Negatively, we may not act merely heteronomously, only to satisfy our sensuous nature; and positively, as self-determining agents, we must act autonomously. Since the Law of Autonomy is a purely rational norm, it also is objective and holds universally for all rational agents. It therefore requires us not only to obey it in our own actions but also to recognize the right and obligation of every other person to do the same.

In his discussions Kant is occasionally so caught up with his polemic against the heteronomous theories of his predecessors that he may seem to overstress the negative role of the second formula. It is true that the fundamental Idea of a "person" is purely formal, so that the concept of persons "must be conceived only negatively"; it must ignore any positive, empirical information that might distinguish one person from another and so provide the information necessary for acting heteronomously. But that is not equivalent to saying – as Kant seems then to say – *only* that persons are "an end against which we should never act" (*Gr.* 82/437; see 68–69/430; *M.M.* 395, 449–50). Because each person has intrinsic worth just by *being* a person (see *Gr.* 82/437), the second formula must legislate positive as well as negative duties. (See *M.M.* 464–65.) As Kant states elsewhere, it obviously is morally insufficient to fulfill only the negative command not to infringe on the dignity of others merely by avoiding them, for we can do that simply because we are indifferent to or disdainful of them. We must go *beyond* negative duties "to make man as such [our] end," both by striving for our own virtue and by acting justly, benevolently, and beneficently toward others (*M.M.* 395; see *Gr.* 69/430). This positive injunction is stressed in the version of the second formula that reads: "Act according to a maxim of *ends* which it can be a universal law for everyone to have" (*M.M.* 395). However, because it mandates respect for persons independently of any empirical information, the moral law suffers one ineluctable limitation: It is by itself unable to discriminate *between* persons in the matter of wide and positive duties. (See *Gr.* 82/437.)

Several other comments need to be made about the relation between the first and second formulas. First, because the ultimate "moral fact" for us is our awareness of the Law of Autonomy in the form of an imperative, that law is logically prior to any ends it generates or identifies as having objective moral worth. In that sense the first formula is always more fundamental than the second. Moral ends *are* objects of moral willing, but they are still not ultimate. The Law of Autonomy remains "the sole determining ground [*Bestimmungsgrund*] of the pure will" and so *the* ground both for identifying morally obligatory ends and for our obligation to respect, and, when appropriate, to promote them (*Pr.R.* 109; see 109–10). Moreover, the first formula is able to generate obligatory objective ends just because it is purely formal and abstracts from all subjective ends, that is, ends based on desires. The notion of "person" that it generates and grounds in a completely a priori way is as formal a notion as the norm of universality itself. Finally, although Kant clearly held that all our duties can be derived from the second formula, he still believed that the first formula is the better guide for moral judgment. (See *Gr.* 66/429, 80–81/436.) It is not unusual, therefore, for him to explain and defend what respect for persons means and requires of us by appealing to the practical principle of contradiction as stated in the Formula of Universal Law. (See, e.g., *M.M.* 393, 395, 417–18, 422, 437, 450–53.)[3] Questions concerning which specific actions are and are not permissible by the criterion of the second formula, and what it means to treat a person "merely as a means," therefore, often can be clarified by appealing to the first formula.

Nonetheless, because of its welcome emphasis on people – or "persons" or "humanity," as Kant usually puts it – the second formula still proves to be the most attractive version of the Categorical Imperative to many readers. Kant's doctrine concerning the supreme and equal value of persons as persons enunciates a fundamental moral, political, and religious principle presupposed in the ordinary moral judgments of virtually everyone today. It has a majesty that can so fire the moral sensibilities of his readers that whatever problems there may be in using it as a norm, Kant's second formula seems obviously the right view to most people.

Persons and things

The best-known version of the second formula is: "Act in such a way that you always treat humanity, whether in your own person or in the person of any other, never simply as a means, but always at the same time as an end" (*Gr.* 66–67/429). When he explains this formula, Kant writes movingly of the radical difference between persons and mere things.

If things have any value at all, Kant believes, it is only an extrinsic, conditional, and subjective value. That is, things – whether natural objects (products of nature) or artifacts of our own making – are rightly regarded as only relatively good, as valuable only insofar as someone happens to desire them and regard them as valuable. (See *Gr.* 65/428, 77–78/434–35; *M.M.* 434–36.) Things therefore have a price, determined by what people will give and take in exchange for them; and when something can be replaced by something else of equivalent value, it clearly has no unique, absolute, intrinsic worth. If things can be measured in terms of money, then money is regarded as the ultimate standard of value. (See *M.M.* 434–35.)[4]

It makes sense to talk about things as having value in this sense; but what can it mean to say that "man, and in general every rational being, *exists* as an end in himself" and is "necessarily an end for everyone" (*Gr.* 64/428, 66/429; see also *H.H.* 114; *Pr.R.* 87; *M.M.* 383, 394–95, 410, 447)? Kant is obviously not trying to offer a scientific or theoretical description of human beings. His claim on behalf of the dignity of persons is an evaluative claim that does not and cannot rest on any empirical information or on any prior empirical conditions in human desires and inclinations. (See *Gr.* 69–70/430–31.) In that sense, it "admits of no proof" (*M.M.* 395; see *Gr.* 69–70/430–31). The notion of persons is a pure practical Idea of reason, already an enunciation of ordinary moral consciousness.

This is an ethical Idea that with the possible exception of the Stoics and of Plotinus, was absent from Greek moral philosophy.[5] Kant inherited this notion from the Christian theological tradition, but he could not incorporate it into a purely rational philosophy without significant revision. He therefore had to struggle to find new language by which to express his claim. The expressions he finally adopted – each person is "an end in himself" and "an object of free choice" – are not only stylistically ugly but to a degree infelicitous as well. He also uses the terms "end" and "object" to refer both to goals we want and aim to produce by acting as well as to whoever or whatever might be subject to our control, while here he is not concerned with persons as "ends" or "objects" in either of those senses.[6] Persons are "self-existent" (*selbständig*), having intrinsic and objective worth simply by the fact that they exist, apart from any and all subjective prudential considerations. (See *Gr.* 82/437.)

As Kant explains, things and brute animals are only contingently desired (or feared) by and so only possibly valued (or given a negative value) by someone. By contrast, just by their existence, persons necessarily, always, and universally *should* be regarded as having objective, absolute, and intrinsic worth, whether or not they also happen to be desired because they contribute in some way to anyone's happiness. (See *Gr.* 64/428, 70/431.) We should not regard or treat ourselves or any other person *only* or *merely* as a possible object of our desires.

Persons can be and often are regarded as having conditional value, too, insofar as they are regarded as useful, likable, lovable, or admirable. (See, e.g., *Pr.R.* 76–77.) Because we are dependent beings, we do have both the need and the right, subject to moral limitations, to attend to our own needs and the needs of those we care about, and to do so we often must use others; likewise, other people frequently have to use us to achieve their purposes. (See, e.g., *Cr.J.* 172.) Kant was always sensitive to the political reality of how important other people can be to the effective exercise of freedom, and he defines prudence in the sense of "worldly wisdom" as the "skill of a man in influencing others in order to use them for his own ends" (*Gr.* 42n/416n). So we can and necessarily often do treat others as means to our ends, as good insofar as they are useful to us. When we think of people in terms of their skills and abilities, as in business, we often regard them as more or less "marketable" and their time as having a price. (See, e.g., *Gr.* 77–78/435; *M.M.* 434; *Anthr.* 292.) Kant does *not* hold that this is morally wrong. (See *Lect.* 343/120.) However, thinking of our ability to set our own ends only in terms of greater utilitarian advantages means regarding ourselves only as having extrinsic value, and that *is* wrong. (See *M.M.* 434.) What the second formula stipulates is that we may not treat others or allow ourselves to be treated *only* as instrumentally valuable, *merely* as a means to satisfy someone's desires, *merely* as a source of pleasure that is in other respects morally permissible. (See *Pr.R.* 83; *M.M.* 434–35, 450, 462–64.)

Unlike mere things, persons have a status that, as we have seen, Kant calls "humanity" in the sense of a moral personality, in contrast to an individual's empirical or psychological personality. (See *Pr.R.* 85, 162; also *Pu.R.* A365.) According to Kant, the latter is "merely the power to become self-conscious of our self-identity" through temporal or other changes, whereas moral personality refers to a rational agent's ability to act freely, that is, independently of the mechanisms of nature. (See *Pr.R.* 87; *M.M.* 222.) Such agents are regarded as "persons" rather than as "things" because they are by nature free and rational, able and obligated to set goals, to recognize the existence of objective ends, to make genuine choices, and to enact and act on genuinely universal laws of conduct for themselves and all others. (See *Gr.* 76/434, 78–79/435, 82–84/437–39; *Pr.R.* 28–30, 67–68; *Cr.J.* 434; *Rel.* 22–23/27–28; *M.M.* 223, 441, 464.) It is because of being under the moral law that each and every person has an intrinsic, inalienable, unconditional, objective worth or dignity (*Würde*) as a person. (See *Gr.* 79/435–36; *Anthr.* 292.) By virtue of that law we are elevated above being merely part of the natural world. (See *Pr.R.* 86–87; *Cr.J.* 442–43.) We have an absolute and irreplaceable worth, for our value is not dependent on our usefulness or desirability. It "has no price or no equivalent for which the object of esteem could be exchanged" (*M.M.* 462; see 434; *Gr.* 64/428; 77–79/435–36). We may never renounce our right to respect, and we ought never act in such a way as to reduce either ourselves or others to the status of mere things.

As we saw in Chapter 1, Kant's entire moral philosophy can be understood as a protest against distinctions based on the far less important criteria of rank, wealth, and privilege, and perpetuated by religious and political force and fear. (See, e.g., *M.M.* 344–46; *Ed.* 498/119.) Kant's is an ethics of the people, of moral egalitarianism. Nowhere is this more clearly evident than in his second formula. "Respect" is radically different from the notion of "honor," which rests only on societal roles and prudential distinctions. (See *Lect.* 407–12/185–91.) Respect is an attitude due equally to *every* person, *simply* because each is a person, a rational being capable of moral self-determination, regardless of social position, occupational role, learning, wealth, or any other special qualities or talents he or she may or may not possess. (See, e.g., *H.H.* 114; *Pr.R.* 76–77; *M.M.* 434–35; *Lect.* 349/126–27, 461–63/242–44.) Every person possesses moral reason and thereby the ability to achieve the highest achievable good, a good will. To be "a man of principle," that is, an autonomous agent, is possible to a person with "the most ordinary human reason" and is of greater worth than having the greatest talent (*Anthr.* 295). Consequently, everyone should respect everyone else, and everyone should "value himself on a footing of equality with" everyone else (*M.M.* 435; see *Pr.R.* 81n).

Given the political power of both the ecclesiastical authorities and the hereditary aristocracy at the time he was writing, it must have taken some courage for Kant to propose what many of his readers would have regarded as a radical and dangerous political doctrine. Kant felt it necessary, for example, to defend every person's right to morally proper self-respect against the objection that such an attitude smacks of arrogance and self-conceit and violates the ordinary person's obligation to be humble in the presence of civil and religious authority. (See *Rel.* 184n/172.) He also attacked the use of titles typical of a society divided into the titled and powerful on the one hand and the politically powerless peasantry on the other, noting scornfully that the observance of such class distinctions is "a pedantry in which the Germans seem to outdo any other people" (*M.M.* 437; see *Anthr.* 130–31, 319). Some of his remarks were directed explicitly at the peasants, who had been acculturated to believe that they should recognize and be content with their "place" in society: "One who makes himself a worm cannot complain if people step on him" (*M.M.* 437; see 465).

Respect for persons

In his analysis of the nature of morality, Kant showed that a moral agent must be free and autonomous, and in the first formula he set out the Law of Freedom and Autonomy. In the second formula his fundamental appeal is to the *self-awareness* of moral agents. In terms of the phenomenal-noumenal distinction, Kant argues that when we think practically, we find we *must* regard ourselves as noumenal agents, free from the domination of causal laws, both able and obligated to act autonomously, on the basis of our own reason. (See, e.g., *M.M.* 434–35.) This is necessarily "the way in which every other rational being conceives his existence on the same rational ground which is valid for me" (*Gr.* 66/429; see 100–101/447–48).

The second formula therefore requires each of us to regard ourselves and every other person as having a dignity that provides the ground for self-esteem or self-respect (*Selbstschätzung*) as well as the moral right to respect (*Achtung*) from all others. (See *M.M.* 462.) Respect, then, signifies an emotional attitude we owe persons as well as just and courteous conduct displaying that attitude. As we saw in Chapter 10, morality cannot ultimately be based on feelings, only on reason alone, but respect or reverence is a special kind of moral feeling that arises irresistibly within us upon recognition of the existence, the nature, and the demands of the moral law. (See, e.g., *Gr.* 13/399; *M.M.* 214.) As a consequence, we do not have a duty simply to *have* respect for the moral law in persons. Despite the way in which the aristocracy of Kant's time treated the peasants, Kant still insisted that no one can avoid experiencing moral respect for others as persons. (See, e.g., *Pr.R.* 77; *M.M.* 399.) What the second formula requires of us all, he maintained, is that we cultivate and act on that disposition. We can be coerced to behave justly toward others, but the internal attitude of respect cannot be mandated by any external authority, which is why Kant calls this obligation by the special title of "a duty of virtue." (See *M.M.* 383, 435.)

Because we are only contingently moral, however, we may not *want* to recognize that everyone else is our moral equal, and Kant therefore describes respect for persons as "necessary" in the sense of being morally obligatory for us. We have an unconditional duty to recognize the dignity of persons independently of and, if necessary, contrary to any feelings of attraction or aversion based on empirical information. (See *Gr.* 64/428, 80/436; *M.M.* 380–81, 385, 395–96, 448.) All contingent facts about individuals – and our subjective, affective relationships with them – are completely irrelevant both to their inherent value and to the respect we owe them. This is what Kant is getting at when he maintains that the moral idea of a person must "be conceived only negatively" (*Gr.* 82/437–38). Unlike the emotions of affection and love, the moral law neither shows any preference for nor excludes any particular persons or groups. (See *Lect.* 357–60/135–38.) "Being a person" is a pure practical Idea of reason that is defined in a *completely impersonal, formal manner,* so that it in effect is equivalent to the requirement of universality in the first formula. (See *Pu.R.* A365.)

Kant unfortunately does not discuss how we are to go about identifying who bears a moral personality; we obviously must apply that Idea to anyone who in our judgment has the power of pure practical reason. He does say that the only beings we in fact know have the status of persons are human beings, so that it is only to them that we actually have moral duties. (See *M.M.* 241, 442–43.) But once we recognize that, we need not know people personally or know anything else about them as individuals to know how we should regard and treat them. The respect owed persons is owed not to the individuals as such but to the individuals as the bearers of the moral law. (See *Gr.* 16n/401n, 78–79/435; *Pr.R.* 77–78, 131–32.)

The disinterested and impersonal character of the notion of personhood can hardly be stressed too strongly. (See, e.g., *Pr.R.* 21, 110.) It will, as we shall see in Chapter 17, provide the moral basis for a society in which justice is unaffected by personal relationships and the law is administered in a completely impartial manner. For that reason Kant's doctrine has been described as "an ethics for relations between strangers."[7] Earlier Western philosophers had thought of morality as originating within the personal and private relationships of the family and extending outward from there to the public order. Kant, by contrast, situates morality primarily within human public life, which he defines in a formal and impersonal way.

Yet actions have specifically ethical worth only when they are motivated by reverence for the moral law. (See *Gr.* 86/440.) We may therefore have special grounds for respecting individuals who exemplify the moral law in their lives, for example, by fulfilling their duty to develop their talents. (See *Anthr.* 292.) We also may lose respect even for talented individuals whose acts lead us to judge that they have a morally bad character. (See *Pr.R.* 78.) But the fundamental respect owed persons is not based on any individual merit or achievement such as morally good character: "I cannot deny all respect to even the immoral man as a man, even though by his deed he makes himself unworthy of his humanity" (*M.M.* 463; see 448; *Gr.* 16n/401n). However immoral a person may have become and regardless of how hateful his vice may be, Kant insists that such a person still "sees himself as subject to the law of duty, no matter how obscure his ideas about it may be"; he "can never lose all his disposition to good" (*Anthr.* 324 and *M.M.* 464; see *M.M.* 379n; *Gr.* 77/435, 112–13/454–55; *Rel.* 45/41). None of us is morally perfect but we all still possess the intrinsic and innate basis for respect, what Kant calls the "subjective ground" for the possibility of morality – our "humanity" or autonomy in the sense of possessing the *power* of moral reason (*Wille*), the consciousness of being free and so of having a moral personality, that is, the *capacity* to develop a morally good will (*Gr.* 70/431; see 64/428, 79/436, 82/437, 86–87/440, 112–13/454–55; *Pr.R.* 77, 87, 131–32; *Cr.J.* 442–43; *Rel.* 18–19/23; *Anthr.* 324).[8]

Besides stressing the objective and intrinsic worth of persons, the second formula has another, equally important function. It emphasizes *why* we must be moral: to live up to the dignity we have by virtue of being rational beings, to sustain the right we and all other persons have to moral self-esteem. Whenever we immorally cater to our inclinations, we violate our integrity by treating ourselves and others as mere things, as of only instrumental value. (See *M.M.* 420, 435, 450.) Kant therefore sums up the command of the second formula, stated positively, as "Live according to your nature"; that is, act out of respect for yourself as a moral being. (See *M.M.* 419.)

To give the second formula content, we must apply it, as we did the first formula, to the only persons of whom we have any knowledge – ourselves and our fellow human beings. Although the notion of a "moral person" remains completely impersonal, moral reason recognizes that all human agents are both imperfectly rational agents and also moral-physical beings; moral reason also recognizes that all human agents fall into two classes, the agent himself and all others. So the duties we have toward persons can be organized in terms of these classifications. Our positive duties to ourselves concern mainly our own moral perfection, Kant believes, whereas our positive duties to others concern mainly their happiness. (See *M.M.* 385, 398.)

Self-respect

It may seem strange and even self-contradictory, Kant points out, to hold that we have absolute obligations to ourselves, for in other circumstances a person obligating another can also excuse the latter from that obligation. (See *M.M.* 417.) But since all duty involves self-constraint, the ability to excuse ourselves from duties to self would in effect destroy all duties. (See *M.M.* 417–18.) Any conceptual difficulty here can be resolved, Kant argues, by pointing out that, when thinking of duties to self, we regard ourselves simultaneously both as supersensible and as free beings, whose pure rational reason legislates the Law of Autonomy, and natural, sensuous, phenomenal beings, subject to that law.

When he considers the positive and wide duties we have toward ourselves as contingently moral agents, Kant writes that "it is not enough that an action should refrain from conflicting with humanity in our own person as an end in itself: it must also *harmonize with this end*" (*Gr.* 69/430; see *M.M.* 395, 453). What is required positively of us is that we must strive constantly for virtue, by adopting the maxim to do always what we ought, from the motive of duty. (See *M.M.* 387, 446.)

This positive (and, as we saw in Chapter 10, wide) obligation also entails negative duties to ourselves considered as imperfect moral agents, and Kant focuses on three such violations – lying, avarice, and servility. (See *M.M.* 420, 428–37; *Lect.* 399–405/178–84.) Whether considered as isolated actions or, far worse, as settled dispositions, all three are directly contrary to and violate the inherent dignity we have as moral agents – what Kant calls "the dignity of humanity [*Menschheit*] in our own person" (*M.M.* 429; see 403, 420, 429–30). Both lying and miserly avarice attack a person's self-respect. The latter violates our self-respect both by regarding our existence as valuable only as a means to the accumulation of mere things and also by not using such things as are necessary and helpful to our acting dutifully and benevolently. (See *M.M.* 432–34, 452.) Finally, since servility characterizes any attitude or action by which we treat ourselves merely as a means to curry another's favor, it thereby disavows the respect we should have for ourselves; in that sense it underlies every immoral action. (See *M.M.* 434–37.) Kant's discussion of servility reflects again his protest against the class consciousness of eighteenth-century Germany. "Be no man's lackey," he advises. "Bowing and scraping to others" is beneath one's dignity (*M.M.* 436–37).[9]

As we saw in the preceding chapter, when Kant considers what is positively required of us as moral beings with a sensuous or physical nature, he holds that each of us has three morally obligatory natural ends: self-preservation, preservation of the species, and the development and use of our abilities to help us attain our goals. (See, e.g., *M.M.* 421.)[10] Since the moral law obliges us to recognize our own absolute, intrinsic worth as rational agents, it also requires each of us to protect our life and develop our abilities, not for any prudential advantage this may give us but to "live up to," "be worthy of," and "promote" our being persons, our having "humanity." (See *M.M.* 387, 391–92, 444–45; *Gr.* 69/430.)

These positive and wide obligations also entail strict or negative obligations to ourselves as moral beings with a physical nature, again forbidding us to treat ourselves or to consent to be treated merely as means. Kant therefore reconsiders the same examples he used in the *Groundwork* to explain the first formula, but this time from the point of view of self-respect. If we were to adopt the maxim of committing suicide to escape from a painful condition, Kant argues, we should do wrong by regarding ourselves merely as things, as means to a prudentially tolerable quality of life, and we therefore would not respect ourselves as intrinsic ends. (See *Gr.* 67/429.) Destroying one's ability to *be* an end-in-oneself for prudential reasons clearly constitutes an attack on proper self-respect. (See *M.M.* 423; *Lect.* 342–44/119–21.) (Likewise, the immoderate consumption of food and drink and the use of drugs such as opium are wrong because they weaken our ability to act rationally and morally; see *M.M.* 420, 427–28.)

In the *Metaphysics of Morals* Kant uses another argument based on the second formula to judge the maxim of committing suicide, this time because a person no longer feels of any use to anyone. Kant grants that suicide does require some courage and "strength of soul" and that in such characteristics "there is always room for reverence for humanity in one's own person" (*M.M.* 422 and 425; see *Anthr.* 258). Nonetheless, a maxim of committing suicide out of duty is still self-contradictory, for it affirms both that we are subject to duty and that we also should withdraw from all duty. (See *M.M.* 422–23; *Lect.* 373/151.) "Man cannot [i.e., may not] renounce his personality as long as he is a subject of duty, hence so long as he lives," even, for example, to avoid the madness at that time inevitably caused by rabies (*M.M.* 422; see 423).[11]

The third example in the *Groundwork* concerns the development of our talents. Kant maintains that not adopting or acting on a maxim of developing one's abilities does not necessarily imply using oneself merely as a means and so may not directly conflict with one's self-respect. (Perhaps he was thinking of relatively uneducated peasants he knew, who were severely limited in what they could hope to make of themselves but who still possessed moral reason and so the possibility of moral virtue.) But even if such conduct may be "compatible with the maintenance of humanity as an end in itself," it is still not compatible "with the *promotion* of this end" (*Gr.* 69/430). Consequently, as a deliberate policy, such neglect is morally unacceptable.

Finally, in the *Metaphysics of Morals,* Kant once again condemns sexual activity "for mere animal pleasure, without regard for its purpose," because doing so is contrary to the natural law and therefore means using oneself or another merely as a thing, merely as a means to the gratification of one's desires. (See *M.M.* 424–26.)

Our own happiness

Since Kant so often treats the Categorical Imperative mainly as a negative criterion, determining what we must not do, it is easy to forget that, when not contrary to the moral law, the pursuit of pleasure and happiness is not only natural but also morally permissible. (See, e.g., *Gr.* 69/430; *M.M.* 451.) Even more strongly, Kant insists that, in the absence of moral objections, we have a right to tend to our own happiness and welfare: "No one has a right to demand that I sacrifice my own ends if these are not immoral" (*M.M.* 388; see *Pr.R.* 61). We cannot totally renounce our concern for our own well-being, nor should we try to do so. As we shall see when we examine the third formula, it also is Kant's doctrine that happiness is not only our highest natural good but also an essential part of our total final good.

Nonetheless, Kant holds that we do not have a *direct* duty to promote our happiness, but only because, given his analysis of the notion of "duty," it does not make sense to say that we can be under an imperative to do what already is "subjectively necessary" for us to do. (See *M.M.* 222.)

Since every man (by virtue of his *natural* impulses) has *his own happiness* as his end, it would be contradictory to consider this an obligatory end. What we will inevitably and spontaneously does not come under the concept of *duty,* which is *necessitation* to an end we adopt reluctantly. Hence it is contradictory to say that we are *under obligation* to promote our own happiness to the best of our ability. (*M.M.* 386; see 387, 451, see also *Gr.* 12/399; *Pr.R.* 37; *Rel.* 6n/6)

We may have an *indirect* duty to tend to our own happiness, however, and that kind of duty may arise in one or more of four ways. First, quoting Kant, "some [natural] qualities are even helpful to this good will itself and can make its task very much easier" (*Gr.* 2/393).[12] Second, because "adversity, pain, and want are great temptations to transgress one's duty," we have an indirect duty "to ward off poverty as a great temptation to vice" (*M.M.* 388; see *Pr.R.* 93). Put more positively, so that we can more easily attend to our moral obligations, "to provide oneself with such comforts as are necessary merely to enjoy life . . . is a duty to oneself" (*M.M.* 452; see also 216). Third, if we are convinced that we lack the happiness we deserve, we have the right and indirect duty to try to increase our happiness accordingly. (See *Pr.R.* 110–11.) Finally, if the concept of happiness becomes so indefinite and incoherent that the principle of self-love loses its power to motivate us, for example, to tend to our health by eating properly and exercising, then an action that otherwise would be only prudentially good may be morally obligatory as an indirect duty. (See, e.g., *Gr.* 11–13/399.)

But in all such cases, "it is not my happiness but the preservation of my moral integrity that is my end and also my duty"; so "the end is not the agent's happiness but his morality" (*M.M.* 388). We only have a direct obligation to do our duty, but to fulfill our positive duty to strive for moral perfection we also may find ourselves indirectly or incidentally obliged to promote what otherwise would be considered only a prudential matter – either a means to or part of our notion of happiness.

Respect for others

As a practical version of the law of consistency, the second formula of the Categorical Imperative is also a law of justice, commanding us to respect all other human beings. Just as we have a right to self-respect and to the respect of all others, so too they have an equal right to our respect. Simply by virtue of being a person, every person is "equal with all others" (*M.M.* 451, 468).

When he discusses the respect we owe others, Kant's first concern is that we not confuse the *moral* attitude of respect with the *prudential* honor and respect traditionally given the aristocracy and the powerful:

The concept of the respect we are obligated to show other men . . . is only a negative duty. I am not obligated . . . to show [others] positive high esteem. The only reverence to which I am naturally obligated is reverence for the law as such; and to reverence the law is man's universal and unconditional duty to others, which each of them can demand as the respect originally due him. But it is not a duty to hold other men as such in honor or to give them some service in this way. (*M.M.* 467–68; see also 449, 464–65; *Ed.* 498/119)

What the Law of Autonomy requires of us is to recognize that all other persons have objective value and that they therefore are, negatively, "the supreme limiting condition of all subjective ends" (*Gr.* 70/431). Our strict duties to all persons are emphasized in the version of the Formula of Respect for the Dignity of Persons that states, "A rational being, as by his very nature an end and consequently an end in himself, must serve for every maxim as a condition limiting all merely relative and arbitrary ends" (*Gr.* 80/436). This means we should treat others as morally responsible agents, and their acts as explicable in terms of their rational choices, and this in turn requires us to respect the autonomy of other persons. We must restrict what we do in the pursuit of happiness by refraining from using anyone merely as a means, that is, by acting in ways that would endanger or violate anyone else's autonomy and self-respect. (See *Gr.* 82/437; *M.M.* 424, 449.)[13] Whenever we do use others to promote our own welfare, we may not denigrate them to promote our own desires; we may not refuse to recognize that they have a dignity equal to ours by virtue of the presence of the same Law of Autonomy in their reason as in our own.

In his second example in the *Groundwork,* that of making false promises considered from the viewpoint of the second formula, Kant points out that, like physical violence and theft, such promises use another person *only* as a thing, as a means to the agent's end, treating the other person in a way to which he could not assent if he properly respected himself. (See *Gr.* 67–68/429–30.) Lying promises wrong others by violating their right to be treated with respect so as to "be able to share in the end of the very same action" (*Gr.* 68/430). Kant here tacitly appeals to the second of his "dialectical rules" for arriving at the truth, including moral truth: the rule to think from the standpoint of every other person, as a rational, not just as a desiring, being. Once again, this means acting only on maxims that can be willed as universal laws in a morally good world.

Some commentators have therefore concluded that Kant is simply offering a variation of the Golden Rule.[14] But Kant himself explicitly argues against interpreting the Categorical Imperative in this way. When stated as a negative norm (and so in its strictest form), he maintains, the Golden Rule has crucial flaws: It cannot ground duties to self, since it is concerned only with how we treat others; and it cannot ground either positive or negative duties to others, for in regard to the former it does not insist on either the respect owed others or duties of benevolence to them, and in regard to the latter, it is vague enough to be understood as merely a norm of prudential reciprocity. (See *Gr.* 68n/430n.)

Kant's stress on the goal-setting nature of reasoning also underlies his discussion of the coordinate *positive* and wide obligations we have toward others. Respect for others necessarily means making their ends, insofar as possible, our own. (See *Gr.* 69/430.) He again points out that every human being has two necessary ends or goals: As a moral being, each person is obligated to strive for his or her own moral well-being, that is, virtue; and as a moral being with a physical nature (or "humanity"), everyone inevitably wants his or her natural well-being, that is, happiness.

We do not have a positive obligation to assume responsibility for anyone else's virtue, for each person's moral character ultimately can only be that person's own responsibility. Only the individual person can respect him- or herself and adopt the end of virtue. No one can do such things for anyone else. (See *M.M.* 393–94.) Kant writes, "It is contradictory to say that I should make another person's [moral] *perfection* my end and consider myself obligated to promote this," for that would require me to do "what only the other person himself can do" (*M.M.* 386). We have only a negative obligation not to tempt others by scandalous example to act immorally, but this is a wide obligation, for its observance requires the exercise of good judgment, since some people can be scandalized by morally right yet unconventional conduct. (See *M.M.* 394, 464.)

We should not take Kant *completely* at his word here. As Allen Wood has pointed out, Kant was correct in holding that no one can *make* another person virtuous, but "this is *not* what is in question." The real question is "whether I can have an effect on the moral character of another," and the answer is that of course we often can do so.[15] Kant himself stated that he wrote the *Groundwork* to help others make their moral judgments correctly. (See *Gr.* vii–viii/389–90, 22–24/405, 81/437.) Moreover, the "Casuistical Questions" in the *Metaphysics of Morals,* as well as his various writings on moral education, show that Kant himself surely meant to try to contribute to the moral development of others. Since he obviously felt a deep positive obligation to promote the pursuit of virtue by others insofar as he could do so, it is puzzling why he refused to include this obligation among our duties to others. (See *M.M.* 477–85.)

Even when we do not use others for our own purposes, we still have an obligation of "inner freedom" to show positive respect for them as moral-physical beings by adopting their end of happiness, insofar as we can, as if it were our own. (See *M.M.* 450, 488.) As we have just seen, we usually do not have a duty to care about and try to promote our own happiness because we will inevitably do so. But we do not necessarily care about the happiness of others. Unless we happen to have strong altruistic feelings, we can easily be tempted to disregard the legitimate interests of others in the pursuit of our own happiness. Since the Categorical Imperative allows us to adopt only maxims that are fit to serve as universal laws, we are morally entitled to pursue our own otherwise morally permissible happiness only if we also empathically identify with, and contribute to the extent we can to, others' pursuit of morally permissible happiness. (See *Pr.R.* 34; *M.M.* 387–89, 393, 451.) So the moral obligation to contribute to the happiness of others rests on the impersonal Idea of personhood and not on their happiness's being of any personal concern to us. (See *Gr.* 89/441.)

Kant summarizes this obligation as a "law of love" but then quickly adds that we need to understand the term "love" rightly.[16] What is meant here by "love" is *moral* love, which is *not* a feeling or inclination, "for it is not possible for man to love someone merely on command" (*Pr.R.* 83). As Kant interprets it, sympathy (*Sympathie*) is merely emotional empathy with others, and we do not have a duty to have such feelings nor can our duties to others be based on feelings. (See *M.M.* 456; *Lect.* 413–14/192–93; *Ed.* 487/97–98.) Rather, moral love (like moral respect) is a practical attitude of the will toward others, regardless of whether we feel any affection for them so that we take pleasure in their happiness and feel pain because of their suffering. (See *Gr.* 13/399; (*M.M.* 401, 448–50, 452, 456.) Although moral love may seem only a wide, imperfect variation of respect, it does go beyond the command of *strict* justice (*Recht*) that we not violate the autonomy or freedom of others (their rational will). It positively requires us to develop kindness (*Leutseligkeit*), that is, a "habit of harmony with all other men," by being concerned about the matter of their will, namely, their wishes, desires, and needs (*Lect.* 452/232; see *Gr.* 13/399; *M.M.* 230).

More specifically, moral love requires that we bear a genuinely benevolent attitude toward all other human beings – that, regardless of whether we like others, we adopt a maxim of benevolence that does not allow us to be completely indifferent to others but instead requires us to will and take satisfaction in their well-being and happiness. (See *M.M.* 393, 449–51.) Stated negatively, the obligation of benevolence forbids us to refuse to wish anyone well. Again, according to the moral requirement of universal law, it is morally permissible for us to be benevolent toward ourselves only if we also are benevolent to every other human being as well. (See, e.g., *M.M.* 441, 451.) Misanthropy, therefore, is contrary to our obligation of benevolence. (See *M.M.* 402, 450.)

Admittedly, Kant believes, benevolence alone is not much. Although we must take an interest in the well-being of all others, the "interest I take in [them] is as slight as an interest can be. I am only not indifferent with regard to [them]" (*M.M.* 451). Moreover, a law of mere well-wishing does not actually help anyone. (See *M.M.* 451–52.) The biblical injunction "Love your neighbor as yourself" means, as Jesus immediately explained, that we should do good to them. (See *Gr.* 13/399; *M.M.* 450–51; also Matt. 5.44, 22.39.) So benevolence must be practical, that is, show itself in our adopting a maxim of beneficence – of *acting* benevolently – not from inclination or affection for others but from duty. That is, we should make the morally permissible ends of others (which can be summed up under the title of their happiness) our own obligatory end by actually promoting and contributing to their well-being, without thought of gaining anything by doing so. (See *M.M.* 387–88, 391–93, 401–2, 441, 449–52.)

The ground for the obligation of beneficence, like that of benevolence, lies in the requirement of the second formula that morally acceptable maxims must be able to serve as laws in a moral world in which persons are given the respect they deserve. When Kant considers the fourth example in the *Groundwork* from the point of view of the second formula, he admits that the maxim of neither asking for nor giving help is not necessarily intrinsically self-contradictory; a world in which that maxim would hold as a law is possible. But we do not fully respect others as we should if we do not make their interests our own and help them insofar as we can, and we therefore are morally obligated to sacrifice part of our own well-being for others. (See *Gr.* 69/430.) Although a maxim of mere benevolence and of not interfering with, or acting against, anyone's pursuit of happiness does not directly conflict with our obligatory respect for others, it still does not sufficiently promote that end. (See *Gr.* 69/430; *M.M.* 393–95, 453, 469.) As we already saw in the case of benevolence, the requirement of universal law states that we are morally entitled to be beneficent to ourselves only if we are also beneficent to others.

Everyone's right to happiness is subject to the moral restriction that it be "in exact proportion to morality" (*Pr.R.* 110–11). But since we cannot know the measure of our own virtue, much less that of others, only an omniscient being could use that norm to decide how to act beneficently. The only usable *moral* norm available to us in acting beneficently is the familiar application of the Categorical Imperative to *individual* maxims of actions to determine whether a particular contribution to the happiness of another is morally permissible.[17] This means that we need to be very careful about refusing to help others we are tempted to judge to be not morally worthy of our help.

Except in the case of small children and the mentally ill, when we make the ends of others our own and help them achieve their desires, respect requires us to take into account what *they* need and want, what *they* count as making them happy. (See *M.M.* 388, 393, 468.) But we still are not obligated to follow their wishes if we disagree with their judgments, as long as they do not have a strict claim in justice to a particular kind of help (*M.M.* 388; see also 454).[18]

The *positive* obligation of benevolence is a wide and imperfect duty, and, like all such obligations, requires us only to adopt and act on the *maxim* of practical benevolence. Although this obligation specifies no definite limits, we clearly are not obliged to sacrifice all our own well-being in order to promote that of others. When made a universal law, Kant writes, the maxims that we should completely sacrifice our happiness for the happiness of others or, alternatively, that we should exhaust our own resources until we can no longer help others but instead need their help are self-contradictory. (See *M.M.* 393, 454.) Since each of us has limited resources and power, we also cannot contribute equally to the well-being of every human being, nor are we obligated to do so. Finally, universal benevolence does not require us to be benevolent toward everyone equally except by minimal well-wishing.[19] Only God, having infinite power, has the resources to be equally beneficent toward everyone.

It is true that we may have special moral obligations to individuals, for example, the duty to show gratitude toward those who have acted beneficently toward us. (See *M.M.* 454–55.) But any special obligations of beneficence we may have only to some individuals cannot be specified ahead of time, in an a priori way:

Since [the actual ways in which we exercise beneficence] are not principles of obligation for men as such to one another, they cannot really comprise a part of the *metaphysical* first principles of the doctrine of virtue. They are only rules modified according to the differences of the subjects to whom we *apply* the principle of virtue (on its formal side) in cases that arise in experience (the material). (*M.M.* 468; see also 393, 452)

Unlike the demand of justice, the positive obligation to beneficence is indeterminate in the sense that it specifies neither the ways in which nor the extent to which we must follow it and contribute to the well-being of different individuals or groups. (See *M.M.* 469, 393.) The actual use of the maxim of beneficence depends too heavily on empirical factors, such as the extent of our resources and the severity of the needs of others, to admit of any a priori and universal claims. (See *M.M.* 448, 468.)

If we were to interpret moral egalitarianism as a strict but positive duty, we would then be forced to hold that all empirical information about individuals and all emotional and familial ties are morally irrelevant to our personal decisions about how to fulfill the duty of beneficence.[20] But Kant again shows his common sense as well as his sensitivity to ordinary moral convictions by holding that we can make such decisions rationally and rightly *only* by taking empirical facts and possible consequences into consideration. In his view, for example, in an either/or case, all other things being equal, it would be morally permissible for a person to choose to save the life of a family member rather than the life of a stranger.

As we have seen several times, the exact ways in which a person may fulfill his or her positive duties, here the duty of beneficence, may and must be left up to that person's judgment, to be decided only on the basis of prudential considerations, including even a cost-benefit analysis when we judge that that is prudentially appropriate. So, Kant argues, "in acting I can, without violating the universality of my maxim, vary the degree greatly according to the different objects of my [moral] love" (*M.M.* 452).

Kant therefore does not try to tell us what features about others we *must* regard as relevant to a decision about whom to help or how, because such decisions rest with our judgment of each individual situation. He does suggest that differences in social rank, age, sex, health, economic situation, education, and even personality traits all may be legitimately taken into account. (See *M.M.* 468–69.) He also states that, in general, we are obligated to show greater benevolence toward those closest to us (*M.M.* 451; see also 452). But he leaves the term "nearer" (or "closer" – *näher*) undefined, so that, as appropriate to the circumstances, it may include physical proximity, emotional closeness, blood kinship, ideological agreement, and even cultural similarities.[21] The only more specific comment he makes is that, since we are closest to ourselves (in every sense), we are *not* bound literally to love others as we love ourselves; "even according to duty" we are morally permitted to tend to our own needs first (*M.M.* 451). Since we are now in the area of prudential judgments, we are not obligated to ignore our personal concerns about ourselves and those we love, and what will be most important in any individual case will depend on the particular facts of that case.

208

Problems

Although the Formula of Respect for the Dignity of Persons carries us a good way toward clarifying and organizing many of our moral duties, it still leaves us with some serious problems.

One problem arises out of the very fact that the notion of "respect for persons" involves an emotion, albeit a moral emotion. When we become involved in disputes over whether a particular course of action means treating someone *only* as a means and therefore not respecting his or her dignity, it is all too easy to fall into what may be called "moral sentimentalism" by using the phrase "respect for people," along with its powerful emotional connotations, not as a purely rational argument but as an emotional sledgehammer. Although Kant does not explicitly address this problem, unquestionably it lies behind his recommendation that we clarify what respect for people means by using the "strict method," that is, the purely formal first formula of the Categorical Imperative. (See *Gr.* 80–81/436.)[22]

Moreover, there remain problems about how to distinguish, as Kant does, between persons doing harm and persons doing wrong. This difficulty relates to the morally ambiguous status of natural goods, such as physical and psychic health, safety, and welfare. Clearly, as the only always absolute good, virtue always takes precedence over any natural good, but, as we have seen, depending on the situation, what is naturally good may be amoral, morally permissible, morally forbidden, or either indirectly or directly morally obligatory. Consequently, it is not possible, in the abstract, to give a single, correct answer to questions such as, What is the value of human life? In Kant's theory, human life is not automatically equivalent to personhood; and insofar as it is simply a natural good, it is not in itself an absolute good. In most cases, the promotion of virtue may require, as we have seen, the protection of one's life and health; but in some other circumstances endangering and even sacrificing one's life may be morally obligatory.

However rightly Kant's second formula stresses the notion of self-respect and respect for others, applying that norm often means we must distinguish between those instances in which human life may be regarded only as a natural good and those in which it must be regarded as a moral good. Other situations require us to judge the difference between harm (which may be amoral or even a moral good) and moral wrong. The ineluctable role of judgment in such matters means that there can be and have been deep differences of opinion on important moral issues among ethicists within the Kantian tradition.

Technological advances (as in genetic engineering) are giving us new and powerful research techniques and opening new choices to us. But the same new scientific information and technological progress that give rise to new moral problems in medicine and the law, sometimes referred to as "wrongful birth" and "wrongful life" decisions, seem impotent to help us resolve these problems. How *do* we rationally arbitrate between different judgments about when it is morally permissible for us to endanger and even terminate human life, either in those cases in which there are compelling prudential reasons for doing so or in those in which there are conflicting grounds of moral obligation? Some ethicists believe, for example, that, when considering terminal illness that will inevitably rob a person of all capacity for moral judgment as well as dignity, Kant's own discussions of suicide (including the example of the person with rabies) are clearly inadequate, that there are stronger grounds to support the view that we have not only a right but an obligation to terminate human life, whether one's own or another's, out of respect for moral autonomy.

Finally, the resolution of many of those same moral problems requires us to decide who is or is not to be considered a person.[23] What is the status of the claim "This is a member of the class of persons"? There are no empirical facts that can function as identifying criteria for the purely rational Idea of a person. Kant insists that we must respect all persons because of their ability to be autonomous, to enact universal moral laws, even if they do not actually behave autonomously. (See, e.g., *M.M.* 241, 442.) He thinks we are entitled, for our practical purposes, to attribute noumenal freedom to others like us if they are "given [to us] as an object of experience" (*als Gegenstand der Erfahrung gegeben sein; M.M.* 442). But he does not tell us how we go about deciding in borderline cases whether a particular entity may or should be regarded as a human being but not a person – or as a person even if not a human being. Among the problematic cases are not only fetuses but also the severely and profoundly retarded, the irrevocably senile or comatose, and animals with verbal ability, such as chimpanzees and porpoises.

Some philosophers today even argue for "plant rights" and "animal rights." Kant himself clearly did not believe in such rights, certainly not if such claims are based only on an ability to feel pleasure and pain, which in themselves are only naturally good and evil. (See *M.M.* 442; *H.H.* 114.)[24] As Kant saw it, plants and animals have no intrinsic, unconditional worth; they are here only to serve our purposes. (See *Cr.J.* 426–27.) But he also says we still have duties *toward* them that are in reality duties we have *to* ourselves; and on that basis he holds that unnecessary and painful scientific experiments on animals "are to be abhorred" (*M.M.* 443; see *Lect.* 413/191, 458–60/239–41). Because children do not possess the developed power of reason required for the imputation of personal responsibility, in at least one passage Kant seems to imply they are not moral beings. (See *Ed.* 492/108.) In another, however, he holds that they should be treated as moral beings, albeit without the full rights of citizenship. (See *M.M.* 314–15.) He holds that states have the right to "charge the people with the duty of not letting [children] perish knowingly"; and he calls infanticide "murder" and "the unlawful killing of another person." (*M.M.* 326–27.)[25] He also argues that it is only because some of his contemporaries were not sufficiently morally enlightened that they considered the killing of illegitimate children (children therefore born outside the protection of the law) not to be a capital offense (*M.M.* 336–37). But he is silent on questions concerning the moral status of fetuses.

That people may not necessarily agree with one another even when they use the same moral principle is not a problem specific to Kant's theory but can and does arise in every moral theory. However, it still is true that Kant seemed to promise more than other philosophers, particularly in the matter of adjudicating morally problematic maxims. (See, e.g., *Gr.* 20–21/404.) As it turns out, in helping us resolve many of the most troubling contemporary moral problems, this promise seems to remain largely unfulfilled.

15
The Formula of Legislation for a Moral Community

The first formula of the Categorical Imperative commands us to act autonomously, to recognize our responsibility to be moral lawmakers in the sense of adopting only maxims fit to serve as the formal structure of an ideal teleological moral world. The second formula commands us to recognize that all persons have objective value and so are obligatory "matter," requiring us to limit our pursuit of private ends both by self-respect and by respect for others. The third formula is the most comprehensive variation of the Categorical Imperative, combining the Ideas of form and matter stressed in the first and second formulas. (See *Gr.* 80/436.) Because this formula also calls attention to the nature of the total final good we are to promote, Kant returns again and again to discussions of the Ideas emphasized in it. Yet, because the Idea of the highest good "arises out of morality and is not its basis," Kant still tells us to use the first formula as our ultimate moral norm (*Rel.* 5/5; see *Gr.* 81/436). As a consequence, he offers only a few variations of the third formula, one of which is: "All maxims as proceeding from our own making of law ought to harmonize with a possible kingdom of ends as a kingdom of nature" (*Gr.* 80/436).[1]

We have seen how often Kant insists that our reason is essentially a teleological faculty; we need ends toward which to direct our rational activity. (See, e.g., *Pu.R.* A797/B825, A815/B843; *Rel.* 4/4.) But not just *any* ends will do. In our search for both truth and goodness, we are not satisfied with partial, conflicting, or only contingent answers. It is the nature of reason to seek and to rest content finally only with an end that is objective, systematically complete, absolute, and necessary. "The unconditioned is the ultimate goal at which [reason] aims" (*Cr.J.* 401; see *Pu.R.* A797/B825).

As we have also seen, the most fundamental epistemological question is, What can I know? We further have seen that, for our theoretical purposes, we must regard the empirical, phenomenal world not only as causally determined but also as "Nature," that is, as a dynamic and systematic, teleological and self-organizing whole. When we turn to our practical concerns, Kant holds that the most fundamental question is, What ought I to do? This, as we have seen, is a question only moral reasoning can answer, and the answer to it is that one ought to be virtuous, by adopting and acting on the Law of Autonomy.

The next question is, If I do what I ought to do, what may I then hope? Or, put more generally and impersonally, What should be the result of human moral agents' acting rightly? (*Pu.R.* A805/B833; see *Rel.* 5/4; *Anthr.* 227).

Only the answer to that question, which Kant addresses most fully in his *Religion,* can give full meaning to our lives. (See *Pr.R.* 108–9; *Rel.* 6n/6; *T&P* 280n.) Western philosophy traditionally had regarded this question as falling within the province of theoretical wisdom. Kant, however, has argued that only moral reason has the ability and the right to identify the final end (*Endzweck*) of human life, an end that includes and, when necessary, conditions all our other ends. (See, e.g., *Pu.R.* A840/B868; *Pr.R.* 87ff; *Cr.J.* 453–56; *Rel.* 6n/6.)

The third formula therefore commands us both to think of "what sort of [ideal] world [morally virtuous people] would create, under the guidance of practical reason, were such a thing in [their] power" and also to "make the highest good possible in the world your own final end" (*Rel.* 5/5 and 6n/7; see *Pr.R.* 43; *Cr.J.* 450, 453). Our own moral reason fulfills the first task by presenting us with the Idea of a kingdom of ends as the morally ultimate end for all human beings. The first two formulas do not deny the social nature of human beings, but their stress is mainly on the individual who has duties both toward self and other individuals. By contrast, the third formula explicitly identifies the Idea of the moral world as *social* in nature, a world in which the human species collectively achieves its ultimate goal as a species, as "humanity." (See *Pu.R.* A814/B842; *Gr.* 70–71/431–32; *Rel.* 97–98/89; *Anthr.* 277.) As we shall also see when we examine his philosophy of history in the next chapter, Kant contends that the collective destiny of the human species is not reducible to individual members living at any particular time. The third formula therefore indicates that the complete good and the final goal toward which we must strive is not merely an aggregate of the moral accomplishments of individuals but is also a collective goal, a moral community or "kingdom of ends," in which "the purest morality throughout the world [is] combined with such universal happiness as accords with it" (*T&P* 279; see *Pr.R.* 110–11; *Cr.J.* 453).

To contribute to the end of the species as a whole, insofar as we can do so, by furthering the coming of the kingdom of ends is a special duty, unlike any other (*T&P* 279–80n and *Rel.* 97/89; see *Gr.* 80/436; *Pr.R.* 4–5, 120). It is "a duty which is *sui generis,* not of men toward men, but of the human race toward itself. For the species of rational beings is objectively, in the idea of reason, destined for a social goal, namely, the promotion of the highest [*Höchste*] as a social good [*als eines gemeinschaflichen Guts*]" (*Rel.* 97/89).[2] Because the highest good is "the entire object [*das ganze Objekt*] of pure practical reason, reason commands us to contribute everything possible to its realization: Make the highest good possible in the world your final end!" (*Pr.R.* 119 and *Rel.* 6n/7; see 126).

Finally, to be a genuinely comprehensive end, "the necessary unity of all possible ends," the ideal world that moral reason projects must span the epistemological distance between the noumenal and the phenomenal viewpoints, between freedom and nature, uniting them in a systematic harmony. (See *Rel.* 5/5; *Cr.J.* 429–54.) We clearly cannot understand how this can be accomplished, but nonetheless our moral reason insists that the ideal consequences of our acting dutifully is "a possible kingdom of ends as a kingdom of nature," a unification of the moral world and the world of nature so as to create "the world in its full perfection as a beautiful moral whole" (*Gr.* 8on/ 436n and *M.M.* 458; see *Gr.* 74/433).

A moral community

In the ideal world, the kingdom of ends, at which moral reasoning aims, the Categorical Imperative is, of course, the ultimate norm that defines the formal relations between persons. (See *Gr.* 74–75/433.) The kingdom of ends must be a community in which "each individual is his own judge" and the members obey only laws they can rationally prescribe for themselves. (See *Rel.* 95/87.) Consequently, each person is both head and subject of that world, for each is subject only to laws to which he or she can rationally assent as legislator, laws mandated by or permitted by the Law of Autonomy or, alternatively, by the Law of Respect for the Dignity of Persons (*Gr.* 75/433). As the first formula stresses, those maxims are universals because they do not rest on any individual's or group's special interests. (See *Gr.* 72/432.) As the second formula emphasizes, the dignity of each person rests on the capacity to adopt and act on universal laws, and each person's virtue depends on obeying those same laws.

Kant holds that this moral union can and should exist in three distinct forms, although he may not always seem to distinguish clearly between them. (Some have taken this as evidence that Kant often is not so much expressing a finished doctrine as working toward one.) First, Kant states, the ideal moral world ought to be "a practical idea, which really can have, as it also ought to have, an influence upon the sensible world" (*Pu.R.* A808/B836). So the Idea of a moral community defines the associations between people in this world and does so in two forms, each of which can only approximate the ideal: first, in a political or juridical way, both in just states and in a world community of such states; and, second and more perfectly, in a nonpolitical ethical community. Kant portrays the third and perfect form of the kingdom of ends as occurring in a future life, by which he generally seems to mean a life beyond death. (See *Gr.* 127/462–63.)[3]

As the ideal for all social unions, the Idea of the moral community first must underlie the structure of the just political state. The existence of the political state is critical, for Kant was convinced that human moral life cannot flourish outside civil society. But not even the best civil arrangements on either a national or an international level or both can completely satisfy the requirements of moral reason. As we shall see in the next chapter, juridical obligations should enforce the negative requirement that our outer behavior be legally correct, that is, follow the letter of the moral law by not violating the external rights of others. But the laws of a state cannot address our inner duties of ethical motivation (acting from the motive of duty) and ethical ends (positively respecting all persons). (See *Rel.* 95/87–88; *Anthr.* 332n.) Moreover, because the citizens of a state remain in an "ethical state of nature," indifferent to or hostile to others, laws concerning external rights must all be coercively enforced by the state.

Juridical societies are not the only societal goal of moral reason in this world. Kant sees only one hope for widespread success in promoting the spread of moral virtue and fidelity in virtue and in combating what, in his *Religion,* he calls "the radical evil in human nature," that is, our propensity to unethical attitudes and unsociable actions toward others. That hope lies with "the establishment and spread of a society in accordance with, and for the sake of, the laws of virtue, a society whose task and duty it is rationally to impress these laws in all their scope upon the entire human race" (*Rel.* 94/86). The "ethical society" Kant envisions is a visible community whose members are committed to going beyond the requirements of mere legality to obey the moral law because it is the moral law and to respect all persons because they are worthy of such respect. Kant consequently stresses the *positive,* voluntary, systematic harmony of purposes within such a community. Moreover, since it is based on the Law of Autonomy, the ethical community should be characterized by universality. It should be "cosmopolitan" and extend beyond civil and national boundaries so as to be able to influence "the whole of mankind" (*Rel.* 96/88).

Kant admits that not everyone already living a virtuous life feels a great personal need to identify with others in an ethical community. But he believes the final social good "cannot be achieved merely by the exertions of" individuals concerned only with their own moral progress (*Rel.* 97/89). It is not enough for individuals to live in a merely "accidental" agreement with others who also are striving to live virtuously. (See *Rel.* 94–95/85–86.) There is a "moral need" for a *union* of the entire human species "held together by cosmopolitan bonds" (*Rel.* 97–98/89; *Anthr.* 333). For one thing, it is part of our nature as sensible beings to need some visible representation of what is unobservable, here the unseen moral world, the invisible kingdom of God. (See *Rel.* 192/180.) For another, both our individual moral destinies and continual progress in moral enlightenment are inextricably tied to our relations with others. Without a public union with one another, a union held together by ethical bonds, people are too prone to remain in an ethical state of nature and, therefore, to tempt one another to act immorally rather than to support each other's moral striving. (See *Rel.* 94/85, 97/88, 151/139, 158/146.)

There are several limitations even on this ideal community, each of which we already have seen and each of which helps Kant to avoid an unrealistic utopianism. First, we are bound to respect our fellow humans, but we still are not required to like them all nor are we morally worse if we find we cannot do so. Second, we should retain a healthy mistrust of any efforts to ban all possible disagreements or competition between individuals and groups in the name of moral harmony and social cooperation, as so many historical religious communities have done. (See *Rel.* 95/86.)[4] Like a republican political union, an ethical union must respect freedom of thought and discussion, both of which are essential for the exercise of reasoning, for the pursuit of truth and virtue. The "dialectical rules" for arriving at the truth and the public forum of open debate remain the only ways in which to expose and peacefully dispose of historical errors and ensure insofar as possible a harmony based on common rational consent. (See *Pu.R.* A738–39/B766–67; *Cr.J.* 294; *Rel.* 114/105, 122–23/112–13; *T&P* 305; *M.M.* 307, 327; *Anthr.* 228; *Logic* 57/62–63.)

Moreover, while an ethical community aims to go beyond the requirements of justice, it stands in danger of becoming a tyranny unless it also recognizes and obeys the requirements of public justice. Therefore it may not legislate rules that conflict with duties already legitimately imposed on its members as citizens. No state has the right to intrude into the internal life of an ethical community, but a state may legitimately restrict any activity that "might prejudice the public peace" (*M.M.* 327).

Unlike the state, an ethical commonwealth explicitly recognizes the importance of moral motives. But it may not use statutory laws to try to compel its members to act from the motive of duty. Such an inner duty must be freely self-legislated, and any effort to coerce it externally is self-contradictory and tramples on autonomy in the name of the moral law. (See *Rel.* 101–2/93, 115/105, 122/112, 157/145.) This is also true of the duty of the members of an ethical society not only to respect all persons as moral ends but also to show that respect by acting justly toward them and by making the happiness of others their own end. (See *Rel.* 95/87.) Kant says remarkably little about this latter obligation, probably because, as we have seen, the fulfillment of wide duties cannot be systematically and completely set out in a metaphysics of morals. Instead, he concentrates most of his attention on a formal structural analysis of the ethical society. But we do know that we should not exhaust our own resources in helping others so that we instead need their help, and, as Kant makes clear in his political theory, no community should assume a paternalistic role, which would deny respect for the individual or discourage each person's obligation to take responsibility for living his or her own life autonomously. (See, e.g., *T&P* 290–99.)

The ethical community: a church

Kant obviously intended his title, a "kingdom [or realm] of ends" (*Reich der Zwecke; Gr.* 74/433), to have religious overtones, recalling the Kingdom of God proclaimed in the Gospels. Kant's other names for it have even stronger religious connotations: *corpus mysticum,* or "mystical body," which he borrowed from Saint Paul's title for the invisible church, and *regnum gratiae,* or "kingdom of grace" (in contrast to the kingdom of nature), a phrase he borrowed from Leibniz. (See *Pu.R.* A808/B836, A812/B840.)

Kant held that in this world the otherwise invisible ethical society should in fact take on the visible form of a church, for, as he repeatedly claimed, "morality leads ineluctably to religion" and especially to Christianity (*Rel.* 6/5; see 6n/7; *Pr.R.* 129). The moral law does so, Kant writes, by leading us to regard it as universally binding and as worthy of reverence as if it were divine legislation. (See *Gr.* 71/431.) In this way we are led to think of God, "who is worthy of adoration only because of His holiness and as Legislator for virtue" (*Rel.* 183/171). Only God can know the human heart, and since the members of an ethical society must observe inner as well as outer moral duties, it is fitting that such a community be *thought of* as a "people of God," whose obedience to the moral law is not coercively enforced like civil obedience (*Rel.* 99/91; see 98–100/90–91; *Pr.R.* 127–28). Moreover, Kant was also convinced that the grace of God is somehow (however incomprehensibly) necessary to make such a community fully actual. (See esp. *Rel.* 100/92.)

Kant therefore defined the essence of religion as consisting in "the performance of all human duties as [if they were] divine commands" (*Rel.* 110/100). But thinking of God as moral ruler of this community does *not* mean believing that ethical laws actually historically originated as commands of God, for taking God to be the author of those laws or his will to be the basis of duty would reduce obedience to those laws to heteronomy. (See *Pr.R.* 129; *M.M.* 227.) Understood correctly, then, the moral law and the "bare idea of a moral Lawgiver for all men" are analytically equivalent (*Rel.* 6n/6; see 181–82/170). Our duties still are laws of, for, and between human beings as rational agents. (See *Pr.R.* 129; *M.M.* 227.)

Every rational agent, Kant therefore writes, belongs to the kingdom of ends "as its head, when as the maker of laws he is himself subject to the will of no other"; but a member may regard himself *always* as the sovereign of this moral realm "only if he is a completely independent being, without needs and with an unlimited power adequate to his will," namely, if that member is God (*Gr.* 75/433–34; see *Pr.R.* 82–83). So Kant calls the ultimate moral ideal of the Kingdom of God "the highest derived good," for only God should be regarded as the highest "original" or independent good (*Pu.R.* A814/B842; *Orient.* 139; *Pr.R.* 125, 132).

Nevertheless, every member of this kingdom must still have equal and full rights of citizenship. Since the Idea we have of God and of God's will originates in our own reason, Kant writes, and since "there is no reason under the law of equality why obedience to duty should fall only to me and the right to command only to him [God]," we still have the right to regard ourselves as sharing the headship of the kingdom of ends with God insofar as we are legislators in that world (*P.P.* 350n). If we were only subject to that legislation, we would have no dignity as persons, for we would be reduced to the status of things, of slaves. (See *Pr.R.* 131–32; *M.M.* 227, 241, 439–41, 486–87.)

As we shall see in Chapter 18, Kant believed that the historical churches had tended to contaminate the pure moral virtue of their members. (See *Rel.* 171/158, 177–78/165–66.) But he still did not want churches or their traditions to disappear, for he believed they are the vehicles necessary to convey pure moral and religious faith. (See *Rel.* 103/94, 106/97, 135n/126.) Nor did he think that religion should be reduced to morality. He did not entitle his book *Religion of Pure Practical Reason Alone,* but *Religion within the Limits of Reason Alone.* He did hope, however, that through the influence of the Enlightenment, ecclesiastical faith eventually would be purified of all morally perverse institutional accretions. (See *Rel.* 121–22/112.) Then everyone would recognize the moral law as supreme over all institutions, including and especially the church.

Kant had another reason for thinking of the moral ideal in religious terms: The *full* achievement of the final necessary end of pure practical reason – the kingdom of ends in its third, fullest, and most perfect form – requires God actually to be its head. (See *Gr.* 85/439.) "This duty will require the presupposition of another idea, namely, that of a higher moral Being through whose universal dispensation the forces of separate individuals, insufficient in themselves, are united for a common end" (*Rel.* 98/89). Christianity alone, not any philosophers, had depicted the concept of that final highest good (the Kingdom of God) correctly, as consisting of both holiness *and* happiness, not only for individuals but for the human species as a whole. The *complete* final good attainable by human beings (our *bonum consummatum* or *summum* or *perfectissimum* or *höchstes Gut* – our highest good) is a synthesis of both holiness (our *bonum supremum* – supreme good – *das oberste Gut*) and happiness and well-being proportionate to our virtue. (See *Pu.R.* A810/B838; *Pr.R.* 110, 113, 125–26, 129; *Rel.* 6/5, 104/95.) Because we cannot actually attain this good by ourselves, we need the assistance of a "holy Author of the world." (See *Pr.R.* 127–29, 127n.) (Likewise, only through a Kingdom possessing the power of God can "nature and morality come into a harmony"; see *Pr.R.* 128–30.)

This last part of Kant's theory will require further analysis. For now, it is enough to say that, in both its forms in this world, as a political, juridical union and as an ethical society, the kingdom of ends is clearly humanly possible, at least in an imperfect form. It is possible in that it is conceivable as the effect of people acting on the Law of Autonomy and thereby also fulfilling the demand of the third formula. (See *Pu.R.* A808/B836; *Gr.* 80n/436n, 83–84/438; *Pr.R.* 43; *T&P* 282; *M.M.* 405.) "The moral law demands that the highest good possible through our agency should be realized" (*Rel.* 5/5). We therefore are obligated to strive with all our power to bring the world, "so far as possible, into conformity with the idea" of a moral community (*Pu.R.* A808/B836; see *Pr.R.* 43; *T&P* 279–80n).

The supreme good and the complete good

Kant's inclusion of happiness in the final comprehensive human good raises a number of questions.[5] The first concerns his justification for including happiness in our final good at all.

As we saw in Chapter 4, "happiness" is the term Kant uses to refer comprehensively to our well-being taken as a whole. Although our tendency to regard and pursue happiness as our predominant good is the chief rival and impediment to moral virtue, our natural desires and inclinations are not of themselves morally evil, nor are they the cause of moral evil, which can be attributed only to our own will. Kant insists that "natural inclinations, *considered in themselves* are *good*," even if only naturally good (*Rel.* 58/51).

Therefore, conflicts between self-love and the moral law, between happiness and virtue, are a contingent and *not* a necessary matter: "This *distinction* of the principle of happiness from that of morality is *not for this reason an opposition* between them, and pure practical reason does not require that we should renounce the claims to happiness; it requires only that we take no account of them whenever duty is in question" (*Pr.R.* 93, emphasis mine; see also 35).[6] Because we are dependent as well as rational agents, happiness and virtue are both genuine practical goods for us. We have both a subjectively unavoidable interest in our own natural well-being or happiness and an objectively obligatory interest in our moral well-being or virtuous character. (See *Rel.* 6n/6.) As different as these two interests and their grounds are, we cannot renounce either.

Good moral character or a good will is the one unique, incomparable, unconditional, intrinsic, and supreme good. (See, e.g., *Pr.R.* 128.)[7] It therefore is "the supreme condition" of our worthiness to pursue and have whatever else may be good (*Pr.R.* 110, 120). For its sake, then, the moral law has the right to issue commands "even to the detriment of all my inclinations" and in individual instances "can even reduce happiness to less than zero without nature proceeding contrary to its purpose" (*Gr.* 15/401 and 7/396).[8] But our moral reason still does not command us to renounce our own happiness *completely*. Indeed, it should not try to do so, for we are incapable of obeying such a command; we can never rid ourselves of all our needs and desires; we cannot totally give up our concern for our own well-being. (See, e.g., *Gr.* 12/399; *Pr.R.* 25; *Rel.* 45n2/41, 58/51; *T&P* 278.)

Because we all have needs to be met, it clearly is rational for us to adopt the principle of self-love to meet those needs (though we also are rationally obligated to subordinate that principle to the moral law). That, Kant declares, is why we rightly take talents, many personality traits, various skills, and the "gifts of fortune" to be (naturally) good in the sense that they all can contribute to our well-being. (See *Gr.* 1–2/393–94, 7/396.) We must reason practically to satisfy our concern for our own welfare, and, Kant writes, we have an "inescapable responsibility" and even an occasional indirect moral duty to do so. (See *Gr.* 12/399; *Pr.R.* 61, 110–11.) In the preceding chapter, we saw that Kant also insisted that we have the right to morally authorized happiness, and in Chapter 13 we discussed his doctrine that we have a moral obligation to develop our abilities in morally acceptable ways, the promotion of which turned out to be important both to morality and, as Mill and Bentham later also claimed, to happiness.

Despite his many claims to the contrary, Kant can be misread and has often been misinterpreted as holding that there is only one good, namely, moral virtue, and as having had no regard at all for human needs and desires. (See, e.g., *Gr.* 1/393, 7/396.) But he does not try to argue for a moral theory that would rule happiness out of the best human life. In fact, he characterizes such a view of morality as "misanthropic." (See *Lect.* 77–78/303–5.) The natural good, which includes both happiness and natural perfection, is neither absolutely good nor absolutely bad; instead, it is, in the abstract, morally ambiguous, and, in the concrete, it can be morally permissible, morally obligatory (at least indirectly), or morally forbidden.[9] We are required "to take no account of happiness when duty is in question," but "no one has a right to demand that I sacrifice my own ends if these are not immoral" (*Pr.R.* 93 and *M.M.* 388). Kant therefore insists that the contention that the virtuous person "should not give happiness any consideration whatsoever, even where such consideration is neither forbidden by nor contrary to duty, completely contradicts my statements" (*T&P* 281).

Negatively, then, there are no moral objections to our striving for happiness as long as we do not do so in ways contrary to the moral law. Positively, our moral reason recognizes in an objective and disinterested way that we are not only persons having intrinsic worth but also finite beings with needs to be met, and it insists on the *strict right* of all human beings not only to strive for but also to *attain* that happiness to which their moral worth entitles them. (See *Pu.R.* A805/B833, A809–10/B837–38, A813–14/B841–42; *Pr.R.* 34–35, 110, 116, 119, 121–22; *T&P* 278–79; *M.M.* 449–50, 481–82.) Our respect for the moral law on which that desert is based transcends merely subjective interest in getting our share of happiness and exhibits an impartial and impersonal respect for all human beings. It enables us to judge that *everyone* should have the happiness he deserves, even if this were to mean that we ourselves may not be morally good enough to get the happiness we might like to have. (See *Gr.* 104/450; *Pr.R.* 124; *Rel.* 5–6/5.)[10]

"The mere fact of deserving happiness can by itself interest us," Kant believes, "even without the motive of getting a share in this happiness" (*Gr.* 104/450). So in this case happiness, which originally is the aim of merely individual, prudential self-love, is transformed into a universal and impersonal goal, thereby enabling it to become an objective, moral end that is also a duty. Subsumed under that goal, our own self-love is transformed into a moral self-love, whereby we desire only that happiness we are worthy to enjoy. (See *Pr.R.* 115; *Rel.* 45n2/41–42; *T&P* 279n.)

Kant concludes, then, that a good will is the *supreme good* (*bonum supremum*), far exceeding in value any natural good we may merit. But because it is not our only good, by itself it also is not our *summum bonum,* our complete final end. (See, e.g., *Pu.R.* A 813/B841; *Gr.* 7/396; *Pr.R.* 110; *T&P* 279.) The final complete good for each human being, our "necessary end," consists in both our obligatory end – good moral character – and our natural and inevitable end – happiness, but happiness exactly commensurate with our character (*Pu.R.* A809–10/B836–37; *Pr.R.* 108–110, 128–29, 143; *Cr.J.* 450, 453; *Rel.* vii/4; *Lect.* 247/6, 304/77–78). Moral philosophy, therefore, is a doctrine "of how we are to be *worthy* of happiness" (*Pr.R.* 130; see also 61, 109–11, 121; *Gr.* 1/393–94; *T&P* 278, 278n, 283, 283n, 288; *M.M.* 481–82). That does not, of course, mean that moral philosophy is a doctrine about how to achieve happiness, nor does it mean that moral character should ever be considered to be instrumentally good as a means to happiness. (See *Pr.R.* 130.) "Just as it is its own end, [virtue] must also be considered its own reward"

(*M.M.* 405; see also 396–97, 406). But the full answer to the question What ought I to do? is, "Be virtuous, by doing that through which thou becomest worthy to be happy" (*Pu.R.* A809/B837).[11] The answer to the next question, If I do what I ought to do, for what may I then hope? is "the happiness I deserve." But it is also much more than that. That answer directs us to Kant's contention that morality leads inevitably to religion, by way of the postulates of pure practical reason. We shall discuss those postulates presently. The movement toward religion will take us through Kant's philosophy of history to the culmination of his philosophy in religion within the limits of reason alone.

We need now to discuss another question Kant raises about our final comprehensive good. He points out that there must be a necessary unity between, and not merely a harmonious but accidental coexistence of, its constituents. (See *Gr.* 84–87/438–40; *Pr.R. 4,* 108–13, 124, 140; *Cr.J.* 435ff, 453; *T&P* 278; *Lect.* 78/304–5.) Therefore, there must be such a unity between morality and happiness that all possible conflicts between them can be resolved in a necessary or a priori fashion.

The relationship between virtue (*das Gute*) and happiness (*das Wohl*) would be necessary if it were analytic, and then the pursuit of one would also be the pursuit of the other, and the maxims for attaining each would be identical. (See *Pr.R.* 111.) But given Kant's definition of happiness and his analysis of morality, they are two very different kinds of good, and the claim that happiness *is* virtue, and vice versa, is obviously false. (See *Pr.R.* 112–14.)[12]

Since their relationship is necessary but not analytic, it therefore must be synthetic, and their union a synthetic a priori relation. (See *Rel.* 6n/7.) That would be true if there were a synthetic a priori *causal* relationship between them so that virtue would always produce happiness "as something different from the consciousness of virtue" (*Pr.R.* 111). In a purely noumenal world, for example, it might be possible for morality to be completely "self-rewarding"; but this is pure speculation. (See *Pu.R.* A809–10/B837–38.) In this world, which we do know, we do not automatically achieve happiness just by acting virtuously, nor do we become morally virtuous just by pursuing and experiencing pleasure: There is no causal relationship between morality and happiness. (See *Gr.* 84/438; *Pr.R.* 113–15, 119, 124–25, 128, 145–46.)

Relating these two different interests and functions of practical reason in a necessary fashion still must be done by reasoning showing that there is "a totality of all ends within a single principle" (*T&P* 280n; see *Pr.R.* 113–15).[13] As we have seen again and again, that principle is the Law of Autonomy, which appears to us in the form of a categorical imperative and commands us both to recognize that morality and happiness are heterogeneous goods and to resolve all conflicts between them by systematically subordinating the principle of self-love to the Law of Autonomy. Then, as we have just seen, the principle of self-love is able to achieve the status of an objective law, a law that, insofar as human beings are virtuous, they *deserve* happiness as a conditional end, which now has satisfied the condition for its being objectively good. It is now sanctioned by the moral law and its promotion commanded as part of our total final good. (See *Gr.* 104/450; *Pr.R.* 34–35, 73, 78; *T&P* 280n.)

Not a norm of moral judgment

The third formula presents us with a moral vision of our final and comprehensive destiny both as individuals and as a species, thereby satisfying the demand of reason in general and of moral or pure practical reason in particular for an ultimate goal. By doing so, Kant wrote, it vivifies the meaning of the Categorical Imperative and so can help "secure acceptance for the moral law" (*Gr.* 81/437; see *Pr.R.* 43, 107; *T&P* 279n). Moreover, as we have repeatedly seen, the Categorical Imperative always needs to be applied within the context of an ideal teleological moral world. (See *Gr.* 80n/436n.) Nonetheless, Kant also holds that we are best advised *not* to use the third formula as our ultimate moral norm. Were we to do so, we could be tempted to take the rationally required *consequence* of conscientiousness to be *either* the criterion *or* the motive for our moral judgments. This would mean taking an object of the will, albeit an objectively necessary object, as ultimate and prior to the moral law, and that would turn autonomy into heteronomy. (See *Gr.* 93–95/444; *Pr.R.* 109, 125–26; *Rel.* 4–6/4–5; *P.P.* 377.)[14]

Moreover, we have no experience with the perfect realization of the Idea of the kingdom of ends, and so we have no idea of exactly how it would function nor should we try to imagine how it might do so. We cannot hope to understand how God would interact with its members or how justice would work or how the world of nature might become part of "a beautiful moral whole." All such matters are simply beyond our ken.[15] Consequently, Kant holds that using the Idea of the highest good as a moral norm too easily encourages a kind of irrational mysticism by appealing for moral guidance to nonsensuous intuitions of an invisible kingdom of God. (See *Pr.R.* 84–86.) Living before the proliferation of utopian schemes and communities of the late eighteenth and the nineteenth centuries, Kant also thinks that few people can be attracted to this kind of thinking for very long. (See *Pr.R.* 70–71, 109–10.) It is true that we do have experience with political states and religions, but, as we know, morality may not be based on experience but only on the rule of pure practical reason.

Kant therefore insists that when we make our moral judgments, we still should "proceed always in accordance with the strict method" by using the first formula as our moral norm and the law-governed natural world as its "type" (*Gr.* 81/436). The only criterion for moral choice as well as the ultimate ground for moral motivation *and* the only foundation for the kingdom of ends remains the moral law. As our only norm for moral judgments, it "completely abstracts from . . . every end one may have," *including* both the kingdom of ends and any expectations of happiness we may deserve in relation to our moral character (*T&P* 280; see *Gr.* 85/439, 127/462–63; *Pr.R.* 109–10; *Cr.J.* 451, 471n; *Rel.* 3–4/3, 6n/5–6, 139/130; *Lect.* 284–85/53–54). Kant writes that "though the highest good may be the entire *object* of a pure practical reason, i.e., of a pure will, it is still not to be taken as the *determining ground* of the pure will; the moral law alone must be seen as the ground for making the highest good and its realization or promotion the object of the pure will" (*Pr.R* 109; see *Rel.* 5/5).

Once we understand that the highest good is grounded in the moral law, however, we *then* can legitimately regard the Idea of the highest good as a *type,* a way of representing the "necessary highest end of a morally determined will and a true object thereof," and in the sense that it is based on the moral law, we may, Kant believes, even regard it as the "determining ground" of moral willing (*Pr.R.* 115 and *Rel.* 6n/7; see *Pr.R.* 109–10). But as *a norm* for moral judgments, the highest good "can be completely disregarded and set aside" (*T&P* 280). Moreover, our inculpable inability to carry out our intention to bring about "what does not lie altogether in our own power" as individuals, namely, any of the forms of the kingdom of ends, does not affect our moral worth, which still depends only on what "lies entirely in our own power" – intentions formed in obedience to the Law of Autonomy. (See, e.g., *Gr.* 85/439–40; *Cr.J.* 471n.)

The postulates of God and immortality

It is our own reason that commands us to obey the moral law and to hope for happiness commensurate with our obedience. Accordingly, it is our duty to "strive" toward the attainment of the highest good, to "realize" it "as far as it lies within our power to do so" (*Cr.J.* 450 and *Pr.R.* 143n; see *Pr.R.* 4, 119, 122, 125, 143). Goals that function as ideals do not actually have to be attainable to function as direction-giving norms. Plato's republic, for example, did not have to become actual to provide a standard against which to measure existing states. But as Kant sees it, in this case it would be self-contradictory for pure practical reason to command us to strive toward what is impossible, for the highest good is an end whose existence is *required* by moral reason. If the highest good were "impossible according to practical rules, then the moral law which commands that it be furthered must be . . . directed to empty imaginary ends, and consequently inherently false" (*Pr.R.* 114; see 109–110). Kant therefore must address the conditions required to make the *achievement* of the final highest good *actual.*

By acting dutifully, we each can be virtuous; and each of us can also promote the highest good insofar as we contribute both to our own morally licit happiness and to that of others. But there is no way to guarantee that everyone will strive for virtue, and no one can achieve virtue for anyone else. Even if everyone did achieve virtue, none of us can fully obey the moral law by actually achieving moral perfection or holiness. Finally, even if we could achieve holiness, that still would not be enough for us to attain our highest good completely. For in this world at least, virtue (conceived of as progress toward holiness) is not a sufficient condition for any individual – much less for everyone – actually gaining happiness proportionate to virtue. (See *Gr.* 84/438;

Pr.R. 113–14, 122–26, 144–45; *Cr.J.* 453; *M.M.* 482.) When virtue does result in happiness, it is only an occasional and contingent matter. (See *Pr.R.* 115.)

Just as moral virtue is possible only under the presupposition that we are free, so also the attainment of the kingdom of God – universal holiness and universal happiness – is possible only in a "mediated" way, through the existence and intervention of the supreme cause and moral ruler of that kingdom. (See *Pu.R.* A809–10/B837–38; *Gr.* 127/462–63; *Pr.R.* 114–15, 119, 125, 129–30, 132–34, 143n; *Cr.J.* 450, 452; *Rel.* 6n/7.)[16] The total achievement of the highest good requires both the existence and intervention of God as well as the immortality of the human soul (*Pu.R.* A807–11/B837–39, A828/B856; *Orient.* 139; *Rel.* 5–8/4–7, 98/89, 104/95; *T&P* 279).

In Chapter 10 we saw that by a postulate of pure practical reason Kant means a self-consistent but theoretically indemonstrable proposition that our moral reasoning not only entitles us but obligates us to assume to be true. (See *Pr.R.* 4, 119, 132, 145.) As we also saw, Kant claims we must assume the postulate of personal immortality for it to be possible for us to obey the moral law by at least making unending and dutiful progress toward the obligatory end of moral perfection. We now have another reason for assuming the postulate of immortality in the sense of the soul's persisting after death: Since our present world so often does not serve the demands of justice, it is morally necessary that there be a God who will provide a future, different, law-governed world that *will* necessarily work harmoniously with our moral intentions. (See *Pr.R.* 132, 145–46.)

That there is a God and that we are immortal are claims about what objectively is the case, but they are not theoretical *dogmas*. (See *Pr.R.* 132; *Rel.* 6n/5–6.)[17] What we can know theoretically is limited to what we can perceive with our senses. If there is life after death and a God, such reality lies beyond all our possible experience and so outside the purview of science. Such claims are problematic, that is, theoretically insoluble in principle. (See *Pr.R.* 132; *Rel.* 153n/142.) Science does not have the right to affirm or to deny either God's existence or the immortality of the human soul. (See *Pr.R.* 125–26, 132, 140–41, 144.) But because neither of these Ideas is self-contradictory, their reality and that of the highest good are theoretically at least possible (*Pu.R.* A828–30/B856–58; *Pr.R.* 144–45).

Now the same moral law that commands us categorically to act dutifully also posits the ultimate kingdom of ends as the rationally necessary consequence of dutiful actions. It is that same law of reason that insists that each person has a strict right to happiness proportionate to virtue and that the human race as a collective whole will achieve its moral destiny in that kingdom. As we saw in Chapter 7, the reality of human freedom is "proved" by the a priori fact of the moral law in our consciousness. (See *Pr.R.* 4–5.) Now that same law demands the reality of its proper end. We therefore must *believe* that the conditions for the possibility of that end are really possible; that is, we must believe that their existence is as certain as that of the moral law within us. (See *Pr.R.* 109–10, 113–15, 124–25, 142–45.) For our necessary moral purposes, then, we may have a rational hope, a "moral certainty," and a purely practical faith (*Glaube* and *Vernunftglaube*) in the objective reality of our own immortality and the existence of God, who will contribute what we cannot to our complete final good, who "reassures and guarantees this endeavor" (*Rel.* 183/171; see *Pu.R.* A829/B857; *Gr.* 127/462–63; *Pr.R.* 125–26, 132, 144–46; *Cr.J.* 450–51; *M.M.* 482).

Although Kant calls this a "moral argument for the existence of God" and refers to it as a "moral proof," he also states that he did not intend that it be "an objectively [i.e., theoretically] valid proof of the existence of God"; "it is not meant to demonstrate to the skeptic that there *is* a God" (*Cr.J.* 447, 450, 450n). Rather it is directed to the person who already acknowledges his or her moral vocation, to show that person that there is a subjective yet still rational ground to "adopt the assumption of this proposition as a maxim of his practical reason, if he wishes to think in a manner consistent with morality" (*Cr.J.* 450n; see also 459–85). So we go too far if we claim that "it is morally certain there is a God"; what we may say is "*I* am morally certain there is a God" (*Pu.R.* A829/B857).

On the basis of the attributes the supreme being must have to be able to fulfill the demand of moral reason, Kant does claim that we can arrive at "an exactly defined concept of this Being" (*Pr.R.* 139).[18] God must be an omnipotent person to be able to bring the future world into harmony with moral willing. We therefore must conceive of God as a beneficent ruler and sustainer and a just judge, as omniscient, omnipresent, eternal, and, above all, holy. (See *Pu.R.* A814–18/B842–46; *Gr.* 85–86/439, 75/434; *Pr.R.* 108–9, 125, 131n, 137; *Cr.J.* 444, 447; *Rel.* 139–40/130–31.)

As we have seen, the practical postulate of God's existence does not extend our knowledge in a theoretical way. (See, e.g., *Pr.R.* 134–35.) But it does go far beyond the corresponding regulative Idea of theoretical reason, which treats God only as the necessary first cause, sufficiently powerful to account for the world and the system of laws we find in it. Theoretical reasoning cannot tell us whether God had a final purpose in creating the world or, if he did, what it might be. However, pure practical reason reveals God both as a moral Person and as a moral Legislator, a "*living* God," whose final purpose in creation is the human species and its moral destiny. (See *Cr.J.* 438, 441–43, 448n.) Kant therefore denies he is a deist, whose god is "a blindly working eternal root of all things" (*Theol.* 96–97). He classifies himself as a theist, one whose God is a living, personal Being.[19]

Kant insists that the highest (derived) good and so also the postulated conditions for its actual attainment – God, immortality, and freedom (insofar as the last is regarded as a postulate rather than as a moral fact) – are integral to morality. The moral law obligates us absolutely, and it specifies that there is a necessary connection between its commands and the effects of those commands, so that the denial of one or all of its postulates implies the denial also of the existence of pure practical reason and of the moral law itself. (See *Pr.R.* 114; *Cr.J.* 447, 471, 531, 553.)

As we have seen, Kant asserts that were we to deny what pure practical reason postulates as its necessary moral goal and as the conditions necessary for that goal, we consistently should also regard the moral law itself as an "empty figment" (*Pr.R.* 114; *Pu.R.* A811/B839; see A828/B856). But the moral law is established by itself in our moral consciousness, independently of its postulates, including any end postulated "as its material condition" (*Cr.J.* 450; see *Pr.R.* 126, 143–44). To deny its necessary conditions or end, therefore, would mean falling into a "practical absurdity" (*Pr.R.* 113ff; *Cr.J.* 452; *Theol.* 160). For example, failure to believe in the existence of God, who is the necessary condition for the fulfillment of the end of the moral law, would make our belief in the categorical nature of that law absurd. Nonetheless, the Categorical Imperative would still command our absolute obedience, regardless of consequences; and it would still condemn us if we did not obey it, including its injunction to contribute to the highest good. (See *Pu.R.* A828/ B856; *Gr.* 112/454; *Rel.* 6n/6; but see also *Cr.J.* 451–53.)

A problem

Not many contemporary Kantians are impressed by Kant's moral argument for the existence of God and immortality. In general, most grant that the final highest good is possible in the sense of conceivable and that Kant was right in saying that we do think it is just for a person to have the happiness he or she deserves. But they also argue that simply knowing what our duty is and striving to do it do not of themselves show either that everyone actually will get deserved happiness or that believing in the attainment of the final good is necessary to morality.[20] They hold that we could know that the highest good is actually attainable only if we could know on independent grounds that there is a God who guarantees its achievement. Some also hold that the introduction of a *summum bonum* and of the conditions necessary for its existence undermines the nonconsequentialist character of Kant's moral theory along with the categorical authority of the moral law.

Although these criticisms are widely held, it may still be possible to throw some further light on Kant's doctrine of the highest good if we attend to two crucial distinctions that such objections tend to ignore.

We first need to recall the distinction between a metaphysics of morals that holds for all rational agents as such and a metaphysics of morals for human beings, who are dependent and imperfectly rational agents. The first is pure a priori in nature and applies to whatever rational beings there may be. Here, for example, we found the Law of Autonomy and the analytic consequence of that law that a perfectly rational agent is necessarily also a holy being. By contrast, the metaphysics of morals for human beings must include not only what the pure analysis has shown about the nature of moral agency as such but also mixed a priori claims. As we have seen time and again, if morality is to apply to human beings, it must take into account a good deal of empirical information about human agency – what Kant usually called "anthropology."

We also need to remember Kant's belief that as our ultimate practical goal, the "kingdom of ends" takes three different forms: the form of a political union and the form of an ethical society, both of which are to exist in this world, and the form of the perfect kingdom of God, which he portrays, somewhat ambiguously, as taking place in a "future world." Kant himself clearly understood what is required for each to be possible and therefore what kinds of obligations each imposes on us.

One of Kant's most informative discussions of our obligation to promote the kingdom of ends in one form or another in this life occurs in his *On the Proverb: That May Be True in Theory but Is of No Practical Use*. There he first defends the need of moral reason as a teleological faculty to have an ultimate end or object *in this world,* one "that includes the totality of all ends within a single principle (a world as the highest good possible through our cooperation)" (*T&P* 280n). "This end," he states elsewhere, "is the *summum bonum,* as the highest good *in this world* possible through freedom" (*Cr.J.* 450). Living under an absolute monarch, Kant would not have underestimated the difficulties in peacefully bringing about a state with a republican form and, eventually, a world federation of republics. So, he writes, the moral law imposes only a "duty to strive with all one's abilities to ensure that such a relationship (a world conforming to the highest moral ends) exists." Given the proper circumstances and the cooperation of others, a republican state *is* possible; it *can* become a reality, even if only in an imperfect form. If we can contribute to bringing this about, then we are obligated to do so. In striving to fulfill this duty, Kant writes, "man thinks of himself on an analogy with the deity" as creating such a political body, not from subjective need (as Hobbes had argued), but because of the command of the objective moral law "to bring about the highest good outside" oneself (*T&P* 279–80n).

Similar remarks can be made about the Idea of an ethical society. As the historical religious communities show, ethical societies can be formed and maintained by cooperative efforts, even if only in an imperfect form. Accordingly, if we can do so, we are obligated to promote and participate in such an association, which Kant envisions as a universal church founded on the moral law, a genuinely religious kingdom of God on earth.

As for the Idea of the highest good in its complete and final form in a future life, what are we bound to do? First, Kant in effect holds, we can and must form the *Idea* of such a possible final good.[21] The Law of Autonomy in the form of the Categorical Imperative commands us to adopt the principle of "moral teleology," making that final good our own end, the final object of our own moral willing. Given what we know about both the capabilities and the limitations of human moral agents, that means striving toward it with all our strength. But because we must admit that the complete fulfillment of that Idea requires the intervention of God in a different kind of world than the one we now inhabit, we also are obligated to fulfill one other duty that we can do, namely, believe in and hope for the conditions necessary for that fulfillment. (See *Pu.R.* A823/B851; *Pr.R.* 143; *Cr.J.* 446, 450–51.) But we clearly are not obligated to try to do what simply is not possible for us –

make that possibility fully actual. As Allen Wood points out, to *adopt* a particular end and to strive for it do not commit a person actually to *achieve* that end or to believe that it is achievable without help. Adopting an end may require an agent only to believe that that end *is* somehow achievable.[22]

If we interpret Kant in terms of these distinctions he makes, it then is possible to make perfectly good sense of his various claims about the kingdom of ends. Problems with Kant's doctrine of the kingdom of ends now come down to one question: Does the acceptance of the *justice* of the Idea of a kingdom of God, both in this world and in the next, and the more fundamental commitment to morality also *require* a person to believe in the eventual actual achievement of the final kingdom of God and, accordingly, the reality of its necessary conditions – God and immortality?

In one passage Kant allows that some morally good people simply may not be able to convince themselves of God's existence, though they still do not judge that they thereby are freed of the moral law. (See *Cr.J.* 302, 451.)[23] But in the main he is convinced that we have a subjective yet "an absolutely necessary need" to answer that question in the affirmative (*Pr.R.* 143). It is true that the moral law commands our absolute obedience, without regard for the consequences of our doing so. It also is true that the moral law "subsists of itself (even without the concept of God)" (*Rel.* 183/171). But belief in God *can* serve "as the means of strengthening" moral resolve, for it "reassures and guarantees this endeavor (as a striving for goodness, and even for holiness) in its expectation of the final goal with respect to which it is impotent" (*Rel.* 183/171).

Kant's ultimate argument, then, has an interest all its own, for it anticipates the contention of atheistic existentialists of the twentieth century. (See e.g., *Cr.J.* 458–59.) If there is no God, some would later say, if there is nothing beyond this world, it is tempting to wonder what *difference* it makes whether or not we act morally. What is the *point* in concerning ourselves with a "moral vocation" or in struggling for a just political state or an ethical society? Acting morally requires us to ignore any personal benefits from doing so, but if there is no final meaning to moral willing, it then becomes too easy for us to conclude that we are "free from all moral obligation" (*Cr.J.* 452; see *Lect.* 54/285; *Rel.* 6n/6–7). We may come to believe that it ultimately makes no difference; "one wide grave" will engulf us all, and "just and unjust, there is no distinction in the grave" (*Cr.J.* 452). Moral behavior might still generally seem the most prudential thing to do, to help us get what we want. But we would no longer be tempted to concern ourselves with purely moral requirements or with our own moral worth. (See, e.g., *Cr.J.* 447–53.)

Is Kant right in thinking that moral interest requires religious faith to be the effective spring or incentive (*Triebfeder*) of purpose and action? (See *Pu.R.* A813/B841; *Pr.R.* 143.)[24] Is belief in God subjectively necessary for most of us, to help sustain our pursuit of moral virtue (still without that belief motivating us)? These are questions that must be left to the judgment of the reader. Clearly, Kant himself wanted to hold (1) that pure reason can be practical in and of itself, (2) that morality is therefore completely independent of institutional religion, but also (3) that religion within the bounds of reason alone is profoundly important to our moral life. As we have seen, he understood his entire Critical philosophy to be a defense of both pure morality and religion.[25]

I V
Kant on history, politics, and religion

16
Autonomy and the state

Immanuel Kant's entire life was spent under absolute hereditary monarchs who retained their thrones by means of conscripted armies as well as the mutually advantageous support of a hereditary nobility with power, wealth, and privileges never shared by the peasants. (See, e.g., *Conflict* 89/161; *Ed.* 448/15.) Frederick II (Frederick the Great) ruled Prussia during most of Kant's adult life, from 1740 to 1786. Although Frederick in fact enjoyed despotic power, his official view of himself was as the "first servant of his people."[1] Most of his subjects would probably have been surprised to learn that they lived in an enlightened age, but Frederick prided himself on his commitment to the Enlightenment. Even today he is usually described as a benevolent and enlightened monarch who compares favorably with all the Prussian kings before him and most after him.

While still the crown prince, Frederick had been encouraged by Voltaire to pen a "refutation" of Machiavelli's *Prince*, which Voltaire then edited and had published in The Hague. Later, in his *Memoirs,* Voltaire wrote: "If Machiavelli had had a prince for disciple, the first thing he would have recommended him to do would have been to write a book against Machiavellism!"[2] Voltaire's rationale was simple: Since Machiavelli had advised a prince to use his power, whenever possible, under the mantle of virtue, a wise student of Machiavelli should publicly attack his tutor's infamous amoralism. Shortly after Frederick's work was published, he unexpectedly inherited the throne. For reasons about which we can only speculate, he immediately ordered Voltaire to buy up and destroy all the copies of his book that Voltaire could find.

Kant is effusive when he addresses and writes about Frederick, who did exhibit an exceptional tolerance for freedom of speech and for philosophical and religious controversy – as long as his subjects obeyed him. "*Argue* as much as you want and about what you want," Kant quotes Frederick as saying, "*but obey!*" (*Enlight.* 37). But Kant was not politically naive, and he did not overestimate Frederick's capacity for tolerance. In his political writings Kant carefully refrained from commenting on Frederick's youthful foray into political philosophy, and he does not so much as refer to Machiavelli by name, even in those essays in which Machiavelli is plainly on his mind. Nonetheless, Kant's political philosophy – and also his ethical theory, regarded politically – was a radical movement away from totalitarianism, toward a state that would recognize the dignity of the ordinary citizen no less than that of the wealthy and the powerful, the gifted and the educated. The very first words of Chapter 1 of the *Groundwork,* for example, state that good moral

233

character is far more valuable than, and totally independent of, any advantages or privileges that any individuals may happen to enjoy.

As a brief examination of the chronology of Kant's publications shows, his works on political theory appear throughout the Critical period, revealing his continuing preoccupation with the historical dimension of human moral and political life. But Kant knew he had to be cautious about arguing for views not congenial to the state that employed his services.[3] So, despite the fact that Kant himself regarded them as setting out some of his most important doctrines, he wrote his explicitly political treatises so that they often looked like only occasional pieces. He uncharacteristically adopted a self-deprecating tone, suggesting, particularly in a superficial reading, that the ideas proposed should not be regarded as very important. Who, he in effect asks, could take seriously what a philosopher thinks about such things? What does such a person know about affairs of the world? As a result, those writings have often been regarded only as marginally significant, and it is not unusual to see them described as "minor" works.[4]

Other factors have tended to diminish Kant's influence outside Germany – in general the strong nationalistic flavor (which Kant himself tried to avoid) of most German political thinking, and in particular the (often unappealing) transcendental idealism underlying his political theorizing. Today, thanks largely to the influence of Harvard professor John Rawls, Kant's contributions to the "classical" liberal political tradition are widely discussed in the English-speaking world.[5]

The liberal tradition is a diverse movement, but John Gray has well summarized its specific conception of the person and society:

It is *individualist,* in that it asserts the moral primacy of the person against the claims of any social collectivity; *egalitarian,* inasmuch as it confers on all men the same moral status . . . *universalist,* affirming the moral unity of the human species and according a secondary importance to specific historic associations and cultural forms; and *meliorist* in its affirmation of the corrigibility and improvability of all social institutions and political arrangements.[6]

It is not difficult to see how Kant's political thought contributed to this view. Against the old despotisms he set the ideals already enunciated in John Locke's *Second Treatise on Civil Government* and proclaimed (if not respected in action) by the French Revolution: freedom and equality. Kant himself stressed the ideal of justice rather than that of fraternity, for fraternity tends to be based on emotional ties leading to partiality, whereas justice as fairness is impersonal insofar as it is based on reason alone. Kant emphasized that only a state that recognizes these ideals of reason will respect the dignity of every person within it.

Problems confronting Kant's political theory

Before examining Kant's political theory, we need to understand problems he had to try to resolve with it.

First, it is a fundamental task for any political theory to justify any political authority. This is a problem only if we look at the state from the outside, so to speak.[7] Once a person is a member of a state, already living by the rules of that political system, a question such as What entitles the state to tax me? can be answered simply by pointing out that the agreements within the state permit the government to do so. But a person who feels alienated from or has not yet adopted this internal point of view may ask a very different question: What entitles a state to engage in coercive functions which limit personal freedoms, while the very same sort of conduct is regarded within the state as immoral when exercised by individuals against other individuals? Like every other political theorist, Kant needed to show what justifies the state doing what individuals may not do.

Second, there are special problems for Kant arising out of his own moral theory. As we have seen, morality *is* autonomy – the ability and obligation of a person to act on rational principles of his or her *own* adoption. Likewise, immorality involves the heteronomous yielding of one's freedom to something or someone outside one's own reason. It would seem that autonomy is incompatible with submission to any government, and that the exercise of coercion by a state will always violate the prepolitical, moral rights of individuals.[8]

Finally, even if Kant can show that there need be no conflict between morality and political authority, he still faces the further problem of the alleged right of the state to regard itself as supreme – and civil obligations as having precedence over all other, even competing moral, obligations. This was, for him, not only a theoretical question but also a very practical one, since he was writing under monarchs who, benevolent or not, had no intention of giving up any of their power.

Kant's philosophy of history

To understand Kant's political theory, we need to begin with his philosophy of history.[9] This part of his philosophical system – and it is an integral part of that system – has generally been ignored by those who criticize Kant's moral theory as excessively ahistorical.

Kant holds that, for the sake of our moral purposes, we must be able to make sense out of human history and of our place in it. If we regard history as meaningless and if we think of the historical record of the human race's gross immorality toward itself, it is all too easy to be tempted to moral despair – to abandon morality and its goals as empty illusions. (See, e.g., *H.H.* 120–21.)[10] As we have seen, any theoretical explanation of historical events must regard them all as sequences of causally related facts, devoid of value. (See *Idea* 18–19; *Cr.J.* 442.) This view of history surely gives us no reason to believe that the world will ever improve morally, or that the kingdom of ends will ever be realized. But Kant holds that we must not yield either our faith in enlightened reason as the instrument of progress in history or our belief that what morality commands is possible. So, he argues, we *must* use the Idea of teleology in order to interpret human history as having meaning and purpose. (See *Conflict* 81/145; *Idea* 17–18, 29–30; *P.P.* 360–62, 362n, 368.)[11]

To regard history in this manner – "transcendentally" – is to view the history of mankind as a teleological process that can be related as a narrative with a beginning, a middle, and an end. This teleological Idea is not drawn *from* experience, for nothing in experience can "adequately correspond to an Idea" (*M.M.* 371; *Pu.R.* A318/B372). Therefore, we may not try to explain any particular event *theoretically* as actually having been caused by some naturally purposive process, nor may we use this standpoint to try to predict the course of history. (See *Conflict* 83–84/149 and 151.) But we may and must use that Idea to guide our moral-practical thinking, and we may even identify past and present historical events symbolically, as examples, however partial and inadequate they may be, of that Idea, to show its practicality. (See *Pu.R.* A328/B385; *Cr.J.* 351.) (The teleological principle may be compared to the "invisible hand" of economic forces to which Adam Smith had appealed in his *Wealth of Nations*.)

Kant rejects any attempt to base morality on revealed religion, but he also argues that the moral law itself provides a rational basis for our believing in a personal God who "favors" the freedom and moral vocation of the human race as a species and who providentially will see to it that our ultimate obligatory moral ends are realized.[12] We *must* trust that the world *can and will* progress morally under the providential guidance of a Moral Ruler having the same moral end for us that our own reason projects – and also having the power to accomplish fully what we may be unable to do (see *Pu.R.* A814/B842). History, then, is a process in which, under the wise guidance of Nature (regarded as Providence), the human species as a collective whole is evolving – erratically but constantly and, as far as many, perhaps most, individual human beings are concerned, largely unintentionally and unwillingly toward fuller expressions of freedom, rationality, and morality. (See *Pu.R.* A801/B829; *Idea* 17–31; *H.H.* 115, 116n; *Cr.J.* 436n, 443; *T&P* 307–12; *P.P.* 360–68; *Anthr.* 328; *Conflict* 82–83/147 and 149, 88–89/159 and 161.)[13]

There is a certain poignancy to the fact that, however highly Kant esteemed human reason, his estimation of human beings themselves led him finally to place his trust not in human reason but in divine wisdom and goodness to see to it that the human race as a species reaches its ultimate goal in history. (See *T&P* 310; *Conflict* 93–94/169 and 171.)

When we look at history transcendentally, Kant points out, we find that, paradoxically, Nature brings forth good even from evil, by using the very moral failures of individuals to advance the race morally. (See *Anthr.* 328.) This means, again, that the human race, taken collectively as a species, is not just the sum of its members. (See *Anthr.* 328.) Individuals may tend to be interested mainly or only in their own happiness, but moral progress, not happiness, is the goal of Nature. (See *Cr.J.* 426n.) Even when individuals attend only to their desires, they may still, in Nature's plan, indirectly promote the freedom and moral progress of the species by adopting merely legal maxims. (See *Rel.* 47/42.) So a transcendental philosophy of history also means examining history impersonally, that is, from the standpoint of the human race collectively rather than in terms of the moral successes or failures of individuals at any given time. (See *Idea* 18–19; *Conflict* 79/141.) The species will eventually achieve its destiny, but only gradually and with many temporary setbacks, through countless obstacles and "innumerable generations" (*Anthr.* 324). Kant kept the liberal faith in meliorism: Progress "can never be completely reversed" (*Anthr.* 324).

If we are tempted to regard this part of Kant's philosophy as a peculiar aberration of the eighteenth-century German Enlightenment, it may be helpful to recall the enormous importance and influence of other philosophies of history, especially those of Christianity, Islam, and Marxism. They have given millions of people a vision with which to transcend their individual lives, to see themselves as part of a historical process giving them both meaning and value, and they have thereby been motivated to try to change the world.

Kant's teleocosmos is a purely rational, moral version of the Christian redemptive history of the human race. In his philosophy of history, the process begins with the human race's being culturally and morally "immature," that is, suffering from a "bondage to instinct" and showing a habituated, heteronomous unwillingness to "come of age" and think autonomously. (See *T&P* 305–6.)[14] The process itself involves a transition from this animal-like "state of nature" to the formation of civil society. Rousseau had held that "civilization does not comply with nature's end" (*Lect.* 466/248). But Kant argues that moral consciousness presupposes some cultural development, and that cultural development is possible only when, under the protection of a state, the constant threat of death by violence has been minimized (*End* 332; see *M.M.* 391–92; *Anthr.* 324). Only within the juridical structure of a state can human beings enjoy those conditions necessary for the protection and exercise of their freedom. (See *M.M.* 306.) Only then do human beings have the possibility of achieving that complex of goals that they have by their very nature: self-preservation, cultural development, and moral virtue (*Idea* 22).[15]

Kant therefore holds that "man is a being meant for society" (*M.M.* 471; *Anthr.* 322–24). But he also maintains that the movement toward social order cannot be explained, as Aristotle, Rousseau, and Shaftesbury had thought, simply by saying that we are by nature social and political creatures. It is true, he believes, that we tend naturally to associate with other people, but by virtue of the character of the human species, we equally tend toward antisocial attitudes and behavior.

We have by nature, Kant proposes, three predispositions or drives (*Anlagen*): to animality, to humanity, and to personality. The first two, which are grounded in self-love, are aimed at the promotion of our natural good, our welfare. (See *Rel.* 26–28/21–23.) They concern the satisfaction of our needs and desires, of our "animality" (as physical beings – self-preservation and the preservation of the species) and of our "humanity" (as social beings – our natural self-development). (See *Anthr.* 270; *Rel.* 26/21.) The third, the predisposition to moral personality, rests on the moral law in our reason and on our consciousness of being obligated to respect it.

Because we all also have a natural propensity to evil, we tend to pervert the drive to animality by such vices as gluttony and drunkenness, and most especially we all tend to pervert the predisposition to sociability (*Geselligkeit*) by being "unsociable." (See *Rel.* 28–34/23–30.) We are not satisfied merely with our own well-being and with being equal to others; we want to achieve superiority over others. So everyone tends to subordinate the demands of morality to the desire to treat others merely as a means to get what one wants, and everyone tries to control others, to keep them from frustrating the desire to have everything one's own way. (See *Rel.* 27/22; *Idea* 20–21; *Anthr.* 268, 277.) Since our moral character depends only on our manner of willing, simply having this propensity to evil does not make us evil. (See *Rel.* 21/17, 28/23, 36/31, 44/40.) Nonetheless, we are all guilty of initially adopting as our ultimate maxim a rule asserting the primacy of the self and refusing to acknowledge that others have a rightful claim to equal dignity and worth. (See *Rel.* 93–94/85; *Anthr.* 272.)

The tendency to immoral social conduct – to what Kant calls "the social (or cultural) vices" of wild lawlessness, envy, jealousy, rivalry, ingratitude, and spitefulness – gives rise to constant conflicts between individuals and groups. (See *Rel.* 27/22.) But Nature – or "the design of a wise Creator" – uses this very discord and its consequent misery to promote the moral progress of the human species, particularly through cultural development. (See *Idea* 20–22.) People as passively content as sheep and as placid as cattle have no reason either to set new goals or to work to achieve them. They need to be forced by frustration and unhappiness to overcome their natural tendencies to sloth and cowardice (*Idea* 22; see 21–22; also *Enlight.* 35; *Anthr.* 322, 325).[16]

Kant therefore concludes that progress in the past toward the formation of the state has resulted, not so much from human wisdom or intention, but from human beings acting on egoistic impulses (*Anlagen*). These impulses paradoxically are possible only to social beings with some cultural development, yet they also make people the most unsocial of social creatures. There are, Kant writes, three such egoistic impulses: love of possessions and money (insatiable avarice); love of power together with a fear of domination by others; and ambition, that is, a craving for the good opinion of others, however undeserved. (See *Idea* 21–22; *M.M.* 307; *Anthr.* 267–68, 272–74; *Ed.* 492/107.) In the original state of nature these impulses give rise to either continuous conflict or at least the constant potential for conflict and violence. Only the devastating effects of conflicts can *force* people eventually to submit to the authority of a political body within which they can be protected from others and also more effectively vie for superiority over each other. (See *H.H.* 120; *P.P.* 348–49; *Anthr.* 330.)[17]

The plan of Nature (or divine Providence) does not intrude on the freedom of individuals and may therefore seem to show little concern for the individual. Everyone can become aware of the moral law in his own reason, but the individual pursuit of virtue remains precarious, for everyone is infected by the tendency to evil. Even within society everyone is still in an ethical state of nature, and each person is in "danger of being contaminated and corrupted by evil or inept guides and examples" (*Anthr.* 327; see 325–28). The attainment of morally certified happiness is equally uncertain, for its pursuit is frequently frustrated by natural disasters and human violence. Fortunately, at least for the most part the progress of the human species does not depend on the achievements, either natural or moral, of any particular individuals. For example, the cultural progress of the human race requires the accumulation of great stores of knowledge, much of it acquired slowly by trial and error. But what individuals can in fact contribute to human knowledge is severely limited by the brevity of the human life span. (See *Idea* 18–20.)

Nonetheless, this does not mean that we may passively leave everything in the hands of God. The plan of Nature does help us make sense out of the past, but now that that plan has been understood, it is no longer the only vehicle for moral progress. Our power of pure practical reason gives us the responsibility to work to shape the future to the vision of the highest good in the world, a vision that reason projects as an obligatory goal. Given our present stage of moral enlightenment, we now are morally obligated "to promote the approach to this goal with all our prudence and moral illumination (each to the best of his ability)" (*Anthr.* 329; see *H.H.* 123). We each have a share in promoting the collective goal that is a unique duty "of the human race toward itself" (*Rel.* 97/89). As we saw in Chapter 15, we have a particular duty to promote the visible social unions of a just state and an ethical community. As difficult as these may be to achieve fully, we must have faith that such ideals are attainable, a faith that "denotes trust in God that He will supply our deficiency in things beyond our power, provided we have done all within our power" (*Lect.* 320–21/95).

The genesis of the state

Kant's account of the origin of the state out of universal and mutual antagonism and hostility at least initially seems very similar to Thomas Hobbes's account in the *Leviathan*. As Hobbes had described it, the state of nature is simply too precarious an existence; it forces people to live in a constant state of war, because everyone must presume that everyone else is at least a potential enemy. (See *Rel.* 97n/89.) In such a lawless situation, even if those with greater power do not actually mistreat those with less, even if sheer force does not always determine what is "just," there are still neither rights nor justice in a juridical sense, for there is no impartial and effective tribunal competent to judge differences and conflicts between people and to enforce what is right. (See *Rel.* 33/28, 33n/28; *P.P.* 346, 355; *M.M.* 256, 312, 346–47.) What determines what is "right" is only an individual's prudential estimate, which does not require him to wait until others attack him before he attacks them. (See *M.M.* 305–8.) In such a condition, therefore, people tend to provoke each other to act unjustly. (See *Rel.* 93–94/85, 97/88–89.) Rousseau was badly mistaken in thinking of such a state of nature as an innocent paradise. (See *Anthr.* 327–28.) Rather, it is "in the highest degree wrong" (*M.M.* 307).

When the decision finally *is* made to enter into a social contract for a civil society, it is motivated by fear, particularly fear of future and even worse conflicts. (See *P.P.* 364–65, 371.) Egoistically motivated individuals, even a "population of devils," need only be intelligent enough to recognize finally that it is in their own best interest to agree, however reluctantly, to limit their own freedom by entering into a civil union with laws that will protect them and thereby help them achieve their goals. (See *Pu.R.* A752/B780; *Idea* 22, 25–26; *P.P.* 366.)[18] "Thanks to Nature," Kant writes, even though the original motive for agreeing to the formation cf the state is selfishness – the source of all moral evil – the human species can and does thereby make progress toward moral autonomy and harmony. (See *Idea* 21–22; *P.P.* 366–67, 375–76; *M.M.* 315.)

Neither Hobbes nor Kant intended that this now familiar notion of an original contract should be taken as a historical account of the origin of the state. But Hobbes had thought that, since people enter a state out of their desire for self-preservation and to promote their own advantage, the best state needs to be a leviathan, a powerfully authoritarian government. Against Hobbes, Kant argued that the rational ideal of a "juridical association of men under public laws in general" cannot be justified solely by prudential considerations. (See *M.M.* 355.) He held that only an Idea of reason can adequately ground the contractarian nature of a state and justify both the legitimacy of coercive public laws and the obligation of people to obey them. (See *T&P* 297; *M.M.* 251, 318–19, 339–40.) That Idea of reason must be the practical Idea of freedom, although, for political purposes, the Idea is limited to the prohibition, according to a universal law, of external interference with others' pursuit of what they regard as good. Kant, therefore, concluded that the role of government should be limited to protecting the citizens' freedom.

Kant's most significant contribution to the development of classical liberal theory, therefore, is his claim that the *justification* of the state ultimately must rest on *moral* grounds, on the innate freedom of each person, and on the obligation of each to recognize and respect the freedom of every one else. According to the Idea of the social contract, each person should elect to live in a juridical condition that can peacefully institutionalize the external exercise of human freedom equally by everyone. (See *M.M.* 315–16; *Rel.* 97/89.) It is the moral law that makes the formal structure of the state something more than a more peaceful state of nature. That law, which in its third formula projects a civil form of the kingdom of ends as a moral Idea, both justifies the state and defines the nature of a good state.

Kant does not think that the transition from a state of nature to a state of juridical freedom can be easy. It is not unusual for states to arise from acts of extreme violence, but there may well be no alternative in a previous state of nature. So Kant holds that the historical genesis of a particular state is irrelevant to the moral justification of its legal authority. Moreover, human nature being what it is, we cannot expect that moral motivation will lead people to form a civil society (or, later, to make them good citizens). "The first attempts will indeed be crude and usually will be attended by a more painful and more dangerous state than that in which we are still under orders and also the care of others" (*Rel.* 188n/176). Each person remains in "an ethical state of nature" and is an "irrational beast," still wanting everything to go his or her own way, never abandoning the tendency to live as if still in a state of nature, "always ready to break forth in hostility towards his neighbors" (*Anthr.* 327).

At first, Kant writes, movements toward a just state tend only to produce despotism, with rulers – including religious rulers – who are no better than anyone else in this regard and probably worse. Kant anticipated the famous saying of the English liberal, Lord Acton, when he wrote that "the possession of power inevitably corrupts the free judgment of reason" (*P.P.* 369; see *Rel.* 33/28–29, 95/87). Typically rulers tend to be corrupt, to treat their subjects only as things, and to see freedom of the people only as a danger to their own power (*Idea* 23; *H.H.* 120; *P.P.* 344, 371). But this is not a reason for delaying the transition to a just civil state, for the only way in which people can learn to govern themselves is by actually trying to do so. Justice is not served by putting off emancipation to some indefinite future. (See *Rel.* 188n/176.)

How, Kant asks, can it be possible to build anything perfectly straight "from such crooked wood?" (*Idea* 23; see *Rel.* 100/92). How can people bring about exactly "what they themselves are in need of?" (*Anthr.* 325). If we had to rely on people forming a just state from moral motives, he writes, the problem would be insoluble. People – especially those having the most power in a state – cannot be counted on to act morally rightly. They are too caught up in the "cultural vices" of pursuing their own desires at the cost of injustice. Here again Kant's teleological principle comes to the rescue. Fortunately, the same selfishness and animosity that forced people originally to enter into a civil union will also lead them both to promote and to obey a just constitution, even though each person is still secretly inclined to exempt himself from the laws of that union: "The powers of each selfish inclination are so arranged in opposition that one moderates or destroys the ruinous effect of the other. The consequence for reason is the same as if none of them existed, and man is forced to be a good citizen even if not a morally good person" (*P.P.* 366). An effective civil constitution will balance out the conflicts between private interests so that they will check one another, and everyone will at least "behave publicly just as if they had no evil attitudes" (*P.P.* 366). The historical process within which these dynamics operate obviously cannot be smooth and gradual. Instead, "man is constantly deviating from his destiny and always returning to it" (*Anthr.* 325). At any given moment there always remains the threat of regression to "revolutionary barbarism" (*Anthr.* 326). But even if, as time goes on, individuals are no better morally than their ancestors, the human race as a species will still, if erratically, "make continual progress toward the better" (*Anthr.* 325).

Autonomy and political coercion

Kant therefore holds that a state may use coercion to ensure that the rule of law (*Wille*) will protect and promote freedom and autonomy. Outside a civil society is *only* the brute force and lawless violence of the state of nature. Clearly submission to the authority of a state and the usually imperfect rule of civil law is both prudentially and morally preferable to the lawless rule of mobs and the violent resolutions of conflict. (See *P.P.* 372–73, 373n; *M.M.* 312, 315–16, 355.) Because individuals who persist in living in a lawless state of nature constitute a threat to the security of the state, Kant also argues that the state has the right to compel them to give up their lawless freedom and obey its laws. (See *M.M.* 307, 312.)[19]

Because the ultimate justification of the state is based not on advantage but on the moral law, the moral rightness of juridical coercion can be shown, Kant argues, by appealing to the criterion of practical consistency, the first formula of the Categorical Imperative. The principle setting out the legitimate use of coercive power by the state, Kant believes, is analytically true and thus self-evident: "We need only the principle of contradiction to see that, if external compulsion checks the hindering of harmonious outer freedom in accordance with universal laws (and is thus an obstacle to the obstacles to freedom), it could harmonize with ends as such" (*M.M.* 396). For whatever "counteracts the hindrance of an effect promotes that effect and is consistent with it" (*M.M.* 231). There simply is "no other remedy" for egoism and the injustices it causes than "to subject the private interest (of the individual) to the public interest (of all united) . . . to a discipline (of civil constraint)" (*Anthr.* 329).

It turns out, then, paradoxically enough, that, instead of being a threat to freedom in the sense of autonomy, political authority is both compatible with and absolutely necessary to autonomy, by preventing obstacles to its external exercise. (See *M.M.* 230–32.) It is the Law of Freedom, in the form of what Kant calls the "Principle of Right" (*Recht*), which legitimates coercion by the state. Such coercion, used to protect everyone's outer exercise of freedom equally by outlawing coercion by individuals, is the only permissible limitation on the freedom of the individual.[20] No other coercion may be exercised legitimately by the state. Most particularly, coercion may not be used to discourage the free and open discussion necessary for people to reach a rational consensus – the only alternative to a unity enforced by tyrannical power.

Given Kant's view of the innate and unsociable drives in human nature, the rule of law apparently does not mean that people within a juridical society will live together in perfect harmony, nor does it seem that the state should try to do away with all competition between them, for that would mean the end of progress in the development of reason within the state. (See *Cr.J.* 433.) Rather, the state should allow everyone the greatest amount of latitude for the competitive pursuit of morally permissible goals, but within a lawful common life. (See *Idea* 22.)

We might hope that the historical process will progress from external coercion by the state to a "golden age" in which the law of freedom will be internalized by each person and enforced only by self-constraint. (See *H.H.* 122.) But since human beings are not only imperfectly rational by nature but also infected by a propensity to evil, we can have confidence that the libertarian ideal is an "empty yearning" that Kant never seriously considered a genuine political possibility. Such an ideal may be the bond within a voluntary ethical community or church, but Kant was convinced that the demands of justice must be clarified, promulgated, and enforced politically. Political freedom in this world will always require the coercive support of the state. Without a juridical society with sufficient force at its disposal to compel its citizens to obey its laws, Kant is convinced that most people would tend to revert to a state of nature, which is "in the highest degree wrong" (M.M. 307).

There are, Kant states, four possible combinations of freedom, law, and power. Power without either freedom or law is barbarism, the state of nature; law and power without freedom are despotism; and law and freedom without power are anarchy, only a step away from barbarism. A civil constitution requires not only freedom and law but also coercive power. (See Anthr. 330–31; Conflict 32/53, 34n/57n.)

Crime and punishment

Within the state, the essence of crime is its violent and lawless violation of the fundamental social contract; crime occurs when individuals illegitimately use coercion against others, thereby encroaching on freedom in ways contrary to the consent on which civil communal living rests. For the most part Kant's views about both the justification of and the norm for the civil punishment of crime are fundamentally retributivist. An individual's unlawful deeds make that person deserving in strict legal justice of punishment, that is, the loss of happiness. (See Pr.R. 37; M.M. 321ff, 460.)[21] Justice may be mitigated by benevolence, but the criminal still owes *society* a strict debt to restore the reciprocal contractual relationship between obedience to the law and benefits received from living under the law. When, but only when, guilt and the proper punishment have been determined does Kant permit the introduction of utilitarian considerations based on experience, for example, the deterrence value of punishment and its possible contribution to the rehabilitation of the lawbreaker. (See M.M. 235–36, 331–37.)

When Kant addresses the question of judging legal guilt, he necessarily limits such judgments to considerations of a person's external behavior and that person's empirical or psychological personality and history. There is no way to determine with any certitude an individual's purely internal moral character. (See, e.g., Lect. 450–51/230–31.) Kant writes:

The real morality of actions, their merit or guilt, even that of our own conduct, thus remains entirely hidden from us. Our imputations can refer only to the empirical character. How much of this character is ascribable to the pure effect of freedom, how much to mere nature, that is, to faults of temperament for which there is no responsibility, or to its happy constitution (*merito fortunae*), can never be determined; and upon it therefore no perfectly just judgments can be passed. (Pu.R. A551n/B579n; see also A553–55/B581–83)[22]

Even though Kant acknowledges that we cannot hope to achieve (or know if we have achieved) the Idea of perfect and certain justice in any of our legal verdicts, he does argue that there is but one guide offered by reason "in accordance with universal laws grounded a priori" for us to use to determine the punishment appropriate for the harm done. That is the Old Testament law of strict reciprocity and just retribution (the *jus talionis*), *returning like for like*. (See *M.M.* 331–35.) The only just penalty for murder, for example, is death; but because even severe punishments may not deny a man the respect still due him as a person, Kant holds that, for the heinous crime of rape, castration and not rape constitutes just punishment. (See *M.M.* 333, 366, 463.)

No right to revolution

States typically claim they are the highest practical tribunal, subject to no higher available authority, with the right to hold that civil responsibilities override all other obligations. Contrary to John Locke's doctrine of the sovereignty of the people and their right to revolution, Kant appeals to the importance of law-abidingness to justify an absolutistic view of the citizens' duty to obey even tyrannies. The ultimate rational end of a civil society is its own self-preservation, for "it is only by the state constitution that civil society maintains itself" (*Anthr.* 331). To be *within* a state, Kant therefore concludes, *means* accepting its authority. The mandate "Obey the authorities!" is an unconditional moral as well as civil injunction (*Rel.* 8/7; see 99n/90; *T&P* 299).

Regardless of provocations by an unjust ruler, Kant argues, any supposed right to revolution would be a right to revert to the lawless state of nature, where only power, not justice, rules, and where there are no safeguards at all for freedom. No constitution can consistently grant genuinely sovereign power to the executive and also give citizens the right to revolt or the right to punish the executive for criminal activity. (See *T&P* 299; *P.P.* 344, 382–83; *M.M.* 317, 320.) A maxim permitting revolution, "if made universal, would destroy all civil constitutions, thus annihilating the only state in which men can possess rights" (*T&P* 299; see 299–304; *M.M.* 312, 319–23, 339, 355, 372).[23] Further, such a maxim is contrary to the notion of the lawfulness of practical maxims and so is self-contradictory and impermissible, although rebellion is sometimes understandable and perhaps even morally excusable. (See *M.M.* 319–20, 372–73.)

Kant further holds that we generally should not even allow ourselves to become involved in questions about the historical origin of the authority of the state, which could imperil our willingness to be obedient to its laws. (See *M.M.* 318–19, 371.) Likewise, he argues that, although citizens have the right to complain about injustice, freedom of speech and public criticism of the government need to be limited so as to exclude the abuse of freedom by the advocacy of rebellion. (See *M.M.* 319.) Kant does allow the possible legitimacy, within a limited constitutional state, of passive resistance to unjust laws when obedience to them would be morally corrupting; we may not obey civil laws that command what the moral law forbids. (See *M.M.* 322, 371;

Rel. 99n/90, 153n/142.) What is always morally permissible, however, is the right of an aggrieved citizen to emigrate and so withdraw from a civil contract, for a person is not a piece of property the state may retain at will. (See *M.M.* 338.)

Finally, Kant argues that, since revolution is always a heinous wrong for the individuals participating in it, the people actually living under an unjust government must never give up their hope that significant reforms can occur gradually and nonviolently. (See *P.P.* 353, 372; *M.M.* 339–40, 355; *Conflict* 92–93/167 and 169.)

Kant's discussions of civil disobedience and of the right to revolution are obviously inadequate, both in terms of his own moral theory and in terms of the judgments of ordinary moral reasoning. They are incomplete and misleading because they are framed only within the limits of the laws of a state that will not allow the possibility of armed rebellion against itself or even tolerate civil disobedience.[24] If civil laws are regarded as morally ultimate, then Kant has committed himself to an empirical "moral relativism" with political boundaries – an utterly untenable view condemned by his own analysis of the moral law as holding universally.

Kant has based his political theory on the a priori moral law that promulgates "human" and not merely "civil" responsibilities and duties.[25] The natural law provides moral criteria that are neither culturally nor constitutionally relative but that hold within every state and extend beyond the boundaries of the state to international law. It is the natural prepolitical law that provides the basis for legitimate conflict of grounds between an individual's civil and moral responsibilities. During Kant's lifetime, one of his followers did in fact argue that Kant's own theory not only permitted but required people to rebel against a government that in effect reverts to the original state of nature by denying them their political freedom and equality. They should do so in order to achieve an end that is also a duty – a just state. But Kant refused to even acknowledge the existence of the essay.[26]

There seems no other way to understand, if not excuse, Kant's strange stance in this regard except to remember that he was writing under despots. Even the benevolent Frederick required absolute obedience, and Kant could be quite sure that whatever he wrote about the obligations of a subject to his sovereign would be scrutinized carefully at court. It seems safe to speculate that Kant here was acting on the rule he had cited in a letter written in 1766 to his friend Mendelssohn: "I am absolutely convinced of many things that I shall never have the courage to say."[27] We therefore may presume that Kant did not say all that he could have said and knew needed to be said. As a consequence, anyone appealing to his political theory must "fill in" obvious deficiencies in his theory regarding political dissent and disobedience.

17
Civil justice and republicanism

The third formula of the Categorical Imperative reminds us that because we are social beings with intertwined moral destinies, we have a special obligation to promote and participate in a political form of the kingdom of ends.[1] But just as moral motives could not be counted on to motivate people to leave the state of nature, so also they cannot be counted on to motivate citizens to obey civil laws. (See *P.P.* 371.) Even the best possible state must therefore exercise coercion to enforce its laws, by attaching penalties to their violations. (See *M.M.* 219, 228.) But only external actions can be legislated by a state, not their inner structure. Kant therefore distinguishes, particularly in his *Metaphysics of Morals,* between the "doctrine of right" (*Rechtslehre*), or jurisprudence, and the "doctrine of virtue" (*Tugendlehre*), or ethics, strictly speaking. Both are parts of moral philosophy, for each rests finally on the Law of Autonomy, but they are differentiated mainly by the kind of constraint possible in each. (See *M.M.* 220.)

The doctrine of virtue concerns what Kant calls "duties of inner freedom" and "duties of virtue" (*Tugendpflichten*). These are obligations to respect morally obligatory ends and to do one's duty from the specifically ethical motive of dutifulness. (See, e.g., *M.M.* 214, 219–20, 231, 239, 379–83, 389, 394, 406, 410; *Lect.* 273/34–35.) They therefore depend on our own voluntary self-legislation and self-constraint. (See, e.g., *M.M.* 238n; *Lect.* 273/34–35, 433/212.) Because it is not possible for there to be a coerced exercise of free choice, no one can *make* another person be virtuous. "It is a contradiction to command someone not just to do something but also to do it willingly" (*End* 338; see *Pr.R.* 83). (It is, however, possible to influence another's intentions; see *Conflict* 22/33.)

Since only a person's behavior can be constrained by the state, civil laws can legislate only "duties of outer freedom" or "juridical [*rechtskräftig*] obligations." (See *M.M.* 205, 214, 219, 383, 390; *Lect.* 340/117.) Civil law does require obedience, but it does not and cannot require obedience from any particular motive, nor can it require the citizenry to have some particular purpose in mind when obeying its laws. (See *M.M.* 214, 218–20, 225, 227, 231–32, 239, 241, 375, 379–92, 394, 417–18, 434; *T&P* 179n.) It cannot insist, for example, on any single political conception of the highest final good for the human species. The laws of a state in effect can coerce the citizens to be law-abiding and act *as if* they were virtuous, but the state cannot make its citizens *be* morally virtuous.[2] Consequently, although the ultimate criterion for civil justice is the Categorical Imperative and civil obedience is morally obligatory, the *enforcement* of the civil law can appeal to and rest only on prudential incentives. It must be "based on empirical principles of human nature, not blushing to draw its maxims from the usages of the world" (*P.P.* 371).

The principle of right (*Recht*)

Probably no term bears more weight in moral and political theorizing today than "right," which Kant gave a place of honor in his political theory. In German the word *Recht* can mean either "right" or "law," and Kant plays on this ambiguity throughout his political writings. But in all of his discussions of rights, Kant always regards "duty" as the more fundamental notion. To say that a person has a right (a juridical "right of man" – *das Recht der Menschen*) is to say that he or she is able "to obligate others to a duty," that is, has a legally enforceable claim against others, limiting how they may behave toward him or her (*M.M.* 239). Likewise, for every juridical duty a person has, there is a corresponding right in the sense of legal entitlement possessed by the person or persons to whom that individual has that duty.[3] Finally, civil rights are all *negative* entitlements of justice, limiting through legal coercion how people may behave toward each other. (See *M.M.* 232, 239–40, 379, 383; *T&P* 289–90.)[4]

In Kant's political writings the term "law" (*Gesetz*) usually denotes the existing "complex of laws concerning external obligations, taken as a whole" (*Lect.* 272/34; see 273/34). The empirical fact that laws have been enacted by and are enforceable by the state does not, of course, thereby make them just. (See, e.g., *T&P* 289.) The moral acceptability of an existing statute depends on its conformity to the Categorical Imperative, especially the Formula of Universal Law. (See *M.M.* 229–30; *T&P* 289–90.) According to that formula, a person's claim to rights, requiring others to limit their actions in certain ways, also requires that person to act on the same limiting maxim, acknowledging that everyone else has the same rights.

The fact that civil laws are limited to enforcing the manner in which people behave toward one another means that when the Formula of Universal Law is used politically, it can be used only in a restricted form, to judge whether actions are morally "legal" or "lawful."[5] As we have seen, a morally legal action conforms to the letter of the moral law, considered apart from a person's purpose and motive for doing it. (See *M.M.* 214, 218–25, 230, 381, 396.) In its restricted form, the first formula is what Kant calls "the Universal Principle of Right" (or Justice – *Recht*). It states that "every action is right [*recht*] that in itself or in its maxim is such that the freedom of the will [*Willkür*] of each can coexist together with the freedom of everyone in accordance with a universal law" (*M.M.* 230; see 229–31, 249, 314, 382; *Pu.R.* A316/B373; *Rel.* 98n/90; *T&P* 289–90).

Kant holds that since it is a variation of the first formula, this principle is recognizable by reason alone. Further, since it is also contained analytically in the notion of what it is to be a person, to have "humanity," the Principle of Right may also be understood as a restricted variation of the second formula of the Categorical Imperative, mandating us to treat everyone "in accordance with their dignity" (*Enlight.* 42; see *M.M.* 238–39). Stated as an imperative, that principle is: "Act externally in such a way that the free use of your will [*Willkür*] is compatible with the freedom of everyone according to a universal law" (*M.M.* 231). Although this is the norm for judging the rightness of civil laws, it also follows that individual citizens cannot be required by the state to make this principle their motive for obeying its laws.

To summarize, according to Kant's liberal political philosophy, the function of civil law is to ensure a juridical condition that protects each person's freedom by protecting everyone's freedom. (See *M.M.* 227.) Just as Kant had championed the dignity of individual persons in the second formula by focusing on the impersonal moral law within them, so in his political theory he defends the rights of each citizen by focusing not on specific individuals and their desires but on a system of impersonal laws, a system of negative legislation that provides the purely formal juridical condition for the political social union. (See *T&P* 292.)

Kinds of laws

The laws imposed by a state are of two kinds. Those of the first kind are derived from "natural right" (or "natural law" – *Naturrecht*), requiring freedom in the negative sense of "independence from the constraint of another's will, insofar as it is compatible with the freedom of everyone else in accordance with a universal law" (*M.M.* 237). Kant holds that "natural right" is in fact the Principle of Right, obligating even those in the state of nature; it is the only innate (*angeboren*) or prepolitical right (*Recht*) we have. (See *M.M.* 237–42.)

By limiting the way in which people may treat one another, the natural law grounds our right to *have* rights. Specifically juridical laws derived from it specify primarily negative rights, forbidding us to engage in behaviors that cannot also be exercised by all others. (See *M.M.* 224, 237–38, 297.) Rights based on the natural law are determined by the very nature of kinds of actions – their universal form – and so, like the Principle of Right itself, can be recognized by reason alone. (See *Lect.* 273/34.) Specific natural rights (*natürliche Rechte*) include innate equality with all others; the right to one's physical, psychological, mental, and moral integrity; the right to be one's own master; the right to obey only laws to which we have given our consent; the right to acquire property; and the right to treat others as we like as long as we do not violate their freedom. (See *M.M.* 238, 238n, 250, 314.)[6] Because all such rights and laws specifying them hold universally, they provide the formal structure of a genuinely universal political code and therefore should be recognized in every political system.

Even though natural rights are not originated by the state, the public enactment of laws recognizing these rights is still crucial. In the state of nature where force and inclinations rule, natural rights exist only provisionally and lack both effective promulgation and enforcement. (See, e.g., *M.M.* 243, 306–7, 308n, 312–13, 343; *Anthr.* 329.)

The second kind of laws is "positive laws" (*positive Gesetze*) or merely "statutory" laws. In contrast to natural laws, these are laws only when and because they are enacted into law by the will of the legislator. (See *M.M.* 224, 229; *Lect.* 262/21–22.) These laws specify what is forbidden and required in matters that are in themselves arbitrary or morally indifferent, pertaining, for example, to rules of the road and the exact procedures for acquiring and transferring property.[7] Although they therefore may vary from place to place and time to time, positive laws still should not be contrary to the natural law. Since the state has a natural right to obligate its citizens to civil obedience, even positive laws must be recognized as civic duties (and, from the point of view of morality, as moral duties, too). (See *M.M.* 224–25, 227, 237, 256; *Rel.* 99n/90.)

The Principle of Publicity

To have a juridical society, laws must be promulgated publicly, and in his *Perpetual Peace* Kant offers another version of the Law of Autonomy – what he calls the transcendental Principle of Publicity (*das transcendentale Princip der Publicität*) (*P.P.* 382) – to determine what is and what is not politically right: "All actions that affect the rights of other men are wrong if their maxim is not consistent with publicity" (*P.P.* 381). (Publicity is also essential to enlightenment; see *Conflict* 89/161.) We have seen that the moral acceptability of maxims must be judged in an a priori fashion – on the basis of their *form*. Because the Principle of Publicity also concerns only the "form of universal lawfulness" (*P.P.* 386), it is but another version of the first formula. Morally acceptable laws must have what Kant calls the form of publicity; that is, they must be *capable* of being stated publicly.[8] Put affirmatively, the principle is: "All maxims that require publicity (in order not to fail of their end) agree with both politics and morality" (*P.P.* 386).[9] The end referred to here is the aim of the state adopting and acting on the law.

Kant reasons as follows: Maxims contrary to strict or negative obligations contradict themselves when made universal laws. Therefore, if a state (or a person) cannot openly divulge the purpose of a particular law (or maxim) without defeating its purpose, the law (or maxim) is unjust. Kant also states it this way: "If I cannot *publicly acknowledge* it without thereby inevitably arousing everyone's opposition to my plan, then this necessary and universal, and thus a priori foreseeable, opposition of all to me could not have come from anything other than the injustice with which it threatens everyone" (*P.P.* 381).[10]

The Principle of Publicity may therefore also be regarded as a variation of the second formula, which prohibits behaviors violating the dignity of others. (See also *Pr.R.* 87; *M.M.* 306.) No one should be treated according to a maxim that if made public law could not also "arise from the law of the passive subject" (*Pr.R.* 87) or, alternatively, that has a purpose that person

249

could not rationally share. (See *Gr.* 68/429–30.) This principle, Kant argues, is "only negative, i.e., it only serves for the recognition of what is not just to others" (*P.P.* 381). It is still true, however, that negative duties ground positive rights. Moreover, as we know, maxims or laws that do not violate the Categorical Imperative are not thereby obligatory but only permissible.

As we have seen, the Categorical Imperative may be used to judge the acceptability of maxims only within the context of a juridically moral condition, either actual or only ideal. Kant gives the example of a tyrant who openly states an unjust intention without worrying about the Principle of Publicity. (See *P.P.* 385.) Testing his or her maxim within the context of an ideal moral world does, of course, show that, when also considered as a universal law, the tyrant's maxim generates a contradiction and so is unjust. But a tyrant exercises power within a context of lawless, arbitrary choices and thereby simply ignores the principle and its verdict. The tyrant's only concern is to have enough power to overcome all possible opposition.

"Private morality"

Kant borrowed the expression "private law" (*Privatrecht*) from Roman law as a technical term to designate laws concerning only the relations between individuals (e.g., property and family laws), in contrast to public law (*öffentliches Recht*) in which the state is an interested third party. (See *M.M.* 242, 245, 264.)[11] In a state of nature there can be legitimate societies (conjugal, paternal, etc.) and thus also private law in Kant's technical sense. In fact, apart from an existing juridical society that "actively binds together the different physical or moral persons, there can be only private law" (*P.P.* 383 [Beck]). But once a juridical society exists, private laws obviously should be enacted into public laws (*M.M.* 306).

Within a juridical union, there can still and necessarily must be a "private will," that is, each individual's pursuit of his or her "private ends." (See *Gr.* 74/433; *Pr.R.* 87.) But the pursuit of happiness is not a completely private matter, for everyone may still act – make contracts, buy and sell property, and so on – only in ways that are permissible *within* the restrictions of public law. (See *Pu.R.* A810/B838; *Pr.R.* 87; *Gr.* 36/412.) As we have seen, specifically ethical duties (that is, one's inner motives and purposes in acting), as well as each individual's decisions about how to fulfill positive moral obligations, also cannot be made part of public law. But rather than competing with the public law, specifically ethical obligations support and supplement the public law, even if they cannot become an explicit part of it.

The point is that, within the Kantian system, there can be no notion of "private morality" as a distinct and legitimate part of morality *competing* with public morality, restricting the range of the norm of universality, and concerned only with what, in today's vocabulary, we might refer to as a person's private life – what a person does apart from any public roles and in the privacy of his or her own home, alone or with friends. One's private conduct is always limited by the one ultimate and public moral principle, the Categorical Imperative. For Kant, it would be precisely the decision to make one's private will (one's inclinations) either exempt from public morality or supreme in any practical matter that would make a person morally evil. So, within the Kantian moral and political theory, "private morality" in the sense specified is the essence of egoistic, antisocial, self-centered immorality, in effect a decision to revert to the state of nature, to living lawlessly.

Kant has placed political justice under the broader heading of morality but still has claimed that "all [external] duties, simply because they are duties, belong to ethics" (*M.M.* 219). He also has maintained that all negative natural laws regarding external freedom hold universally and so should be incorporated into the laws of every state. It therefore follows that Kant believes not only that civil laws inconsistent with negative moral laws need to be changed but also that the civil law should prohibit the same behaviors forbidden by the natural law. (See *M.M.* 306–7.)[12] The basis for civil legislation, again, is the natural law, not prudence.

Kant, however, is not naive about political realities, and he also maintains that morality does not require us to be foolish in dealing with inconsistencies between the moral and civil law. "It would be absurd to demand that every defect be immediately and impetuously changed," for the stability of the bonds of civil society also need to be taken into account (*M.M.* 372). On the one hand, he condemns the "despotizing moralist," who ignores all the "rules of political prudence" by precipitous legislative changes that in effect show a lack of respect for the electorate. (See *M.M.* 355.) On the other hand, he also scorns the "moralizing politician," who makes legislative reform impossible by constantly talking about the inability of human nature to do what is right, all the while acting only for his or her personal advantage and thereby effectively undermining the Principle of Right (*M.M.* 374; see 373–79).

Whenever changes in legislation are necessary to make civil law conform to the moral law, Kant writes, the electorate should be encouraged to a change of heart so that the necessary changes can eventually be made with their consent. The changes eventually *must* be made. Morality *may* recognize that prudence has an important role in statecraft, but morality still holds primacy: "Right [*Recht*] must never be accommodated to politics but politics always accommodated to right."[13] As he also writes, "The rights of men must be held sacred, however great the cost of sacrifice may be to those in power. Here one cannot go halfway, cooking up hybird, pragmatically-conditioned rights (which are somewhere between the right and the expedient); instead all politics must bend its knee before morality" (*P.P.* 380).

Morality and politics

The most common objection to using moral criteria in civic decision making is the contention that moral ideals are simply impractical: The hard realities of the political world cannot take moral considerations into account. (See *P.P.* 370–86; *T&P* 276–77.) Kant admits that we often experience both private and public conflicts between prudential and moral interests. But moral reason enjoys primacy, and Kant predictably insists that "true politics cannot take a single step without first paying homage to morals." In fact, he refuses to call political decisions dictated only by prudential concerns "practice," since "that would imply that it rested on rational maxims" (*P.P.* 379; *T&P* 275). Only moral reasoning is rational through and through. He therefore contends that, objectively or in theory, there can be no genuine conflicts between morality rightly understood and politics as "a practical doctrine of right" (*P.P.* 370).

In his argument Kant focuses on the problem of attaining a stable peace. The politician who tries to use prudential considerations quickly finds they cannot offer any certainties. (But Jeremy Bentham later still claimed it is possible to assess the consequences of any policy in exact quantitative terms.) Even though the ultimate moral criterion, the Categorical Imperative, ignores the desirability of peace, it still much more effectively promotes peace just because of its a priori recognition of the freedom and equality of everyone concerned. So it turns out that the most practical political judgments are not prudential guesses that only seem to promote peace by trying to take into account the desires of various individuals and groups, but those decisions that conform to the ultimate political Principle of Right. (See *P.P.* 343, 377–78.)

Kant's philosophy of history, which led him to contend that moral progress within a state often emerges from morally corrupt prudential behaviors, is a perspective only for the spectator of world history. It is not a standpoint anyone may adopt as a maxim on which to act as a citizen. Moreover, as culture has continued to develop, people have become increasingly aware both of the injustice that egoism causes and of the fact that they belong to a species with a moral "vocation, as reason represents it to [them] in the ideal" (*Anthr.* 329–30). However wickedly people may tend to behave, mankind still is not completely evil; each person is "also endowed with a moral predisposition" (*Anthr.* 329; see *P.P.* 355; *Rel.* 27/22–23). Each person therefore shares responsibility for promoting the ends of moral reason within civil society. The moral law commands them each to do so, while at the same time it is Kant's faith that they can be confident that Providence eventually will accomplish what they cannot.

The ideal state: a republic

Obviously not every political arrangement conforms to the Idea of a kingdom of ends on earth. A morally acceptable political union, as we have seen, must be based on the Principle of Right. Only a state conforming to the principle of classical liberalism can be fully acceptable to persons who view themselves as autonomous agents. Only then is an "enduring constitution possible" (*P.P.* 374; see 373–79). A stable government also must be strong enough to allow its citizens the greatest freedom possible to develop and exercise their ability to think – and still protect the peace, both internally and externally. (See

P.P. 373.) Kant believed that achieving such a state is at least as difficult as leaving the state of nature.

In the transition from the state of nature to a morally acceptable society, the most fundamental theoretical problem is how to arrange political power so as to protect the citizenry, insofar as possible, from misuse of power by the state itself. Kant argues that such protection can be secured best only when the functions of the government are kept separate and when the legislative power rests with the people. (See *M.M.* 338–42.) A just government, therefore, should have three distinct branches, each independent and supreme in its own proper function – the legislative, the executive, and the judicial. (See *M.M.* 313, 316–18.)[14]

The legislative power must belong in the hands of a popularly elected assembly, for, Kant argued, if people are to be bound by civil law and yet retain their autonomy, they can be subject only to laws of their own willing. (See *M.M.* 223; *Conflict* 91/165.) Freedom and equality therefore can flourish only within a state in which sovereign authority rests finally with the consent of the people, whose will must also guide the decisions of the chief executive. Kant offers a specifically *political* conception of the moral, autonomous will – what he calls the general legislative will (*Wille*) of the people (*M.M.* 306; see 223).[15] He uses various expressions to designate this Idea of reason: the "distributive unity" of the people, the "general will," the "collective will," and the "united will" of the people. (See *Idea* 24; *Enlight.* 40; *T&P* 294–305; *Rel.* 98/90; *P.P.* 351–53, 371, 383; *M.M.* 256, 313, 328, 338.)[16] But it is clear that what he refers to here as the ground for both political authority and obedience to it is not an empirical political consensus but the Law of Autonomy residing in the will of the people. "All right and justice is supposed to proceed from this authority," and because the Law of Autonomy is the ultimate norm for justice and for respect of persons, the united will "can do absolutely no injustice to anyone." (See *M.M.* 313; *T&P* 292.)

For legislation to enunciate the general will, it is not necessary that everyone actually agree to it. It could happen that a substantial percentage of the population dislike a law, say, of taxation, but only because it lessens their consumable income.[17] By itself that would not mean that such a law violates the general will. The Law of Autonomy is a prescriptive law, determining how people *should* agree if they all fulfilled that law. For a law to be just, therefore, it is only necessary that "it is possible that a people *could* agree to it" *if* they were to follow their reason rather than their desires (*M.M.* 297, emphasis mine; see 297–98). With regard to especially complex and difficult decisions, "unanimity cannot be expected of an entire people" and perhaps not even a majority in the case of a direct vote by a large population. The general will of the people may come down to "a majority of those delegated as representatives of the people" (*T&P* 296). (But Kant neglected to discuss how it is possible to arrange a representative government so as not to violate the responsibility of each person to judge the moral rightness of prospective legislation, a responsibility one would think should not be delegated to anyone else.)

253

What will keep a representative government from degenerating into a democratic tyranny that ignores the rights of minorities is the requirement that both the executive and judicial branches be constitutionally insulated from direct popular pressures that could reintroduce arbitrary privileges on behalf of some individuals or groups. (See *P.P.* 351–53.)

So Kant concluded that the "one and only legitimate constitution," the one that best satisfies the requirements – of autonomy, of universal law, and of respect for persons – imposed by the Categorical Imperative, is that of a republic. Little wonder, then, that he admired the representative constitutions already adopted on a secular foundation by the French Republic and, some ten years earlier, in 1787, in North America under the influence of Enlightenment thinkers such as Jefferson, Paine, and Franklin (*M.M.* 340; see also 340–42, 351; *P.P.* 349–50, 366; *Conflict* 85–86/153 and 155). Such governments rest on the free, rational consent of the people. By minimizing tendencies toward despotism in a pure democracy, they are also best able to protect everyone's freedom and maintain the peace (see *Conflict* 91/165).[18]

Principles of a republican government

Civil laws are just and the civil rights of each person are properly respected, Kant believes, when those laws are based on three a priori principles of representative government.[19] These principles explicitly enunciate Kant's classical liberalism.[20] Again, his limited-government political theory emphasizes both political liberty and the contractual consent of citizens regarded as free, equal, and autonomous individuals, and it restricts civil laws to either universal negative principles of justice or laws compatible with such principles.

The first principle concerns "the freedom of every member of society as a human being" to pursue happiness, each in his or her own way (*T&P* 290). This version of what is often called "the neutrality principle" follows from the primacy of moral over prudential interests: "No one can compel me (in accordance with his beliefs about the welfare of others) to be happy after his fashion; instead, every person may seek happiness in the way that seems best to him," as long as his doing so does not violate anyone else's right to pursue happiness, "under a possible universal law" (*T&P* 290; see *Pr.R.* 119). In Kant's interpretation, this principle, which is also a fundamental tenet of classical liberalism, is implicit in the first formula of the Categorical Imperative for which Kant now gives a new variation: "So act that you can will that your maxim could become a universal law, regardless of the end" (*P.P.* 377). As did Locke and the American Constitution, Kant represents what is right (and therefore also what is just) as more fundamental than, and thus as defined independently of, the notion of the "good," that is, of any particular conception of social welfare or of individual self-realization.

As a political norm, then, the principle of freedom "has nothing whatsoever to do with the ends that men have by nature (the objective of attaining happiness)" (*T&P* 289). Civil laws conforming to that law are *limitations,* concerned with our quest for happiness *only* insofar as they set the formal limits on what anyone may do in its pursuit. (See *M.M.* 375.) Moreover, like the notions of "culture" and "self-realization," "happiness" is a subjective and imaginative notion that varies from person to person and cannot function as an objective rational principle holding universally. (See *Anthr.* 331.) As we also saw in Chapters 5 and 15, the moral law does not and cannot specify exactly what and how much we must do to fulfill our personal wide duties to others. Consequently, there also is no rational way in which the state can or should try to formulate or enforce positive, universal laws about how it should contribute to the happiness of the citizens, much less laws that would also be compatible with the freedom of everyone. (See *T&P* 290, 298.)[21]

So, even though the official mythology rests the genesis and justification of the state on prudential grounds, the state, once founded, has no positive obligation to assume responsibility for anyone's pursuit of happiness. The purpose of civil law is "not as it were, to make the people happy against their will, but only to make them exist as a commonwealth," that is, to preserve the state constitution once it exists (*T&P* 298–99; see *Anthr.* 331). Moreover, the well-being of the state consists in the construction of a constitution according to justice, not according to a barometer of the happiness or material well-being of its citizens. (See *M.M.* 318.) Therefore, no one holds a rightful claim against the state for failing to be sufficiently concerned about his or her personal happiness. (See *M.M.* 318; *T&P* 289.) What each person does have a right to is the freedom to *pursue* his or her own happiness in lawful ways. (See *M.M.* 382.)

It was also Kant's respect for the freedom and dignity of persons that led him in his political theory to credit each person with both the capacity and the responsibility to identify the nature of the best human life and to tend to his or her pursuit of that life. Kant excoriates any paternalistic model of government that would violate the freedom or dignity of its citizens by authoritarian edicts, telling them what they *must* believe about the meaning of life or how they *will* be happy, "like immature children unable to distinguish between what is truly useful or harmful to them" (*T&P* 290; see 290–91; *M.M.* 316–17, 454; *Anthr.* 209).[22] He also believes that a welfare state would exacerbate the natural human tendencies to selfishness and sloth and, by doing so, encourage people to remain in perpetual "tutelage" – the immoral unwillingness to develop one's own capabilities.[23]

The second principle of a republican form of government mandates "the equality of each member with every other as a subject" (*T&P* 290). It requires each person to recognize and protect the right of everyone to the external exercise of freedom compatible with the Principle of Right (*M.M.* 231; see 230, 314). By definition a law must be universal in form, and the principle of juridical equality requires that laws apply to everyone equally, with no exceptions made in favor of any individuals or groups such as a hereditary nobility or an ecclesiastical foundation with perpetual proprietorship of lands. (See *H.H.* 114; *T&P* 293–94; *P.P.* 350n, 351n; *M.M.* 324–25, 367–70.) Under this principle, each person has exactly the same rights as every other person – and the same right to protect those rights through the coercion of public law (*M.M.* 232; see 232–33; *T&P* 291–93).[24] No one has a rightful claim to some special, innate privileged political status. No one may take away or diminish another's rights (unless that person has committed a crime), nor may any person voluntarily surrender his or her own rights (*T&P* 292–93).

The principle of equality of civil rights, however, is not a principle of egalitarianism in the actual distribution of goods or of power, for egalitarianism of that sort is not possible without continual violations of freedom and justice. Since each person is responsible for his or her own happiness, Kant sternly resists any move in the direction of a welfare state that would aim at egalitarian economics. (See *P.P.* 376, 379.) Maintaining that each person has exactly the same legal rights, Kant argues, is not inconsistent with the sorts of substantial inequalities in possessions, power, and opportunities that arise in every society from a combination of talent, industry, and luck. (See *T&P* 291–93.) Such differences, Kant contends, can be dealt with – insofar as the state is obligated to deal with them at all – simply and justly by a formal legal requirement of a fundamental equality of opportunity for all. (See *M.M.* 256, 315; *T&P* 293.) In fact, since the principle of equality concerns only the form of law and not the matter or object of desires, Kant rephrases that principle as: "Every member of the commonwealth must be permitted to attain any degree of status (to which a subject can aspire) to which his talent, his industry, and his luck may bring him; and his fellow subjects may not . . . hinder him or his descendants" (*T&P* 292). Kant included the last phrase, since he saw no violation of rights in people bequeathing their personal possessions to whomever they might wish (*T&P* 292–93).[25]

The third and final principle of a republican government states that both the authority of the government and the legitimacy of its laws rest with the rational consent of the governed. This requires the recognition of "the independence of every member of the commonwealth as a citizen . . . that is, as a co-legislator" of the laws of the state (*T&P* 290, 294; see *M.M.* 223, 314, 345–46). Since civil laws lay down what is allowed and forbidden for everyone, the justice of a proposed law can be determined by using the norm of the general will to ask, Can the people consent to such a law and impose it on themselves, no matter how much pain it may cost them? (See *P.P.* 349n; *Enlight.* 39; *T&P* 297, 299.)[26] Kant's analysis of the notion of the general will here again shows that it is an Ideal that does not require the *actual* consent of every person. People are not entitled, for example, to engage in criminal conduct simply because they want to do so, nor do opinions based on ignorance or emotion deserve respect.

Perpetual peace and a league of nations

Like his philosophical ancestors the Stoics, Kant believed that moral reason "voices its irresistible veto: there should be no war" (*M.M.* 354). Perpetual international peace – the permanent cessation of warfare and not merely a temporary truce between wars – should be our ultimate political goal on earth. (See *P.P.* 343.) However independent nations may try to be of one another, they also "cannot do without associating peacefully with one another" (*Anthr.* 331). In his most famous political essay, *Perpetual Peace,* published first in 1795 and in a revised and enlarged edition a year later, Kant describes individual states as "moral persons," with the same external rights and obligations as all other persons. He argues that in their external relations to one another, nations were all originally (and are still) in a nonjuridical and lawless state of nature, either actually at war – each trying to force the other to yield to its will – or continually preparing for war. Despite any public pronouncements to the contrary, such behavior shows a fundamental disregard for the rule of law and morality, for, more than war itself, the "never-ending and constantly increasing arming for future war" prevents nations from attending to what is genuinely worthwhile (*H.H.* 121; see *P.P.* 345, 347, 367; *Idea* 24; *Rel.* 34/29–30, 96/88; also *M.M.* 343–45).

Kant's proposal for a lasting peace closely follows an earlier proposal for a federation of European states made by the Abbé de Saint-Pierre in the latter's 1713 *Projet de paix perpétuelle.* The Abbé's plan required enormous imagination, particularly at the time he wrote, as well as a "cosmopolitan" vision, transcending all forms of provincialism – geographic, temporal, and nationalistic. The only way to ensure international peace and security, he wrote and Kant echoed, is for nations to organize into a league of nations and agree to authorize that institution to arbitrate international disputes by means of a system of common international laws "established on a moral basis," that is, conforming to the natural law (*Cr.J.* 433; see *M.M.* 311–12, 344; *Lect.* 470–71).[27]

Of course, nations, like individuals, will resist yielding their power to an international commonwealth. So Kant thinks it probable that Nature again will have to allow the devastation of war to continue until, out of sheer exhaustion and fear of even further destruction, nations will finally be willing to "give up their brutish freedom" (*Idea* 24–25; see *Cr.J.* 432–33; *T&P* 310–13). There are, however, other prudential considerations that Nature can use to promote peace. As international trade increases, nations will become increasingly economically dependent on one another. In their concern for profits, they may decide that it is in their best self-interest "to promote an honorable peace," to negotiate disputes in order to avoid risking their own prosperity (*P.P.* 368). Moreover, international competition will induce countries to promote the education of their citizens so they can compete more effectively with other nations.

From the point of view of the plan of Nature for the human race as a whole, then, not only war and the fear of war but also materialism and avarice, exploitation and social stratification all may turn out to be "indispensable means to the still further development of human culture" (*H.H.* 121; see *Cr.J.* 432). This is highly desirable, since few people want the self-discipline that the development of reason requires. But they can be motivated by the unsocial desire to surpass others, especially when this motive is broadened into a nationalistic motive. (See *Idea* 22.)

With the growth of culture may emerge greater moral pressure for peace.

Kant cannot resist the hope that moral reason may be able to play a larger role in preventing an international state of nature from continuing indefinitely. People sufficiently enlightened may be able to influence their governments to act justly toward other nations. If they cannot actually prevent warfare, they may still be able to insist that nations set limits to what is allowable in battle. Moreover, they also can encourage victorious nations to allow the vanquished to rebuild their juridical condition, if possible, as a republic. (See *P.P.* 343–48; *M.M.* 343–51.)[28]

The Idea of a lasting international peace, Kant writes, requires not only that the individual governments eventually adopt a republican constitution, each promoting distributive justice, but also that the league of nations itself have a republican constitution. (See *Idea* 29; *P.P.* 354–57; *M.M.* 350–55.) But even under an international commonwealth, individual nations will still show the same competitiveness as do individual citizens within states. Therefore, such a league must have sufficient military power so that it can arbitrate conflicts by laws of justice rather than allowing open hostilities.[29]

So great are the obstacles in the way of achieving such a league and perpetual peace that Kant occasionally seems to waver in his conviction that they are genuinely attainable. But no matter how difficult they may be to achieve, these are still regulative Ideas that reason projects as necessary moral ends (*Anthr.* 331). Just because a goal has not yet been attained does not mean that it cannot be attained. (See *T&P* 309–10.) Moreover, Kant writes hopefully, "perpetual peace is *insured* (guaranteed) by nothing less than the great artist *nature*" (*P.P.* 360). We therefore must regard peace as a genuine possibility and not just a fantasy. (See *Rel.* 34, 34n/29–30; *P.P.* 357; *M.M.* 350–55; *Anthr.* 331.)

Kant's moral and political theories

The connections between Kant's political and ethical philosophies are obvious enough. A transformed interpretation of Rousseau's political principle of self-legislation is the foundation of both Kant's political and moral philosophies. There is little profit in trying to decide whether Kant's political views were an outgrowth of his moral views, or whether his political convictions came first in the development of his thinking and led to his moral doctrines, or whether the two more or less evolved together. Far more important is how the two so mirror each other both in vocabulary and in structure that it can be argued that Kant's ethics is as much a political as a moral theory.[30]

For example, internal moral conflict for the individual finds its external counterpart in the conflicts within civil society between what is expedient and what is right and between citizens, as well as in conflicts between nations. The moral law appears, in a necessarily restricted form, as the political Principle of Right, and like the moral law, civil law is also by its very nature coercive. Although legitimate political coercion involves external coercion rather than the self-restraint of moral virtue, its legitimacy still rests finally on self-constraint, on our recognition of the rights and dignity of all persons

– a moral foundation – and entails that the laws of a nation must be just in the sense of protecting the greatest possible freedom for everyone. Just as the Categorical Imperative is the impersonal norm for the maxims of individuals, the Principle of Right also requires that the laws of a state be impersonal and be applied evenhandedly to everyone, without distinctions between classes based on differences in position or wealth.

One of the best ways in which to understand the Categorical Imperative is to think of it as the antithesis of tyranny. Tyrants use other people as their property, merely as things for their own private purposes, and have no respect for the rights or intrinsic worth of their subjects nor for their individual pursuit of happiness. By contrast, the Law of Autonomy forbids us to use anyone in such a fashion; we may not even use ourselves merely as a means to satisfying our desires. But within this limitation moral reason recognizes that each person has a legitimate right to be concerned about and pursue his or her own happiness, and that each person's pursuit of happiness therefore is to be protected insofar as it does not deny anyone else's right to do so as well. Like the moral law, civil law functions mainly as a negation, limiting our actions by the right of others. Civil laws should be enforced only to defend the primacy of lawfulness over lawlessness, not to promote any particular individual's or group's best prudential interests.

It is unfortunate that Kant's political writings are not usually read alongside his ethical writings, since each illuminates the other. Clearly, Kant's political philosophy belongs at the center of his moral philosophy, just as his moral philosophy provides the center for his entire Critical enterprise.

The value of the political life

Finally, what, for Kant, is the value of politics? Clearly, political life is a prudential and an instrumental good, for people commonly assent to the civil constitution, as they assent to other social unions, in order to attain what they want – here the security to pursue such goods as associations with others, possessions, power, and recognition. (See *T&P* 289.) But political activity can be and ought to be more than that. A life in which we act justly in our external relations with others is possible only within a civil society. Such a life is therefore always both a means to and a necessary condition for human moral life. It also enforces at least an important part of our moral duties. (See *Conflict* 91–92/165 and 167.)

What the public law cannot command as an incentive but what is always up to each individual is the recognition that the just demands of public law are moral duties. (See *T&P* 289, 292.) Civil rights are publicly legislated and enforced moral rights, the right (*Recht*) of people under public coercive laws that derive entirely from the Law of Autonomy.

Moreover, a just state, a world federation of states, and lasting peace are all part of the moral end of humankind on earth, the kingdom of ends. We can and should therefore regard civic life as an integral part of human moral life. The good citizen should obey the laws of the state because to do so is a moral duty, and the "moral politician" should put politics at the service of morality and seek, above all, justice. (See *P.P.* 372, 377.) The life of both the citizen and the politician, then, should be made an intrinsic good, an end in itself, and such a life, lived dutifully, is not only our moral duty but also unconditionally good. (See, e.g., *Rel.* 99n/90.) In one sense, in fact, political ends are higher than the final goal of individuals, for the promotion of the political kingdom of ends rests on a social and *sui generis* duty, not of individuals to individuals, but of the human race to itself. (See *Rel.* 97/89.)

Kant's political philosophy has occasionally been criticized on the grounds that he did not accord it a sufficiently high place in his total philosophy. Kant could have given the state no higher place in his philosophy than he gave it: A just state is an essential part of our necessary moral goal on earth – the kingdom of ends in political form; and obedience to the laws of such a state is a moral duty, as sacred as if they were divine commands. (See *Rel.* 99n/90.) As one form of the kingdom of ends on earth, a just state is a necessary object of moral reason and of human life. Moreover, the limitations of politics are not limitations that Kant arbitrarily imposed on it. Rather they are limitations that every political philosopher has found inherent in the very nature of the state – at least every philosopher who has held that the worth and dignity of its citizens are based on their very nature rather than on the state itself. Finally, by insisting that we must think of our moral destiny as part of a larger whole encompassing first all our fellow citizens and then all mankind, our reason gives political life a place of particular honor within the pursuit of the meaning of human moral life.[31]

18
Kant's philosophy of religion

It is fitting that the study of Kant's practical philosophy should conclude with his philosophy of religion, since it was his conviction that morality leads inevitably to religion. (See *Pr.R.* 129; *Rel.* 6/5.) This claim proved so disappointing to antireligious Enlightenment thinkers that, according to an often repeated story, it was cynically suggested that Kant had put religion into his system in his old age only to spare the feelings of Lampe, his devout man-servant. But a close reading of his Critical writings clearly shows that, despite Kant's disaffection with the emotionalism of Pietism, he had always retained a profound belief in a personal God who providentially cares for the human species he has created. Friedrich Paulsen goes so far as to claim that "the real purpose of the critical philosophy, the philosophy of Kant, is . . . to restore the agreement between faith and knowledge" to show how it is "possible to be at once a candid thinker and an honest man of faith."[1] Indeed, in his second preface to his *Critique of Pure Reason,* Kant had written that such a critique would "above all" have the "inestimable benefit" of forever silencing "all objections to morality and religion" (*Pu.R.* Bxxxi).

Kant was also criticized for introducing God into his system only as a *deus ex machina,* an ad hoc solution to problems he could solve in no other way. This is an excessively harsh verdict, however, for Kant did no more than what virtually every other philosopher before him had done – conclude that the answers to our most ultimate philosophical questions can be found only in transcendent Being. The chief difference between Kant and his predecessors lay in Kant's insistence that, even if these are theoretical questions, they may be addressed only by moral-practical reasoning.

In the preceding chapters we have seen almost every positive thing Kant had to say about religion. His claims have all been based on the same fundamental contention: To live our lives rationally – and the moral law within us apodictically commands us to do so – we must accept what that moral law requires us to accept, whether as necessary presuppositions, as necessary procedural assumptions, or as necessary goals. Belief, then, in a personal God, in divine providence, in the immortality of the human soul, and in divine grace is both specified by and based entirely and only on reason. Kant was convinced that we cannot live our lives in a fully rational way without a practical faith in these unavoidable religious requirements of our own reason.

What was mainly left for Kant to do in his *Religion Within the Limits of Reason Alone* was to develop those themes he already had introduced and to construct a negative critique of historical religions. Religious belief may not be based on heteronomous reasons – not on emotions, whether of loneliness or fear or even hope, and certainly not on the philosophically weakest of all supports, the appeal to authority, whether natural or supernatural. But throughout this discussion, it should be kept in mind that Kant regarded religion itself as so important that he believed treating it with ridicule or contempt a "dreadful offense." His negative criticisms are directed only at "particular absurd duties" that had come to be associated with historical religions, and his aim was to defend and clarify what he regarded as religion in its only pure, authentic form – religion within the bounds of moral reason. (See *Lect.* 314/88.)

"The philosopher of Protestantism"

Richard Kroner notes that "Kant has often been called the philosopher of Protestantism; this is true, if one takes seriously the emphasis he put on conscience as the highest tribunal of the moral and religious consciousness."[2] But, as Kroner then points out, "The moral freedom of man is not merely a freedom from nature, but also a freedom from external supernatural powers. No one before Kant had ever exalted man so much; no one had ever accorded him such a degree of metaphysical independence."[3] This independence is rooted in the moral demands of both the Enlightenment and the moral law that each person renounce all "tutelage" and think for himself or herself.

The epistemic foundation for Kant's examination of historical religions had been laid in his first *Critique.* Knowledge is a human accomplishment, and we may claim to have knowledge of the existence and nature of reality only insofar as we can encounter it in our experience: "We shall entitle the principles [for understanding reality] whose application is confined entirely within the limits of possible experience, *immanent;* and those, on the other hand, which profess to pass beyond these limits [and so are merely speculative], *transcendent*" (*Pu.R.* A295–96/B352; see A308–9/B365, A327/B383, A638/B666, A643/B671, A845–46/B873–74). Kant thereby limited the knowledge claims of both science and speculative theology to the world of sensory experience. Such experience gives us no metaphysical insights into supersensuous or supernatural reality. (See *Rel.* 194/182.) Any theoretical claims to some unique access to the supernatural are all equally transcendent. (See *M.M.* 488–89.)

We have seen that the moral law requires us to *think* of God as a Person. But because our experience is limited to appearances of finite reality, God is simply inaccessible to us. (See *Rel.* 174/162; *M.M.* 489; *Conflict* 57/103.) We therefore can have absolutely no theodicy, *no knowledge* of God – of his existence, of his nature, or of his will. We only generate contradictions and paradoxes when we try to understand, for example, how God might be both merciful and just toward us. (See *M.M.* 489.) We can "understand nothing of such transcendent relationships of man to the Supreme Being" (*Rel.* 72/66; see 195n/183; *M.M.* 487–91). So Kant argues:

All attempts to employ reason in theology in any merely speculative manner are altogether fruitless and by their very nature null and void, and . . . the principles of its employment in the study of nature do not lead to any theology whatsoever. Consequently, the only theology of reason which is possible is that which is based upon moral laws or seeks guidance from them. (*Pu.R.* A636/B664; see A814–18/B842–46)

Moreover, since we have no knowledge of God, we also have no duties *to* God; our duties to others concern only the "moral relations of men to men" (*M.M.* 491; see 488).

The orthodox view in which Kant had been reared held that religion is and must be the foundation of morality, and it defined "moral virtue" as fidelity to God's will: We may never oppose our will to God's. But, Kant responds, it is only from our own reason that we come to have even the Idea of God. (See *M.M.* 443; *Rel.* 168n/157; *Orient.* 142.) "Where do we get the concept of God as the highest good?" he asks. "Solely from the *Idea* of moral perfection which reason traces a priori and conjoins inseparably with the concept of a free will. . . . Even the Holy One of the gospel must first be compared with our ideal of moral perfection before we can recognize him to be such" (*Gr.* 29/408–9; see *Rel.* 104/95, 141/132–33; *Lect.* 277–78/40).

We therefore need not – indeed must not – look to religion for knowledge of the moral law or for a motive to obey the law. Autonomy cannot be grounded on anything but our own reason. If we define "morality" as conformity to God's will even as supposedly revealed, we risk falling into heteronomy. By thinking of God as the rewarding and avenging power behind the moral law, we turn that law into a rule of prudence, and we then can be motivated to obey it only by the hope of reward and the fear of punishment. (See *M.M.* 484, 478; *Lect.* 278/41, 282–83/51–52, 307–8/81–82; *Ed.* 493–95/ 109–15.) This destroys the moral value of our actions.

Orthodoxy also claimed that Holy Scripture is the ultimate source of religious truth, before which human judgment must bow. Once again Kant disagrees, arguing that since the only purpose of reading Sacred Scripture is "to make men better," the Bible must be interpreted according to the moral law, not the moral law according to Scripture. (See *Rel.* 87/81, 110–11/100– 1, 110n/101–2, 132–33/123.) We may regard the contents of the Bible as authentic revelation only if its moral teaching agrees with what we already know on purely rational grounds to be morally right. (See *Rel.* 104/95, 113– 14/103–5.) This means we often must interpret the Bible "symbolically" rather than literally if we are to show that it proclaims the same moral law as our own reason and offers a genuinely religious meaning and hope to human moral striving. (See *Conflict* 40–41/69 and 71, 46–47/81 and 83.)[4]

Lewis White Beck summarizes Kant's view succinctly and well:

There is no such thing as a theological morality, i.e., a system of moral rules derived from knowledge of God. There are three reasons for this. First, we do not have the knowledge. Second, if we did have it and used it as a moral premise, the autonomy of morals would be destroyed. Third, moral laws are not dependent upon any lawgiver, as if a difference in the nature of God (or the non-existence of God) would make any difference in the determination of duty.[5]

So, as he had done when defending both the reality of our moral nature and the primacy of pure practical reason, Kant inverts the traditional view. The Enlightenment ideal of freedom convinced him that no one can be morally good who does not have the "courage to stand on his own feet" by following his own reasoning. (See *Rel.* 184/172.) Our own moral reason – pure practical reason – is the only foundation of authentic religious belief and practice. (See *Rel.* 202/190.) The claims of religion, then, must be limited to what is consistent with our own moral reasoning, to "the bounds of reason alone" (*M.M.* 488). Although "the doctrine of religion is an integral part of the general doctrine of duties," the task of delimiting rightful religious claims is an application of ethics rather than being ethics itself (*M.M.* 487; see 487–88). "I must first know that something is my duty before I can accept it as a divine injunction" (*Rel.* 154/143).

In this sense, Kant argues, moral obligations are logically independent of religion and even of the existence of God. "For its own sake morality does not need religion at all (whether objectively, as regards willing, or subjectively, as regards ability [to act]); by virtue of pure practical reason it is self-sufficient" (*Rel.* 3/3). Yet, insofar as we find it difficult to make the claims of moral obligations "tangible to ourselves" without thinking of the Idea of God and of his will, we may hold, on the basis of reason alone, that we have a moral duty to be religious in the sense of "recognizing all our duties *as if* they were divine commands" (*als göttliche Gebote*), and we may use this thought to enliven and strengthen our moral resolve (*M.M.* 443; see also 487; *Rel.* 153/142; *Conflict* 36/61).[6] Since the Idea of God originates in our own reason, the duty to be religious in this sense is not heteronomous but is a duty we have to ourselves. (See *Pr.R.* 129; *M.M.* 443–44, 486–87.) "It does not follow that the law-giver is the author of the law" any more than God is "the author of the fact that the triangle has three sides" (*Lect.* 283/52; *Ed.* 494/112). We still recognize moral obligations and ideals as holy only by a criterion we ourselves first recognize, without looking outside ourselves.

On the basis of what reason alone can determine, Kant concludes, the only correct formal definition of religion is "the sum of all duties *as if* they were divine commands," and the sole function of religion is to strengthen the good will (*M.M.* 487; *Rel.* 105/96). Moral religion "must consist not in dogmas and rites, but in the heart's disposition to fulfill all human duties as divine commands" (*Rel.* 84/79).

In the judgment of many believers, then, Kant's moral religion rejected almost everything constituting the essential message of Christianity.[7] Kant was clearly on the side of deism in basing religion on reason rather than on supernatural revelation. It also was believed that he in effect had revived the ancient heresy of a British monk, Pelagius (c. 360–c. 431), whose views about the possibility of justification without a need for grace had been attacked by Saint Augustine and condemned by the Council of Carthage in 411.[8] To understand the opposition of orthodox Christianity we will need to look at three doctrines that received particularly close examination in Kant's *Religion*

Within the Limits of Reason Alone: the nature of the church, the doctrine of Original Sin, and the doctrines of justification and grace.

We will begin with Kant's discussion of the nature of the church. The spiritual authority of the church is a prime target for Kant, since the moral law inevitably conflicts with any ecclesiastical structures claiming to have divinely authorized moral authority.

The church

The ethical community – the kingdom of God – mandated in the third formula of the Categorical Imperative is based on the single, universal Law of Autonomy. The most fundamental characteristic of that kingdom is therefore its universality; there can be only one such kingdom. (See *Rel.* 101–2/93, 115/105, 122/112, 157/145.) Moreover, because the moral law, which defines the nature of the ethical community, requires the observance of inner, ethical duties, the members of that kingdom must be united in an inner, ethical "service of the heart." (See *Rel.* 192/180.) This, then, is a realm made up of all those trying to give the moral law primacy in their lives. "The kingdom of God," Kant quotes Jesus as saying, "is within you" (Luke 17.21).

Nonetheless, as we saw in Chapter 15, the invisible kingdom of God still needs to be organized as a visible community, a church, in order to function as an effective "vehicle for" promoting a pure moral faith. (See *Rel.* 103/94, 105/96, 118/109, 151/139.) Therefore, Kant writes, although there is only one true religion, there may be many different "ecclesiastical faiths" (*Kirchenglauben*) – visible, historical forms of the one invisible universal church. (See *Rel.* 107/98; *Conflict* 48–53/85–95.) But as part of the same ethical community, individual denominations still may appeal only to the moral reason of their members. As we have seen, specifically *ethical* duties cannot be mandated with penalties for their violation, whether by the state or by a church, without contradicting the very nature of those duties. Therefore, the relations between the members of a church must be similar to those in a republic or commonwealth, in which they all obey only laws to which they first have assented. Beyond that, reason alone cannot tell us exactly what juridical form a church must take.

Like any other community, each visible denomination requires statutory laws regulating the administration and "public business" of the church. Of themselves, different sets of statutory laws are "all equally good" insofar as they promote or at least do not impede the moral interests of the members. Any differences between them are "morally indifferent" and not worth making "a stir about" (*Rel.* 106/97 and 167–68/156; see 105–9/96–100, 115/105, 132n/123, 152/139–40).

The "service of a church," Kant holds, is therefore twofold – first and most important, the observance of universal ethical duties based on reason alone and aimed at virtue, and secondarily, the fulfillment of those duties necessary to maintain the church as a visible community. The affairs of the church do require administrators, but they are properly only ministers in the literal sense, not officials or dignitaries. (See *Rel.* 179/167–168.) Since the most effective way in which the church can transmit pure religion may be through Scripture, there also should be at least a small learned body of scholars or clerics to explain the moral meaning of the Scriptures and the historical creeds of the church to its members, as well as to defend the church from its enemies. (See *Rel.* 107/97–98, 164–65/152–53.)

Most individual churches, however, also have claimed a supernatural title to their members' obedience to statutory laws and observance of rituals, on the basis of a divine revelation containing special material duties to God. They therefore have insisted that their members fulfill special statutory duties in order to obtain salvation. Once this happens, Kant writes, a church becomes a theocratic tyranny, relying on incentives of fear and hope based on superstition. Such a church is despotic in spirit, whether its actual structure is monarchical, aristocratic, or democratic. (See *Rel.* 99–100/91, 102/93.) Contrary to all the ideals of the Enlightenment, the members of the church are then kept "in strict and perpetual tutelage" by a clergy claiming that they alone have rightful authority over the interpretation of the Scriptures and over even the very reason and thought of the laity (*Anthr.* 209–10 and *Rel.* 180/168). This hierarchy proclaims itself to be the "uniquely authorized guardian and interpreter of the will of the invisible Legislator." (See *Enlight.* 35–36.)

Just as Kant rejected political despotism because it does not respect the freedom and dignity of each person, so also he rejects religious tyranny for exactly the same reason. "Religious truth does not require force for its support; it should rely on reasoned argument. Truth can defend itself. . . . Freedom of investigation is the best means to consolidate the truth" (*Lect.* 455/235; see 454–55/234–35; *Enlight.* 41; *Orient.* 144). By contrast, whether in the form of doctrinal dogmatism or political establishmentarianism or both, religious despotism demands a debasing and groveling subservience in order to perpetuate itself by enforcing unity without freedom. (See *Enlight.* 41; *Rel.* 133n/124.)

If statutory religious authority is allowed to claim primacy over reason and the moral law, there is nothing to limit its sectarian demands. (See *Rel.* 172/160.) Then, Kant sarcastically notes, the principle seems to be that the more we believe, whether true or not, supposedly the safer is our salvation and the more pious is our belief. (See *Rel.* 188/176, 195n/183.)

Finally, because statutory religious obedience is coerced under the promise of eternal rewards and the threat of eternal punishment, it is the worst kind of tyranny. By promoting heteronomy, it makes moral virtue and genuine religion impossible. (See *Rel.* 172/160, 182/170, 190/178; *Anthr.* 332n.) It encourages either slavish subjection to sheer power or prudential – hypocritical and dishonest – conformity. Such an abuse of sectarian power, if effective, crushes the very freedom necessary for moral autonomy and indeed for being religious. Consequently, Kant concludes that churches that resort to authoritarian bribes and threats become instruments of the Antichrist, by actually working against the ultimate moral end of the human race. (See *Rel.* 133n/ 124; *End* 338–39.)

What of the claim by a church that its authority is warranted by divine revelation? Clearly, Kant writes, God can, if he so wishes, somehow enter human history at a particular time and place to found and organize his kingdom and to promulgate a pure moral code. If he has done so, those to whom he has revealed himself may somehow know this. But we will still have no criteria that we can judge to be objectively sufficient to certify that any particular claim to revelation can "be made known publicly" and believed universally (*Rel.* 137/129; see 187/175). Since no experience or intuition we can have can ever be adequate to the concept of God our own reason forms, it is unclear how we could ever be sure that any revelation came from God, and we cannot be morally obligated by uncertainties or even probabilities. (See *Rel.* 186–87/174–75, 189/177; *Conflict* 63/115.) We can only decide whether a claimed revelation contradicts the concept we already have of God or the moral demands of pure practical reason. (See *Orient.* 142, 153n.)

The orthodox response is that miracles are the ultimate validation of genuine revelation. But Kant's adoption of Newtonian physics meant that he held that the laws of the universe must be exceptionless. If there could be exceptions, there would be no laws. In effect, Kant repeats Hume's earlier argument: Because miracles by definition violate the objective laws of natural causation, we obviously cannot understand how they might be possible. (See *Rel.* 194/183.) We have no rational way to know *what* causes anomalous events, much less that any such events actually are miraculously caused by God. (See *Rel.* 63/56, 84–88/79–84.) Although "we need not call in question any of these miracles and indeed may honor the trappings" that help publicize the genuine moral doctrine in them, "it is essential that . . . we do not make it a tenet of religion that the knowing, believing, and professing of them are themselves means whereby we can render ourselves well-pleasing to God" (*Rel.* 85/79–80). No belief in a historical event can provide the warrant for or constitute a saving religious faith. (See *Rel.* 181/169.)

Moreover, there is no rational principle by which to distinguish between all the various and conflicting claims to a unique divine revelation or miracles on its behalf. (See *Rel.* 176/164; *Lect.* 454/234–35.) For this reason, differences in statutory religious beliefs are not grounds for hating or persecuting anyone; and beliefs other than our own should be tolerated, even if we think them mistaken. Such toleration should not be thought of as treason against God. If there is no objective way to arbitrate between differences in sectarian beliefs, there "is no such thing" as treason against God (*Orient.* 144–45; *Lect.* 454/ 234–35).

Finally, because every historical revelation occurs at a particular place and time, it cannot be known by, and believed by, everyone. Therefore, *no* historical faith can provide the foundation for a truly *universal* invisible kingdom of God. (See *Rel.* 102/94, 179/167.) Kant does not deny that Christianity may be *regarded* as a revealed faith, with genuine moral teaching. But allegiance to the Christian church must rest on a pure rational faith, that is, on the commitment of its members to the Christian church only insofar as it promotes the moral law. (See *Rel.* 164/151.) In the case of conflicts between the moral law and ecclesiastical statutory laws, the latter must always yield. (See *Rel.* 186/174.)

By contrast, the commands of the inner moral law, which is certain in and of itself, *can* be known and publicly shared by everyone throughout all history, for that law is present in each and every person's reason. (How far moral enlightenment has progressed in individual cases is irrelevant to the fact that every person has sufficient rationality to be considered a moral being.) It is certain that God speaks and speaks to everyone alike *only through the moral law,* so only that law can serve as the basis of genuine universality, an essential attribute of the kingdom of God. (See *Rel.* 155–57/143–45.) Moreover, only through that law can we have certainty about what we must do that will be pleasing to God. Therefore, only by obedience to that law can we be sure that we are offering God the "true veneration which he desires" (*Rel.* 104–5/96; see 115/105).

In Kant's philosophy of religion, then, authentic religious faith is only "that certainty which can be maintained by the moral will."[9] Kant walks a thin line when he allows that this is a "merely natural" religion but insists it is *not* religious naturalism. (See *Conflict* 44–45/77 and 79.) Naturalism, as he defines it, "denies the reality of all supernatural divine revelation," whereas a "pure rationalist" is a person who recognizes at least the *possibility* of divine revelation. Nevertheless, for all the reasons already given, religious rationalism – to which Kant apparently subscribes – does hold that "to know and accept [any purported revelation] as real is not a necessary requisite to religion" or to personal salvation and so may be ignored; "natural religion alone [is] morally necessary, i.e., as a duty" (*Rel.* 154–55/143).

Kant believed that the claimed revelation of virtually every church will contain *some* moral doctrines that can be known by reason alone, and in this regard Christianity, "as far as we know, is the most adequate" (*Conflict* 36/61). Among all historical faiths, Christianity best embodies the essence of a pure, rational ethical religion, discoverable behind the symbolism of its various dogmas and rituals. (See *Rel.* 155–57/143–45.)

In Kant's interpretation, then, Jesus came to found the "first true church," the first world religion "in the face of a dominant [Judaic] ecclesiastical faith" based only on statutory laws (*Rel.* 158–59/146–47). His essential message was the public promulgation of a "pure rational faith," a "moral religion" consisting of the same moral law that all persons already find in their own hearts – mandating the pursuit of virtue through precepts of holiness and offering the hope of attaining what those precepts command. (See *Rel.* 128–29/118–20, 159–63/147–51, 167/155.)

Original Sin

Orthodox Lutheran theology interpreted the Book of Genesis as teaching that all human beings are conceived in a state of "Original Sin," that is, tainted by an "evil principle" making them "radically evil" or "evil by nature" (*Rel.* 32/27). When our historical first parent, Adam, acting on behalf of all his descendants, violated the will of God, his sin estranged the entire human race from God. We all now enter the world suffering from total moral depravity, unable by ourselves to do anything that will make us pleasing to God and restore the original relationship with him. Personal immorality results in even further estrangement from God, a moral disaster that every person causes but that no human being can repair. Only God, by his freely given grace and forgiveness, can restore the original, lost relationship.

Kant held that in many ways the traditional doctrine of Original Sin simply *cannot* be true – and yet, as we have already seen in Chapter 9, he also was convinced that in other ways it *is* true.

To begin with, the traditional understanding of sin and its interpretation of the meaning of Original Sin cannot be correct, for, as we have seen, basing morality on the will of God destroys morality by making it only a species of heteronomy. As a consequence, sin may not be defined as wronging "the infinite and inaccessible ruler of the world," a view of sin that is rationally incoherent anyway. (See *Rel.* 72/66; *M.M.* 489.) Rather, sin is the choosing of one's own inclinations over one's duty, and the evil in doing so consists in violating one's own free nature and dignity as a person. (See, e.g., *Ed.* 448/15.)

Further, Kant continues, moral evil cannot be attributed to a preexisting and transmissible condition within human nature, such as a trait inherited from our first parents, independently of any choices we ourselves have made. (See *H.H.* 123.) The consequences of natural causation may be natural good or evil (pleasure or pain) but never moral good or evil. (See *Rel.* 20–22/16–18, 22n/17–19.) A causal explanation of moral evil destroys the possibility of *any* free moral choice and therefore of any responsibility and of moral character of *any* kind (*Rel.* 37–41/32–36, 44/40).[10] If it were true, we could not still be obligated, as the traditional doctrine holds, to try to be pleasing to God, for we would be utterly unable to do so. As we saw in Chapter 9, Kant concludes that we therefore cannot be innately corrupt in the sense of being unable to do anything morally good.

Reason, however, does generate an account that shows the actual moral truth in the Genesis account. (See *H.H.* 109–15.)[11] The story of Adam is an allegory of how each of us is born fundamentally good but is later tempted by sensuous incentives. Each of us in fact yields to such temptation, and that is the sense in which we are all said to suffer from an innate propensity to evil (while still possessing a propensity to good). In Chapter 15, we saw that Kant also contends that our tendency to the social vices requires an equally specieswide solution.[12] A political union can behaviorally discourage that tendency by prudential punishments, but the only genuine remedy is a truly universal, ethical society, a kingdom of virtue (*Rel.* 94/86). Only an ethical community is by its very nature dedicated to the affirmation of the good principle – to promoting the spread of that principle and fidelity to it.

This is precisely why Kant insisted on the importance of the church as the kingdom of God on earth, despite the manifold ways in which various forms of that church historically also had fallen into errors that impeded rather than promoted moral virtue. (The church could not even state the Categorical Imperative clearly, distinguishing properly between moral and prudential considerations; see *Gr.* 68n/43on.) Again echoing his commitment to the Enlightenment, Kant held that moral philosophy has the crucial task of cleansing the church of specifically religious forms of heteronomy – authoritarianism, mysticism, superstition, and fanaticism.[13]

Grace and justification

Along with its understanding of the meaning of Original Sin, Pietism had held that we must rely totally on the mercy of God both for his forgiveness and for our moral conversion. Justification – the restoration of the lost relation with God – requires unmerited grace through faith in Christ and in his vicariously atoning sacrificial death on our behalf.

But Kant's analysis of morality as autonomy led him to reject the traditional doctrines of vicarious atonement and of salvation through faith alone as antitheses of morality. "No thoughtful person can bring himself to believe" that we need only have faith that someone else has vicariously atoned for our guilt for that guilt to be annihilated. (See *Rel.* 116–17/107, 200/188.) The orthodox interpretation of vicarious atonement is rationally incoherent, he wrote, for no one can assume either the guilt for another's evil disposition or the loss of happiness due to it: "This is no *transmissible* liability which can be made over to another like a financial indebtedness" (*Rel.* 72/66).

Moreover, the doctrine of justification by faith alone leaves individuals only a slothfully passive piety, only a sniveling and slavish self-abnegating need for help. Their freedom and therefore even the possibility of morality are completely taken away. (See *Rel.* 51/47, 184/172–73, 184n/172–73.) Such a doctrine encourages them to throw themselves on God's mercy without doing what his justice requires – improving their way of life. (See *Rel.* 193–94/181–82; *Conflict* 41–42/71 and 73.) "To this end man busies himself with every conceivable formality, designed to indicate how greatly he *respects* the divine commands, in order that it may not be necessary for him to *obey* them" (*Rel.* 201/189). No wonder, he continues, we hear the common complaint that religion contributes little to the improvement of moral conduct. Piety, that is, a "passive respect for the law of God," must be combined with virtue if it is to be a genuinely religious disposition. (See *Rel.* 201/189; *Lect.* 314–15/89.)

As we saw in Chapter 9, Kant argues that the only meaning that can rationally be given to "justification" is each person's own radical moral self-redemption. Interpreted morally, the doctrine of atonement can only mean that one must strengthen one's resolve to "stand on one's own feet." But a saving faith does involve two other elements:

. . . the one having reference to what man himself cannot accomplish, namely, undoing lawfully (before a divine judge) actions which he has performed, the other to what he himself can and ought to do, that is, leading a new life conformable to his duty. The first is the faith in an atonement (reparation for his debt, redemption, reconciliation with God); the second, the faith that we can become well-pleasing to God through a good course of life in the future. Both conditions constitute but one faith and necessarily belong together. (*Rel.* 116/106)

What we can and must do is act as if everything depends on us alone. (See *Rel.* 52/47.) That means that "the only real way in which we may please God is by our becoming better men. . . . It is a good life alone that makes [us] worthy of happiness" (*Ed.* 494/112). "There exists absolutely no salvation for man apart from the sincerest adoption of genuinely moral principles into his disposition" (*Rel.* 83/78). Therefore, "whatever, over and above good life-conduct, man fancies that he can do to become well-pleasing to God is mere religious illusion and pseudo-service of God" (*Rel.* 170/158; see 169–70/157–58).

Interpreted morally, Kant maintains, the Christian religion teaches that the change of ultimate principles that can be effected is so radical that even though it is the same person before and after, Scripture describes the first as the "old man" and the second as the "new man" (Col. 3.9–10). It is the "new man" in us, scripturally personified in the Son of God, who bears the guilt of the "old man" and who as "savior" accepts the punishment due the "old man" for the latter's moral wrongs. (See *Rel.* 74, 74n/68–69.) The biblical references to the sanctifying presence of the Holy Spirit symbolize our hope of continuing steadfastly in a morally good disposition. (See *Rel.* 70–71/65.)

The biblical account of Jesus' life provides an extraordinarily powerful moral example and symbol of a "manifestation of the good principle, that is, of humanity in its moral perfection" (*Rel.* 82/77; see 62/55, 80,80n/74–75, 128/119–20; *Conflict* 39/67). Likewise, his sufferings and death symbolize how we can overcome and "atone" for evil and in that sense be symbolically reconciled with God. (See *Rel.* 74/68–69.) The evil principle, symbolized by the prince of darkness, may not be conquered once and for all, but the life of Jesus shows how the good principle can triumph, even if at the cost of great physical sufferings and the mortification of self-love. (See *Rel.* 82–83/77–78.)

Nothing further in the biblical account can be understood or have any moral value for us. The foundation for our taking Jesus as an example of the good moral disposition is still and always our own morally legislative reason, which generates both the original archetype or ideal of holiness and the incentive to strive for it. (See *Rel.* 61/55, 119/109–10.)

Nonetheless, no matter how hard we try, we know full well that we cannot make adequate reparation for our previous sinful actions. We can only hope that they may somehow be "wiped out" by our moral conversion "to a new mode of life" (*Rel.* 184/172). Such a hope is morally crucial.[14] If the magnitude of past moral failings is great and if they still must count against our achieving our final goal, it is all too easy to despair and give up any effort to strive for the goal. Moreover, as we have seen in Chapter 10, the goal that the moral law apodictically commands us to attain in order to be "reconciled with God"

271

is holiness, and what that law commands always is and must be possible. Yet, as finite creatures, we never can be wholly adequate to that command. We can achieve virtue, but not holiness.

In his concern to protect human freedom, responsibility, and autonomy, Kant first argues that faith in religious "mysteries" is a dangerous permission to admit any and every kind of superstitious nonsense. (See *Rel.* 194/182.) But in the end he is driven to admit that we must cultivate religious trust – that if we do all that is in our power, God will help us realize our *summum bonum,* by somehow doing for us (through "grace") whatever we cannot do for ourselves. (See *Rel.* 75–76/70, 137/129, 143/134; *Lect.* 320/95.) This is also why Kant held that morality inevitably leads to religion and to the hope that religious faith can offer.

We cannot avoid being conscious of our inability to understand as much as we would like of such a crucial area of our moral life; once again we find ourselves at the very limits of reason. (See *Rel.* 45n/50, 52/47.) As we saw in Chapter 10, we cannot understand how to reconcile freedom and responsibility with God's providing for our inadequacies, and we therefore should not try to do so. (See *Rel.* 117–18/108, 144/135; 188–89/177.) For us, these must remain completely incomprehensible religious mysteries. Because of this "peculiar weakness of human nature," people find it difficult to believe that "steadfast diligence in morally good life-conduct is all that God requires of men, to be subjects in his kingdom and well-pleasing to him" (*Rel.* 102/94). Kant is not unsympathetic with the heartfelt desire of people to try to gain further insight into their transcendent relation with God. But this desire has also commonly led people to turn to the "parerga," or ornamental embellishments, of visible religion and to fall into the "stupidity of superstition and the madness of fanaticism." (See *Rel.* 51–53/47–48.)

One such error – "illuminationism" – is to believe every claim anyone makes to have access to some special arcane revelation from God. (See *Orient.* 145.) Another error – superstition – constantly looks to experience for miracles. A third, the fanaticism of "thaumaturgy," falls into the religious illusion that devotional exercises can be a *means* of grace. Kant, of course, maintains that the various ecclesiastical devotions (sometimes based on a claimed revelation) are "all one and all equal in value." That is, whatever they consist of – washings, praying, fasting, almsgiving, sacrifices, penances, pilgrimages, or Tibetan prayer wheels – none of them has any moral value in itself. Either they are salutary insofar as they help to promote an authentic moral disposition, or they are superfluous, worthless, and even pernicious. (See *Rel.* 173/161, 176–77/164–65, 193–94/182; *Ed.* 495–96/113–15.)[15]

Neither revelations nor miracles nor devotional practices have any power to make us good and pleasing to God, and belief that they do is only a "superstitious illusion" that makes fetishes of morally impotent rituals. (See *Rel.* 193–95/181–83; *Ed.* 88/100.) The illusion here, Kant writes, lies in thinking that one can become morally good through means such as rituals, which, of themselves, "can produce no effect at all according either to natural laws or to moral laws of reason" (*Rel.* 193/181; see 174/162, 178/166, 184n/172, 193–94/181–82). This encourages the absurd belief that it is possible to become a good person without fulfilling the one certain condition for becoming a good person and so for pleasing God – obeying the moral law. (See *Rel.* 173/161; see also 170–74/158–62, 175n/163.)

The consequence of this illusion is a "damnable" insistence on what Kant terms "pseudo-service," that is, the claim that salvation depends on such activities as accepting a denominational creed, obeying canon laws, and participating in the devotions of any particular form of the church. (See *Rel.* 153/140–41, 165/153, 168, 168n/156, 178–79/166–67, 187/176.) In fact, Kant sarcastically remarks, "The less [such practices] are designed for the general moral improvement of man, the holier they seem" (*Rel.* 169/157).

Conclusion

Notwithstanding the harshness with which Kant criticizes theological religion and historical forms and practices of the church, it would be a mistake to conclude either that he reduced religion to morality or that he held religion to be merely an adjunct to the moral life. Morality and religion do have exactly the same content (or matter), but there is a formal distinction between them: Religion is grounded in the legislation of the moral law, not the other way around. (See *Conflict* 36/61.) The moral and therefore also the religious consciousness of the ordinary person are basically correct and are worthy of deep respect. God's existence is the most profound "fact" of human life, albeit a fact we cannot *know* but *about* which we may still have moral certitude based on the demands of the moral law that also grounds rationally necessary hope and faith.

Kant's transcendental philosophy of history, which also is grounded in faith and trust in God's plan for the human species, means that each person's struggle for virtue takes place against a cosmic background of eternal significance. Despite human moral frailties and frequent moral failures, as long as we try to do all that we can, we may view our own eventual destiny and that of the human species optimistically. Only through such a religious faith embodied in our participation in the kingdom of God – first here on earth and later after death – does human ethical life take on its complete form as a social ideal, a moral community not unlike a family under a common moral Father. (See *Rel.* 102/93.)

Kant's philosophy of religion, therefore, represents his resolution of the enormously difficult challenge of fidelity both to the faith of the Enlightenment in the power of human reason and to the faith of the ordinary person in God and the importance of religion, particularly the Christian faith. There *is* essential moral truth in the Christian doctrines of the sanctity of the individual conscience, of Original Sin, and of justification by grace as well as by moral works. On the one hand, there is no need to regard religion only as an impediment to rational progress, as so many Enlightenment thinkers held; and on the other hand, there is no need for truly religious people to see reason as a dangerous enemy of faith. As Allen Wood has written, the "true originality and lasting value of Kant's moral defense of faith" lie not merely in showing that reason and faith are *compatible* with each other; Kant shows that they *require* each other.[16]

A price has to be paid by both sides, however. Again, on the one hand, we modern human beings have to yield our illusory ambition to be God, for our reason mandates that not everything can be understood by science or permitted in the name of progress. On the other hand, the stultifying and heteronomous shackles used historically by both tyrannical governments and churches must be broken. In God's plan, known only through the moral law within us, we find that we can fulfill our vocation to be human only by standing on our own feet, conscious of our dignity as rational creatures. Only by doing so will we be entitled to hope that with the help of our Creator, we can and will achieve our full final destiny, both as individuals and as a species.

For some time it has been common for commentators and Kantian scholars either to ignore Kant's fundamentally religious orientation or to reject it as an unfortunate aberration.[17] But in his moral writings Kant again and again insists that the moral law itself requires us to believe in God. This may not be the familiar God of the Gospels, but it is the God of traditional Christian apologetics – a living, holy, omnipotent, and caring Person. Kant rejects only speculative and dogmatic "explanations" and misleading pictorial depictions of how God interacts with his creatures. All such matters are transcendent, beyond the capabilities of human reason. We are left with a pure moral faith, a faith that is fundamentally religious but that does not *need* to understand what it must postulate for its own purposes. (See *Rel.* 139/130.) "As simple and profound as it is," Wood writes,

there is nothing original or extraordinary in the outlook of moral faith as it is presented by Kant. This faith is, finally, no more than the courage to struggle toward the attainment of one's moral ends, sustained through hardship and apparent failure by a loving trust in God as the wise and beneficent Providence in whose hands all will be well. . . . The outlook of moral faith is not in any sense a *solution* to the dialectic of man's situation, but is only a rational means of *facing* the inescapable tension and perplexity which belong essentially to us as finite rational beings. We know already that the road we travel is a dark and a difficult one; we should not expect philosophy to tell us otherwise. In Kant's view, philosophy has succeeded if it has given clarity and rationality to the difficult wisdom and hard-won virtue whose validity we recognize already.[18]

In Chapter 1 we saw that Kant began his long philosophical journey as a young student at the University of Königsberg, facing profound tensions between his Pietistic faith in God and his Enlightenment faith in reason. Now, at the end of this journey, we see how he resolved those tensions. As it turned out, it was not a victory either for those who scorned or for those who remained committed to orthodox religious faith. Keith Ward points out that Kant has offered us an ethics that is "unmistakably Christian in origin" and that Kant, therefore, develops within a deeply religious context; but because it is expressed "in a radically humanistic terminology," that ethics remains to the orthodox Christian an "unsatisfactory and incomplete" expression of the personal relation between God and his creatures.[19]

Appendixes

Appendix 1:
Kant's two-viewpoints doctrine

In this brief discussion I intend only to try to clarify, particularly for readers not already experts in Kant's theory, some of the kinds of problems typically associated with Kant's noumenal-phenomenal distinction.[1]

Kant used two different methods in his moral writings. In one, the analytic method, he studied the "common knowledge" of morality of ordinary people, to make clear what is contained there. In the other, the synthetic method, he drew on doctrines and definitions he had already developed to explain the nature of human morality. Depending on which method he is using, Kant tends to use the terms "freedom" and "heteronomy" in two very different senses.[2]

"Morally indifferent" freedom

When he reflects on ordinary moral thinking, Kant holds, in effect, that there are three kinds of agents and actions:[3]

First, there are those changes caused by nonrational agents, such as chemical reactions and the movements of animals. They are all the effects of – reactions or responses to – stimuli from other causal agencies that are the effects of still other causes, and so on, and so they are all governed by laws of causal necessity. (See *Gr.* 97/447.)

Second, there are those actions, examined in Chapter 4, performed by rational agents to attain pleasure or avoid pain. In such conduct, we act on maxims of conduct that can help us satisfy our needs and inclinations. Consequently, whatever the moral legality of prudential actions, Kant calls them all "empirically conditioned" and "heteronomous," because we are pathologically affected yet still independent of pathological, causal determination. That is, our incentives for acting all lie with our desires and inclinations, but we do not for that reason constantly suffer from pathological compulsions in the usual psychological sense of that term. A particular desire or inclination can serve as an incentive only "so far as the individual has incorporated it into his maxim" of action, thereby making it a reason for that particular action (*Rel.* 24/19).[4] As an exercise of what earlier has been called practical or psychological freedom, this evidences the minimal sense of what Kant calls the "causality of reason"; it is also as much freedom as anyone before Kant had thought we can have.

279

Finally, there are the actions of morally good agents, that is, agents who have and exercise the power of pure practical reason. An agent is morally good or autonomous when that agent acts cognitively and conatively independently of "everything empirical and hence [of] nature generally," entirely and only on the agent's own rational norms and incentives (*Pr.R.* 97). This is the only genuine exercise of absolute spontaneity or transcendental freedom.

Although he was the first to propose that we might be transcendentally free, Kant does seem to set out faithfully our common belief that *both* morally *and* prudentially (even if also immorally) motivated actions are reasoned and purposive as well as free in some sense or another. Moreover, as we have seen, Kant himself had earlier insisted that the notion of a will always implies the ability to exercise causal power and that the notion of causality makes sense only when it occurs according to a rule or law, so that the notion of a "lawless" will of any kind is simply incoherent.[5] The alternative, as Hume saw, is that anything can follow from anything, and if that were true, there would be no way to identify *anything* as a cause. Our actions can be an exercise of causal power, then, only if they are done according to some rule or other, and they are an exercise of our will if they are done according to a rule of our own adoption.

This same point can be put another way. We have seen that every rule or maxim of an action "contains an end" that is the purpose of that action (*M.M.* 395). An end, according to Kant, is "an *object* of free choice," and "the power to set an end – any end whatsoever – is the characteristic of humanity (as distinguished from animality)" (*M.M.* 384, 392; see also 434). Moreover, "since no one can have an end without *himself* making the object of choice [*Willkür*] into an end, it follows that the adoption of any end of action whatsoever is an act of *freedom* on the agent's part, not an operation of *nature*" (*M.M.* 385; see 381, 383, 384, 389).

Throughout this analysis, then, Kant interprets rational agency and freedom broadly, as not necessarily identified with the moral law. (See *Pu.R.* A802/B830; *M.M.* 379n; *Lect.* 346–47/124.) When we are tempted to act wrongly, Kant says that the moral law appears to us "as a moral imperative *limiting* our freedom" (*M.M.* 437, emphasis mine; see also, e.g., 396; *Gr.* 69–70/430–31; *Lect.* 345/122–23). Again reflecting ordinary moral judgments, Kant clearly holds that if a person adopts and acts on immoral rules, that person is immoral precisely because that choice was made consciously, freely, and responsibly (although Kant of course considered morally right actions to be rational in a significantly fuller sense).

As we saw in Chapter 9, Kant describes the ultimate moral quality of human character as depending on a noumenal disposition to adopt either the Law of Autonomy or the principle of self-love as fundamental and then to subordinate the other to it. In either case, moral character is determined by the practical principle a person adopts. Insofar as the "act of establishing character" is ultimate, however, neither morally good nor morally evil character can be explained or understood.

Autonomous freedom

Kant insisted that it is both necessary and legitimate for us to regard ourselves as noumenal *and* phenomenal beings. (See, e.g., *Gr.* 110–11/453, 113/455; *Pr.R.* 97–98.) The two-viewpoints doctrine is necessary in order to defend the claim that freedom (and so also morality) "is at least *not incompatible with* nature" (*Pu.R.* A558/B586). We can *think about* both viewpoints, but we cannot *take* both simultaneously. So, we can avoid self-contradictory and incoherent claims by saying that "in one and the same event, in different relations, both [freedom and natural causal determination] can be found" (*Pu.R.* A536/B564).

It is also *because* we must regard ourselves as both noumenal and phenomenal beings, Kant writes, that we find we may not regard ourselves as having a nature that is either holy or only causally determined. (See *Gr.* 110/453–54.) Further, because we are noumenal beings and because the noumenal must be regarded as in some sense the ground of the phenomenal, even when we are regarded as "natural beings (*homo phaenomenon*)," we may also be regarded as moral agents who "can be determined by the *causality* of [our] reason to actions in the sensible world" (*M.M.* 418).

But the two-viewpoints doctrine also forced Kant to adopt a quite different view of both freedom and heteronomy, namely, to reduce the three kinds of causal agencies to only two. "When we are dealing with what happens, there are only two kinds of causality conceivable by us; the causality is either according to *nature* or arises from [transcendental] *freedom*" (*Pu.R.* A532/B560; see A547–48/B575–76, A800–804/B828–32). The difference between these two viewpoints is so radical, Kant goes on, that each must be regarded as a different and incommensurable kind of "nature," each with its own kind of laws (*Pr.R.* 43; see also *Gr.* 36/412). As a consequence, theoretical reasoning can recognize the existence of the noumenal point of view that includes the notion of transcendental freedom, but it cannot describe it except in terms of negations.

The consequence of Kant's two-viewpoints doctrine is that it simply does not allow for the possibility of some third, middle, ground, some partial freedom – or what is now sometimes called "soft determinism." (See, e.g., *M.M.* 226.) For our theoretical purposes we must take the viewpoint that every phenomenal agent is completely bound by causal natural laws; for our moral purposes, we must take the viewpoint that all human agents have pure practical reason, enabling them to be transcendentally free. (See *Gr.* 108–9/452; *M.M.* 239.)

Transcendental freedom "must be thought of as independence from everything empirical and hence from nature generally" (*Pr.R.* 97). "An act of freedom cannot (like a natural effect) be derived and explained according to the natural law of the connection of effects with their causes, all of which are appearances" (*M.M.* 431; see also *Pu.R.* A533–34/B561–62; *Gr.* 101/448; *Pr.R.* 96–97). Since that is so, a free action must be the autonomous exercise of power by an agent who is not subject to any prior causal determination. Therefore, a free action *must* be determined only by the Law of Freedom, the Law of Autonomy (see *Gr.* 98/447, 104–5/451; *Pr.R.* 15, 93–94, 97–98, 104–7, 114, 158–59; *M.M.* 213, 217–18, 381, 481).[6]

So Kant denies that "freedom of the will" (*Willkür*) may be defined "as the capacity to choose [*wählen*] to act for or against the law (*libertas indifferentiae*), as some people have tried to define it" (*M.M.* 226).[7] This common opinion, he writes, is mistakenly based on an appeal to what we learn from experience, namely, that people in fact do engage in both morally right and wrong behavior. (See *M.M.* 226–27.) But experience can tell us nothing about freedom, which is an Idea of reason; and what reason tells us, Kant argues, is that only those actions are morally good that are radically free, that is, completely self-determined by practical reason (*freie Willkür;* see e.g., *Pu.R.* A534/B562, A802/B830; *Pr.R.* 72).

But, as Kant particularly stressed in the second *Critique, this* view of freedom seems to mean that all immorally heteronomous actions must be regarded as behavior that is completely determined by causal laws that taken together form the "mechanism of nature" (*Pr.R.* 95–97; see also *Pu.R.* A418–19/B446–47; *Gr.* 108–9/452–53; *M.M.* 378). Even in his earlier *Lectures on Ethics,* Kant states: "Our actions are determined either practically, i.e., in accordance with laws of freedom, or pathologically, in accordance with laws of our sensuous nature" (*Lect.* 255/14). What lies under causal laws cannot be free actions, as Kant says a little later: "The man who does a thing because it is pleasant is pathologically determined" (*Lect.* 257/16).

Insofar as we regard a human agent as acting heteronomously, Kant writes, we must regard that agent as being as causally determined as the movements of a clock, whether we think of the agent as a material machine or, like Leibniz, as a "spiritual machine (an *automaton spirituale*)" (*Pr.R.* 97). Merely psychological freedom is "in essence no better than the freedom of a turnspit, which when once wound up also carries out its motions of itself" (*Pr.R.* 97; see *M.M.* 213). "Choices" of what Kant describes as "the ends man sets for himself according to the sensuous impulses of his nature" are like "animal choice (*arbitrium brutum*)," that is, *both* pathologically affected *and* determined, compelled behavior and not free choices at all.[8] Immoral actions must therefore signal a lack of will, "a lack of power"; and Kant in fact does describe immorality as akin to madness, and moral repentance as giving rise to "the consciousness of our restored freedom" (*M.M.* 227 and 485; see 384, 420).

All the desires of the heteronomous agent have been shaped and determined by past conditioning over which he now has no control so that, according to this strand of Kant's thinking, what the agent now does is "inescapably necessary" (*Pr.R.* 97–98; see 96–98; *M.M.* 213). Moreover, insofar as thinking has a causal role in prudential action, this kind of "practical reason" or "will" – along with all other related notions such as deliberation, motives, purposes, and practical rules – must also be regarded as causally conditioned. For their determining ground (*Bestimmungsgrund*) lies in an indeterminately long chain of temporally prior causal connections (*Pr.R.* 96; *M.M.* 223). Phenomenal psychological mental events are "a merely internal concatenation of ideas of the mind" (*Pr.R.* 96), and, like the inferences made by a computer, they all, ideally at least, can be exhibited empirically. Causally speaking, therefore, all such reasoning must be regarded like chemical reactions, and this apparently is why Kant holds that technical-practical reasoning cannot be part of a practical philosophy of freedom. (See, e.g., *M.M.* 213, 217–18, 418.)

In Chapter 4 we saw that Kant concluded that prudential activity gives us no grounds at all to think we are radically superior to brute animals, and now we can understand more fully why he took that view. We may have wanted to protest that our ability to think about and choose how to act to meet our needs shows we are free, with a dignity that raises us above brute animals. But Kant's identification of freedom and autonomy leads him to maintain that there is no significant difference between the actions of non-rational agents and those of heteronomously motivated rational agents. Insofar as we are taken up only with prudential concerns, Kant regards us as merely natural beings, with the same "slight," "low," and "insignificant" value as other animals, namely, extrinsic value determined by utility. (See e.g., *M.M.* 434–35.)

The consequences of the phenomenal-noumenal distinction seem to be disastrous for Kant's moral theory. Dichotomizing human life into the mutually exclusive realms of absolute freedom and absolute determinism seems to destroy any possibility that, at least insofar as his moral theory requires that distinction, it can offer a coherent explanation of human moral life, together with all its complex shadings and subtleties.[9]

For example, there can be no moral evil, because heteronomous behavior is simply amoral. Moreover, Kant's analysis of duty as fidelity in the face of opposition seems simply incoherent. The internal moral conflict characterizing human moral life seems to be not just incomprehensible but impossible, for such a conflict would seem to require an *ontological* dualism where Kant at least *seems* to say there is only an epistemological distinction, a difference only of viewpoints. (See, e.g., *Pu.R.* Bxxv–xxviii, A38/B55, A45/B63.) Appearances do not have an "absolute reality"; they are not things-in-themselves but only "representations, connected according to empirical laws" (*Pu.R.* A537/B565). Since Kant holds that we must regard the noumenal as the ground of the phenomenal, we also are sure to be puzzled about how a noumenal agent cannot be subject to causal determinism but can still be "influenced by" phenomenal desires so as to act immorally, thereby losing noumenal freedom. We also seem to lose the possibility of acting from mixed motivation or of acting from greater or lesser freedom and responsibility. (See, e.g., *M.M.* 228; *Lect.* 291/62.)

Finally, there no longer seems to be any possible justification for morally permissible prudential behavior. If all prudential action "reduces the will to a mechanism destructive of freedom," the moral law could never approve of our reducing ourselves or anyone else to the level of mere animate things (*Pr.R.* 38; see *Gr.* 93–95/443–44; *M.M.* 378).

Heteronomous freedom

It is certainly true that Kant *wanted* to maintain the claim of ordinary moral consciousness that we are responsible for immoral actions. He writes that "all moral evil springs from freedom; otherwise it would not be *moral* evil" (*Lect.* 295/67). And again, the "subjective grounds of choice . . . must itself always be an expression of freedom (for otherwise the use or abuse of man's power of choice [*Willkür*] in respect of the moral law could not be imputed to him nor could the good or bad in him be called moral)" (*Rel.* 21/16–17). And again, when a person acts immorally, he still is "in possession of his freedom," so that he "can rightly say of any unlawful action which he has done that he should have left it undone" (*Pr.R.* 98; see 98–100; *Lect.* 267/28). "The action is ascribed to the agent's intelligible character; in the moment when he utters the lie, the guilt is entirely his own. Reason, irrespective of empirical conditions, is completely free, and the lie is entirely due to its default" (*Pu.R.* A555/B583). So he still also interprets immoral action as a heteronomous mode of freedom. (See, e.g., *Rel.* 20–22/16–17; *T&P* 282.)

Some authors have argued that Kant eventually amended his analysis of freedom to permit including heteronomous actions by distinguishing between two senses of "will." This distinction coincides with the difference between the Law of Freedom and the choice of whether to act on that law, and so with taking practical reason to be both a cognitive and a conative power. *Wille* (*voluntas*) is pure practical reason in the sense of being the legislative source of the Law of Autonomy; it is the same in every rational agent, and because it does not itself act, it is neither free nor determined. (See, e.g., *Pr.R.* 32, 55; *M.M.* 213, 226, 335.) *Willkür* (*arbitrium*) is our ability to choose (*wählen*), that is, to express an arbitrary preference. As Kant describes *Willkür,* it can follow the law of *Wille* or not, and so can vary from person to person. (See *M.M.* 213.)

Kant himself does not consistently observe this terminological distinction. Sometimes he characterizes *Wille* as synonymous with free will rather than being neither free nor determined. (See, e.g., *Pr.R.* 55.) At other times he describes *Wille* as both a legislative and an elective power. He clearly needed to distinguish between the legislative and the elective functions of the will to avoid holding that every choice is morally good just because it is free. But distinguishing the cognitive from the conative functions of pure practical reason in this manner does not seem to indicate how immoral heteronomous conduct can be a mode of freedom.[10]

Allen Wood defends Kant as well as possible by arguing that Kant did not simply equate freedom with autonomy but regarded freedom as the *capacity* (*Vermögen*) to act autonomously, "something which can be present even when we fail to exercise it (as we do in heteronomous action)."[11] It follows that "both autonomous and heteronomous action, therefore, are actions of a free being, though only autonomous action actualizes the capacity in which freedom consists." Heteronomous action "cannot be motivated by reason, because [such action] is not autonomous, and it cannot be motivated by sensuous inclinations as natural causes, since such causes (on Kant's view) are incompatible with freedom (with the capacity to act autonomously)." Kant therefore traced "heteronomous action not to a sensuous motive or incentive (*Triebfeder*) but instead to a fundamental maxim or rule made by the free will, to the effect that it prefers incentives of inclination to those of reason."

"This solution," Wood admits, "has the oddity that there can be no motive for the adoption of such a maxim, since the maxim itself concerns the order of priority to be given to all motives which might influence the will." But this problem is quite different from "the outright incoherence into which Kant would have fallen if he had failed to distinguish freedom (the capacity to act autonomously) from autonomous action itself."

The inexplicability of adopting the ultimate evil maxim is not surprising, since, as we saw in Chapter 9, the adoption of an ultimate good maxim is also an inexplicable exercise of spontaneity. (See *Rel.* 19/15, 21n/17, 25/20, 43/38.) But even though Kant on occasion holds just what Wood represents him as holding, Kant himself also discusses moral evil in language that seems to indicate that he simply could not make up his mind exactly how to regard it. Occasionally he describes moral evil as amoral heteronomy: "The less a man can be compelled by natural means the more he can be constrained morally (through the mere thought of the law), so much the more free he is" (*M.M.* 382n). In his *Anthropology* he first describes Sulla as evil because of his "firm maxims" of violence, and then denies that evil can be traced to a principled decision: "There is really no evil from principles; it comes only from abandoning principles" (*Anthr.* 293–94).

When we try to make sense of what Kant says, we may find ourselves wanting to adopt a new version of Plato's "Third Man Argument" by looking for a more ultimate self behind the phenomenal-noumenal viewpoints, being pulled and tugged between them and ultimately determining our decisions. But this strategy makes no sense within Kant's philosophy. In fact, Kant himself rejects any description of human beings as being somewhere between the angels and the beasts. "The bisection of a being composed of heterogeneous elements really produces no determinate concept." (See *M.M.* 227, 461.) Unfortunately, this may seem to be exactly the effect of Kant's bifurcation of human beings into two utterly heterogeneous viewpoints.

We also may look for a more nearly ultimate self that will help us "make sense of," that is, achieve *some* understanding of, the relationships between the two viewpoints. But this is a deep mistake, for the doctrine of the two viewpoints was never intended by Kant to be a theoretical *explanation* of *how* we can be both free and determined, or *how* we can be morally good or morally evil. It was Kant's response to the charge that it is irrational, because self-contradictory, to hold that we are both natural and moral beings.

However, it is still not difficult to see one of the main reasons why Kant's theory has generated some very harsh criticism. Even if we do not misuse the two-viewpoints doctrine by trying to turn it into an explanation, it may seem to generate more problems than it purports to solve. Apparently because he was convinced that there is simply no other way in which to defend the reality of our freedom and moral agency, Kant persisted in maintaining two apparently incompatible theses: (1) Freedom *must* be defined as a power to act completely independently of all heteronomous influences; and (2) human moral agents can be and are responsible for acting freely but immorally, "though we still cannot conceive of the possibility" of their doing so (*M.M.* 226). He was clearly bothered by this problem, but he had no solution to it, and he admits as much at least in one place: "The solution given here to the difficulty will be said to have so much difficulty in it, however, that it is hardly susceptible of a lucid presentation. But is any other solution, which anyone has attempted or may attempt, any easier or more comprehensible?" (*Pr.R.* 103). Kant is surely right on this point. It is arguable that no one has been able to propose a more satisfactory solution to the difficulty of reconciling freedom and determinism. Any attempt to "reconstruct" Kant's doctrine by construing freedom as, in Kant's terminology, "morally indifferent" proves to generate at least as many problems as it solves.[12] If we are looking for theoretical insights, it may just not be possible to understand how to reconcile those dichotomous beliefs that ordinary moral understanding takes for granted. The difficulties seem to be both unavoidable and irresolvable.[13] If we cannot find morally significant actions in the world of experience, if we cannot understand how a noumenal cause can be the ground of *any* action in the phenomenal world, we can hardly hope to understand how freedom can exhibit itself in immoral actions – or moral actions, for that matter. (See *Pu.R.* A555–56/B683–84; *Gr.* 110/453; *Pr.R.* 99; *Rel.* 40–41/34–35, 58n/45.)

Despite an underlying doctrine that may at times seem incoherent, the Kantian analysis of morality continues to dominate Anglo-American moral philosophizing. Insofar as his moral theory is able to stand on its own, independently of the harsh contrasts generated by the noumenal-phenomenal distinction, Kant's analysis of ordinary moral awareness exhibits a sensitivity toward human morality that many people today still believe is substantially correct. It is easy to understand why philosophers within the Kantian tradition tend to concentrate on those parts of Kant's moral theory that they believe accurately reflect our ordinary moral awareness.

Appendix 2:
Kant's philosophy of moral education

Because the Enlightenment placed its faith above all else in the power of reason, education was considered the hope of the future. (See *Ed.* 444/8.) Becoming enlightened requires, externally, the removal of institutional restraints on free inquiry and, internally, what Kant calls "the most important revolution within man," the renunciation of dependence on external authority and a willingness to think for oneself (*Anthr.* 229). Nature has brought man to the place where he now is responsible for himself and his future. "Man can only become man by education. He is merely what education makes of him" (*Ed.* 443/6; see *Anthr.* 323–24).

Kant believed that, in the main, education had been badly mismanaged by those groups controlling it – civil rulers and the church – for they had been far more interested in inculcating blind obedience than in promoting autonomy. (See *Ed.* 448–49/16–17, 450–51/20–21; *Conflict* 19/27.) But, reflecting the optimism typical of the Enlightenment, he wrote that "it is only now that something may be done in this direction [promoting enlightenment through education], since for the first time people have begun to judge rightly, and understand clearly, what actually belongs to a good education" (*Ed.* 444/7–8). The development of the ability to reason depends on education in freedom, a systematic process in discipline that can be directed only by "enlightened experts" (*Ed.* 449/17; see 441/2–3, 444/8; *Anthr.* 325; *Lect.* 470–71/252–53).[1] "It is through good education that all the good in the world arises" (*Ed.* 448/15).

Kant was convinced that, since education is an art, a philosophy of education needs to be based on an empirically tested theory of child development. Only empirical testing and observation can tell us which educational techniques are in fact the most effective. (See *Ed.* 445–46/9–11, 451/21–23.) Moreover, the process of education needs to take into consideration the individual differences in students (*M.M.* 483; see *Ed.* 446–47/10–11, 455/31, 456/34, 468/44, 466/58, 485/93, 492–94/108–10; *Lect.* 468–69/250–51; *Anthr.* 324). He therefore was vitally interested in new theories about child development as well as in educational experiments being carried out at the "Philanthropist" Dessau Institute, founded by J. B. Basedow, an admirer of Rousseau. (See *Ed.* 444/6–7, 451–52/21–25.)[2] With Rousseau, Kant believed that "since Nature has made nothing in vain," the best methodology would follow the guidance of man's first educator, Nature, insofar as possible.

Since young children do not know what profession they will choose and thus what skills they will need, the schools need to teach them many different things. (See *Gr.* 41/415; *M.M.* 445.) In general, though, Kant believed that an adequate education requires students to develop their natural physical, emotional, intellectual, and social potentialities. (See *Ed.* 441/2–3, 445/9.) For this reason, he divided "physical" (in contrast to specifically moral) education into nurturing and physical training (tending and feeding the child), discipline (*Zucht* and *Asketik* – which must begin before instruction), and the development of understanding, judgment, and reason through instruction in the various fields of knowledge, including logic, mathematics, the physical sciences, geography, and history. (See *Ed.* 441/1, 456/33–34, 469/64–66, 475/76–78; *Lect.* 467/248–49; *Orient.* 146n.)[3] Moreover, we also need to develop our powers of memory, imagination, and taste, all of which contribute to our ability to learn. Genuine enlightenment requires learning how to think for oneself, and that requires an early beginning and a long learning process. (See *Orient.* 146n.)

Because the ultimate end of human life is virtue with the happiness proportionate to virtue, the ultimate purpose of education is not theoretical but practical: to "make the objectively practical reason also subjectively practical" (*Pr.R.* 151; see *Ed.* 445/10). The measure of education, then, is its effectiveness in teaching students "how to live as . . . free being[s]," thereby promoting their ultimate goal (*Ed.* 455/30). But education first must equip students with the technical skills and self-discipline they need to learn to work to achieve their prudential goals (*Ed.* 471/69). To fulfill their destiny to be "worthy of the nature of man," they then must be taught to use their skills and talents in morally right ways, and that requires both the development of judgment and the moral discipline necessary to act as duty demands. (See *Ed.* 444/8, 450/20.)

Because so much depends on each individual's talents and the possibilities open to each person, however, there is a good deal of leeway in the manner in which each person may obey the injunction to "cultivate your powers of mind and body so that they are fit to realize any end you can come upon" (*M.M.* 392). As Kant has said, wide and imperfect duties do not specify exactly how or to what extent we are to fulfill them, that is, exactly how we should frame our physical and mental development. We have a duty only to adopt the general maxim to do so, and we enjoy a good deal of leeway in deciding how to obey it. (See *M.M.* 392, 433n, 445–46.)

Given Kant's conviction that ethical development requires the support of an ethical community, the ideal educational agency should be the church, but he also thought that, in general, public education would be best because it would attract the most competent teachers. Yet he was fearful that a state system of education would be too vulnerable to abuse by the sovereign. (See *Ed.* 448–49/15–18, 454/29.)

Much of Kant's philosophy of education would fall today under the heading of developmental psychology. In this brief appendix I will concentrate only on his discussions of specifically moral education. These discussions deal mainly with children and young adults, for Kant regarded those who were sixteen years old as ready for parenthood and adult life.

What students most need to learn, he wrote, are moral sentiments, the only moral incentives for a morally good life. Students must learn

. . . to substitute abhorrence for what is revolting and absurd, for hatred; the fear of their own conscience, for the fear of man and divine punishment; self-respect and inward dignity, for the opinions of men; the inner value of actions, for words and mere impulses; understanding, for feeling; and joyousness and piety with good humour, for a morose, timid, and gloomy devotion. (*Ed.* 493/108–9; see *Lect.* 46–47)

He organized this task into three related parts. The first two he called didactic, for one aims systematically to clarify the students' conception of morality and of virtue and the other to help students develop their moral judgment. The third or "ascetic" aims to help the student to practice virtue, insofar as that is possible, by developing "the capacity for the will to virtue" (*M.M.* 411). Throughout Kant's discussions, however, it should be kept in mind that he also held that no one can *make* another person virtuous. Further, as we saw in Chapter 9, the actual adoption of a good moral disposition requires a revolutionary, noumenal change of heart. But the educator can only deal with phenomenal character and from that point of view the adoption of a good disposition is a very gradual process.

A moral catechism

The first task of moral education is to help students become sensitive to the presence of the moral law within them. The moral law itself "is already present in a sound natural understanding and requires not so much to be taught as merely to be clarified" (*Gr.* 8/397). Therefore, "without the least attempt to teach it anything new, we merely make reason attend, as Socrates did, to its own principle" (*Gr.* 21/404; see *M.M.* 483).

The only objective basis for morally virtuous character is the moral law itself, and the only subjective basis is respect for that law. There can be only one correct general way to help students develop sensitivity to, and intensify their respect for, the moral law – appealing *only* to that law in all its purity, to the Idea of duty alone, and to the students' own sense of worth. (See *Gr.* 33–34/410–11, 33n/411n; *Pr.R.* 152–53, 156.) We can learn how to appeal to the students' own reason most effectively only by trying various approaches. Since this method "has never yet been widely used," we cannot look to past educational theories to tell us exactly what to do (*Pr.R.* 153).

What is clear is that we may not try to make morality attractive by holding up rewards, whether in this life or in the next, or try to make immorality unattractive by portraying it as harmful rather than as disgraceful. (See *M.M.* 482–83.) Likewise, it is a mistake to try to base morality on any feelings, even on what may seem to be moral emotions such as feelings of nobility. All such tactics, as we have seen, turn morality into prudence. (See *Pr.R.* 151.) As we saw in Chapter 3, Kant condemned those moralists who had not carefully isolated that moral motive, but instead had appealed to both moral and prudential motives. They had injured their students by confusing the students' thinking about the nature of morality and caused them to waver between two radically different kinds of motives. (See *Gr.* 30–34/409–11.)

Nonetheless, Kant allows that two kinds of students may need a special introduction to moral education proper: the young, whose ability to reason is still weak and needs to be developed, and those with a morally depraved character who habitually ignore the moral law. For these, Kant permits an initial appeal to prudential considerations of advantage or of fear of harm, for, as experience shows, it is often in our interest to act morally rightly. (See, e.g., *Pr.R.* 152; *M.M.* 216, 482–83.) Once these two classes of students have developed some interest in morality, moral education proper must not then base the pursuit of virtue on any such prudential considerations but may appeal only to the moral motive of dutifulness. (See *Pr.R.* 152; *M.M.* 482.)

Kant discusses two different methods for teaching the foundations of morality. The first of these is the "dogmatic" way, that is, lectures by the instructor. (See *M.M.* 179.) This seems to have been the method Kant himself most commonly used in his university classes, since the students' notes we have from his course on ethics over a period of several years show that he must have read aloud from substantially the same lecture notes year after year. Yet according to one of his students, he did so "to all appearances, as though he himself had just begun to consider the question," and only after comparing different views finally came to a "definitive conclusion of his treatment of the subject."[4] He taught in this way because he thought that simply lecturing did not sufficiently require students to think. It tended to allow students passively to record and memorize what he had said and repeat it back to him in what he disparagingly called merely historical or mechanical knowledge. (See *Pu.R.* A836–37/B864–65; *Ed.* 450/20, 477/81.)

The second method consists in questioning students and appealing to their understanding to develop the right analysis of morality. Such questioning, Kant writes, can take two different forms. (See *M.M.* 411.) One is what he called "the catechetical method," which he thought to be probably the best method for beginning students, who do not know enough even to know what questions to ask. (See *M.M.* 478.) Using a ready-made moral catechism chiefly addresses the students' memory. The second form, which challenges their reasoning, imitates the method of the Socratic dialogue, while not encouraging sheer argumentativeness in the students. The instructor acts as a midwife for the students' reason, using questions and cases to initiate a dialogue with the students to help them clarify their thinking. (See *M.M.* 411, 478–79.) The instructor tries to elicit the nature of morality from the students (who are ordinary moral reason personified). When their answers are sufficiently precise, they then can be written down as a "moral catechism" to be memorized.

Kant thought that nothing is more helpful in promoting both moral understanding and moral conduct than such a catechism, supplemented by casuistical discussions. (See *Ed.* 490/103–4; *M.M.* 480–82.) He also insists that the moral catechism must precede any religious catechism, for a religious catechism will tend to teach that vice is wrong because it is forbidden by God rather than because it is detestable in itself. Doing this generates feelings of fear on the one hand and hope of reward on the other, thereby producing a prudential, not a moral, code of conduct. (See *M.M.* 478–79, 484; *Ed.* 450/ 20–21, 493–95/110–12.) When religious ideas permeate a culture, as was the case in Königsberg, the topic of religion cannot be avoided, but morality "must come first and theology follow" (*Ed.* 495/112).

Developing moral judgment

Once the students are clear about the nature of moral virtue, they then must turn their attention to the specific duties they have, and they must develop their power of judgment by making it "as it were, a habit" to judge their own actions and those of others according to the moral law (*Pr.R.* 159; see *Ed.* 488–89/100–2). They need to learn how to use the form of natural laws as a "typic" of the form of moral maxims, and they also need to distinguish the different ways in which they are morally obligated. As we have seen, in some cases the moral law requires a person only to adopt a maxim for positive duties while in other cases it obligates a person to perform or avoid performing a particular action. (See *Pr.R.* 159.) They also need to discuss whether various actions were probably done from the motive of duty so as to have genuine moral worth. (See *Pr.R.* 159.)

They need to learn all this, Kant writes, "partly in order to distinguish the cases to which [various moral rules] apply, partly to procure for them admittance to the will of man and influence over practice for man" (*Gr.* vii/ 389):

> By the mere habit of frequently looking upon actions as praiseworthy or blameworthy, a good foundation would be laid for righteousness in the future course of life. . . . It is entirely proper to extol actions which display a great, unselfish, and sympathetic disposition and humanity. But in them we must attend . . . to the subjection of the heart to duty. (*Pr.R.* 154–55 and 155n; see 159–60)

The more adept individuals become in making judgments about actual cases, the more they tend to take an interest in morality. (See *Pr.R.* 166; *M.M.* 484.) The more, also, they learn to respect "the dignity of humanity." Later that respect by itself will be able to motivate them consistently to act as they ought (*Ed.* 489/101–3).

The case method (or "casuistry") can also be used to help students develop their ability to reason morally and quicken their interest in morality. (See *M.M.* 484; *Rel.* 48–50/44–45.) For adults as well as children, Kant writes, the most effective way to clarify and vivify the motive of duty may be to take advantage of their natural liking for both stories and argumentation. (See *Pr.R.* 153.) Once they have developed the foundation of morality into a moral catechism, the educator then can tell stories in which moral and prudential considerations conflict and the fulfillment of duty costs the person much in the way of pleasure and happiness. (See *Pr.R.* 156, 160–61.) "Examples are the go-cart of judgment; and those who are lacking in the natural talent can never dispense with them" (*Pu.R.* A134/B173–74). But even those of ordinary intelligence can show an impressive ability to distinguish subtly and precisely between the two kinds of motives, and they quickly learn to assess a person's entire moral worth by the quality of that person's motives. (See *Gr.* 8/397, 21–22/404; *Pr.R.* 152–54, 162.) Moreover, the "vivid presentation of the moral disposition in examples" helps students become increasingly conscious of their freedom, their own power to act independently of all inclinations and regardless of circumstances (*Pr.R.* 160; see 160–61; *M.M.* 483–84).

What should be avoided when using stories or cases is any appeal to sentimental heroics, romantic daydreams, or "so-called noble (super-meritorious) actions" (*Pr.R.* 155). Such appeals are injurious, for thinking of oneself as deserving merit subtly introduces self-love and thus contaminates the pure motive of dutifulness; they also have no lasting "genuine [moral] effect" (*Pr.R.* 157). Morality must be based on the "dry and earnest idea of duty," not on emotional moods or enthusiasms, which die as quickly as they are aroused. (See *Pr.R.* 157.) Moreover, cases should mainly concern the "common and everyday responsibility" the students have as children (*Pr.R.* 155; see *Lect.* 467–68/249).

In his "Ethical Doctrine of Elements" in the *Metaphysics of Morals* Kant tries to follow his own advice by including a section on "Casuistical Questions" at the end of each "Article." But his own cases are often quite dramatic and far removed from "the observance of the commonest duty" (*Pr.R.* 157). After his discussion of suicide, for example, Kant suggests discussing such breathtaking moral problems as "hurling oneself to certain death in order to save one's country," voluntarily "offering oneself as a sacrifice for the welfare of the whole human race," and, after contracting incurable hydrophobia, killing oneself to avoid harming others later (*M.M.* 423–24).

Practice in moral discipline

Since morally virtuous character consists essentially in adopting the morally right intentions, there is little need to teach anyone the means for obeying the moral law; "in this respect whatever [a person] wills to do he also can do" (*Pr.R.* 37).

Still, the very notion of "virtue" as moral strength shows both that virtue is not innate and that we do not become virtuous simply by learning what virtue is. (See *M.M.* 477.) Nor is the acquisition of phenomenal virtue easy. "Affected as he is by so many inclinations," a person "has not so easily the power to realize the Idea *in concreto* in his conduct of life" (*Gr.* vii/389). So "virtue cannot be learned through the mere presentation of duty or through admonitions, but must rather be cultivated (by discipline) and practiced by being put to the proof of combat with the inner enemy in man" (*M.M.* 477). The third stage in moral development, therefore, consists in what Kant calls "moral asceticism," the "vigorous, spirited, and courageous practice of virtue" (*M.M.* 484; see 410–11, 484). In the sense that it teaches us freedom in its negative sense of controlling our "animal impulses," "discipline changes animal nature into human nature" (*Ed.* 441/2; *M.M.* 485). Actually to become virtuous, we first must adopt the ultimate moral disposition to act always as we should, and we then must act on that intention, denying the demands of our desires when they conflict with the rule of moral reason. (See *M.M.* 477.)

As we might expect, Kant takes discipline in general to be mainly negative in nature – a Stoic-like regimen, a "severe education" in strengthening the body and controlling and frustrating desires so as to foster and promote self-restraint and self-control. (See *Rel.* 459/39, 463–64/45–46; *Ed.* 449/18, 464/46; *Lect.* 467/249.) Children must learn as early as possible to control their natural unruliness and to avoid acting capriciously (*Ed.* 464/47, 481–82/86). Such discipline initially may only teach children to be obedient and to act rationally in prudential matters, even if that means acting according to another person's reason. For the most part, this is not specifically moral training, since it generally amounts to pitting one desire (for pleasure) against another (to escape the pain of punishment). (See *Ed.* 453/26–27, 482/87–88; *Lect.* 360–61/138–39.) But even that is at least preparatory to moral training proper ("moral culture"), for it aims not at "breaking their self-will" but at preventing children from developing either a "spoiled" or a "slavish" character (*Ed.* 465/48; see 459/52, 461/49). This is a necessary stage for children in learning to overcome impediments to freedom so that they eventually will be able to fulfill their duties on their own. (See *Ed.* 442/3–4, 482/86–87.)

Only through effort and practice can individuals learn for themselves to combat their radical tendency to evil and to do so in the only meritorious manner (as we saw in Chapter 10) – with a brave cheerfulness accompanying their awareness of their "restored freedom" (*M.M.* 485). They must develop strength of will so that they are willing to and in fact do set aside the influence of inclinations both on their moral judgments and on their decisions. This means that "to establish morality, we must abolish punishment" (*Ed.* 481/84). Students must learn not to rely on any inducements for moral conduct except the moral law itself. It also means that moral strength of will must not be confused with mere habituation, which produces only "a permanent inclination" rather than a regularity in conduct based on a principled decision. (See *M.M.* 479.)[5]

Children first learn how to act by imitating others, and so the instructor should endeavor to be "a model and impulse to imitation" for his students, especially when they are very young (*Pr.R.* 158; see 162; *M.M.* 479–80; *Ed.* 453/27). Examples also show students that they in fact can do what the Categorical Imperative commands, and so encourage them to obey its commands even when "everything that nature can present as an incentive [is] in opposition to it" (*Pr.R.* 158; see *Gr.* 30/409; *M.M.* 479–80, 479n). However, since morality requires individuals to be autonomous, their character must be based on their *own* maxims, formed according to the standard of the moral law in their *own* reasoning, not according to the way others act. (See *M.M.* 480; *Ed.* 475/77.) They can select what qualifies as an example of good conduct only if they first have norms, given by their own reason, for identifying such conduct. What other people do "must first itself be judged by moral principles in order to decide if it is fit to serve as an original example – that is, as a model" (*Gr.* 29/408; see *Pu.R.* A315/B371–72). For these reasons, as we saw in Chapter 4, the moral law cannot be derived from or based on examples, even the exemplary conduct of others, and in this sense "imitation has no place in morality" (*Gr.* 29–30/409; see *M.M.* 480–82).

Notes

Preface

1 John Rawls, *A Theory of Justice*, 251n29.
2 Lewis White Beck, *Essays on Kant and Hume*, 61.
3 Such questions could be raised, for example, of such authors as Bruce A. Ackerman, Ronald Dworkin, Charles Fried, R. M. Hare, Friedrich A. Hayek, John Rawls, Marcus George Singer, and Paul W. Taylor.

1. Introduction

1 Hans Saner, *Kant's Political Thought: Its Origins and Development*, 212. The major part of Saner's book is devoted to an eminently readable historical account of Kant's views about and participation in polemics. Two other accounts in English of Kant's life are Friedrich Paulsen's *Immanuel Kant: His Life and Doctrine* (1899) and Ernst Cassirer's magnificent work, *Kant's Life and Thought* (1918).
2 The chronology of Kant's major publications after the first (1781) edition of the *Critique of Pure Reason* is as follows:
   1783 – *Prolegomena to Any Future Metaphysics*
   1784 – *Idea for a Universal History from a Cosmopolitan Point of View*
   1784 – *An Answer to the Question: What is Enlightenment?*
   1785 – Review of Herder's *Ideas for a Philosophy of the History of Mankind*
   1785 – *Groundwork of the Metaphysic of Morals*
   1786 – *Speculative Beginning of Human History*
   1786 – *Metaphysical Foundations of Natural Science*
   1786 – *What Is Orientation in Thinking?*
   1787 – *Critique of Pure Reason*, second edition
   1788 – *Critique of Practical Reason*
   1788 – *On the Use of Teleological Principles in Philosophy*
   1790 – *Critique of Judgment*
   1793 – *Religion Within the Limits of Reason Alone*
   1793 – *On the Proverb: That May Be True in Theory but Is of No Practical Use*
   1793 – *Critique of Judgment*, second edition
   1794 – *The End of All Things*
   1795 – *Perpetual Peace*
   1797 – *Metaphysics of Morals*
   1797 – *On the Supposed Right to Tell Lies from Benevolent Motives*
   1798 – *Anthropology from a Pragmatic Point of View*
   1798 – *The Conflict of the Faculties* (Part II is "An Old Question Raised Again: Is the Human Race Constantly Progressing?")
   1800 – *Logic*
   1803 – *Education* (*Pedagogy*)

3 One unpleasant incident marred the tranquility of Kant's later life, when he incurred the displeasure of the imperial censor for views he stated in his *Religion Within the Limits of Reason Alone*. See Chapter 18.

4 Cassirer, *Kant's Life and Thought,* 84.

5 Cassirer again: "From the very beginning, the goal of [Kant's] life was not 'happiness' but self-sufficiency in thinking and independence of will," exactly the qualities he encouraged in his students (16).

6 Cassirer, 412–13; see also 414.

7 See Robert Paul Wolff, *The Autonomy of Reason,* 24–26, 93.

8 In the first part of his *The Critique of Judgment,* Kant extended the critique of theoretical reason begun in his *Critique of Pure Reason,* to defend the objectivity of aesthetic judgment.

9 The first chapter or section (*Abschnitt*) of the *Groundwork* has generated so much confusion that an early discussion of Kant's strategy there may prove useful. Kant had stated in the preface that he wrote this book with but one aim in mind: "to seek out and establish [i.e., defend] the supreme principle of morality" (*Gr.* xiii/ 392). This aim, of course, makes sense only if Kant was convinced there was a need to state clearly and defend the objective validity of the ultimate moral norm. In the first chapter his method for identifying that *principle* is through an analysis of the nature of morally good *character* – "a good will," which, Kant maintains, in the reasoned judgment of ordinary people is the only thing intrinsically and unconditionally good. He then proceeds by in effect raising three questions about the nature of human morally good character. He calls his answers to these questions his "propositions."

I. What makes a person morally good (have a "good will")? Not the good things one is able to accomplish but one's intentions (see *Gr.* 3/394). (Unfortunately, Kant neglected to identify the first proposition, and there is no consensus about exactly which claim belongs here.)

II. After an introduction concerning the difference between acting from a desire for happiness and from the motive of duty (*Gr.* 8–13/397–99), Kant in effect asks, If Proposition I is correct, then what kind of intention makes a person morally good? The answer is, one's intention to act (consistently, i.e., on a rule or maxim of acting) from duty (*Gr.* 13/399).

III. The third question, then, is, What does it mean to adopt the maxim to act "from duty"? And the answer to that is, the intention to do whatever morality obligates one to do, out of the motive of respect for the ultimate standard or law of morality (*Gr.* 14/400).

Finally Kant asks, What is this ultimate law of morality that can give rise to such respect as to outweigh every other motive? Since it is not a rule for being effective in achieving some end or other, that law must concern a purely formal characteristic of the maxim of an action, namely, that it can be a maxim on which any and every person may rationally act. Without much explanation, Kant states this formal principle as: "I ought never to act except in such a way that I can also will that my maxim should become a universal law" (*Gr.* 17/402; also 19/403).

Kant appeals to ordinary moral awareness to support his analysis, which is simple and straightforward, even if very compressed and badly in need of the explanations he offers in the second chapter. But Kant has distracted many readers by claiming that the third proposition is "an inference from the two preceding" (*Gr.* 14/400). This has led them to think that the second also must be an inference from the first, and this means that they have regarded the first chapter of the *Groundwork* as an enthymematic "argument." They then have made various creative suggestions for those premises necessary to make the argument explicit and perhaps even valid. (See, e.g., Robert Shope, "Kant's Use and Derivation of the Categorical Imperative," 264–68.) But doing this misses the point of what Kant actually was trying to do: to "unpack," so to speak, what there is about morally good character that leads people to regard it as uniquely good (*if* there is such a thing as morally good character).

The "inferences" here are not inferences in the sense of what we mean today by a logical inference. Instead, Kant's analysis consists of a chain of reasoning that begins with the conviction of ordinary people that we can be morally good even when we do not accomplish great things in the world, and proceeds to the contention that moral character therefore must be a quality intrinsic to the person: A person's character must depend on that person's intentions. Kant then analyzes a good person's intentions as all based on the resolve to act dutifully. His inclusion of the notion of respect here has frequently puzzled readers, but Kant meant only to stress how important moral sentiment is at least to *human* virtue. Finally, from his analysis of dutifulness or respect for the moral law, he elicits the ultimate moral norm by which ordinary moral judgment determines the moral quality of a person's maxims of conduct.

10 So the expression "ordinary people," as used throughout the rest of this book, should be taken as an honorific title, not a denigrating expression. Kant did not foolishly believe that everyone's moral judgments are all correct, and he was acutely aware of how often people deliberately do the morally wrong thing. He also admitted that ordinary moral language does not always offer the precision we need in philosophical analysis; see, e.g., *Pr.R.* 58–59, 163. But he still thought that the ultimate data of moral philosophy – beginning with the inner experience of moral obligation – must be found in what he called "ordinary moral consciousness."

Although consensus alone is not a sufficient condition of the validity of a particular moral or scientific claim, it still can be a sign of truth, for "objective validity affords the ground for a necessary universal agreement" (*Pr.R.* 13; see also 91–92; *Pu.R.* A820–22/B848–50). Kant had great respect for scientific consensus; in moral matters, with which everyone must be acquainted, he had even more respect for common convictions.

In a recent paper, "Cultural Development and Progress in Kant's Philosophy of History," Sharon Anderson-Gold points out that Kant did not believe that this examination of ordinary moral (or religious) consciousness will necessarily reveal the *ground* for the apodictic nature of moral demands. (See *Gr.* 20/403.) That requires a *critique* of practical reason, which Kant held to be possible only in an advanced stage of moral enlightenment. (See, e.g., *Gr.* xi–xii/391, 23–24/405; also the next section of this chapter.)

However, any attempt to understand morality in terms of or to base it on anything but itself would only destroy morality. Kant's critique of practical reason therefore analyzes what the concept of "a moral agent" must mean and then shows that human agency can be understood (insofar as it can be understood) only in terms of our actually being moral agents. There is an inevitable circularity here (as in every moral theory), but the circularity need not be vicious as long as the critique of practical reason and the analysis of morality are done with sufficient care.

A unique source of information about attitudes toward life and about human nature commonly accepted during Kant's lifetime is a long poem, *The Seasons* (1818), by a Lithuanian writer and pastor, Kristijonas Donelaitis, who had attended the University of Königsberg from 1736 to 1740. For example, since "no one can escape the troubles of this world" (37), "you, O futile man, must learn to be content" even "if at times your meals are lean, Or solid food is scarce, or if your soup is thin" (31). I owe this relatively unknown reference to my colleague Ignas Skrupskelis.

11 See Paulsen, *Immanuel Kant,* 335–41.

12 If our life were such that we always enjoyed a perfect coincidence between pleasure and morality, Kant thought, we would have no way in which to discriminate between them and we would be unable to recognize even the existence of morality.

13 From a Hegelian stance, Peter Laska writes, "Because this external control of natural desire by reason is necessary, the practical consequence of the Kantian critique is an internalized master-slave relation as the means to a moral life and moral community." See his "Kant and Hegel on Practical Reason," 133.

This Hegelian critique is echoed in the hostile comment of Max Stirner: "Protestantism has actually put a man in the position of a country governed by a secret police. The spy and eavesdropper, 'conscience,' watches over every motion of the mind, and all thought and action is for it a 'matter of conscience,' that is, police business. This tearing apart of man into 'natural impulse' and 'conscience' (inner populace and inner police) is what constitutes the Protestant" (Max Stirner, *The Ego and His Own: The Case of the Individual Against Authority,* 89).

14 By contrast, other practical rules – prudential rules – hold only conditionally, that is, on the condition that we desire whatever it is that a particular rule can help us get. They lose their hold over us simply by our renouncing the relevant end.

15 For a more detailed history of Pietism and its influence on Kant, see John Macquarrie's "Pietism" and Lewis White Beck's *Early German Philosophy: Kant and his Predecessors,* particularly 156–59.

16 In an undated fragment probably written about 1765, Kant attributes the recovery of this conviction (which he had lost, apparently while under the influence of Leibniz's writings) to Rousseau: "There was a time . . . when I despised the masses, which know nothing. Rousseau has set me right. This blind prejudice disappears; I learn to honor men." (See Paul Arthur Schilpp, *Kant's Pre-Critical Ethics,* 46.) Although it has become customary, following Cassirer, to note Kant's debt to Rousseau, it also needs to be pointed out that Kant came to disagree deeply with Rousseau about both human nature and the philosophy of history. For a useful discussion of these differences, see Sidney Axinn's "Rousseau *versus* Kant on the Concept of Man."

17 See "Grace and Justification" in Chapter 18. Yet, without some such training in intensive self-reflection, could Kant have engaged in the equally intense introspection later required by his transcendental philosophical method?

18 A more cynical view is found in Voltaire's *Candide.* Voltaire saw people like Kant and Fichte as representing those who came from the poorest economic background, were able to achieve middle-class status through the university system, but were prevented by the repressive political structure from rising any higher in power and influence. So, according to Voltaire, they used morality as a weapon to level their social superiors. *If* there is any truth in this view, it may partly explain Kant's disdain for the aristocratic Greek philosophers.

Some commentators have argued that Kant's moral opinions about such matters as sex and suicide are not valid "deductions" from or applications of the ultimate moral norm. Kant, they write, was only trying to justify the prephilosophical views of his social class, and his doing so unfortunately has allowed critics to burlesque that moral norm and its use. Although it is clear that Kant did wish to justify his prephilosophical views, he did not think this a philosophical failing. Later I shall maintain that Kant's examples in fact do show exactly how he thought the Categorical Imperative should be used.

19 Quoted by both Paulsen, *Immanuel Kant* (28), and Cassirer, *Kant's Life and Thought* (17–18), from Rink, *Ansichten aus Immanuel Kants Leben*, 12–13. See also "The Spirit of Virtue" in Chapter 10.

Much of what Kant most respected in Pietism he also found in Stoicism, which he had learned from reading both Christian Wolff and Alexander Baumgarten. In 1783 Kant's friend Christian Garve translated Cicero's Stoic treatise *De officiis* (*On Duties* – 44 B.C.) into German (as *Ciceros Abhandlung über die menschlichen Pflichten in drei Büchern*) along with a commentary (*Anmerkungen zu Ciceros Buch von den Pflichten*). The late Klaus Reich argued that the *Groundwork* (which was published two years later) shows considerable Stoic influence because Kant had read Garve's works just before writing it; see Reich's "Kant and Greek Ethics (II)," esp. 447–51. Kant did not agree completely with the Stoics (see, e.g., *Gr.* 2–3/393–94), but he believed they "had chosen their supreme practical principle, virtue, quite correctly" and deserved respect (*Pr.R.* 126).

20 See *Gr.* 25–34/406–11 and Chapters 4 and 5, this volume, for Kant's arguments against basing morality on experience.

21 For a recent critique of the "Kantian program of analyzing the invariant presuppositions contained in the 'moral knowledge of ordinary human reason,' " see Paul Stern, "The Problem of History and Temporality in Kantian Ethics." Stern raises complex issues that are also addressed by Sharon Anderson-Gold in her "Cultural Development and Moral Progress in Kant's Philosophy of History." As we shall see in Chapters 5 and 11, Kant did hold that the moral law itself is a "fact of pure reason," but he also held that we human agents have a phenomenal or empirical/historical aspect even in our moral lives. He wrote that we become *aware* of the moral law only by becoming aware of internal moral conflict, so that we have to regard ourselves both as noumenal (nontemporal) and phenomenal (temporal-historical) beings. On this topic, see also this chapter's note 10, Chapters 15 and 16, and Appendix 1.

22 We can note here at least in passing that Kant did not think psychology could be a science in the strict sense. (See *Pu.R.* A847–49/B875–77.) See Mary J. Gregor, "Translator's Introduction" to Kant's *Anthropology from a Pragmatic Point of View*, x–xv; and her *Laws of Freedom*, 1–33; also Theodore Mischel, "Kant and the Possibility of a Science of Psychology."

23 In his article "Enlightenment," Crane Brinton tells how the French *Encyclopédie* epitomized antipathy toward traditional religion with the statement "Reason is to the *philosophe* what grace is to the Christian" (520). My discussion of the Enlightenment is indebted to this article, to Beck's *Early German Philosophy: Kant and His Predecessors,* and Ernst Cassirer's classic work, *The Philosophy of the Enlightenment.*

24 For an examination of how Kant's pre-Critical work reflects the influence of Wolff and Leibniz, see Keith Ward, *The Development of Kant's View of Ethics.*

25 D. Brown, *Understanding Pietism*, 153.

26 See Ward, *Development of Kant's View of Ethics,* 21–22, 175–77. But see also Schilpp, *Kant's Pre-Critical Ethics,* 169–70; also Chapter 9, this volume, note 5.

2. The context for Kant's moral philosophy

1 Here I have followed a suggestion made in a seminar by John Silber to translate *aufheben* as "set aside" rather than "deny" knowledge (Kemp Smith's translation). No amount of theoretical knowledge can help us either understand or defend morality, and no knowledge of what is can tell us what ought to be. So we can set our knowledge aside when we turn to ethical philosophy. (Of course Kant did deny that we can have knowledge of supersensible reality, and he also held that we need empirical knowledge to understand specifically human morality.) See also Lewis White Beck, "Kant's Theoretical and Practical Philosophy."

2 In a letter to Marcus Herz in 1772 (nine years before the first edition of the first *Critique*), Kant wrote that he had already achieved as much clarity about ethical theory as he had in his analysis of theoretical knowledge. See Arnulf Zweig, *Kant: Philosophical Correspondence 1759–99*, 71; Ernst Cassirer, *Kant's Life and Thought*, 126–27.

3 The problem in this chapter is to include what is necessary to understand Kant's moral writings without either seriously oversimplifying the materials or overwhelming readers not acquainted with Kant's *Critique of Pure Reason*. Those who wish more information than I provide about Kant's theoretical philosophy or about the history of philosophy immediately preceding and concurrent with Kant can find such materials in several of the books listed in the bibliography – for example, Lewis White Beck's monumental *Early German Philosophy: Kant and His Predecessors;* C. D. Broad's *Kant: An Introduction;* Henry E. Allison's *Kant's Transcendental Idealism: An Interpretation and Defense;* W. H. Werkmeister's *Kant: The Architectonic and Development of his Philosophy;* John R. Silber's "The Context of Kant's Ethical Thought"; Paul Guyer's *Kant and the Claims of Knowledge;* and Ermanno Bencivenga's *Kant's Copernican Revolution.* See also Beck's "Kant's Theoretical and Practical Philosophy," as well as his introduction to his *Immanuel Kant's Critique of Practical Reason and Other Writings in Moral Philosophy.*

4 In general, Kant uses the word "ground" (*Grund*) to specify the reason sufficient for something else (its "consequent"). Depending on the context, it therefore can mean either the "justification for saying x" or the "cause of x" or the "nature of x." The uses are closely related. In the first sense, the ground for a particular claim is the support for the correctness of that claim. In the latter two senses, the ground for a particular claim about x is something about x that accounts for x's being what it is; the "something about x" may be the cause of x or the nature of x. When applied to human actions, the ground of an action is the reason or motive for (and therefore also the end or purpose of) that action.

On the meaning of "objective," see this chapter, note 7.

5 Kant did not write *only* to refute Hume; he also studied and eventually disagreed with many other authors, including Rousseau and "dogmatists" like Leibniz and Wolff. (See. e.g., Ernst Cassirer, *Rousseau, Kant, Goethe.*) However, references to Hume in Kant's writings show that Hume was very much on Kant's mind. For example, Kant called Hume "perhaps the most ingenious of all the skeptics" and a "representative" of them all (*Pu.R.* A764/B792 and A856/B884; see also *Pr.R.* 12–13, 51–57). He also acknowledged that Hume's analysis of causal necessity had had a crucial influence on him: "My recollection of David Hume was the very thing which many years ago first interrupted my dogmatic slumber and gave my investigations in the field of speculative philosophy a quite new direction" (*Proleg.*

260). On this latter topic, see Keith Ward, *The Development of Kant's View of Ethics,* and Henry E. Allison, *The Kant-Eberhard Controversy.*

6 Knowledge of the world requires contributions by both the person and the object world, while, as we shall see, in general the objectivity of moral claims depends only on conditions in the moral agent.

7 This characterization holds for both theoretical and practical claims. Practical claims are called "subjective" when they are "regarded by the subject as valid only for his own will" and "objective" (or laws) when they are "valid for the will of any rational being," even if they are not recognized as such by every person (*Pr.R.* 19; see also *Pu.R.* A53–55/B78–79, B139–42, B168, A189/B233–34, A214/B261, A820/B848; *Pr.R.* 19–20, 36, 62, 162; *Gr.* ivff/388ff, 28–29/408–9, 34–35/411–12, 62–63/426–27, 94/444; *Rel.* 6n/6). The norm of objectivity is reflected in the requirement that mathematical proofs and scientific experiments must in principle be replicable.

To some extent, how Kant uses the term "objective" depends also on the context. For example, with regard to theoretical knowledge of the world, our *concepts* are objective if they conform to the formal conditions of experience; namely, (1) the concept itself as logically self-consistent, and (2) its referent can be found in experience so that the concept is "usable." But what makes *temporal sequences* in experience objective is their "schematized" or rule-governed character. (See *Pu.R.* A189; *Rel.* 64n/59.) We can look at the various people in a family portrait in any order we choose, for example. But according to the rule of ground and consequent, schematized temporally as the rule of cause and effect, the younger members of a family are generated by, rather than generate, the older members, and each person still has an objective temporal place within the family. (See *Pu.R.* A113–14, A189–211/B232–56.)

Two other notes about Kant's terminology: First, although he often used the terms "speculative" and "theoretical" synonymously, Kant also called theoretical thinking "speculative" in a narrower sense to designate thought about concepts of objects "which cannot be reached in any experience" and which are the proper subject matter of metaphysics (*Pu.R.* A634/B662; see A841/B869, A845/B873).

Second, the term "transcendent" refers to the *use* of Ideas of reason and is not synonymous with "transcendental," which refers only to the Idea itself. A transcendental Idea is used transcendently when a person ignores the limits of knowledge and claims either that the Idea gives knowledge of reality beyond all our possible experience or that that person has had empirical experience with the referents of those Ideas. (See, e.g., *Pu.R.* A296/B352–53.) The word "transcendent" contrasts with "immanent": An "immanent idea" is one that may be used legitimately to refer to appropriate objects in experience. (See, e.g., *Pu.R.* 643–44/B671–72.) Kant's strong doctrine here aroused antipathy among adherents to all those religions that claimed to have immediate converse with God; on this, see Chapter 18, especially note 7.

8 A transcendental deduction is not a "proof" as we commonly use that term today, for there is no point in proving what we already accept – for example, our own experience. It also is not a proof in the sense of inferring a conclusion from given premises, for the concepts and rules involved may be ultimate and so not based on anything more fundamental.

Positively, this kind of argument proceeds by asking what *must* be postulated in order to account for the admittedly "given" (whether given theoretically or practically). (See *Pu.R.* A786–91/B814–19; *Proleg.* 274–75.) Negatively, the method shows that the consequence of denying those conditions would be to deny the undeniable. So, for example, Kant argues that Hume's empiricism has the untenable consequence of undermining what no one wishes to deny – the possibility of science.

Kant's methodology here also has ancient roots in the history of Western philosophy. The dialectical arguments we find in Plato's dialogues commonly consist of a reflective analysis of what beliefs are necessarily presupposed by other beliefs, and Aristotle's "demonstration by way of refutation" is another version of the same type of argument. (See *Metaphysics* 1008b8–10b10.) Such arguments maintain that the denial of a certain claim results in either a contradiction or an absurdity. See Kant's defense of human moral agency in Chapter 7; also Wolff, *The Autonomy of Reason: A Commentary on Kant's Groundwork of the Metaphysics of Morals,* 26; S. Körner, "The Impossibility of Transcendental Deductions"; Dieter Henrich, "The Proof-Structure of Kant's Transcendental Deduction"; and Barry Stroud, "Transcendental Arguments."

In trying to summarize Kant's aim and methodology with some clarity, I have unavoidably understated the enormous difficulty of his undertaking. Critically reflecting on what we can legitimately claim to know has been a main philosophical task from the time of the Greeks, but Kant's critique was far more radical than anything attempted before him, so much so that his philosophy came to be known as "*the* Critical philosophy," even in his own lifetime.

9 What we know a priori can be either "mixed" (with empirical concepts) or "pure." For example, the claim "Every change has a cause" is a mixed judgment, for, Kant writes, "alteration is a concept which can be derived only from experience"; but it is also a priori, because universal in scope and necessarily true (*Pu.R.* B3). Pure a priori knowledge, by contrast, has "no experience or sensation whatsoever mixed with it" and so can only be learned by reflection, not from experience (*Pu.R.* B11; see A20/B34). The rules of general logic are examples of pure thought; they are completely formal and hold necessarily for all thinking. Logic therefore is "propaedeutic to," that is, preliminary to all other thinking, which must presuppose it and conform to its rules; see *Pu.R.* Bix, A50–54; *Gr.* i–iii.

In the *Groundwork* Kant argues that even the metaphysics of specifically human morality must consist of "pure" concepts and rules – "pure" in the sense of being "based on reason alone and holding universally" in contrast to "empirical," that is, based on experience and holding only generally. (See, e.g., *Gr.* vii/389, 32/410, 32n/410n.) These claims, which are confused and hyperbolic, have given rise to considerable controversy over exactly how "pure" Kant thought moral philosophy can and must be. On this question see this chapter, note 13.

10 The Latin terms "a priori" and "a posteriori" are so much part of the Kantian vocabulary that I will not italicize them. Strictly speaking, they function as adverbial expressions modifying verbs such as "learned" and "known," but it has become common for English-writing translators and commentators to use them as adjectival expressions modifying "knowledge."

11 Although he held that our ability to think is and can be only a single power, Kant also conformed to the custom of his day by adopting the vocabulary of "faculty psychology," that is, by attributing different mental activities to different mental faculties or powers. According to Kant, we have three cognitive powers: sensibility, understanding, and reason.

Sensibility (*Sinnlichkeit*) enables us to have perceptions or empirical sensations and also contributes the "forms" of space and time that do not originate in our senses but are presuppposed in our sensory knowledge, making it possible. (See *Pu.R.* A19–49/B33–73.)

Our understanding (*Verstand*) contributes those concepts or categories (such as substance) and rules (such as the rule of ground and consequent) that are necessary for us to have coherent empirical knowledge. (See *Pu.R.* A65–136/B89–173; *Proleg.* 322; *Gr.* 108/452, 114/455; *Pr.R.* 9n.)

Reason (*Vernunft*) is concerned mainly with regulating the use of the concepts and rules of the understanding. In its "empirical" use as the faculty of judgment, it has two functions. First, reason applies these completely abstract concepts and rules by means of "schemata" (imagelike concepts provided by the imagination) to sense perceptions, organizing them so we can have coherent experiences. (See *Pu.R.* A118–20, A120n, A124–25, A137–47/B176–87, A833–34/B861–63.) Judgment (*Urteilskraft*) also has the function of deciding whether a given case falls under a particular rule or, coordinately, whether a given rule applies to a particular case. (See, e.g., *Pu.R.* A133/B172; *Cr.J.* 179; *Anthr.* 199; *Logic* 131–33/135–37.)

In its pure (or "real") use, reason engages in the metaphysical quest for finalities by going beyond the limits of experience (and so also of the understanding) to think of the world as a complete systematic whole and to seek completeness and systematic unity of explanation. (See *Proleg.* 331–32; *Pu.R.* A326ff/B382ff, A650ff/B678ff.) In doing so it generates what Kant called "Ideas" (*Ideen*), discussed later in this chapter. (See *Pu.R.* A310–38/B366–96; *Pr.R.* 136.) Finally, it is reason that distinguishes between the sensible and the intelligible world. (See *Gr.* 108/452.)

In the "Metaphysical Deduction" in his first *Critique,* Kant set out to identify all these various mental contributions and, in the "Transcendental Deduction," to determine their legitimate uses as well as their limitations. None of these mental contributions can be derived from experience; for example, we never actually see the exercise of causal power but only successions of events.

12 William James, *The Principles of Psychology,* 462. See also *Pu.R.* Bix, Bxxiv, Bxla, Bxxx, A1–2/B1–3, A11–12/B25–26, A104ff, B234, A353; *Gr.* 105–6/450–51; *Pr.R.* 4n, 107.

13 The parallels between theoretical and practical knowledge are not as neat as Kant tries to make them out to be in the preface of the *Groundwork.* (See i–iii/387–88.) The foundation (or metaphysics) of ethics *in general* must be based only on reason and so be "pure," but the foundation of ethics *for human beings* must take into account how the human will is "affected by nature," and *that* we can learn only from experience. (See, e.g., *Pu.R.* A15/B29, A54–55/B79; *Gr.* 35/411–12; *M.M.* 216–17.) So the metaphysics of human morality cannot be completely "pure" but must consist of mixed a priori claims, for example, that morality necessarily appears to us as our *duty* because we have desires and inclinations and are only contingently rational.

Kant clearly held that moral philosophy may not *base* any laws of conduct on experience and in that sense does not have an "empirical part" like science. In fact, the *Groundwork,* at least on one level, is but a single long argument against basing morality on experience. Kant, however, also clearly holds that, in order to produce substantive ethical principles for human beings, the application of the moral law always "presupposes . . . objects as given" empirically (*Pr.R.* 65; see also Chapter 11). So there is and must be this second "empirical part" of moral philosophy, which he calls "practical (or pragmatic) anthropology." (See *Gr.* ii/387 and v/388; *Pu.R.* A550/B578.) By that expression he mainly means the (empirical) descriptive study of how, in his ordinary life, man in fact acts and "interacts with other men in pursuit of his ends," thereby facilitating or impeding his moral destiny (from Mary J. Gregor, "Translator's Introduction" to Kant's *Anthropology from a Pragmatic Point of View,* xx–xxi). Nonetheless, Kant also confusingly describes anthropology as a study of "what man as a free agent makes or can *and should* make of himself" (*Anthr.* 119, emphasis mine; see 246; *Lect.* 244/2). Moreover, he states that the fourth question philosophy must seek to answer is, "What is man?" and that this question lies within the province of anthropology (see his 1793 letter to Stäudlin in Arnulf Zweig, *Kant: Philosophical Correspondence 1759– 99,* 205).

In the same section of the preface to the *Groundwork,* Kant also writes about the "matter" or "objects" of moral reasoning and moral knowledge. Unfortunately, he can be distressingly loose with those terms; on this, see note 10 in Chapter 6. Sometimes he uses the term "the object" of human moral thinking to refer to empirically observable behavior. But he also defines "the object" (or "matter") as consisting in the formation of morally right intentions, which do not appear in the world of experience and are not observable phenomena. So the meaning of the terms "object" and "matter" must be carefully determined from the context in which they occur.

Finally, in the same preface, Kant uses the terms "ethics" and "moral philosophy" synonymously. Later, however, in his *Metaphysics of Morals* he restricts the terms "the doctrine of virtue" (*Tugendlehre*) or "ethics," properly speaking, to those moral duties concerning motives and ends that cannot be enjoined by public law, in contrast to "the doctrine of law" (or *Rechtslehre*), which has to do only with behaviors that can be so coerced. He then uses the expression "moral philosophy" (*Moralphilosophie* and *Sittenlehre*) to refer to both of these. Once again he is not always faithful to his own vocabulary in his various books and articles. (See *M.M.* 214, 219, 379.) Except when I am specifically discussing his political theory, I generally will use the expressions "moral philosophy" and "ethical theory" interchangeably.

14 Even today there is no consensus about such knowledge. The distinctions Kant makes between kinds of knowledge claims, which initially seemed clear, tend to become more and more murky under continued analysis, even within the development of Kant's own system. See, for example, Newton Garver, "Analyticity and Grammar." For a valuable discussion of Kant's response to criticisms of his analytic-synthetic distinction, see Henry E. Allison, *The Kant-Eberhard Controversy,* particularly 36–75. See also Lewis White Beck, "Kant's Theory of Definition," "Can Kant's Synthetic Judgments Be Made Analytic?" "On the Meta-Semantics of the Problem of the Synthetic A Priori," and "Remarks on the Distinction between Analytic and Synthetic."

15 Several comments need to be made at this point. First, I need to thank Donald Livingston and Michael Costa for reminding me that here I am presenting only Kant's interpretation of Hume's analysis of human knowledge. Hume's own distinction was not between judgments, that is, between kinds of statements with a truth-value, but between mere relations of ideas and matters of fact; see his *Enquiry,* Section 4. The former can be known with certainty, hold independently of the way the world is, and tell us nothing about the world. Claims about matters of fact do inform us about the world, but they can give us only contingent and, at best, probable knowledge.

Second, Kant understood Hume as holding that mathematical judgments are all analytic (and argued that he should have classified them as synthetic but a priori; see, e.g., *Proleg.* 272; *Pr.R.* 13, 52). Hume scholars still debate the exact status of mathematical judgments in Hume's theory. Some hold that Kant's interpretation of Hume was essentially correct, but also maintain that the expression "synthetic a priori" would not have meant for Hume what it meant to Kant. On this, see Dorothy P. Coleman, "Is Mathematics for Hume Synthetic A Priori?" Others have argued that Kant was either confused or mistaken about Hume, because mathematical judgments do not seem to be either analytic or synthetic to Hume. For this view, see Donald W. Livingston, *Hume's Philosophy of Common Life,* 49–52.

   Although he admitted that the difference between a priori and a posteriori claims had been recognized by other philosophers, Kant still claimed that the distinction between "analytic" and "synthetic" judgments had "never previously been considered" (*Pu.R.* B19). In his article, "Analytic and Synthetic Judgments before Kant," Lewis White Beck surveys what Locke, Leibniz, Wolff (and so also his follower Baumgarten, whose books Kant used in his classes), and Crusius in fact had held, and concludes that Kant's claim was unjustified. In a later article, "The Originality of Kant's Distinction between Analytic and Synthetic Judgments," Henry E. Allison finds some truth in Kant's claim; see also his *Kant-Eberhard Controversy,* especially 57–59, 141. In any case, the understanding of the difference between synthetic and analytic statements is now quite different from Kant's; see Beck, "Can Kant's Synthetic Judgments Be Made Analytic?"

   Finally, there are problems with the clarity of Kant's manner of distinguishing between synthetic and analytic judgments; see, e.g., Allison's *Kant's Transcendental Idealism,* 72–78, as well as Beck's relevant articles.

16 For a still helpful discussion of Kant on causality, see A. C. Ewing, *Kant's Treatment of Causality.*

   Mathematics must be included in this paragraph because Kant held that mathematical knowledge is synthetic (connecting logically distinct concepts) but that the necessity in it requires it to be known a priori. (See, e.g., *Pu.R.* A712ff/B741ff; *Proleg.* 268–72; *Pr.R.* 52.) His analysis of mathematics and geometry is not obviously relevant to his moral theory; I will subsume it tacitly under what is said about theoretical knowledge.

   Although Kant himself was not reluctant to use the term "experience" (*Erfahrung*) to refer to our inner moral and aesthetic awareness, to avoid any possible confusion I shall generally use that word only to refer to the sensory awareness that provides the basis for our empirical knowledge of objects.

17 Kant began the preface to the first edition of his *Critique of Pure Reason* with precisely this problem: "Human reason has this peculiar fate that in one species of its knowledge [theoretical knowledge] it is burdened by questions which, as prescribed by the very nature of reason itself, it is not able to ignore, but which, as transcending all its [theoretical] powers, it is also not able to answer" (*Pu.R.* Avii; see also Ax, Bix–xv). One of the virtues of Lucien Goldman's *Immanuel Kant* is the way in which Goldman stresses the importance of the concept of "totality" throughout Kant's writings.

18 Kant was well aware that merely *saying* that our theoretical knowledge is limited by what we can perceive would not win over those who still believed in the old-style metaphysics. He therefore constructed the best available theoretical arguments both for and against freedom, immortality, and God, showing that we only involve ourselves in insoluble contradictions ("paralogisms" and "antinomies") and inco-

herence (an "indeterminate idea") by doing so. He regarded this negative part of his critique of the powers of reason to be so important that he devoted over a third of his entire first *Critique* to it – Book II of the "Transcendental Dialectic" (A338–704/B396–732). He characterized the difficulties generated there to be "the most fortunate perplexity in which human reason could ever have become involved," for they show conclusively that the old rationalistic metaphysics was mistaken. (See *Pr.R.* 107, 138–39.) This realization, Kant wrote to his friend Garve, marked the beginning of his Critical philosophy. On this see also Beck, *A Commentary on Kant's Critique of Practical Reason,* 24–25. The solution Kant offered to dissolve the problems he had generated is his phenomenal-noumenal distinction, mentioned earlier in this chapter and discussed at greater length in both Chapter 7 and Appendix 1. This distinction allows for the possibility of a kind of causality defined not by natural deterministic laws but by the law of freedom.

19 Beck, *Early German Philosophy,* 486; see also 487–88. In his "Dreams of a Spirit-Seer" (1766, *KGS* II, 315–73), Kant had caricatured the mystical claims of Swedenborg with a somewhat heavy-handed humor, seeing in them a paradigm of the pretensions and fallacies of the claims of the old metaphysics to knowledge of a supersensible world.

20 See Beck, *A Commentary on Kant's Critique of Practical Reason,* 46n, 227, 245, 263n. Within the Critical philosophy, metaphysics consists entirely of synthetic propositions attainable in an a priori fashion, and is divided into metaphysics of nature and metaphysics of morals (see *Pu.R.* Axx, Bxxiv, B18, A841/B869).

21 Calling them "Ideas" signals the debt Kant admitted owing to Plato, especially Kant's denunciation of any effort to base a moral theory on anything but reason; see also Chapter 9, note 5. In his *Critique of Pure Reason,* Kant first examined three theoretical Ideas of reason – soul, world, and God – before introducing the three practically postulated Ideas of freedom, immortality, and God. For further discussion, see also Beck, *Commentary,* 264ff; J. D. McFarland, *Kant's Concept of Teleology,* especially Chapter 2; and John R. Silber, "The Metaphysical Importance of the Highest Good as the Canon of Pure Reason in Kant's Philosophy." These two triads will also be discussed further in Chapters 7 and 8.

22 Against the contention, mentioned at the beginning of this chapter, that the New Science is the enemy of human freedom and of religion, Kant argued that the Ideas of freedom, the human soul, and God (all rightly understood) are necessary presuppositions for the very possibility of science!

For a discussion of the "regulative" use of Ideas, see Stanley G. French, "Kant's Constitutive-Regulative Distinction"; also "Limitations of Theoretical Reason" in Chapter 8.

23 See Chapters 5 and 7.
24 See Chapters 5 and 11.
25 See Chapters 6 and 14.
26 See Chapter 14.
27 See Chapters 9 and 10.
28 See Chapter 15.
29 See Chapters 10 and 15.
30 See Chapters 8, 10, and 15.
31 See Chapter 16.
32 See Chapter 17.
33 See Chapter 18.
34 Transcendental deductions are of two kinds. If the argument begins with a "given"

object in experience, Kant calls it an "objective deduction"; if it begins with the nature of reason in the thinking subject, he calls it a "subjective deduction." The argument in support of Ideas of reason is of the latter kind. (See *Pu.R.* Axvi–xvii, A92–94/B125–26, A336/B393, A666/B694, A669–71/B697–99.)

35 See Kroner, *Kant's Weltanschauung*, 39–40. Moreover, our scientific beliefs concern only appearances, whereas the moral law gives us access to the noumenal world, which is more real than mere appearances; see *Cr.J.* 468, 474. The three postulates of God, immortality, and freedom also are the proper objects of metaphysical inquiry (see *Pu.R.* B395n, A798/B826), so the elucidation and defense of morality also fulfill, insofar as that is possible, our metaphysical quest for ultimate meaning in our life.

36 See Chapter 3, note 2.

37 It is difficult – perhaps, finally, impossible – either to conceive of or defend Kant's philosophy (particularly insofar as it is *critical* in character) apart from the doctrine of the two viewpoints. But I shall refer to that doctrine as sparingly as possible and concentrate instead on Kant's analytic exposition of ordinary moral consciousness. For one thing, there is little agreement about how to understand the phenomenal-noumenal distinction or about what we may and may not say about the noumenal world. See, for example, George Schrader, "The Thing in Itself in Kantian Philosophy," and Ralf Meerbote, "The Unknowability of Things in Themselves."

Under *any* interpretation it is so difficult to sustain faithfully the doctrine of the two viewpoints that nearly all present-day Kantian ethicists tend to adopt Kant's conceptual analysis of morality without paying much attention to this part of his doctrine. They set aside problems concerning the compatibility of freedom and determinism, which Kant intended the doctrine to allow, and they defend the reality of morality by simply following his appeal to ordinary moral awareness. Once physicists officially decided that there are areas of indeterminacy in the world, the scientific view of the world apparently no longer seems such a danger to the contention that we are moral agents as it did to Kant.

Nonetheless, as it turns out, abandoning the metaphysical and epistemological context for Kant's ethical theory and trying to construct a moral theory solely on the basis of an analysis of ordinary moral language, turns out to mean, for Kant, the destruction of morality. Moreover, it also requires us to ignore what Kant himself considered necessary for the defense both of human morality and of some of his other most crucial claims, including the postulates of pure practical reason, the importance of the concept of the final good, and the essentially religious nature of his enterprise and of the human race's ultimate destiny.

This much needs to be said now. Throughout my exposition I will take the view that the noumenal-phenomenal distinction rests on the limits of our theoretical insight and therefore remains always an epistemological, not an ontological, distinction. I do not believe that Kant ever held that there are two different worlds – the one we experience and another one behind the world we experience. In general, I think Nicholas Rescher may have offered as clear an analysis as may be possible in his "On the Status of 'Things-in-Themselves' in Kant."

3. The nature of human action

1 As we would expect, given that Kant did not adopt a precise theory of action, he is not always consistent in using his own technical terminology, and he occasionally

words his claims in such a way that they can be read as completely inconsistent with his actual doctrines. Consequently, my interpretations of his theory of action and, later, of his moral theory may seem to be incompatible with individual passages in his writings. I shall call attention to some such examples later, in notes.

2 In his book *The Categorical Imperative: A Study in Kant's Moral Philosophy,* the renowned Kantian scholar H. J. Paton repeatedly expresses this same view. He writes, "There is much to be said for the view that if [Kant] had set forth in detail a sound philosophy of action, this would have been a great help toward understanding his moral philosophy" (33; for similar comments, see also 32, 83, 108, 123, 193, 260, and 275–76).

3 A person is also a spectator when only appreciating the aesthetic qualities of the world.

Although Kant uses the term "practical" in some passages to refer to both prudential and moral interests in contrast to theoretical interests, in most places he means "practical" to be synonymous with "moral" and to contrast with "prudential."

4 This claim may not seem very important now, but it has enormous implications in Kant's moral theory, in which moral "action" refers primarily to the formation of intentions and only secondarily to physical behaviors we can perceive with our senses. Since Kant does not always clearly state how he is using the term "action," many important passages can be systematically misunderstood by an unwary reader. See "Relating the Two Viewpoints" in Chapter 7.

5 Although Aristotle had used the term "practical reason" (to designate what later philosophers called the "will"), that expression had dropped out of philosophical usage and was virtually reinvented by Kant. On this, see Lewis White Beck, *A Commentary on Kant's Critique of Practical Reason,* 37.

Kant sometimes uses two different terms to distinguish between two powers or functions of practical reason or the will: *der Wille* to designate its cognitive power – the moral law within us; and *die Willkür* to designate its conative power – our ability to choose how to act. (See *M.M.* 213.) For further discussion of this division of our "faculty of desire," see Chapter 5 and Appendix 1.

6 Kant writes that whenever we act, it is "inescapable" that we should "have regard, in every action, to the consequence thereof, in order to discover therein what could serve [us] as an end . . . which consequence, though last in practice . . . is yet first in representation and intention" (*Rel.* 6n/6; see also *Pr.R.* 20). All morally assessable behaviors have consequences and we typically engage in moral assessment only after we have become interested in the consequences of a particular action, but what makes an action morally right is its intrinsic nature, regardless of any possible consequences. (Since two people can pursue the same state of affairs from different motives, we should not collapse "motive" and "end" into one another.)

Kant's moral theory clearly is "teleological" (from the Greek word meaning the study of ends) because practical reason is by its very nature goal directed. But the use of labels can be more misleading than helpful. In metaethical language, today "teleological" is usually contrasted with "deontological" (meaning the study of obligation), and in *that* sense Kant's theory is not teleological but deontological, for Kant takes the notion of moral obligation to be fundamental and the notion of moral "good" to be derivative from it (rather than the other way around). For further discussion of these types of moral theorizing, see Frankena, *Ethics,* 12–33. The fact that Kant's theory is also "nonconsequentialist" should signal both the religious roots of his theory and his tendency still to rely on divine justice and providence to remedy any untoward consequences of our acting dutifully.

7 See Chapter 11, note 21. In his monograph, "The Primacy of Practical Reason," for example, G. J. Warnock interprets Kant as arguing that "moral action aims at no end at all" because the worth of moral action does not depend on what it produces (254–55). In his famous essay "Does Moral Philosophy Rest on a Mistake?" H. A. Pritchard writes somewhat ambiguously but also gives the impression of committing the same error. Although Kant did hold that the moral value of rational action does not depend on its empirical consequences, he also insisted that completely aimless behavior is not rational and so cannot be morally significant. On this, see Lewis White Beck, "Sir David Ross on Duty and Purpose in Kant"; also Mark Timmons, "Kant and the Possibility of Moral Motivation."

8 Neither Aristotle nor Kant thought that our reason can be practical in the sense of causing us to act, totally without any need for motivational power supplied by desires. For Kant's doctrine, see Chapter 10; for Aristotle's doctrine, see my *Morality and the Good Life: A Commentary on Aristotle's Nicomachean Ethics*, 62–63, 85–88. In his *Commentary on Kant's Critique of Practical Reason*, Beck writes that "Kant rejected the Aristotelian thesis that reason alone cannot move us" (41). Whether this claim is correct depends on how it is interpreted; see this chapter, note 10.

9 Again, notwithstanding a common interpretation to the contrary, Kant does hold that human morality requires the presence of emotions. Note that here Kant is analyzing specifically human morality. Whether this analysis would also hold for other kinds of rational agents would depend on how they were structured metaphysically.

10 So Beck's claim in this chapter, note 8, is correct if interpreted to mean that moral desires – which must interest us in being morally good – must be generated by and be based only on the purely rational moral norm. For further examination of Kant's views of the role of emotions in human morality, see Chapters 9 and 10.

11 But see Chapter 9, note 1. See also Kerferd and Walford, *Kant: Selected Pre-Critical Writings and Correspondence with Beck*, 31–32.

12 Kant's use of the term "pathological" does not imply that our desires and inclinations are diseased or perverse. He apparently derived the term from the Greek word "pathos," and uses it to mean both emotional states, which are physically felt, and our susceptibility to experiencing such states. On this, see also Chapter 4.

13 Kant points out that "the concept of causality carries with it that of *laws* in accordance with which, because of something we call a cause, something else – namely, its effect – must be posited" (*Gr.* 97–98/446, emphasis mine). The rule- or law-governed nature of causality will be crucial to his analysis of freedom and morality: Just as the world of nature is governed by physical laws, so also the moral world is governed by the law of freedom.

14 Kant seems to use the term "maxim" in two different senses. Sometimes he uses "maxim" to refer to *any* practical rule that is "subjective" in the sense that it is a rule a person (or "subject") possibly can or in fact does adopt, *whatever* the moral quality of the action and *whatever* the person's motivation may be. (See, e.g., *Pr.R.* 20; *M.M.* 389.) Given this definition, subjective maxims are also objective principles or laws if they are fit to hold for every rational being, that is, when they are rules on which any rational agent could act. (See *Pu.R.* A812/B840; *Gr.* 15n/400n.) Other times Kant restricts the term "maxim" to a rule that is "subjective" in the sense that it is based on subjective factors such as a person's inclinations and even a person's ignorance so that it holds only for that person, in contrast to objective principles, which ignore all purely subjective considerations and therefore

are fit to hold for all rational agents. (See, e.g., *Gr.* 51n/420n; *M.M.* 225, 389; *Pr.R.* 19–20.) Many students of Kant have found Onora Nell's discussion of maxims helpful; see her *Acting on Principle: An Essay on Kantian Ethics,* particularly 34–42.

Since Kant's various formulations of the ultimate moral principle uniformly mandate the form that our maxims *should* have (whether or not they do), I will use the term in the first sense, as meaning any rule of conduct which people actually do or possibly can adopt and use and which may or may not also qualify as a morally acceptable rule or law.

15 On this crucial difference, see also Chapter 5.

16 Kant peculiarly insists that *all* imperatives originate in reason alone because they all express "an objective law of reason" (*Gr.* 413). If we understand all maxims as merely subjective principles, Kant writes, it then follows that maxims "are not imperatives," not even hypothetical imperatives (*Pr.R.* 20). But clearly, many imperatives originate in and express sheer emotions. Moreover, there seems to be no good reason why a morally good agent could not express his intention, or maxim, in the form of an imperative addressed to himself, particularly since, as Kant insists, it is moral fanaticism to believe we can ever be so confirmed in virtue that we no longer experience morality as an imperative. But perhaps I am missing Kant's point here.

17 This analysis is stressed particularly in the *Groundwork.* By contrast, in his *Metaphysics of Morals* Kant carefully distinguishes between ethical and juridical duties. The former require the motive of duty, while a person's motives are irrelevant to the fulfillment of civic duties, which are and can be described and prescribed only in behavioral terms. See also Chapters 6, 16, and 17.

4. Prudence: taking care of our own interests

1 Pleasure and pain are not themselves sensations, as Dwight Van de Vate, Jr., has noted in "A Kantian Paradox" (unpublished). "They are not on a par with colors or sounds or tactile sensations. Rather, pleasure and pain are adverbial classifications" of a range of diverse feelings, some pleasurable and others painful. Kant's analysis of the various kinds of "affects" and passions in his *Anthropology* shows a good deal of sensitivity to the complexity of this topic. (See Books II and III.) For purposes of moral theorizing, however, he thought the simplified account given in this and the previous chapter would be sufficient.

2 In his *Nicomachean Ethics,* Book 9, Chapter 8, Aristotle had argued that conflating the notions of "self-love" and "selfishness" (as Kant did) was a common mistake, yet still a mistake because it is "not in harmony with the facts." According to Aristotle, the morally best person "is an egoist or self-lover in the truest sense." Kant makes a bow in this direction when he states that selfishness becomes morally acceptable "rational self-love" when it is subordinated to the moral law. (See *Pr.R.* 73.) By contrast, "self-conceit" or arrogance (*Eigendünkel*) has no place in the life of moral virtue and needs to be suppressed as completely as possible.

Today the theory that claims that *all* human conduct can be explained by a Kantian-like analysis of prudential action is called "psychological egoism" or "psychological hedonism." For a discussion of that theory, see William K. Frankena, *Ethics,* 22. Kant's claim that prudentially motivated actions are at best nonmoral and at worst immoral will be familiar to those brought up to think that actions performed merely to satisfy our own desires cannot be morally admirable and that selfishness is a, if not *the,* fundamental moral vice.

3 This analysis applies also to technical principles. Kant holds that the ultimate formal principle of prudence is analytically true in the sense that a fully rational agent with needs who wills something as an end implicitly at least also wills whatever that agent knows is necessary to get that choice. When stated in any substantive form, its actual use requires empirical content and usually at least an implicit appeal to the principle of causality, making it a synthetic claim. Further, if that principle is stated as either a practical principle or an imperative for agents like human beings, who can act imprudently, this is a second reason why it and all its more particular rules must be synthetic (and a priori) propositions. See "The Derivation" in Chapter 11.

Robert Paul Wolff points out that in the *Groundwork,* Kant confuses the difference between the ultimate prudential principle and substantive hypothetical rules and therefore represents our determining what desire(s) and what hypothetical rule(s) the person actually has acted on as empirical questions (44–50/417–20). On the basis of his theoretical philosophy Kant does hold that we must theoretically understand *all* human actions as founded on desires, but this does not mean that it is easy for us to know which desire has motivated a person or which rule a person has used. See Wolff, *The Autonomy of Reason: A Commentary on Kant's Groundwork of the Metaphysics of Morals,* 142–46. As Aristotle had pointed out, however, assuming a person is acting rationally, once we know his aim (the final cause of his acting), we can understand why he is doing what he does. (See, e.g., *Physica* 194a27–5a3; *De partibus animalium* 639b17–19.)

4 But see Chapter 5, note 9. Kant's labeling different kinds of imperatives as hypothetical and categorical should be understood as based on the *manner* in which each binds the will of an agent, a difference that *may or may not* be reflected in the logical form of individual imperatives. Particular hypothetical imperatives oblige only those people wanting the ends set out in those imperatives.

5 In 40–41/414–15 of the *Groundwork* Kant also calls rules of skill "problematic imperatives," because it is only possible and in that sense problematic that we will want the ends to which such imperatives are relevant. Later he decided that the notion of a "possible imperative" is incoherent; every imperative commands an action, even if it does so only conditionally. (See the first introduction to *The Critique of Judgment* 200, 200n.) Generally I will refer to *all* hypothetical imperatives as prudential, because the main contrast Kant will make is between reasoning and principles that are prudential in nature and those that are moral in nature. (See *Gr.* 44n/416n.)

6 Science can offer us objectively valid principles because scientific explanations exclude consideration of the purely personal desires and inclinations of individuals. Philosophers of science refer to this characteristic of science by saying that science is "value neutral."

7 By contrast, Kant argues, if there are objective practical principles, they necessarily and always bind every rational agent insofar as that agent is rational, for they are based on reason alone. (See *Gr.* vi–vii/389, x–xi/391, 15n/400n, 34/411, 38/413; *Pr.R.* 60–61.)

8 As mentioned in the opening section of this chapter, in the *Groundwork* Kant is so concerned to show the superiority of moral to prudential reasoning that he thoroughly exaggerates the limitations of prudential planning (and he also reflects

his reverence for Nature as an Idea of reason), claiming we would have a better chance of being happy if we were still guided by instinct. (See *Gr.* 4–7/395–96.) In other works Kant takes the more sensible view set forth at the beginning of this chapter. Those who read only the *Groundwork* never see this side of Kant and are misled by the hyperbole there. Nonetheless, for all the reasons given, Kant still did not believe that anyone can achieve any lasting happiness, for it is part of our very nature always to be torn by ambivalence. On this see Sidney Axinn, "Ambivalence: Kant's View of Human Nature"; also John E. Atwell, *Ends and Principles in Kant's Moral Thought,* 23–24.

9 In his discussions Kant usually does not separate the analysis of prudence from his assessment.

10 For a discussion of the importance of this kind of appeal in Kant's moral philosophy, see "Kant's Respect for Ordinary Moral Thinking" in Chapter 1.

11 In this and the following section we are concerned only with whether there is something intrinsic to prudential behavior that justifies the use of moral predicates, and Kant concludes that of itself such behavior is simply amoral. However, when taken *in relation to* genuine morality, much more will need to be said. For a fuller discussion of the relation between prudential and moral interests and ends, see Chapters 5, 9, and 15.

12 Kant's list of "nonmoral goods," here taken from the *Groundwork,* reflects traditional Stoicism; on this see Chapter 1, note 9.

There is a problem here. Prudential maxims are motivated .by desires, which tend to assume habitual patterns and generate repetitious conduct. From the point of view of prudence, such habituation is desirable, insofar as it facilitates our choices (the power of *Willkür*) and thereby promotes our happiness. But in Kant's moral theory this is a negative, for habituation belongs to the natural or phenomenal determination of the will, and the more a person becomes habituated, the less freedom he has (*M.M.* 407, 409). On this, see the discussion of virtue in Chapter 9, note 9.

13 Here Kant agrees with Aristotle, who had pointed out that skills and abilities all are capacities for moral opposites and that gifts of fortune are merely instrumentalities in the moral life. (See, e.g., *Nicomachean Ethics* 1.9.1099b27–28; 5.1.1129a12–17.) Without a morally good disposition, a person could be a worse scoundrel just for being talented. (See *Gr.* 1–2/393–94; *M.M.* 394.) But Aristotle analyzed emotional characteristics such as self-control as an integral part of *moral* character, disposing a person to act typically only one way, namely, morally well (or badly), whereas Kant's theoretical philosophy led him to treat such traits as capacities for moral opposites. Kant's contention was that a good will or morally good character is ultimately a nonemotional, principled decision. On this see Chapter 9.

John E. Atwell points out that Kant was mistaken when he described the various natural goods as "bad and hurtful" when they are not used in morally right ways. (See *Gr.* 1–2/393–94.) Such things cannot become bad, for only *persons* can be morally good or bad. See Atwell's *Ends and Principles in Kant's Moral Thought,* 14–15.

14 See "Merely Pathological Desires" and note 2 in Chapter 9.

15 See John R. Silber, "The Copernican Revolution in Ethics: The Good Reexamined."

16 Ignoring this difference was the fundamental error, in ancient times, of both the Stoics and Epicureans; on this, see Chapter 15, note 12.

17 Kant anticipates a common criticism of twentieth-century positivists when he writes that the basic error here consists in believing that only the claims of science (theoretical reason) can be cognitively significant. If all human behavior were reducible to physiological changes, the notions of freedom, dignity, and morality would be meaningless. (See *M.M.* 378.)

18 See Chapter 3, note 6. Lewis White Beck makes the important point that after Kant banished these principles from the foundations of moral volition, he then reinstated them all, but as subject to the Categorical Imperative; see *A Commentary on Kant's Critique of Practical Reason,* 107.

19 For Kant's understanding of the Idea of "perfection" in a practical, human context, see Chapter 6, note 15. Kant particularly had Aristotle's notion of "the mean" in mind here; for his criticism of that criterion, see Chapter 5, note 17. Kant's criticism here is directed only at efforts to make the notion of "good" be the foundation of morality. He does not deny that there are genuine goods, including genuinely moral goods, but he insists that their identification as "good" must rest finally on the single, unique foundation of the Categorical Imperative. On this see Chapters 6 and 13.

20 It might seem then that Kant's *Anthropology from a Pragmatic Point of View,* which mainly concerns our theoretical knowledge of man as a natural, prudential being, would be irrelevant to his account of morality. In one of his discussions of a person's responsibility for telling a malicious lie, for example, Kant argues that empirical information is irrelevant not only to the foundation of morality but also to the assessment of a person's moral character. Even if we believe we can account for the lie on the basis of the person's previous way of life, we "can regard the past series of conditions as not having occurred. . . . The action is ascribed to the agent's intelligible [noumenal, supersensible, moral] character . . . irrespective of all empirical conditions of the act" (*Pu.R.* A555/B583). Moreover, as Frederick P. Van de Pitte, following Erdmann, suggests in his fine study, *Kant as Philosophical Anthropologist,* it is likely that, as he wrote his specifically moral treatises, Kant excerpted those materials from his lectures on anthropology that were directly related to his ethical theory, so that by the time his lectures were published "there was very little material left to deal with" (109). Nonetheless, as the passages I quote throughout this book show, Kant's *Anthropology* contains a wealth of material that provides valuable background information for understanding Kant's ethical theory. As Van de Pitte points out, Kant's entire Critical philosophy is anthropological in the sense that "it is concerned with the nature and destiny of man" (31). See also *Logic* 25; Kant's letter to Stäudlin in Zweig (ed.), *Kant: Philosophical Correspondence 1759–99,* 205; and Chapter 2, note 13.

21 Our ability to reason theoretically and to be self-conscious of our continuing existence over time does make us more useful, of more extrinsic value. (See *M.M.* 223.) We may be able to charge more for our time and services, but this only shows that, in this respect at least, money, not theoretical reasoning, is the more final standard of value. (See *M.M.* 434.)

5. Morality: living autonomously

1 The word "determine" is used here rather than "decide," because, according to Kant, the nature of morality is not something about which we make a decision. Its nature is "given" by our reason, and our task is only to understand and respect it.

In one sense, "moral" means "capable of acting in morally significant ways," in contrast to "amoral" or "nonmoral." In another sense, "moral" means "morally good (character)" or "morally right (action)" in contrast to "immoral" or "morally wrong." The two meanings obviously should not be conflated, because immorality is part of morality in the first sense but not in the second. Kant uses "moral" primarily in the second sense, although here he is using it in the first sense. He also sometimes uses the term to contrast with *both* amorality and immorality. To stay as close to Kant's own presentation as possible, I will occasionally use "moral" and "morality" in the same ambiguous way.

2 As we shall see in Chapter 7, the defense of morality rests on our moral self-awareness.

3 See also Chapter 9.

4 Later Kant made a verbal distinction between the cognitive power of pure practical reason (*Wille*) and its conative power (*Willkür*). The conative power of pure practical reason will be discussed again in the next chapter and in Chapters 9 and 10. The remainder of this chapter will concern mainly practical reason as a cognitive power. See also W. H. Walsh, "Kant's Concept of Practical Reason."

5 Hardly any topic in Kant's moral theory has proved so controversial as how best to understand his doctrine concerning the nature of freedom and of autonomy. One of the best treatments is Bernard Carnois's *Coherence of Kant's Doctrine of Freedom.*

In his *Kant's Transcendental Idealism: An Interpretation and Defense* (310–29) as well as in two articles, "Practical and Transcendental Freedom in the *Critique of Pure Reason*" and "The Concept of Freedom in Kant's 'Semi-Critical' Ethics," Henry E. Allison discusses the differences between Kant's conception of freedom in the Dialectic and in the Canon of the first *Critique.* Allison points out that, in the Canon of the first (the 1781 or "A") edition of the first *Critique,* Kant held that what he there called "practical freedom" did not require the introduction either of transcendental freedom or of the moral law as the *ratio cognoscendi* of freedom. As Lewis White Beck also points out (see his *Commentary on Kant's Critique of Practical Reason,* 11, 14), Kant first explicitly identified autonomy as the principle of freedom only in 1785 in the *Groundwork* and then later developed that view further in the "fully critical" theory of the second *Critique* (1788) and *Religion* (1793). Unfortunately, in this book I cannot adequately go into this and other ways in which Kant's thinking developed and changed. But see Allison, *The Kant-Eberhard Controversy;* Paul Arthur Schilpp, *Kant's Pre-Critical Ethics;* Keith Ward, *The Development of Kant's View of Ethics;* and Hans Saner, *Kant's Political Thought: Its Origins and Development.*

6 The Stoics, to whom Kant's theory is indebted in other ways as well, had also characterized the virtuous man as having autonomy (*autarkeia*), and Rousseau had at least suggested the meaning of autonomy when, in his *Social Contract,* he wrote: "Obedience to a law which one has prescribed to himself is freedom." (See Beck, *Commentary,* 200n72.) Rousseau was preoccupied, as was Kant, with the problem of protecting human freedom within the authoritative structure of the state. Kant's analysis of civil law as the expression of the general will is also indebted to Rousseau. On Kant's debt to Rousseau, see Frederick P. Van de Pitte, *Kant as Philosophical Anthropologist,* 49–57. For further discussions of autonomy, see Chapters, 9, 12, and 16; also Thomas E. Hill, Jr., "Autonomy in the *Groundwork.*"

7 Kant does not consider the possibility that there may be species of rational beings

other than humans, with different sets of substantive moral rules; on this see Chapter 11, note 18.

8 This is not to say that moral rules are not *also* material rules, for, as we saw in Chapter 3, Kant insists that *all* rational actions must have an end or object.

9 I am using the expression "the Law of Autonomy" as a synonym for both "the Categorical Imperative" and "the moral law." Later I use the title "Formula of Autonomy" to refer only to the first formula (*not* the third, as Paton does).

10 The meaning of "categorical" here should not be interpreted merely as a remark about grammatical form, namely, that a moral imperative has no explicit condition. Given the rules of modern statemental logic, p is equivalent to "$p \vee \mathord{\sim} q$," which in turn is equivalent to "$q \to p$," where q can stand for anything. On such an interpretation, any categorical imperative can be made into an indefinitely large number of explicitly conditional imperatives!

As Jeffrie G. Murphy has pointed out, the imperative, " 'If you make a promise, then keep it' is a categorical moral demand, according to Kant, even though it is expressed in a hypothetical grammatical form." Murphy rightly holds that, strictly speaking, the terms "categorical" and "hypothetical" describe not the logical form of the imperatives in question but the manner in which those imperatives bind an agent. (See his *Kant: The Philosophy of Right*, 46; also *Gr.* 44/417; also Beck, *A Commentary on Kant's Critique of Practical Reason*, 87–88, 117.) Hypothetical imperatives, Kant writes, present "a possible action to be practically necessary as a means to the attainment of something else that one wills (or that one may will)"; a categorical imperative, by contrast, "declares an action to be objectively necessary in itself without reference to . . . any further end" (*Gr.* 40/414–15). According to Kant, any analysis that makes ends of any kind to be fundamental turns autonomy into heteronomy.

Kant points out that the force of expressions like "should (not)," "is (not) permissible," and so on depends on the *grounds* determining them. (See *Pr.R.* 11n.) So, saying "It is never permissible to put your elbows on the table" expresses a rule of formal etiquette in a categorical fashion. Even so, all rules of etiquette remain prudential, hypothetical counsels, for there are many occasions when we rightly judge that we are not bound by them. They therefore have a quite different force than categorical moral rules. Philippa Foot unfortunately did not discuss this passage in her article, "Morality as a System of Hypothetical Imperatives." For a careful analysis of Kant's doctrine, see Lewis White Beck, "Apodictic Imperatives."

11 An objective practical principle would never appear as an *imperative* to a perfectly rational being (like God). Kant calls such a being "holy," for the very nature of such a being is always and necessarily to act on the Law of Autonomy. (See *Gr.* 86/439; *M.M.* 227, 379.) On this see Chapter 9.

12 Some commentators have argued that the cases Kant presents in his "Casuistical Questions" in the *Metaphysics of Morals* seem to suggest that he believed that perfect and negative duties can admit of "morally necessary exceptions." See, e.g., H. J. Paton, "An Alleged Right to Lie: A Problem in Kantian Ethics," and *The Categorical Imperative: A Study in Kant's Moral Philosophy*, 147; also John E. Atwell, *Ends and Principles in Kant's Moral Theory*, 42.

However, whenever Kant uses the case method, his usual procedure is to present the conflict between morality and prudence in the most dramatically vivid way possible. His examples are all contructed as clashes between morality and prudence in which one must yield to the other. He does this because he believes the greatest danger to the purity of morality is to be found just in those cases in which we apparently can accomplish the greatest imaginable benefits by moral compromise. Because he always condemns making moral decisions on the basis of consequential considerations, it would seem that interpreting his casuistical cases any differently would be completely contrary to his intentions.

13 We have narrow duties to ourselves, but most of our narrow and negative duties concern what Kant calls duties of "outer freedom," which restrict the ways in which we behave toward others. (See *Gr.* 53n/421n; *M.M.* 240.) Considered apart from whatever motives and aims we might have for such behavior, they are enforceable by an external agency such as the state. As we shall see in Chapters 16 and 17, Kant calls these "juridical" (*rechtskräftig*) and "legal" duties, and he places them under what he calls "the doctrine of law" (*Rechtslehre*). (See *M.M.* 390, 406.)

All our moral duties, including juridical duties, are "ethical" in that they are required by the moral law and should be done because they are so required. But in his discussions of political obligations, Kant also uses the term "ethical duty" in a restricted way to designate only those duties that are *not* juridical. (See *M.M.* 218–20, 394.) In this restricted sense, ethical duties concern duties of "inner freedom": the duty to adopt and act on the motive of dutifulness, and "duties of virtue." These latter involve the duty to recognize and respect persons, whose freedom and rationality give them an inherent dignity. (See, e.g., *M.M.* 383, 394–95, 410.) By their very nature, ethical duties in the narrow sense require an "inner legislation" or self-constraint not subject to control by any external agency. It is incoherent to say that anyone can be compelled to adopt freely any particular motive or goal.

14 As we shall see in Chapter 10, there is an important exception to the claims made here about positive duties: the obligation to pursue holiness, Kant writes, is a positive duty, but one without any latitude.

15 In *Gr.* 53n/421n Kant writes, "I understand here by a perfect duty one which allows no exception in the interests of inclination," seeming to imply that in wide or imperfect duties we may make such exceptions. This is an unfortunate choice of wording, for a decision, say, to donate to the Cancer Fund but not to the Heart Fund does not mean making an exception to the wide duty of beneficence. Kant later wrote that "a wide duty is not to be taken as a permission to make exceptions to the maxim of actions, but only as a permission to limit one maxim of duty by another" (*M.M.* 390).

16 There is no way in which to determine exactly how anyone (much less everyone) should interpret wide duties. Saying "I have now done enough" clearly is a judgment call, requiring a good deal of moral enlightenment and sensitivity. This may explain why Kant claims, unfortunately without clarification, that the failure to fulfill adequately one's wide duties shows only a "want of moral worth" while actually fulfilling wide duties is morally meritorious. (See *M.M.* 227, 390.)

When I once suggested that Kant might thereby have been indicating that he believed this is the arena for acts of supererogation, Sharon Anderson-Gold pointed out to me that if works of supererogation are defined as "beyond all duty," under that description they clearly cannot be considered part of morality within the Kantian system. (In his *Lectures on Ethics,* Kant maintains that we have a misshapen conscience if we worry constantly about how to fulfill our positive obligations; see 356/134.) Nonetheless, in our ordinary moral judgments we often do take people like Mother Teresa to be morally heroic, even if we also think that we are not morally obligated to follow their example. Thomas E. Hill, Jr., argues that there is a place for supererogatory acts in Kant's theory; see his "Kant on Imperfect Duty and Supererogation." But Marcia Baron controverts that view in her "Kantian Ethics and Supererogation."

17 Because wide duties permit and require discretion and attention to the contingent details of the given situation, we might have expected Kant to have recommended that we use Aristotle's notion of the "mean" as a guide. Instead, he writes that the mean is completely unhelpful as a guide. It defines the difference between actions by means of a degree (between too much and too little) and yet does not specify what that degree is. This is a superficial wisdom, he writes, which cannot offer us any definite principles for guidance. (See *M.M.* 404, 433n.)

Kant then goes on to argue that the notion of the mean also cannot be used to distinguish between virtue and vice. The difference between moral and immoral maxims lies not in the degree to which a person follows a maxim, but solely in the moral quality of the maxims, as is shown by the fact that the maxims for each kind of conduct necesarily conflict with each other. Between truthfulness and lying, for example, there is no mean, and virtue is not a matter of observing the mean between opposing vices, for that would make it "a diminished, or rather a growing, vice" (*M.M.* 432, 432n; see also 404–5, 404n, 433n).

18 Because even negative obligations do not prescribe exactly how a person should behave, there always will be an ineluctable role for judgment (see *M.M.* 205). Still it is true that negative duties allow us much less leeway than positive duties. (See *M.M.* 394.)

19 Strictly speaking, then, H. J. Paton is correct when he writes that "a good man has the duty at all times of acting on maxims which can be willed as universal laws," but such a claim needs to be interpreted very carefully. (See *The Categorical Imperative*, 141.) See also Bruce Aune, *Kant's Theory of Morals*, 8–9; and Henry E. Allison, "Morality and Freedom: Kant's Reciprocity Thesis," 415–16.

20 The Categorical Imperative is identified in the political context of the citation here as the "sovereign Will." Both Aristotle and Kant took the practical syllogism to be a reflective reconstruction of what is usually an informal reasoning process. Neither thought anyone actually deliberates in neat logical steps. On this, see my *Morality and the Good Life: A Commentary on Aristotle's Nicomachean Ethics*, 63–71.

21 On the "administrative model" of practical thinking, see Andrew Harrison, *Making and Thinking: A Study of Intelligent Activities*. The distinction I am drawing here is exactly parallel to the distinction between act and rule utilitarianism: the former holds that the Greatest Happiness Principle should be applied to proposed actions so as to generate individual decisions; and the latter holds that that principle should be applied to act types so as to generate policies (expressible in maxims or administrative principles). Although this distinction is commonly recognized in commentaries on John Stuart Mill's theory, it has not generally been used in discussions of the Categorical Imperative.

22 In his *Kant on Moral Practice* (53–99), Rex P. Stevens discusses how to bridge the gap between moral theory and moral practice, between the cognitive and conative functions of pure practical reason. He finds it helpful to conflate the notions of moral judgment and moral character.

23 Some authors believe Kant did not adequately discuss the criteria of relevance to be used in applying the Categorical Imperative. See Onora Nell (O'Neill), *Acting on Principle: An Essay on Kantian Ethics*, 142–43. However, determining relevance

requires an exercise of judgment that Kant repeatedly states cannot be schematized into a formal procedure. If Kant does not say very much about relevance, it is because he does not think there is much that can be said. As Aristotle would have held, practical wisdom is a critical faculty, a creative faculty, and an imperative faculty. As a critical faculty, it can construct policies and rules on which to act, and that is the limit of moral philosophy proper. As an imperative faculty, it can make our deliberations issue in action, and that is the realm of moral character and moral education. As a creative faculty, it must bridge the cognitive distance between principles and actions, and that is the role of judgment. Clearly, Kant tacitly believed that criteria of relevance can be checked in any instance against the judgment of ordinary moral reasoning. A person trying to evade the spirit of morality would hardly be willing to use this appeal. For further discussion of this issue, see also Chapter 11, note 20; also Nelson T. Potter, Jr., "How to Apply the Categorical Imperative," 404–13.

In a recent article, Barbara Herman argues convincingly that the exercise of moral judgment requires familiarity with and the use of what she calls "rules of moral salience," acquired as part of our normal socialization process. These rules identify what may be called a "moral range" of features about a situation moral judgment must take into account. See her "The Practice of Moral Judgment." On this same point, see the next section of this chapter.

24 The main emphasis in contemporary moral theorizing has been placed, as in Kant's writings, on cases of moral conflict. Such conflicts have been regarded as displaying most clearly how the logic of moral language operates, particularly in the kind of deliberation over possible moral maxims. Likewise, the main point of doing moral philosophy has been taken to be the clarification of moral terms and an examination of the various justifications offered for morality in general and particular substantive rules in particular. (For Kantians, of course, this requires a rational justification.) Because this aim seems appropriate for a course to help legislators think about the grounds for just legislation, the natural evolution in contemporary ethical theorizing has been toward considering moral questions in terms of legal questions, such as is often done in the journal *Philosophy & Public Affairs*.

By contrast, in his *Ethics* Aristotle was concerned mainly with the kind of deliberation that leads to actions. He wanted to set out the most effective way to educate people to make the best choices in their everyday lives, and he placed very little trust in the power of reasoning alone to accomplish this. He considered moral education to be an initiation into a kind of life rather than as learning the logic of moral argumentation.

Contrasting the Aristotelian and the Kantian models of moral philosophy shows that each is a response to a different problem, so that they also are somewhat different enterprises. In choosing between these two models, a moral philosopher might decide that the most pressing issues today are sufficiently similar to the skepticism Kant faced as to justify imitating his theory in purpose and spirit. A moral educator, however, might prefer to emphasize the Aristotelian model, supplementing it, perhaps, with those parts of the Kantian model that can be helpful in dealing with questions that typically arise in a pluralistic society.

25 Kant thus rejects "probabilism" (and, tacitly, probabiliorism as well). Probabilism was and is the view of some Catholic moral theologians that, when it is not possible to determine with certainty what is morally right or wrong, it is morally permissible to do what is only *probably* permissible, even though a contrary opinion may be even more probable. Kant advocates a version of what is called "absolute tutiorism,"

the moral view that we should not do what is *possibly* wrong or even *probably* right, because he is convinced that we can attain *certitude* by our moral reasoning alone and, moreover, that we are morally obligated to do so. (See, e.g., *Rel.* 186n1/ 174, 187/175.)

26 When Kant offers his four examples in the *Groundwork*, he writes, "These are some of the many actual duties – *or at least of what we take to be such*" – that can be derived from the Categorical Imperative (*Gr.* 57/423, emphasis mine). But rather than admitting here that he might be wrong, he is probably only saying that, since he has not yet defended the reality of human moral agency, at this point in the argument these are only putative duties. In favor of the latter interpretation, in his *Metaphysics of Morals* he shows no doubts at all about what he takes to be our "actual duties."

27 These are just the procedures an egoist refuses to use. A "logical egoist" refuses "to test his judgment by the understanding of others"; an "aesthetic egoist" is content with his own idiosyncratic taste; and "the moral egoist is a man who limits all ends to himself, sees no use in anything except what is useful to him and, as a eudaemonist, locates the supreme determining ground of his will merely in utility and his own happiness, not in the thought of duty" (*Anthr.* 129–30; see 128–30). A moral egoist would not generalize one of his own substantive maxims, for it would be counterproductive for him to do so.

To discuss one's judgment with others, Kant writes, means checking the correctness of one's own reasoning, not looking heteronomously either for the approval of others or for what might be called "philosophical precedents": "In philosophizing we need not [and, indeed, should not] appeal to the judgment of others to corroborate our own, as jurists appeal to the judgment of legal experts" (*Anthr.* 129). Nonetheless, Kant does hold that thinking, even thinking for oneself (*Selbstdenken*), is virtually impossible without the ability to communicate and discuss one's thinking with others. The pursuit of objectivity requires us to respect that impartiality available only by subjecting our thinking to the inspection and criticism of others. See, e.g., *Enlight.* 36–37; *Orient.* 144–45; see also "The Principle of Publicity" in Chapter 17.

28 Given the reverence we must have for the moral law, Kant writes that an analysis of our moral self-awareness should show that we at least "in an obscure way" think of our conscience "as a subjective principle of responsibility before God" (*M.M.* 439; see also *Cr.J.* 445–46).

29 In a clearly pre-Critical section of his *Lectures on Ethics*, Kant identifies conscience as an "instinct to pass judgment" on ourselves. But there he also seems closer to our ordinary moral thinking, for he holds that both habitual immoral conduct and casuistic hairsplitting can corrupt a person's conscience so that eventually it "loses all its authority." (See *Lect.* 356–57/134.)

6. Morally obligatory ends

1 Note that this question requires a transcendental deduction of the conditions necessary for the possibility of moral agency and moral actions. As we shall see in the next chapter, when Kant does ask how we might explain (theoretically) how pure reason has this power to be practical, he concludes that we simply cannot do so.

2 The notions of "good" and "evil" are Ideas of reason; see Chapter 2; also Beck, *A Commentary on Kant's Critique of Practical Reason*, 87–88. Moral reasoning is

justified in adopting such Ideas of reason, Kant writes, simply because it has the right to adopt whatever Ideas it needs in order to function.

Kant's most systematic treatment of obligatory ends occurs in the section entitled "The Concept of an Object of Pure Practical Reason" in the second *Critique,* although his doctrine concerning such ends is found throughout his ethical writings. See also this chapter, note 10, and Chapters 13–15; also Nelson Potter, "Kant on Ends That Are at the Same Time Duties."

3 On this issue, see Chapter 2, notes 9 and 13. What Kant needed to say, to be perfectly precise, is that some objective ends (e.g., physical well-being and cultural development) are properly ends for us and any other agents like us (if there are any) because we are imperfect and moral-physical beings. Such ends would not be appropriate to a perfect being like God or spiritual beings like angels. In that sense, objective ends need not be ends for *every* rational being, but all rational agents would agree, insofar as they are rational, that such ends are objective ends for us.

4 At the time he was writing, the internal forum was the area in which Kant and his fellow Germans enjoyed the most freedom. Kant here anticipates the doctrine for which Sartre would later become famous – that unjust political restrictions may elicit from the human spirit a deep appreciation of the power and value of internal freedom; see *Rel.* 123/113. Nonetheless, many readers think Kant is wrong to deny all moral value to the good consequences of an action.

5 In the first *Critique* Kant defines the notion of causal power in such a way that he here could distinguish between the exercise of free causal power in intentions and their physical effects in the world; on this see Chapter 3.

6 Kant is usually interpreted as holding that "should" (*sollen*) implies "can" (*können*). Although he nowhere makes this claim in so many words, this is clearly his doctrine. He writes, for example, that "since reason commands that such actions should take place, it must be possible for them to take place," "for reason will not command the impossible" (*Pu.R.* A807/B835 and *Anthr.* 148). Also, we "know that we *can* do [what the moral law commands] because our reason acknowledges [that law] as its law and says that we *ought* to do it," and man "must judge that he *can* do what the law commands unconditionally that he *ought* to do" (*Pr.R.* 159 and *M.M.* 380; see *Cr.J.* 472). Again: "We must not determine ethical duties according to our estimate of man's power to fulfill the law; on the contrary, we must estimate man's moral power by the standard of the law, which commands categorically. Hence we must appraise this power on the basis of our rational knowledge of what men should be . . . not on the basis of our empirical knowledge of men as they are" (*M.M.* 404–5). Moreover, "it would not be a duty to pursue a certain effect of our will . . . if it were not possible to do so" (*T&P* 277; see also *Pr.R.* 36; *Rel.* 41/36, 50/46, 62/55). And finally, "it would obviously be absurd, after granting authority to the concept of duty, to pretend that we cannot do our duty, for in that case this concept would itself drop out of morality (*ultra posse nemo obligatur*)"; that is, no one is obligated to do what is not possible (*P.P.* 370; see also *Pu.R.* A476/B504).

The aphorism is occasionally taken to mean either that having a moral obligation *p* either entails or means having the physical ability *q* to carry it out ("*p* → *q*"). On this reading, empirical inability also means no moral obligation ("~*q* → ~*p*"). As the examination of "moral action" in this chapter shows, however, this is not Kant's doctrine. Since moral obligations are not conditioned by physical possibilities, the preceding interpretations of the aphorism would reduce Kant to making either the tautological claim that "should and can" imply "can" or the equally trivial claim that "should" means "should try to" or the erroneous claim that, for example, my lack of money relieves me of the obligation to repay a debt.

Kant in fact is making three different and important claims in these passages. First, the mere fact of physical ability or inability does not necessarily add to, or detract from, a person's moral obligations or moral quality. (This presupposes that a person is not culpably responsible for inability.) As Beck argues, in this sense "success" and "failure" are not moral categories. (See his *Commentary*, 115.) Second, as we shall see in the next chapter, the positive assurance of our freedom rests epistemologically on the prior appearance in our awareness of the Categorical Imperative and its more particular commands. Because we do not and cannot have an intuition of our motives, we can never *know* that we have actually acted from the moral motive of dutifulness. But we may still have a rational faith that we *can* act from the motive of duty, a faith based on that command. Finally, the inexorable nature of the moral law means that its necessary objects, including the highest good, *must* be achievable. As we shall see in Chapters 10 and 15, this end requires us also to adopt the postulates of immortality and God.

7 The meaning of *Gr.* 37/412–13 is problematic: "If reason [*Vernunft*] solely by itself is not sufficient to determine the will [*Wille*], . . . if, in a word, the will [*Wille*] is not *in itself* completely in accord with reason [*Vernunft*] (as actually happens in the case of men) . . ." Since he had just defined will (*Wille*) *as* practical reason (*praktische Vernunft*), Kant's taking the contingent moral goodness of human beings to be a lack of power on the part of pure reason would seem to make immoral conduct inculpable. Some commentators have argued that it was just to avoid this problem that Kant later distinguished between two senses of "will" – *Wille* and *Willkür*; on this, see Appendix 1. But immediately after setting out this distinction, Kant denies that freedom of the will (*die Freiheit der Willkür*) should be understood as the ability to choose (*das Vermögen der Wahl*) to act either morally or immorally. (See *M.M.* 226.)

8 Since the concept of virtuous action is an Idea of reason, "possible objects of experience," namely, observable legal behaviors, "may serve as examples," but they are never completely adequate to the original Idea. (See *Pu.R.* A315/B371–72.) Although we can never be sure a person is acting from the moral motive of dutifulness, such behaviors do show that those external actions required by the moral law are possible. (See *Gr.* 30/409.)

9 Since Kant may seem to stress our powerlessness in dealing with the world more frequently than he does our ability to develop and extend our power and skills, he can be misread as licensing well-intentioned incompetence. This interpretation, however, is clearly contrary to his explicit statements that good intentions must issue in right conduct if that is within our power, and that we have an obligation to develop our talents so that we can carry out our duties in the world. Given his commitment to the Enlightenment, Kant had no time for stupidity, foolishness, or simple imprudence. (See *Anthr.* 210–11.) See also "Culture and Morality" in Chapter 13.

10 The notion of "object" is an Idea of reason. Because he did not begin with a reasonably developed philosophy of action, Kant is sometimes distressingly loose in his use of terms. Usually he equates "end," "object," and "matter"[*Materie*]. For example, "An end [*Zweck*] is an object [*Gegenstand*] of the power of choice (of a rational being), through the thought of which choice is determined to an action to produce this object" (*M.M.* 381; see also 380–81, 384; *Gr.* 38/413; *Pr.R.* 57).

But in other places he defines an object (*Gegenstand*) of the will (*Willkür*) as a "thing I have the physical power to use" (*M.M.* 246). He then lists three such objects external to the individual person – things, particular actions another person has promised, and other persons under one's authority, for example, "a wife, a child, a servant" (*M.M.* 247–48).

To further complicate things, in his *Critique of Practical Reason,* Kant also defines *"the"* object (*Objekt* or *Gegenstand*) or end (*Zweck*) of pure practical reason not only as moral reason itself (65–66) but also as free actions (44), as supersensible nature (44), as perceptible actions in the world (45, 65), as the moral law (44, 73, 110), as good and evil (58–76), as unending progress toward holiness (122), as the relation of pure practical reason to good actions (60), and as the highest good (4, 108–10, 119). He also calls the ideal moral world (the kingdom of ends) the object (*Gegenstand*) or final end (*Endzweck*) of moral reason (*Pu.R.* A808/B836; *M.M.* 405; *Cr.J.* 450, 453). Finally, he describes moral perfection as an obligatory end, and persons as ends (*Zwecke* and *Endzwecke*) in the sense of being both objects of respect and limitations on prudential ends. (See, e.g., *Cr.J.* 434–35, 448n; *M.M.* 384–86.)

All these various meanings for *"the* object of pure practical reason" *are* coherently related in Kant's ethical theory, and showing their relationships is part of the aim of this and the following chapters. But because on any particular occasion we need to determine how he is using the terms "object" and "end" from the context in which they occur, it is understandable that he can be and has been misunderstood on this matter. Moreover, different readers may easily come to various and equally plausible interpretations of what Kant meant to say.

11 For a detailed discussion of moral virtue, see Chapters 9 and 10. See also Christine M. Korsgaard, "Two Distinctions in Goodness." Kant's claim in the quotation in the text on behalf of the good will is hyperbolic. When the good will requires us to sacrifice our natural welfare, it certainly cannot be considered good by the criterion of prudence.

12 We will examine this part of Kant's theory in detail when we study the second formula of the Categorical Imperative, the Formula of Respect for the Dignity of Persons, in Chapter 14.

13 Although we only have moral duties *to* other human beings, we do have duties *with regard to* other beings. (On this distinction, see Paul D. Eisenberg, "Kant on Duties to, and Duties Regarding, Oneself or Others.") But these actually are still duties to ourselves. For example, we should not wantonly destroy beauty in nature and we should not unnecessarily inflict pain on animals, not because pain and destruction are moral evils (in themselves they are natural evils), but because such conduct tends to weaken our moral disposition. (See *M.M.* 442–43; *Lect.* 413/191, 458–60/239–41.)

As far as moral philosophy is concerned, we do not have special duties *to* God, even on the basis of a purportedly divine revelation. (See *M.M.* 227; *Rel.* 153n/142.) We have and can have no theoretical basis for claiming to *know* that God actually does exist or has revealed his will to someone. (See *M.M.* 241, 439.) Moreover, "God can receive nothing from us; we cannot act for Him, nor yet upon Him" (*Rel.* 153n/142). But because we cannot avoid thinking of the moral law as holy, we can say we have a formal duty to be religious in the sense of thinking of all our duties as if they were divine commands, thereby strengthening the motive of dutifulness. (See *Pr.R.* 129.) It is only "because we have an inward obligation

NOTES TO PAGES 68-70

to" the moral law that we are justified in regarding it as a divine command; if we literally looked on actions "as obligatory *because* they are the commands of God," our obedience to them would then be heteronomous and without moral value (*Pu.R.* A819/B847, emphasis mine). Since the Idea we have of God and of his will originates in our own reason, religion, understood correctly, is actually a duty we have to ourselves. (See *M.M.* 227, 241–44, 439–40, 442–44, 486–87.) As long as we realize that, Kant argues, it is not heteronomous for us to imagine morality as the submission of our will to God's will, for that is only a way of describing self-discipline, our submission to our own reason. (See *Pu.R.* A813–14/B847.) For a somewhat different interpretation, see George A. Schrader, "Autonomy, Heteronomy, and Moral Imperatives."

14 In the first part of the *Groundwork* Kant defines the good will as the *only* thing "good without qualification," and his discussions of other practical ends there are limited to subjective, prudential goods. There is no preparation for his later claims that personhood and the total final good are absolute goods. It is small wonder that readers are bewildered about how these claims fit together. Some interpreters have held that Kant's insistence on other morally obligatory ends is to a large extent a mistake on his part. I hope the relation between these various goods will become clearer as we discuss them in later chapters.

15 As we shall see in Chapter 10, we actually have an obligation to be holy, but holiness is not a status we can attain by our own efforts alone. Virtue is *our* highest possible moral accomplishment.

16 See "Obligatory Natural Ends" in Chapter 13. Kant defines human "perfection" in this context, not as a quantitative whole but as a qualitative or formal notion, meaning "the adequacy of a thing's qualities to an end" (*M.M.* 386; see also *Pr.R.* 41). Although a person could have only one perfection in the first sense, there are an indefinite number of qualitative perfections. Moral perfection consists only in conscientiousness, whereas natural perfection usually includes the mastery of different skills as well as knowledge of different fields of inquiry; and what we need to learn depends at least partly on "what sort of life we should like to lead" (*M.M.* 445; *Pr.R.* 41). Kant clearly does not hold that we are morally obligated to pursue *every* morally permissible goal or the fullest realization of *every* purpose of which a person may be capable.

17 In this section I have avoided discussing Kant's often confusing efforts to place particular duties under one or another category even when they do not perfectly fit his given definition of that category. Such problems are conscientiously discussed in Mary J. Gregor's *Laws of Freedom* (95–127), a book that should not have been allowed to go out of print. Onora Nell (O'Neill) suggests distinguishing between the obligation and the requirement of various kinds of duties. Using this terminology, ethical duties, for example, should be thought of as wide in obligation but narrow in requirement, demanding acts and omissions that cannot be externally legislated. See her *Acting on Principle*, 44–58. See also Thomas E. Hill, Jr., "Kant on Imperfect Duty and Supererogation."

18 Kant also lists several "special" duties we may acquire, for example, the duty to be grateful and show gratitude to those who have been our benefactors (see *M.M.* 454–56, 459).

19 See *M.M.* 429–41.

20 See *M.M.* 392–93, 399, 405–9, 446–47.

21 See *M.M.* 386–87.

22 See *M.M.* 419, 422–28; *Gr.* 53–54/421–22, 67/429.
23 See *M.M.* 391–93, 419, 421–28, 444–46; *Gr.* 55–56/422–23, 68–69/430; also "Obligatory Natural Ends" in Chapter 13.
24 See *M.M.* 388.
25 See *M.M.* 388.
26 See *M.M.* 394.
27 See *M.M.* 394; but see also "Respect for Others" in Chapter 14.
28 See *M.M.* 387–91, 395; *Gr.* 69/430.
29 See *M.M.* 448–49.
30 See *M.M.* 449–50, 458–61, 464–65; *Gr.* 69/430.
31 See *M.M.* 401–2, 450–52.
32 See *M.M.* 449; *Gr.* 54–55/422, 67–68/429–30.
33 See *M.M.* 393n, 452–54; *Gr.* 56–57/423.
34 See *M.M.* 390, 460, 465–68.
35 See *M.M.* 326; also Chapter 17, note 12.
36 See Edmund L. Pincoffs, "Membership Obligations and the Limits of Moral Obligation," especially 31–36.
37 H. J. Paton, "An Alleged Right to Lie: A Problem in Kantian Ethics," 198. But see also Lewis White Beck, "Apodictic Imperatives," 156n38. Onora Nell (O'Neill) rightly compares Kant's distinction between "rules of obligation" (*leges obligandis*) and "obligatory rules" (*leges obligantes*) to the modern distinction, introduced by W. D. Ross, between prima facie duties and actual duties. See her *Acting on Principle*, 133; also W. D. Ross, *The Right and the Good*, 19–47.
38 For a suggestive analysis of the use of these terms, see James K. Mish'Alani, " 'Duty,' 'Obligation,' and 'Ought.' "
Note that the obligation to keep one's promises is not the same as the obligation not to make lying promises; on this see Chapter 12.
There are only two other places of which I am aware where Kant specifically discusses "a clash of determining grounds." The first concerns the rule that sexual intercourse is permissible only when its natural end of procreation (within marriage) is intended by a couple, which may conflict with the obligations of couples to each other by virtue of the marriage contract when the wife is pregnant, sterile, or "feels no desire" (*M.M.* 426). Kant does not try to settle this "casuistical question," but his respect for that contract by which people reciprocally obligate each other "to the use of one another for pleasure" in marriage, seems to make him lean toward allowing, in his inimitable manner of putting things, "the animal inclinationsa playroom" (*M.M.* 426; see also 424). On this, see also Chapter 13, note 5.
The second occurs in a footnote in *T&P*. There Kant discusses a case in which what he calls absolute and conditional (a term we would not expect him to use) "duties conflict with one another" (*T&P* 300n). Preventing evil to the state is an example of an absolute duty; preventing harm to an individual is an example of a conditional duty – that is, it is a duty only if an individual has not done something that deserves the withdrawal of natural well-being. So, Kant writes, it is one's duty to inform on a traitor, even one's father or son. This raises difficult questions about when a natural good is or is not to be considered also a moral good. On this problem, see Chapter 12, note 10.
In his political theory Kant takes the ground of the obligation of civil obedience to be so strong as to override what otherwise might be morally justifiable civil disobedience. On this, see Chapter 16.

7. The defense of morality

1 For a discussion of contemporary moral skepticism (based more on conceptual considerations than on a deterministic view of the universe), see Christine M. Korsgaard, "Skepticism about Practical Reason."

2 In this and the next chapter we encounter a stylistic problem that seems to defy a totally successful resolution. When Kant examines different kinds of reasoning, he typically writes of idealized, abstract faculties such as "practical reason" and "theoretical reason." Impersonal "faculty talk" has the advantage of avoiding extraneous questions about possible idiosyncratic features of individuals. (Today in logic texts the same problem is dealt with by discussing only rules.) The consequence, however, is that *people,* who after all are the focus of human morality, are conspicuously absent from many of Kant's discussions. Since faculty psychology is no longer in style, almost everyone writing on Kant has tried, with varying degrees of success, to avoid using faculty talk.

3 Substantive technical imperatives are also synthetic propositions because they at least implicitly appeal to the principle of causality. (See *Gr.* 45/417.) Kant ignores this when he claims in *Gr.* 48/419 that if we knew with certainty what would make us happy, "the imperative of prudence would be an analytic practical proposition." He also does not stress that prudential imperatives are also subjectively a priori for agents who may genuinely want an end but are only contingently rational about paying the price necessary to get it.

4 In several places, e.g., *Gr.* 98–99/447, Kant seems to hold that the *Law* of Autonomy, of itself, is a synthetic a priori, not an analytic, judgment. On this, see "Problematic Texts" in Chapter 11.

5 If we understand the expression "all rational beings" to mean "beings with pure practical reason," then Kant of course does hold it is analytically true to say such beings are under the moral law.

6 In his "Morality and Freedom: Kant's Reciprocity Thesis," Henry E. Allison argues that Kant's conception of psychological freedom in the first edition of the first *Critique* means that an agent does act on some emotion or other but the agent has the freedom to decide which desire to act on and so also the ability to reject any particular desire – not merely to react automatically to the strongest desire (409–12). Allison also holds that this view is incompatible with Kant's position in the second *Critique.*

7 There is a theological version of the same argument against human freedom, Kant writes. If God is the cause of our existence and being (as the very notion of God seems to require), then it would seem that we are simply marionettes, for all our actions would in fact be God's actions. But the argument does not follow if we adopt the phenomenal-noumenal distinction and regard God and all other rational beings as noumena, not subject to temporal existence or the rules of temporal causal succession, both of which hold only for phenomena. Kant admits that it is difficult to make this solution lucid, but he still contends that this is the only way in which human freedom and responsibility can be defended. (See *Pr.R.* 100–103; *Rel.* 49n/45.)

8 I thank Tom Hill, Jr., for his suggestions about the contents of this section. Although he and I do not agree exactly on our interpretations, his criticism has helped me improve what I wanted to say.

Note that actuality is a sufficient proof of possibility, but that logical possibility tells us nothing about actuality. (See *M.M.* 382.)

9 In his *Critique of Pure Reason* Kant held that the necessity in all synthetic a priori propositions originates in a necessary connection of both the subject concept and the predicate concept with a *third* term, an *"x,"* as he mysteriously put it. With regard to synthetic theoretical propositions known a priori, it turned out that the referent of the *"x"* (and grounding their necessity) is the rational consciousness of the knowing person, or, more technically, "inner sense and its a priori form, time" (*Pu.R.* A155/B194; see also A9–10/B13–14, A259/B315, A753/B761, A766/B794; *Gr.* 112/454). The claim "A human agent (the subject concept) ought to be an agent who never violates the Law of Autonomy (the predicate concept)" is a synthetic principle learned a priori. The third term *"x,"* accounting for the necessity we find in that principle, refers to the practical self-consciousness of the acting person who must regard himself as a member of the supersensible world. This is the ground of "the *positive* concept of freedom" of which we have "an Idea a priori" in our practical consciousness (*Gr.* 99/447, 110–11/453). At this stage in his thinking, then, Kant saw the defense of morality by a transcendental deduction as resting on our consciousness of freedom, which the doctrine of the two viewpoints shows is both unavoidable and allowable.

10 Since Kant is best known for the effort he spent to defend our right to think of ourselves as free and moral beings, it often is forgotten that, as a leading proponent of the Enlightenment, he was equally concerned to promote science. Even though he did not believe that psychology could ever become a full-fledged science, he did want to defend the right of theoretical thinkers to try to understand our mental life in causal terms insofar as they can do so. In fact, on many occasions he insisted that it is not possible, on the basis of experience, to show that *any* action has *not* been causally determined. (See e.g., *Gr.* 25–28/406–8, 48–49/418–19.) For that reason, he would have had a good deal of sympathy for philosophers working in cognitive science today and thinking of our mental processes in causal language.

See, for example, Daniel C. Dennett's *Elbow Room.* Dennett writes that Kant "could not see how a human act could be *both* the effect of physical causes and also the execution of a decision of a rational will" (27). As I hope that this chapter makes clear, the function of the doctrine of the two viewpoints is precisely to *insist* that we both may and must still take *both* points of view. The two viewpoints are mutually exclusive, and Kant does hold that no one can "see" (understand) exactly how they are related to each other. But because we cannot *take* both viewpoints simultaneously, he also holds that neither denies or constitutes an attack on the other. Obviously, however, we can *think about* them both at the same time, as we are doing at this moment. (See also this chapter, note 14.) It should be added that the noumenal point of view was never meant by Kant to function as an explanation.

Other Kantian claims are still also echoed today. For example, like Kant, Dennett holds that "abandoning the participant attitude is practically inconceivable" (47), and, following Nozick, he regards his scientific, naturalistic vision of human agency not as a proof but as a kind of (what Kant might call a "regulative") explanation to help us "see how something we want to believe in could be possible" (49).

11 Kant's point in introducing the self-consciousness of the theoretical thinker, as I understand it, is only to show – contrary to the contention of some Enlightenment skeptics – that there are *no* good reasons, even from the side of science, for attacking the possibility of our being free and moral beings. Rather, as theoretical thinkers,

we have every legitimate reason to hope that our claim to transcendental freedom can somehow be defended. (See, e.g., *Pr.R.* 3, 7.)

In his concern both to explain again that, for moral agents like us, freedom and moral obligation are not mutually exclusive concepts, Kant interposes a discussion of moral interest, which has seemed to some readers to be irrelevant to his argument. (See *Gr.* 102–3/449.)

12 The almost casual way in which Kant includes the words "in the order of efficient causes" makes it easy to overlook this phrase, but it is just this phrase that shows that the so-called problem with a "kind of circle" arises only from thinking of the defense of morality as meaning a defense of a *theoretical* claim that freedom is the *cause* of morality.

13 There are almost as many different interpretations of *Groundwork* III as there are commentators. Part of the problem, as Allison has pointed out, is how to understand Kant's claim that freedom and morality are "reciprocal" concepts without immoral conduct then being regarded as compelled and so as amoral. See Thomas E. Hill, Jr., "Kant's Argument for the Rationality of Moral Conduct"; also Henry E. Allison, "The Hidden Circle in *Groundwork* III" and "Morality and Freedom: Kant's Reciprocity Thesis." Although I have disagreed here with some of Allison's claims, his books and articles have kept me from committing several serious errors, and I gratefully acknowledge my debt to him. Some commentators argue that Kant's argument in *Groundwork* III is salvageable but only in a reconstructed form. See, for example, Brendan E. A. Liddell's *Kant on the Foundation of Morality,* 236–43, and Ralph C. S. Walker's *Kant,* 147–48.

14 When we think of ourselves as under obligation to the Law of Autonomy as an imperative, Kant continues, we are regarding ourselves as "belonging to the sensible world and yet to the intelligible world at the same time" (*Gr.* 110/453). Only this dual citizenship can explain why we are not necessarily either holy or amoral beings. (See 110–13/453–55.)

15 There is a virtual consensus today that Kant's argument in *Groundwork* III fails. In his *Kant's Theory of Mind: An Analysis of the Paralogisms of Pure Reason,* Karl Ameriks argues for the interpretation that the second *Critique* represents "an apparent total reversal of positions"; see 211; also 189–233. But I am inclined to believe that Kant himself held that his deduction in *Groundwork* III did succeed within limits. He already had admitted in *Groundwork* III what he then repeated in *Pr.R.* 47 and 94, that in this instance a defense is as much as a deduction can accomplish.

It apparently is true, however, that Kant still found this defense to be unsatisfactory in the sense that it addressed the question of right but not the question of fact. (See *Pu.R.* A84/B116.) Just as we may be rationally satisfied in a theoretical way only by having the reality of an object pointed out in our experience ("There it is!"), so it is more rationally satisfying if, in a somewhat analogous way (we have no intuitions of a noumenal law), we can "point to" the moral law in our moral experience. And this is just what Kant offers in the second *Critique* – "the fact as it were" of the moral law, a move foreshadowed in the first *Critique;* see A806–7/B834–35.

16 Consequently, the moral law provides the ultimate ground for our *entire* moral life, including particular moral principles, morally permissible and morally obligatory ends, moral emotions, and our actual moral judgments. (See, e.g., *Gr.* 60/426, 109/452–53; *Pr.R.* 106.)

17 Beck, *A Commentary on Kant's Critique of Practical Reason,* 166–70; also his "The Fact of Reason: An Essay on Justification in Ethics." Throughout the rest of this book I will take the moral law in our consciousness to be *the* fact of and for pure reason.

18 T. C. Williams therefore interprets Kant as holding that we become aware of the moral law through specific moral judgments arising from the spontaneous activity of pure practical reason, rather than through a direct apprehension of the ultimate moral norm itself; see his *Concept of the Categorical Imperative,* 105–7.

19 This is one of the important meanings of the dictum "Ought implies can"; see Chapter 6, note 6.

   In several places Kant claims that the reality of our moral agency can be "verified," "proved," and "established" by the moral "intentions or maxims" that are acted on *in concreto* by those who "acknowledge the law as binding upon them" (*Pr.R.* 47, 56; see also 3, 56, 105–6; *Cr.J.* 468; *M.M.* 221, 225). It might seem that this argument is hyperbolic, for we can be certain only that we have tried to do our duty by acting on a morally acceptable maxim. (See, e.g., *M.M.* 392–93.) But it is enough for Kant's argument that we are aware that we have *tried* to act from the right intention, for, as Beck has pointed out, the categories "success" and "failure" are not moral categories; see his *Commentary on Kant's Critique of Practical Reason,* 115.

20 It apparently was this "identity" that led him to claim in the third *Critique* that it is *freedom* that is the "one idea of reason . . . to be found among the matters of facts. . . . the only one of all the ideas of pure reason whose object is a matter of fact and must be included among the *scibilia* [knowable matters of fact]" (*Cr.J.* 468).

21 In the second *Critique* Kant had to defend himself against attacks from two quarters. On the one hand, empiricists complained that he was claiming that moral reason can enlarge our theoretical knowledge of reality; and, on the other, rationalists charged that, if moral insights do not enlarge our theoretical knowledge, practical reasoning can only make assertions lacking any objectivity.

22 On this topic, see Nicholas Rescher's careful analysis of Kant in his "Noumenal Causality." According to Kant, this same reasoning permits the application of Ideas of reason to noumenal beings as moral agents for *moral* purposes only, and also justifies the right of moral reason to think of those attributes necessary for God to be the moral ruler of the world. See *Pr.R.* 56–57; also "The Postulates of God and Immortality" in Chapter 15. But Kant's use of the category of causality here should not be interpreted as indicating that he thought that the noumenal and phenomenal worlds are ontologically distinct.

8. The primacy of morality

1 The antinomies of the first *Critique* can be understood as representing just such conflicts between empirical reasoning and pure practical reasoning. (See A426–76/B454–504.)

2 Kant himself is chiefly concerned here with religious ideologies, for he judges that that is where irrational subjectivity is most likely to appear and infringe on the rights of reason; hence his use of the terms "fanatics" and "zealots." (See, e.g., *Enlight.* 41; *Orient.* 142–45, 143n, 146n.) Standard historical cases of such errors include the persecution of Galileo by the Inquisition, the demand of Stalinist Russia that the science of genetics conform to the mandates of Marxism, and efforts of

Christian fundamentalists to censor school libraries and curricula. These are errors not of pure practical reason (which has no authentic interest in not respecting the legitimate claims of science) but of empirical practical (prudential) reason, here brutalizing science and freedom of inquiry for the sake of power but in the *name* of morality. (See *Pr.R.* 120–21.)

3 Kant states that he had himself at one point in his thinking fallen into the error of supposing that knowledge is the highest human activity, an error from which Rousseau's writings rescued him. (See *KGS* XX, 44.)

4 As Hannah Arendt points out, this philosophical view carried over into Christianity as the religious tradition that the contemplative life is superior to the active life. Both the Greeks and Christians thought of contemplative activity as transforming mortal humans into the likeness of immortal divinity, but Christianity added the belief that the ultimate goal of life is the attainment of the "beatific vision," the sheer contemplation of God in eternity. See Arendt's *Life of the Mind,* I, 6–7, 92–98, 129–32, and II, 27–28.

5 On Aristotle's failure, see Chapter 9 of my *Morality and the Good Life: A Commentary on Aristotle's Nicomachean Ethics,* especially 170–85.

6 Few topics in Kant's theory have been discussed so infrequently as the primacy of practical reason. Consequently I am grateful to Lewis White Beck for assuring me that an earlier version of this chapter was substantially accurate. I have since expanded the chapter, and Professor Beck should not be blamed for errors I may have introduced.

7 For further discussion of this topic, see Keith Ward, *The Development of Kant's View of Ethics,* 172–73; also Christine M. Korsgaard, "Aristotle and Kant on the Source of Value," especially 500–505; also my "The Kantian Model of Moral-Practical Reason," 83–85.

8 In his 1966 Dawes Hicks Lecture on Philosophy, "The Primacy of Practical Reason," G. J. Warnock contends that Kant's primacy doctrine "cannot be adequately supported, or even explained, within the confines of [his] own moral theory" (263). Professor Warnock claims that Kant fails to show that moral reason has either conative or cognitive power superior to that of theoretical reason: Conatively, our ability to make decisions on the basis of reasons is not radically different from our ability to form beliefs on the basis of reasons; and cognitively, the theoretical use of reason does not have the "disadvantage of committing its practitioners to mere assumptions [like the postulates of pure practical reason] for which no support is conceivably forthcoming" (262–63). Warnock's monograph is valuable for helping us focus on the question, Does the primacy of moral reason have adequate support within the confines of Kant's theory? On Warnock's thesis, see also Victoria S. Wike's *Kant's Antinomies of Reason: Their Origin and Resolution,* 161–66.

9 It may seem misleading to claim that pure practical reason has superior *cognitive* power, since rational *belief,* which is what is authorized by pure practical reason, is not theoretical *knowledge.* Kant himself, however, legitimates this usage of "cognitive." He argues that pure practical reason *can* achieve a kind of knowledge – and he uses the word *Erkenntnis* – of what is the case, for example, of God's existence, albeit not theoretical knowledge, which requires a ground in sensible objects and yields explanations only in terms of causal laws. (See, e.g., *Pu.R.* B395n, A818/B846; *Orient.* 141; *Pr.R.* 50, 103, 105, 133.)

10 Nathan Rotenstreich takes this view in his "Is There a Primacy of Practical Reason?" (247–59), and his position is supported by a number of other commentators. He

continues his argument in Chapter 6 of his *Experience and Its Systematization: Studies in Kant.*

11 See "Ideas of Reason" in Chapter 2; also "The Concepts of Pure Reason" in *The Transcendental Dialectic* of the first *Critique* (A310–38/B366–96).

12 See also J. D. McFarland, *Kant's Concept of Teleology.* Also Stanley G. French, "Kant's Constitutive-Regulative Distinction." Any attempt to use Ideas of reason both theoretically and constitutively, yet without objects in experience to which to apply them, inevitably gives rise to conflicts within reason. (See, e.g., *Pu.R.* A327/B384, A405–567/B432–595, A666/B694.) The fact that we have no rational way to arbitrate such conflicts shows why any claim to theoretical knowledge of supersensible reality should be rejected and why the old metaphysics needed to be abandoned. For a discussion of Hegel's criticisms of Kant's use of Ideas, see John E. Smith's "Hegel's Critique of Kant."

In *The Development of Kant's View of Ethics,* Keith Ward holds that "Kant does not regard the idea of God as *merely* regulative and immanent. He never wavers in his belief that there must be a transcendental 'ground of the order of the world' (A696/B724). . . . though this ground must remain completely unknown to us, as it is in itself" (81).

13 Any argument for freedom that appeals to prudential reasoning suffers exactly the same problem. It may not seem to make sense to talk about empirical practical *reasoning* unless we presume we are rational, able to think about which desires to satisfy and how to satisfy them. But the rationality in empirical practical reason is supplied by theoretical reason. So if the only practical thinking we could do were prudential, it would not make sense to claim that practical reasoning has primacy over theoretical reasoning. (See *Pr.R* 120–21.)

As I pointed out in the preceding chapter, I do not believe that Kant tries to defend morality in *Groundwork* III by appealing to theoretical reason. He does state there that freedom *is* a presupposition of theoretical reasoning, but he also argues that it is a mistake to try to offer a theoretical defense of freedom, for that would have to be a causal account of how freedom can be possible.

14 Kant points out in his *Critique of Judgment* that when Nature is regarded as a systematic whole it appears to us as a work of art, eliciting both wonderment and pleasure, particularly for the transcendental philosopher. Such remarks must surely reflect the aesthetic satisfaction Kant himself experienced as his critical philosophy began to assume the shape of an organic whole. Moreover, the extension of his critique of reason in the third *Critique* enabled Kant to develop a critical aesthetics with the same teleological principle as Nature and morality. (See especially *Cr.J.* 189, 228, 235, 298; also Ernst Cassirer, *The Philosophy of the Enlightenment,* 275–360.)

15 Metaphysics "has as the proper object of its inquiries three ideas only: *God, freedom, and immortality*" (*Pu.R.* A337n/B395n, A798/B826). These are just the Ideas of reason that moral reasoning must use and legitimately may assume as postulates. Keith Ward argues that, without the postulates, the primacy of moral reason could not be defended; see his *Development of Kant's View of Ethics,* 83. The speculative Ideas of theoretical reason prepare for the practical Ideas, thereby indicating an underlying unity of the two uses of reason (see *Pu.R.* A329/B385–86):

• The theoretical Idea of freedom is only a negative and thus incomplete notion, which prepares for the corresponding moral Idea of freedom, which moral reason defines both negatively and positively;

- The theoretical Idea of the human soul as a permanent substance prepares for the moral Idea of an immortal soul;
- The theoretical Idea of the world, or Nature, as a systematic natural whole prepares for the moral Idea of the kingdom of ends, which is a systematic whole encompassing both the natural and supersensible or moral worlds; and finally,
- The theoretical Idea of God simply as deistic First Cause prepares for the moral Idea of God as a Person with all the other attributes that moral reason determines are necessary for such a being.

16 Pure practical reason does not entitle us to claim, "There *is* a God," but it does give us the right to assert, "I *believe* in God's existence." (See *Pu.R.* A769/B797.) See also Mary-Barbara Zeldin, "Principles of Reason, Degrees of Judgment, and Kant's Argument for the Existence of God."

17 Although the world of Pietism may seem far removed from the concerns of this chapter, belief in both the primacy of moral practice and the religious Ideas that pure practical reason supports were important themes of Kant's early religious education.

Kant's view here also foreshadows, as it historically helped to engender, modern pragmatism, which sought to integrate thought and action by finding what Charles Sanders Peirce described (in his essay "What Pragmatism Is") as "an inseparable connection between rational cognition and rational purpose." As we have seen, Kant avoids accepting nonsense in the name of practical value by insisting that the denial of the special rights of science stunts and perverts practice. It is in this way, I think, that we should interpret Kant's claim that the "chief object" (*Hauptzweck*) of science is (in Kemp Smith) the "happiness of all mankind" (*die allgemeine Glückseligkeit*), an expression to be read within the context of A840/B868 (*Pu.R.* A851/B879).

There is this problem, however: Ward, in his *Development of Kant's View of Ethics,* describes Kant as "attempting to develop a rationalist vision of the universe as an intelligible coherent whole; but one which is dynamic, centered on moral willing and commitment, rather than static, centered on the contemplation of metaphysical perfection, as that of Wolff had been" (132) – and that of Leibniz, Aristotle, and Plato, for that matter. Yet Kant's delineation of the supersensible moral world of freedom seems as atemporal and static as the life of contemplation recommended by his rationalistic predecessors.

18 See "Culture and Morality" in Chapter 13.

19 See "A Problem" at the conclusion of Chapter 15.

20 On the one hand Kant holds that any claim that the final end of creation is "human beings [actually] living in conformity with" the moral law presumes more insight into the noumenal world than we in fact can have. (See *Cr.J.* 448n.) But on the other, as we shall see in Chapter 15, he also holds that moral reason still projects a social, specieswide goal – what he calls "the kingdom of ends," in which the human species as a collective entity can and does achieve its complete final end, the *summum bonum,* which is a "totality of all ends within a single principle" – both our virtue (our supreme good, our *bonum supremum*) and our happiness limited by, or proportionate to, our virtue. (See *Pu.R.* A813–14/B841–42; *Gr.* 7/ 396; *Pr.R.* 110–15; *Rel.* 97/89; *T&P* 279, 280n; *Anthr.* 277.) Kant also holds that the Idea of the final good requires also the unity of freedom and Nature in a systematic, harmonic whole. (See *Rel.* 5/5.) *That* this will occur is a religious faith justified by moral reason; *how* it can occur is completely incomprehensible to us.

21 It is ironic how frequently Kant is described as completely indifferent to human happiness.

It should be noted, though, that this is not the happiness of any particular individuals, but rather well-being as a social and cosmopolitan good. (See *Cr.J.* 431–33, 436n; also Chapters 16 and 17.)

22 In confirmation of Kant's claim, every now and then we read stories like that about a postdoctoral fellow at the Max Planck Institute for Biochemistry near Munich, who in 1977 admitted that his reports about the effects of opiates on nervelike cells were fraudulent. In 1981 a similar case of fabrication of data involved a postdoctoral fellow at Harvard Medical School. The terms used in such instances – "fraud," "deception," "truthfulness," "honesty," "integrity," etc. – are moral and not scientific terms. All the motives given in such instances fall in the class of desires and inclinations, just as Kant said. See also *False Prophets* by Alexander Kohn.

23 Rotenstreich, "Is There a Primacy of Practical Reason?" 253.

24 In his political theory, Kant calls the first formula of the Categorical Imperative the "Principle of Publicity"; see Chapter 17.

25 For further discussion of the Categorical Imperative as an imperative of consistency, see Chapter 11. On scientific anomalies, see Thomas S. Kuhn, *The Structure of Scientific Revolutions.*

26 See Lewis White Beck, *A Commentary on Kant's Critique of Practical Reason,* 47–51; also W. H. Werkmeister, *Kant: The Architectonic and Development of His Philosophy,* 173–202.

27 When we engage in philosophical reflection, Kant writes, we find ourselves unavoidably asking four questions. The first, What can I know? is theoretical and speculative; the second, What should I do? is a moral question; and the third, If I do what I ought to do, what may I then hope? is a religious question that can be answered only by moral reason (insofar as it can be answered; see *Pu.R.* A804–6/B832–34; *Logic* 25/29). The fourth question, What is man? is an anthropological query.

9. Moral character: Part I

1 There is no guarantee that we will always act morally, and in individual cases we cannot judge securely the moral quality of even our own motivation. Still, Kant believes, ordinary people can easily distinguish between moral and prudential incentives. (See *Gr.* 21–22/404; *Pr.R.* 92–93, 152, 163; *T&P* 286–87.) Only sophisticated philosophers seem to have difficulty recognizing differences a child can see, granted that a child with only "a crude and unpracticed judgment" may still err. (See *Pr.R.* 30, 92, 155, 163; *Rel.* 48/44.)

2 Note the abstractness imposed by the qualification "in itself." Actually, no action occurs as an isolated event but instead is situated within a person's ultimate moral commitment. On this, see the next chapter.

In the example of a grocer who treats his customers honestly in *Gr.* 8–9/397, Kant distinguishes between morally correct (legal) actions done from an immediate desire and such actions done in a more calculated way as part of a long-range program of self-interest. He holds that we have more difficulty in identifying the specifically prudential quality of the motivation in the first kind of action, because, although all prudentially motivated actions are only instrumentally good, those motivated by an immediate inclination more closely resemble actions motivated by duty, which causes us to take an immediate interest in an action as good in itself. (It may be added that, on the basis of the information he gives, Kant's presumption that the grocer acted out of self-interest lacks support.)

3 Except in his specifically political treatises, Kant usually uses the term "law" to refer only to the *moral* law and not the civil law, and in nonpolitical contexts he uses the expressions, "lawfulness," "the merely lawful character of the act," and "legality" to refer to behaviors not forbidden by the Categorical Imperative. (See, e.g., *M.M.* 214, 219.)

4 The first formula here is restricted in that it is applied only to behaviors; see also Chapters 12 and 17. Kant's doctrine here may be more clearly put by John Rawls, whose first principle of justice, stated in provisional form, reads: "Each person is to have an equal right to the most extensive basic liberty compatible with a similar liberty for others"; see his *Theory of Justice*, 60.

5 There is some evidence to suggest that *"Bewegungsgrund"* (literally, "reason for moving") was first used as a technical term by Christian Wolff to translate the Latin *ratio* in the sense of the reasoned or principled motive underlying an action. Typically, having insisted on the importance of this distinction, Kant elsewhere uses *Bewegungsgrund* to refer to prudential motivation and *Triebfeder* to refer to moral motivation. (See, e.g., *Pr.R.* 21; *M.M.* 376.)

6 Throughout this section and chapter the expression "merely pathological feelings," although awkward, is intended to allow for there being other emotions that are pathological but also specifically moral in nature. These latter are discussed in the next chapter.

7 George Schrader, "The Constitutive Role of Practical Reason in Kant's Moral Philosophy," 74–75. In this superbly reasoned article, Schrader questions Kant's tenet that all desires can be morally innocent. Schrader points out that a desire, say, to cheat someone, already is intentional, that is, constituted by the will *as* an instance of cheating. Therefore (as Aristotle had also held), a person's moral judgment about such a desire is not "the measuring of an intrinsically neutral action against an external moral standard" but already "the activity of the will in assessing its own volition" (80). Only by understanding moral judgment in this way, he continues, can Kant avoid many problems with action descriptions (such as those raised by Onora Nell (O'Neill) and mentioned in Chapter 5, note 23).

The contention that Kant's analysis of desires and inclinations is radically inadequate to the facts of human moral life leads to an even more fundamental discussion of his theory. As is well known, nothing is more important to any philosophical theory than its initial claims. Lenn Evan Goodman pointed out to me that when Kant defined human beings as essentially or authentically "rational" – and desires as "pathological" and so as "outside," and alien to, our essential self – he "turned the tables" on those philosophers, such as the Epicureans, who had identified man's essential, authentic self as the *desiring* self. Virtually everything else Kant then says about autonomy, heteronomy, and the ultimate moral norm is deeply affected by that initial stance. For a sustained argument against Kant's consequent views on the nature of morality, see Lawrence A. Blum, *Friendship, Altruism, and Morality*.

8 See Sidney Axinn, "Ambivalence: Kant's View of Human Nature."

9 Like Aristotle and Plato before him, Kant wishes to avoid any analysis that might attack the fundamental soundness and endanger the very existence of reason itself. (See *Pr.R.* 120; *Rel.* 35/30, 45/50.) He therefore is careful not to portray this conflict as *within* reason itself; rather, it is "an opposition of inclination to the precept of

reason (*antagonismus*)" (*Gr.* 58/424). Because we have two different practical interests and incentives, conflict between them is an inevitable but still contingent "fact" of human morality.

As long as we reason correctly (observe the appropriate criteria of correctness), the *rules* generated by the various uses of reason do not conflict. The rules formulated by prudential reasoning, for example, do not conflict with one another, but simply set out the means to different pleasures; conflicts occur between our desires for different pleasures. Moreover, prudential rules do not directly conflict with moral rules; rather, each kind of rule addresses different interests, which can conflict. As we saw in Chapter 7, in concrete situations apparently conflicting moral rules do not both bind a person.

10 For this reason Kant makes the otherwise startling claim that "right-thinking persons" find themselves wishing to be completely free of desires so they might be purely rational agents: "Even the feeling of sympathy and warmhearted fellow-feeling . . . is burdensome to right-thinking persons" (*Pr.R.* 118; see also *Gr.* 65/428; *Anthr.* 252). We act irrationally only because we have desires; we have desires only because we have needs; and it would be better not to have any needs at all. Such comments show how firmly Kant is situated within the intellectualistic philosophical tradition dating to the Greeks. Similar remarks, as in Plato's *Phaedo,* signal a recurrent yearning to be more than human.

For an examination of the influence of the *Phaedo* on Kant's thinking, see Klaus Reich, "Kant and Greek Ethics (I)." In his 1763 competition essay, Kant had seemed to ally himself with the "moral sense" school of Hutcheson and Shaftesbury, and based morality on feelings. But by 1770, in his inaugural dissertation, Kant was denouncing empiricism in ethical theorizing. See Kerferd and Walford, *Kant: Selected Pre-Critical Writings and Correspondence with Beck,* 32-34 and 59-60.

11 Kant argued that the foundation of ethics *in general* must be completely pure and a priori, but he also allowed that the elucidation of *human* morality must take into account "the concepts of pleasure and pain, of the desires and inclinations, etc., all of which are of empirical origin" (*Pu.R.* A15/B29). So although the concept of duty as rational self-constraint is an Idea of reason, it necessarily is also a "mixed" concept, formed of both rational (or a priori) and empirical elements and applying only to contingently rational agents like us. (See *Gr.* vi–vii/389, 28/408, 32–33/410; *Pu.R.* A801n, A841–42/B869–70; *M.M.* 219, 379, 480–81.) In *M.M.* 376 Kant does describe the idea of duty as "purified of everything empirical (every feeling)," but he can mean only that, as a motive, duty does not include any merely pathological feelings nor rely on any of them for its efficacy. Moral philosophy for human agents must *take into account* empirical conditions, but it is not thereby *based* on those conditions. See also Chapter 2, note 13, and Chapter 11, especially notes 17 and 18.

12 Acting from the moral motive of dutifulness is *not* itself a duty in the second sense. Otherwise we would involve ourselves in an infinite regress, to have a duty to act from duty, and so on. This attitude of conscientiousness, Kant writes, also leads us to think of our duties as being as sacred as if they were God's commands, even if we are "not able to affirm that the existence of God is wholly certain" (*Rel.* 195n/183; see 153–54/142–43, 195/183–85). So another word for "conscientiousness" is "religion," properly understood. (See *M.M.* 439–40.) See also Chapter 6, note 13, and Chapter 18.

13 Kant holds that there are two kinds of characteristics or dispositions concerning our choices (*Willkür*) – those that are free and therefore moral, and those formed

by frequent repetition. He argues that a *habitus* in the Aristotelian sense causes us to *want* to act certain ways and so actually causes the *loss* of freedom. Such psychological habituation (Kant calls this *"assuetudo"*) reduces our moral personality to the level of heteronomy, to "a physical inner necessitation" (*Anthr.* 149; see *M.M.* 380n, 383–84, 407, 409). Consequently, he holds that any effort to develop virtue by training our desires, as Aristotle had recommended, is destructive of freedom and so is self-defeating. Virtue must be based not on sensuous desires but only on the distinctively moral emotion of respect for the moral law, an emotion in turn generated by that law. (See *M.M.* 407, 409.) Kant also argues that moral character based on "resolute and firm principles," not psychological habituation, can best prepare a person to deal with the varying moral situations of life (*M.M.* 383–84). (Aristotle had argued, to the contrary, that habituated character traits can be flexible enough to be more effective guides in situations than principles alone.)

Their different analyses of the role of emotions in human moral life lead to a corresponding difference in the moral ideals Aristotle and Kant present. Aristotle judged Kant's morally best person, the virtuous person, who is equivalent to Aristotle's morally strong person, to be only the second best, not the best person we can aim to become. Kant, on the other hand, thought Aristotle's ideal of moral excellence – and his analysis of practical wisdom, too – was merely fantasy: We cannot habituate our emotions to love what is right (rather than what is merely pleasurable), as Aristotle had claimed, and even if we could, we should not do so. For further discussion of these differences between Aristotle and Kant, see my "Kantian Critique of Aristotle's Moral Philosophy: An Appraisal."

Finally, given Kant's analysis of morality as duty, his theory leaves no room for a separate category for supererogatory actions, that is, morally "noble" actions above and beyond the call of duty. (See, e.g., *Pr.R.* 155, 157.) If we want a theory that gives a special place to morally heroic actions, we need something like Aristotle's theory. On this topic, see also Chapter 5, note 16.

14 We are responsible for developing moral strength, but we do not have a duty to *acquire* the power to be virtuous, for we already have that power because we possess pure practical reason. (See *M.M.* 397, 405.)

15 It was just such inclinations that helped mislead other moral philosophers into confusing morality with happiness and claiming that such desires can provide the motivation for moral conduct. As we have seen, their error served only to undermine morality.

16 The doctrine in this section needs to be balanced by what Kant says about morally permissible and morally indifferent actions as well as what he says about positive, wide duties of benevolence. For the former, see Chapter 10, for the latter Chapters 5 and 14.

17 Today there is a good deal of disagreement over how to understand Kant's treatment of both moral and nonmoral desires. Some commentators, for example, argue that Kant's various statements about desires and inclinations are not as self-consistent as I am interpreting them; see, e.g., John R. Silber's introduction to Kant's *Religion within the Limits of Reason Alone*, lxxxvi. Recently, others have argued, on the basis of remarks such as those found in *M.M.* 402 and *Rel.* 21n/9n, for a quasi-Aristotelian interpretation of Kant: that he held it not only permissible but even morally obligatory to encourage emotions like love and benevolence, which can support the motive of duty. For one proponent of this latter view, see Henning Jensen, "Kant on Overdetermination, Indirect Duties, and Moral Worth." Paul

Dietrichson also maintains that the "emergence" of an inclination to obey the moral law is a sign of virtuousness; see his "What Does Kant Mean by 'Acting from Duty'?" 329–30. For a similar view, see Thomas Auxter, *Kant's Moral Teleology*, 149–79. Barbara Herman also discusses "overdetermination" in her "On the Value of Acting from the Motive of Duty."

Such discussions continue a controversy over the role of inclinations in human moral life, begun between Kant and his contemporary Friedrich Schiller (1759–1805); on this controversy, see Hans Reiner, *Duty and Inclination: The Fundamentals of Morality Discussed and Redefined with Special Regard to Kant and Schiller.*

18 Kant suggests that the only hope for widespread success in the struggle against radical evil is not simply through the efforts of individuals but especially "through the establishment and spread" of an ethical society, a kingdom of virtue (*Rel.* 94/86). On this, see Chapter 15; also Sharon Anderson-Gold, "Kant's Ethical Commonwealth: The Highest Good as a Social Goal."

19 It may seem helpful to think of the difference between the phenomenal and noumenal viewpoints as reflecting the different purposes of an agent and of a spectator. (See "A Brief History" in the preceding chapter.) Lewis White Beck discusses this possibility in *A Commentary on Kant's Critique of Practical Reason* (see 191–94). In *The Actor and the Spectator*, Beck also suggests thinking of citing the causes of and giving the reasons for an action as two distinct kinds of explanations, each depending on rules (but of different kinds), for there is a sense in which reasons can be considered causes, albeit a unique kind of cause. (See, e.g., 78 and 97.) See also Stephen Körner, "Kant's Conception of Freedom." In his "Empirical and Intelligible Character in the *Critique of Pure Reason*," however, Henry E. Allison points to serious difficulties in correlating the causes-reasons distinction closely with Kant's doctrine of the two viewpoints. For one thing, Kant never intended the noumenal point of view to be a (nonempirical) kind of explanation.

20 As we have seen, Kant defines moral virtue as strength of soul and regards it as a paradigmatic exercise of freedom and rationality. (See, e.g., *M.M.* 382n.) But that very analysis makes it difficult for him to handle moral evil. For example, he apparently feels forced to hold that moral evil is a lack of power. The evil person may be like a "madman" with more physical strength than a sane person, but to be evil is to lack rational strength. (See *M.M.* 226–27.) Moreover, a person must choose evil knowingly and freely in order to be responsible for that choice, but Kant also regards the choice of evil as fundamentally irrational. So, on the one hand, Kant describes Sulla as evil because of the latter's "firm maxims" of violence; and, on the other, he virtually denies there can be an ultimate principle of heteronomy: "Man never sanctions the evil in himself, and so there is really no evil from principles; it comes only from abandoning principles" (*Anthr.* 293–94; see *Rel.* 21/17). Finally, because, apart from the Law of Autonomy, a person cannot act on completely consistent maxims, Kant also holds that evil character tends to be self-destructive. (See *P.P.* 379; *Conflict* 81/145.)

John R. Silber argues that historical individuals like Hitler and his ministers suggest, to the contrary, that there can be evil people whose lives evidence unusual rational strength. Silber therefore finds this part of Kant's analysis of character to be inadequate to the facts of our moral life; see his introduction to Kant's *Religion*, cxxv, cxxviii–xxx; also his "Kant at Auschwitz."

21 Kant shows some cynicism about how widespread virtue actually is: "Perhaps there are but few who have attempted this revolution before the age of thirty,

and fewer still who have consolidated it firmly before they are forty," and then they do so only because they have become "sick and tired of the precarious state of instinct" (a merely prudential basis for the ultimate moral decision?) (*Anthr.* 294).

22 In his paper, "Empirical and Intelligible Character in the *Critique of Pure Reason*," Henry E. Allison argues that, at best, all we can infer from an individual's behavior is that person's empirical character.

23 Because he held that good intentions are best indicated by a consistent pattern of actions throughout a person's lifetime taken as a whole, Kant is very skeptical about the genuineness of "death-bed conversions." (See *Rel.* 69n/63–64, 77–78, 78n/71–72.)

24 For Kant's discussion of the civil imputation of responsibility, see "Crime and Punishment" in Chapter 16.

25 In Kant's analysis, even the morally worst person still possesses moral reason. Accordingly, vice cannot cause invincible ignorance that might excuse such a person from moral responsibility for his evil actions.

Therefore, Kant holds, although human beings can give themselves up to "diabolical vices," they can never actually have a diabolical (i.e., a *totally* evil) character. (See *Rel.* 27/22.) That would require the *complete* rejection of the moral law *because* it is the moral law and the deliberate and defiant choice of the evil principle for its own sake, simply because it is evil. (See *Rel.* 35/30, 37/32.) Since the moral law is ineluctably present in the human will, Kant holds that it is not possible for anyone totally to reject it. When individuals do choose to do evil, they choose to subordinate the moral law to the principle of self-love. (See *Rel.* 27–28/22–23.) As we saw in Chapter 4, this latter principle is in its own way a rule of rationality and so of self-preservation, but only a partial and incomplete principle.

In "Kant's Rejection of Devilishness: The Limits of Human Volition," Sharon Anderson-Gold defends Kant's analysis by pointing out that actions so enormously evil as to seem diabolical in origin can be adequately explained without resorting to diabolical agency. The specieswide propensity to evil shows itself mainly in the social vices. When large numbers of "ordinary" people are willing to cooperate with wrongdoing for petty reasons "no more interesting than job security, personal advancement, or greater material rewards," the cumulative effect can be enormous evil (46). This view echoes Hannah Arendt in her *Eichmann in Jerusalem: A Report on the Banality of Evil;* see also her *Life of the Mind,* I, 3–6.

10. Moral character: Part II

1 Kant may seem to deny this doctrine, for example, when he contends that human moral reason must be practical without "an intervening feeling of pleasure or displeasure even if this pleasure is taken in the [moral] law itself" (*Pr.R.* 24–25; see also 71). Here, however, he is discussing *heteronomous* desires, that is, the anticipation of pleasure or contentment from doing what the moral law requires. He of course denies that such desires are moral in nature. (See *Lect.* 225/37.)

Kant was determined to combat every kind of empiricism in ethical theory, here that type of hedonism or "eudaemonism" that confusedly argues that our motive for acting virtuously is anticipation of the contentment we feel after having acted dutifully. That claim, Kant argues, is incoherent, involving an internal contradiction. Moral contentment can only follow from our consciousness of having acted dutifully, and we can act dutifully only if we *set aside* all consideration of effects that may follow from doing so. If we could recognize our duty and be moved to do it only to feel good afterward, we could never act dutifully and therefore could never experience moral contentment. On this see, *Pr.R.* 116 and *M.M.* 377–78.

2 Kant uses the term "subjective" in two very different senses. In one sense, "subjective" refers to the subject or human agent (or conditions in that agent) and contrasts with what is "given" from outside the agent in some sense or other, such as objects given in experience. In the second sense, that is "subjective" that is arbitrary and thus peculiar to individual agents, in contrast to what is objective and holds necessarily and universally for all rational agents or at least for all human agents. Moral emotions are subjective in the first sense, for they reside in the human moral agent. They are also subjective in the second sense because their strength can vary from person to person. But because they are generated by the objective moral law, they are not *completely* subjective in the second sense, as are our likes and dislikes.

John R. Silber points out that all incentives appear alike from a theoretical standpoint; they are all regarded as merely pathological in nature. See his introduction to Kant's *Religion Within the Limits of Reason Alone,* cviii–cix. If all the internal conflicts we experience were simply between homogeneous desires for pleasure, then all human rational conduct would be merely prudential in nature. But Kant argues that, in our self-awareness, we can distinguish between conflicts involving only pathological desires and conflicts between such desires and duty; and, further, that we also recognize that the demands of dutifulness or conscientiousness are radically different from the insistencies of mere desires.

3 According to Kant's doctrine of the two viewpoints, no contradiction is generated by saying that, from the theoretical viewpoint, all emotions must be regarded as causally determined phenomena whereas, from the viewpoint of the moral agent, moral emotions must be regarded as freely generated by reason. But Robert Paul Wolff protests that since "feelings of any sort are events of the phenomenal world" it is futile for Kant to try to distinguish between moral and nonmoral feelings; see his *Autonomy of Reason: A Commentary on Kant's Groundwork of the Metaphysics of Morals,* 83.

4 Saying that we have a duty to acquire moral feelings would generate an infinite regress – having a duty to have a duty, and so on. (See *M.M.* 402–3.)

5 Although they may legitimately appeal to moral emotions to try to motivate their students, moral educators must still teach their students to guide their judgment only by the Categorical Imperative. (See *M.M.* 376.)

6 An illusion, in general, is the "kind of false impression that persists even though . . . our understanding declares it impossible" (*Anthr.* 149). Here the "inner practical illusion" consists in taking a subjective element (moral sentiments) to be the ultimate objective ground of moral action. (See *Anthr.* 274.) Kant claims that both Epicurus and Francis Hutcheson fell into this error. (See *Gr.* 91n/442n.) For Kant's discussion of Epicurus, see Chapter 15, note 12. As Lewis White Beck contends, Kant was not fair here in his criticism of the British moralists, who actually had distinguished carefully between interested and disinterested pleasure. (See Beck, *A Commentary on Kant's Critique of Practical Reason,* 105–6; also his "Kant's Theoretical and Practical Philosophy," 47–49.)

7 As we shall see in more detail in Chapter 14, moral respect is not based on a person's talents or accomplishments. It is our moral personality – the moral law within us – that gives us an intrinsic, objective dignity. Nonetheless, reason is a teleological faculty, and, as the third formula of the Categorical Imperative makes

clear, we also live up to that dignity by contributing to the final total good of the human race.

8 Moral contentment presupposes that we have a sturdy hope that we have done our duty because it is our duty. This feeling should not be confused with bliss, which requires consciousness of complete moral self-sufficiency. (See *Pr.R.* 118.)

9 If they are not understood to be only partial statements of Kant's beliefs, statements such as this can easily give rise to the common misinterpretation that Kant has no regard at all for human welfare and happiness. Those who read mainly the *Groundwork* can end up with a very skewed understanding of Kant's views on moral emotions. Others have criticized his insistence on moral emotions in other works as only a sign of geriatric sentimentality. This seems to be one topic on which Kant is damned, whichever position he takes. For his doctrine concerning the final relation between virtue and happiness, see Chapter 15.

10 It would seem that neither the antinomies arising out of the old way of doing metaphysics nor perverse moral practices can be errors of moral reason itself, even though Kant examines them both in the second *Critique* under the title of the "Dialectic of Pure Practical Reason." Within his theory, pure practical reason, unlike speculative reason, does not tend to "presumptuously overreach itself" but is our highest moral court. (See *Pr.R.* 3, 15–16.) Any dialectic here must therefore be caused either by the ambitiousness of speculative reason or by empirical practical reason, intruding craftily under the guise of morality, for reasons of power and/or pleasure, into the moral realm. Note that moral fanaticism is detectable only by pure practical reason reflecting on and critiquing extreme claims. (See *Pr.R.* 16.) As it turns out, Kant eventually finds most such errors are abuses of the good moral predisposition by historical religions and political leaders. (See, e.g., *Anthr.* 332n; also Chapter 18.) But Kant did not sufficiently analyze the errors of those who seem to have a good will but still give moral goodness a bad name either by their stupidity or by their desire to use morality only to control the conduct of others.

11 As Barbara Herman puts it, since Kant insists that we have *two* legitimate goals, happiness as well as virtue, Kantian morality leaves a "space" for nonmoral reasons and for the morally permissible pursuit of happiness. See her "Integrity and Impartiality," 245–46.

It is regrettable that Kant emphasized morally obligatory and forbidden actions to the neglect of morally permissible actions. He aimed to set out what he called "common and everyday responsibility," and it does seem that a good deal of that life consists in acting in morally permissible ways.

12 Note that the discussion is limited to actions already determined to be morally permissible. As we saw in Chapter 5, all the expressions of a good will may be good, but they also may be not morally right when they are, for example, based on erroneous judgments.

13 In the *Groundwork,* Kant then immediately explains what a good will is – but only for sensuous and imperfectly rational human agents – without explicitly noting that he is making a crucial transition by doing so.

14 In *Pr.R.* 32 Kant defines a holy will as one "incapable of any maxims which conflict with the moral law," but his description of moral perfection in the passages quoted seems to indicate that here he may have been thinking of the absence of constraint as a sufficient condition for holiness rather than holiness itself, which then would consist simply in acting always on the Law of Autonomy because it is the Law of Autonomy.

15 As Mary J. Gregor points out, Kant uses "wide duty" here quite differently from his official definition of such duty, for there still is no latitude in the duty to strive for holiness. (See her *Laws of Freedom,* 172–73; also *M.M.* 446.)

16 It might seem, Kant writes, that virtue is superior to holiness, because virtue can be measured by the strength of the obstacles it can overcome whereas a holy being faces no such internal obstacles. But this contention, Kant writes, confuses the subjective conditions by which we measure *our* strength with objective strength. (See *M.M.* 383, 396–97.) A holy or superhuman being could also be considered morally strong simply in the sense of always and spontaneously acting rightly. (See *M.M.* 405.)

   If a holy being does not experience moral conflict, a critical reader might want to ask how such an agent could be a moral being at all. Frederick Van de Pitte seems simply to concede that there is no morality for a divine will. (See his *Kant as Philosophical Anthropologist,* 57.) So, too, does Hardy E. Jones in his *Kant's Principle of Personality,* 124.

17 See Chapter 7.

18 Strictly speaking, Kant's use of temporalities here is incoherent, since the exercise of freedom is noumenal and is not temporally conditioned. From a phenomenal point of view, our moral goal appears unattainable; but from a noumenal viewpoint, the transformation to a perfect disposition to fulfill the moral law apparently must be regarded as instantaneous.

   Most modern Kantian scholars in the Anglo-American tradition find so many problems with Kant's postulate of immortality that they have tended simply to ignore it, as well as his doctrine that we have a duty to strive for moral perfection. In his "Primacy of Practical Reason," G. J. Warnock sums up one common argument for dispensing with the postulate of immortality (and that of God as well): "It may well be the case that moral perfection, as perhaps for that matter perfect physical health, is not attainable in the course of any finite span of terrestrial existence; but why is it necessary to believe that it is attainable at all? If it is said that its being attainable is implied by the proposition that we ought to attain it, we may reply that that implication is easily avoided by substituting the proposition that we ought to *strive* to attain it, a proposition which seems to have just as good a claim to express the substance of the moral conviction in question. . . . and if so, then it is not necessary to believe in any supernatural arrangements for its realization" (261). Lewis White Beck concurs with this position; see his *Commentary on Kant's Critique of Practical Reason,* 269–70. So too does John Silber. (See his "Kant's Conception of the Highest Good as Immanent and Transcendent," 472–76.)

19 See Allen W. Wood, *Kant's Moral Religion,* 226–48; also Michel Despland, *Kant on History and Religion,* 281–82. For Wood's defense of Kant against the claim that he introduced God into his moral theory only so we can get the happiness we *want,* see *Kant's Moral Religion,* 166–70.

11. The categorical imperative

1 Kant's distinction between the groundwork of a metaphysics of morals and a metaphysics of morals itself is similar to the distinction often made today between metaethics and normative ethics. In terms of the latter distinction Kant in effect holds that the Categorical Imperative is *both* the ultimate metaethical principle

underlying the logic of our ordinary moral judgments (those made rightly, of course) *and* the ultimate normative ethical principle for judging maxims and motives.

2 Most commentators follow the influential lead of H. J. Paton, who held that Kant offers five formulas – three main formulas, with the first and third each having a significant variation. (See his *Categorical Imperative: A Study in Kant's Moral Philosophy,* 129.) In this exposition, as I understand Kant, he thought he was offering three and only three formulas of the one Categorical Imperative. On this topic, see also Bruce Aune, *Kant's Theory of Morals,* 35; T. C. Williams, *The Concept of the Categorical Imperative,* 22–35; and Keith Ward, *The Development of Kant's View of Ethics,* 125–26.

Some commentators have argued that the different formulas are not logically equivalent. Again, I will interpret the different formulas as I think Kant conceived of them. He at least intended that all three versions should be equivalent, though each has its own emphasis and function.

The late Klaus Reich contended that there is one fundamental or "general principle" and three "particular formulas"; see his "Kant and Greek Ethics (II)," 453. (By contrast I hold that the "general principle" is the first formula.) Reich also pointed out the close parallel between Kant's three formulas and three Stoic rules recommended by Cicero to resolve conflicts between reason and desires.

Finally, it is worth noting that Kant seemed to make a point of stating the Categorical Imperative at least a little differently every time he repeated it.

3 As we have seen in Chapter 10, Kant argues that human morality has a crucial emotional side that must be taken into account. Accordingly, we should not be surprised that he would try to bring this formal norm "nearer to feeling" (*Gr.*80/436).

4 Readers familiar with H. J. Paton's work will notice that I give different names to the three formulas than does Paton. This is the first time I have used the expression "Formula of Autonomy," which I will use only as a title for the first formula. Paton instead gives this title to one verson of the third formula; see his *Categorical Imperative,* 129–32. (In the preceding chapters, I have used the expression "the Law of Autonomy" as synonymous with "the moral law," whether that law occurs only as a principle or as an imperative; see Chapter 5, note 9.)

5 Readers unfamiliar with the literature should be aware that most other commentators disagree, to a greater or lesser extent, with my analysis in this and the next four chapters. Some argue that Kant simply does not make as much sense as I may seem to claim for him; others offer quite different analyses of the Categorical Imperatives. T. C. Williams, for example, argues that, regardless of what Kant actually tried to do, since everyone has found the Categorical Imperative "untenable" as a test of maxims, it therefore must be only a statement of the fundamental moral disposition of conscientiousness. (See his *Concept of the Categorical Imperative,* 22–35, 116–18.) Jonathan Harrison's "Kant's Examples of the First Formulation of the Categorical Imperative" and "The Categorical Imperative" and J. Kemp's "Kant's Examples of the Categorical Imperative" raise other interesting and difficult problems with the Categorical Imperative. Here I have had to remind myself that I am limiting myself to offering an exposition, with some prima facie textual plausibility, of what Kant said. For other criticisms of the Categorical Imperative, see Marcus George Singer, *Generalization in Ethics,* particularly 217–99; also the essays in *Morality and Universality: Essays on Ethical Universalizability,* ed. Nelson T. Potter and Mark Timmons.

6 Two comments need to be made here. First, when Kant occasionally describes such an agent as "possible," he is maintaining that the Idea of such an agent is not self-contradictory; the existence of such an agent is at least logically possible. Further, he uses this description only in passages that occur before he has defended our right to take ourselves to be such agents, so that at that stage of his analysis the existence of such agents is still only a possibility. Second, he occasionally claims that we ought to be able "to derive our [moral] principles from the general concept of a rational being as such," meaning that the moral law can be derived by analyzing the moral nature of *whatever* agents there may be who possess pure practical reason and are obligated by that law (*Gr.* 35/412). But as we have seen, first in Chapter 3 and later in Chapter 7, Kant also objects to this same way of putting things, because the expression "rational agent as such" had been preempted by philosophers like Christian Wolff to refer to agents with only empirical practical reason, with no idea of the moral law or ability to follow it. When, by contrast, he offers his own analysis of the concept of a "rational being" in *Gr.* 36ff/412ff, Kant begins by defining such a being as having freedom in its positive sense, with "the power to act in accordance with his idea of laws" (*Gr.* 36/412; see 63–64/427).

7 In this derivation I am not concerned with two other problems: how it is possible for us to be agents with pure practical reason; and how individuals should use the Categorical Imperative in judging maxims. We have already seen Kant's defense of our moral agency – and its limits – in Chapter 7; and the second has been discussed in Chapter 5 and will be addressed later in this chapter and in Chapters 12–15.

As we saw in Chapter 2, in his first *Critique* Kant had defined knowledge learned in an a priori fashion as "knowledge absolutely independent of all experience" (*Pu.R.* B3). He also said such knowledge can be either pure or mixed: The former uses Ideas or rules furnished only by our own reason as in logic, and the latter also uses concepts learned from experience. As long as his analysis concerns only perfectly rational beings and agents, Kant's claims remain "pure," for we never encounter such perfection in our experience. However, once he turns his attention to dependent and imperfectly rational agents like us, his elucidation of morality must consist of a priori but mixed concepts and principles. (See, e.g., *M.M.* 216.)

I should note here that my claims in the text about how to understand the analyticity and/or syntheticity of both the prudential and moral norms are also moot. For a careful analysis of some of the issues here, see Henry E. Allison, "Morality and Freedom: Kant's Reciprocity Thesis"; also the relevant articles by Thomas E. Hill, Jr., whose analyses are a model of careful Kantian exegesis. I also wish to thank my colleague Davis Baird for his criticisms of this chapter, although he of course should not be held responsible for my analysis.

8 See also "A New Exposition of the First Principles of Metaphysical Knowledge" (1755) in *KGS* I, 385–416, especially 387–91. Kant calls this "the principle of contradiction," but today the more common practice (which I will follow) is to refer to it as "the principle of noncontradiction." A second and positive formal criterion given by reason alone, Kant writes, is the principle of sufficient reason, using the categories of ground and consequent. (See *Logic* 51–53/57–58.) This principle underlies Kant's transcendental deductions. Although the logical relation of ground and consequent is analytically true, when schematized as the principle of causality, it becomes synthetic. (See Kant's two letters to Reinhold in Arnulf Zweig, *Kant: Philosophical Correspondence 1759–99*, 136–50.)

9 It might seem that this sentence should read, *"Besides freedom,* there is but one condition necessary for the existence of reason." However, since Kant interprets the law of freedom as but a practical version of the principle of noncontradiction, strictly speaking such a qualification is redundant.

10 Stated as the principle of consistency, this is a positive requirement. Since this principle enjoys the power it has because it is purely formal, Kant denounces any reformulation that would add empirical ("synthetic") qualifications, such as "at one and the same time." (See *Pu.R.* A151–53/B191–93.) The application of this principle to temporal judgments, Kant notes, can alter the meaning of at least one of the concepts so as to make the connection between the concepts synthetic, not analytic.

Kant's discussion here is deliberately ahistorical and sets aside issues related to the historical progress of reason in which contradictions may be a fortunate stimulus to the development of rational insight. On this, see, e.g., Chapter 2, note 18, and Chapter 16; also Hans Saner, *Kant's Political Thought: Its Origins and Development.*

11 Kant generally tries to avoid distracting questions about empirical, psychological possibilities and complications. For example, we can hold contradictory beliefs without realizing it, say, because we have not thought through their implications. It is just to avoid such problems that Kant tends to use impersonal language rather than writing about people who are thinking theoretically or practically.

12 Kant distinguishes between the logic of "willing" (or "genuinely wanting" or "choosing") and that of merely "wishing" this way: Willing includes the notion of striving to attain what one sees as good, whereas merely wishing means desiring something without "using our power to produce the object" (*Anthr.* 251; see *Gr.* 44–45/417).

13 Because the ultimate principle of prudence is analytically true, it holds objectively for all finite, rational agents as rational (abstracting, of course, from all moral considerations). Individual prudential imperatives are synthetic a priori principles insofar as they contain causal laws that can be learned only empirically, but they hold only subjectively because their binding force depends on a person's desires and willingness to act rationally so as to satisfy them. (See *Gr.* 45/417.) On this, see also Chapter 4, note 3, and Chapter 5, note 10. Kant seems to confuse these issues in *Gr.* 50n/420n when he apparently attributes the analyticity of the principle of prudence to the "perfect will" of a rational being acting on it.

14 Henry E. Allison, "The Concept of Freedom in Kant's 'Semi-Critical' Ethics," 107; see also his "Morality and Freedom: Kant's Reciprocity Thesis," 417–18. Note the restricted meaning of "as such"; on this, see note 6, this chapter.

15 See also *Pu.R.* A534/B562, A802/B830; *Gr.* xiv/392, 8/395, 35/412, 59/425, 86/439, 97–98/446–47, 100–101/448, 104–5/451; *Pr.R.* 15, 93–94, 97–98, 104–7, 114, 158–59; *M.M.* 213–14, 217–18, 227, 379, 381, 481. There is also some slippage in Kant's use of "moral," which contrasts sometimes with "amoral" and other times with "morally evil." On the problem of the meaning of "freedom," see Lewis White Beck, "Five Concepts of Freedom in Kant"; also Appendix 1, and the discussion of "reciprocal concepts" in Chapter 7 ("Kant's First Argument: Part I").

16 The argument here seems to be that "if we can, then we should." A more typically Kantian contention would be that "should implies can"; for a discussion of that claim, see Chapter 6, note 6. Then the argument would appeal (as does the argument in the second *Critique*) to the appearance of the Categorical Imperative in our

practical awareness. Since it is our own reason commanding us, we must be both able and obligated to obey it.

17 So, for example, Kant defines a law as "an objective principle for any rational being," but then claims "it is a principle on which he *ought* to act – that is, an imperative" (*Gr.* 51n/420n). This, even though he already had clearly stated that with regard to a perfectly rational or holy being (like God), the notion of obligation is meaningless and inappropriate.

18 When he gets caught up in his argument against empiricism in ethical theorizing, Kant occasionally claims that not only the Categorical Imperative but also all moral concepts and principles are and must be *pure* a priori claims, empty of all empirical content. (See, e.g., *Gr.* v–vi/389, 35/411–12.) But the Law of Autonomy is, of course, a synthetic a priori norm when applied to us. Moreover, generating specific, substantive moral rules always requires us to apply the Categorical Imperative to maxims that can be known only empirically. For further discussion of this point, see Allen Buchanan, "Categorical Imperatives and Moral Principles."

Problems about the "purity" of moral rules may also arise from the manner in which Kant somewhat misleadingly contrasts hypothetical imperatives with the Categorical Imperative. Even if we know that acting rationally in prudential matters imposes on us the requirement that we should do what we know is necessary and within our power to get whatever we genuinely want, Kant states, this does not give us any substantive information about what to *do*. We also must know *what* we want and *how* to get it. By contrast, he writes, we need only conceive of the Categorical Imperative and we know at once what it commands. (See *Gr.* 51/420–21; *Pr.R.* 25.) What it commands is that, regardless of what we might want, we should act only on maxims fit to serve as universal laws. But Kant is not (or at least should not be) thereby also claiming that the Categorical Imperative by itself can generate any of our *particular* concrete duties. It still needs to be *applied* to empirical matter in order to have any content.

On occasion Kant seems to contribute to further confusion by claiming that because the "ground" of morality, the Law of Autonomy, holds for all rational agents and/or because all specific norms for human morality (such as "Do not steal" and "Do not lie") apply to *us* universally and categorically, those same substantive moral rules also apply universally to all other rational beings (if there are any), whoever they may be, insofar as they too are rational. (See, e.g., *Gr.* vi/389.) "Moral laws have to hold for every rational being as such" (*Gr.* 35/412). But it is not too difficult to imagine a world of rational agents in which the very notions of theft and lying would be meaningless. Let us suppose that such agents communicate intuitively and so cannot lie, and are immaterial in nature and so have no use for property. Clearly it would not be rational for them to adopt moral norms about lying and the possession of property. It follows that different species of rational beings might have somewhat different sets of substantive moral rules. But regardless of how different from us other species might be, they all would be bound by the Law of Autonomy, and each set of substantive moral rules would apply universally to all rational beings of the same species. Even if Kant did not explicitly recognize all this, there is nothing in his theory to have prevented him from doing so.

19 Although Kant occasionally may appear to waver on this point, we cannot have a moral theory at all for human beings unless we also have an anthropology, that is, some view of what it is to be a human being and, further, how human perfection should be understood, that is, what it is to be a well-functioning human being.

This point is important for Kant's use of morally obligatory natural ends, as well as for his discussions of the importance of cultural development; on these matters see Chapter 13. What we think about the purity of the moral law will determine whether we think the content ("humanity") of the second formula makes that formula substantively different from the first formula because the second is explicitly concerned with specifically *human* morality.

20 Onora (Nell) O'Neill, "Consistency in Action," 170–71. See also 162–67.

21 These requirements are adapted from the characteristics of a moral law, as analyzed by Paul W. Taylor in his "On Taking the Moral Point of View."

22 See Barbara Herman, "The Practice of Moral Judgment." See also the relevant discussions in Onora Nell (O'Neill), *Acting on Principle*.

23 In this context Kant distinguishes between "rational willing" and "wanting" or "wishing" this way: Rational willing means assenting to impersonal laws, regardless of the consequences to ourselves personally; wanting, whether efficacious or not, means desiring the pleasure an object promises, and then the identification of the object depends on discriminations on the basis of its particular, empirical characteristics. For further discussion of rational willing, see Keith Ward, *The Development of Kant's View of Ethics*, 113–18.

R. M. Hare offers the famous example of the Nazi fanatic who is "willing" to be killed himself if he were to find out he is Jewish. (See, e.g., his *Moral Thinking: Its Levels, Method, and Point*, 169–87.) Asking the fanatic how he distinguishes Jews from non-Jews and why he does so will show, as Hitler demonstrated in *Mein Kampf*, that this kind of "willingness" is based on personal hatred appealing to purportedly empirical data, not on impersonal willing. This may seem too facile a response to Hare, but it still seems faithful to Kant's thinking. For further discussion of the impersonal nature of the criterion of universality, see Chapter 14.

24 In the introduction to his *Utilitarianism*, John Stuart Mill claimed that Kant was a covert Utilitarian. "[Kant] fails, almost grotesquely," Mill claimed, "to show that there would be any contradiction, any logical (not to say physical) impossibility, in the adoption by all rational beings of the most outrageously immoral rules of conduct. All he shows is that the *consequences* of their universal adoption would be such as no one would choose to incur."

Mill oversimplifies Kant's theory. As we shall see in Chapters 12 and 13, Kant does show that some immoral intentions do contradict themselves as universal maxims, but he also allows that others do not. These latter still cannot be chosen rationally because they contradict other maxims we must adopt, and in that sense Kant in fact does hold that "the *consequences* of their universal adoption would be such as no one would choose to incur." Mill seems to believe that *no* consideration of consequences is available to Kant, because Mill tends to think of any assessment of consequences as prudential, using the norm of desirability, whereas Kant maintains that moral assessment of a maxim is independent of whether anyone might *want* the result of its adoption, whether by one person or by everyone.

In this discussion it is important to remember that, although he is not a consequentialist in Mill's sense, Kant still insists both that practical reason is goal-directed and that all maxims are teleological in nature. On this point, see Thomas Auxter, *Kant's Moral Teleology*, 1–3; also Michael J. Sandel's introduction to his *Liberalism and the Limits of Justice*.

25 In Chapter 13 we shall see how properly to test this particular maxim and others like it.

12. The Formula of Autonomy or of Universal Law: Part I

1 Kant offered more variations of the first formula than of the other two combined:

"I ought never to act except in such a way that I can also will that my maxim should become a universal law" (*Gr.* 17/402).

"Should I really be content that my maxim . . . should hold as a universal law (one valid both for myself and others)?" (*Gr.* 19/403).

"Can you also will that your maxim should become a universal law?" (*Gr.* 20/403).

"Act only on that maxim through which you can at the same time will that it should become a universal law" (*Gr.* 52/421).

"Act as if the maxim of your action were to become through your will a universal law of nature" (*Gr.* 52/421).

"Act always on a maxim of such a will in us as can look upon itself as making universal law" (*Gr.* 72–73/432).

"Never perform an action except on a maxim such as can also be a universal law, and consequently such that the will can regard itself as at the same time making universal law by means of its maxim" (*Gr.* 76/434).

"Maxims must be chosen as if they had to hold as universal laws of nature" (*Gr.* 80/436).

"Act on the maxim which can at the same time be made a universal law" (*Gr.* 81/437).

"Act always on that maxim whose universality as a law you can at the same time will" (*Gr.* 81/437).

"Act on a maxim which at the same time contains in itself its own universal validity for every rational being" (*Gr.* 82/437).

"So act as if your maxims had to serve at the same time as a universal law (for all rational beings)" (*Gr.* 84/438).

"Never choose except in such a way that in the same volition the maxims of your choice are also present as universal law" (*Gr.* 87/440).

"So act that the maxim of your will could always hold at the same time as a principle establishing universal law" (*Pr.R.* 30).

"Ask yourself whether, if the action which you propose should take place by a law of nature of which you yourself were a part, you could regard it as possible through your will" (*Pr.R.* 69).

"Act according to a maxim which can at the same time be valid as a universal law" (*M.M.* 226).

"Act externally in such a way that the free use of your will is compatible with the freedom of everyone according to a universal law" (*M.M.* 231).

"Could a maxim such as yours harmonize with itself if everyone, in every case, made it a universal law?" (*M.M.* 376).

"So act that the maxim of your action could become a universal law" (*M.M.*

"So act that the maxim of your action could become a universal law" (*M.M.* 389).

"Act so that you can will that your maxim ought to become a universal law (no matter what the end may be)" (*P.P.* 377).

2 Readers familiar with H. J. Paton's views will recognize that I am, in effect, holding that he is mistaken in thinking there is a "sharp" difference between what he calls the "Formula of Universal Law" and the "Formula of the Law of Nature." (See *The Categorical Imperative: A Study in Kant's Moral Philosophy*, 146.) I believe Kant regarded the latter only as a variation of the first formula. (See, e.g., *Gr.*

80/436.) For a careful discussion of problems that Paton's view generates, see Nelson T. Potter, Jr., "Paton on the Application of the Categorical Imperative." See also Leslie A. Mulholland, "Kant: On Willing Maxims to Become Laws of Nature."

I also have taken Kant's discussion in *Gr.* 73–74/432–33 as referring to his first formula. For those interested in such matters, this means that I regard Paton's Formula III (and Bruce Aune's fourth formula) as only another version of the first formula, so that what I take to be the third formula is what Paton calls Formula IIIa. This also means interpreting Kant's remark in 70/431 about the "third practical principle" (which he there also contrasts with the Formula of Universal Law) to refer to a considerably abbreviated version of what he identifies as the third formula in 80/437.

In *Gr.* 19/403, even if Kant is referring to *moral* contentment, his wording is still unfortunate, for it seems to make moral sentiment the norm of moral judgment; on this, see "Moral Sentiments" in Chapter 10.

3 Understood as a political norm, the Principle of Right (*Recht*) limits only our "external relations" with others (*P.P.* 377; see *M.M* 231; Chapter 17). The cause of this restriction lies not with the first formula, which can still be used in its unrestricted form, but with what it is possible for a state to legislate. (See *P.P.* 377.) John Ladd points out that the word *Recht* "carries with it the connotation of moral rightness" and "applies *only* to the moral component of [civil] law in general"; see his introduction to his translation of *The Metaphysical Elements of Justice*, xvi–xvii.

4 Taking the origin of the formulation of all civil law to be heteronomous means that morally acceptable political arrangements must be either anarchistic (Robert Paul Wolff) or libertarian (Robert Nozick). (See George A. Schrader, "Autonomy, Heteronomy, and Moral Imperatives.") In Chapters 16 and 17 we shall see that Kant himself rejected both anarchism and libertarianism; he held that it is possible for a constitutional democracy (not unlike that proposed by John Rawls) or a government that is at least republican in spirit to accord with rational self-coercion.

5 Kant has no misgivings about using the heteronomous laws of the natural world as a model for moral laws, since the formal structure of the laws of *both* worlds originates in our own thinking. In that sense, then, even natural laws are not something outside of and alien to our own reason.

There can, of course, be a radical difference and incompatibility between the *kind* of "laws of nature" involved in different worlds. The laws of a possible moral world of freedom could not hold in the same manner as physical laws do in the causally determined world of experience. Were they to do so, they would transform the world of freedom into a deterministic world, thereby destroying morality. (See *Gr.* 84/439; *Pr.R.* 44.) For this reason and following Kant's definition of "nature," I generally have avoided using the expression "law of nature" and instead have discussed maxims as laws in a possible moral world. Since reason is an intrinsically purposive power, the laws of an ideal moral world must be teleological, with mutually compatible ends. But, as we saw in Chapter 8, Kant also held that we must use the principle of teleology regulatively to investigate the natural world. (He may have been tacitly considering natural laws as purposive and as given a systematic harmony by Nature.) For further discussion of laws of nature, see Paul Dietrichson, "Kant's Criterion of Universalizability," 177–86; also Thomas Auxter, *Kant's Moral Teleology*, especially 57–80.

6 Not even universal obedience to the Formula of Universal Law would mean that our relations with others would be *completely* harmonious, however. The Cate-

gorical Imperative does not forbid us, for example, to compete for jobs or future spouses or whatever else might be in short supply. As we shall see when we examine his political theory, Kant did not think that all competition and conflict between individuals or groups is either morally wrong or prudentially undesirable. What the Categorical Imperative does require is that all parties to a conflict treat each other fairly, as they could will that they themselves be treated. Not everything "goes" in the competitive pursuit of the things we want.

7 Kant's use of an ideal world as a norm for how we humans should act in a far-from-ideal world has given rise to the consequentialist criticism that his moral theory is excessively idealistic. (See, e.g., Thomas E. Hill, Jr., "Kant's Utopianism." See also this chapter, note 30.)

8 Even some of Kant's adherents have thought he was particularly inept in constructing examples of how to apply the Categorical Imperative. They argue that too many of his examples obscure rather than clarify the application of that moral norm. Throughout this exposition I will take the view that Kant's examples are quite helpful in showing us how he thought the Categorical Imperative operates. On this topic see W. I. Matson, "Kant as Casuist." See also Kant's own discussion of these matters in his 1793 piece, *On the Proverb: That may Be True in Theory but Is of No Practical Value.*

9 Hegel later argued that because the Categorical Imperative is a purely formal test, it can rule out internally inconsistent and conflicting maxims but not all immoral maxims. (See his *Philosophy of Right,* par. 135.) In other words, it can as easily certify a self-consistent body of false claims as a self-consistent body of true claims. Coherence is just as necessary a condition for good fiction as it is for truth. For further discussion of Hegel's criticisms of Kant's moral theory, see T. O'Hagen, "On Hegel's Critique of Kant's Moral and Political Philosophy" and other essays in *Hegel's Critique of Kant,* ed. Stephen Priest.

10 Kant should not have added that those who overhastily believe such promises "would pay me back in like coin" (*Gr.* 19/403). Consideration of adverse consequences is a prudential, not a moral, matter, leading to what Kant calls an "impure will."

11 See Christine M. Korsgaard, "Kant's Formula of Universal Law," for further discussion of these three ways of interpreting a practical contradiction. Also Onora Nell (O'Neill), *Acting on Principle: An Essay on Kantian Ethics,* 63–84; and Allen W. Wood, "Kant on False Promises." Kant himself does not distinguish between kinds of contradictions in this exact manner.

12 As a matter of fact, according to Kant we are *not* morally free to give up a world with promises and contracts. Kant holds that we have a serious moral obligation to make and keep whatever promises are necessary to have a just state. (As we shall see in his response to Constant, Kant held that a law permitting lies would make a just state impossible.) Moreover, there are many morally permissible transactions between individuals that presuppose formal or informal promises, such as business contracts, marriage contracts, and friendships.

13 Kant holds that the prohibition against lying is a negative duty to *self,* but this aspect of lying will not be discussed until Chapter 14.

14 It is now a commonplace that there are many different kinds of speech acts and that the communication of factual information is the point of only a few of them. Kant's theory can accommodate this insight without difficulty, for he allowed that some speech acts, such as flattery and novel writing, are fabrications but not lies. (See *Lect.* 450/229–30; *Anthr.* 24n.) For Kant's most detailed discussion of language

as a form of social intercourse, see *Anthr.* 152. In effect, Kant held that the notion of lying makes sense only when the purpose of speech is explicitly understood to be the communication of factual information.

15 Nonetheless, equating "not lying" and "truth telling" is a common error still committed by even the very best authors. Examples can be found without a great deal of effort.

16 Kant seems to forget this when, in his *Metaphysics of Morals,* he strangely insists that the socially conventional excuse, "I'm sorry; he's not in," is a lie. (See *M.M.* 431.)

17 We are not, however, free simply to abandon the practice of making truthful statements. Kant maintains that even when no particular individual is injured, both lies and the refusal to engage in truthful intercourse violate the "general right of mankind" by setting us "in opposition to *the* condition and means through which any human society is possible" (*Lect.* 447/227, emphasis mine; see 444/224, 447–49/227–29). As we shall see in Chapter 17, by destroying the value of contracts, lying directly undermines any guarantees of civil rights as well as the very possibility of a just political system. Like the assurances of a tyrant, even a benevolent tyrant, lies typically aim at manipulating others by treating them merely as tools for the liar's purposes. It is because lying "vitiates the source of [civil] law itself," as well as the possibility of all enlightenment, that Kant holds that lying must be ranked as among the worst moral evils. Lies all wrong "mankind generally" (*M.M.* 431).

18 Arnulf Zweig, *Kant: Philosophical Correspondence 1759–99,* 188–90. See also the letter to Kant, 174–75. I wish to thank John Marshall for reminding me of these letters. Also recall Kant's remark to Mendelssohn: "I am absolutely convinced of many things that I shall never have the courage to say" (Zweig, 54).

19 Kant seems to take a harsher view about the distinction between untruths and lies in *M.M.* 429 when he claims that *every* deliberate untruth (*jede vorsätzliche Unwahrheit*) morally deserves to be called a lie (*Lüge*).

20 This brief piece can be found in the *KGS* VIII, 423–30. My page references are to the translation in Lewis White Beck's *Immanuel Kant: Critique of Practical Reason and Other Writings in Moral Philosophy,* 346–50. The words in the title, "from Altruistic Motives," translate the German *aus Menschenliebe,* which may also be rendered as "out of love of one's fellowmen." The exchange between Kant and Constant may be important in helping to clarify Kant's moral and political philosophy, but it apparently has not been considered important in understanding Constant. It is not even mentioned in at least one study of Constant as a political philosopher – Guy H. Dodge's *Benjamin Constant's Philosophy of Liberalism: A Study in Politics and Religion.*

21 Beck, *Immanuel Kant,* 346. Kant himself was under the impression that he had in fact somewhere said what Constant had attributed to him, although it seems that no one has been able to find such an assertion in any of his previous published works.

22 Beck, ibid., 347. Oddly enough, there is one passage in student notes, taken over fifteen years earlier from Kant's lectures on ethics, in which Kant may seem to take a position very similar to Constant's: "The forcing of a statement from me under conditions which convince me that improper use would be made of it is the only case in which I can be justified in telling a white lie" (*Lect.* 449/228; see also 444–52/224–32). Kant here seems to endorse the view that lying may be a legitimate form of self-defense, but it may be that he is actually only discussing that contention, for a few lines later he insists that a "white lie" is still a lie and "a lie is a lie, and

is in itself intrinsically base whether told with good or bad intent. . . . formally a lie is always evil" (*Lect.* 449/229). In the main, Kant's lectures seem to be consistent with his contention in his response to Constant that the negative duty not to lie makes no distinctions between persons by allowing us to lie to those who do not "have a right" to the truth.

Kant's "Critical turn" in philosophy is generally dated around 1769–1772. The students' notes we have from Kant's lectures on ethics date from 1780 to 1785. That they show few changes from year to year may indicate that Kant did not have the time to revise his lecture notes because he was too involved in finishing work for publication. (The first edition of the *Critique of Pure Reason* appeared in 1781 and the second edition in 1787; the first edition of the *Groundwork* was published in 1785.) This would tend to confirm Keith Ward's view that the notes probably represent an intermediate state between Kant's pre-Critical and his Critical views about ethics. (See *The Development of Kant's View of Ethics*, 67–68.) That and the fact that these are student notes means that they must be read with caution and measured against Kant's mature doctrines.

23 See H. J. Paton, "An Alleged Right to Lie: A Problem in Kantian Ethics," 191–93, 196–98, 201–2; also John R. Silber, "Procedural Formalism in Kant's Ethics," 223. Paton argues, mistakenly I think, that the Kantian system allows us to make "necessary" exceptions to narrow moral duties "because of some over-riding duty" as well as exceptions to wide duties "in the interests of inclination." On these topics, see "Narrow and Wide Duties" in Chapter 5 and "Conflicts between Moral Rules" in Chapter 6.

24 Note that Kant simply ignores questions that would be relevant to doing casuistry. He does not, for example, point out that the person being questioned would certainly be aware that his own life could be in danger, particularly if he were suspected of lying. But he does not discuss such questions as, Is a person under a strict moral obligation to protect the life of another at the possible cost of his own? Do we have more serious moral obligations to friends than to people we do not know? Kant ignores the given fact that the person providing sanctuary to his friend knows in advance that the potential murderer will show up looking for his intended victim. It would seem that the potential murderer would conceal his intention and try to get a truthful answer by stealth, but Kant chooses rather to interpret the case as involving coercion. He does not discuss the possibly diminished responsibility of a person acting under coercion.

25 John E. Atwell is one of the few commentators to recognize that Kant treated Constant's article as a *political* treatise; see his *Ends and Principles in Kant's Moral Thought*, 193–202. (See also his bibliography.)

26 Beck, *Immanuel Kant*, 347; see also 348–49.

27 See "Morality and Politics" in Chapter 17. Kant's response could be anticipated, for both his moral and political theories are built on the denial that the correct assessment of acceptable action types can be based on consequential considerations, even when one's interest in consequences is not based on self-interest. (See *Gr.* 10/398.) To Kant, disregarding this doctrine, even in extreme cases, *completely* undercuts both morality and politics by reducing them to merely prudential theories.

28 See Beck's translation, 349. Kant maintains that we are not responsible for either the good or the bad consequences following from fulfilling our strict duty or from omitting some particular action that falls under a wide obligation. He also holds without explanation that we deserve recognition for the good consequences of mer-

itorious actions (those fulfilling wide duties) and that we are blamable for the bad consequences of immoral actions. (See *M.M.* 228, 431.) Finally, he holds that the harm we bring on ourselves by immoral action may be only a prudential matter. (See, e.g., *M.M.* 429.)

As we saw in Chapters 4 and 5, Kant first drew a sharp distinction between the natural good (human life and happiness) and the moral good (virtue, doing one's duty). What is naturally good (pleasure, our welfare) may be morally evil, and what is naturally harmful – the diminishing or destruction of actual or possible happiness – may be morally good. So, for example, protecting the state is an unconditional duty that we may have to fulfill at the cost of much natural good, including our own life and happiness and that of those we love. (See *T&P* 300n; *M.M.* 306–7.) But in the course of developing his moral theory Kant also describes natural goods as having what he calls "conditional moral value." As we shall see in the next chapter, we sometimes have a duty to promote or protect what is naturally good (e.g., our cultural development) and avoid causing natural harm (e.g., by excessive drink or by suicide). Likewise, an action that causes unjust harm to others is a moral wrong. (See *T&P* 300n; *M.M.* 235–36.) But Kant does not seem to offer any *principled* way of deciding in specific cases when the natural good must *also* be considered morally good and obligatory and when natural harm must *also* be considered a moral wrong. This gap in his moral theory is bound to lead to serious disagreements between reasonable people when applying his theory to specific cases.

29 Beck's translation, p. 348.

30 Christine M. Korsgaard, "The Right to Lie: Kant on Dealing with Evil," 325, 349; also her "Kant's Formula of Universal Law," 43. See also Thomas E. Hill, Jr., "Moral Purity and the Lesser Evil."

Aristotle had argued that it is simply not possible for practical rules, however well formed, to take into account all possible exceptional cases. He therefore would have argued that morality should not be tied quite so tightly to universal rules as Kant later thought. Laws cannot totally define the notion of "right action," and justice cannot coexist with exceptionless laws. In extraordinary circumstances we must make exceptions to our normal moral and civil rules in order to act morally rightly. Following the usual rules needs no explanation, but breaking them in exceptional cases must be justifiable. Such justifications can be "checked out" against the judgment of people (including judges) who are not personally involved in the case at issue. The term Aristotle used here was *epieikeia* or "equity"; see my *Morality and the Good Life: A Commentary on Aristotle's Nicomachean Ethics*, 78n44.

By contrast, Korsgaard argues for the view that a moral theory must be explicitly two-tiered, because "the results may be very bad" if a theory does not sometimes allow or even require us "to do something that from an ideal perspective is wrong" ("The Right to Lie: Kant on Dealing with Evil," 327). So, for example, "the maxim of lying to deceivers is universalizable . . . in order to counteract the intended results of their deceptions" (330).

Kant argues against our having an "objective" right to lie when "necessary" in exceptional cases. However, as Atwell points out, Kant does acknowledge that the judiciary has the right to decide not to punish those guilty of violations of the law, without such decisions establishing a new civil right to lie from the motive of benevolence. (See, e.g., *T&P* 300n; *M.M.* 234–36, 334.)

For my own criticism of Kant's exceptionless rules (from an Aristotelian point of view), see "The Kantian Model of Moral-Practical Reason," especially 102.

31 Beck's translation, p. 348. See, e.g., Sissela Bok's discussion in her *Lying: Moral Choice in Public and Private Life,* 37–42.

32 There are echoes between, on the one hand, Kant's two kinds of tests and, on the other, his distinction, when discussing empirical knowledge, between "logical possibility" and "real possibility." (See, e.g., *Pu.R.* A218–26/B265–74.) In the former, something is logically possible that can be thought without contradiction; in the latter, something is (or is not) possible as the consequence of there being something else, here a complex of compatible laws defining the moral world.

33 Here we need to appreciate how thoroughly Kant agreed with Hobbes's contentions that life outside the state completely lacks justice and that justice within the state is always in jeopardy. On this see Chapter 16.

34 Note that this claim would not necessarily hold in a moral world of rational agents who do not share our needs and dependencies. That is why there is reason to qualify general claims here by expressions like a "moral world of human beings." In this instance what is "rational" is not a *purely* rational matter but certainly *is* what is rational for agents who need others to achieve obligatory or rationally permissible and justified ends, such as our necessarily desired end of happiness and our moral right to happiness not contrary to the moral law. (This view of rationality also underlies Kant's various postulates of pure practical reason.)

35 Kant is not arguing here for a merely prudential trade-off; on this, see Julius Ebbinghaus, "Interpretation and Misinterpretation of the Categorical Imperative"; Paul Dietrichson, "Kant's Criteria of Universalizability," 196–97; and Lewis White Beck, *A Commentary on Kant's Critique of Practical Reason,* 162. See also Chapter 14. For another discussion of the fourth example, see Barbara Herman, "Mutual Aid and Respect for Persons," especially 577–99.

36 For example, Keith Ward holds that "a distinction must be made" between helping others in distress and helping others attain their purposes. (See his *Development of Kant's View of Ethics,* 118–19.)

13. The Formula of Autonomy or of Universal Law: Part II

I wish to thank Thomas M. Seebohm and Gerhard Funke, editors of *Proceedings: Sixth International Kant Congress,* for permission to use the examples in this chapter; variations of them appeared in my essay "The Categorical Imperative and the Natural Law."

1 Quite commonly commentators characterize Kant's theory as "deontological" in contrast to "teleological." This description may mislead those who do not know Kant's theory into thinking he has no regard for human ends, which is far from the truth. The Categorical Imperative may not *presuppose* any particular ends, but it clearly must identify what is objectively and morally good and so *should* be ends for us all.

2 In *M.M.* 396, Kant notes that the Law of Autonomy (used in the *Doctrine of Law* as the principle of outer freedom) is analytic but that the addition of obligatory natural ends (in the *Doctrine of Virtue*) makes more specific moral principles incorporating those ends synthetic, for the inclusion of obligatory "matter" goes beyond merely making explicit what is contained in the notion of a moral agent.

3 We already know that these ends will not be morally obligatory just because they are naturally good in the sense of being pleasurable. Because what is good in that sense is based on desires, it can only be subjectively good, a matter of individual

preference but not an adequate, reliable ground for either universal rules of conduct or objective ends. (See *Pr.R.* 21, 28.)

4 John R. Silber exemplifies this reluctance to admit those strands of thought in Kant that identify him as belonging to the natural-law tradition. See, e.g., "The Importance of the Highest Good in Kant's Ethics," 188–90. In her *Laws of Freedom,* Mary J. Gregor holds that Kant could have gotten along without introducing teleological arguments. Typically, the view is that Kant had all he needed if he had simply used natural laws as a formal model of lawfulness in the first formula and then used the second formula to judge all the cases in which he appeals to obligatory natural ends.

In "Kant's Formula of Universal Law," Christine M. Korsgaard suggests that Kant's use of natural ends to generate teleological contradictions might be replaced by showing that the problematic maxims generate a "practical contradiction"; one could not achieve one's purpose in a world in which one's maxim is made a universal law. This is the sort of contradiction Kant discusses in his political writings when he appeals to the version of the first formula that he called "the transcendental principle of the publicity of public law." (See *P.P.* 382; also Chapter 17.)

5 Kant's use of the principle of finality also reflects his conviction that our metaphysical proclivities are inevitable, and his use of that principle in moral judgment exemplifies his reintroduction of metaphysics and of belief in God in the form of what Beck calls a "practical-dogmatic metaphysics." We first "ascribe everything to Nature, and afterwards Nature herself to God" (*Ed.* 494/111). In this way, Kant argues, morality leads inevitably to pure, moral religion. (See *Pr.R.* 129; *Rel.* 6/5.) So Kant is not embarrassed to say that, for purely practical purposes, Nature "represents the invisible reason (the ruler of the world) that looks after the human race by a power higher than human reason" (*Anthr.* 276).

6 Likewise, the Ideas of God, immortality, and freedom are "immanent and constitutive" for pure practical reason (*Pr.R.* 135). "Insofar as the *belief* in the transcendental object of the ideas of God and immortality are subjectively necessary for . . . belief in the practical possibility of the highest good," these Ideas have an immanent *practical* use (Allen W. Wood, *Kant's Moral Religion,* 151).

7 For Kant's philosophy of history, see Chapter 16. See also Emil L. Fackenheim, "Kant's Concept of History." On Kant's belief in God, see "The Postulates of God and of Grace" in Chapter 10, "The Postulates of God and Immortality" in Chapter 15, and Chapter 18.

8 Note that, having banished the traditional interpretation of the natural law from the foundation of ethics, Kant immediately reinstates that law, transformed however, by grounding specific obligatory natural goods in the Categorical Imperative, the law of pure practical reason as it appears to us. This is not the first time Kant has used this tactic to avoid falling into heteronomy; see Chapter 4, note 18.

For a brief discussion of transcendental deductions, see Chapter 2. Kant's argument for morally obligatory natural ends also presupposes his defense both of the use of Ideas of reason in the first *Critique* and of moral reason itself in the second *Critique.* These topics are discussed in Chapters 2, 6, 7, 8, and 16.

Kant holds that even when we can neither prove nor disprove the existence of something, we may still find it necessary to assume its existence for the sake of a theoretical explanation or for the sake of giving us either a pragmatic or a moral goal. "If it is a moral end," he states, "it is one that duty requires us to adopt as a maxim"; that is, we must "act in accordance with the Idea of such an end," however theoretically problematic it may be, "as long as its impossibility cannot be demonstrated either" (*M.M.* 354). So, for example, even if there has never been a time when there has not been war and even if abolishing war completely may be "just a pious wish," that is irrelevant to our moral obligation to work for perpetual peace, which is an Idea given by reason and which we therefore are obligated to adopt as an end and to work to *make* real. (See *M.M.* 355; *Ed.* 444/8.)

9 Moreover, without such ends, we are too likely to yield to the influence of sensuous ends grounded in our desires. (See *M.M.* 381.)

10 Yet he also defines instinct as "the inner necessitation of the appetitive power to take possession of this object even before we know we know it (like the sexual instinct) [*der Begattungstrieb*]" (*Anthr.* 265). Instincts cannot identify obligatory ends, since the latter must be consciously and freely chosen, independently of desires, and moral character cannot be based on instinctive conduct.

11 Kant may not be using the most appropriate word, then, when he calls the vices of gluttony, drunkenness, lasciviousness, and wild lawlessness "beastly," for he takes these to be perversions of what natural instincts alone (which beasts typically have) would promote – self-preservation and preservation of the species. (See *Rel.* 26–27/22.)

12 For the Stoic roots of the negative principle, see Klaus Reich, "Kant and Greek Ethics (II)," 456–57.

13 Kant's inclusion of procreation here is problematic. It is not clear why the preservation of the race should be classed, along with self-preservation and self-development, as an end that pure practical reason identifies as morally obligatory for each *individual*. In fact, nowhere does Kant actually make this claim, even though he always includes the preservation of the race as an end of our "animality." But if we individually have no positive duty to procreate (and it seems clear that Kant thought he personally had no such obligation), does it then make sense for him to argue that we each have *negative* duties concerning our individual sexual conduct? Why is this not, like the duty to contribute to the highest good of the species, "a duty which is *sui generis,* not of men toward men, but of the human race toward itself"? (*Rel.* 97/89; see also Chapter 15).

14 "Perfection" for rational-physical beings like us, Kant writes, is qualitative or formal rather than quantitative perfection. (See *M.M.* 386–87, 424, 444; *Gr.* 55–57/423, 68–69/430.) We do not need to try to know literally *everything* in order to fulfill our obligation of self-development.

Kant particularly stresses the specifically social character of the drive toward self-development or culture. Arising out of our "predisposition" or "tendency" (*Anlage*) to humanity, its achievement requires "community with other men." (See *Rel.* 26–27/21–22.)

15 Duties only legislate what we find onerous and what we therefore may be reluctant to do. However, Kant does hold that we may have an *indirect* duty to tend to our own happiness when the "press of cares" and "unsatisfied wants" tempt us to neglect our duties, but at such times "the end is not the agent's happiness but his morality" (*Gr.* 11–12/399 and *M.M.* 388). Moreover, this is only an occasional duty, not a continuing duty to obey a maxim to cultivate and promote natural perfection, a maxim we apparently can never fulfill to the extent that we may say we no longer need to be concerned about it.

16 Many of Kant's readers find his treatment of suicide unsatisfactory. If, for example, a person can foresee that, under torture or due to dementing illness (such as Alzheimer's disease), he or she eventually will lose all rationality and behave in ways seriously incompatible with self-respect, the historical continuity of the self would

seem to entail *some* present responsibility for either allowing or preventing such a state to occur, even if it is something that will happen *to* a person rather than the effect of the exercise of his or her own agency. Kant himself held that we may not deliberately choose to destroy our present moral personality; but he apparently thought us morally obligated passively to allow other forces to do so.

As we shall see in the next chapter, Kant's arguments against suicide and the neglect of one's talents still appeal to teleological considerations, but in the form of persons as morally obligatory ends.

17 In terms of the second formula, a maxim completely to ignore or to be indifferent to the obligatory natural end of self-development would mean denying one's dignity by using oneself merely as a means to pleasure; in terms of the third formula, such a maxim would mean neglecting our duty to strive for our final good. (See *Gr.* 55/423; *M.M.* 425.)

18 When he appeals to the second formula, Kant uses a different argument against "self-abuse": Just as we may not use others *merely* as a means to our own sexual pleasure, so also we may not use our own bodies *merely* for that purpose. Doing so, Kant maintains, violates the dignity of "humanity in one's own person" and makes a person "loathsome." (See *M.M.* 424–25.) In his lectures on moral education Kant is untrue to his own moral theory, by listing all the supposed consequences of masturbation, such as a weakened intellect and premature old age. (See *Ed.* 497/117.) Whenever Kant discusses what he regards as perverse sexual practices, he becomes uncharacteristically and spectacularly emotional. He sounds much more like a Pietistic preacher than a moral philosopher. In such passages, his emotional tone does not conceal the superficiality of his views. For Kant's most detailed discussion of sex, see *Lect.* 384–92/162–71.

19 Kant tolerates intercourse within marriage but "without regard for its end" when the wife is pregnant or sterile, because of the "legal contract in which the two reciprocally obligated each other," thus allowing the "animal inclinations a playroom" (*M.M.* 425, 426).

Kant certainly had a low opinion of sexual intercourse even within marriage, which he describes as "permissible (but in itself, admittedly, merely animal) physical union of the two sexes" (*M.M.* 425). It is hard to avoid concluding that he would have preferred that Nature had provided some alternative method of procreation. Throughout his various discussions of sex, Kant simply assumes that all erotic behavior, even within marriage, means using a person, either oneself or another, *merely* or *only* as a thing. (See, e.g., *M.M.* 276.) As we shall see in the next chapter, Kant does not object to our using persons for our own purposes as long as we do not *merely* do so. It is morally permissible, for example, to hire a person to do work, as long as one also respects that person as a person. It is unclear why Kant did not argue in a similar fashion when considering sexual activity. Instead, he takes the crass attitude that any time a man is sexually attracted to a woman, the fact that "she is a human being is of no concern" to him (*Lect.* 384–85/163–64). In view of this, Kant's defense of marriage as "a union of wills" concerning a reciprocal "use of each other's sexual organs" seems unconvincing. (See *Lect.* 388/167; *M.M.* 278.) It should still be immoral for marriage partners to allow themselves to be treated merely as erotic objects. (See *Lect.* 387/167.)

It may be mean-spirited to recall that Kant remained a lifelong bachelor, but he clearly will never be remembered as a great romantic. Perhaps he was revealing something of himself when he wrote: "It is by marriage that woman becomes free; man loses his freedom by it" (*Anthr.* 309).

20 Of course, variations of "natural law" ethics predate Christianity. For example, in his *De officiis* Cicero wrote that Nature has implanted in "all living creatures" the "fundamental instinct" to preserve themselves, their lives, and their physical well-being. See Klaus Reich, "Kant and Greek Ethics (II)," 450–51.

21 The risks are even greater when we use the second formula with its emotion-laden notion of dignity.

22 The notion of culture is an integral part of Kant's philosophy of history as well as his political philosophy. See Chapters 16 and 17. Also *Cr.J.* 431; Emil L. Fackenheim, "Kant's Concept of History," 389.

23 On that ultimate end, see Chapter 15. For a discussion of Kant on moral education, see Appendix 2.

24 See Chapters 9 and 18 for Kant's doctrine of the innate human propensity to evil, and Chapter 15 for his discussion of the vices of culture and of the consequent need for an ethical community.

14. The Formula of Respect for the Dignity of Persons

1 Following the influential lead of H. J. Paton, most writers call this version the Formula of an End in Itself. I cannot imagine an uglier title, especially for an idea of such great strength. The fact that Kant himself occasionally writes inelegantly is hardly justification for us to imitate him on that score. The following are all variations of the second formula. Many of them in the *Groundwork* occur within Kant's discussion of the third formula, which, as we will see, concerns the "kingdom of ends."

"Act in such a way that you always treat humanity, whether in your own person or in the person of any other, never simply as a means, but always at the same time as an end" (*Gr.* 66–67/429).

Each rational being "should treat himself and all others, *never merely as a means, but always at the same time as an end in himself*" (*Gr.* 74–75/433).

"A rational being, as by his very nature an end and consequently an end in himself, must serve for every maxim as a condition limiting all merely relative and arbitrary ends" (*Gr.* 80/436).

"So act in relation to every rational being (both to yourself and to others) that he may at the same time count in your maxim as an end in himself" (*Gr.* 82/437).

"A subject of ends, namely, a rational being himself, must be made the ground for all maxims of action, never merely as a means, but as a supreme condition restricting the use of every means – that is, always also as an end" (*Gr.* 83/438).

"Do not make yourself into a mere means for others, but be at the same time an end for them" (*M.M.* 236).

"Act according to a maxim of *ends* which it can be a universal law for everyone to have" (*M.M.* 395).

"Man is obligated to regard himself, as well as every other man, as his end" (*M.M.* 410).

"Man cannot be used merely as a means by any man (either by others or even by himself) but must always be treated at the same time as an end" (*M.M.* 462).

2 Kant introduces this doctrine in the *Groundwork* before he has presented his defense of morality in that book, so he postulates it there only as an unsupported assertion. (See *Gr.* 66n/429n.) But he also sets out this doctrine so that it can serve as an introduction to that defense, which rests on our self-awareness as moral agents. Pepita Haezrahi thinks that defense is inadequate in "The Concept of Man as End-

in-Himself," whereas Hardy E. Jones defends Kant against her objections in *Kant's Principle of Personality*, 22–26.

3 Kant certainly would not object to the fact that many people are most immediately attracted to the second formula; that was exactly why he offered it. This attraction also has its dangers, however, for it opens the possibility that if we take either the notion of persons or our feeling of respect for persons to be basic, we will fall into sentimentality. Kant regards it as a moral weakness (*Schwäche*) to be motivated merely by an emotion, even by sympathy for another's plight (see *Anthr.* 236); for then, in the name of "respect for persons," we would try to judge the moral acceptability of actions by how well we *feel* they promote that end. As we have repeatedly seen, making feelings of whatever kind or ends of any kind (even objective ends) into the ultimate basis for moral judgment renders our judgments merely prudential and heteronomous. (See, e.g., *Pr.R.* 38, 44–45, 83–85, 109–110; also "Moral Sentiments" in Chapter 10.)

This error could be supported by misunderstanding Kant's claim in *Gr.* 64/428 that persons are "the ground of a possible categorical imperative" as saying that the Categorical Imperative itself can be *based* on the objective value of persons. On this reading, the second formula also would be more fundamental than the first. Only some paragraphs later does Kant explain what he meant: If there were no persons, no rational beings for whom the principle of autonomy held, there would be no such principle, no morality, and then "the existence of such a world would have no worth whatever" (*Cr.J.* 449; see 442–43, 448–49; *Gr.* 65–66/428). In *that* sense, "the basis of moral law is to be found in the subject," that is, "a subject capable of an autonomous will"; see Michael J. Sandel, *Liberalism and the Limits of Justice,* 6. Persons are "objective ends," that is, morally necessary ends for everyone, but they are also the "subjective ground" of morality in the sense that they are the self-legislating subjects in whom the moral law resides. (See *Gr.* 70/431.) (For Kant's use of "subjective" in two very different senses, see Chapter 10, note 2.) On "humanity" as the ground of the second formula, see also Christine M. Korsgaard, "Kant's Formula of Humanity"; and Thomas E. Hill, Jr., "Humanity as an End in Itself."

As we saw in Chapters 5, 6, 9, 10, and 11, the ontological and epistemological foundation of morality is always and only the Law of Autonomy, appearing to us as a categorical imperative. "The ground for every enactment of practical law lies *objectively in the rule* and in the form of universality (according to our first principle)," and it is only that rule that identifies which ends are morally obligatory and so provides the ultimate ground for holding in the second formula that persons are such ends (*Gr.* 70/431; see also *Pr.R.* 16). That is why the principle that "rational nature exists as an end in itself" can only be a restatement of the first formula (*Gr.* 66–67/428–29). For a somewhat different interpretation, see Leslie A. Mulholland, "Value and Ontology in Kant's Concept of the End in Itself."

4 In an old movie, *The Train,* starring Burt Lancaster, French Resistance fighters decide they must prevent the Nazis from taking the art treasures of the Louvre away to almost certain destruction. They succeed, but only at the cost of lives on both sides. Kant does not explicitly consider cases such as this, in which some *things* – such as art objects (which, even for Kant, may be regarded as symbols of or the embodiment of cultural and spiritual values), endangered species, or a fragile environment – have no natural substitute and for that reason are regarded as irreplaceable and beyond all price. In the *Groundwork* he does refer to some things having an "affection price" (*Affektionspreis*) and not just a "market price"

(*Marktpreis*). (See *Gr.* 77/435.) In his *Anthropology* he explains this distinction by pointing out that a pleasant temperament is valued in the former sense because "people can be desirable just for the pleasure they give rather than their utility" (*Anthr.* 292). On this, see also H. J. Paton, *The Categorical Imperative: A Study in Kant's Moral Philosophy,* 189.

5 Paton also points out that Kant borrows the distinction between "price" and "dignity" from the Stoics. (See his *Categorical Imperative,* 189; also Seneca, *Epistulae* 71, 33.) As John Rist has shown, however, no ancient philosopher thought of human beings as *all* having inherent worth simply by virtue of their ontological status as human beings. The Stoics came closer than most with their doctrine that all rational beings have a divine spark within them. Mainly the value that gives individuals dignity was regarded as something that had to be achieved and could also be irrevocably lost. (See John Rist, *Human Value: A Study in Ancient Philosophical Ethics,* 1, 30–32, 41, 46–47, 70, 112–13, 151–52.)

In the Christian tradition, of course, the dignity of each human being is based on the claim that each person has worth because he or she is loved by God – a heteronomous, if divine, basis. Kant could use the expressions "children of God" and "God's creatures" only symbolically, to indicate the universal subjection of everyone to the moral law. (See *M.M.* 473; *Rel.* 142/133.)

6 In their *Respect for Persons* (pp. 13–15), R. S. Downie and Elizabeth Telfer argue that to speak of persons as "ends" in the sense of what can be desired or brought about is to make a "category mistake."

For a listing of the various ways in which Kant uses the terms "end" and "object," see Chapter 6, note 10. Underlying his discussions of the second formula is his contention, in his philosophy of history, that according to the teleological principle, the final goal of Nature is "humanity," that is, the existence and perfection of human beings who, as rational beings, do not exist for the sake of anything further and in that sense are of intrinsic and absolute value. On this, see *Cr.J.* 371, 434–35.

7 See Stephen Toulmin, "The Tyranny of Principles," 35. See also note 21, this chapter.

8 That is what Kant had to have meant in *Gr.* 113/455 and *Cr.J.* 443 by the expression "a good will" (or "willing" – *Willen*): Man is still "subject to" and "under" moral laws even if he does not actually have good character (*Cr.J.* 448n).

9 See Thomas E. Hill, Jr., "Servility and Self-Respect" and his later "Self-Respect Reconsidered."

10 Whether or not we agree with Kant here, it is clear that we simply cannot have a moral theory for human beings unless we take *some* view or other of what it is to be a moral, human being and, also, what perfection can mean for beings imperfect by nature, that is, what it is to be a reasonably well-developed human being.

11 See Chapter 13, note 17. We should not interpret Kant's second formula to mean that it is *always* immoral to risk human life, for we may have to do so in order to act according to duty; on this, see *Gr.* 77/434–35; *M.M.* 483. Even if Kant had not held that a person survives his death, he could not have distinguished between prudence and morality (or virtue), had he considered human life or any other natural goods (health, talents, etc.) to be of absolute, intrinsic value. (See *Lect.* 373/152.) He explicitly defended capital punishment. (See *M.M.* 331–37.) And as much as he hated war, he still offered rules for conducting warfare when it cannot be avoided. (See *M.M.* 343–50.)

12 This indirect obligation to promote our *happiness* should not be confused with our direct obligation to promote our natural *perfection*. Moreover, Kant's remarks here need to be read within the context of his doctrine on mixed motivation; on that topic, see Chapter 9.

13 Opposed to our strict obligation to respect others are both attitudes and actions such as envy, ingratitude, malice, pride, vengefulness, giving scandal, calumny, slander, ridicule, contempt, and arrogance that "demands from others a respect which it denies them" (*M.M.* 465; see also 458–61, 464–68, 474; *Lect.* 435–44/ 214–23). Such attitudes and behaviors not only violate the rights of others but also may make it more difficult for them to maintain their own rightful self-respect.

14 See, for example, Sir David Ross, *Kant's Ethical Theory*, 44–45. Kant's footnote in *Gr.* 68/430 helps clarify how "treating another only as a means" is equivalent to pursuing an end another person "does not share" and to which that person "cannot possibly [morally] agree." Since people can want, adopt, pursue, and share immoral ends, those ends with which we should identify are only those that others may adopt as autonomous or fully rational agents. Elsewhere he describes those ends as "possible by a law which could arise from the will of the passive subject itself," that is, by the legislation of that person's own pure practical reason (*Pr.R.* 87). For further discussion of this point, see Hardy E. Jones, *Kant's Principle of Personality*, 32–67.

15 Allen W. Wood, *Kant's Moral Religion*, 75–76. See also Appendix 2 for Kant's doctrine concerning the importance of moral education.

In his *Religion* Kant came to hold that people either help or impede each other's pursuit of virtue. He concluded that the only solution to the universal proclivity to evil is through a moral community in which people deliberately join together to promote a public moral climate. Such a community is constituted by concern for the moral welfare of others. But, as Mary J. Gregor points out, even this concern should not be so intrusive as to violate respect for others; see her *Laws of Freedom*, 186. On the topic of an ethical community, see Sharon Anderson-Gold, "Kant's Ethical Commonwealth: The Highest Good as a Social Goal."

16 Note the historical antecedent of moral love in Christian *agape*. Kant contends that, strictly speaking, even the term "moral love" is inappropriate, for duty always implies constraint, which is incompatible with acting from desires. (See *M.M.* 401.) By contrast, being "a friend of man" means recognizing the equality of all human beings and acknowledging one's obligation to be both benevolent and beneficent to them, "as if all men are brothers under one universal father who wills the happiness of all" (*M.M.* 472–73).

Moral love, Kant writes, must not be confused with two other kinds of love. Sexual passion seeks carnal pleasure 'from the use of another person," and love in this sense "really has nothing in common with moral love, though it can enter into close union with it under the limiting conditions of practical reason" (*M.M.* 426). Simple affection is a feeling of pleasure at the very thought of another person, but a feeling that stops short of carnal enjoyment. This is not morally significant either, Kant writes. For one thing, it is merely a pathological feeling, and such feelings are in themselves not morally valuable. Moreover, it is "logically impossible" to have a duty to have or not have such feelings, for we cannot generate or get rid of feelings just by willing to do so or just because we think we have a duty to do so. (See *M.M.* 401–2.) Emotions such as affection cannot be forced, and the very notion of dutifulness implies self-constraint according to the requirements of the moral law. (See *M.M.* 401.) So even though we often do learn to feel affection for those we help, we do not have a duty to have such affections. (See *M.M.* 402.)

In his pre-Critical *Lectures on Ethics* Kant offers a long and touching discussion of friendship, one that seems deeply indebted to Aristotle's discussions in the *Nicomachean Ethics*. Like Aristotle, Kant divides friendships into those based on utility, pleasure, and character. By the time he composed his Critical moral writings, however, he apparently had decided he did not need to devote a great deal of special attention to the topic of friendship. His brief portrayal of friendship in the *Metaphysics of Morals* treats it simply as a microcosm of human moral life. (See *M.M.* 469–71.) He defines friendship as "the union of two persons through equal and mutual love and respect" (*M.M.* 469). Because it spans our emotional and moral interests, friendship paradigmatically embodies the tension between those interests. Emotional love, he writes, tends to draw people closer together, thereby threatening their respect for one another, while moral respect limits intimacy by requiring us not to become "too familiar" with one another and by occasionally demanding actions, such as the duty of regretfully "pointing out the other's faults to him," which, however respectfully done, may still endanger affection (*M.M.* 470; see 449, 463; but see also *Lect.* 452/232). Kant goes so far here as to claim that the ultimate basis of friendship should lie with *duty,* in moral benevolence rather than in feelings of affection or considerations of mutual advantage. To have moral worth, what we do for our friends must be done because it is our duty, not because we care for them. (See *M.M.* 393.) (So Kant rejects his earlier view that "love from inclination is also a moral virtue"; *Lect.* 417/190.) Even if such a friendship does not make us completely happy in this world, Kant concludes, it still makes us worthy of being happy. (See *M.M.* 449, 469.)

17 Thomas Auxter argues that even this restriction may be indefensible; see his *Kant's Moral Teleology,* 120–24; also Lewis White Beck, *A Commentary on Kant's Critique of Practical Reason,* 245; also Thomas E. Hill, Jr., "Kant's Anti-moralistic Strain."

18 Whatever help we give to others, however, we may not violate the respect due them. Although helping others does obligate them to gratitude, any help we give them should be given in such a way, for example, privately, as to allow them to keep their self-respect. (See *M.M.* 448, 450, 453–54.) Moreover, as his political liberalism also indicates, Kant believed that helping others should not undermine their ability or deny their obligation to be self-determining.

19 See "Narrow and Wide Duties" in Chapter 5. People today often regard duties of benevolence as the ground for "rights." Claims about "rights" most frequently occur in reference to social and medical services provided citizens by the state, especially when those services have already been supported by public funds. We will discuss Kant's views on rights when we discuss his political theory in Chapter 17.

20 For further discussion, see Thomas E. Hill, Jr., "Kant's Utopianism," 921–22; and Barbara Herman, "Mutual Aid and Respect for Persons," 590–602.

21 Within the Kantian system none of these provides a *moral* ground for special obligations. Kant always insists that "merely pathological" emotions such as affection may not be taken as the *basis* of *moral* discrimination, that love between persons is always merely an "animal" attraction, and that insofar as we perform morally legal acts for the benefit of those we love *because* of our affection for them, our actions have *no* moral worth. For one argument contending that Kant and those who follow him in this matter are fundamentally mistaken, see my "The Kantian Model of Moral-Practical Reason." For other authors who share that view, see the

references at the end of that article. For a defense of Kant's views, see Barbara Herman, "Integrity and Impartiality" and "Rules, Motives, and Helpful Actions."

Our circumstances today are so different from Kant's – what we now do can have effects on a global scale, the definitions of "heroic" and "extraordinary" measures have become unglued, and so on – that appeals to "nearness" are far more indeterminate and less useful than they must have seemed to Kant.

22 On this problem, see also note 3, this chapter.

23 For an incisive discussion of this issue, see Edmund L. Pincoffs, "Membership Decisions and the Limits of Moral Obligation," especially 38–48.

24 See the dialogue between Alexander Broadie and Elizabeth Pybus on the one hand and Tom Regan on the other in *Philosophy* 49, 51, and 53.

25 In one passage (*M.M.* 336–37) Kant questions the state's political right to invoke capital punishment against a mother who murders an illegitimate child to preserve her honor, since the child "crept surreptitiously into the commonwealth (much like prohibited wares)" and laws forcing the mother to acknowledge the child would have the effect of disgracing her. Kant thinks there is a parallel between this and the example of a military officer who kills another in a duel to preserve his honor. In both cases Kant seems to be considering only the political implications of honor. But his contentions, which certainly sound morally odd today, also raise interesting questions about the relation between a priori demands of morality and the historical recognition of those demands within historical cultural beliefs.

15. The Formula of Legislation for a Moral Community

1 Because he did not intend his readers to use this formula as the moral norm in choosing maxims, Kant offered only three other variations of the third formula:

"The supreme limiting condition of all subjective ends [is] the Idea of the will of every rational being as a will which makes universal law" (*Gr.* 70/431).

"Every rational being must so act as if he were through his maxims always a lawmaking member in the universal kingdom of ends" (*Gr.* 83/438).

"Act on the maxims of a member who makes universal laws for a merely possible kingdom of ends" (*Gr.* 84/439).

Under the third formula H. J. Paton includes some variations that I regard as restatements of either the first or the second formula. On this, see Chapter 12, note 2.

2 On the duty of the human species to itself, see Sharon Anderson-Gold, "Ethical Community and the Highest Good." For various ways in which Kant identifies the object or end of pure practical reason, see Chapter 6, note 10.

3 One of the finest discussions of Kant's doctrine of the final highest good can be found in Yirmiahu Yovel's *Kant and the Philosophy of History*, 29–121. On the basis particularly of Sections 87 and 88 of the third *Critique*, Yovel argues that Kant came to hold that the highest good is to be realized in the future but in this world. The task of the human race is to realize *in history* a synthesis of the worlds of freedom and nature. I have decided still to portray Kant as positing the final form of the kingdom of ends in a life after death, because this is the position he seems to take in all his other writings. Moreover, placing the realization of the final kingdom of God in this world seems to undercut at least one of Kant's arguments for the postulate of immortality, a postulate he nowhere indicates he is willing to give up. In other respects the two views are similar. Both require the postulate of divine intervention to make the final moral community possible, to

overcome evil and make holiness attainable, and to accomplish the systematic integration of the moral and the sensible worlds. Both also locate the highest good in an equally remote "future life," and both require us to use that good as a regulative Idea.

4 Kant holds that "even according to duty" we may tend first to our own happiness, so he apparently also believes that we are morally permitted to engage in competitive activities in which our own success would necessarily detract from the happiness of others. In competitive situations (situations in which natural goods are in short supply), we are still not obligated to *feel* empathically toward rivals, but we also may not ignore the claims of justice (first formula) or of respect for persons (second formula). Justice is then usually defined explicitly or tacitly by "the rules of the game," which ban conduct considered to be unfair treatment of any of the competitors. In his political theory Kant makes it clear that fairness should not be equated with equality of results.

5 In order to retain in the second *Critique* the same organization he had used in the first *Critique,* Kant claims that these questions arise from "the self-contradictions of pure practical reason" (*Pr.R.* 89), and he addresses them under the title "Dialectic of Pure Practical Reason" (*Pr.R.* 106). But the "dialectic" here does not involve contradictions, only problems needing clarification.

6 Any dialectic here is not *within* practical reason but between moral reason and inclinations (see *Gr.* 58/424), for the rules given by moral reason and the rules given by technical reason do not contradict each other. Moral rules tell us how to act virtuously, and technical rules tell us how to get what we want. Each kind of rule addresses a different kind of interest, and each remains correct by its *own* criterion even when each recommends a course of action incompatible with the other. So when there is opposition, it is between the two *interests* of practical reason, one grounded in reason alone and the other in desires.

7 See Chapters 7 and 9. In *Gr.* 7/396 and *Cr.J.* 435 Kant calls the good will "the highest good" (*das höchste Gut*) in the sense of the supreme good. In *Pr.R.* 110, he prefers to reserve the title "the highest good" for the complete final human good.

Morally good character is not good in every possible respect. When morality requires us to renounce a particular pleasure, virtue can be considered prudentially bad, that is, undesirable from the viewpoint and by the criterion of our natural welfare. But this is a judgment that the primacy of morality requires us to ignore; virtue or a good will must still be considered the supreme and incomparable human good.

8 Such statements, taken in isolation from other things Kant says, have frequently given rise to claims that he has no concern for needs or feelings. Actually, in Kant's theory, human needs, feelings, and well-being are connected with morality in various important ways: Because of the presence of desires, the moral law necessarily appears to us as an imperative, as our duty, rather than simply a practical principle; prudential maxims provide the empirical material of morality; moral emotions are necessary for agents like us so that we will act dutifully; the promotion of the happiness of others is a moral duty; the moral law recognizes that we necessarily seek our own happiness and does not require us to renounce that quest; and happiness is an essential part of the highest human good in which it is joined necessarily to virtue.

9 The naturally good is sometimes called morally good when it is morally permissible. For discussions of the morally permissible, see Chapters 5 and 10.

10 The lack of virtue makes a person unworthy of happiness. (See *M.M.* 481; *T&P* 283.) And doing evil makes a person deserving of the withdrawal of happiness (punishment) in exact and just proportion to that evil. (See *Pr.R.* 37–38.) For our practical purposes, Kant writes, it may seem salutary to embrace the view "in which *some* are chosen for blessedness, but all others are condemned to eternal damnation" (*End* 329; see 330; also *Pr.R.* 128; *Rel.* 69/63, 161/149). But we do not know what such a future world might be like, and we cannot judge our own moral worth with any certainty, much less that of others (*End* 329–30). Moreover, were we to be motivated to perform morally legal actions out of fear of or hope of eternal consequences, that would destroy all moral merit (*End* 338–39).

11 Within the context of Kant's theory, there may still seem to be something anomalous about his counting happiness (in his sense) as an intrinsically if only conditionally good end. Even when the pursuit of happiness is not contrary to morality, happiness remains, on Kant's own account, radically distinct from and inferior to virtue. Can pleasure ever be morally permissible when pursuing it for its own sake always means choosing a radically inferior good in preference to doing some always available wide duty? Similar considerations have led Leslie Mulholland to argue that, since Kant allows that a person can be both virtuous and still have unsavory desires, that person should not hope for happiness achievable only at the cost of virtue. See his "A Paradox in Kant's Concept of Virtue." It also might be argued that Kant would have been more consistent had he included prudential considerations only insofar as they are at least indirectly part of our moral duty, and left it up to God "to bring it about that each receives whatever [happiness] his actions are worth" (*Rel.* 139/91).

Such questions originate in the separation Kant makes between reason and desire, on the one hand, and virtue and happiness, on the other, and his consequent rejection of the Aristotelian view that some desires can be so integral a part of human *moral* personality that the morally best person is the one who has broken down the separation between virtue and pleasure and has achieved an integrity between what is morally good and what is pleasurable.

12 Understanding this relatively obvious point, Kant believes, represents a tremendous advance in clarity. He claims that the Greek philosophers all committed the error of treating morality and happiness as analytically identical notions, because they all confused the difference between happiness and moral contentment. They then differed among themselves only on how to express the fundamental principle for attaining that single goal. (See *Pr.R.* 111–13, 115, 126–27, 141.)

The Epicureans, Kant explains, held that "to be conscious of one's maxims as leading to happiness is virtue" (*Pr.R.* 111). For them, happiness is the single ultimate good for human beings. But happiness, at least as Epicurus understood it, consists, not in sensuously based pleasure but in the moral feeling of contentment following on the awareness of virtue and of control over the inclinations. (See *Pr.R.* 115; *Lect.* 148/7.) However attractive this view may seem, it bases both the rule and the incentive of morality on a feeling (albeit a moral feeling) and so turns the ultimate moral rule into a rational but prudential rule, recommending self-control and moderation as the best means to obtain a certain kind of feeling. Trying to base virtue on the feeling of moral contentment, Kant argues, is also counterproductive, for it in effect makes the achievement of genuine moral contentment impossible. (See *Pr.R.* 24, 111–12, 115–16, 126.)

Epicurus also erred, Kant writes, by presuming, in effect, that those whom he wished to attract to virtue were already virtuous, for his appeal could be meaningful only to those who had already felt moral contentment. (See, e.g., *Pr.R.* 38, 116.) That Epicurus and more modern philosophers could make this kind of mistake, Kant argues, shows that "even the most experienced person cannot entirely avoid . . . an optical illusion in the self-consciousness of what one does [act dutifully] in contradistinction to what one feels" passively for having done so (*Pr.R.* 116–17). On the notion of an "illusion," here "an illusion of the inner sense," see *Pu.R.* A396; also Chapter 10, note 6.

The Stoics, on the other hand, who, more than any other philosophical school, were the spiritual ancestors of Kant's moral theory, erred, Kant believes, by holding that, whatever the external conditions of one's life, "to be conscious of one's virtue is happiness" or *eudaimonia* (*Pr.R.* 111; see also 111–12, 126–27, 141; *Lect.* 248/7). Kant admires the Stoics for insisting (correctly) that virtue (which they called "true wisdom") is the ultimate human goal and for holding that the principle of morality both is the condition of the highest good and is based on reason, independent of all merely prudential grounds. (See *Pr.R.* 111–12, 126–27, 127n; *Rel.* 57n/50.)

But by confusing moral contentment with happiness, Kant contends, they, like Epicurus, also dropped our ordinary notion of happiness out of their system and replaced it with a notion of a completely internal happiness. (See *Pr.R.* 88, 126–27; also Chapter 10, this volume.) They also erred in two other respects. First, they did not appreciate that the pursuit of virtue does not begin from a morally neutral state but with a will already disposed to act from a morally perverse maxim. Consequently, they mistakenly regarded human beings as needing only to tame their inclinations in order to achieve virtue. (See *Rel.* 57, 57n/50.) Second, they exaggerated human self-sufficiency, that is, the power of the moral willing of the sage to achieve happiness. (See *Pr.R.* 126–27.) As we have seen, moral possibility and physical possibility are radically different from each other, and being virtuous does not inevitably produce happiness. Such a causal relation is not absolutely impossible, but, given the world we know, it can only be contingently the case. The Stoics would have been correct, Kant believes, had they distinguished between moral action and physical action and regarded the former as limiting the exercise of the latter. (See *Pr.R.* 114–15.)

Strangely enough, in his survey of the Greek schools of thought, Kant lists the Cynics, Epicureans, and Stoics, but does not place either Plato or Aristotle in any of his categories of ethicists. He notes merely that they differed between themselves "only as to the origin of our moral concepts" (*Pr.R.* 127n). Apparently he thought of Plato as relying on reason alone and Aristotle on reflective experience.

13 Kant used this same argument to insist on a necessary unity of theoretical and practical thinking; see Chapter 8.

14 Kant apparently believed that Christian Garve had fallen into this error, and he argues against him in *T&P* 278–89. See also Thomas Auxter, "The Unimportance of Kant's Highest Good," and Lewis White Beck, *A Commentary on Kant's Critique of Practical Reason*, 244–45.

15 Kant held that the claim of orthodox Christianity – that the final end of human beings both in this world and in the next is personal communion with God – is but another form of fanaticism. (See *Lect.* 98–103/323–27.) Direct knowledge of (rather than just faith in) God after death would destroy our freedom and with it morality. (See *Pr.R.* 147–48.) In *The End of All Things,* Kant discusses the speculative notion of human life after death, a notion "found in one guise or another among all reasoning peoples in all times" (*End* 327). Although pure practical reason

may, for its own purposes, *try* to offer some insights about eternal life, we tend only to generate puzzles and contradictions when we make this effort. (See *End* 327–28; see also *Pr.R.* 128–33; *Rel.* 161/148.)

Since the idea of eternal life is not empirically derived but an Idea of reason, it must refer to a supersensible or noumenal duration, about which theoretical reason may say nothing without falling into contradictions (*End* 327, 332–34). If we try to make sense of the notion of eternity, even if only for our moral purposes, we find we can only think of eternity as duration without time and so without progress as we know it in our experience, and that seems like a "thoughtlessness" equivalent to annihilation. Life after death apparently must allow an "unending progression" in a dutiful disposition, yet a progression that "remains permanently the same" (*End* 334).

Sometimes Kant thinks of life after death as purely noumenal, with happiness but without desires. (See *Pu.R.* A809/B837.) But other times he apparently thinks of it as being in many ways just like our existence now. (See *Pr.R.* 114–15.) For it would seem that such an existence would have to be an intelligible world and a phenomenal, temporal, sensuous world in order to permit the continuing resolution of moral conflict, which, for us, must underlie "an infinite progression to the ultimate purpose," and to allow for the possibility of both happiness and moral contentment. (See, e.g., *Pu.R.* A809–11/B837–39, A814/B842; *Pr.R.* 61, 115; *Rel.* 67–68/60–62.)

Because we cannot arrive at any clear insights, Kant wisely concludes we had best "leave to Providence the outcome of the means selected toward the best ultimate purpose . . . if we do not prefer to relinquish our ultimate purpose altogether" (*End* 336–37; see also 335; *Pu.R.* B421; *Pr.R.* 145; *Rel.* 161/148). "For practical [i.e., moral] purposes, we can be quite indifferent as to whether we shall live as pure spirits after death or whether our personal identity in the next world requires the same matter that now forms our body" (*Conflict* 40/69).

16 For the need of divine assistance (or "grace") to augment our effort to obey the command of moral reason to be perfect, see also Chapters 10 and 18. The help of God is also necessary to "manage" how the *ethical* state of nature can be overcome so people will work together in a universal ethical community to achieve the total final end of the species, although, again, it is not clear how God could give such assistance without destroying human freedom. (See *Rel.* 139/130.)

17 Because these claims go beyond the sheer analysis of concepts and state that the necessary conditions for obedience to the moral law actually do exist, Kant holds that they are synthetic a priori propositions. (See *Rel.* 6n/5–6.)

18 But we also must be careful, Kant warns, not to claim that we can *actually* describe God's attributes by using psychological concepts that can be learned only empirically. (See, e.g., *Pu.R.* A600–602/B628–30.) Given the limitations of our reason, we are forced to talk about God's relationship to his creation in terms of a "symbolic anthropomorphism." But it is morally dangerous to try to reason analogically to a natural theology concerning that which lies forever outside our experience; any claims to *know* God in that manner are illusory. (See *Pu.R.* A697/B725, A700/B728; *Proleg.* 356–57; *Orient.* 138–40; *Pr.R.* 137–39; *Cr.J.* 353, 456–58; *Rel.* 64n/59, 168–69/156–57, 182–83/170–71.) As we shall see in Chapter 18, thinking of God in anthropomorphic terms too easily leads to our thinking of God as a heavenly version of an earthly tyrant, to be placated in various ritualistic ways.

Norman Kemp Smith believes that Kant, toward the end of his life, considered – how seriously is a matter of dispute – the possibility that our practical reason in the sense of *Wille* and its law, the Categorical Imperative, might be a kind of direct inner revelation of God. (See Kemp Smith's *Commentary to Kant's 'Critique of Pure Reason,'* 636–41; also *Cr.J.* 445–46, 479. See also Keith Ward, *The Development of Kant's View of Ethics,* 160–66.)

Allen W. Wood has provided a pair of companion volumes that address the topic of Kant's theodicy. The first is a translation (with Gertrude M. Clark) of Kant's *Lectures on Philosophical Theology;* the second, *Kant's Rational Theology,* is a commentary on those lectures. The latter supersedes an earlier (1929) study by F. E. England, *Kant's Conception of God.* See also Kant's pre-Critical essay (published first in 1762, with editions in 1770 and 1794), *The One Possible Basis for a Demonstration of the Existence of God,* trans. Gordon Treash (KGS II, 63–163).

19 The only discussion of which I am aware of Kant's calling himself a "theist" is Allen W. Wood's "Kant's Deism."

20 See, e.g., Beck, *Commentary,* 242–44; G. J. Warnock, "The Primacy of Practical Reason," 261. Also Yirmiahu Yovel, *Kant and the Philosophy of History,* 115–21, 125–26, and Thomas Auxter, *Kant's Moral Teleology,* 81–101. Also Chapter 10, note 18. For a defense of Kant, see Mary-Barbara Zeldin, "The Summum Bonum, the Moral Law, and the Existence of God."

21 This Idea belongs to a metaphysics of morals; but whether we think that the Idea of the highest good for human beings consists of pure or of mixed a priori concepts depends on whether we think it makes sense to speak of a purely rational being as enjoying "bliss" without the introduction of empirically derived notions of feelings and happiness.

22 See Allen W. Wood, *Kant's Moral Religion,* 94–95.

23 "If a man lacks knowledge of God, he does not necessarily lack morality in his actions" (*Lect.* 311/86). Nor does he lack religion understood as conscientiousness. Kant believed that this was in fact the case with Spinoza, who did not believe in God or immortality, yet, as far as Kant could judge, was a "righteous" (*rechtschaffen*) person. (See *Cr.J.* 452.)

24 For criticisms of Kant's views on these matters, see W. H. Walsh, "Kant's Moral Theology"; also Ralph C. S. Walker, *Kant,* 138.

25 See Keith Ward, *The Development of Kant's View of Ethics,* 87.

16. Autonomy and the state

1 See Paul Sonnino (ed.), *Frederick of Prussia: The Refutation of Machiavelli's Prince or Anti-Machiavel,* 34.

2 Quoted by Max Lerner in his introduction to the Modern Library translation of *The Prince and the Discourses,* xli.

3 Kant's publications, after all, were subject to scrutiny and possible condemnation by the imperial censor, and his *Religion Within the Limits of Reason Alone* did in fact result in an imperial edict not to write on religion again. On this, see Chapter 18, note 7.

4 For some indications of how lightly Kant's political philosophy has been regarded, see "Liberalism" in *The Encyclopedia of Philosophy;* also Hannah Arendt, *Lectures on Kant's Political Philosophy,* 8.

5 See, for example, Ernest J. Weinrib, "Law as a Kantian Idea of Reason," and Peter Benson, "External Freedom According to Kant," and, indeed, the entire

conference on Kantian legal theory at which these papers were read. Papers from the conference have been published in the *Columbia Law Review* 87 (April 1987).

Classical liberalism has been espoused by a wide range of thinkers: in Scotland, by David Hume, Adam Smith, and other members of the Scottish Enlightenment; in England, by John Locke, Edmund Burke, and Herbert Spencer; in France, by Baron de Montesquieu, Alexis de Tocqueville, and Benjamin Constant; in Germany, by Friedrich Schiller and Wilhelm von Humboldt; and, in the United States, by James Madison, John Marshall, and Daniel Webster. It must be sharply distinguished from the "revisionist" liberalism held by Voltaire, Jeremy Bentham, James Mill, John Stuart Mill, T. H. Green, and Bernard Bosanquet. Based mainly on utilitarianism, this latter is the progenitor of state interventionist policies typical of the modern welfare state and today is often regarded as "the only sound basis" for legislation; see George P. Fletcher, "Why Kant," 422. On the difference between the two kinds of liberalism, see Friedrich A. Hayek, "The Principles of a Liberal Social Order." Also Michael J. Sandel, *Liberalism and the Limits of Justice*, especially 1–7.

6 John Gray, *Liberalism*, x. I wish to thank my colleague from the Department of Government and International Affairs, Charles B. Weasmer, for conversations about the liberal tradition.

7 See P. H. Nowell-Smith, "What Is Authority?"

8 Some contemporary authors have argued that consistency should have led Kant to be either an anarchist or a libertarian. Both ideologies claim their philosophical roots in Kant; they heavily stress the autonomy of the individual and argue that any coercive intrusion on the responsibilities of individual persons is heteronomous and immoral. See, for example, Robert Nozick, *Anarchy, State, and Utopia*. Robert Paul Wolff argues that since he is unable "to discover a form of political association which could combine moral autonomy with legitimate authority," "philosophical anarchism would seem to be the only reasonable political belief for an enlightened man" (*In Defense of Anarchism*, 19, 70). In this and the next chapter we shall see why Kant, although also considering himself an enlightened man, did not draw this conclusion but rather considered the choice of anarchy to be a reversion to the state of nature; see also *H.H.* 112–13.

9 See Gerhard Funke, "Concerning Eternal Peace – Ethics and Politics." There are a number of English translations of Kant's writings on the philosophy of history and political philosophy. One collection is *Immanuel Kant: On History*, edited by Lewis White Beck and translated by Beck, Robert E. Anchor, and Emil L. Fackenheim. That book includes *What Is Enlightenment? Idea for a Universal History from a Cosmopolitan Point of View*, reviews of Herder's *Ideas for a Philosophy of the History of Mankind*, *Conjectural Beginning of Human History*, *The End of All Things*, *Perpetual Peace*, and *An Old Question Raised Again: Is the Human Race Constantly Progressing?* Another collection, *Perpetual Peace and Other Essays*, includes most of the same material, translated by Ted Humphrey, along with *On the Proverb: That May Be True in Theory but Is of No Practical Use*. Unless otherwise identified, I have used Humphrey's translations. A third collection, *Kant's Political Writings*, contains an excellent introduction by Hans Reiss, but unfortunately the translations by H. B. Nisbet lack the standard German pagination.

The few remarks that Paton makes about Kant's doctrine of moral progress in his *Categorical Imperative: A Study in Kant's Moral Philosophy* (194–95) show how little attention typically was given to Kant's philosophy of history before Emil

Fackenheim's seminal study "Kant's Concept of History" (1956). Since then, there has been a growing appreciation of the importance of this part of Kant's philosophy and its significance to his entire philosophical system, including his moral philosophy. See, for example, Michel Despland's *Kant on History and Religion;* William A. Galston's *Kant and the Problem of History;* and Yirmiahu Yovel's *Kant and the Philosophy of History.* In his dissertation as well as in several articles Sidney Axinn has stressed the significance of Kant's radical separation of the distributive and collective senses of human beings.

10 See Allen W. Wood, *Kant's Moral Religion,* 157–60.

11 For the technical meaning of an "Idea of reason," see Chapter 2. Ideas are transcendent; that is, "no appearance can be found in which they can be represented *in concreto.* They contain a certain completeness to which no possible empirical knowledge ever attains" (*Pu.R.* A567–68/B595–96). Nonetheless, just as we represent the ideal perfect circle by approximations on drawing boards, it is possible, permissible, and sometimes necessary for our *practical* purposes to regard some Ideas as instantiated, if only imperfectly, in the empirical world. (See, e.g., *Pu.R.* A328/B385, A538–41/B566–69.) So, for example, in Chapter 7 we saw that Kant holds we may and must regard our actions in the world as manifestations of our noumenal moral character and its actions.

In Kant's philosophy of history and his political philosophy, the Idea of Nature, the teleological view of history, and the Idea of the original social compact are all normative practical Ideas of reason. For our practical purposes only, they have the function of helping us understand history and make definite other practical Ideas that are obligatory goals, that is, the kingdom of ends on earth in the form of legitimate state authority, the republican form of government, a league of nations, and perpetual peace. (See, e.g., *Idea* 27; *P.P* 360–62, 374; *Pu.R.* A316–17/B373–74; *Conflict* 85–86/153 and 155, 90–91/163 and 165; *T&P* 297; *M.M.* 313, 315, 354–55.)

12 See Chapter 18. Kant, of course, was familiar with the Christian theological philosophy of history in which each person has a role in a historical drama with a beginning (Creation and Fall), a middle (the Redemption and each person's individual participation in it), and an end (eternity with God). But in the spirit of the Enlightenment he determined he needed to write a new, purely rational yet still religious moral teleocosmos that would be compatible with and provide a context for a nontheological moral political theory. In his *Religion Within the Limits of Reason Alone* he therefore interpreted the Christian histodrama symbolically so that it would be consistent with his moral theory.

13 In most of his writings Kant seems to identify Nature and Providence, but in different ways. For example, in *M.M.* 419, Nature's aim is limited to what a person can become as a merely natural being; but a moment later Nature's aim *includes* moral perfection. This distinction is also made in the third *Critique.* On this, see Michael Despland, *Kant on History and Religion,* 73.

14 In *Perpetual Peace* Kant writes that "with advancing civilization reason grows pragmatically in its capacity to realize ideas of law. But at the same time the culpability for the transgressions also grows" (*P.P.* 380). Kant held that personal moral responsibility depends on the development of culture and the emergence of moral consciousness. He therefore may be interpreted as holding that in the beginning, when prehistorical humanity had not yet freed itself from "bondage to instinct," there apparently was no blame for moral immaturity. For Kant's rational version of the story of the Garden of Eden and of the Fall, see *H.H.* 110–15.

15 See also Chapters 6 and 13.

16 Michael Despland points out that Kant's use of the expression "stepmotherly nature" in *Gr.* 3/394 was borrowed from Leibniz and ultimately from Pliny to describe a parent who deliberately denies her children the warmth of her love in order to impel them out of the maternal nest so they will begin to assume responsibility for their own lives. See Despland, *Kant on History and Religion,* 314n66.

17 As Hans Saner has argued, this same theme – that the antagonism and discord that arise from subjectivity stimulate progress toward peace and objective unity – actually constitutes the *Leitmotif* for Kant's conception of the nature of philosophy as polemical thinking. In the realm of theoretical reasoning, the antinomies and parallelogisms that pure reason generates in its illegitimate use give rise to a genuine critique of theoretical reason, showing both its legitimate use and its limits. Conflicts in the realm of practice show the subjective character of prudential reason and the need and right of pure practical reason to establish the conditions for peace in practical reasoning based on its own ultimate principle. Finally, the potential conflicts between theoretical and practical reason again must be subjected to a critique that establishes the primacy of moral-practical reason. See Saner, *Kant's Political Thought: Its Origins and Development,* especially 303, 312–13.

  Saner also points out parallels between Kant's philosophy of history and the theological Christian histodrama. In the latter, the original Fall from grace (*O felix culpa!*), while clearly a moral tragedy, unintentionally prepared for the next act in the drama – the Incarnation and Redemption; and in that sense, Kant argues, "it was a gain" (*H.H.* 115).

18 Kant may be overstating his case here, for, if the devil has a totally evil character, as Kant holds in *Rel.* 27/22, devils might enter into such a compact if it were in their individual self-interest, but they would be incapable of *keeping* their word. They would tend to be in a constant state of lawless rebellion and would all inevitably end up in permanent incarceration. (But then who would guard them – or guard the guards?)

19 James Dickey's novel *Deliverance* gives a graphic description, supporting Kant, of people continuing to live in the state of nature. Kant here clearly disagrees with Rousseau, who had extolled the prepolitical noble savage uncontaminated by society. People act lawlessly when they either choose to remain in a state of nature or in effect return to the state of nature by acting lawlessly within the state. They are not entitled to such "freedom," for freedom in the sense of autonomy requires a juridical condition within which the Law of Freedom is enforced. When people live by violence, they therefore may be dealt with legitimately by force to safeguard lawful freedom. (See *P.P.* 372.)

20 It is difficult to state this claim both correctly and clearly, because in various contexts in his political writings Kant uses the term "freedom" to mean either morally indeterminate freedom *or* heteronomous freedom *or* transcendental and moral freedom.

21 See Jeffrie G. Murphy, "Kant's Theory of Criminal Punishment." In his "Kant's Retributivism," Don E. Scheid maintains that Kant is not a thoroughgoing retributivist, as he is commonly described. In "Does Kant Have a Theory of Punishment?" Murphy reconsiders his earlier analysis (with which my brief summary generally agrees) and concludes that Kant did not provide a self-consistent, acceptable theory of punishment.

22 See Thomas E. Hill, Jr., "Kant's Anti-Moralistic Strain"; Appendix 1, note 4; also "Relating the Two Viewpoints" in Chapter 7 and "The Nature of Moral Char-

acter" in Chapter 9. For our practical purposes, Kant holds we must regard phenomenal actions as free.

23 Kant, of course, has been proved wrong here, for both the Declaration of Independence and the Virginia Constitution of 1776 insist on the right of the people
to revolt against injustice.

Kant's last major work was a collection of three essays, entitled *The Conflict of
the Faculties* (1798). In the second essay, "An Old Question Raised Again: Is the
Human Race Constantly Progressing?" Kant writes that the French Revolution is
an "intimation" of and "demonstrates" the inevitable and constant moral progress
of the human race (*Conflict* 84/151). Earlier, in his *On the Proverb: That May Be
True in Theory but Is of No Practical Use*, he also had written that "one can offer
a great deal of evidence showing that the human race as a whole has in our age,
by comparison with all earlier ones, bettered itself morally" (*T&P* 310; see *Idea*
28). It may be difficult at first to understand how Kant could take this view, given
that he did not believe any people has the moral right to revolution, and given
that he regarded the executions of the king and queen and the Reign of Terror
"with horror" (*M.M.* 321n). We now can understand how he could do so.

Since the French Revolution meant in effect that the people reverted to mobs
living in a state of nature, with universal, uncontrolled antagonisms and hostilities
between individuals and groups, it was to be expected that there would be bloodshed
and chaos, without justice or respect for rights, at least until after the Republic
was finally established. Kant would have been surprised had the period during
and immediately following the Revolution been anything else. It would take such
atrocities to convince people that it was in their best interest to submit to the power
of the new state. In the end Nature could see to it that it would be "a gain" that
would force the French to establish a state that would uphold freedom by means
of the ideals of the Revolution. Rather than being an embarrassment to Kant's
theory of history, then, for the transcendental *spectator* viewing events and the
human race as a collective whole, the French Revolution showed that moral progress
can result from immoral conduct. (See *Conflict* 85/153.)

The ultimate sign of moral progress, Kant argues, is not the historical event of
the Revolution itself (which might have resulted only in tyranny) but the fact that
moral enlightenment had progressed to the point where an attitude (*Denkungsart*)
of disinterested sympathy for those seeking justice and freedom had become so
widespread. (See *Conflict* 84–89/151–61.) Moral progress as a social goal still depends finally on the widespread adoption of the moral disposition underlying that
way of thinking. Nonetheless, Kant insists that people living under a monarchy
(as Kant was) are still not entitled to "even only cherish the secret wish of seeing
it changed," much less become active participants in doing so (*Conflict* 86n1/155n1).

For a more detailed discussion of Kant's views on revolution in general and the
French Revolution in particular, see Sidney Axinn's classic article "Kant, Authority,
and the French Revolution." Axinn dramatically contrasts the differences between
considering the French Revolution from the viewpoint of the individuals and groups
historically involved and from the viewpoint of the human species as a collective
whole. Kant's distinction between the distributive and collective senses of "mankind"
allows him also to hold that, if tyranny can be overthrown only by violence, in
Nature's plan revolutions still can contribute to the moral progress of mankind.
See also Hannah Arendt, *Lectures on Kant's Political Philosophy*, 44–59; John E.
Atwell, *Ends and Principles in Kant's Moral Theory*, 174–93; and Thomas Seebohm, "Kant's Theory of Revolution."

24 In her report of Adolf Eichmann's trial for the murder of millions of Jews, Hannah Arendt recounts that at one point in his trial Eichmann "declared with great emphasis that he had lived his whole life according to Kant's moral precepts, and especially according to a Kantian definition of duty" (*Eichmann in Jerusalem: A Report on the Banality of Evil*, 135–36). As Arendt points out, there were these verbal similarities: Eichmann believed that a law is a law and there can be no exceptions, that he had done his duty as a soldier, that he had obeyed the law of the land, and that he had obeyed his particular orders. But there was one critical difference. Eichmann had distorted the first formula into what came to be called the "categorical imperative of the Third Reich"; namely, "Act in such a way that the Führer, if he knew of your action, would approve it." In place of a person's judgment, which Arendt points out rules out blind obedience, Eichmann had substituted what he himself called the "obedience of corpses" (135–36). Under further questioning, he admitted that he had known he had ceased to live by Kantian principles "from the moment he was charged with carrying out the Final Solution."

At his trial for "supervising the murder of 'at least 400,000 persons' " the former SS commandant of the Nazi death factory at Treblinka, Franz Paul Stangl, tried to use the same defense. "I have nothing on my conscience," he said. "I did nothing but my duty" (*Time*, May 25, 1970, 41).

There is one (perhaps pre-Critical) passage in Kant's *Lectures on Ethics* that may seem to support this attitude. When discussing legal responsibility, Kant asks: "Can we hold a man responsible for something which he does on the authority of law?" And he answers: "In so far as he is not a free agent, but is coerced by the law, he is not responsible: responsibility for the action, regarded as a legal action, lies with the lawgiver" (*Lect.* 289/58). But this discussion addresses only the question of *legal* responsibility *within* a given state, and Kant adds that, insofar as the agent "acts as a free agent he is accountable" (see also *Rel.* 99n/90).

Against Eichmann, Julius Ebbinghaus argues that "the *maxim* by means of which a man makes this transference, if he subjects himself in every possible exercise of his own will to the arbitrary will of another, cannot possibly have the character of a law for *his* will, and therefore cannot possibly be a categorical imperative; for such a law would make him have no will of his own at all – and consequently he would also cease to be a person." See his "Interpretation and Misinterpretation of the Categorical Imperative," 219.

25 By contrast, the way in which Plato had appropriated the term "justice" represented an extreme reaction against any tendencies to liberalism in Greek thought; on this see John Gray, *Liberalism*, 2–4; also Karl R. Popper, *The Open Society and Its Enemies*, I, 102–3. Aristotle was certainly not a champion of egalitarianism, but he did set out four criteria for judging the moral acceptability of a state: justice, respect for the dignity of the citizens, a sense of moral community with others, and freedom. See my *Morality and the Good Life*, 131–32.

26 See Lewis White Beck, "Kant and the Right of Revolution," 173–74.

27 Arnulf Zweig, *Kant: Philosophical Correspondence 1759–99*, 54.

17. Civil justice and republicanism

1 There are a number of recent commentaries on Kant's political theory, including Jeffrie G. Murphy, *Kant: The Philosophy of Right* (1970); Hans Saner, *Kant's Political Thought: Its Origins and Development* (1973); Susan Meld Shell, *The Rights of Reason: A Study of Kant's Philosophy and Politics* (1980); Patrick Riley,

Kant's Political Philosophy (1983); and Howard Williams, *Kant's Political Philosophy* (1983).

2 Kant is not proposing a novel doctrine here. Plato and Aristotle, as well as most other political theorists before Kant, also had reluctantly concluded that, since many citizens cannot be counted on to act rightly from moral motivation, individual moral responsibility must be replaced in the public forum by externally enforced behavioral norms consistent with moral principles. On this see, e.g., my *Morality and the Good Life: A Commentary on Aristotle's Nicomachean Ethics,* 114–38, esp. 130–31.

Nature, Kant writes, has implanted in us a tendency at least to *act* politely, affectionately, and respectfully toward others. (See *Anthr.* 151; *Lect.* 456–57/236–37.) Insofar as this is only role playing, Kant writes with as much humor as he ever shows in his writing, it may be only "small change" in comparison with the "real gold" of genuine virtue. But it does at least tend to make the semblance of genuinely moral attitudes "fashionable," and the very effort by people to affect the "illusion" of virtuous character can develop into genuine benevolence, bringing conduct "as near as possible to the truth" (*M.M.* 473; see *Lect.* 445/224–25; *Anthr.* 151–53, 244). What moral virtue itself can add in one's relations with others is genuinely moral respect for others as persons, an attitude of benevolence toward them that manifests itself in civility, affability, propriety, courtesy, hospitality, and gentleness.

3 To say that someone has duties but no rights is to deny that person freedom and reduce him or her to the level of a slave. (See *M.M.* 241.) Autonomy imposes the condi ɪ that laws must be rationally acceptable to the will of the subjects. This requirement, Kant writes, applies "even to the divine will with respect to the rational beings in the world as its creatures, since the condition rests on the personality of these beings, whereby alone they are ends in themselves" (*Pr.R.* 87). Since Kant has insisted that every person has inalienable dignity just by existing, it is certainly puzzling that he also allows that, for some unspecified crimes, a person can lose that dignity and a judge may sentence him or her to be a slave (*servus in sensu stricto*) and, within limits, to be treated as a thing. (See *M.M.* 330, 333.)

4 Kant also recognizes nonpolitical rights, the "rights of humanity" (*das Recht der Menschheit*), which concern specifically ethical duties, that is, duties of virtue, and cannot be legislated by the state. (See *M.M.* 390–91.)

5 This way of using the term "action" was discussed at the end of Chapter 3 and the beginning of Chapter 9. The distinction between juridical and ethical duties has also been discussed in "Narrow and Wide Duties" in Chapter 5 and in "A System of Obligatory Ends" in Chapter 6.

6 So Kant holds that lies are to be considered political injustices only when they violate specific civil rights of others. (See *M.M.* 238, 238n.) Ethically, of course, all lies are violations of "the dignity of humanity" and are morally wrong. (See e.g., *M.M.* 429.)

7 I have not tried to include a detailed discussion of Kant's doctrine about property rights; see *M.M.* 245–308. (Ladd's translation of the *Rechtslehre* unfortunately omits much of this material.) But it should be noted that the monarchic governments with which Kant was most familiar often restricted the ownership of land to the crown, the nobility, and the established church. Kant therefore was led to conclude that Locke was right in holding what some regard as Locke's greatest contribution to liberalism: the contention that full political freedom is not possible without the

private ownership of property, protected under the laws of the state. Kant therefore considered that, like the right to freedom, the general right to acquire property must be an innate natural right. (See *M.M.* 237, 239.)

However, with Rousseau and contrary to Locke, Kant also held that property belongs originally to the united will so that the *actual* ownership of property is an acquired right. This is why the right to hold secure (noumenal) *title* to rather than simply (phenomenally) possess any specific property depends on contracts enforced by the state; positive civil law must supply the rules concerning the rightful ownership of property. For further discussions, see Howard Williams, *Kant's Political Philosophy*, 77–96, and Mary J. Gregor, *Laws of Freedom*, 49–63.

8 Kant understood the need for confidential relations both between individuals and between nations, and he allows that there may be legitimate "secrets" in politics – things "which ought not to be known publicly" (*Rel.* 138n/130). What still must conform to the Principle of Publicity is the maxim that certain kinds of transactions, e.g., diplomatic negotiations, need to be carried out in a confidential manner.

9 Although Kant himself does not make this point, the Principle of Publicity obviously may be used to apply the first formula in order to judge the moral acceptability of maxims.

10 Kant uses this norm to argue against both the right to revolution and sheer political expediency (*P.P.* 382–85).

11 Kant therefore calls crimes against individuals "private" and criminal offenses directed against the public order "public." (See *M.M.* 331.) See Ladd's introduction to his translation of *The Metaphysical Elements of Justice*, xxii. Kant also distinguishes between the public and private spheres in a related yet still somewhat curious way: "By the public use of one's own reason I understand the use that anyone as a *scholar* makes of reason before the entire *literate* world. I call the private use of reason that which a person may make of it in a *civic post* or office that has been entrusted to him" (*Enlight.* 37). He argues that the public use of reason even by ordinary citizens should never be restricted but that we have no "private" discretion in carrying out bureaucratic roles "under the direction and in the name of another" (*Enlight.* 38; see *T&P* 304). If, however, a person finds he cannot continue in a particular role in good conscience, "he would have to resign" (*Enlight.* 38; see 38–39). (See also R. S. Downie and Elizabeth Telfer, *Respect for Persons*, 65–93.)

12 Some authors, for example, Jeffrie G. Murphy, argue that, even on Kantian grounds, the state need make no laws about so-called victimless crimes, such as homosexual activities of consenting adults. While such activities may be distasteful to a significant percentage of the population, they do not attack anyone's freedom or violate what is usually called the harm principle. (See Murphy, *Kant: The Philosophy of Right*, 103–8.) Kant's views are that homosexual activity is seriously immoral and that like the lie that "harms" no one, immoral action is *always* an attack on the "rights of humanity."

During the 1984 U.S. presidential campaign, a number of candidates maintained that they personally opposed abortion but, in view of a lack of public consensus on the morality of abortion and in the name of freedom of choice, did not support enacting public laws against abortion. In response, Roman Catholic bishop John Malone issued a Kantian-like statement that "the implied dichotomy between personal morality and public policy is simply not logically tenable in any adequate view of both." Consequently, Bishop Malone concluded, it is not rational for candidates to say that "their personal views should not influence their policy decisions"

(Columbia, S.C., *State,* August 10, 1984, 5A, cols. 1–5). Without intending to weaken his previous statement, he added that "there is room for sincere disagreement . . . over how moral principles should be applied to the current facts." Kant would also have had some sympathy with the contention that civil law should reflect a moral consensus of the electorate.

In this regard it may also be noted that in cases of conflict between civil law (even if only positive civil law) and supposedly "divine statutory law," that is, ecclesiastical regulations based on a claimed revelation, Kant holds that our duty is always to obey the civil law. The latter is clearly a duty, whereas there never can be sufficient evidence for historical religious claims to accredit them as certain duties. (See, e.g., *Rel.* 99n/90–91, 153n/142.) In the case of a proposed prohibition against abortion, one crucial question concerns the ground of such a law: Is it based on the natural law or on religious statutory law?

13 *On a Supposed Right to Lie from Altruistic Motives, KSG* VIII, 429; Beck (ed.), 350.

14 We saw in Chapter 5 how Kant likens the three branches (or functions) of government to a practical syllogism. (See *M.M.* 313.) He extends this analogy to argue against vesting both the legislative and executive powers in any single person or group. (See *P.P.* 352.) Contrary to Hobbes, he also holds that the power of the ruler is not absolute; the people have "inalienable rights" that no ruler may violate (*T&P* 303).

15 See Rousseau's *Social Contract,* Book 1, Chapters 5–8, and Book 2, Chapters 1–6; also Patrick Riley, *The General Will before Rousseau: The Transformation of the Divine into the Civic.*

16 Deliberations of both the electorate and the judiciary should follow the dialectical rules for arriving at truth; see "Erroneous Moral Judgments" in Chapter 5. Public debate is the most effective way to ensure that the Principle of Publicity is respected.

17 Rousseau had discussed this problem in his *Social Contract,* Book 2, Chapter 3. As we see here, Kant's norm of the general will is an a priori Idea of reason rather than a merely empirical norm. (See *M.M.* 250.)

18 Kant also thought that a representative form of government would most effectively promote international peace, for the citizens would, even from a prudential point of view, be less willing to wage war than would be absolutist governments with little regard for the lives of their subjects. (See *H.H.* 114; *P.P.* 351, 371; *M.M.* 341, 345–46.)

A constitutional hereditary monarchy as in Britain and Canada *can* be as republican in spirit, that is, in its "manner of governing," as a government that is literally a republic (*Conflict* 88/159; see *T&P* 297, 304; *M.M.* 340–41, 351–52). But Kant in fact had his doubts (perhaps reflecting a Prussian nationalism?) about the republican spirit of the British monarchy (see *Conflict* 90/163). Although he had no sympathy for absolutist forms of government, he thought it might be possible for an unenlightened citizenry to have a better chance for freedom under a strong central government than in a democracy ruled by a tyrannical majority. In his essay *What is Enlightenment?* Kant praised enlightened monarchs like Frederick the Great, who demanded absolute obedience in conduct but still promoted education and permitted freedom of discussion (*Enlight.* 40–41).

19 See also *On a Supposed Right to Lie from Altruistic Motives* (*KSG* VIII, 429), in Beck (ed.), 349–50. Kant calls these "pure rational principles," but insofar as they include empirical information about what it is to be a *human* moral agent, they are mixed a priori principles; on this, see Chapter 2, note 9.

20 See Chapter 16, note 5.

21 We have an excellent example today of how lack of clarity, whether in moral thinking in general or about moral theories in particular or both, can generate what are often labeled "moral dilemmas." Dilemmas are problems that have only equally unsatisfactory alternative solutions. Today, however, the term is widely misused to cover a heterogeneous variety of cases, including those that are simply problematic, those in which some alternatives (e.g., the use of fetal tissue) may be aesthetically repulsive but not necessarily morally wrong, and those in which no solution is completely free of negatives but different solutions have negatives of various weights. To label a moral problem a "dilemma" from the beginning tends to beg the question at issue. There is a good deal to be said for trying to gain clarity about why a particular problem *is* a problem.

Be that as it may, confusion is often caused by the fact that people concerned with normative political issues begin with a welfare-state view ("revisionist liberalism" in the English tradition of James and John Stuart Mill), which maintains that the state is obligated to contribute positively and significantly to the happiness and welfare of the citizenry. They then appeal to a "Kantian" moral egalitarianism to argue that everyone has a strictly equal moral and legal entitlement to, for example, all the exotic and enormously expensive medical techniques available (which often have been developed with the help of federal funds). They also contend that exactly those sorts of prudential and "socially discriminatory" considerations are both inappropriate and immoral when used in public-policy decisions, which Kant held that we may and must use in our private lives in order to decide rationally how to fulfill our positive duties to others.

As we saw, Kant's theory, with its stress on the impersonality of the notion of "persons," usually cannot offer *any* substantive moral guidance for decisions about *how* to fulfill positive duties. Some of those trying to use Kant's impersonal notion of "person" in a utilitarian view of politics have therefore suggested that distributive justice must require something like a lottery. At least, they argue, that decision process begins by treating everyone alike. But the proposal is self-defeating, since it only postpones unequal treatment and does so in a way Kant would have abhorred – by a completely nonrational decision process. Luck, Kant wrote, "cannot become a matter of universal legislation" (*T&P* 296).

The fact that society today has not been able to reach a consensus on such problems as the public allocation of scarce and expensive medical resources would have been no surprise to Kant, who foresaw exactly why such a consensus cannot be reached rationally and why any "agreement" finally will depend on sheer coercion, that is, on arbitrary (and Kant would say, tyrannical) governmental edicts. Kant would have argued that the government should not have gotten involved in such matters of positive distribution of welfare in the first place.

For a sustained critique of the use of such an "attenuated conception of the person" to try to support a liberal political theory, see Victor J. Seidler, *Kant, Respect and Injustice: The Limits of Liberal Moral Theory.*

22 Kant was suspicious of any form of governmental largess, for he believed that one of the main causes of widespread need is "the injustice of the government," which, by favoring some, actually causes others to need help (*M.M.* 454; see 453–54).

23 Kant did allow one significant exception: The state may tax citizens "to provide the means of sustenance for those [such as orphans] who are unable to provide the most necessary needs of nature for themselves" (*M.M.* 326). This exception does not fit in with his political theory, and he does not try to justify it in his

Doctrine of Justice, where he mentions it. In his *Reflections,* Kant in fact admits that this is fundamentally an ethical duty, one based first not on the fact that the needy are citizens but on the fact that they are human beings; see Howard Williams, *Kant's Political Philosophy,* 197. Like any other positive ethical obligation, this duty requires prudential judgment, and for that reason there are no guarantees that *whatever* arrangements are made will work out to the satisfaction of everyone, including the needy themselves.

24 Kant insists on one exception here also: A ruler cannot be a ruler, he holds, and still be subject to coercive laws (or to punishment for breaking them). (See *T&P* 291, 298–304; *M.M.* 317, 319–20.) Kant may have been misled here by thinking, on the one hand, of the kingdom of ends with God as the sovereign and, on the other, of revolution as the usual means of deposing tyrants. (See *M.M.* 317, 341.) But no contradiction is necessarily generated by laws specifying legal criteria and procedures for impeachment for malfeasance in office.

25 Since the actual possession of property is derivative from the united or general will, Kant apparently *could* have held that estates could be confiscated and redistributed by the state, acting on behalf of that general will, but his conviction that private property is essential to freedom and justice led him to limit his discussion of this possibility. (See *M.M.* 291–92, 324–25, 368–70.) His own experience of living under a despot, even a benevolent one, led him to believe that, whenever possible, the power of the state should be limited.

26 In his essay, *What Is Enlightenment?* Kant held that he lived in a time that was only in the *process* of becoming enlightened. (See *Enlight.* 40.) Nowhere is this better confirmed than by Kant's insistence that in the state "not everyone is equally qualified to have the right to vote," but only those whom he called "active citizens." By contrast, "dependents" include "anyone who must depend for his support (subsistence and protection), not on his own industry, but on arrangements by others (with the exception of the state)," and "all such people lack civil personality" (*M.M.* 314–15; see *T&P* 294–96). Kant strangely argues that this rule of enfranchisement is compatible with the Principle of Right (which still requires that laws be impartially formulated) as long as everyone can "work up from this passive status to an active status" (*M.M.* 315). However, "dependents" include not only minors, servants, and all other wage earners, but also all women. Although he regards "legal tutelage" as degrading, Kant does not tell us how women can get free of their tutelage and "work up" to an "active" status. (See *Anthr.* 209.)

When Kant discusses women, he almost invariably remarks on their ability to dominate men and manipulate them for their own purposes, a "trait" he apparently also felt he had to try to "justify" – as part of Nature's aim in perpetuating the human race and encouraging the development of culture. (See, e.g., *Anthr.* 303–11.) In general, Kant's views about women and marriage, which his champions today maintain were advanced for his time, are still best ignored and forgotten. But Kant is not unique in the fact that he reflected some such prejudices of his own day; philosophers commonly have done so from the beginning of the history of Western thought.

27 For a fuller discussion of Kant's doctrines, see Howard Williams, *Kant's Moral Philosophy,* 244–71; also Patrick Riley, *Kant's Political Philosophy,* 114–31.

28 This does not mean that Kant ever sanctioned war, which he regarded as an unmitigated evil, but he was realistic enough at least to try to *limit* that evil when nations do go to war.

29 However, Kant mainly thought of the league of nations as a completely voluntary confederation rather than as a kind of super republic able to enforce laws coercively. See F. H. Hinsely, *Power and the Pursuit of Peace*, 66; also *M.M.* 344.

30 A good deal of Kant's ethical vocabulary is borrowed directly from the political arena. So pervasive is this vocabulary that people reading his ethical writings for the first time frequently confuse his references to law (*Gesetz*) – the moral law – as references to civil law.

31 See also Robert B. Pippin, "On the Moral Foundations of Kant's *Rechtslehre*." For another point of view, see George P. Fletcher, "Law and Morality: A Kantian Perspective."

18. Kant's philosophy of religion

1 Friedrich Paulsen, *Immanuel Kant: His Life and Doctrine*, 4, 7. See also James Collins, *The Emergence of Philosophy of Religion*, 89–211, and Keith Ward, *The Development of Kant's View of Ethics*, 95–96.

2 Richard Kroner, *Kant's Weltanschauung*, 35–36.

3 Ibid.

4 "We can use, as an example," Kant proposes, "the myth of the sacrifice that Abraham was going to make by butchering and burning his only son at God's command. . . . Abraham should have replied to this supposedly divine voice: 'That I ought not to kill my good son is quite certain. But that you, this apparition, are God – of that I am not certain, and never can be, not even as this voice rings down to me from (visible) heaven' " (*Conflict* 63n/115n). The blind obedience supposedly modeled in the Old Testament by Abraham is part of a tyrannical form of religion, certainly not of a religion our reason can accept as divinely revealed.

In his *Kant and the Philosophy of History*, Yirmiahu Yovel argues that, because Kant intended his *Religion* to change the consciousness of his readers, his apparent biblical exegesis is used only as "a fictitious common ground between the critic and his audience," aimed at turning the believers' own book against their beliefs (214; see also 214–22).

5 Lewis White Beck, *A Commentary on Kant's Critique of Practical Reason*, 279.

6 The virtuous disposition of respect for, and obedience to, the moral law, therefore, may be understood religiously as godliness – both as similar to fear of God (e.g., the dutifulness of a subject) and as similar to love of God (e.g., the dutifulness of a son). (See *Rel.* 182/170.)

I confess that I am not sure how the claims in this paragraph of the text can be reconciled. There is no problem about the origin of the content of morality, but if pure practical reason is "self-sufficient," it would seem that any use of religious beliefs to support moral motivation is unnecessary, risks heteronomous dependency, and would inevitably result in what Kant elsewhere calls an "impure will."

7 Kant knew that his *Religion Within the Limits of Reason Alone* would arouse a furor, even though the basis for everything he would say there had been set out both in his previous writings and in his well-attended lectures on ethics. On the one hand, the fact that he intended to argue that religion has real and ultimate rational value would shock those who held that religious faith is simply an impediment to enlightenment. On the other hand, the fact that he would offer what he called "a symbolic interpretation" of the Bible and of Christian belief – what in today's terms might be called a demythologized interpretation of Christianity

– would be a scandal to many religiously orthodox believers and to traditional biblical theologians.

The first part of *Religion* was published as a separate essay in 1792 (and approved by an imperial censor), the first edition of the entire work in 1793 (and approved by the philosophical faculty at the University of Jena after the imperial censor Hillmer refused to do so), and a second edition was issued in 1794. These dates are politically important, for Frederick the Great, benevolent champion of the Enlightenment, had died in 1786. He had been succeeded by his nephew, Frederick William II, who had immediately begun to move against the Enlightenment in Prussia through a censorship commission.

Although Kant had little confidence that arguments would carry much weight with Frederick William, the now sixty-nine years old philosopher did devote a good deal of space in the first edition to instructing the imperial censor about his responsibilities. Even Kant himself came to regard his language there as "in a way rather violent." (See Zweig, *Kant: Philosophical Correspondence 1759–99*, 205–6.) He pointed out that he (Kant) was not writing as a theologian about biblical interpretation but as a philosopher writing a philosophy of religion, granted that this might involve interpreting parts of the Bible in an unorthodox manner. An imperial censor, he argued, should protect the progress of scholarship and freedom of inquiry by respecting the legitimate internal criteria of the individual disciplines involved. (See *Rel.* 8–11/7–10, 43n/39.)

Court gossip of impending action against him must have reached Kant's ears, and in the concluding paragraph of his essay *The End of All Things*, also published in 1794, an obviously furious Kant went even further. First he prophesied that imposing Christianity by "dictatorial authority" rather than allowing it to attract people by its own "gentle spirit" will only cause people to dislike and resist it. Then he boldly proclaimed that the day such an authoritarian imposition occurred would also be the beginning of "the (perverse) *end of all things,*" a time ruled by the Antichrist on the basis of fear and selfishness.

Such sentiments could have elicited but one response from an "unenlightened" monarch, and, as Friedrich Paulsen tells the story (see 49–50), Frederick William ordered his Minister of Spiritual Affairs, Johann Wöllner, to put an end to "the disgraceful writings of Kant." So it happened that on October 12, 1794, Kant received an imperial cabinet order informing him that "our most high person has long observed with great displeasure how you misuse your philosophy to distort and disparage many of the cardinal and basic teachings of the Holy Scriptures and of Christianity. . . . We demand that you, . . . in keeping with your duty, apply your authority and talents to the progressive realization of our paternal purpose," namely, the public promotion of Lutheranism by the government (from Mary J. Gregor's translation of Kant's *Vorrede* to his *Conflict of the Faculties* 6/11).

Unrepentant, the seventy-year-old philosopher replied with another strong defense of the right of scholars to engage in free and open inquiry. However, because he also had no other choice but to submit, given his own political philosophy, he did conclude his letter by declaring, "As Your Majesty's most loyal subject, . . . I will hereafter refrain altogether from discoursing publicly, in lectures or writings, on religion, whether natural or revealed" (*Conflict* 10/19). He privately defended his own integrity by pointing out that he had not recanted anything he believed; and although "all one says must be true, it does not follow that it is one's duty to tell publicly everything which is true."

When Frederick William died three years later, in 1797, Kant regarded himself as released from his promise and quickly returned to the subject of religion in his *The Conflict of the Faculties* (1798). Kant had written at least the first part of this little book in 1794 to defend the rights of the philosophy faculty against attacks by the theology faculty, but he had postponed publishing it until after Frederick William's death. In the preface to that book, he maintained that he had used the phrase "Your Majesty's most loyal subject" to indicate that his promise had been made personally to Frederick William and obligated him only during the latter's lifetime (10n/19n). Today this claim may seem hypocritical, but only if we forget that under an absolute monarchy a citizen's allegiance was to the *person* of the emperor. In a footnote to his *Anthropology*, published that same year (1798), Kant could not resist taking one last swipe at the late Frederick William II, by decrying the misuse by despots of "man's moral predisposition for political ends" (*Anthr.* 332n).

It was not just authoritarian Protestants who found Kant's philosophy of religion abhorrent. Despite the fact that Kant's strongest attacks had been on Lutheran theology (although he does not mention Luther by name), a century later it still seemed to some Catholic theologians and members of the Catholic hierarchy that Kant's philosophy gave "the strongest support to the drive towards 'subjectivism' implicit in Luther's doctrine of faith," so that Kant became "the *bête noire* of Roman Catholic apologetic." (See Gabriel Daly, *Transcendence and Immanence: A Study in Catholic Modernism and Integralism,* 8.) According to Daly, the condemnation of "Modernism" by Pope Pius X in 1907 traced a host of doctrinal errors to Kantian "transcendental skepticism" and "epistemological relativism," which had attacked "the rational foundations of Catholic belief," "had opened up a chasm between itself and Christian belief," and therefore needed to be "regarded as totally incompatible with Catholic theology" (2, 45-46). "What [the Catholic theologians] did genuinely fear," Daly writes, "was a system of philosophical inquiry which placed the knowing and willing subject at the core of man's approach to God" (49).

8 Pelagius had denied the traditional doctrine of Original Sin and affirmed that it is possible to become pleasing to God by one's own efforts without the help of baptism or divine grace; see John A. Mourant, "Pelagius and Pelagianism." As we have seen, Kant did believe, albeit in an unorthodox way, in both Original Sin and grace, but with Pelagius he clearly subordinated religious dogma to ethics. He wrote, for example, that "the doctrine of the Trinity, taken literally has *no practical relevance at all*, even if we think we understand it; and it is even more clearly irrelevant if we realize that it transcends all our concepts" (*Conflict* 38-39/65-67).

9 Richard Kroner, *Kant's Weltanschauung,* 52.

10 In his classic article "Kant and Radical Evil," Emil L. Fackenheim argues that Kant's doctrine of radical evil "represents a shift in doctrine," which Kant made, not because he wished to fashion a rationally justified version of the doctrine of Original Sin, but because he finally had come to realize how serious a problem moral evil was in his philosophical system. Kant's doctrine of the two viewpoints seemed to make it impossible for him to account for the possibility of a free but evil will. In Kant's doctrine, human agents could only choose between the alternatives of acting freely and morally or of falling into naturally determined and therefore amoral behavior. As Fackenheim writes, "Evil exists. The philosopher must explain it; he cannot explain it away" (346; see 345). Contrary to his previous

379

contentions (see, e.g., *M.M.* 226), Kant finally was "convinced that moral freedom can have no other meaning than the freedom to choose between good and evil. And he finds it necessary to introduce the doctrine of radical evil so as to make freedom, in this sense, intelligible" (Fackenheim, 340–41).

Fackenheim comments that when Kant embraced the view that freedom requires a choice between good and evil, he did so "at the risk of leaving it philosophically unintelligible" (343). So it does not seem merely coincidental that in *Religion* Kant is willing to set aside the distinction between noumena and phenomena, expressions he casually dismisses in the preface to the second edition as "used only because of the schools" (*Rel.* 14/13).

11 Kant therefore maintains that, for moral purposes, he has the correct interpretation of the Genesis account of the Fall, rather than theologians like Augustine who claimed that we all are born in an inherited state of sin. (See *Rel.* 41–44/36–39.)

12 See Sharon Anderson-Gold, "Kant's Ethical Commonwealth: The Highest Good as a Social Goal." One of the effects of the propensity to evil, Kant argues, is the tendency of people to *want* to be duped into accepting those "doctrines which demand the least self-exertion and the least use of their own reason, and which can best accommodate their duties to their inclinations," as, for example, "the doctrine that they can be saved merely by an implicit faith" or the belief that "their performance of certain prescribed rites will itself wash away their transgressions" (*Conflict* 31/51).

13 See "Moral Fanaticism" in Chapter 10.

14 See Allen W. Wood, *Kant's Moral Religion*, 232–48.

15 Christian ecclesiastical faith, Kant writes, traditionally has been expressed in four kinds of devotional exercises: private prayer, Sunday church services, the communion service, and baptism (see *Rel.* 193/181). All of them can be salutary, that is, helpful in quickening a genuine moral disposition, thereby promoting goodness of heart. But because they are not helpful to everyone, they also "cannot be a duty for everyone." Rituals are not a *means* of grace by which God is directly served and his favor gained. As for prayer, God does not need information about us; we cannot actually commerce with him; we cannot ingratiate ourselves with him as with an earthly potentate, by giving him honor and glorification; and we have no reason to believe (prudentially) that we can influence his providential plans by our wishes. (See *Rel.* 51/47, 103/94, 115/106, 185/173, 195–200/183–88; *Lect.* 323–30/98–106.) Again, nothing can substitute for morally upright conduct.

16 Allen W. Wood, *Kant's Moral Religion*, 254; see also Kant's letter to Stäudlin, in Zweig, cited in note 7.

17 Wood, *Kant's Moral Religion*, 2; see 249–54. When Wood's book was published in 1970, he stood virtually alone within Anglo-American tradition in insisting that the Critical philosophy itself is "a *religious* outlook, a profound conception of the human condition as a whole, and of man's proper response to that condition." Other commentators have since followed Wood's lead, e.g., Michel Despland.

18 Wood, ibid., 250–51.

19 Keith Ward, *The Development of Kant's View of Ethics*, 167; see also 167–68, 171–74.

Appendix 1. Kant's two-viewpoints doctrine

1 For discussions of problems with Kant's doctrine of the two viewpoints, typical in the literature, see Robert Paul Wolff, *The Autonomy of Reason;* also Ralph C.

S. Walker, *Kant*, 147–50; and Keith Ward, *The Development of Kant's View of Ethics*, 168–71.
2 See "Freedom" in Chapter 5. Although it is repetitious to mention this, it is still worth noting how often Kant uses the word "moral" in his various works in such a way that it can be interpreted to mean either "morally good" or "morally significant," whether morally good or not. As a consequence, many of his discussions of morality can be read so as to seem consistent with either view of heteronomy.
3 This division may underlie Kant's claim in his *Religion* that human nature includes predispositions to all three kinds of agency: predispositions, first, "to *animality* in man, taken as a *living* being"; then, "to *humanity* in man, taken as a living and at the same time a *rational* being" whose reason is dependent on pathological desires for both its ends and its motivation; and last, "to *personality* in man, taken as a rational and at the same time an *accountable* being" (*Rel.* 26/21). Sometimes, however Kant seems also to believe that the predisposition to animality is taken up into and incorporated into the predisposition to humanity.
4 See also Henry E. Allison, *Kant's Transcendental Idealism: An Interpretation and Defense*, 327. For Allison's discussion of "the radical shift" in Kant's theory "brought about by the introduction of the conception of autonomy," see his "The Concept of Freedom in Kant's 'Semi-Critical' Ethics."
5 This important doctrine has already been set out in various places – for example, in Chapter 3, in the analysis of Kant's theory of human action; in Chapter 4, in the analysis of "empirically conditioned reason"; and in Chapter 5, in the analysis of pure practical reason as a "causal power to act in accordance with [one's own] idea of laws" (*Gr.* 35/412).
6 Kant had adumbrated this claim in his *New Exposition of the First Principles of Metaphysical Knowledge* in 1755 (*KGS* I, 398–405; 75–87 in Lewis White Beck et al., *Kant's Latin Writings*).
7 Moreover, defining freedom as moral indeterminism would entail that God would be "equally capable of doing good or evil, if His actions are to be called free" (*Rel.* 49n/45).
8 Nonetheless, Kant still denies that we *have* an "animal will," which not only "can be pathologically necessitated" but "cannot be determined save through sensuous impulses, that is, pathologically" (*Pu.R.* A534/B562, A802/B830; *Pr.R.* 97; *Lect.* 267/28). Kant insists that the human will is an *arbitrium sensitivum* and an *arbitrium liberum;* it is sensuously "affected" but *not* pathologically "necessitated" (*Pu.R.* A534/B562).
9 Some commentators, such as H. J. Paton, while admitting that Kant held that "a free will is equivalent to an autonomous will," still maintain that he did not hold "the absurd view" that only morally good actions are free and all other actions wholly determined. (See *The Categorical Imperative*, 208, 211–12, 214–15; but also 276–77. See also Thomas E. Hill, Jr., "Kant's Argument for the Rationality of Moral Conduct," 7–8.)

Few people are willing to adopt the all-or-nothing view of freedom. Civil law, for example, holds that human agents should be presumed to be free enough to be responsible for their actions. But it also recognizes the possibility of internal or external compulsions, any of which can mitigate that freedom.

Kant takes an untenably harsh view of the imputation of responsibility only when he is writing with the noumenal-phenomenal distinction in mind. (See, e.g., *Pu.R.* A551n/B579n.) When he discusses moral and legal responsibility at least implicitly from the point of view of ordinary moral judgments, he uses distinctions that the doctrine of the two viewpoints does not allow. (See *Pu.R.* A554–55/B583; *M.M.* 227–28, 390, 431; *Lect.* 62.)

10 I have often included the German word in the English translations of Kant's text, not only to make clear what Kant wrote but also to show that insisting on the significance of this distinction is often not helpful in interpreting him. See the introduction to *Interpreting Kant,* ed. Moltke S. Gram, especially 7–8; also "*Wille* and *Willkür* in Kant's Theory of Action" by Gram, 69–84. But see also John R. Silber, "The Importance of the Highest Good in Kant's Ethics," 180–83, and Lewis White Beck, "Kant's Two Conceptions of the Will in Their Political Context."

11 These citations are taken from Wood's review of G. Prauss's *Kant über Freiheit als Autonomie* (Frankfurt: Klostermann, 1983), in the *Journal of Philosophy* 81 (May 1984), 271–72. See also Wood, "Kant's Compatibilism."

12 The extraordinary difficulties one encounters in trying to "reconstruct" Kant's doctrines show how tightly his theory is constructed. Whenever Kant does *not* argue for an alternative position, it is not presumptuous to hold that there is some very good reason for his not doing so. For example, taking *Willkür* to be the basis for freedom and freedom to be the ground of human dignity seems to lead to the unsavory consequence of moral laissez-faireism, in which morally wrong actions such as theft and rape would have to be construed as manifestations of human dignity. On this, see Jeffrie G. Murphy, *Kant: The Philosophy of Right,* 82–88.

13 See Lewis White Beck, "Kant's Theoretical and Practical Philosophy," 36–42.

Appendix 2. Kant's philosophy of moral education

1 The main sources for Kant's philosophy of moral education are his "Methodology of Pure Practical Reason" at the end of the *Critique of Practical Reason* (151–61); "The Ethical Doctrine of Method" at the end of the *Metaphysics of Morals* (477–90); "Duties Arising from Differences of Age" at the end of his *Lectures on Ethics* (466–70/247–51); and what purports to be a compilation of Kant's lecture notes, edited by Theodore Rink and published in 1803, the year before Kant died, under the title *Immanuel Kant über Pädagogik.* (See *KGS* IX, 437–99.) This latter was translated into English by Annette Churton and published as *Education* in 1960. For a critique of the work of both Rink and Churton, see Lewis White Beck, "Kant on Education," 192–97.

It is seldom recognized today how influential Kant's views on education have been; see William K. Frankena, *Three Historical Philosophies of Education,* 79–80.

2 For several brief essays Kant wrote in praise of such schools, see *KGS* II, 447–52, and X, 191. Kant devoted a good deal of time to trying to raise money for the Dessau Institute. (See Beck, "Kant on Education," 189–91.)

3 As Beck points out, this division echoes the stages of Nature's plan for human development in Kant's philosophy of history. (See Beck, "Kant on Education," 199.) *Education* offers several different divisions of the educational process, not all of which are compatible with one another. I have ignored these differences, for nothing of great importance hangs on them.

4 Quoted by Roger Scruton in *Kant,* 4.

5 As we saw in Chapter 9, habituation limits freedom, so Kant counsels that children "must be prevented from forming any habits, nor should habits be fostered in them" (*Ed.* 468/45). Yet he also thought that the formation of character requires

the adoption of maxims that will issue as a methodical regularity in eating, sleeping, working, and recreating, according to a rule or plan; and "having once made a rule [children] must always follow it" (*Ed.* 481/85; see 463/45–46, 480/83). Kant's biographers commonly note the regularity of his own conduct. Although there may not seem to be any behavioral differences between habituated conduct and regular conduct according to a rule, Kant argues the two are radically dissimilar in their ground.

Bibliography

Translations of Kant's works

Unless otherwise noted, all page references are to *Kants gesammelte Schriften,* abbreviated as *KGS,* edited under the auspices of the Königliche Preussische Akademie der Wissenschaften – Berlin: Walter de Gruyter, 1902–

An Answer to the Question: What Is Enlightenment? (1784, *KGS* VIII). Ted Humphrey, *Immanuel Kant: Perpetual Peace and Other Essays,* 41–48.
Anthropology from a Pragmatic Point of View (1798, *KGS* VII), Mary J. Gregor. The Hague: Nijhoff, 1974.
The Conflict of the Faculties (1798, *KGS* VII), Mary J. Gregor. New York: Abaris, 1979. (Part II, *An Old Question Raised Again: Is the Human Race Constantly Progressing?* is reprinted from the translation by Robert E. Anchor, in *Immanuel Kant: On History,* Lewis White Beck, ed.)
Critique of Judgment (1790, *KGS* V), James Creed Meredith. Oxford: Oxford University Press, 1952.
Critique of Practical Reason (1788, *KGS* V), Lewis White Beck. Indianapolis: Bobbs-Merrill, 1956.
Critique of Pure Reason (1781, 1787, *KGS* IV and III). Norman Kemp Smith, *Immanuel Kant's Critique of Pure Reason.* London: Macmillan, 1956. References give the page numbers first of the 1781 (A) edition and then of the 1787 (B) edition.
Education (1803, *KGS* IX), Annette Churton. Ann Arbor: University of Michigan Press, 1960. References to this book give first the *KGS* pagination and then that of the translation, which unfortunately does not include the *KGS* pagination.
The End of All Things (1794, *KGS* VIII). Ted Humphrey, *Immanuel Kant: Perpetual Peace and Other Essays,* 93–105.
Groundwork of the Metaphysic of Morals (1785, *KGS* IV), H. J. Paton. New York: Harper & Row, 1964. References to this book give the page numbers first to the second edition published during Kant's lifetime and (after the slash) the edition published after his death and in *KGS* IV.
Idea for a Universal History with a Cosmopolitan Intent (1784, *KGS* VIII). Ted Humphrey, *Immanuel Kant: Perpetual Peace and Other Essays.* Indianapolis: Hackett, 1983, 29–40.
Lectures on Ethics (1780–85), Louis Infield. 1930. Reprint. Indianapolis: Hackett, 1981. The dates given after the title represent the semesters when Kant probably gave these lectures, which were published posthumously. When citations are given to this book, the numbers before the slash refer to the pagination of that version of the lectures included in *KGS* XXVII, consisting of class notes from the winter semester 1784–85; the pagination after the slash refers to Infield's translation of *Eine Vorlesung Kants über Ethik,* a compilation from three other

BIBLIOGRAPHY

sets of student notes (from 1780, 1781, and 1782), ed. Paul Mentzer. Berlin: Rolf Heise, 1924.

Lectures on Philosophical Theology (c. 1783–84, *KGS* XXVIII, 2), Allen W. Wood and Gertrude M. Clark. Ithaca, N.Y.: Cornell University Press, 1978. The dates after the title represent the semesters when Kant probably gave these lectures, which were published posthumously.

Logic (1800, *KGS* IX), Robert S. Hartman and Wolfgang Schwarz. Indianapolis: Bobbs-Merrill, 1974.

The Metaphysics of Morals (1797, *KGS* VI)
John Ladd, *The Metaphysical Elements of Justice*. Indianapolis: Bobbs-Merrill, 1965.
Mary J. Gregor, *The Doctrine of Virtue*. Philadelphia: University of Pennsylvania Press, 1964, 1971.

On a Supposed Right to Lie from Altruistic Motives (1797, *KGS* VIII). Lewis White Beck, *Immanuel Kant: Critique of Practical Reason and Other Writings in Moral Philosophy*, 346–50.

On the Proverb: That May Be True in Theory but Is of No Practical Use (1793, *KGS* VIII). Ted Humphrey, *Immanuel Kant: Perpetual Peace and Other Essays*, 61–92.

The One Possible Basis for a Demonstration of the Existence of God (1763, *KGS* II), Gordon Treash, trans. and ed. New York: Abaris, 1979.

Perpetual Peace: A Philosophic Sketch (1795, *KGS* VIII). Ted Humphrey, *Immanuel Kant: Perpetual Peace and Other Essays*, 107–43.

Prolegomena to Any Future Metaphysics (1783, *KGS* IV), Lewis White Beck. Indianapolis: Bobbs-Merrill, 1950.

Religion Within the Limits of Reason Alone (1793, *KGS* VI), Theodore M. Greene and Hoyt H. Hudson. New York: Harper & Row, 1960. References to this book give first the *KGS* pagination and then that of the translation, which unfortunately does not include the *KGS* pagination.

Speculative Beginning of Human History (1786, *KGS* VIII), Ted Humphrey, *Immanuel Kant: Perpetual Peace and Other Essays*, 49–60.

What Is Orientation in Thinking? (1786, *KGS* VIII), Lewis White Beck, *Immanuel Kant: Critique of Practical Reason and Other Writings in Moral Philosophy*, 293–305.

Collections

Beck, Lewis White, ed. and trans. *Immanuel Kant: Critique of Practical Reason and Other Writings in Moral Philosophy*. 1949. Reprint. New York: Garland, 1976.

Immanuel Kant: On History. Indianapolis: Bobbs-Merrill, 1963.

Kant's Latin Writings (1755–88, *KGS* I, II, XV). In collaboration with Mary J. Gergor, Ralf Meerbote, and John A. Reuscher. New York: Peter Lang, 1986.

Humphrey, Ted, trans. *Immanuel Kant: Perpetual Peace and Other Essays on Politics, History, and Morals*. Indianapolis: Hackett, 1983.

Kerferd, G. B., and D. E. Walford, trans. *Kant: Selected Pre-critical Writings and Correspondence with Beck* (1763–93, *KGS* II, X, XI). Manchester: Manchester University Press, 1968.

Reiss, Hans, ed. *Kant's Political Writings*. Trans. H. B. Nisbet. Cambridge: Cambridge University Press, 1970.

Zweig, Arnulf, ed. and trans. *Kant: Philosophical Correspondence 1759–99* (*KGS* X–XII, XXII). Chicago: University of Chicago Press, 1967.

BIBLIOGRAPHY

Books on Kant

Acton, H. B. *Kant's Moral Philosophy*. London: Macmillan, 1970.
Allison, Henry E. *The Kant-Eberhard Controversy*. Baltimore: Johns Hopkins University Press, 1973.
　Kant's Transcendental Idealism: An Interpretation and Defense. New Haven, Conn.: Yale University Press, 1983.
Ameriks, Karl. *Kant's Theory of Mind: An Analysis of the Paralogisms of Pure Reason*. Oxford: Clarendon Press, 1982.
Arendt, Hannah. *Lectures on Kant's Political Philosophy*. Ed, with an interpretative essay by Ronald Beiner. Chicago: University of Chicago Press, 1982.
Atwell, John E. *Ends and Principles in Kant's Moral Thought*. Dordrecht: Nijhoff, 1986.
Aune, Bruce. *Kant's Theory of Morals*. Princeton, N.J.: Princeton University Press, 1979.
Auxter, Thomas. *Kant's Moral Teleology*. Macon, Ga., Mercer University Press, 1982.
Beck, Lewis White. *A Commentary on Kant's Critique of Practical Reason*. Chicago: University of Chicago Press, 1960.
　Early German Philosophy: Kant and His Predecessors. Cambridge, Mass.: Harvard University Press, 1969.
　Essays on Kant and Hume. New Haven, Conn.: Yale University Press, 1978.
　Kant Studies Today. LaSalle, Ill.: Open Court, 1969.
　ed. *Proceedings of the Third International Kant Congress (1970)*. Dordrecht: Reidel, 1972.
　Studies in the Philosophy of Kant. Indianapolis: Bobbs-Merrill, 1965.
Bencivenga, Ermanno. *Kant's Copernican Revolution*. New York: Oxford University Press, 1987.
Blum, Lawrence A. *Friendship, Altruism, and Morality*. London: Routledge & Kegan Paul, 1980.
Broad, C. D. *A Commentary on Kant's Critique of Practical Reason*. Chicago: University of Chicago Press, 1963.
　Kant: An Introduction. Ed. C. Lewy. Cambridge: Cambridge University Press, 1978.
Carnois, Bernard. *The Coherence of Kant's Docrine of Freedom*. Trans. David Booth. Chicago: University of Chicago Press, 1987.
Cassirer, Ernst. *Kant's Life and Thought*. 1918. Trans. James Haden. New Haven, Conn.: Yale University Press, 1981.
　Rousseau, Kant, Goethe. Trans. J. Gutman, P. O. Kristeller, and J. H. Randall, Jr. Princeton, N.J.: Princeton University Press, 1945.
Despland, Michel. *Kant on History and Religion*. Montreal: McGill-Queen's University Press, 1973.
Downie, R. S., and Elizabeth Telfer. *Respect for Persons*. New York: Schocken, 1970.
England, F. E. *Kant's Conception of God*. 1929. New York: Humanities Press, 1968.
Ewing, A. C. *Kant's Treatment of Causality*. 1924. Hamden: Archon Books, 1969.
Frankena, William K. *Three Historical Philosophies of Education*. Glenview, Ill.: Scott, Foresman, 1965.
Funke, Gerhard, ed. *Proceedings of the Fourth International Kant Congress (1974)*. Berlin: Walter de Gruyter, 1976.

BIBLIOGRAPHY

Galston, William A. *Kant and the Problem of History*. Chicago: University of Chicago Press, 1975.

Goldmann, Lucien. *Immanuel Kant*. 1945. Trans. Robert Black. London: NLB, 1971.

Gram, Moltke S., ed. *Interpreting Kant*. Iowa City: University of Iowa Press, 1982.

Gregor, Mary J. *Laws of Freedom*. New York: Barnes & Noble, 1963.

Guyer, Paul. *Kant and the Claims of Knowledge*. Cambridge: Cambridge University Press, 1987.

Jones, Hardy E. *Kant's Principle of Personality*. Madison: University of Wisconsin Press, 1971.

Kemp, John. *The Philosophy of Kant*. London: Oxford University Press, 1968.

Kemp Smith, Norman. *A Commentary to Kant's 'Critique of Pure Reason,'* 2d ed., rev. 1923. Atlantic Highlands, N.J.: Humanities Press, 1962.

Kennington, Richard, ed. *The Philosophy of Immanuel Kant*. Washington, D.C.: Catholic University of America Press, 1985.

Körner, S. *Kant*. Baltimore: Penguin Books, 1955.

Kroner, Richard. *Kant's Weltanschauung*. 1914. Trans. and ed. John E. Smith. Chicago: University of Chicago Press, 1956.

Liddell, Brendan E. A., trans. and commentator. *Kant on the Foundation of Morality*. Bloomington: Indiana University Press, 1970.

McFarland, J. D. *Kant's Concept of Teleology*. Edinburgh: University of Edinburgh Press, 1970.

Murphy, Jeffrie G. *Kant: The Philosophy of Right*. London: Macmillan, 1970.

Nell (O'Neill), Onora. *Acting on Principle: An Essay on Kantian Ethics*. New York: Columbia University Press, 1975.

Paton, H. J. *The Categorical Imperative: A Study in Kant's Moral Philosophy*. 5th ed. London: Hutchinson, 1965.

Paulsen, Friedrich. *Immanuel Kant: His Life and Doctrine*. 2d ed. 1899, Trans. J. E. Creighton and Albert Lefevre. New York: Ungar, 1963.

Potter, Nelson T., and Mark Timmons. *Morality and Universality: Essays on Ethical Universalizability*. Dordrecht: Reidel, 1985.

Reiner, Hans. *Duty and Inclination: The Fundamentals of Morality Discussed and Redefined with Special Regard to Kant and Schiller*. Trans. Mark Santos. The Hague: Nijhoff, 1983.

Rescher, Nicholas. *Kant's Theory of Knowledge and Reality: A Group of Essays*. Washington, D.C.: University Press of America, 1983.

Riley, Patrick. *Kant's Political Philosophy*. Totowa, N.J.: Rowman & Littlefield, 1983.

Rink, Friedrich Theodor. *Ansichten aus Immanuel Kants Leben*. Königsberg: Goebbels & Unzer, 1805.

Ross, Sir David. *Kant's Ethical Theory*. Oxford: Oxford University Press, 1954.

Rotenstreich, Nathan. *Experience and Its Systematization: Studies in Kant*. The Hague: Nijhoff, 1965.

Saner, Hans. *Kant's Political Thought: Its Origins and Development*. Trans. E. B. Ashton. Chicago: University of Chicago Press, 1973.

Schilpp, Paul Arthur. *Kant's Pre-Critical Ethics*. 2d ed. Evanston, Ill.: Northwestern University Press, 1960.

Scruton, Roger. *Kant*. Oxford: Oxford University Press, 1982.

Seebohm, Thomas M., and G. Funke, eds. *Proceedings: Sixth International Kant Congress (1985)*. In press.

387

Seidler, Victor J. *Kant, Respect and Injustice: The Limits of Liberal Moral Theory*. London: Routledge & Kegan Paul, 1986.

Shell, Susan Meld. *The Rights of Reason: A Study of Kant's Philosophy and Politics*. Toronto: University of Toronto Press, 1980.

Stevens, Rex P. *Kant on Moral Practice*. Macon: Mercer University Press, 1981.

Van de Pitte, Frederick P. *Kant as Philosophical Anthropologist*. The Hague: Nijhoff, 1971.

Walker, Ralph C. S. *Kant*. London: Routledge & Kegan Paul, 1978.

 ed. *Kant on Pure Reason*. Oxford: Oxford University Press, 1982.

Ward, Keith. *The Development of Kant's View of Ethics*. Oxford: Basil Blackwell, 1972.

Werkmeister, W. H., ed. *Reflections on Kant's Philosophy*. Gainesville: University Presses of Florida, 1975.

 Kant: The Architectonic and Development of His Philosophy. La Salle, Ill.: Open Court, 1980.

Wike, Victoria S. *Kant's Antinomies of Reason: Their Origin and Resolution*. Washington, D.C.: University Press of America, 1982.

Williams, Howard. *Kant's Political Philosophy*. Oxford: Basil Blackwell, 1983.

Williams, T. C. *The Concept of the Categorical Imperative*. Oxford: Oxford University Press, 1968.

Wolff, Robert Paul. *The Autonomy of Reason: A Commentary on Kant's Groundwork of the Metaphysic of Morals*. New York: Harper & Row (Harper Torchbooks), 1973.

 ed. *Foundations of the Metaphysics of Morals with Critical Essays*. Trans. L. W. Beck. Indianapolis: Bobbs-Merrill, 1969.

 ed. *Kant: A Collection of Critical Essays*. Notre Dame, Ind.: University of Notre Dame Press, 1968.

Wood, Allen W. *Kant's Moral Religion*. Ithaca, N.Y.: Cornell University Press, 1970.

 Kant's Rational Theology. Ithaca, N.Y.: Cornell University Press, 1978.

 ed. *Self and Nature in Kant's Philosophy*. Ithaca, N.Y.: Cornell University Press, 1984.

Yovel, Yirmiahu. *Kant and the Philosophy of History*. Princeton, N.J.: Princeton University Press, 1980.

Other books

Arendt, Hannah. *Eichmann in Jerusalem: A Report on the Banality of Evil*. Rev. and enlarged ed. New York: Penguin Books, 1965.

 The Life of the Mind. 2 vols. New York: Harcourt Brace Janovich, 1978.

Beck, Lewis White. *The Actor and the Spectator*. New Haven, Conn.: Yale University Press, 1975.

Bok, Sissela. *Lying: Moral Choice in Public and Private Life*. London: Quartet Books, 1980.

Brown, D. *Understanding Pietism*. Grand Rapids, Mich.: Eerdmans, 1978.

Cassirer, Ernst. *The Philosophy of the Enlightenment*. 1932. Trans. Fritz C. A. Koelln and James P. Pettegrove. Princeton, N.J.: Princeton University Press, 1968.

Collins, James. *The Emergence of Philosophy of Religion*. New Haven, Conn.: Yale University Press, 1967.

Daly, Gabriel, O.S.A. *Transcendence and Immanence: A Study in Catholic Modernism and Integralism*. Oxford: Clarendon Press, 1980.

BIBLIOGRAPHY

Dennett, Daniel C. *Elbow Room.* Cambridge, Mass.: MIT Press, 1984.
Dickey, James. *Deliverance.* Boston: Houghton Mifflin, 1970.
Dodge, Guy H. *Benjamin Constant's Philosophy of Liberalism: A Study in Politics and Religion.* Chapel Hill: University of North Carolina Press, 1980.
Donagan, Alan. *The Theory of Morality.* Chicago: University of Chicago Press, 1977.
Donelaitis, Kristijonas,. *The Seasons.* Trans. Nadas Rastenis; ed. Elena Tumas. Los Angeles: Lithuanian Days, 1967.
Edwards, Paul, et al., eds. *The Encyclopedia of Philosophy.* 8 vols. New York: Macmillan, & Free Press, 1967.
Foot, Philippa. *Virtues and Vices and Other Essays in Moral Philosophy.* Berkeley: University of California Press, 1978.
Frankena, William K. *Ethics.* 2d ed. Englewood Cliffs, N.J.: Prentice-Hall, 1973.
French, Peter A., Theodore E. Uehling, Jr., and Howard K. Wettstein. *Midwest Studies in Philosophy.* Vol. 3, *Studies in Ethical Theory.* Minneapolis: University of Minnesota Press, 1978.
Gray, John. *Liberalism.* Minneapolis: University of Minnesota Press, 1986.
Green, O. H., ed. *Respect for Persons.* New Orleans: Tulane University Press, 1982.
Hampshire, Stuart. *Public and Private Morality.* Cambridge: Cambridge University Press, 1978.
Hare, R. M. *Moral Thinking: Its Levels, Methods, and Point.* Oxford: Oxford University Press, 1981.
Harrison, Andrew. *Making and Thinking: A Study of Intelligent Activities.* Indianapolis: Hackett, 1979.
Hartshorne, Charles, and Paul Weiss, eds. *Collected Papers of Charles Sanders Peirce.* Vol. 5. Cambridge, Mass.: Harvard University Press (Belknap Press), 1965.
Hayek, Friedrich A. *Studies in Philosophy, Politics and Economics.* Chicago: University of Chicago Press, 1967.
Hegel, Georg Wilhelm Friedrich. *Philosophy of Right.* Trans. T. M. Knox. Oxford: Oxford University Press, 1952.
Hinsley, F. H. *Power and the Pursuit of Peace.* Cambridge: Cambridge University Press, 1963.
James, William. *The Principles of Psychology.* Vol. I, 1890. Cambridge, Mass.: Harvard University Press, 1981.
Kohn, Alexander. *False Prophets.* Oxford: Basil Blackwell, 1987.
Körner, Stephan. *Practical Reason.* New Haven, Conn.: Yale University Press, 1974.
Kuhn, Thomas S. *The Structure of Scientific Revolutions.* 2d ed. Chicago: University of Chicago Press, 1970.
Lieb, Irwin C., ed. *Experience, Existence and the Good: Essays in Honor of Paul Weiss.* Carbondale: Southern Illinois University Press, 1961.
Livingston, Donald W. *Hume's Philosophy of Common Life.* Chicago: University of Chicago Press, 1984.
Machiavelli, Niccolò. *The Prince and The Discourses.* Trans. Luigi Ricci, E. R. P. Vincent, and Christian E. Getmold. Intro. by Max Lerner. New York: Random House, 1950.
Manier, Edward, William Liu, and David Solomon, eds. *Abortion: New Directions for Policy Studies.* Notre Dame, Ind.: University of Notre Dame Press, 1977.
Mill, John Stuart. *Utilitarianism.* Indianapolis: Hackett, 1979.
Nozick, Robert. *Anarchy, State, and Utopia.* New York: Basic Books, 1974.
O'Malley, Joseph J., Keith W. Algozin, and Frederick G. Weiss, eds. *Hegel and the History of Philosophy.* Proceedings of the 1972 Hegel Society of America Conference. The Hague: Nijhoff, 1974.

Popper, Karl R. *The Open Society and Its Enemies.* 2 vols. 5th ed. rev. Princeton, N.J.: Princeton University Press, 1966.

Priest, Stephen, ed. *Hegel's Critique of Kant.* Oxford: Oxford University Press, 1987.

Pritchard, H. A. *Moral Obligation and Duty and Interest: Essays and Lectures.* Oxford: Oxford University Press, 1968.

Rawls, John. *A Theory of Justice.* Cambridge, Mass.: Harvard University Press (Belknap Press), 1971.

Raz, Joseph, ed. *Practical Reasoning.* Oxford: Oxford University Press, 1979.

Riley, Patrick. *The General Will Before Rousseau: The Transformation of the Divine into the Civic.* Princeton, N.J.: Princeton University Press, 1986.

Rist, John. *Human Value: A Study in Ancient Philosophical Ethics.* Leiden: Brill, 1982.

Ross, W. D. *The Right and the Good.* 1930. Oxford: Oxford University Press, 1967.

Rousseau, Jean-Jacques. *The Social Contract.* Trans. and intro. Maurice Cranston. Harmondsworth: Penguin Books, 1968.

Sandel, Michael J. *Liberalism and the Limits of Justice.* Cambridge: Cambridge University Press, 1982.

Singer, Marcus George. *Generalization in Ethics.* 1961. With a new Preface. New York: Atheneum, 1971.

Sonnino, Paul, trans. and ed. *Frederick of Prussia: The Refutation of Machiavelli's Prince or Anti-Machiavel.* Athens: Ohio University Press, 1981.

Szrednick, J. T. J., ed. *Stephan Körner: Philosophical Analysis and Reconstruction.* Dordrecht: Nijhoff, 1987.

Stirner, Max. *The Ego and His Own: The Case of the Individual Against Authority.* Trans. Steven T. Byington; ed. James J. Martin. New York: Libertarian Book Club, 1963.

Sullivan, Roger J. *Morality and the Good Life: A Commentary on Aristotle's Nicomachean Ethics.* Indianapolis: Hackett, 1980.

Wolff, Robert Paul. *In Defense of Anarchism.* New York: Harper & Row, 1976.

Articles on Kant

Allison, Henry E. "The Concept of Freedom in Kant's 'Semi-Critical' Ethics." *Archiv für Geschichte der Philosophie* 68 (1986): 96–115.

"Empirical and Intelligible Character in the *Critique of Pure Reason.*" Unpublished.

"The Hidden Circle in *Groundwork* III." *Proceedings: Sixth International Kant Congress (1985).* In press.

"Morality and Freedom: Kant's Reciprocity Thesis." *Philosophical Review* 95 (July 1986): 393–425.

"The Originality of Kant's Distinction between Analytic and Synthetic Judgments." In Kennington, *The Philosophy of Immanuel Kant,* 15–38.

"Practical and Transcendental Freedom in the *Critique of Pure Reason.*" *Kant-Studien* 73 (1982): 271–90.

Anderson-Gold, Sharon. "Cultural Development and Moral Progress in Kant's Philosophy of History." Read at the University of South Carolina, Columbia, April 3, 1987. In press.

"Ethical Community and the Highest Good." Proceedings: Sixth International Kant Congress (1985). In press.

BIBLIOGRAPHY

"Kant's Ethical Commonwealth: The Highest Good as a Social Goal." *International Philosophical Quarterly* 26 (March 1986): 23–32.

"Kant's Rejection of Devilishness: The Limits of Human Volition." *Idealistic Studies* 14 (January 1984): 35–48.

Atwell, John E. "Are Kant's First Two Moral Principles Equivalent?" *Journal of the History of Ideas* 32 (July–September 1971): 273–84.

Auxter, Thomas. "The Unimportance of Kant's Highest Good." *Journal of the History of Philosophy* 17 (April 1979): 121–34.

Axinn, Sidney. "Ambivalence: Kant's View of Human Nature." *Kant-Studien* 72 (1981): 169–74.

"Kant, Authority, and the French Revolution." *Journal of the History of Ideas* 32 (July-September 1971): 423–32.

"Rousseau *versus* Kant on the Concept of Man." *Philosophical Forum* 12 (Summer 1981): 348–55.

Baron, Marcia. "Kantian Ethics and Supererogation." *Journal of Philosophy* 84 (May 1987): 237–62.

Beck, Lewis White. "Analytic and Synthetic Judgments before Kant." In W. H. Werkmeister, *Reflections on Kant's Philosophy,* 7–27. Also included in Lewis White Beck, *Essays on Kant and Hume,* 80–100.

"Apodictic Imperatives." In Beck, *Studies in the Philosophy of Kant,* 177–99.

"Can Kant's Synthetic Judgments Be Made Analytic?" In Beck, *Studies in the Philosophy of Kant,* 74–91.

"The Fact of Reason: An Essay on Justification in Ethics." In Beck, *Studies in the Philosophy of Kant,* 200–14.

"Five Concepts of Freedom in Kant." In Srzednick, *Stephan Körner: Philosophical Analysis and Reconstruction,* 35–51.

Introduction. *Immanuel Kant: Critique of Practical Reason and Other Writings in Moral Philosophy.* 1949. Trans. and ed. L. W. Beck. New York: Garland, 1976, 1–49.

"Kant and the Right of Revolution." *Journal of the History of Ideas* 32 (1971): 411–22; reprinted in Beck, *Essays on Kant and Hume,* 171–87.

"Kant on Education." In Beck, *Essays on Kant and Hume,* 188–204.

"Kant's Theoretical and Practical Philosophy." In Beck, *Studies in the Philosophy of Kant,* 3–53.

"Kant's Theory of Definition." In Beck, *Studies in the Philosophy of Kant,* 61–73.

"Kant's Two Conceptions of the Will in Their Political Context." In Beck, *Studies in the Philosophy of Kant,* 215–29.

"On the Meta-Semantics of the Problem of the Synthetic A Priori." In Beck, *Studies in the Philosophy of Kant,* 92–98.

"Remarks on the Distinction Between Analytic and Synthetic." In Beck, *Studies in the Philosophy of Kant,* 99–107.

"Sir David Ross on Duty and Purpose in Kant." In Beck, *Studies in the Philosophy of Kant,* 165–76.

Bennett, Jonathan. "Kant's Theory of Freedom." In Wood, *Self and Nature in Kant's Philosophy,* 102–12.

Benson, Peter. "External Freedom According to Kant." *Columbia Law Review* 87 (April 1987): 559–79.

Broadie, Alexander, and Elizabeth Pybus. "Kant's Treatment of Animals." *Philosophy* 49 (1974): 375–83.

"Kant and the Maltreatment of Animals." *Philosophy* 53 (1978): 560–61.

BIBLIOGRAPHY

Buchanan, Allen. "Categorical Imperatives and Moral Principles." *Philosophical Studies* 31 (1977): 249–60.
Dietrichson, Paul. "Kant's Criteria of Universalizability." In Wolff, *Foundations of the Metaphysics of Morals with Critical Essays*, 163–207.
"What Does Kant Mean by 'Acting from Duty'?" In Wolff, *Kant: A Collection of Critical Essays*, 314–30.
Ebbinghaus, Julius. "Interpretation and Misinterpretation of the Categorical Imperative." In Wolff, *Kant: A Collection of Critical Essays*, 211–27.
Eisenberg, Paul D. "Kant on Duties to, and Duties Regarding, Oneself or Others." In Beck, *Proceedings of the Third International Kant Congress* (1970), 275–80.
Fackenheim, Emil L. "Kant and Radical Evil." *University of Toronto Quarterly* 23 (July 1954): 339–53.
"Kant's Concept of History." *Kant-Studien* 48 (1956–57): 381–98.
Fletcher, George P. "Law and Morality: A Kantian Perspective." *Columbia Law Review* 87 (April 1987): 533–58.
"Why Kant." *Columbia Law Review* 87 (April 1987): 421–32.
Foot, Philippa, "Morality as a System of Hypothetical Imperatives." In Foot, *Virtues and Vices and Other Essays in Moral Philosophy*, 157–73.
French, Stanley G. "Kant's Constitutive-Regulative Distinction." In Beck, *Kant Studies Today*, 375–91.
Funke, Gerhard. "Concerning Eternal Peace – Ethics and Politics." In Werkmeister, *Reflections on Kant's Philosophy*, 91–108.
Garver, Newton. "Analyticity and Grammar." In Beck, *Kant Studies Today*, 245–73.
Haezrahi, Pepita. "The Concept of Man as End-in-Himself." In Wolff, *Kant: A Collection of Critical Essays*, 291–313.
Harrison, Jonathan. "The Categorical Imperative." In Wolff, *Foundations of the Metaphysics of Morals with Critical Essays*, 245–52.
"Kant's Examples of the First Formulation of the Categorical Imperative." In Wolff, *Foundations of the Metaphysics of Morals with Critical Essays*, 208–29.
Henrich, Dieter. "The Proof-Structure of Kant's Transcendental Deduction." In Walker, *Kant on Pure Reason*, 66–81.
Herman, Barbara. "Integrity and Impartiality." *Monist* 66 (April 1983): 233–50.
"Mutual Aid and Respect for Persons." *Ethics* 94 (July 1984): 577–602.
"On the Value of Acting from the Motive of Duty." *Philosophical Review* 90 (July 1981): 359–82.
"The Practice of Moral Judgment." *Journal of Philosophy* 82 (August 1985): 414–36.
"Rules, Motives, and Helping Actions." *Philosophical Studies* 45 (May 1984): 369–77.
Hill, Thomas, E., Jr., "Autonomy in the *Groundwork*." Paper read at the University of South Carolina, Columbia, April 4, 1987. In press.
"Darwell on Practical Reason." *Ethics* 96 (April 1986): 604–19.
"Humanity as an End in Itself." *Ethics* 91 (1980): 84–99.
"The Hypothetical Imperative." *Philosophical Review* 82 (October 1973): 429–50.
"Kant on Imperfect Duty and Supererogation." *Kant-Studien* 62 (1971): 55–76.
"Kant's Anti-moralistic Strain." *Theoria* 44 (1978): 131–51.
"Kant's Argument for the Rationality of Moral Conduct." *Pacific Philosophical Quarterly* 66 (January/April 1985): 3–23.

"Kant's Utopianism." *Proceedings of the Fourth International Kant Congress (1974)*, 919–24.

"The Kingdom of Ends." In Beck, *Proceedings of the Third International Kant Congress (1970)*, 307–15.

"Moral Purity and the Lesser Evil." *Monist* 66 (April 1983): 213–32.

"Self-Respect Reconsidered." In Green, *Respect for Persons*, 129–37.

"Servility and Self-Respect." *Monist* 57 (January 1973): 87–104.

Jensen, Henning. "Kant on Overdetermination, Indirect Duties, and Moral Worth." In Seebohm, *Proceedings: Sixth International Kant Congress (1985)*. In press.

Kemp, J. "Kant's Examples of the Categorical Imperative." In Wolff, *Foundations of the Metaphysics of Morals with Critical Essays*, 230–44.

Körner, Stephan. "Kant's Conception of Freedom." *Proceedings of the British Academy* 53 (1967): 193–217.

"The Impossibility of Transcendental Deductions." In Beck, *Kant Studies Today*, 230–44.

Korsgaard, Christine M. "Aristotle and Kant on the Source of Value." *Ethics* 96 (April 1986): 486–505.

"Kant's Formula of Humanity." *Kant-Studien* 77 (April 1986): 183–202.

"Kant's Formula of Universal Law." *Pacific Philosophical Quarterly* 66 (January/April 1985): 24–47.

"Morality as Freedom." *Kant's Practical Philosophy Reconsidered: Proceedings of the Seventh Jerusalem Philosophical Encounter*, December 28–30, 1986. In press.

"The Right to Lie: Kant on Dealing with Evil." *Philosophy and Public Affairs* 15 (Fall 1986): 325–49.

"Skepticism about Practical Reason." *Journal of Philosophy* 83 (January 1986): 5–25.

"Two Distinctions in Goodness." *Philosophical Review* 92 (April 1983): 169–95.

Laska, Peter. "Kant and Hegel on Practical Reason." In O'Malley et al., *Hegel and the History of Philosophy*, 129–40.

Matson, W. I. "Kant as Casuist." In Wolff, *Kant: A Collection of Critical Essays*, 331–36.

Meerbote, Ralf. "The Unknowability of Things in Themselves." In Beck, *Proceedings of the Third International Kant Congress (1970)*, 413–23.

Mischel, Theodore. "Kant and the Possibility of a Science of Psychology." In Beck, *Kant Studies Today*, 432–55.

Mish'Alani, James K. " 'Duty,' 'Obligation,' and 'Ought.' " *Analysis*, n.s., 134 (1969): 33–40.

Mulholland, Leslie A. "Kant on War and International Justice." *Kant-Studien* 78 (January 1987): 26–41.

"Kant: On Willing Maxims to Become Laws of Nature." *Dialogue* 18 (1978): 92–105.

"A Paradox in Kant's Concept of Virtue." Paper read at the University of South Carolina, Columbia, April 3, 1987. In press.

"Value and Ontology in Kant's Concept of the End in Itself." In Seebohm, *Proceedings: Sixth International Kant Congress (1985)*. In press.

Murphy, Jeffrie G. "Does Kant Have a Theory of Punishment?" *Columbia Law Review* 87 (April 1987): 509–32.

"Kant's Theory of Criminal Punishment." In Beck, *Proceedings of the Third International Kant Congress (1970)*, 434–41.

393

O'Hagan, T. "On Hegel's Critique of Kant's Moral and Political Philosophy." In Priest, *Hegel's Critique of Kant,* 135–59.

O'Neill, Onora (Nell). "Consistency in Action." In Potter and Timmons, *Morality and Universality,* 159–86.

Paton, H. J. "An Alleged Right to Lie: A Problem in Kantian Ethics." *Kant-Studien* 45 (1953–54): 190–203.

Pippin, Robert B. "On the Moral Foundations of Kant's *Rechtslehre*." In Kennington, *The Philosophy of Immanuel Kant,* 107–42.

Potter, Nelson T., Jr. "How to Apply the Categorical Imperative." *Philosophia* 5 (October 1975): 395–416.

"Kant on Ends That Are at the Same Time Duties." *Pacific Philosophical Quarterly* 66 (1985): 78–92.

"Paton on the Application of the Categorical Imperative." *Kant-Studien* 64 (1973): 411–22.

Pritchard, H. A. "Does Moral Philosophy Rest on a Mistake?" In Pritchard, *Moral Obligation and Duty and Interest: Essays and Lectures,* 1–17.

Rawls, John. "Kantian Constructivism in Moral Theory." *Journal of Philosophy* 77 (September 1980): 515–72.

Regan, Tom. "Broadie and Pybus on Kant." *Philosophy* 51 (1976): 471–72.

Reich, Klaus. "Kant and Greek Ethics," trans. W. H. Walsh. 2 parts. *Mind* 48 (July/October 1939): 338–54, 446–63.

Reiss, Hans. Introduction. *Kant's Political Writings.* Ed. Hans Reiss. 1970, 1–40.

Rescher, Nicholas. "Noumenal Causality." In Beck, *Proceedings of the Third International Kant Congress (1970),* 462–70. Revised and reprinted in Rescher, *Kant's Theory of Knowledge and Reality,* 17–30.

"On the Status of 'Things-in-Themselves' in Kant." *Synthese* 47 (1981): 288–99. Revised and reprinted in Rescher, *Kant's Theory of Knowledge and Reality,* 1–16.

Rotenstreich, Nathan, "Is There a Primacy of Practical Reason?" In Lieb, *Experience, Existence and the Good: Essays in Honor of Paul Weiss,* 247–59.

Scheid, Don E. "Kant's Retributivism." *Ethics* 93 (January 1983): 262–82.

Schrader, George. "Autonomy, Heteronomy, and Moral Imperatives." *Journal of Philosophy* 60 (January 1963): 65–77.

"The Constitutive Role of Practical Reason in Kant's Moral Philosophy." In Werkmeister, *Reflections on Kant's Philosophy,* 65–90.

"The Thing in Itself in Kantian Philosophy." In Wolff, *Kant: A Collection of Critical Essays,* 172–88.

Seebohm, Thomas M. "Kant's Theory of Revolution." *Social Research* 48 (1981): 557–87.

Shope, Robert K. "Kant's Use and Derivation of the Categorical Imperative." In Wolff, *Foundations of the Metaphysics of Morals with Critical Essays,* 253–91.

Silber, John R. "The Context of Kant's Ethical Thought." *Philosophical Quarterly* 9 (July & October 1959): 193–207, 309–318.

"The Copernican Revolution in Ethics: The Good Reexamined." *Kant-Studien* 51 (Fall 1959): 85–101.

"The Ethical Significance of Kant's *Religion*. Second introduction to *Religion within the Limits of Reason Alone*. Trans. Greene and Hudson, lxxix–cxxxiv.

"The Importance of the Highest Good in Kant's Ethics." *Ethics* 73 (1962–63): 179–97.

BIBLIOGRAPHY

"Kant at Auschwitz." *Proceedings: Sixth International Kant Congress (1985).* In press.

"Kant's Conception of the Highest Good as Immanent and Transcendent." *Philosophical Review* 68 (October 1959): 469–92.

"The Metaphysical Importance of the Highest Good as the Canon of Pure Reason in Kant's Philosophy." *Texas Studies in Literature and Language* 1 (Summer 1959): 233–44.

"The Moral Good and the Natural Good in Kant's Ethics." *Review of Metaphysics* 36 (December 1982): 397–437.

"Procedural Formalism in Kant's Ethics." *Review of Metaphysics* 28 (December 1974): 197–236.

Smith, John E. "Hegel's Critique of Kant." In O'Malley et al., *Hegel and the Philosophy of History,* 109–28.

Stern, Paul. "The Problem of History and Temporality in Kantian Ethics." *Review of Metaphysics* 39 (March 1986): 505–45.

Stroud, Barry. "Transcendental Arguments." In Walker, *Kant on Pure Reason,* 117–31.

Sullivan, Roger J. "The Kantian Critique of Aristotle's Moral Philosophy: An Appraisal." *Review of Metaphysics* 28 (September 1974): 24–53.

"The Kantian Model of Moral-Practical Reason." *Monist* 66 (January 1983): 83–105.

Taylor, Paul W. "On Taking the Moral Point of View." In Peter A. French, Theodore E. Uehling, Jr., and Howard K. Weltstein, *Midwest Studies in Philosophy,* vol. 3. Minneapolis: University of Minnesota Press, 1978, 35–61.

Timmons, Mark. "Kant and the Possibility of Moral Motivation." *Southern Journal of Philosophy* 23 (Fall 1985): 377–98.

Van de Vate, Dwight, Jr. "A Kantian Paradox." Unpublished.

Walsh, W. H. "Kant's Concept of Practical Reason." In Körner, *Practical Reason,* 189–212.

"Kant's Moral Theology." *Proceedings of the British Academy* 49 (1964): 263–89.

Warnock, G. J. "The Primacy of Practical Reason." *Proceedings of the British Academy* 52 (1967): 253–66.

Weinrib, Ernest J. "Law as a Kantian Idea of Reason." *Columbia Law Review* 87 (April 1987): 472–508.

Wood, Allen W. "Kant on False Promises." In Beck, *Proceedings of the Third International Kant Congress (1970),* 614–19.

"Kant's Compatibilism." In Wood, *Self and Nature in Kant's Philosophy,* 73–101.

"Kant's Deism." Read at Marquette University, November 1987. In press.

Zeldin, Mary-Barbara. "Principles of Reason, Degrees of Judgment, and Kant's Argument for the Existence of God." *Monist* 54 (April 1970): 285–301.

"The Summum Bonum, the Moral Law, and the Existence of God." *Kant-Studien* 62 (1971): 43–54.

Other articles

Brinton, Crane. "Enlightenment." In Edwards et al., *Encyclopedia of Philosophy,* vol. 2, 519–25.

Coleman, Dorothy P. "Is Mathematics for Hume Synthetic A Priori?" *Southwestern Journal of Philosophy* 10 (October 1979): 113–26.

BIBLIOGRAPHY

Cranston, Maurice. "Liberalism." In Edwards et al., *Encyclopedia of Philosophy*, vol. 4, 458–61.

Hayek, Friedrich A. "The Principles of a Liberal Social Order." In Hayek, *Studies in Philosophy, Politics and Economics,* 160–77.

Korsgaard, Christine M. "Skepticism about Practical Reason." *Journal of Philosophy* 83 (January 1986): 5–25.

Macquarrie, John. "Pietism." In Edwards et al., *Encyclopedia of Philosophy*, vol. 6, 311–12.

Mourant, John A. "Pelagius and Pelagianism." In Edwards et al., *Encyclopedia of Philosophy*, vol. 6, 78–79.

Nowell-Smith, P. H. "What Is Authority?" *Philosophic Exchange* 2 (1976): 3–15.

Peirce, Charles Sanders. "What Pragmatism Is." In Hartshorne and Weiss, *Collected Papers of Charles Sanders Peirce*, vol. 5, 272–292.

Pincoffs, Edmund. "Virtue, the Quality of Life, and Punishment." *Monist* 63 (April 1980): 172–84.

"Membership Decisions and the Limits of Moral Obligation." In Manier et al., *Abortion: New Directions for Policy Studies,* 31–49.

Rawls, John. "Justice as Fairness: Political not Metaphysical." *Philosophy & Public Affairs* 14 (Summer 1985): 223–51.

Sullivan, Roger J. "Some Suggestions for Interpreting *Eth. Nic.* 10.7–8." *Southern Journal of Philosophy* 15 (Spring 1977): 129–38.

Toulmin, Stephen. "The Tyranny of Principles." *Hastings Center Report* 11 (December 1981): 31–39.

Index of names

Index of subjects

absurdity, practical, 226
action, 23–30
  and behavior, 30, 67, 92, 117, 129
  causally determined, 24, 279, 282–83
  empirical consequences of, 41–42, *see also*
    moral philosophy
  goal-directed, 24–26, 309n7
  identification of individual, 162
  immoral, 284–85
  and intention, 30, 66–67, 117, 280
  legal, 30, 117
  moral, 17, 66–68, 92, 133, 321n8, 368n11
  morally indifferent, 138–39, 282
  perceived changes as effect of, 24
  presupposes interest, 26–27, 131–32
  prudential, 31–43, 279
  role of rules in, 28–29
  theory of, 23–29
  transcendentally free, 46, 80–81, 281
aesthetic of pure practical reason, 135–37
agency, 24–25
  rational, 25–26, 78, 153–54, 309n7,
    319n1, 342n6, *see also* practical reason
analytic method, *see* methodology of moral
  philosophy
anarchism, 347n4, 367n8
anthropology, 304n13
  and Categorical Imperative, 159–60,
    344n19
  and human destiny, 313n20
*Anthropology from a Pragmatic Point of
  View*, 313n20, 379n7
anthropomorphism, symbolic, 225, 365n18
antinomies
  of pure practical reason, 143
  of theoretical reason, 305n18, 328n1
apathy, moral, 136
appearances, *see* phenomena
architectonic, value of, 71
asceticism, 137, 292–93
atonement, vicarious, 270
autonomy
  compatibility of, with political coercion,
    235

  contrasted with heteronomy, 46–48, 80,
    149
  as freedom, 46, 154–55, *see also* freedom
  as legal term, 46
  positive and negative aspects of, 46, 80,
    91, 120
  power of, as ground of moral worth, 107–
    8
  as psychological term, 46
  self-consistency and, 178–79
  as self-constraint, 165–66
  as self-legislation, 46–47, 80, 158
  Stoic use of term, 314n6
  as universal legislation, 47, 166–67
  see also Autonomy, Law of
Autonomy, Law of, 47–50, 139, 154–55,
  158–59
  derivation of, 151–52, 165
  as descriptive law, 48–50, 77–78,
    325n4
  formula of, 48, 154–55, 165
  as ground for moral life, 133–34, 194,
    327n16
  as imperative, 49–50, 77–79, 140, 156, *see
    also* Categorical Imperative
  lack of reason excuses from, 49
  as law of freedom, 46, 48, 89, 155
  and moral law, 315n9
  Natural Law and, 58–59
  as objective practical norm, 110–11
  positive and negative aspects of, 46, 80,
    91, 122
  as prudential norm, 163–64
  as *ratio cognoscendi* of freedom, 90
  as sole "fact of pure reason," 88–89
  as "supreme principle of right," 165

behaviorism, 3, 9
belief, *see* faith
benevolence and beneficence, 206–8
bliss, 140, 339n8
bonum summum, see good, highest
bonum supremum, see good will, as supreme
  good